Testimonios

Testimonios

Early California through the Eyes of Women,
1815–1848

Translated with introduction and commentary by
Rose Marie Beebe and Robert M. Senkewicz

HEYDAY BOOKS, BERKELEY, CALIFORNIA

THE BANCROFT LIBRARY, UNIVERSITY OF CALIFORNIA, BERKELEY

Library of Congress Cataloging-in-Publication Data
Testimonios : early California through the eyes of women, 1815-1848 / translated, with introduction and commentary, by Rose Marie Beebe and Robert M. Senkewicz.
    p. cm.
  Includes bibliographical references and index.
  ISBN 1-59714-032-5 (cloth : alk. paper)
  ISBN 1-59714-033-3 (pbk. : alk. paper)
  1. California—History—To 1846—Biography. 2. Hispanic American women—California—Biography. 3. Women pioneers—California—Biography. I. Beebe, Rose Marie. II. Senkewicz, Robert M., 1947-
 F864.T327 2006
 920.72'089680794—dc22
                   2006002549
Cover Art: Alfred Sully (1821–1879). *Monterey, California Rancho Scene*, c. 1849. Water-color on paper. Courtesy of the Oakland Museum of California, Kahn Collection.
Cover and Interior Design: Lorraine Rath
Printing and Binding: Sheridan Books, Inc.
Published in collaboration with The Bancroft Library, University of California, Berkeley.

Orders, inquiries, and correspondence should be addressed to:
      Heyday Books
      P. O. Box 9145, Berkeley, CA 94709
      (510) 549-3564, Fax (510) 549-1889
      www.heydaybooks.com

Printed in the United States of America

10 9 8 7 6 5 4 3 2 1

We lovingly dedicate this book to the memory of two of our professors at Santa Clara University:

Fr. Norman F. Martin, S.J. (Professor of History)
Dr. Andrew I. Rematore (Professor of Spanish)

Their wisdom, guidance, and inspiration will be with us always. We are truly grateful.

Contents

Acknowledgments

We have been fortunate to have been assisted by many generous people as we have worked on this project. At the very beginning, Malcolm Margolin of Heyday Books and Charles Faulhaber, Director of The Bancroft Library, agreed that this enterprise was worthwhile. We thank them for working together to make it happen.

We are grateful for grants from the offices of Diane Jonte-Pace, Associate Provost for Faculty Development at Santa Clara University, and Thomas Turley and Barbara Molony, successive Chairs of the History Department there. These grants supported an undergraduate research assistant. We also thank the Historical Society of Southern California for a Haynes Grant, which supported travel to repositories in southern California. We are also very appreciative of the support given our project by Josef Hellebrandt, Chair of the Santa Clara University Department of Modern Languages and Literatures, and Marie Brancati of the College of Arts and Sciences.

At The Bancroft Library, we have been aided by Peter Hanff, Deputy Director, and Teresa Salazar, Curator of the Bancroft Collection of Western Americana. The staff behind the desk during the years we researched this endeavor are too numerous to mention individually. We continue to be thankful for the unfailing goodwill and patience of each of them, even while they were preparing to remove large portions of the collection to a temporary location during the retrofit of the Bancroft's permanent home.

In the course of our travels, we were assisted by the staffs of many repositories and libraries throughout the state. In the Bay Area, we are indebted to Anne McMahon, Archivist at Santa Clara University, Cindy Bradley and Carolee Bird of Orradre Library's interlibrary loan service, Dan Murley of the Healdsburg Museum, and the staff of the California Historical Society in San Francisco. Along the central coast, Joyce Hermann and Wally Ohles shared their knowledge and resources at the Ríos-Caledonia Adobe in San Miguel. In Santa Bárbara, Patricia Livingston and Lynn Bremer of the Santa Bárbara Mission Archive-Library and Lee Goodwin and Mary Louise Days at the Santa Bárbara Trust for Historic Preservation generously made their collections and their own deep expertise available to us. In the Los Angeles area, Janet Fireman and John Cahoon at the Seaver Center for Western History Research allowed us to consult their extensive photographic collections, and Peter Blodgett steered us to the right people and resources at the Huntington Library. In San Diego, Iris Engstrand generously took time to guide us through the collections at the San Diego Historical Society.

We also wish to thank the University of Wisconsin Press for giving us permission to use a number of biographical sketches and notes that we originally composed for Antonio María Osio's *The History of Alta California,* which they published in 1996.

We were fortunate to be able to call upon the assistance of a number of generous and knowledgeable individuals. Carmen Boone de Aguilar of Mexico City found the information on the Real Casa de Expósitos that greatly helped us reconstruct the first few years of Apolinaria Lorenzana's life. Randy Milliken and Ed Castillo shared their own research on Isidora Filomena, and John Johnson and Victor Golla helped us with some indigenous terms she used. Russ Skowronek assisted us in deciphering some technical archaeological terms. Mike Mathes helped clear up some obscure Latin American references in the testimonios. Phil Valdez shared his knowledge of Dorotea Valdez, and Louise Pubols assisted us on matters relating to the de la Guerra family. Leon Hooper, S.J., found and sent us photographs from Georgetown University, and Harry Crosby was an invaluable resource on many items relating to Baja and Alta California.

At Santa Clara University, Denisse Rubio, a history major, served as an excellent research assistant and greatly helped us in many aspects of this project. Ricardo Salgado, another student, assisted in the transcription of Angustias de la Guerra's *recuerdos* and her journal. Two other students, Holly Kearl and Francesca Zanfini, provided bibliographic and other assistance.

At Heyday Books we were lucky enough to benefit from the superb editing skills of Jeannine Gendar and Lisa K. Manwill and the creative artistic abilities of Lorraine Rath and Rebecca LeGates.

Our greatest debt is to Susan Snyder of The Bancroft Library. She was an extremely supportive colleague during this entire process. Her enthusiasm for the project was matched only by her deep knowledge of the resources available at The Bancroft Library. She guided us through the Bancroft's rich collections of documents, graphics, maps, and photographs. She opened all sorts of doors for us, and many of the photographs that appear in the volume and the sources that appear in our notes were first called to our attention by Susan. We cannot imagine having been able to complete this volume without her. Along with many other readers, we profited from Susan's wonderful book *Bear in Mind* and we are glad that another volume from her is on the way. Thanks for everything, Susan!

Finally, no expressions of thanks would be complete for us without mentioning our faithful and wise companion Ollie. He constantly reminded us that playing with him and taking him for walks are necessary parts of any research agenda. His advice helped keep us fresh and renewed as we worked on this project.

Prologue

Sometime in 1793, a baby girl was brought to the main entrance of a large structure, the Real Casa de Expósitos (the Royal House for Abandoned Children), at No. 3 Puente de la Merced in Mexico City. The individual placed the baby girl on the turnstile of the revolving window next to the entrance and pulled on a hanging rope, which rang a bell inside. Then he or she left.[1]

The porter, whose room was next to the main door, turned the revolving window toward the inside and picked up the infant. First he checked the girl to see if any identifying information, such as a letter or a locket, had been left with her. He then turned the girl over to the *ama mayor,* the woman in charge. She estimated the child's age and then took the child to the chaplain. The chaplain, in the presence of the *ama mayor,* brought out two separate record books. One was the Spanish Register and the other one was a register for Indian Children and Other Castes. In these books he listed the day, month, and year that the girl arrived, her sex, and her race. The chaplain and the *ama mayor* agreed to place this girl in the Spanish Register and to categorize her as *"española"*—Spanish. Next to this information was a space for noting birthmarks or unusual physical characteristics. When a letter or other documentation was left with a new arrival, it would be copied word for word in the record book. If the person who dropped off a child indicated in some fashion that there was a sibling at the Casa, that information would be recorded as well. All of the information in the record books was safeguarded for the future, should a child's family wish to reclaim her or him.

The girl's last name had already been determined. It was Lorenzana, in honor of Francisco Antonio Lorenzana y Butrón. In 1793, this man was thousands of miles away, in Toledo, Spain, where he was the cardinal archbishop of the city and the leading Roman Catholic churchman in the country. But in 1767, when he was the archbishop of Mexico City, he had founded the Real Casa de Expósitos. All the children were named Lorenzana in his honor. For the first name of this girl, the chaplain and the *ama mayor* agreed on Apolinaria.

After these administrative duties had been completed, the girl was handed back to the *ama mayor,* who then selected one of the four wet nurses employed at the Casa to feed and care for her.

Apolinaria lived at the Casa for seven years. Life for the children there was highly structured, to the point of being monastic. The boys and girls lived in separate dormitories, and their activities were separate as well. Girls learned a variety of skills: reading, arithmetic, grammar, sewing, embroidery, how to make artificial flowers, geography, music, and the catechism. Boys received a similar education, except that, when they were old enough, they would be taught a craft that might help them obtain a job. The following routine was typical for girls who were between six and eight years old:

From April 1 until the end of October, the girls got up at 6:00 a.m. From the end of October until April 1, they arose at 7:00 a.m. As soon as the children got up, the teacher had them kneel, cross themselves, recite the Act of Contrition, the Creed, the Salve Regina, and the Alabado. Then they made their beds, cleaned their room, washed up, and combed their hair. Next they went to Mass. After Mass, they ate breakfast.

At 8:00 they went to the *sala,* the main room. There they knelt, crossed themselves, recited the Lord's Prayer and the Ave María. Then they began to work quietly at their sewing projects. The teacher watched over them. She kept a cane and some leather straps in her hand to punish any girl who misbehaved. At 11:00, the girls put down their sewing. Each girl picked up her primer or another book and began to study the lessons for the day. At 12:00, the girls put their books away, knelt, and prayed the Alabado. After that, they waited to be called to lunch. When lunch was finished, they would return to the *sala* for a period of quiet playtime until 3:00, when they resumed their lessons, which continued until 4:00. At 4:00, the teacher sent the oldest girl of the group to get bread from the *ama mayor* for the afternoon snack. The teacher distributed a piece of bread to each girl. After they were done with their snack, they resumed their sewing. They did not stop until between 6:00 and 7:00 in the evening. Then they went to the dormitory and turned down their beds. If there was any free time left, the girls were allowed to go out into the patio until the bell rang, signaling that it was time to say the Rosary. At the sound of the bell, the girls all lined up and waited for the teacher to lead them into the chapel. The girls knelt next to the chaplain, to his right. They remained kneeling while the catechism was being recited. When that was finished, they returned to the *sala* and resumed sewing until the teacher determined that it was time for dinner.

Dinner was usually eaten at 8:30. After dinner they were allowed to play quietly. Bedtime was no later than 10:00. Before changing into their bedclothes, the girls had to kneel, cross themselves, pray the Lord's Prayer and say one Ave María, one Gloria to their guardian angel, and another to the patron saint for whom they were named. After they finished these prayers, they changed into their bedclothes, blessed themselves with holy water, and went to bed. The teacher watched over them as they did all this. As soon as the girls were all in bed, she went to her own room, which was right next to the girls' dormitory. She either took the light with her or extinguished it.

Between 1777 and 1794, the Casa admitted 1,056 children. Of these, 509 children died and only 75 children were adopted by families; at the end of 1794, there were 472 children under the care of the Real Casa de Expósitos. Within one year, 601 more children were admitted. The high mortality rate continued, and 405 died during that same year. Apolinaria was one of the fortunate children who survived. During 1795, 107 children were placed with families.

By September 1799, the Casa was in deep financial trouble and was having tremendous difficulty supporting the 180 children under its care. A unique solution was proposed to alleviate the fiscal problems and, at the same time, place some of the children in homes. The viceroy of New Spain, Don Miguel José de Azanza, agreed to a plan whereby a group of healthy boys and girls who were at least ten years old would be sent to help colonize California. Apolinaria Lorenzana, even though she was only seven years old, was one of the children chosen to participate in this venture.

On November 7, 1799, five boys and eleven girls were removed from the Real Casa de Expósitos and placed in the Real Hospicio de Pobres (Royal Hospice for the Poor) of Mexico City. There they waited until January 28, 1800, when they traveled to San Blas to board the frigate *Concepción* for California. The children were accompanied by the girls' teacher from the Casa, María de Jesús Lorenzana. She, too, had been abandoned at the Casa and had lived her entire life there. María was not just a teacher to the children; she was probably more like their mother. That may be why the director of the Casa had María give up her position and travel to California with them. She was expected to remain with the girls in Monterey.

The following children boarded the frigate *Concepción* at San Blas and headed for California:

Names of Boys	*Race*
José Victor Lorenzana	*Mestizo*
Juan Vicente Lorenzana	*Indio*

José María Macedonio Lorenzana	*Mestizo*
Manuel Felipe de Jesús Lorenzana	*Español*
José María de los Dolores Lorenzana	*Español*

Names of Girls	**Race**
María Francisca Ignacia Lorenzana	*Española*
María Josefa Pasquala Lorenzana	*Española*
María Vicenta Lorenzana	*Mestiza*
María Margarita Lorenzana	*India*
María Toribia Lorenzana	*Española*
María de Jesús Valeriana Lorenzana	*Española*
María Ana Josefa Leonarda Lorenzana	*Española*
María Alexa Josefa Lorenzana	*Española*
[A]Polinaria María Guadalupe Lorenzana	*Española*
Leonarda Joaquina Lorenzana	*Española*
María Gertrudis Lorenzana	*Española*

Seventy-eight years later, in 1878, the memory of landing in Monterey after a long, difficult sea voyage still haunted Apolinaria Lorenzana. In Monterey, she saw her friends being distributed to families "as if they were puppy dogs." She, too, would be left with a family but her new home would be in Santa Bárbara. Her other friends would be sent to San Diego. One can only imagine how frightened these children must have been.

Apolinaria lived for many years with the family of Lieutenant Raymundo Carrillo in Santa Bárbara. Lieutenant Carrillo witnessed the adverse effects that the "orphan project" had on the children of the Real Casa de Expósitos. In a report he said, "I do not believe that there are any advantages to be gained in trying to increase the population here by sending more children such as these. It places a financial burden on the royal treasury to keep them here and to care for them. The inhabitants do not want to take them in, because they have growing families of their own. These children are so unhappy, and it seems pointless to take them away from the capital and expose them to hardship. They are too young, and there seems to be little hope that they will be able to contribute anything, since there is no one here who can teach them a craft that might, in time, make them useful to the country."[2]

But Apolinaria Lorenzana became more than merely "useful" in California. She taught herself to write, and she taught other girls the kinds of skills she had learned at the Casa. She eventually became the glue that held Mission San Diego together. She managed many of its temporal affairs, acting at times as its purchasing agent and negotiating prices with hardened ship captains in the port. She acquired ranchos, and she hired other people to manage them so that she could continue to attend to her duties at the mission. A much loved and respected figure, she became known throughout southern California as *La Beata,* the pious woman.

After the Americans invaded, her life changed. The mission was already in ruins and her beloved priests were dead. Then her land was stolen from her. By the 1870s, she lived in the Santa Bárbara area, supported by the charity of her friends. Compared to her mission days, she lived an almost hidden life, an existence reminiscent of the obscurity which attended her birth and her delivery to the Real Casa de Expósitos.

In 1878 Apolinaria Lorenzana's life intersected with a research project that had been conceived three hundred miles to the north, in San Francisco. The project was large and sprawling. Its execution was messy. Its results were often deeply flawed. Yet because of that project—and only because of it—are we able to hear the voices of Apolinaria Lorenzana and twelve other women who lived and worked with her in Mexican California.

Introduction

Henry Cerruti left San Francisco for Sonoma on March 24, 1874. His task was to try to forge a personal relationship with Mariano Guadalupe Vallejo so that Hubert Howe Bancroft could induce Vallejo to contribute to his proposed *History of California*. Vallejo had himself begun to write a lengthy history of California, but his manuscript and notes had been destroyed in the fire that consumed his house in 1867. Bancroft hoped to use Vallejo's well-known interest in history to obtain from him a dictation of his reminiscences and, even more important to Bancroft, the large trove of documents from the Mexican period that Vallejo had saved from the fire.

On the steamer that took him north across the bay, Cerruti encountered a group of Californios. He found them "grouped in a corner not far distant from the barroom of the steamer…quietly engaged discussing the topics of the day." He invited them into the bar for a drink. He related, "After they

This posed picture was meant to represent Mariano Guadalupe Vallejo working with Henry Cerruti on the Bancroft project. Vallejo is standing in the center, with Cerruti seated at the left of the photograph. Between them is José Abrego, whom Cerruti interviewed in Monterey in June 1874. To the right of Vallejo is Rosana Leese, daughter of Rosalía Vallejo. On the extreme right is Vicente P. Gómez, who conducted ten interviews with Californios for Bancroft. Courtesy of The Bancroft Library, University of California, Berkeley

had swallowed their allotted share, I begged of them to supply me with information as to the ancient times of California, and Mr. Guillermo Fitch and Blas Piña, both intelligent persons endowed with a good dose of common sense, came forward and volunteered to dictate a few pages."

In the course of his conversation with Fitch, Cerruti asked him about his mother's family, the Carrillos. Fitch replied that the family had come from Baja California. Two of his mother's sisters had married the Vallejo brothers, Mariano and Salvador. He added that a third sister, Ramona, had married Romualdo Pacheco, who had been killed in battle in 1831 by a soldier named Avila. The mention of Romualdo Pacheco piqued Cerruti's interest, for the son of that man, who was also named Romualdo Pacheco, was currently serving as lieutenant governor of California. Cerruti asked Fitch if he knew anything else about Pacheco's life. He recorded Fitch's reply: "He said that he did not remember anything else, but if I would be so good as to visit Healdsburg, his mother, Doña Josefa Carrillo de Fitch, would be very happy to lay before me as many facts as she could recall."[1] Cerruti did not follow up on Guillermo Fitch's invitation for a year and a half. But on November 24, 1875, he and Mariano Guadalupe Vallejo went to Healdsburg and paid a call on Josefa Carrillo. She was the sixth woman he would interview for Bancroft.

Woman and child at the Vallejo home in Sonoma, nineteenth century. Courtesy of the Autry National Center

It was at this adobe chapel in San Diego, the Church of the Immaculate Conception, that Thomas Savage was first introduced to Juana Machado and Felipa Osuna, in January 1878.© San Diego Historical Society

From October 1877 until June 1878, Thomas Savage, another member of Bancroft's staff, undertook a journey through California to obtain documents and interviews for the history project. He appears to have included only three women in his list of potential interviewees. They were Eulalia Pérez of San Gabriel, Angustias de la Guerra of Santa Bárbara, and María Inocenta Pico of San Luis Obispo. Savage had already interviewed Pérez when he arrived in San Diego in January 1878. He went to the Catholic church in Old Town. He introduced himself to the priest on duty there, explained who he was, and asked for permission to copy the old mission books that were there. The priest told him that the permission of the pastor, Father Antonio Ubach, would be necessary, and that he was away. However, he said that he would be happy to arrange for some old residents of San Diego to talk to Savage. With nothing else to do, Savage agreed to this proposal. The priest brought two women to Savage, Juana Machado de Alipás de Writhington and Felipa Osuna de Marrón. Savage spoke first to Juana Machado and then to Felipa Osuna. Thus the number of interviews with women climbed to nine. Savage would interview three more, and a third colleague, Vicente Perfecto Gómez, interviewed another. Of the seventy-eight interviews that Bancroft's staff ultimately completed with Spanish and Mexican residents of pre–gold rush California, thirteen were with women.

These interviews were part of an effort organized by Hubert Howe Bancroft to support his project of writing an exhaustive history of California. The task came to fruition between 1884 and 1890, when seven hefty volumes of Bancroft's *History of California* were finally published.

As the above two vignettes make abundantly clear, interviewing women for Bancroft's *History* was often an afterthought. In nineteenth-century America, men were usually regarded as the true makers of history, and this view was, if anything, even more pronounced in the male-dominated society that gold rush California had produced. Yet these thirteen women had important perspectives and insights into the development of their native land. In this volume, we present all thirteen of the women's interviews together for the first time. We have translated each one, including those previously translated, into English.

In these interviews, the women talked about themselves and their experiences. In a literary sense, these interviews are *testimonios:* what Rosaura Sánchez has described as a "mediated narrative by a subaltern person interviewed by an outsider."

Testimonios contain autobiographical information, but they are a very different genre from autobiography. In an autobiography, the author has complete control over the content, scope, and style of the work. A testimonio is different in that it is not a self-generated work.[2] The memories contained in the interviews in this volume were filtered in a specific way. These women did not sit down and compose memoirs in a leisurely and relaxed fashion. They were sitting in a room, with perhaps one other family member present, answering questions directed at them by a man they had just met. The dynamics of the interviews we are presenting here depended on three factors: the woman, the man, and the situation.

The Women

They were a diverse group. Some of them, such as Rosalía Vallejo, and the de la Guerra sisters, Teresa and Angustias, were members of the elite. Their families had long and well-known histories in California. Some were not themselves of the elite, but bore the names of elite families. María Inocenta

Pico fit into this category. Most of the women were from prominent landowning families. This group included María Antonia Rodríguez, Josefa Carrillo, Catarina Avila, Juana Machado, and Felipa Osuna. Some had spent the greater part of their lives working in a number of capacities at the missions. This was the background of Eulalia Pérez and Apolinaria Lorenzana. One of them, Isidora Filomena, was an indigenous woman whose husband had been an important ally of the Mexicans in the Sonoma area in the 1830s and 1840s. We think that the final woman, Dorotea Valdez, was a mestiza, the daughter of a Mexican father and an indigenous mother. We will provide more information on each of them in the introductions to their respective testimonios.

The Men

They were also a diverse group. Henry Cerruti was mercurial and volatile. Vicente Gómez was something of a character. Thomas Savage was the most professional and workmanlike of the three. Since these men are recurring characters in our story, we shall summarize their careers here.

Virtually all of what we know about Cerruti came from his own pen, and there is no guarantee that he was a reliable source of information on his

Henry Cerruti affecting the sophisticated air which so captivated Hubert Howe Bancroft.
Courtesy of The Bancroft Library, University of California, Berkeley

own life. He said that he was born in Turin, Italy, in 1836 and that his parents were relatively well-to-do. According to him, he ran away from home at the age of fourteen and took a steamer to Gibraltar. He ended up in Latin America, where he held a diplomatic post as a Bolivian consul in Colombia. He resigned from that position in 1870 to join the forces of Bolivian president Mariano Melgarejo, a general who had seized power in 1864. Melgarejo was notorious for corruption and for persecuting Bolivia's indigenous population, qualities that led to massive uprisings against his rule. Cerruti claimed that he had commanded some of Melgarejo's forces and had been forced to flee after surrendering a town to the opposition. He escaped first to Chile and then to the United States. He came to California in 1873 and, on the strength of a letter of recommendation from *San Francisco Examiner* editor Philip A. Roach, Bancroft hired him in October.

How much of this story was even remotely true is difficult to ascertain. Bancroft himself characterized Cerruti as loose with the truth, remarking that "with him, lying was a fine art," but he employed Cerruti nevertheless. Bancroft was susceptible to tall tales told by those who were seeking employment, especially if they promised access to segments of the past that required linguistic skills he did not possess. For example, he was taken in by Ivan Petrov, who claimed to be able to open up the Russian experience in California to him, but whose "interviews" with former Russian colonists in Alta California were at times imaginative reconstructions with only a slight historical basis. Perhaps this is why Bancroft was inclined to accept Cerruti at face value.[3] He was fascinated by his new employee's ability to talk endlessly on a variety of topics. He was also intrigued by what he called Cerruti's "chameleon-like" ability to shift his opinions according to the company he was in. Cerruti worked for Bancroft for three years. It seems, however, that a profound instability lay at the root of his flamboyance. True to his persona, Cerruti speculated grandly in mining stocks. When the speculation failed, his financial situation became perilous. On October 9, 1876, in his room at the Union Hotel in Sonoma, he took a lethal dose of drugs. Since Bancroft was away, Thomas Savage represented him at Cerruti's funeral.[4]

Vicente Perfecto Gómez was born in Mexico. He probably came to California with his father in 1830, but he was soon sent back to Mexico to receive some formal education. He returned to California in 1842 as a clerk to Governor Manuel Micheltorena. This service in the government made him a popular witness in land cases in the 1850s, as intricate questions of land ownership were sorted out—or not—in the transition from Mexican to U.S. rule in California. His own claims were rejected, and he seems to have supported himself as a clerk in the Monterey area. He worked for Bancroft in the mid-1870s, becoming well known among his fellow staff members for his elaborate stories about early California. They were instructed to write them down, and these efforts resulted in the production of his own testimonio, *Lo que sabe* ("What he knows").[5]

Thomas Savage was born in Havana, Cuba, in 1823. His father, originally from New England, was a merchant there, and Savage grew up learning both English and Spanish. He served in the U.S. consulate in Cuba for over twenty years. After his retirement he spent some time in Central America before coming to San Francisco in 1873. Four months after his arrival, Bancroft hired him. Bancroft later wrote, "For many years, Mr. Savage was my main reliance on Spanish-American affairs....With good scholarship, ripe experience, and a remarkable knowledge of general history, he brought to the library strong literary tastes, a clear head, and methodological habits." After the publication in 1890 of the seventh and final volume of Bancroft's *History of California,* a dispute arose between Henry Lebbeus Oak, the supervisor of the library, and Bancroft. Oak claimed that Bancroft had not given sufficient credit to his staff (especially Oak) for their part in writing the *History.* In an essay titled "Estimate of the Authorship of Hubert H. Bancroft's Works," Oak wrote of Savage, "His manuscripts required in part some condensations, etc., but large portions have also been printed as written. Volume III of *California* may be regarded as entirely his work."[6]

The Situation

Our attempt to translate and recover what these thirteen women said and what they meant requires us to recognize the filters through which their words traveled on their way to us.

One set of filters involved the setting. First, Bancroft's employees had a graduated list of priorities, and interviewing people was not at the top of that list; their primary aim was often to obtain documents. One documentary source that Bancroft wished to mine was the rich collection of official documents that constituted the overall Spanish and Mexican government archives. In the first decade of the American possession of California, a number of archival collections had been gathered together from around the state. Since their major use at the time was as evidence in sorting through the confusing thicket of rival land claims, a good portion of these documents had been deposited in the office of the United States Surveyor

General in San Francisco. Savage's 1879 manuscript "Report of Labors in Archives and Procuring Material for History of California," which we reproduce as an appendix to this volume, summarizes the way in which Bancroft's staff obtained access to these documents.[7]

The missions were another source of documents. The Bancroft staff attempted to copy information from the baptismal, marriage, and death records of as many missions as they could. They also sought to copy the annual or biennial mission reports, the surviving correspondence of the missionaries, and any other miscellaneous material they could find. When Cerruti visited Teresa de la Guerra, he was especially concerned with obtaining the papers of her late husband, William Hartnell, who had served as inspector of the missions in the late 1830s.

Private individuals proved to be another rich source. People who had held political or military office in Spanish or Mexican California sometimes ended up with copies of important official documents. These were often kept with other family papers in trunks or in the corners of houses throughout the decades after the American invasion. Mariano Guadalupe Vallejo had collected an extensive number of such documents, and acquiring them was the principal object of Cerruti's 1874 sojourn in Sonoma. Savage also inquired after such documents at virtually every stage of his 1877 to 1878 journey. A major purpose of Savage's visit to Santa Bárbara, where he spoke with Apolinaria Lorenzana and Angustias de la Guerra, was to find out what official documents the important de la Guerra family might still have in its possession.

The many Anglo-Americans who had settled in California in the 1820s and afterward were generally engaged in some form of commerce, and their records, from Thomas O. Larkin and others, were eagerly sought by Bancroft. When Cerruti and Vallejo visited Josefa Carrillo in 1875, they were principally seeking the business records of her late husband, Henry Fitch.

Given this focus on various sorts of textual documents, one has to be impressed with the major commitment that Bancroft and his staff made to oral history. As we have seen, Cerruti initiated his interviews on his 1874 trip to Sonoma. He continued interviewing until July 1876, when he conversed with Félix Buelna in San Francisco. In all, he conducted eighteen interviews. Six were with women: Isidora Filomena, Rosalía Vallejo, Dorotea Valdez, María Antonia Rodríguez, Teresa de la Guerra, and Josefa Carrillo. Vicente Gómez's first interview was in March 1875 with Florencio Serrano in Monterey. He interviewed for two years, ending with his

June 1877 conversation with Juan Bojorques in Santa Clara. He conducted a total of ten interviews. One was with a woman: Catarina Avila. Thomas Savage's first interview was with Marcelino García at Salinas in March 1877, and his final one was a conversation with Justo Larios in June 1878 at Gilroy. In all, he conducted fifty interviews with Californios. Six were with women: Eulalia Pérez, Juana Machado, Felipa Osuna, Apolinaria Lorenzana, Angustias de la Guerra, and María Inocenta Pico.[8]

The interview process itself introduced another set of filters. Cerruti, Gómez, and Savage generally came to the interviews they conducted with a series of prepared questions. The men consciously attempted to direct all aspects of the conversation.[9] The women were, to put it mildly, not invited to engage in free association! The quality and scope of the questions depended on how much the men knew about the women and how thoroughly they had prepared themselves for the encounter: knowledge and preparation varied tremendously. When Savage sat down with Angustias de la Guerra, for instance, it is obvious that he was well acquainted with many of the events in which her family had been involved and about which he wished to question her. Similarly, it is quite clear that Gómez had been instructed to ask Catarina Avila about the 1848 murders at Mission San Miguel. But it is equally clear that on other occasions the interviewer was not expecting a particular interview and was unprepared for it. For instance, Cerruti was not ready for either Rosalía Vallejo or Dorotea Valdez. As we have seen, Juana Machado and Felipa Osuna were suggested as subjects to Savage only after he had already arrived in San Diego. Similarly, Savage interviewed Apolinaria Lorenzana because Angustias de la Guerra, who was unavailable to speak to him herself that day, suggested that he talk to her. All in all, it appears that seven of the thirteen interviews were prepared beforehand.

It is not always easy to discern the actual shape of the conversation. In only two of the testimonio transcripts, those of Rosalía Vallejo and Dorotea Valdez, were the actual questions included. Even so, it is often possible to reconstruct the general direction of the sessions. For instance, at times the women said that they "remembered well" a certain person or event. At these points, they were most likely responding to a specific question: Do you remember so-and-so, or when such-and-such happened? At other points, an abrupt change in subject probably indicates that the interviewer posed a new question.

The transcripts at times reveal the women breaking through the boundaries within which their interviewers sought to limit the conversation. At times we can hear the women objecting to a new theme because they had not yet finished what they wanted to say about a particular topic. For instance, at one point Angustias de la Guerra told Savage that she was "returning to Father Martínez," indicating that she had not yet finished her remarks about him and was not ready to proceed to the new subject he had introduced. At other points, we can hear the women expanding their answers to questions posed by the interviewers, squeezing in topics they wanted to talk about. Thus Isidora Filomena was able to speak at length on the social role of women in her native group.[10] Likewise, Josefa Carrillo took a simple question about Spanish place names and used it to denounce those who had taken over her rancho. Each of these women managed to establish her own voice and impart her own tone as she was being interviewed.

Another filter between the women's words and what we read today came when the interviewer put the words down on paper. After the interview was concluded the interviewer returned to wherever he was staying and wrote up the session. Here the two major interviewers, Cerruti and Savage, differed in what they did. Cerruti apparently kept some notes during the interview itself and tried to polish them relatively soon after the interview. He described his procedure when he recounted his first full day in Sonoma: "About eleven o'clock I repaired to the sitting room, where I wrote in intelligible shape the items I had received from Messrs. Piña and Fitch on board the *Antelope*." The quest for an "intelligible shape" no doubt affected not only how he phrased his narrative, but what he decided was significant enough to be included. Savage, on the other hand, tried to take down a more word-for-word version of what his informants were telling him during the interview. This was how Savage, referring to himself in the third person, described his sessions with José María Amador: "During five or six days he related all events in which he participated, and much other important matter, forming a volume of 229 pages—every word of which was written down by Savage, who for that purpose rode out to the ranch in the morning and returned in the evening to town." But Savage was not a professional stenographer, and as he was trying to make his pen keep pace with the conversation, his own evaluation of what was significant must have influenced which words he put to paper.

The final format of Cerruti's and Savage's transcripts differed dramatically. In Cerruti's interviews, the narrator's voice is that of the interviewer himself. He generally inserted the women's comments into an essay which he composed, and in which he was the major actor. Thus the women's voices were often rendered in the third person: "She told me" or "She said."

But Cerruti often shifted voices within his accounts. That tactic could at times render his prose difficult to follow: most often the "I" referred to himself, the narrator, but sometimes, without any indication he was about to do so, he might quote a woman directly. Before long, the essay would shift again, the "I" once more referring to the narrator.

Savage generally spent a page or two introducing the interview. He described something about the women and the scene, revealed whether anyone else was present, and offered any other details he deemed relevant. Then, in a separate part of the document, he offered his subject's words in the first person. Thus his first interview with a woman began, "I, Eulalia Pérez, was born at the presidio of Loreto in Baja California." The interviewee then proceeded to answer the questions posed by Savage. It is probably the case that when we read a Savage interview, we are closer to the subject's original words than in a Cerruti interview. But "closer" is a relative term, and this is not to say that Savage gave the women free rein. He did not. He posed the questions and tried to dictate the content and pace of the process. The Pérez interview illustrates the process well. In the conversation, it was generally Savage who determined the subjects of the discussion, the amount of time and emphasis given to certain topics, as well as the overall tone. Eulalia Pérez did not talk about whatever came to her mind. She responded to the concrete questions posed to her by Savage and relayed to her by her daughter María del Rosario, who was present. In his "Report of Labors," Savage was explicit about the scope of his questions. He said that Eulalia "was questioned only upon mission life, characteristics of padres, manner and customs of the Californians in her early days, and other topics like these, upon which she could give information, as relating to her daily duties when still able to perform them. With a little perseverance, for the old lady was almost as deaf as a door post, straight answers were received, and they threw considerable light upon such subjects."

A final filter was constructed in San Francisco, when the interviews were again copied, this time at the Bancroft Library. Cerruti and Savage tried to make the final versions as clear and as polished as they could. In the process they no doubt changed some words and the sequence of others, and there is no way of telling how much the final version that was deposited in the library deviated from the conversation that occurred months earlier. In sum, there were at least three stages in a Cerruti interview: his notes during the conversation, his polishing of these notes in his room, and their final copying in San Francisco. Similarly, there were at least three steps to a Savage interview: taking down the transcripts while he was interviewing,

A drawing of Hubert Howe Bancroft's study in San Francisco. Courtesy of The Bancroft Library, University of California, Berkeley

composing the introductions, and making a final copy at the library. Thus what we have to work with now is three steps removed from what the women actually said.

Filters were not an element of the interview process alone. All of these women had lived full lives since the events they described in the interviews had happened—thirty years or more before. Their culture had been turned upside down. They were living, as one Californio wrote in 1851, as "foreigners in their own land."[11] These experiences no doubt affected not only what they remembered, but how they remembered. Some of the women were quite advanced in years when they participated in this project, and as we all know, memories fade with age and time.

Preserving the Voices
Despite the inherent limitations of the process that produced the testimonios, we believe that these interviews, if they are used critically, are wonderful sources for the history of early California. The introductions, notes, and appendices we have included in this volume are intended to help readers approach these documents in a discerning fashion and appreciate the strong voices of the women interviewed.

Over the past decade, writers and scholars, working from a variety of perspectives, have begun to employ women's narratives such as these.[12] The thirteen testimonios presented here have begun to appear in such endeavors as California studies, women's studies, gender studies, ethnic studies, and literary studies.[13] We hope that these translations can be of assistance to writers and scholars in these different disciplines. Just as important, we hope that anyone interested in California's heritage will gain, through these women's voices, a deeper appreciation of the range of personalities and experiences that have helped to create the world we now inhabit. Our aim has been to preserve these women's voices both accurately and fully.

Accuracy is a relative term. Experienced translators know that there is no such thing as a perfect translation, since the words of every language contain nuances that can never be mechanically transported into another tongue, even when the dictionary meaning of two words in two different languages is exactly the same. All living languages are constantly changing. The Spanish spoken by these women in the 1870s was not the same as that spoken by their grandparents in Sinaloa, Sonora, or Baja California. Nor is the English that we currently speak in the United States the same as that spoken over a century ago. Thus, a translation that may have been appropriate for 1900 or 1940 may not be so fitting for 2006. In the translations that follow we have attempted to render the living language these women spoke in the 1870s into the living language we speak today. At the same time, we have attempted to preserve the individuality of the speakers. The Spanish in which Isidora Filomena spoke to Cerruti was quite different from the Spanish in which Angustias de la Guerra addressed Savage. We have tried to represent those differences in our English versions.

Unfortunately, past English renditions of these women's words have sometimes been marred by actual mistranslations. The most spectacular incidence of this occurred in a 1956 translation of Angustias de la Guerra's testimonio. In that text, she was made to say that she and the other women of California favored the American takeover in 1846. What she actually said was that they opposed it![14] In other cases, we have discovered that sentences, even entire paragraphs, of the women's words have been left out of some English translations. We have attempted to rectify those omissions in the present volume. Finally, two of the testimonios, those of Rosalía Vallejo and Dorotea Valdez, were transcribed by the interviewer directly into English. For reasons which we detail in our introduction to these two testimonios, we doubt that Cerruti's English was a reasonable reflection of those two women's words. So we have "retranslated" them.

Those who compare our translations with earlier efforts will soon discover many instances in which we have chosen to translate words or phrases much differently than previous scholars did. We do so with humility and respect. We are quite aware that we are building on the efforts of those who have gone before us. Anyone who has spent even a small amount of time translating any type of document knows that this is an art, not a science. Inaccuracies exist in even the most competent and creative efforts, and we do not regard ourselves as immune from this danger. However, we believe that the translations in these pages are the most accurate overall renderings in English of the words which these thirteen women spoke in Spanish to their interviewers. At the same time, we are acutely aware that, as translators, we are ourselves inevitably filtering them.

A Well-Rounded History

We wish to present these words as fully as we can. So that the testimonios can be more completely understood, we seek to enable readers to appreciate the historical context that these women took for granted.

These testimonios ranged over the entire scope of California's history during the late Spanish and the Mexican periods; virtually every significant military and political event from 1818 to 1847 was mentioned. Starting with the privateer Bouchard's raid in 1818, the women spoke of the transfer of power from Spain to Mexico and the soldiers' resentment of the new Mexican government's inability to pay its soldiers in California consistently. They spoke out about many conflicts between the indigenous Californians and the Mexican authorities and settlers. These included the Chumash revolt of 1824, the revolt of Estanislao in 1829, and a series of Indian attacks in the San Diego area in the late 1830s. They detailed the struggles over secularization of the missions in the 1830s. They offered accounts of the sectional conflicts between northern and southern Alta California in the 1830s and 1840s. Finally, they remembered a series of occurrences connected with the American invasion of 1846 and its aftermath.

All these events formed the backbone of Bancroft's *History of California.* Yet the women tended to recall them in a manner that insisted that the deeds of the military and political elites were inextricably linked with a vibrant social universe peopled by women, children, and ordinary folks. The California that emerged from these testimonios was a complicated place in which the familial intersected with the political and in which the public sphere interacted with the private sphere to create a different kind of society than the one the Americans had brought.

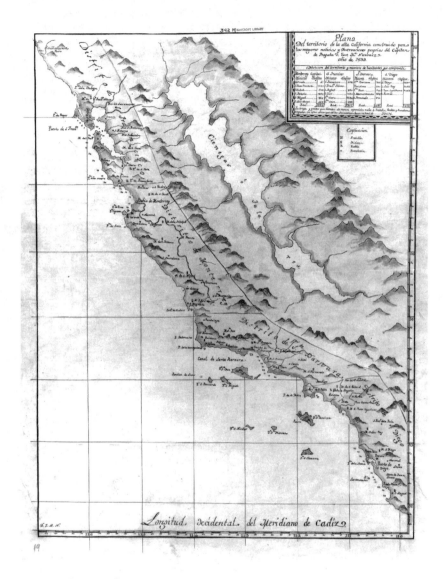

This map of Alta California in 1830, drawn by José María Narváez, depicts the land described by the Californios that Bancroft's staff interviewed in the 1870s. Courtesy of The Bancroft Library, University of California, Berkeley

These testimonios presented California as a place that could not be understood by the conventional categories that were already beginning to dominate the historical understanding of the state's experiences. For instance, María Inocenta Pico argued that secularization could not be understood simply as a power struggle between the missionaries and the rancheros for control of the land. In her telling, at least some of the ranchero families understood that the destruction of the mission infrastructure, which many of the appointed civil administrators oversaw during the late 1830s, hurt people who were trying to set themselves up as rancheros. She also argued that the 1837 movement against Governor Nicolás Gutiérrez was not due to a single cause, but to a complex interplay of local, regional, and personal issues. And even though governors José María Echeandía and Manuel Victoria were on opposite sides of most issues, especially the fate of the missions, Angustias de la Guerra found reasons to be critical of aspects of both of their administrations.

Nowhere was this complexity more manifest than in the women's memories of the American conquest. In their accounts, the lines between those who opposed and those who did not oppose the invasion and its aftermath were constantly shifting. Felipa Osuna recalled how the Californio community in the south was split. Suspicions were rife and recriminations abounded on all sides. Juana Machado remembered that her brother served as a guide for a group of American soldiers. Dorotea Valdez stated that the regular American troops who took Monterey in 1846 were well behaved, but that other American fighters acted "more like thieves than soldiers." Angustias de la Guerra despised the conquest, but in her very next breath felt compelled to say that California was in very bad shape before the invasion.

The way the women reckoned time spotlights the social context within which they recounted historic events, and it enriches history for readers today. Eulalia Pérez remembered that she was almost ready to give birth to a child when an earthquake destroyed the church at San Juan Capistrano. Juana Machado remembered her parents crying when her father was forced to cut his hair when California became a part of Mexico. Angustias de la Guerra said that she was confused about some dates around 1839, but she remembered that when she arrived in Monterey, Juan Bautista Alvarado was already married. She also recalled that she had just given birth when she hid a Californio soldier from the Americans.

In keeping with their social acuity, these women were aware of the ways in which their gender limited their public influence. Juana Machado attributed the success of an Indian attack on Rancho Jamul in 1838 to the reluctance of the male *mayordomo* to believe two women's warnings that an attack was planned. Angustias de la Guerra remembered that she and Adelaida Estrada had doubts about the story of Archibald Gillespie, an American military agent whom consul Thomas O. Larkin was parading around Monterey in 1846 as a merchant who had come to California to recover his health. They brought their suspicions to the military commander, José Castro, but he told them that "we were thinking badly of a man who was ill." According to her, Castro "accused us, and all women, of thinking badly of others, which according to him was something that women did much more so than men." Much of the obvious pride that Eulalia Pérez and Apolinaria Lorenzana exhibited in their interviews with Savage stemmed from their awareness that their own leadership roles in the missions contradicted the normal limitations on women's influence.

At times, such reflections could lead to criticism of the society in which the interviewees had grown up. When she was discussing education, for instance, María Inocenta Pico told Savage, "Many girls did not complete even...basic subjects because their mothers would take them out of school almost always to marry them off. The bad custom existed of marrying off very young girls, whenever men asked for their hands."

The women could also be critical of the society that had replaced their own. Dorotea Valdez told Cerruti that the California birthrate had dramatically declined since the Americans arrived. She was sure she knew why: "Ever since the Americans took possession of this country, sterility has become very common. The American women are very fond of visiting doctors and swallowing medicines. This is a sin that God does not forgive." The women interviewed were aware of Americans' negative views of Californios and Mexicans, and this sometimes sharpened their criticism. Teresa de la Guerra reported that many Californios objected to the book on Mexican California written by her brother-in-law Alfred Robinson. They deemed it a biased effort in which the author had distorted events. Her sister Angustias argued that some of the criticism being directed against Governor Alvarado was unwarranted.

The clearest criticism came from Teresa de la Guerra. She disputed the American claim of having brought progress and civilization to the west coast of the continent, arguing forcefully that Mexican California had already been civilized by the time the foreigners arrived; those who thought that the Californios had "lived in the woods" were arrogant and mistaken.

Each of the women whose testimonios we present here would have vigorously agreed with Teresa de la Guerra's assessment. They rarely engaged in sentimental nostalgia, yet they all remembered Mexican California as a basically good and decent place. The domestic sphere was integrated into public life. The social order was not so acquisitive as the one which had been so dramatically forced on them by the gold rush. Life in the world they had lost was fuller and richer than was life in post-conquest California.

We feel privileged that we have been able to come into contact with these women and humbled to be able to recover and preserve their voices. One of us learned Spanish and English at the same time as a young child; she spoke English at home with her parents, and Spanish at her grandmother's house across the street. Listening over the past few years to the voices of these Californio women, she would often hear the voice of her grandmother, who was born in Cuba and came to the United States as an adult. Her English was never perfect, but she would say to her granddaughter, "*Me puedo defender en inglés*"—I can take care of myself in English. These thirteen women certainly tried to take care of themselves, their families, and their histories with these testimonios. We hope that we have taken good care of their words.

The Present Volume
Finally, a word about the organization of this book. We have decided to present these interviews in the chronological order in which they were given. This order had a great deal to do with the questions which the men posed to the women, and it affected the structure and tone of what the women wanted to say. For instance, Cerruti's negative experience with Rosalía Vallejo affected the manner in which he interviewed Dorotea Valdez and María Antonia Rodríguez over the next few days. Similarly, Savage received unexpectedly rich information from Juana Machado, and this raised his expectations for Felipa Osuna. When her testimonio turned out to be focused differently than Machado's had been, he discounted her views. In sum, we believe that ordering the testimonios in a chronological fashion offers the best way to appreciate the full range of perspectives which the women offered.

In the introductions to many of the testimonios, we have included abbreviated genealogical trees. We hope that these diagrams will make it easier for readers to locate these women as they tended to locate themselves, as heirs to a rich tradition. The diagrams are not intended to be complete; rather we intend them to illustrate the points made in our introductory remarks, which often highlight the inseparability of the family histories of these women and the historic events of their lifetimes.

In our appendices we have attempted to provide additional information to assist the reader in understanding the testimonios. We have included excerpts from Henry Cerruti's manuscript "Ramblings in California," which was edited in 1953 by Margaret Mollins and Virginia E. Thickens and published by the Friends of The Bancroft Library. We reproduce the sections of the manuscript in which Cerruti detailed the interviews he conducted with three of the women: Isidora Filomena, Rosalía Vallejo, and María Antonia Rodríguez. As mentioned above, we have also reproduced the entire manuscript that Savage wrote describing his efforts to obtain testimonios and documents. Since this manuscript has not been previously published, we have reproduced it in its entirety.

We also provide in the appendices the original Cerruti versions of his interviews with Rosalía Vallejo and Dorotea Valdez. Since we have redone those interviews, we thought that readers might be interested in seeing the original documents from which we worked. As for the Spanish pages of the testimonios, The Bancroft Library hopes eventually to place them, and many of the other documents which Bancroft's staff transcribed, on the Web.

We have also provided biographical sketches of many of the figures to whom the women refer in their testimonios. Some of these figures appear in more than one testimonio, and we think that a set of sketches will allow the reader the most straightforward access to this information. We have also included a chronology in which we summarize some important events in the history of Mexican California, a brief time line which covers other events, a list of governors of Mexican Alta California, a glossary, and a bibliography to guide readers who wish to delve more deeply into the testimonios.

Testimonios

Isidora Filomena

INTRODUCTION

When he arrived in Sonoma for the first time, at the end of March 1874, Henry Cerruti took a room at the Union Hotel on the plaza. He spent his first few weeks visiting Mariano Guadalupe Vallejo at his home, attempting to gradually charm him into cooperating with Hubert Howe Bancroft. During his free time Cerruti wandered through the town looking for people to interview. He also struck up a friendship with Mariano's brother Salvador.

Over these first few weeks, Vallejo appeared alternately accommodating and resistant. Around April 8, Cerruti went to interview Isidora Filomena, accompanied by Salvador Vallejo and Captain M. A. McLaughlin. Isidora was the widow of Mariano Guadalupe Vallejo's important ally during the 1830s and 1840s, Suisun chief Sem-Yeto. The chief was better known among the Mexicans by his baptismal name of Francisco Solano. He had been dead for over two decades, and Isidora was living close to the Vallejo residence in a house lent to her by the family. Cerruti did not indicate in his memoirs whether he or one of the Vallejo brothers had first suggested interviewing Isidora. Nor did he state what he intended to try to learn from her.

Cerruti knew two things about Isidora. First, she was less than friendly to the Americans who had taken over the land in 1846. Their arrival had meant the end of the system under which her husband had become one of the most powerful men in northern California. Second, she was widely reported to have a weakness for alcohol. Cerruti therefore made sure to equip himself with a bottle of brandy. His belief that alcohol would enable him to control the conversation and wrest secrets from his interviewees

Salvador Vallejo, brother of Mariano Guadalupe Vallejo, befriended Cerruti soon after he arrived in Sonoma. Courtesy of the California Historical Society, FN-36283

was especially strong when he was talking to Indians and to those he considered to be lower-class Californios.

We do not know what her house looked like. Cerruti called it a "hut." When she let them in, Cerruti reported, "I did my best to engage her in conversation, but to no purpose. She was rather shy." Vallejo spoke up and inaccurately assured her that Cerruti was "one of her people, and an innate enemy" of the North Americans. That seemed to lessen her apprehension, and Cerruti immediately offered her some of the brandy.

Isidora frankly admitted that she was living in very poor conditions. Cerruti noted this and took advantage of it. Fascinated by her accessories and wardrobe, he determined to obtain parts of it cheaply. At one point during the interview, as Isidora was describing the jewelry the Indian women wore before the arrival of the Europeans, he convinced her, through means he did not disclose, to sell some of her jewelry to him. At the conclusion of the interview, he saw an opportunity to come away with an even larger prize. He stated:

> When we were about to depart, the Princess Solano went to her sleeping room and presently came forth holding in her hand a bag containing several strings of beads made out of bones and shells, a belt about six inches wide made from the same material, and many other articles of adornment worn by Indian women in ancient days. She assured me that those things constituted the whole of her wedding dress. I offered to purchase the whole and laid a ten-dollar gold piece on the table, but she laughed at me and felt indignant at my presumption. Nothing daunted, I offered her another drink and begged her to introduce me to her son, who happened to be in the courtyard cleaning fish. She called Bill—the name of the young prince—and he came forward. I had the opportunity of conversing with him, and I found him an intelligent man about thirty years of age, well learned in the art of reading and writing, tolerably well versed in the mysteries of the Catholic Church, of which he is a constant attendant, strongly in favor of local option, and always ready to censure his mother, who is a decided worshiper of Bacchus. Bill has a few thousand dollars deposited in the San Francisco banks, but being very fond of his aged mother, he prefers to remain by her and watch over her in her old age. He greatly deprecates the drunken habits of the Princess but is powerless in effecting a reform.
>
> When Bill returned to his fish-cleaning business I offered the Princess another drink and again broached the subject of selling me her wedding dress. I offered her twenty-four dollars and the rest of the brandy contained in the bottle. She accepted my offer, and I thus became the happy possessor of a sacred relic of days gone by. Having paid the cash and noted in my portfolio the story of the Princess, I retraced my steps towards the residence of Salvador Vallejo, thanked him for having been so condescending with me, and then went home, where I wrote down in an intelligible style the record of my interview with Isidora and her son.

In the midst of such a set of intrusions, with three men crowding her house, deceiving her about the purpose of the visit, plying her with brandy, and casting greedy eyes over the few prized possessions that remained to her, Isidora gave her interview. As was the case with all Cerruti's interviews, her words were embedded within a larger narrative composed by the interviewer. The last two paragraphs are openly Cerruti's own. In them he described her appearance and implicated Salvador Vallejo in her "sale" of the wedding dress to him. He also rendered explicit the judgment which no doubt guided him during the encounter: that she was not a "woman of esteem" and that the respect which she did deserve stemmed mainly from the deeds of her husband.

Faced with such an inhospitable environment, Isidora's performance was truly remarkable. Cerruti's major interest was the career and exploits of Solano, who had helped Mariano Guadalupe Vallejo bring "civilization" to north-central California. At points in the interview we can hear Isidora responding to specific questions about her husband: How were Solano's warriors armed when they went out to fight? What game did the men hunt? What were your people's celebrations like? Yet time and again, Isidora turned the conversation in directions she chose. She described her own influence on her husband's decisions. She placed the experiences of the female members of her group in the foreground as she recounted what the women did, how they dressed, and what they ate. She made clear that, even in her reduced state, she could still direct affairs. For instance, she would send Bill, whom Cerruti had mistaken for her son but who was in fact her husband in a rather loveless marriage, to San Rafael to gather *amole* (soaproot). She spoke all of this in Spanish, a language which was not her own, but which she had learned after she had begun to live with Solano. In the transcript of the interview, Cerruti tried to reproduce her broken Spanish, which he patronizingly termed "charming."[1]

The woman who was able to maintain such initiative had already lived a very eventful life. Her account reached back almost to the beginning of the Mexican experience in the far northern frontier of Alta California. Mission San Francisco Solano, at Sonoma, was founded in 1823. It was intended to declare to the Russians who had established themselves at Fort Ross, and to their indigenous allies in the region, that the Mexican authorities did not intend to cede control of the area. The Mexican governor of Alta California, Luis Antonio Argüello, convinced Father José Altimira, who was unhappy in San Francisco's cold and damp Mission Dolores, to start a new mission. Father Altimira did so without bothering to obtain approval from his religious superiors. Although the Franciscan leadership fumed about this, there was little they could do. They did not want to begin their relationship with the new Mexican government in California on a sour note. So the mission continued to exist. The surrounding peoples were at times quite hostile. The mission was burned in 1827, underscoring the need for a more consistent military presence. In 1833, Mariano Guadalupe Vallejo, who was then stationed at the San Francisco presidio, was ordered to begin plans to establish a military outpost in the region. Vallejo had gained a reputation as a frontier fighter by undertaking a campaign against Estanislao and his band of rebel Indians in the Central Valley four years earlier.[2]

When Vallejo began to move into the region, the indigenous population of the immediate vicinity consisted largely of Suisun people. At the beginning of the nineteenth century, the Suisun homeland north and east of San Pablo Bay served as a protective zone for peoples east of the San Francisco Bay who were fleeing the advance of the mission frontier. When their southern neighbors, the Carquins, moved to Mission San Francisco in 1809, the Suisuns found themselves directly facing Spanish power. An expedition led by Gabriel Moraga fought with them the next year. Moraga brought some Suisun children back with him to Mission San Francisco and they were baptized. By 1815 most of the Suisuns had moved to San Francisco, and the last group of eleven members of the tribe located there by 1821. Scm-Yeto was one of the first children to enter the mission at San Francisco. He was baptized and given the name Francisco Solano on July 24, 1810. The priest who administered the sacrament estimated that he was about eleven years old.[3]

The Suisuns were moved back north in 1824 so that they could form part of the core population of the new mission of San Francisco Solano. By 1826 Francisco Solano was one of the mission Indian *alcaldes*. He was married in 1827 to Helen Saquenmupi of the Aloquiomis, who lived at Pope Valley. She died in 1830 and three years later he married Guida Coulás of the Topayto group from the Lake Berryessa area. Solano was still an *alcalde* in 1836. The next year he was listed first in a census that was taken in October. He headed an eighteen-person household and was recorded as a widower. He married again in 1839. This time his bride was a twelve-year-old girl, María del Rosario Ullumole. No record of Solano's marriage to Isidora appears to exist. The remarkable number of deaths in Solano's family illustrates the high mortality rates suffered by many northern California native groups in the 1830s and 1840s, as introduced diseases, such as smallpox and measles, took a frightful toll.[4]

Solano's prominence in the 1837 census most likely indicates that he and his group of Suisuns had become important allies of Vallejo by that time. The precise nature of the various military campaigns which Vallejo undertook against the northern Indians is difficult to ascertain. The one major source for many of these events is the memoirs that Vallejo provided to Bancroft in the 1870s. In these accounts Vallejo routinely exaggerated the number of Indians against whom he fought, so as to present himself as the heroic and embattled civilizer of the northern frontier. But it seems clear that after 1836 Solano did assist Vallejo in campaigns against a number of Sacramento Valley groups, such as the Yolotoy and Satiyomi. In her testimonio, Isidora associated her being brought to Solano with hostilities between the Mexicans and the Satiyomi; her capture and delivery to him may have resulted from one of these campaigns.

One effect of the growing Suisun and Mexican power was that a large number of Indian laborers were conscripted to work for the Mexicans, especially at Vallejo's nascent ranching operation in Petaluma. For a time, Solano became something of a labor contractor, and he sold some Indian children to rancheros in the San Pablo area. However, Vallejo forced him to cease working independently, and he generally worked together with the Vallejo brothers to obtain Indian workers.

Until the American invasion, Vallejo and Solano were close allies. Solano skillfully positioned himself as the intermediary between the indigenous population and Vallejo. The epidemics which ravaged the area in the 1830s devastated many groups, including those that opposed the Mexicans, and probably increased Solano's personal power.[5] Vallejo, in turn, honored the chief by outfitting a special honor guard of over forty Indians for him. He also presented him with a special horse and an elaborate uniform. He once took Solano and some of his men to Monterey, in order to impress the Mexican authorities with the prowess of his private army. He was also instrumental in obtaining for Solano a grant of land in the Suisun area. The grant probably consisted of a former mission rancho named Santa Eulalia. The petition for the grant spoke of Solano as "chief of the unconverted Indians and born chief of the Suisuns." It stated that "said lands belong to him by hereditary right from his ancestors, and he is actually in possession of it; but he wishes to revalidate his rights in accordance with the existing laws of our republic and of the order of colonization decreed by the Supreme Government." Solano constructed an adobe house on the land, ran some cattle there, and planted some crops as well. When the grant was legally finalized in 1842, Solano sold the land to Vallejo. This was most likely Vallejo's intention in the first place. Solano continued to live there whenever he wanted, and he was given the title of Vallejo's *mayordomo*.[6]

All the while Solano continued to campaign with Vallejo. They organized military expeditions into the Napa Valley and Mendocino in 1843. Vallejo also used Solano to underline his continuing preeminence as more Anglo-Americans arrived in northern California in the 1840s. In 1844, for instance, Englishman Edward Bale, a resident of Sonoma, shot at Salvador Vallejo and then sought refuge in the house of *alcalde* Jacob P. Leese. Solano and a group of his men stormed the house and seized him, ostensibly to lynch him. Vallejo ostentatiously refused to allow that, thereby making the point that Solano's warriors answered only to him.[7]

The Bear Flag rebellion and the American takeover put an end to the world in which this partnership had flourished. No Indian could be a significant public figure in gold rush California, and Solano dropped out of sight. Nonetheless, in 1850 Vallejo, then a member of the state legislature, convinced that body to name a county in the new state after Solano. Vallejo referred to him as "the great chief of the tribes originally denominated 'Suisuns' and scattered over the western side of the [Sacramento] River." But Solano's whereabouts at the time were either unknown or unadvertised. In 1852 Vallejo described him to the Land Commission as "the greatest and principal chief of the whole frontier…civilized and friendly to the Mexican government and the white people." Manuel Vaca told the same commission that the chief had died the year before. Local lore says he died at the site of one of his old encampments, Yulyul, near Rockville. As her testimonio indicates, Isidora remarried after his death. The time and place of her own death are uncertain.[8]

Narrative of the Interview I Had with Isidora, Widow of Prince Solano

MY NAME IS ISIDORA. I am ninety years old. The Indians who knew me when I was the wife of Chief Solano called me "Princess" and they still treat me like a princess. And even some of the white men, such as Remigio Berreyesa, Gonzalo Ramírez, Captain Salvador Vallejo, and many others who from time to time come to Lacryma Montis to visit us still call me Princess.[9] They remember that whenever my husband would get angry, I would do everything possible to calm him down.

Although I was young, I, like the other Indians of my tribe, worshiped the god named Puis, who was a mortal being like myself. He dressed all in

Mariano Guadalupe Vallejo and a native woman at Sonoma. Courtesy of The Bancroft Library, University of California, Berkeley

white feathers but wore black feathers on his head. My people worshiped him as if he were a real god.

Later, I married the great Solano, prince of the Suysunes, Topaytos, Yoloitos, and Chuructas. He became prince of the Topaytos after he conquered them.[10] During his lifetime he inspired fear in everyone, white men and Indians, with the exception of his friend General Guadalupe Vallejo. Solano always refused offers of friendship from Sutter, Yount, and many other blonde men who wanted to be his friends.

The priest Guias (Prince Solano always called Reverend Fray Lorenzo de la Concepción Quijas by the name Guias), who baptized me and gave me the name Isidora Filomena, taught me how to be very charitable toward the poor, very gentle with my husband, and very compassionate toward the prisoners.* This is why I prevented my husband from killing enemy prisoners after he had conquered all of his enemies with the eight thousand men he led. Back then, it was customary to tie the prisoners to trees and shoot arrows at them. I told him, "Leave them with Vallejo. He will make them work the land." Fr. Guias advised the same thing. Solano followed our advice and many poor souls were spared.

I belonged to Solano before I married him and even before I was baptized. I am not a Suysun like he is. I belong to the Churucto tribe.[11] My father's tribe lived near Cache Creek. I do not know the name of the county to which it belongs today. On a trip Solano took there to do some negotiating, he stole me. My father and many Satiyomi went after him, but they could not catch him.

I have already gone downhill. I drink a lot of liquor because I do not have very much land filled with cattle. The blonde men stole everything. They left nothing for poor Isidora, who married Bill after Solano died. Bill is not a very loving man. I did not give birth again. With Solano I gave birth to eight little ones. They all died except for one son named Joaquín, who works the land to make a living. He usually gives me twenty pesos. Commander Vallejo lets me live in a house with some land for free.

When Solano would go off to fight, he would arm his people with flint daggers, flint lances, and flint arrows. All the weapons were made poisonous with herbs. I do not know if there was something else mixed with the herbs. Solano's warriors did not wear a jacket, a shirt, shoes, pants, or a hat. They were not stupid. They wore nothing on their bodies that a white man or another Indian could grab onto. They went into battle buck naked. Only on their head would they put some feathers. The Indians who carried the food would wear an ash-gray feather taken from a wild chicken. The soldiers who fought with lances and arrows would wear white duck feathers. All the chiefs would wear black feathers. In the beginning, Solano would put feathers on his head, but not after all the Indians were ordered to dress like gente de razón. Vallejo gave him a fine weapon and the missionaries gave him a hat and some boots.

We would use our fingers to count, and that is how we counted up to ten. Ten in the Suysun language is pronounced papa cien. We did not have enough fingers to count from ten on up, so we would make piles of sticks. That way we could count up to one hundred. This is how we counted in our Suysun language:

*This footnote was appended to the interview: "He would take communion with brandy and would take a swig to do Mass. He was always drunk."

11

20   panum papa cien
30   punor papa cien
40   emu papa cien
50   etem papa cien
60   cac eta papa cien
70   cala pata papa cien
80   panum buya papa cien
90   eta ele papa cien
100 papa ciem

Before the white men arrived in Soscol, we had lots of food and it was very good and easy to obtain without much work. There were lots of animals to hunt, and the countryside provided lots of wild onions. We called the wild onions *ur*. We also had wild soap that we called *amoles*. It still grows abundantly near San Rafael. I sometimes send Bill there to look for it. That soap cleans better than any soap made by man. It removes all stains and does not burn your body or make your skin hurt.

In my land, everyone of my race had very red skin like mine. All the women were very tall. I was perhaps one of the shortest. Many of us live to be more than one hundred years old. The women's hair never turns white. Men's hair changes color. Our Indians do not have large feet or large hands like the white Germans or the Mexicans. They are tall and their feet and hands are small. They always go barefoot. My tribe and many others would eat quite a bit of fish. One could find many varieties of fish in our rivers. But the fish that was most abundant was the type called salmon. We did not always catch fish with nets. Many times, when the river would be low, we would place poles in the middle of the river and we could catch lots of fish that way. Some of the fish would be eaten fresh and the rest would be dried and put away for the winter.

When the white man arrived, I did not know what liquor was. But Sutter, who was a *gente de razón*, would send *Joaquinero* Indians to trade liquor for hides, pelts, and dried fish. Sutter had an Indian wife. She was not from California. She was a Kanaka Indian who arrived with him on a ship. I do not like the white man very much because he is very tricky and a thief. My *compadre* Peralta and friend Bernales had many cattle. Sutter tricked them and took everything but paid for nothing.[12]

We would have very nice dances. The men would dance with men. The women would dance with women. The men danced naked. After the *gente de razón* came, the women wore a skirt. But before, when there were only

María Luisa Emparán, daughter of Mariano Guadalupe Vallejo, displaying some of the Indian artifacts her father collected. Courtesy of the California Historical Society, FN-36285

Indians here, the women only wore a necklace like this one, around their necks. (She showed me the necklace and sold it to me.) They wore a crown of feathers on their heads and a string of beads we call *abalorios*. They wrapped their body from the chest all the way up to the neck with little beads. The larger beads were made into a sash and tied with a shell at the waist. They wore earrings made of feathers and bills from geese and ducks. They would hang the earrings from their ears with a duck bone that had been filed down with flint until it was very thin.

The food we like the most is *topoc* and *huraja*.[13]

Some Suysun women had sashes with feathers. Many wore nothing more than a pelt that hung in front but did not go around their waist. Churucto Indians would paint their bodies with charcoal and red ochre. This paint was not permanent. We all had houses made of tule and we lived comfortably. We liked to bathe very much because cleanliness makes you strong. We would teach little boys how to hunt. Women did the cooking and took care of the little children.

Solano had good astrologers who knew all about herbs and how to cure illnesses.[14] They could also fix broken arms or legs. My people always had white teeth which they cleaned with a stick called *fresno*.

At the same time Cerruti was interviewing the impoverished Isidora, a romanticized view of Chief Solano as an ally of white settlers was prevalent in the Sonoma area. This banner was employed by the Association of Solano Pioneers. Courtesy of The Bancroft Library, University of California, Berkeley

We did not understand the Satiyomi language because all the Indians from the other *rancherías* spoke other languages.

I was not embarrassed to get drunk, because the *gente de razón* taught me how to drink. When the Kanaka Indian and her husband from the big hacienda at the Sacramento River would bring wine, I always got drunk like the *Joaquinero* Indians.

I have written down what ex-Princess Isidora Filomena de Solano has stated in her own words. I did not consider it appropriate to change the phrases she uttered, which were so charming and were offered with such good intentions. She deserves much respect because of the many ways her husband aided the cause of civilization. The princess was born near Cache Creek, where Woodland is presently located. She has a rather smiling face. She is tall—five feet eight inches. Her feet are very small. Her hands would fit a size six pair of gloves. Her nose is flat and her mouth is small. Her teeth are white and rather big. Despite her advanced age, she walks without bending over.

She wears ladies' boots. She could be considered a woman worthy of esteem if, unfortunately, she did not allow herself to be controlled by the vice of drunkenness.

In return for the aid that Solano gave Señor General Vallejo, Isidora lives near Lacryma Montis on land that belongs to Vallejo. At the request of Major Don Salvador Vallejo, Isidora agreed to sell me her wedding outfit, which consists of a shell belt, a row of bones strung together that she wrapped around the upper part of her body all the way up to her neck, and a tuft of feathers that she wore on her forehead. She no longer had the crown of feathers because it burned in a fire at her tule house. Isidora was very attached to these mementos. Whenever the cords that held together the bones and the shells wore out, she would obtain new cords and restring the bones and shell. She valued that outfit very much because Solano had given it to her. She had planned to be buried in it.

> *Enrique Cerruti*
> *Sonoma*
> *April 9, 1874*

The undersigned were present at the interview which Don Enrique Cerruti had with Princess Isidora Solano. After having read the above, we certify that everything the señor has written down is what Isidora Solano said in our presence and in her own words.

> *Salvador Vallejo*
> *M. A. McLaughlin*
> *Sonoma*
> *April 10, 1874*

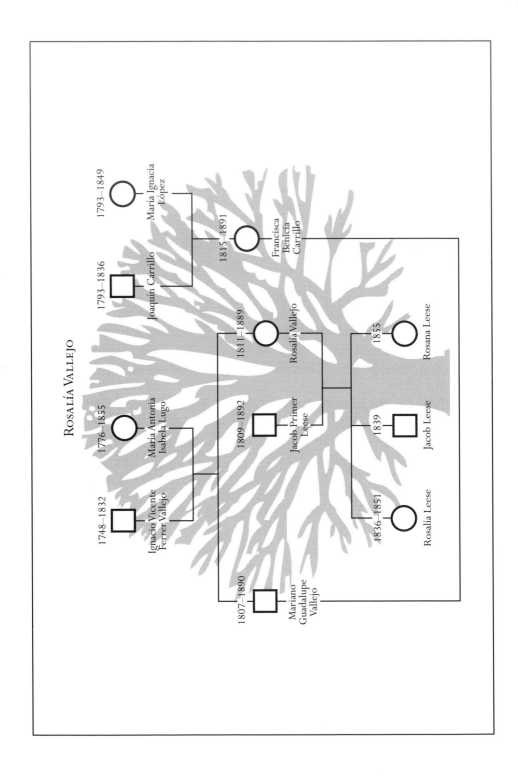

ROSALÍA VALLEJO

1793–1849
María Ignacia López

1793–1836
Joaquín Carrillo

1815–1891
Francisca Benicia Carrillo

1776–1855
María Antonia Isabela Lugo

1748–1832
Ignacio Vicente Ferrer Vallejo

1811–1889
Rosalía Vallejo

1809–1892
Jacob Primer Leese

1807–1890
Mariano Guadalupe Vallejo

1855
Rosana Leese

1839
Jacob Leese

1836–1851
Rosalía Leese

Rosalía Vallejo

INTRODUCTION

*A*fter Vallejo had agreed to cooperate with Bancroft's research, he and Cerruti took a trip to San Francisco to visit Bancroft. Cerruti, armed with several letters of introduction from Vallejo, continued on to the Santa Clara Valley to collect documents and conduct further interviews. The trip did not go as well as he had hoped. Particularly distressing was his visit to the Argüello residence in Santa Clara. The late Luis Antonio Argüello had been the first Mexican governor of Alta California, from 1822 to 1825. Cerruti met with his oldest son, José Ramón. He informed Cerruti that he had burned all of the old papers around the house, since he did not want his abode to be cluttered with that sort of trash. Cerruti was outraged, both by the message and the messenger. He recorded, "Before Mr. Argüello had uttered four words, I felt convinced that I stood in the presence of a self-conceited fool."

Cerruti wired Vallejo and asked him to come down to Santa Clara as rapidly as he could. Vallejo obliged, and he accompanied Cerruti to the Argüello residence. They were graciously received by Soledad Ortega, the former governor's widow. In the course of their conversation she told Vallejo, "Our sweet Castilian tongue has given place to the unpronounceable English jargon—bless the Almighty I have not learned it." She confirmed to both of them that no papers had survived. Thus the visit to the south of the San Francisco Bay seemed to have been a waste of time. Vallejo was no doubt feeling that his prestige was rather on the line, for his first attempt to use his good name to open doors for Bancroft was proving

Rosalía Vallejo. Courtesy of the California Historical Society, FN-25807

pointless. If he were to position himself as the principal link between the Californio community and the Bancroft project, he could not afford to let Cerruti return to San Francisco empty-handed. So he suggested that they continue on to Monterey. There, he assured his companion, they could get some people to agree to interviews and also gather some documents for Bancroft's library.

When the two of them arrived in Monterey, they went to the house of Vallejo's sister Rosalía. As Cerruti recorded the event, his meeting with her did not proceed smoothly. He noticed that the house was decorated with Chinese artifacts: "In her salon I noticed many bureau lamps, tables, pictures, and boxes of Chinese make." This puzzled him, so he questioned her, apparently in a rather brusque manner, about it: "I made bold to inquire the reason why she preferred Chinese furniture to French or American. She replied that in the olden times she was not allowed to choose, that French or American furniture was not to be had in her country, and therefore she had no choice but to furnish her apartments with articles of Chinese make." Rosalía Vallejo, in other words, told him as politely as she could that her financial situation compelled her to make do with very old sets of furniture. She may also have been telling him that she preferred to outfit her house in a manner that affirmed the traditions of her country before the Americans gained control of it.

Apparently oblivious to her implicit messages, Cerruti continued his line of discussion. He recorded, "I engaged Mrs. Leese in conversation for the purpose of discovering her feelings in regard to the changes which had taken place in California since the arrival of the Americans, and to my sorrow I discovered that she disliked the whole race." Rosalía Vallejo's words were sharp. Cerruti summarized them. "She, the sister of the most wealthy Californians, had married an American who had squandered her dowry and then had deserted her, leaving to her charge four young daughters and two sons. She had also, through the decisions of the state courts and through squatters, lost the greater part of her landed property. Aside from these reasons, she had been roughly treated by the Bear Flag party, who in 1846 had imprisoned two of her brothers and her husband and had repeatedly plundered her deposit of provisions." Cerruti then attempted to smooth matters over, but he was forced to admit that he was unsuccessful. "I tried to dispel the prejudices she entertained against the Americans, but my efforts were of no avail. She has suffered too long and too deeply to forget or forgive her wrongs. Her daughters have been educated in the highest branches of grammar and music and speak English very well, but Mrs. Leese always insists that they shall converse in the Spanish language when in her presence. The very sound of the English language causes her to shudder."

The conversation was apparently strained and, perhaps by mutual agreement, it was short. It focused on only one event, the Bear Flag rebellion of 1846. Cerruti already had a good indication of what the Vallejo women thought of this episode. At one of his first meals with the Vallejo family, he had received firsthand evidence that the household had not forgotten the humiliation it had experienced in 1846. He remembered the remarks of Francisca Benicia Carrillo, wife of Mariano Guadalupe Vallejo, at dinner: "The conversation during the meal was quite spirited and occasionally enlivened by some witty repartee of Madame Vallejo, who, whenever a favorable opportunity presented itself, would fire a full broadside at the

Francisca Benicia Carrillo, wife of Mariano GuadalupeVallejo and sister-in-law of Rosalía Vallejo. Courtesy of The Bancroft Library, University of California, Berkeley

Bear Flag crowd, to whom, either justly or unjustly, she attributes the loss of a great part of her husband's estate."

Rosalía Vallejo, who had been in Sonoma when her husband and two brothers were carted away, was not in a forgiving spirit about the revolt. She termed the Bear Flaggers "ruffians" and a "marauding band." She insisted that Frémont's reputation was due to nothing more than "paid writers" and that he was actually a coward. She said that he had sought to have her deliver one of her Indian servants to his soldiers so that they could sexually abuse her.

This was one of the two interviews that Cerruti recorded almost entirely in English. This was hardly a casual decision on his part. Rosalía Vallejo's very last words in the interview were, "Since I have not wanted to have anything to do with them, I have refused to learn their language."This declaration may have reminded him of Soledad Ortega's similar statement just a few days earlier, during his unsatisfactory visit to the Argüello house. In any event, by putting her words into the language which she said she refused to learn, Cerruti was having the last word in this encounter. He literally took her own words away from her.

The English in which Cerruti rendered Rosalía Vallejo's Spanish was stiff and awkward. Part of this was no doubt because English was at least his third language. But his English writing, while it was at times quite overblown, was generally not nearly so stiff as her words came out to be. For instance, after calling Frémont a coward, she was made to say to Cerruti, "Hear me." She undoubtedly said to him something like "*¡Oiga!*" (Listen to me!) Cerruti was probably expressing, either through a gesture, or perhaps frowning or looking at her with an air of obvious disbelief, his skepticism at her characterization of Frémont. In reaction, she snapped back at him. Cerruti's inattention convinced Rosalía Vallejo that nothing would be gained by her continuing to talk to him. "I could tell you about the many crimes committed by the Bear Flag mob," she stated. Then she sarcastically added, "But since I do not wish to detain you any longer, I will end this conversation with this: those hateful men instilled so much hate in me for the people of their race that, even though twenty-eight years have gone by since then, I still cannot forget the insults they heaped upon me."

Cerruti's translation of the interview erased most of that tension. The English which he wrote had the effect of rendering Rosalía Vallejo's statements more abstract and less engaged than they were. We doubt, for instance, that she ever used the Spanish equivalent of "an alarming piece of intelligence" to describe the capture of Sonoma. And we are certain that she would not have employed a tepid word like "misdeeds" to convey her evaluation of the acts of the Bear Flaggers!

Paradoxically, Cerruti's English offers a way back to Rosalía Vallejo's Spanish. At one point he had her say, "Few days after the departure of my husband arrived in Sonoma John C. Frémont." This horrible English syntax, when translated word for word into Spanish, comes out perfectly: "*Pocos días después de la ida de mi marido, llegó a Sonoma John C. Frémont.*" This sentence tells us that Cerruti took Rosalía's Spanish and translated it word for word into formulaic English. This recognition makes it possible to present an English version of her words that we believe represents what she said more accurately than Cerruti's version. We have tried to imagine the Spanish words that lay behind Cerruti's rigid translation. Then we have translated those Spanish words and phrases in a way that better reflects the full engagement, wit, and sarcasm with which we believe Rosalía Vallejo actually spoke.

Rosalía Vallejo had always been a woman of strong opinions and decisive action. In the 1870s, Juan Bautista Alvarado called her "a woman full of spirit." Her antecedents stretched far back into California history. Her maternal grandparents and her father had come to Alta California in 1774, when Fernando de Rivera y Moncada recruited soldiers from northwestern Mexico to accompany him to Monterey. Rivera y Moncada had been appointed military commander of Alta California after Junípero Serra had made an extraordinary trip from Monterey to Mexico City in 1773 and convinced the viceroy to sack Pedro Fages, who had been serving as commander since 1770.[1]

Rosalía Vallejo's mother, María Antonia Isabela Lugo, was born in 1776 in San Luis Obispo. At that time Ignacio Ferrer Vallejo, who had also been recruited for California by Rivera, was serving in the mission guard and working as a carpenter. Ignacio Vallejo married María Antonia Isabela Lugo in 1791, when she was fourteen and a half years old. Rosalía was the couple's tenth child. She was born in Monterey in 1811 and she grew up there. Her father died in 1832, and her brother Mariano Guadalupe, already a rising military officer, became the de facto head of the family.

In 1836 Mariano took her to a Fourth of July party in Yerba Buena, a very small settlement near the tip of the peninsula on San Francisco Bay. At the gathering Rosalía met a recently arrived North American, Jacob P. Leese. She and Leese engaged in a courtship, which Rosalía carried on against her brother's wishes. Her brother apparently wished for a union between her and Timothy Murphy, an Irishman who had arrived in Alta California from Lima in 1828, and who was close to Mariano. The courtship with Leese may have been partly a way of her resisting her brother's dictates.

In February 1837, Mariano Guadalupe Vallejo left Sonoma for Monterey with about fifty soldiers to signal support for Juan Bautista Alvarado, who was attempting to consolidate his position as governor against a group of Californios around Los Angeles and San Diego who opposed him. He remained in Monterey until the middle of April. Rosalía took advantage of his absence to move her own plans forward. According to Alvarado's later reminiscences, she snuck out of Monterey with just two trusted servants and two drivers. She took a series of roundabout roads to Sonoma, where she met up with Leese. They were almost immediately married. Leese said that the marriage "caused a great deal of talk among the people of the country, which was in consequence of its being so sly and not a custom of the country." Vallejo was naturally upset when he arrived home to find the

Jacob P. Leese and Rosalía Vallejo. Their marriage was undertaken against her brother Mariano's wishes. Courtesy of the California Historical Society, FN -25806

newlyweds, but he was powerless to do anything about it. The family calmed him down, and Vallejo soon took Leese under his wing.[2]

Rosalía lived with Leese in Yerba Buena until 1841. Their daughter was the first nonnative child born there. As a brother-in-law of the powerful Vallejo, Leese received a number of land grants. He developed them and tried to take advantage of the important hide and tallow trade. He took possession of Rancho Cañada de Guadalupe, just south of Yerba Buena, in 1839. He later stated, "I first put my cattle on the rancho in December of 1839. At this time I put on about fifty head, but in the following spring I put on about five hundred head." He also remembered that on one occasion before 1842, Rosalía brought the children to the rancho so that they could

Yerba Buena in 1837. RosalíaVallejo and Jacob P. Leese lived there from the time they were married in 1837 until they moved to Sonoma in 1841. Courtesy of the California History Room, California State Library, Sacramento, California

witness the *matanza*. Vallejo also arranged for Leese to receive Rancho Huichica, on the outskirts of Sonoma. He began to place horses and cattle on it in 1839 and built an adobe on the property. Leese and Rosalía and their children moved to Sonoma and occupied the rancho in 1841. At Sonoma they built an adobe on the plaza, and Leese served as *alcalde* of the pueblo.[3]

After the war, they remained in Sonoma for a time, but they moved to Monterey in 1849. Leese had long speculated in real estate in Yerba Buena, and he continued to do so as Yerba Buena evolved into the city of San Francisco. In 1850, Leese swapped property with Thomas O. Larkin; Larkin received some of Leese's San Francisco properties, and Leese received Larkin's Monterey residence, where he, Rosalía, and the children set themselves up. Larkin also purchased an interest in Rancho Huichica.[4]

Leese continued to be involved in various land schemes. The most notable venture was in Baja California, where, in the 1860s, he sought to obtain rights to almost two-thirds of that peninsula. He moved back to New York in 1865, ostensibly to attend to matters relating to this scheme, but it quickly failed. He stayed in the East, in effect abandoning his family. He did not return to California until after his wife died. She had remained in Monterey, living at the Larkin house and supported by her son Jacob. He gave his occupation as "saloon keeper" in the 1870 census, and he was elected county recorder a few years later. Rosalía Vallejo died in 1889.[5]

*AdelaVallejo, the second daughter of Mariano Guadalupe Vallejo and Francisca Benicia
Carrillo. Adela married Levi Cornell Frisbie, brother of one of her father's business associates.
Courtesy of the California History Room, California State Library, Sacramento, California*

Narrative of Mrs. Rosalía Leese, Who Witnessed the Hoisting of the Bear Flag in Sonoma on the 14th of June, 1846

*Q: Mrs. Leese, could you please tell me what you know about the raising of the Bear
Flag in Sonoma?*
A: On June 14, 1846, at about 5:30 in the morning, an old man named
Don Pepe de la Rosa came to my home and told me that a group of seventy-
two ragged desperados had surrounded General Vallejo's house. Many of
those men were sailors from whaling ships who had jumped ship. They
arrested General Vallejo, Captain Salvador Vallejo, and Víctor Prudón.
When I heard this alarming news, I quickly got dressed and rushed out to
the street to see if there was any truth to what the old man had said. The

Adela María Vallejo, the daughter of Rosalía Vallejo's nephew Platón. Courtesy of the Autry National Center

first thing I saw was Colonel Prudón running off to try and rescue Captain Salvador Vallejo—a ruffian named Benjamin Kelsey was trying to murder Captain Vallejo in cold blood. What other word would you use to describe the killing of an unarmed prisoner by a strong brute who had seventy men just like himself right behind him? Kelsey's comrades had dragged Captain Vallejo off to where Doctor Semple and his group were located, but Prudón arrived in the nick of time to save his life.

From appearances, Doctor Semple seemed to be more humane than the rest of that godforsaken bunch. I also saw ex-Commander General Vallejo, who was dressed in the uniform of a Mexican army general. A large group of rough-looking men were holding him prisoner. Some of the men were wearing caps made from the skins of coyotes or wolves. Others were wearing slouch hats full of holes or straw hats as black as charcoal. Most of these marauders had on buckskin pants, but some were wearing blue pants that reached only to the knee. Several of the men were not wearing shirts, and only fifteen or twenty of the whole bunch were wearing shoes.

After talking among themselves for a while, a good number of the men mounted their horses and rode off with the prisoners. General Vallejo, Captain Salvador Vallejo, Colonel Víctor Prudón, and my husband, Jacob Leese, were taken to Sacramento and were left to the tender mercies of that demon John A. Sutter. Although he had married in Europe and had several children, he had left his wife and children behind and was living openly with two black mistresses. These women were from the Sandwich Islands. Sutter had brought them to California on his ship.

After General Vallejo was hurriedly taken away, the marauders who had stayed behind in Sonoma raised a piece of linen cloth on the flagpole located in the corner of the plaza near the old mission church. The cloth was about the size of a large towel, and they had painted a red bear and one star on it. John C. Frémont was the man who had planned this all-out robbery of California. Even though he was an officer in the U.S. army, it is fair to assume that Frémont was afraid to compromise the honor of his government. He was not about to let his thieves steal California while waving the flag that lovers of liberty throughout the world hold dear. This was why he adopted a flag unknown to civilized nations.

John C. Frémont, whose involvement in the Bear Flag events continued to rankle Rosalía Vallejo and her sister-in-law more than a quarter century later. Courtesy of the California History Room, California State Library, Sacramento, California

As soon as the Bear Flag was raised, I was told by the thieves' interpreter that I was now a prisoner. This interpreter's name was Solís. He was a former servant of my husband's. Solís pointed to four ragged desperados who were standing close to me with their pistols drawn. I surrendered because it would have been useless to resist. They demanded the key to my husband's storehouse and I gave it to them. No sooner had I given them the key than they called their friends over and began ransacking the storehouse. There were enough provisions and liquor there to feed two hundred men for two years. A few days after my husband was taken away, John C. Frémont arrived in Sonoma. He said that his sole purpose for coming was to arrange matters to everyone's satisfaction and protect everyone from extortion or oppression. Many paid writers have characterized Frémont with a great number of endearing epithets, but he was a tremendous coward. Listen to me! I have good reason to say this. On June 20, we received news that Captain Padilla was on his way to Sonoma with a squad of one hundred men to rescue us.[6] As soon as Frémont heard about this, he sent for me. He ordered me to write Padilla a letter and tell him to return to San José and not come near Sonoma. I flatly refused to do that, but Frémont

Rosalía Vallejo, Jacob P. Leese, and their children. Their daughter Rosana, who was present when Cerruti interviewed her mother, is at the far right. Their son Jacob, who later assisted Savage in copying documents in Salinas, is immediately to the right of his mother. Courtesy of The Bancroft Library, University of California, Berkeley

was bent on having his own way. He told me that if I refused to tell Padilla exactly what he told me to say, and if Padilla approached Sonoma, he would order his men to burn down our houses with us inside.[7] I agreed to his demands, not because I wanted to save my own life, but because I was pregnant and did not have the right to endanger the life of my unborn child. Moreover, I judged that a man who had already gone this far would stop at nothing to attain his goals. I also wanted to spare the Californio women from more trouble, so I wrote that ominous letter which forced Captain Padilla to retrace his steps. While on alert for Padilla's possible attack, Frémont changed out of his fancy uniform into a blue shirt. He put away his hat and wrapped an ordinary handkerchief around his head. He decided to dress like this so he would not be recognized. Is this the way a brave man behaves? [8]

During the whole time that Frémont and his ring of thieves were in Sonoma, robberies were very common. The women did not dare go out for a walk unless they were escorted by their husband or their brothers. One of my servants was a young Indian girl who was about seventeen years old. I swear that John C. Frémont ordered me to send that girl to the officers' barracks many times. However, by resorting to tricks, I was able to save that poor girl from falling into the hands of that lawless band of thugs who had imprisoned my husband.

During the two months that my husband was held prisoner, I sent him exquisite food and gold, but that despicable Sutter arranged it so my husband never received one dollar. On more than one occasion Sutter had been forced to acknowledge the superiority of Mr. Leese. For an entire week, Sutter made my husband sleep on the bare floor and assigned an uncouth man from Missouri to guard his room. Whenever that guard opened the door, he would insult the prisoners. This band of ungrateful horse thieves, trappers, and runaway sailors had deprived these prisoners of their liberty.

I could tell you about the many crimes committed by the Bear Flag mob, but since I do not wish to detain you any longer, I will end this conversation with this: those hateful men instilled so much hate in me for the people of their race that, even though twenty-eight years have gone by since then, I still cannot forget the insults they heaped upon me. Since I have not wanted to have anything to do with them, I have refused to learn their language.

Monterey
June 27, 1874
By Rosalía de Leese
Rosana Leese[9]

Dorotea Valdez

INTRODUCTION

*C*erruti's interview with Dorotea Valdez took place on the same date as his interview with Rosalía Vallejo. Like that interview, this one was also recorded in English. For reasons which we have explained in our introduction to the Rosalía Vallejo interview, we have "retranslated" Cerruti's language in the Dorotea Valdez testimonio as well.

We know little about Dorotea Valdez. According to her testimonio, she spent a good part of her life as a servant in a series of prominent households in and around Monterey. She was very conscious of having been relegated to the sidelines of her society. She states that, as a woman, she did not have much formal education. She apparently regarded Cerruti's presence as a vehicle for establishing the recognition that had so long been denied her. She invited him to spend as much time with her as he needed.

She stated that her father was Juan Bautista Valdez. He was one of the most significant figures in the exploration of California and the Southwest. He first appears in the documentary record in the 1760s as a member of the presidio company at Loreto, in Baja California. He was a member of the 1769–1770 Portolá expedition, which opened a path between Baja and Alta California and established a Spanish presence at both San Diego and Monterey. Valdez, however, did not remain in Alta California. He returned to Baja California in 1770, and like many Loreto soldiers, he probably moved back and forth between the two Californias in the 1770s.

In 1773 he was sent to Mexico City, where he received documents which the viceroy ordered him to deliver to Juan Bautista de Anza. The orders concerned the project of opening a land route from Sonora to Monterey. Anza was told to add Valdez to his expedition, since he knew the route from San Diego north. When Anza reached San Gabriel, he sent Valdez to San Diego to seek supplies. On Anza's return journey, Valdez was instructed to carry documents concerning the expedition all the way back to Mexico City and deliver them to the viceroy. He did so and made a formal statement to the viceroy's secretary on June 14, 1774. This series of journeys made him the first colonist to make a round trip between Mexico City and Alta California by land.[1]

The documentary record of Alta California is silent about Valdez after this point. We have Dorotea's word that he was in Monterey when she was born in 1793, but we have little information on him or the rest of the family after that.

Cerruti did not mention Dorotea Valdez at all in his memoir, "Ramblings in California." The fact that his interview with her took place on the same day as the interview with Rosalía Vallejo and that it was recorded in English lead us to suspect that she was at Rosalía Vallejo's house, or very close to it, when Cerruti visited. We know from her testimonio that she had been a servant for much of her adult life. Perhaps she was a servant there. In his dictation for Bancroft, Juan Bautista Alvarado stated that Rosalía Vallejo was living in Monterey and that she was attended by her daughter Rosana (who was present at the interview with her mother) and by a female servant who was "very devoted" to her. Perhaps that servant was Dorotea Valdez.

The testimonio offers us another set of clues about this woman. Native Californians were present in her interview in a different fashion than they were in most of the others that Cerruti or Thomas Savage conducted. Valdez had barely begun to describe Governor José Joaquín Arrillaga's funeral, for instance, when she commented on the vast number of neophyte singers who had performed, and remarked, with pride, on the abilities of the lead indigenous singer, José. Another somewhat unique aspect of the interview was that Cerruti asked her about Solano's visit to Monterey. And finally, we note that Cerruti wrote in "Ramblings in California," which was completed well after this interview had been conducted, that Rosalía Vallejo had two Indian girls as servants "whose mother had also been employed in [her] house, and when dying had requested the mistress to take care of her children." While this statement may not have referred to Dorotea Valdez directly, given all of this, we believe it reasonable to suggest that Dorotea Valdez's mother may have been an Indian.[2]

If Dorotea was a mestiza servant with close ties to Rosalía Vallejo, then it is easy to imagine Rosalía insisting that Cerruti interview her. And it is just as easy to imagine Cerruti doing so reluctantly. He asked her a series of basic questions about events in Monterey from 1814 to the 1850s. After asking about Arrillaga's funeral, he asked her about two famous seafaring voyages to Monterey: the arrival of the ship *Asia* in 1825 and the Bouchard raid of 1818. He posed his questions out of chronological order. This may indicate that he was not very prepared for the interview, and it would be consistent with his feeling somewhat coerced into doing it.

After Dorotea Valdez had answered these questions, Cerruti seems to have been struggling for more things to ask her. After inquiring about Solano, he threw in a question about David Spence, who had been a merchant in Monterey since the 1830s and whom he was scheduled to interview the next day. After that he inexplicably asked her about David Jacks, a local real estate mogul who had come into possession of the Monterey pueblo lands in the late 1850s. He seems to have recovered his bearings, for he then asked her about more or less connected events in the 1840s. The first was the rule of Governor Manuel Micheltorena, whose troops had been notoriously rowdy and who had been expelled from Alta California in 1845. The second was the American takeover of Monterey in 1846.

In her interview, Dorotea Valdez offered some highly critical remarks about Mariano Guadalupe Vallejo. Her criticism of Solano's visit to Monterey was obviously a criticism of Vallejo, for he had brought the chief to the capital. She placed the sharpest criticism of the visit in the mouth of Prudencia Amesti, who was actually Vallejo's sister! Dorotea Valdez also presented Vallejo as arrogant, to the point of forcing people to salute his house. She also blamed him for some of the troubles which Governor Micheltorena experienced. In these attitudes, she was clearly reflecting the evaluation of Vallejo that had become increasingly prevalent in Monterey in the later 1830s and the 1840s. The citizens of the capital believed that Vallejo was building a private empire for himself in the north, and they resented that. The progressive estrangement during this period between Vallejo and Alvarado, who exercised his authority from Monterey, symbolized that rift. Dorotea Valdez's testimonio perfectly captured it.[3]

The testimonio seems to have ended a bit abruptly. Dorotea Valdez let loose with a denunciation of Frémont that closely paralleled what Rosalía Vallejo had said about him. She offered the unorthodox opinion that the Bear Flaggers were worse than the despised troops of Governor Manuel

Micheltorena. At that point, Cerruti terminated the interview and consigned her actual Spanish words, along with those of Rosalía Vallejo, to oblivion.

Reminiscences of Dorotea Valdez with Reference to Governor Arrillaga. Arrival of Man of War *Asia*. Destruction of Monterey by the Pirates under Captain Hipólito Bouchard. Appearance of Solano in Monterey. Doings of David Spencer Esq. Conduct of Micheltorena. Some Items about Yankees in General

MY FATHER'S NAME WAS JUAN BAUTISTA VALDEZ. He came to Alta California with Captain Rivera, who was the first settler of San Diego. My father later settled in Monterey, where I was born in 1793. I have witnessed every event that has taken place since that time, but because I am a woman, I was denied the privilege of participating in politics or in business. My education has been very limited, yet my memory is good. I am aware of the fact that you have been sent by a learned man who is focused on the noble objective of writing the true history of this country. I would be very pleased to provide you with my recollections. You may proceed to ask me questions at your leisure.

Q: Do you remember Governor Arrillaga's funeral in 1814?
A: Yes, I do. His Excellency is buried at ex-mission Soledad. His funeral was very impressive. Hundreds of good Spanish citizens attended.[4] Missionaries from four of the missions were there, as well as a great many Indians. All of the soldiers from the Monterey presidio also attended the funeral. José el Cantor and more than four hundred neophytes sang the Miserere continuously.[5] To digress for one moment, even though José el Cantor was a young Indian, he was an excellent singer and understood music. His knowledge of the Latin used in Church was as good as that of any priest.

After Governor Arrillaga was buried, a monument was placed on his grave. Year after year on November 2, hundreds of Indians and white men and women would visit his grave and place flowers on it. Mission Soledad is now in ruins and only a part of the church exists, but I can show you where Arrillaga was buried because I have often prayed in front of his tomb.

Q:Were you in Monterey in 1825 when the Spanish man-of-war, the Asia, *arrived from Peru?*

A: I do not remember the year that event took place. However, I do remember the day that Captain Martínez landed in a large boat with six heavy-set *gachupines*[6] who were sporting shiny cutlasses. Those men were dressed in white pants and wore good shoes. When the lookout at the fort first spotted the *Asia,* Governor Argüello, whose father was Governor Arrillaga, believed that the large ship had hostile intentions. He therefore ordered all the old men, women, and children to go to the woods. He then began to prepare for a good fight. In my opinion, it would have been crazy for him to try and fight against the *Asia.* This ship had more than fifty mounted cannons and a crew of close to one thousand men. Governor Argüello would not have been able to muster more than two hundred men. In addition, the guns at the fort and the soldiers' weapons were of the poorest quality.

When Captain Martínez came ashore and respectfully saluted Governor Argüello, the governor took him inside the presidio. I remember well that during the time the ship was in port, Governor Argüello and Captain Martínez would stroll arm in arm every evening. Two days after the captain of the *Asia* had taken up residence in the presidio, about five hundred or more sailors came ashore and built themselves temporary shelter with the sails from their ship. They also built a large oven in which they baked bread. The sailors were primarily Spaniards who had been fighting along the coast of Peru and Chile for a great many years. They behaved very well and paid for everything they purchased with good Spanish currency. They were also very generous with the Californios and the neophytes and gave them many sacks of sugar. Sugar was very scarce in Monterey. At that time, sugar sold for four bits a pound, and sometimes it even went for one dollar for a pound, and the pound was only twelve ounces.

After the sailors had been on shore for nineteen days, they returned to the large ship and then sailed off to some of the ports on the Pacific. I do not remember exactly whether the ship sailed to Mazatlán or to Acapulco. But this much I do know, she was placed under the command of a Peruvian sea captain named Don Juan Malarín. The Mexican government was satisfied with Malarín's service as commander, so it rewarded him by appointing him first lieutenant of the Mexican navy. Captain Malarín died in 1849, leaving eleven children behind—eight daughters and three sons. All of his children are still alive. Some of them live in Monterey and others in Santa Clara County.

Some of the sailors from the *Asia* were granted permission to remain on shore. It is possible to find some of their descendants among the most esteemed Californio families. I must not forget to mention that during the early days of this country, in fact before the arrival of the Americans, our population increased very rapidly. It was not unusual to see a mother leading twenty-four children to church. And all these children had the same father. I am not exaggerating when I state that the average number of children raised by one mother was usually more than eleven and not less.[7] However, ever since the Americans took possession of this country, sterility has become very common. The American women are very fond of visiting doctors and swallowing medicine. This is a sin that God does not forgive.[8]

Q:Were you in Monterey in 1818 when Captain Hipólito [Bouchard] arrived commanding two pirate ships?
A: I was living at the presidio with Governor Solá's family. I cannot describe the battle that took place, nor the manner in which the presidio of Monterey was sacked. That is because in the early morning of that tragic day, Governor Solá ordered that all the women, children, and old men be taken to the woods. I tell you, they hurried us out of there so fast that most of us were practically naked when we left. Only two people in the whole group were wearing shoes, and none of the women had dresses. I remember one girl who was very clever. She took off carrying a basket filled with boiled beans on her head. It was quite funny to see her long hair streaming in the wind with grease running down her neck and other parts of her body. Governor Solá had sent couriers to the missions closest to Monterey to notify the missionaries that everybody, except for the soldiers, had gone to the Rancho del Rey. The good Fathers and the wealthy people of the surrounding area sent us food and clothing. After spending two days at the Rancho del Rey, we returned to Monterey. Instead of houses, all we found were smoldering ruins. The despicable pirates had sacked our dwellings and then burned everything they could lay their hands on. But our people bravely faced up to an evil that they could do nothing about. With the assistance of carpenters, blacksmiths, and many neophytes, in less than four months our pueblo looked as good as it had before the pirate captain arrived.

Q:Were you in Monterey when the Indians from Sonoma visited there?
A: When Solano visited Monterey, I was living with Señora Prudencia Amesti. I especially noticed how tall that dark-colored savage was, and that

he was dressed like the people of my race. His many followers, however, were dressed like Indians. They wore feathers around their heads, and many of them had tattoos around their wrists, arms, and legs. We did not like having them here, because their behavior was really overbearing. Solano and his Indians all rode fine horses. They all had *jáquimas,* but few of them had saddles.[9] Their hair was long and they carried bows and arrows. Their looks inspired fear in everybody. I firmly believed that they were devils who had been let loose from hell. Not all of the Indians had dark skin like Solano; some had white skin. However, most of them had very red faces. I heard Señora Amesti say that the arrival of these savages in Monterey was a plague sent by God to punish us for our sins. Solano did not stay very long in Monterey. Governor Alvarado and Don Pablo de la Guerra persuaded Solano to return to Sonoma. Pablo de la Guerra was a very influential person in this country at that time and he was also one of the people in charge of the Customs House.

Q: Can you tell me something about Don David Spence?
A: Of course I can. I have known him since 1824, when he arrived from Europe to work for the large business run by the foreigners who purchased goods from the missions. I knew him when he had his own business. I was present at his wedding. I also helped his wife when, within a week's time, she had to bury a granddaughter, a grandson, and Don David's only son. I know about his position as a high official in the Mexican government. I can assure you that I and the people of my country have the greatest respect for him. We consider him to be very honest. I do know, though, that in the early days of California, from 1834 to 1842, Señor Spence did a good amount of smuggling. However, this does not detract one bit from his good reputation. During those days, smuggling was commonplace, and nobody could make a dollar without resorting to some sort of dishonorable practice. This was because every business transaction was done on long credit, duties were high, and money was very scarce. The missionaries, however, had coffers full of money—but the concept of generosity was not fully developed in their brains. After his only son's death, Señor Spence assumed the responsibility for his three grandsons. They are being educated by the Italian priests who have a boys' school in Santa Clara. They are fine boys, full of promise.

Q: Do you know Mr. Jacks?
A: Señor Jacks is the owner of the pueblo. In my opinion, he is a very mean man, a cunning rascal, and a pious hypocrite. He is such a miser that he

The Monterey home of David Spence, as it appeared a year after Cerruti interviewed him. Courtesy of the California History Room, California State Library, Sacramento, California

even denies his own wife and children the comforts of life. At the present time, Jacks considers himself a millionaire. But as soon as the railroad begins to operate, many foreigners will come to settle here. Rest assured, that is when Señor Jacks will receive the punishment he deserves. All we want is for some clever lawyer to take the pueblo land away from him. The American authorities sold land that did not belong to them in order to pay off their debts. This is land that nobody had the right to give away, because it rightfully belongs to every man, woman, and child who was born in our town. When the pueblo owned the land currently owned by David Jacks, people could just go out and gather the wood they needed. Our horses and cattle could graze everywhere and nobody ever bothered them. Ever since this evil man obtained possession of our land, he has placed fences everywhere. Even the famous well where the pirates landed in 1818 is surrounded by a fence. Señor Jacks is a natural-born enemy of everything related to our history. He even tried to gain possession of the crops by the bridge. There is a live oak tree near those crops, and it is under that very tree that Fr. Junípero Serra said his first Mass on June 7, 1770.

Q: Did you ever know General Micheltorena?
A: I knew General Micheltorena. He was a very good man and a much better man than we deserved. However, he had the misfortune of arriving at a

very difficult time. He also had to command an army that was primarily composed of robbers and cowards. Micheltorena was governor for a very short time. He was a weak man and was forced to surrender his army to the Californios. I am sure that Micheltorena would have defeated his enemies if he had been given the chance. This poor man came to our country during a bad period. I heard Micheltorena say that General Vallejo had sent for him and had promised him many things. However, when he arrived, Vallejo refused to support him. I believe every word that General Micheltorena said. Between him and Vallejo, Micheltorena was by far the better and the more popular. Any poor man could obtain land for free from General Micheltorena. Everybody was allowed to speak to him directly on the street. He was fair with everyone who came into contact with him. It was a different story with General Vallejo. Whenever he came to Monterey, he would place some of his Sonoma savages outside the front door of his house, and everyone who passed by had to take off their hats and salute. Mind you, the people were saluting the house, not the general. He was inside and had no idea who was walking past his home.

Manuel Micheltorena was appointed governor of Alta California in 1842. The Californios drove him out in 1845. Courtesy of the California History Room, California State Library, Sacramento, California

General Micheltorena was a tall man. He had very light-colored skin and was always clean-shaven. When he was in California, he was about forty-eight years old but looked considerably younger. In my opinion, General Micheltorena was terribly mistreated. He came to this country at the special request of the most prominent men of California, but no sooner had he arrived than everybody turned against him. In spite of this, he behaved with bravery and prudence, and his surrender should be attributed to his desire to avoid bloodshed. After Micheltorena surrendered in Los Angeles, Pío Pico became governor and José Castro became commander general. The interests and private views of these men were completely opposite. This situation produced bad feelings to an alarming extent among the Californios of the north and the south. Pío Pico used every means within his power to move the Customs House from Monterey to San Pedro, which was the port for Los Angeles. Castro wanted the Customs House moved to San Francisco. Don Pío Pico was conspiring with Forbes to turn the territory into an English protectorate. Meanwhile Castro, with the assistance of General Vallejo, was doing his best to have the country annexed to the United States. To make a long story short, I will conclude by saying that if the Americans had not taken the country in 1846, by 1847 every Californio would have been killed in a civil war due to the bitter hatred that existed. No matter how much preaching was done by good men, nobody was willing to listen to the voice of reason.

Q: Were you in Monterey when Commodore Sloat raised the American flag there?
A: I was living in Soledad when Commodore Sloat arrived in Monterey. However, I do remember hearing that the commodore was in port for several days before he made up his mind to take possession of Monterey. He was hoping that the Californios would rebel against Mexico and seek his assistance to obtain their independence. Señor Larkin had led him to believe that such a thing might happen. I also heard that he raised the American flag because he had been told that an English man-of-war would be arriving in the port, and then the emissaries from England would hand over the country to England.

Commodore Sloat took possession of Monterey on June 6, 1846. Only one hundred and sixty men came ashore. The American flag was raised on the flagpoles at the Customs House, at the government house, and at the fort. Our fort was useless. The soldiers who came ashore behaved very well. But the riffraff who came later with Captain Frémont acted more like thieves than soldiers. Captain Frémont never appeared before us—the enemy. However, his men stole horses, saddles, *aguardiente,* and anything else they could lay their hands on. I have heard the people of my country curse Micheltorena's soldiers, but I can assure you that they were gentlemen compared to the trappers that Frémont brought to Monterey.

Monterey
June 27, 1874

José Abrego, Esq.
Please review these few pages of historical recollections that Dorotea Valdez dictated to me and let me know if what she said is true.

Respectfully,
your obedient servant,
Henry Cerruti

Monterey
June 28, 1874
I believe that the facts that Dorotea Valdez related are very close to the truth.

Your devoted servant,
José Abrego

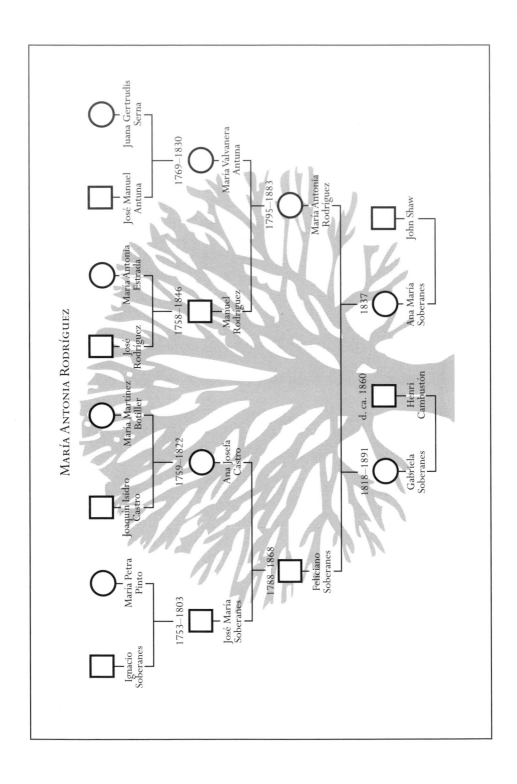

MARÍA ANTONIA RODRÍGUEZ

Juana Gertrudis Serna

José Manuel Antuna

1769–1830

María Valvanera Antuna

1795–1883

María Antonia Rodríguez

María Antonia Estrada

José Rodríguez

1758–1846

Manuel Rodríguez

John Shaw

Ana María Soberanes

1837

María Martínez Botiller

Joaquín Isidro Castro

1759–1822

Ana Josefa Castro

Henri Cambustón

d. ca. 1860

Gabriela Soberanes

1818–1891

María Petra Pinto

Ignacio Soberanes

1753–1803

José María Soberanes

Feliciano Soberanes

1788–1868

María Antonia Rodríguez

INTRODUCTION

*O*n the day after he had interviewed Rosalía Vallejo and Dorotea Valdez, Cerruti went to interview David Spence and José Abrego, two men who had played important roles in the history of Mexican Monterey. While talking to Abrego, Cerruti showed him the rough transcript he had made of his conversation with Dorotea Valdez. He asked if what she had told him was "in consonance with truth and veracity." Abrego replied, in Spanish, that he believed that her testimonio was *"muy cerca de la verdad"*—very close to the truth.

After he finished his conversation with Abrego, Cerruti returned to Rosalía Vallejo's house, where he met Vicente Gómez for the first time. Gómez would, over the next few years, become an important part of the Bancroft effort. After his conversation with Gómez, Cerruti spent some time looking at a large building known as "the barracks" that Abrego had constructed in 1839. When he found that it was closed and he could not get in, he paid a call on María Antonia Rodríguez, widow of Feliciano Soberanes.

María Antonia Rodríguez's family embodied a unique part of California's heritage. Junípero Serra recruited her father, Manuel Rodríguez, a carpenter in Jalisco, to come to California with him as the missionary president was returning through Mexico to California in 1774 after his meeting with the viceroy in Mexico City. Manuel Rodríguez first was stationed at San Diego, and he most likely assisted in the rebuilding of the mission there after the Kumeyaay attacked it in 1775. At some point he went to Monterey, where in 1781 he married María Valvanera Antuna. She was the daughter of a presidio soldier, José Manuel Antuna, and his wife, Juana Gertrudis Serna. They were both from Sinaloa and had most likely been recruited for California in 1774 by Fernando de Rivera y Moncada.

María Valvanera Antuna gave birth to twelve children. María Antonia, her sixth, was born in Monterey in February 1795. María Antonia married Feliciano Soberanes in 1810. Like his wife's grandparents, his parents, José María Soberanes and Ana Josefa Castro, were both from Sinaloa, and they had probably come to California in the same recruiting venture organized by Rivera y Moncada in 1774.[1]

The Soberanes family was already becoming an important local clan. In 1795 one of the first land grants in the area had been awarded to José María Soberanes and Joaquín Isidro Castro, a veteran of the Anza expedition. But after their deaths in the early 1800s, the rancho seems to have been largely abandoned.

María Antonia Rodríguez had fourteen children. Her husband built on his father's prominence and became active in public affairs. After her husband's death, she remained in Monterey. At the time of the interview with Cerruti, she was living with at least one of her daughters, and in 1880 she was living with two of them. She died in 1883.

The background of the interview was a bit clouded. Cerruti did not indicate in "Ramblings in California" why he decided to call on her. In that manuscript he categorized her as the widow of Feliciano Soberanes and the mother of Gabriela Cambustón, who was the widow of Enrique Cambustón, a schoolteacher in Monterey in the late 1830s and early 1840s. Perhaps Cerruti, irritated at the results of his two earlier encounters with women in Monterey, merely wanted the satisfaction of choosing a female subject on his own. He may also have learned that she was less hostile to the Americans than Rosalía Vallejo and Dorotea Valdez had proven to be.

When Cerruti appeared at her door, María Antonia Rodríguez at first thought that he wanted to rent some of her property. Then he began to engage her in conversation. It is not clear from his account whether he ever told her about Bancroft's project. He never included this interview in the "California Pioneers" heading under which he placed the others. And Bancroft never used it in his *History of California*. Cerruti embedded the interview, part in English and part in Spanish, in his "Ramblings in California," which was not published during his lifetime.

Cerruti began the interview by asking open-ended questions about what had happened in Monterey, and she responded by talking about the

Bouchard affair. Then Cerruti got to the heart of his concerns and asked her what she thought of the Americans who had taken over her country. He was not disappointed in her reply: unlike Dorotea Valdez, she said that Governor Micheltorena's troops had behaved much worse than the Americans. While she was critical of Frémont's men, she also termed them merely a "small band." Their behavior did not cloud her overall assessment. She was also excited about current development plans for Monterey, especially the hoped-for arrival of the railroad.

These answers clearly put Cerruti at ease. A discussion of the name "Salinas" led them into a conversation about how salt had been collected. When María Antonia Rodríguez's daughter Anita entered the room, her mother asked her to play the piano for Cerruti. The interview ended with a discussion of the *jarabe,* a dance popular in Mexican California.

In the presentation of the interview that follows, the main text is what Cerruti wrote in English, in "Ramblings in California." The italicized text is our translation of what he wrote in Spanish.

María Antonia Rodríguez, Widow of Feliciano Soberanes

She assured me that the most trying period of her existence took place toward the end of the year 1818, when a pirate named Bouchard and his lieutenant, Gómez, burned and sacked the presidio of Monterey.[2] She could not narrate the manner in which they fought, but she had seen the casemate when it was blown up by Don Ignacio Vallejo by order of Governor Solá. She had followed the family of Lieutenant Estudillo when, by order of the governor, he sallied forth from Monterey in the still hour of midnight; she had camped in the Rancho del Rey under a wagon drawn by oxen and, until supplied with clothing from the good friars, had suffered from cold. "However," she added, "with the help of the Virgin Mary everything ended satisfactorily, and in one short year our town was rebuilt, and since then I have not experienced any great sorrow."

I asked her if she was pleased with the change of rulers, and she replied that though the Americans had taken away from her nearly the whole of her lands, she had no grudge against them—for, she said, "It is the law of nature that the poor should steal from the rich. We Californians in 1846 owned every inch of soil in this country, and our conquerors took away from us the greater part. The same thing, I suppose, has happened over and over again in every conquered nation, and if I compare the American soldiers with the cholos of Micheltorena, the comparison will be highly to the advantage of the former, with the exception of the small band under the leadership of General Frémont, who behaved very badly and stole everything they could lay their hands upon.

"Before the arrival of General Micheltorena, Monterey was a business place, and everybody living in it eked out a comfortable existence, but since then the poor town has lost the whole of its former importance and has dwindled down to its present forlorn condition. However, in three months our railroad will be finished, and with the iron horse we will prosper again. The whole production of the extensive and fertile Salinas Valley will have to be shipped through our port, and many a ship and steamer will come here daily to load grain for European marts."

I next requested her to tell me how the name of Salinas Valley originated, and she assured me that "during the rule of the Spaniards and Mexicans, no such name was known to the natives, but the Americans, who are always ready to introduce changes in everything created, have called the valley of Monterey "Salinas Valley." I admit, however, that they had good ground for effecting the change of name. *I remember when I was a little girl, Governor Solá sent a detachment of cavalry soldiers out to the two small lagoons twelve miles from Monterey at the edge of the sand dune near the ocean. The salt in the lagoons was beginning to set, and the soldiers had orders to make sure that nobody touched the lagoons until the salt was hard and ready to dry out. Once that process had been done, they would put the salt in leather bags and transport it to Monterey. There it would be stored and accounted for as belonging to the royal treasury, which had a monopoly on salt. Nobody was allowed to collect salt in the vicinity of Monterey, even though some smugglers who were working for the Señores Ortega collected several* fanegas *of salt in José Armenta's field.[3] They were caught by surprise, placed in jail, and charged with stealing from the royal treasury. They only spent a few days in jail, because some witnesses testified that the salt found in Armenta's field had been brought there on the back of a burro that Armenta owned. But the governor did not believe the witnesses. He ordered that the thieves be severely punished. When the order was given to re-arrest them, they could no longer be found. Don Juan Ortega, who had many friends, had sent the men to his large house in the country, known as* "Rancho del Refugio."[4]

I then asked Mrs. Soberanes at what price the treasurer sold the salt to the inhabitants, and she stated that they had to pay one and a half dollars for each *fanega,* a very high price indeed in those days, during which, to

Landscape after the slaughter of cattle for hides and tallow, by William Rich Hutton, 1840s. Reproduced by permission of The Huntington Library, San Marino, California

prevent sickness among their cattle, the rancheros gave them a monthly allowance of salt. *The men who make jerky and those who slaughter the animals also use a large amount of salt to cure the meat.* I intended to ask Mrs. Soberanes a great many other questions, but her daughter Anita having entered the parlor she at the request of her mother went to the piano and played an Italian song, and I admit that she played admirably.

After a while Mrs. Soberanes requested her daughter to play the jarabe, once the national dance of the native Californians; she complied with the request, and I admit fulfilled her task to my entire satisfaction. After I had bestowed the praises Mrs. Anita Shaw so richly deserved, her mother proceeded to explain how, in the good old days gone and never to return, the Californians danced the jarabe.[5] *I will give the description in her own words, fearing that it would lose some of its originality if I were to jot it down in English.*[6] The following words were hers:

> *The* jarabe *is a dance that is quite similar to the jig that is all the rage with the Americans from the states of Virginia and Alabama. Only two people dance the* jarabe. *The dancers would stand facing each other, and at the sound of a harp, a* vihuela, *and a violin, they would move their legs in such a way that it was a*

View of ranch hands (many of whom were Indians) preparing tallow, by William Rich Hutton, 1840s. Reproduced by permission of The Huntington Library, San Marino, California

pleasure to watch them. It was customary to reward the best female dancer with a prize. This is how the prize was given: some of the people in attendance would take off their hats and put them on the female dancer's head. She would continue dancing for a while longer, until another dancer would come and relieve her. Many times the men would get carried away with enthusiasm and throw money at the dancers' feet. When this happened, the male dancer would stop dancing. The person calling the dances would then pick up the gifts of money and take them to the woman. A person could get their hat back if they threw a medio or a real. You could also get your hat back with a cuartillo, which was even better, because many young women refused to accept large gifts of money. I remember that in 1842, after Commodore Jones returned Monterey to the Mexicans, there was a dance. That sailor Jones attended with some of his officers. He liked our way of dancing so much that he took off his cap, without anybody telling him to do that, and put it on Doña Ramoncita de la Torre's head. When the time came for him to retrieve his cap, he gave her one hundred pesos. The young Ramoncita refused that gift, but the commodore strongly insisted, and she finally accepted it because he was such a refined gentleman. She accepted his gift in such a gracious manner that the next day, the commodore went to visit her at her home. When he left to go back to his country, he said that he would always remember the beautiful Ramoncita.

Teresa de la Guerra

INTRODUCTION

B y the beginning of 1875, Mariano Guadalupe Vallejo and Henry Cerruti had been working together for a number of months. Vallejo was dictating material to Cerruti, rummaging through his own documents, and encouraging other Californios to give whatever documents they might possess to him so that he could use them in his efforts. They made a number of trips to San Francisco and Monterey in the course of their endeavors.

In January 1875, Vallejo wrote a letter to Teresa de la Guerra and asked if her late husband, William Hartnell, who had lived in Alta California for thirty-two years, had left any papers he might examine. She replied that although many of her husband's papers had been lost over time, Vallejo was welcome to come to her rancho at Alisal and examine them himself. Vallejo brought along Cerruti, who interviewed her on March 12, 1875.

Teresa de la Guerra was the oldest daughter of José de la Guerra y Noriega, longtime commander of the Santa Bárbara presidio and one of the most eminent men in central Alta California. He was born to parents who were members of the lesser nobility in Novales, Spain, in 1779. He went to Mexico City at the age of thirteen to clerk for an uncle who was a businessman there. At the age of nineteen, he decided to enter the army. His background entitled him to enter the officer corps, and he enrolled in the newly formed California service. After almost three years of training in the headquarters of Manuel Cárcaba, the *habilitado general* (overall supply master) for the Californias, José de la Guerra was assigned to Monterey in 1801. He served as *habilitado* there and was made acting commander when

TERESA DE LA GUERRA (ALSO SEE: ANGUSTIAS DE LA GUERRA)

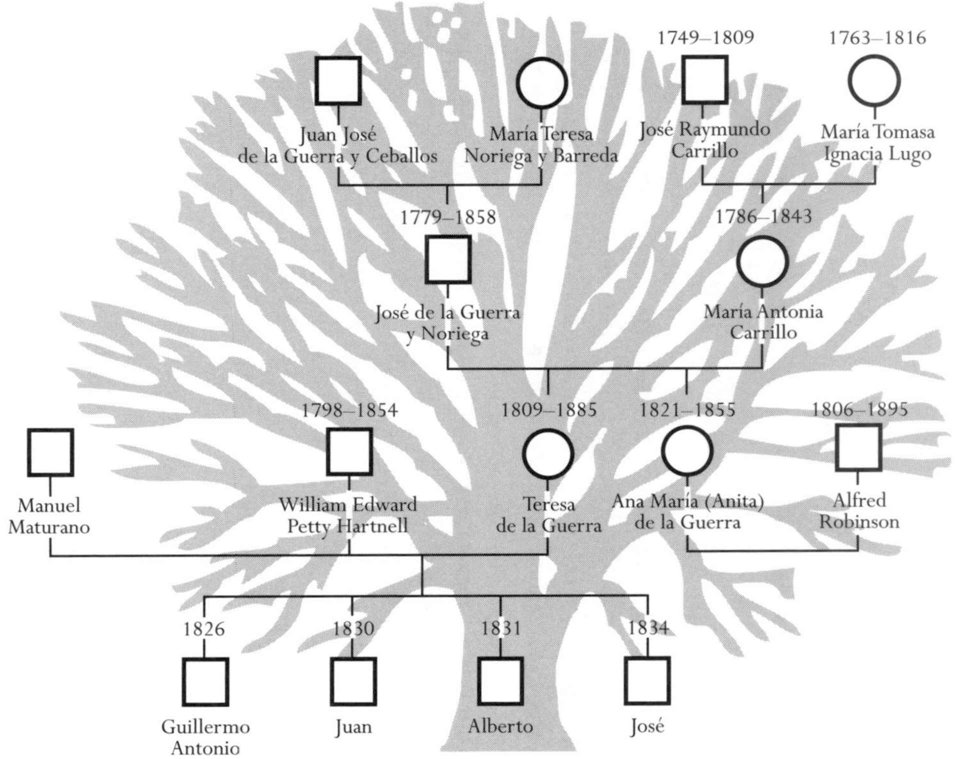

1763–1816
María Tomasa
Ignacia Lugo

1749–1809
José Raymundo
Carrillo

1786–1843
María Antonia
Carrillo

1806–1895
Alfred
Robinson

1821–1855
Ana María (Anita)
de la Guerra

María Teresa
Noriega y Barreda

1779–1858
José de la Guerra
y Noriega

1809–1885
Teresa
de la Guerra

Juan José
de la Guerra y Ceballos

1798–1854
William Edward
Petty Hartnell

Manuel
Maturano

1826
Guillermo
Antonio

1830
Juan

1831
Alberto

1834
José

Commander Raymundo Carrillo was transferred from Monterey to Santa Bárbara in 1802. In 1804 he married his former commander's daughter, María Antonia Carrillo.

María Antonia was the daughter of María Tomasa Ignacia Lugo, who was Rosalía Vallejo's aunt. María Tomasa was born in Sinaloa and came to California with her parents, Francisco Salvador Lugo and Juana María Rita Martínez, with Rivera y Moncada in 1774.

José de la Guerra and María Antonia lived at the presidios of Monterey, Santa Bárbara, and San Diego, where José often served as *habilitado*. He was appointed commander of the Santa Bárbara presidio in 1815. During this period he was able to draw on his contacts in Mexico City to begin a very lucrative commercial career. He soon became a leading merchant. Teresa, born in 1809, was José and María Antonia's third child, after José Antonio, born in 1805, and Rita, born in 1807. Rita's death in 1810 or 1811 left Teresa as the eldest daughter.[1]

Shortly after Mexico obtained its independence from Spain, Anglo-American merchants began to arrive in Alta California to take advantage of the liberalized trading environment. One of the first to set up business along the coast was an Englishman, William Edward Petty Hartnell. After three years clerking in South America for the British firm Begg and Company, Hartnell and another Begg clerk, Hugh McCullough, decided to strike out on their own. They established McCullough, Hartnell, and Company, with Hartnell the resident partner in California. Being the first on the scene, they were able to negotiate contracts with the missions, and they did a brisk business in hides and tallow in the mid-1820s.[2]

Teresa de la Guerra was two and a half weeks shy of her sixteenth birthday when she and Hartnell were married. The marriage, arranged by her father and her new husband, was an attempt to bind together two business enterprises. However, Hartnell experienced very little business success.

Teresa and William Hartnell moved to Monterey, where he was headquartered, and children started coming quickly—their first, Guillermo Antonio, was born eleven months after their wedding. Teresa de la Guerra gave birth at least nineteen times in the next twenty-six years.

Hartnell's commercial enterprises did not go well, and the profitable business alliance that his father-in-law had anticipated quickly soured. In fact Hartnell, far from being an asset to the de la Guerra family, quickly became a liability. He was unable to maintain his competitive advantage as more merchants moved into California. The wreck, in 1829, of the *Danube,* which contained a great deal of his merchandise, sealed his fate.

Hartnell was forced to try other ventures. He became a naturalized Mexican citizen in 1830. He came to an agreement with the Soberanes family for an interest in a rancho, Alisal, that they were beginning to develop. In exchange for Hartnell's labor at harvest time, they agreed to support his receiving a formal grant. Hartnell built a small house on the land and, after borrowing money from his father-in-law, managed to eke out a trying existence for the next few years.

In 1834 Governor José Figueroa granted Hartnell the land he was work-ing at Alisal in exchange for his opening and administering a school on it. Hartnell commenced this venture in partnership with Father Patrick Short, an Irish priest who had recently come from Hawai'i. He contracted Indian labor to expand the adobe on the rancho. Monterey resident David Spence later stated that by 1835 Hartnell "was living there in an adobe house with his family. The house was two stories high…he [also] had a gar-den and a large piece of land fenced in and cultivated. He also had on the place a considerable stock of cattle and horses." But the school meant more work for Teresa, who already had given birth to eight children, of whom six had survived. She cared for the boarding students, who numbered as many as ten at once, while raising her own increasing family.

After the school went out of business, Governor Alvarado appointed Hartnell inspector of the secularized missions in 1839. This task kept him on the road for a considerable amount of time. It was the papers connected to his inspection tours in the early 1840s that Bancroft, Vallejo, and Cerruti were seeking from Teresa de la Guerra. She was able to provide the docu-ments to them.[3]

In the 1840s, Hartnell managed to obtain a few more land grants. One, Todos Santos y San Antonio, was near the former mission of La Purísima. Teresa de la Guerra's brother Francisco later stated that there were about two thousand head of cattle on the rancho and three hundred horses, and that one of her sons, most likely Guillermo, lived there. After the war, the Americans employed Hartnell as an interpreter. He died in 1854.[4]

Five years later, Teresa remarried. Little is known of her new husband, Manuel Maturano. She was listed in the 1860 federal census under the name "Teresa Matman," married to Manuel Matman. According to the cen-sus, he was fifteen years younger than she was. After his death, she had trouble paying her taxes. This situation was not unusual for those who owned landed estates in gold rush California. The California legislatures of

Teresa de la Guerra, painted by Leonardo Barbieri in the 1850s. Courtesy of The Bancroft Library, University of California, Berkeley

the 1850s were dominated by mining and commercial interests, and they taxed personal wealth, which the majority of their constituents held, less heavily than they taxed landed wealth. This policy had a severe impact on those Californio families that had managed to hold on to some of their land during this period, and they bore a disproportionate share of the tax burden.

Teresa de la Guerra's decision to sell some of her property in order to pay her taxes disgusted her brother Pablo, who found out about it on a business trip to San Francisco and vigorously denounced it in a letter to their brother. However, Pablo most likely did not appreciate that Californio families who lived from Santa Bárbara south, as he and his family did, were much less pressured by Anglo encroachments than were those who were struggling to survive farther to the north.

By 1870 Teresa de la Guerra's family had dispersed. Her oldest son, Guillermo, now William, lived near Santa María with his wife, Refugio, and their nine children. He was listed in the census as a sheep raiser. Another son, José, was living at Alisal with his wife, Mary, and five children. He was listed in the census as a farmer. A third son, Alberto, was living nearby, working as a shepherd. A fourth son, Juan, was living in Santa Bárbara with his wife, Angustias, and their three children. He was a music teacher.

Teresa de la Guerra's testimonio reveals the struggles of her difficult life and testifies to the tensions Californio families experienced as they tried to maintain their positions in the years following the American invasion and takeover. Her testimonio shows that many Californios were all too aware that they were being pushed to the sidelines and sensitive to what was being said and written about them. She indicated, for instance, that many Californios thought that a very popular book on Mexican California written by her brother-in-law Alfred Robinson did not do them justice.

Teresa de la Guerra also insisted that her husband's business reversals were not his fault. Rather, she argued, the local authorities and some leading families had favored other merchants to his detriment. In the course of her interview with Cerruti, she sought to turn the conversation to three themes. These were her family, the missionaries, and the visit of Duflot de Mofras.

About her family, she had much to say of her late father and her sisters. She hardly mentioned her brothers. Her tone tended to be one of lament for the lost family wealth her father had amassed. She explicitly evoked the language of patriarchy as she remembered José de la Guerra y Noriega as the "father" of his community, but that represented for her a bygone age. In the present, she complained, "lawyers and squatters" were gobbling up the once grand estates. Her descriptions of her sisters were perhaps tinged with envy and a bit of resentment that some of her younger siblings were living in better material circumstances than she was.

Her recollections of the missionaries were uniformly positive. She praised what she saw as their selflessness and dedication. The prism through which she chose to view the missionaries' labor reflected her status as a Californio living in American California. She insisted that the missionaries had civilized California and that they had done so long before the North Americans arrived. Oversimplifying the fate of California's Indians, she put the matter in terms that the newcomers could readily comprehend: "When the foreigners came here, they found the land free of its primitive ways because the Indians had already disappeared."

Teresa de la Guerra's treatment of Duflot de Mofras was merciless. Eugene Duflot de Mofras was a French diplomat who became an attaché in Mexico in 1839. He was instructed to investigate conditions in Alta California and along the Pacific coast. He spent five months in Alta California in 1841 and 1842. He aroused strong negative reactions in many Californios, including the Vallejo brothers and Governor Alvarado. His memoir of that experience was published in 1844. In Teresa de la Guerra's narrative about the Frenchman, he was an ungracious and boorish interloper. According to her, he thought that the Californios were not as "civilized" as the French, that they "lived in the woods." Yet her account of his actions reveals him to be the truly uncivilized one. (Bancroft refused to believe this story and called it "without foundation.") We suspect that Teresa de la Guerra used her experience with Duflot de Mofras as a way of expressing her strong resentments against all the foreigners who had come to her land with preconceived notions about the inferiority of Californios. She may have been formally speaking about one allegedly uncouth Frenchman, but the real targets of her remarks were the Americans.

Narrative of the Distinguished California Matron Doña Teresa de la Guerra de Hartnell, Dictated on March 12, 1875, at Rancho del Alisal and Approved on the 21st Day of the Same Month and Year at the Same Rancho

On February 26, 1875, I visited the hacienda of the widow of Don Guillermo Hartnell. I presented her with a letter of recommendation certified by Señor General Mariano Guadalupe Vallejo and then proceeded to explain the purpose of my visit. I told her that I would only be asking her for information about California during the period it was an integral part of the Mexican Republic. With the kindness for which she is noted, Señora Hartnell responded that it would give her great pleasure to help me with this project. She told me that she was the daughter of the late retired Captain Don José de la Guerra y Noriega. Her father was born in Novales, in the province of Santander, old Spain. At the age of twelve, he immigrated to Mexico, the capital of the viceroyalty that bears the same name. During his first years in America, her father worked at the business establishment of a maternal uncle. But after ten years in America, he entered the Royal Army as a cadet. After two years of good and loyal service, he was named *alférez de caballería*. After he was invested with that rank, he was sent to the royal presidio of Monterey as a member of the garrison.

Señora Hartnell added that in 1804 her father married Doña María Antonia Carrillo, the eldest daughter of Captain Don Raymundo Carrillo,

William Edward Petty Hartnell, as depicted by Ellwood Graham, ca. 1943. Courtesy of the Hartnell College Foundation, Salinas, California

who was the commander of the presidio of Santa Bárbara at the time. That marriage produced seven boys and four girls. The boys were José Antonio, Juan, Francisco, Pablo, Joaquín, Miguel, and Antonio María. The girls were Teresa, Angustias, Anita, and María Antonia. Teresa, the oldest of the sisters, married Don Guillermo Hartnell. He was a British citizen who had gone to South America as a young man. He lived for a long time in Valparaíso and Callao. In 1822, Señor Hartnell left the port of Callao aboard the British brig *John Begg*. The captain of the ship was Don Juan Lincoln. The ship was loaded with goods from the "House of Juan Begg of Lima" and consigned to the young McCullough and Hartnell, who were passengers on the ship. The two men were headed to California to establish a large house of commerce in the port of Monterey that would be engaged primarily in purchasing hide and tallow from the missionary Fathers of the Alta California missions. McCullough and Hartnell did a very good business during their first years of operation, but later this all changed because of the competition from the American Captain John B. R. Cooper. Governor Argüello favored Cooper and declared himself Cooper's protector. The governor provided Cooper with certain advantages and granted him privileges that were denied to the other merchants. McCullough and Hartnell's business also suffered because of the defection of Don David Spence. Spence had been contracted from Aberdeen to clerk at the firm of McCullough and Company. After living for a few years in California, Spence married Doña Adelaida Estrada. She was the daughter of Don Mariano Estrada, who was the head of the very powerful Estrada family. Spence parted company with his employers and opened his own warehouse, making use of the knowledge of mercantile operations he had acquired in this country. In this way, Spence helped chip away at the foundations upon which Hartnell and his partner had rested their hopes. Two consecutive years of business reversals forced McCullough and Company to liquidate their assets and dedicate themselves to other activities that could provide them with a comfortable living.

After Don Guillermo Hartnell closed the warehouse, he and Reverend Father Short opened a school in Monterey where many young Californios were educated. However, the school's earnings were so low that the two professors could not fulfill their aspirations. So after a few years in operation, they decided to close the school, and Father Short went to Valparaíso. The last time I heard from Father Short was in 1870, and he was still living there.

Governor Alvarado appointed Señor Hartnell to the position of visitor general of the missions, a position that brought him many troubles and few benefits. I believe he accepted the position more to please the governor than for his own personal gain. Since the demands of that job required him to travel constantly, from one part of Alta California to another, he no longer belonged to himself or to his family, but rather to his job. No living soul can imagine how much suffering Don Guillermo Hartnell endured as visitor general of the missions. In those days, there were many individuals who believed they had every right to dispose of the Indians' property, which had been administered exclusively by the missionary Fathers until the time of Governor Figueroa. These people were bolstered in this belief by the fact that they had contributed in some fashion to the ousting of Governors Chico and Gutiérrez. The missionaries had a difficult and delicate assignment, yet they showed abundant proof that their skill in managing the Indians' property went hand in hand with their exemplary Christian faith. They kept the interests of their pupils (or children, as they were referred to before 1840) at heart.

I have heard many people ascribe a thousand denigrating epithets to the Reverend Fathers without being aware of how things were done in the past. May God forgive them. Those people who dislike the ministers of the altar neither know what they are saying nor what they are talking about. If they had witnessed, as I did, the Fathers' day-to-day acts of self-denial; if they had seen them, half sick, ride into the countryside on bad horses equipped with poor saddles, traveling league after league on bad roads in search of a sick or wounded person; if they had seen Reverend Father Narciso Durán, as I did, with his head uncovered and barefoot, teach the Indians how to cultivate the lands with wooden tools, or Father Sánchez instruct the neophytes in the art of pruning the vineyard or some other hard work, I am certain they would set aside their criticism. This criticism is so unjust, and should not be doled out against individuals who during their lifetime made unprecedented efforts to redeem this blessed land from the hands of the barbarous infidels. When the Americans came to this country, they found it already oriented on the path of civilization. But the Reverend missionary Fathers found it filled with hundreds of thousands of Indians thirsty for the blood of Christians. I can still remember the revolt at La Purísima. Pacomio, the great Indian chief, had taken all the necessary steps to carry out a successful combined operation to eliminate all the *gente de razón* living in Alta California. I also remember that in 1838, the Indians were still conspiring against the lives, property, and interests of the Californios.[5] During that year, despite the fact that all the inhabitants were armed, the gentiles burned the Sánchez family rancho, ransacked the Pacheco rancho, and raped all the women at those places. They killed Don Pedro Mejía as he tried to defend the honor of one of his nieces, whom the infidels were trying to offend in his presence. Those were dangerous times that put the resolve of the Fathers' souls to the test. I am confident that no one of my race who has witnessed the conduct of those worthy ministers of God would fail to recognize that civilization is indebted to them for the progress that has been made in this, my native land. When the foreigners came here, they found the land free of its primitive ways because the Indians had already disappeared. In addition, the indomitable missionary had explored the forests, rivers, plains, and hills, always placing himself first in harm's way. And after victory, he would spurn not only the material benefits his role in the triumph could bring him, but also the gratitude of those who were by his side in this conquest.* The Fathers only sought to dedicate themselves to the noble work of attracting souls to the bosom of the Apostolic Catholic religion. This, without exception, was the conduct of the missionary Fathers in Alta California from June 3, 1770, until 1833. There is nothing that can prevent me from making this assertion, because my grandparents and other relatives who are the true founders of this country told me everything I have recounted. And I personally have wit-

---

*Cerruti comments in English that "she alluded to the Yankees, which she styles as foreigners."

nessed many meritorious acts by the Reverend Fathers and have admired their virtues ever since I was an innocent young girl. Here I am today, the mother of twenty boys and five girls, and I have one foot in the grave. However, I still remember the Fathers with the utmost satisfaction.

The second daughter [Angustias de la Guerra] of retired Señor Captain Don José de la Guerra y Noriega married the distinguished Doctor Santiago Ord. He was a citizen of the United States of America, born in Washington, D.C. In January 1847, Dr. Ord came to California as a surgeon and doctor of Company F of the United States artillery. He remained in the service of his government until the end of the war. He later retired from military service. In Monterey, he dedicated his life to the medical profession. This allowed him to live very comfortably and amass a rather large fortune. After becoming a rich man, Dr. Ord made various trips to the United States and traveled to all the important places in the Mexican Republic. He happened to find himself in the capital of Mexico when President Benito Juárez died. Chance had crowned Juárez with the laurels that by rights belonged to Rivas Palacios, Plácido de la Vega, Jesús Gonzales Ortega, Diego Alvarez, and Porfirio Diaz. I remember hearing Dr. Ord say that when that illustrious Indian died, the authorities were having tremendous difficulties obtaining the necessary funds to pay the funeral expenses. There were only forty-eight pesos in cash in the general treasury of the Mexican Republic.

Anita, the third sister, married Alfred Robinson. He was a merchant from the United States of North America (Boston) who had arrived in Monterey in 1827 aboard the North American merchant frigate *Brookline*. This frigate belonged to Don Guillermo A. Gale, also known as "Four Eyes." Señor Robinson came to California as a second supercargo of that ship. He found our country so pleasing that he decided to stay and conduct business in the ports. He spent most of the time traveling up and down the coast aboard Señor Gale's ships, managing his interests as he pleased. Señor Gale and the missionary Fathers had the highest opinion of Don Alfredo Robinson. Even though he was of the Protestant religion, in California he received the holy sacrament of baptism in order to gain the good will of the Catholics of this country. On one of Señor Robinson's trips to the United States, he published an anonymous book entitled *Travels in California*. She could not judge its merits because she is not very familiar with the English language. She did remember hearing her deceased brother, Senator Don Pablo de la Guerra, say to his friends that Señor Robinson's narrative was quite biased.

Richard Henry Dana came to California as a seaman on board the Pilgrim *in 1835. In* Two Years Before the Mast, *he described the festivities that accompanied the Santa Bárbara wedding of Anita de la Guerra and Alfred Robinson. Courtesy of The Bancroft Library, University of California, Berkeley*

If a large number of the events in the narrative had actually happened as he described them, the people involved would not recognize themselves based on Señor Robinson's version, because he had distorted the events so much. She had been told by her husband, her uncle General Mariano Guadalupe Vallejo, and a number of family friends that *Travels in California* seemed more like a book written to gain the goodwill of the important people in this country. It was not a serious history capable of transmitting for posterity a faithful reminder of the events Robinson had witnessed. I asked her what kind of person Señor Robinson was. She told me that as a husband and a father, he was unsurpassable. His strong faith was proverbial and his love for all his family as well as his wife's relatives was exactly what one could hope for. He was always willing to do anything he could to make them happy.

When Howland and Aspinwall and Henry Chauncey had the upper hand in the Pacific Mail Company, because of the Panama railway, they had Señor

Alfred Robinson named agent of the Pacific Mail Company in the Port of San Francisco.[6] He earned praise from the directors of the company and from the public for the way he fulfilled his responsibilities. At the present time, Señor Robinson lives in San Francisco, where he manages the interests of ex-Governor Don Pío Pico. Many other old Californios have also entrusted Señor Robinson with managing their businesses. They know very well that rectitude is the principle that guides Señor Robinson.

Her youngest sister, María Antonia, was married to the Spanish merchant Lataillade. After a few years of marriage she was left a widow with four children. She married again and became the wife of Don Gaspar Oreña, a rich merchant and landowner from the city of Santa Bárbara. She presently lives in Santa Bárbara surrounded by a large family and all the comforts that a colossal fortune and a loving husband can give her.

While Captain Don José de la Guerra y Noriega was alive, he was always held in the highest regard by the inhabitants of Alta California, those from the north as well as those from the south. However, he did have a small dis-

Alfred Robinson, who married Anita de la Guerra in 1836. Teresa de la Guerra reported that some Californios judged Robinson's Life in California *(1846) to be an inaccurate portrait of their history and culture. Courtesy of The Bancroft Library, University of California, Berkeley*

agreement with Commander General Mariano Guadalupe Vallejo in 1838. After giving the situation some thought, the commander backed down and lifted the twenty-four-hour arrest he had placed on the captain.

Before Commodore Stockton arrived in California, her father owned four large ranchos that comprised a total of fifty-three square leagues. Those ranchos were: Cieneguita (25 leagues in size), Conejo (11 leagues), and San Julián. San Julián was known as the Rancho Nacional because it had once belonged to the nation. Governor José Figueroa had designated the rancho as separate from the other national lands so it could be used to rear the cattle and horses that belonged to the troops garrisoned at the presidio of Santa Bárbara. However, in 1837, Governor Don Juan B. Alvarado owed her father money but did not have the funds available to pay him because he had paid the troops in Alta California in advance. Instead, he paid her father back by giving him title to eleven leagues of land, which is the rancho referred to above as San Julián. There was a lot of gossip at that time about that transaction. Some came forward and openly said that Governor Alvarado had given Rancho San Julián to her father as a means of persuading him to side with those who favored California independence. But in her opinion, it was clear that the people who spread such rumors did not know Captain de la Guerra, for if they had any dealings with him or had the opportunity to understand his feelings about the matter, they would not have spread such false notions. Captain de la Guerra y Noriega yielded to Governor Alvarado because he was tired of seeing the Mexicans send governors and officials to this country who were men of very bad principles. I believe that with the exception of the Señores Echeandía and Figueroa, all the rest were very bad individuals. There was one Mexican governor who was crazy and lecherous. He was given the nickname "Oso Chico" [Little Bear], but his real name was Mariano Chico. There were many officials who were cowards and bad people, but the worst one of them all was a man named Rodrigo del Pliego. For example, one time a foreigner who was in the process of killing otters and beavers punched del Pliego. The foreigner then gave del Pliego a small amount of money as compensation for the beating.

I then asked Señora Hartnell the name of the other rancho. She told me that it was a small rancho not worth describing. I informed her that it was extremely important that I know even the most insignificant details about her parents' illustrious family. She then told me that the ranchito was called Las Pozas and it was only six leagues in size. I asked her about the number of cattle, sheep, and horses that her father owned at the time Alta California was swallowed up by the Yankees. She said that her family owned more than fifty-eight thousand head of cattle. She did not remember how many horses and sheep were grazing on their lands, but she thought that it was in proportion to the number of cattle. She had always heard that after Señor Vallejo and Señor Lugo, Señor Noriega was the person who had the most cattle in the nation. During the period of Mexican independence and after an agreement had been reached with the Mexican government, oxen, cattle, horses, and sheep abounded in Alta California. Travelers who would go from one place to another were allowed to kill steers in the fields whenever they needed them for food. The only thing required was that they leave the hide staked so the owner could pick it up when he passed through his property.

With regard to her father, Señor Captain de la Guerra y Noriega, she said that even during the time of the Americans he had been able to keep some of his immense property holdings. However, lawyers and squatters had seized most of it. Her father died in Santa Bárbara on February 11, 1858, at eleven-thirty in the morning. His funeral was the most well-attended funeral that has ever taken place in Santa Bárbara. If you take into consideration the number of inhabitants that were in the city at that time, you could say that it was the most well-attended funeral that has ever taken place in California. Everyone from Santa Bárbara attended the religious service, regardless of their religious or political beliefs or their nationality. There was general mourning. Businesses were closed. The press dedicated entire columns of their newspapers to eulogies celebrating the virtues of the deceased. Even British and Spanish poets tuned their lyres to sing the praises of Captain Don José de la Guerra y Noriega, who had left this life at the age of the patriarchs. He left more than one hundred and twenty-five direct descendants on this earth. They were grief-stricken and wept at the death of this great man who knew how to earn the glorious title of *Padre del Pueblo*. Even though seventeen years have passed since that ill-fated day when Divine Providence snatched from us the best of fathers, the most loyal of friends, and the most honorable of citizens, his many virtues are still fresh in the memory of the grateful people of Santa Bárbara.[7]

Concerning the gentleman and French writer Don Duflot de Mofras, she told me the following. In 1841 Señor de Mofras appeared at Rancho del Alisal while her husband was away in San Diego attending to his responsibilities as visitor general of the missions of Alta California. The Alisal property belonged to her husband, Señor Hartnell. When Señor Mofras arrived at the rancho, he dismounted at the entrance of the house but did not seek the customary permission. Travelers knew that all Californio rancho owners freely offered hospitality to whomever happened to appear at their doorstep; however, the rancho owners appreciated it all the same when people asked permission to stay at their homes. It seems that Señor Duflot de Mofras was aware of our proverbial hospitality. However, although we were not as civilized as the ladies and gentlemen of his country, he was unaware that we had established among ourselves certain customs which gave us no reason to be envious of that lauded French civilization. After tying up his horse, he opened the *sala* door and headed straight to the library. With a brazen boldness that is shocking to think about, he began to scrutinize all the books and papers he could find. She also told me that when it was time for dinner, she followed the promptings of her heart and sent one of her servants to ask Señor de Mofras if there was anything they could get for him. With much arrogance and impudence, Señor de Mofras ordered the servant to unsaddle his horse and put it in the stable. Instead of obeying the order given by the intrusive gentleman, the servant went and told her about this further demonstration of arrogance. After being informed of this very strange behavior, she decided to go personally and question this person who dared give orders to her servants in her own home. She went to the room that housed Señor Hartnell's library. There she found Señor Duflot de Mofras busily inspecting as many papers as he could get his hands on. Even though she caught him in the act, inspecting somebody else's papers is not a crime punishable by law. It is, however, an act condemned by society, which holds meddlesome and unscrupulous people in contempt. She greeted him rather coldly. Her greeting, however, was reciprocated with certain gestures that only people who know one another very well or have very close family ties are allowed to use. She was filled with indignation at being treated with such little decorum in her own home. She told him, "Mind you, Señor, I am the wife of Señor Hartnell and this is my home. You desecrate the rules and sanctity of this domestic sanctuary as well as the respect that women deserve from all well-mannered gentlemen." Señor de Mofras was somewhat frightened after hearing such serious language expressed with such a decisive attitude by a person who "lived in the woods." But after a short while, his cold-bloodedness returned and he responded, "Señor Hartnell, your husband, gave me permission to come to his home; therefore, I expect you to provide me with anything I need. I will be staying here for a few days and I need a room where I can sleep." Since she could not find any way out of such an obligation, and believing that this man was telling her the truth, she could do nothing more than have the room he requested made ready for him. She did, however, harbor some doubts as to the veracity of his words. When it was time to eat, the Frenchman appeared in the dining room and seated himself at the head of the table. The best food available was served. But every time de Mofras was served something, he would make gestures of disapproval and say he did not care for such and such a dish. Señora Hartnell noticed these gestures and reprimanded him, saying, "Señor, what we eat at my table is what my family's rancho provides. If this does not please you, then do what suits you best." That broad hint, coupled with her gesture indicating the location of the door, should have been enough for any man endowed with some honor to understand, and he would have left. Señor de Mofras, however, was very brazen. He did not take into account that he was on shaky ground and that it would be preferable for him to leave rather than stay, and so he stayed in her home.

Señora Hartnell continued with her story. After dinner, she had Señor de Mofras taken to the bedroom that the servants had prepared for him. She did not see him again that night. The following morning she asked that he be called to breakfast, but Señor de Mofras did not answer the repeated knocks on the door of his room. She ordered the servants to force open the door. When the servants entered the guest's room, they found him stretched out on the floor, stark naked and drunk. The bed was in such a state that the odor emanating from it was very different than perfume made from roses or jasmine. I asked Señora Hartnell to what cause she attributed such a shocking state of affairs. She told me that, unfortunately, there was a trunk in Señor de Mofras's room. The trunk contained twenty gallons of fine altar wine that was a gift from her father, Señor Don José de la Guerra y Noriega, who had sent the wine from Santa Bárbara. And because it was mature wine of superior quality, she had ordered it kept in the room designated for visitors. She had feared that if she left the wine in the pantry, where the other provisions were kept, the household servants would quickly finish it off. She had set the wine aside for the exclusive use of the Father who said Mass daily in the private chapel on their hacienda. It was her belief that de Mofras, like any good Frenchman, sniffed out the wine and decided to sample it. He found that it was good and drank so much of it that he was deprived of his senses. She also told me that the young diplomat's drunken state caused a serious illness. He was forced to stay in bed for many days. She felt sorry for him because he was all alone, far from his native land, and far from his mother, brothers, and sisters. She does not remember hearing de Mofras say that he left brothers or sisters behind in France. Seeing him alone and without friends in a strange land, she sympathized with his sad fate. Since she looked upon him as a victim of a serious illness, she took care of him as if he were her child. She comforted him every day with consoling words, she brought him chicken broth, and she lavished attention on him as if he were a beloved son. After many days had passed, Señor de Mofras's health began to improve. When he finally began to feel strong enough, he would order the servants to saddle his horse so he could ride around the area of El Alisal. On one occasion, he left without saying good-bye to Señora Hartnell. She had no news of his where-abouts until Señor Don David Spence happened to arrive at El Alisal. This señor told her that he had seen the French diplomat in Monterey dancing with her sister Doña Angustias.

A month after de Mofras left El Alisal, her husband returned home. She reprimanded him for sending the "French drunk" (the nickname the ser-vants of El Alisal gave de Mofras) to the rancho to stay. Her husband assured her that he had not authorized such a thing. She undoubtedly had been tricked by an audacious and unscrupulous adventurer who resorted to lies to achieve his goal. A few days later, Señor Hartnell went to the room where de Mofras had stayed to take some black clothes out of the trunk. They planned on wearing these clothes to the baptism of one of their chil-dren. He found that the lock had been forced open and the black dress was missing. On one of his trips to Monterey, Señor Hartnell looked into the matter to see if he could discover the whereabouts of Señora Hartnell's dress. He was able to ascertain that Señor de Mofras was the person who had stolen the dress. I asked Señora Hartnell if she knew that de Mofras had later been arrested in San Antonio. She replied that she had heard that Cap-tain Jesús Pico had ordered de Mofras put in jail but she did not know why. I asked her if she thought de Mofras was an uneducated man or not very bright. She replied that she believed that he had studied much more than what the young Californios were being taught. When he was not drunk and was with Europeans, he demonstrated a deep understanding of the rules of good etiquette. But even when he was in his right mind, he would adopt an arrogant tone with the Californios. In her opinion and that of many Cali-fornios, and some foreigners, this arrogant tone demonstrated that de Mofras considered the Californios to be quite inferior to the Europeans. She firmly believes that this idea was deeply rooted in the mind of the agent of the king of France. And it would have been almost impossible to dispel this very unjust opinion he harbored toward the Californios.

I asked her if she had ever read the works de Mofras had written about his travels and residence in California. She responded that she had never read those works. I asked her if she harbored any hatred toward Señor de Mofras. She assured me that her Christian upbringing prevented her from hating human beings. She had no reason to hate him. She had put the events she had described to me behind her many years ago. I asked her if she had any objections to making public what she had recounted to me. She said that she saw no reason why the veil of secrecy should be drawn over a conversation that could not harm innocent people. She gave me complete authorization to make public—collectively or separately—all the historical facts she had recounted. Hubert H. Bancroft's representative had told her that Bancroft was preparing for posterity a history that would reflect times past and she simply wanted to place these facts at his disposal.

> *Enrique Cerruti*
> *Monterey*
> *March 12, 1875*

On March 21, I again visited Rancho del Alisal. I read to Señora Hartnell, in the presence of her esteemed daughter Doña Amelia and General M. G. Vallejo, the twenty pages that record the facts she communicated to me on my first interview on March 12. She found what I wrote to be a faithful account of what she told me and signed her name at the bottom of the page.

> *Enrique Cerruti*

I provided of my own free will the preceding narrative signed by Señor General E. Cerruti and I am signing it today, March 21, 1875.

> *M.ª Teresa de Hartnell*
> *In the presence of David Leese[8]*

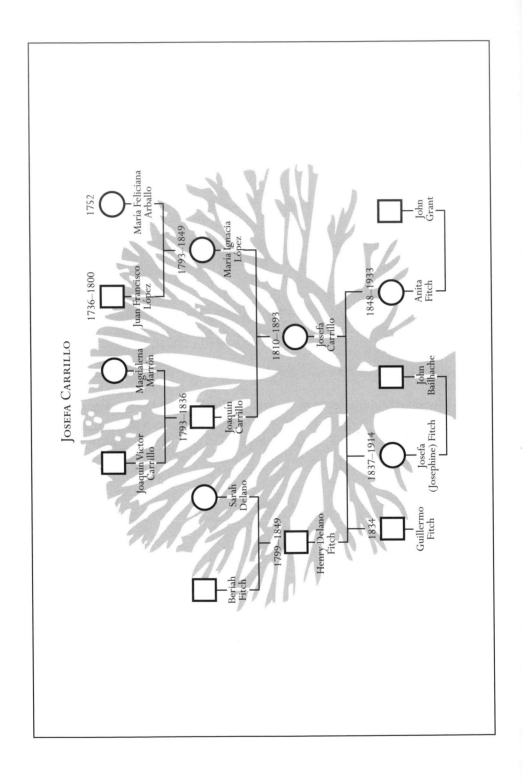

JOSEFA CARRILLO

1752 — María Feliciana Arballo

1736–1800 — Juan Francisco López

1793–1849 — María Ignacia López

Magdalena Marrón

1793–1836 — Joaquín Carrillo

Joaquín Victor Carrillo

1810–1893 — Josefa Carrillo

Sarah Delano

1799–1849 — Henry Delano Fitch

Beriah Fitch

John Grant

1848–1933 — Anita Fitch

John Bailhache

1837–1914 — Josefa (Josephine) Fitch

1834 — Guillermo Fitch

Josefa Carrillo

INTRODUCTION

*C*erruti's last interview with a Californio woman was with Josefa Carrillo. She admitted him into her home on November 24, 1875. In a sense, this brought Cerruti full circle. As we have seen, the very first interview he conducted with a Californio had been with Josefa Carrillo's son Guillermo Fitch on board the steamer that was taking Cerruti to Sonoma for his first meeting with Vallejo. Guillermo had suggested that Cerruti interview his mother, and a year and a half later, Cerruti paid her a visit. He was accompanied by Mariano Guadalupe Vallejo, who wished to obtain some documents relating to the business dealings of Josefa Carrillo's late husband, Henry Fitch.

Josefa Carrillo's family was deeply rooted in the military life of the Spanish colonial frontier, and it included many strong women. Her maternal grandmother, María Feliciana Arballo, had been a member of the 1775 Anza expedition. The widow of José Gutiérrez, she traveled with her two girls, María Tomasa, age six, and María Eustaquia, age four. On the evening of December 17, 1775, the three parties into which Anza had divided the expedition celebrated their rendezvous at San Sebastián, east of San Diego near the Salton Sea. Father Pedro Font wrote:

> At night, with the joy at the arrival of all the people, they held a fandango here. It was somewhat discordant, and a very bold widow who came with the expedition sang some verses which were not at all nice, applauded and cheered by all the crowd. For this reason the man to whom she came attached became angry and punished her.

Josefa Carrillo in the late nineteenth century, when she lived in the town of Healdsburg. Courtesy of the Healdsburg Museum, Healdsburg, California

The commander, hearing of this, sallied forth from his tent and reprimanded the man because he was chastising her. I said to him, "Leave him alone, Sir, he is doing just right," but he replied, "No, Father, I cannot permit such excesses when I am present." He guarded against this excess, indeed, but not against the scandal of the fandango, which lasted until very late.

The widow to whom Font was referring was María Feliciana Arballo. At Mass the next morning, Font used his homily to return to this incident:

I said Mass and in it spoke a few words about the fandango of last night, censuring the performance, saying that instead of thanking God for having arrived with their lives and not having died from such hardship, as the animals did, it appeared that they were making such festivities in honor of the Devil. I do not think that the commander liked this very well, for he did not speak to me once during the whole morning.[1]

María Feliciana did not remain long with the unnamed man who had rebuked her. When the expedition reached San Gabriel, she left it and soon married Juan Francisco López, a native of Baja California who was serving as a member of the mission guard there. Their youngest daughter, María Ignacia, was born at San Diego in 1793.[2]

In 1809, in the presidio chapel at San Diego, María Ignacia married Joaquín Carrillo. Her husband, who was born in San José del Cabo, came from an old Baja California military family. María Ignacia gave birth to thirteen children between 1810 and 1833. Their first child was a girl, whom they named María Antonia Natalia Elija, but who soon became known as Josefa. The family lived for a good amount of time in a house built just outside the presidio by *Comandante* Francisco Ruiz, who was godfather to three of the children.

Like her mother, María Ignacia was strong-willed. In 1835, for instance, she became embroiled in a controversy with her husband. Commander Ruiz had given the family the orchard of the house so that it could be held in trust for his three godchildren. However, Joaquín Carrillo decided to sell it instead. María Ignacio appealed over her husband's head to the governor, José Figueroa, and he disallowed the sale.[3]

Josefa Carrillo was most remembered in California for an event that occurred in 1829. Henry D. Fitch, a native of Massachusetts who had become a merchant seaman at a young age, arrived in Alta California in 1826. He was the master of the *María Ester,* a vessel owned by Enrique Virmond, a European businessman operating a series of trading ventures from his headquarters in Acapulco. Fitch became Virmond's agent in San Diego, and he found himself attracted to Josefa Carrillo, who was twelve years his junior. The attraction was mutual. As we have seen with the de la Guerra family, marrying eligible daughters to Anglo-American men of commerce was becoming an accepted practice among the elite and would-be elite of the territory, and Josefa's father gave his approval to the union. As was the law, Fitch prepared for the marriage by being baptized a Catholic. The baptismal ceremony occurred the day before the scheduled wedding. It took place at the presidio chapel and was administered by Father Antonio Menéndez. This priest had been removed from Mission San Vicente Ferrer in Baja California by Governor José María Echeandía as a result of Indian complaints against him. The governor then placed him at the presidio, where he would have little contact with Indians.[4]

The day after Fitch's baptism, as Menéndez was preparing to preside at the wedding, Domingo Carrillo, Josefa's uncle, and the man who had served as Henry Fitch's godfather the day before, burst into the house with the news that Governor Echeandía had forbidden the wedding. Menéndez immediately left, and the wedding did not take place.

In her testimonio, Josefa Carrillo indicated that Echeandía, who had made San Diego his residence, was a disappointed suitor for her hand. There may have been other reasons for the governor's refusal to allow the ceremony. Technically, Fitch had not completed the requirements for the wedding by becoming a Mexican citizen. Fitch may also have irritated the governor by engaging in the common practice of smuggling in the very seat of power of Alta California. Also, the recent incursions into the territory by fur trappers led by Jedediah Smith may well have made the governor impatient with North Americans.[5]

The very next day, Henry Fitch and Josefa Carrillo left San Diego together aboard his ship the *Buitre*. At the end of June they arrived in Valparaíso, Chile, where they were married by a priest. When they returned to San

Josefa Fitch, the oldest daughter of Josefa Carrillo and Henry Fitch, with her husband, John Bailhache. Courtesy of the Healdsburg Museum, Healdsburg, California

The plaza in Sonoma as it appeared in 1852, shortly after Josefa Carrillo moved her family to the area. Courtesy of The Bancroft Library, University of California, Berkeley

Diego with their young son in July of the next year, they presented church officials with their marriage certificate. Alleged irregularities in the document led to their both being detained in Monterey. Fitch was placed in jail at the presidio, which was commanded by Mariano Guadalupe Vallejo, who, ironically, would marry Josefa Carrillo's sister Francisca Benicia a year and a half later. Josefa Carrillo herself was lodged at the house of merchant Juan Cooper. Eventually they were both transported south to Mission San Gabriel, where an ecclesiastical investigation finally ruled that their marriage, although it had been contracted in an illicit manner, was valid. As a punishment for not following proper form, Fitch was ordered to pay for the installation of a new bell at the pueblo church in Los Angeles. It is not clear if he ever complied.[6]

With their marriage recognized, the couple settled in San Diego. Henry Fitch became a Mexican citizen in 1833. He spent a good amount of time at sea, while his wife raised their growing family. Six more children had been born by 1840, and eventually she gave birth twelve times. Their relationship was at times a stormy one. During one of her husband's absences, Josefa Carrillo apparently lost a good deal of money in some gambling events which she hosted at the store. At the end of 1835, Fitch put in motion an appeal for a legal separation from her, but she promised to restrain her behavior and they continued together. During the 1830s and 1840s, Fitch became a leading citizen of San Diego and held a variety of public offices, including *síndico* and *juez de paz*.[7]

Josefa Carrillo's father died around 1836, and her mother soon moved to the San Francisco Bay region, where her son-in-law Mariano Guadalupe Vallejo arranged to settle her on a rancho, Cabeza de Santa Rosa, north of Sonoma. Fitch received a grant of land, Rancho Satiyomi, in the same area in 1841. During part of the 1840s, he employed Moses Carson, Kit Carson's brother, to manage the rancho for him while he and his family were in San Diego. In 1846 Josefa Carrillo and María del Pilar Salvadora Ortega, wife of Santiago Argüello, received a land grant between Tijuana and Ensenada in Baja California.[8]

Henry Fitch died in January 1849. Josefa Carrillo took control of the store, which was now known as "the store of Doña Josefa Carrillo." She took charge of getting various goods onto ships and sending them to San Francisco to try to take advantage of the population increase there, but it proved a hard task. The death of her mother in Santa Rosa a scant six weeks after her husband's death did not make things easier for her. To help her out, Vallejo sold her a house in Sonoma that his brother-in-law

Benjamin Hayes toured Old Town in San Diego with Josefa Carrillo in 1874. Courtesy of the Seaver Center for Western History Research, Natural History Museum of Los Angeles County, Los Angeles, California

Jacob Leese had sold to him to finance a business trip to China. Josefa Carrillo was able to continue renting the house to its occupant, General Persifor Smith.[9]

Nevertheless, by the middle of 1850 she was still struggling. For instance, merchant John Temple wrote her a sarcastic note telling her that she still owed him money for a pair of shoes she had bought for her daughter. She claimed she had paid for them, but Temple insisted she was wrong. If she did not believe him, Temple continued, "I shall feel pleasure in making you a present of the bill, as I have the satisfaction of knowing I can live without it." Soon after, Josefa Carrillo moved her family north to Rancho Satiyomi.[10]

At the rancho, squatters were occupying parts of her land. In this situation, Josefa Carrillo was forced into the same strategy that plagued many Californio families after the gold rush: she had to sell some of her land in order to try to pay the legal costs involved in defending the rest of it. As we have seen with the family of Teresa de la Guerra, such decisions were never easy to make, and family members would sometimes disagree bitterly about legal strategies as they saw their landholdings being whittled down. Josefa Carrillo had to submit to a series of forced land auctions in 1856. At one such auction, Harmon Heald purchased over one hundred acres. A year later, he christened them "Healdsburg." Josefa Carrillo's daughter Josephine Bailhache sued to have squatters evicted in 1859 and won, but she was forced off part of the land in 1861. In 1870 two of Josefa Carrillo's children sued people who had bought some of the land she had been impelled to sell.[11]

Josefa Carrillo held on to the house on the plaza that Vallejo had sold her. After her first tenant, Persifor Smith, left she leased the house to an Episcopal priest, J. L. Ver Mehr, who operated St. Mary's Academy for Young Ladies there for a year. She also rented to Major Robert Allen, a quartermaster in the U.S. army. For a while the house was owned by someone else, who ran it as a hotel named the Fitch House. In 1874 she made a visit to San Diego. In Old Town, she took Benjamin Hayes on a tour of the house in which she had grown up and showed him the olive, pear, and pomegranate trees in the orchard that *Comandante* Ruiz had given to her family. She continued to live at her old rancho house until her death in 1893.[12]

Cerruti clearly intended for the interview with Josefa Carrillo to focus on the elopement. He began the conversation with a couple of "ice breakers," asking her about her own name, as well as the word "California." Once they got under way, her interview made it clear that she was not at peace with the world in which she had been forced to live. As we have seen with other Californio women who had lost large parts of their lands, she struggled to come to terms with the new order that the Americans had brought. Living on what was once her own Rancho Satiyomi but was now the city of Healdsburg was galling to her, and when Cerruti asked her about the origin of her rancho's name, she let loose with a denunciation of the ways in which the newcomers had butchered a series of native and Mexican place names in the region. For her, such destruction seems to have symbolized a deeper and lasting injury. At the end of the interview she made it clear that she and her husband had forgiven the Mexican ecclesiastical and military authorities who had harassed them when they married. The interview contained no such expression of reconciliation with those who had taken over her land.

Dictation of Mrs. Captain Fitch of Healdsburg

On November 24, 1875, in the city of Healdsburg, I visited Señora Doña Josefa Fitch. She is the widow of Captain Don Henry Fitch, a native of Charlestown, Massachusetts. I asked her about her name and she told me that it was María Antonia Natalia Elija Carrillo de Fitch. All of her relatives and friends call her Doña Josefa de Fitch. Three days after she was born, Señora Doña Josefa Sal del Mercado took her to be baptized. When she returned from the church, Señora del Mercado handed the baby over to her mother. When the mother asked her what name the baby had been given when she was christened, Señora del Mercado said that she could not remember, but for the time being they could call her Josefa. Señora del Mercado's suggestion was taken and ever since then everybody has known her by the name Josefa.

I asked her about the origin of the word "California." She answered that she remembers hearing her mother say that "California" is an Indian word, and in Spanish it means "high hill." This is the real meaning of the word and any of the other many meanings that have been offered by those who have written the books she has read, in English as well as in Spanish, are false and erroneous.

Her mother's name was María Ignacia López de Carrillo, and she spoke the language of the Diegueño Indians perfectly. The Diegueños spoke the same language as the Indians from Santa Catalina, Loreto, Santo Tomás, San

The Fitch family house, which was known as "Sotoyome," as it appeared in the early twentieth century. It was here that Cerruti interviewed Josefa Carrillo in 1875. Courtesy of the Healdsburg Museum, Healdsburg, California

Miguel, El Rosario, Santo Domingo, and all the land that is considered the northern frontier of Baja California and the southern frontier of Alta California. Don Crisóstomo Galindo, a famous corporal of the company who is now one hundred and three years old, believes that what Doña Josefa says is true. He lives in Milpitas, a small town situated near Mission San José.

I asked her about the meaning of the word "Satiyomí." She said that "Satiyomí" is derived from the Indian word *sati*, which means "brave" or "handsome," and *yomí*, which means *ranchería*, or large gathering of Indians. For the time being, the Americans have changed the name from Satiyomí to Sotoyome and, most likely, within a few years some "Yankee savant" will write a newspaper article to prove that the name of this place should be "Santo You and Me."

I asked her why she suspects the "Yankee savants" have such intentions. She said it is based on the following event. Near the city of Napa there was a place known by the Indians and by the Californios as "Violijolmanoli." Dr. Bale, an Englishman by birth who was originally from the city of Manchester, obtained the land title for this place from the Mexican government. In his petition to Governor Alvarado, Bale assigned the name "Carne Humana" to "Violijolmanoli." The odd thing was that he was granted title to the land and the place ended up being identified by the strange name "Carne Humana."[13] In Napa County, in the place known as "Valle de Berreyesa," there is a small river that the Californios and the Indians called "Río Putoy." The Americans, without permission from anyone, named it "Río de los Putos."[14] And Point Quintín, which was named for an Indian who was more of a demon than a saint, was later renamed "San Quentin" by the Americans. They had no right to do this. They believe they know it all. What amazes her most is that all those name changes were made by people who did not have the right to baptize anyone.

I asked her how her marriage to Captain Enrique Fitch had come about. She said that she met Captain Fitch in 1826 when he came to California as commander of the brig *María Ester* to engage in trade for Don Enrique Virmond. Virmond was a gentleman who had a huge fortune and was regularly engaged in large business enterprises with the Mexican government. Since she found the refined manners and handsome presence of the young man from Massachusetts to her liking, when he asked for her hand in marriage, she accepted. In March 1829, Señor Fitch returned to the port of San Diego as commander of the *Buitre*. At that time, San Diego was a port equipped for foreign trade. After Señor Fitch discussed the marriage proposal with my parents, they arranged for an altar to be prepared at home, and they had Reverend Father Fray Antonio Menéndez of the Dominican order come to our home. Dressed with the paraphernalia that ministers of the altar normally wore on such occasions, he proceeded to celebrate my marriage. He had barely begun the ritual when, by order of His Excellency General Echeandía, Señor Don Domingo Carrillo appeared in the *sala*. Carrillo was the assistant to His Excellency. In the name of the "citizen governor," he ordered Father Menéndez to immediately halt the tying of the nuptial knot, under penalty of incurring the wrath of the civil, military, and ecclesiastical authorities. That peremptory command was announced in the presence of a large gathering of people who, by character and upbringing, were used to blindly obeying all governmental orders. The announcement weighed so heavily on the spirit of the poor friar, who had just arrived in San Diego, that he decided to stop my marriage ceremony. He removed his ceremonial robes and left my parents' home as quickly as possible. Shortly after Fray Menéndez left, so too did Captain Fitch. He knew that his friend Don Pío Pico was a man whom you did not have to ask twice if it came to helping a woman, especially if that woman was his relative.[15] So Fitch told Pico everything he wanted Pico to do to help him carry

Henry Fitch. Courtesy of The Bancroft Library, University of California, Berkeley

out his just intentions and thwart the selfish designs of Governor Echeandía.

Echeandía was a man with liberal ideas, but in this instance he allowed his desires to lead him off the path of good sense and thus gave the order to stop the celebration of a function that was sanctioned by civil and ecclesiastical laws. During that time, I, as well as my female friends and relatives, harbored deep resentment toward Governor Echeandía. But a few years later, I forgave him with all my heart, since he was the one who liberated my country from the yoke of the tyrant Victoria. I concluded that his persecution of me and my husband was no more than an act motivated by the despair that had taken hold of his soul. He was convinced that I had shown preference for a rival whom he detested. Pío Pico advised Captain Fitch to board the ship he commanded and prepare to weigh anchor. As soon as it got very dark, Fitch was to send out a small boat for Doña Josefa. Pico would take care of getting her out of the house. Don Enrique Fitch followed his friend's advice. At the appointed hour a fine boat was ready and waiting at the place they had agreed upon ahead of time. In the meantime, Pío Pico came to my home. Using the types of arguments that have great impact on the soul of a young woman in love, especially coming from a person my parents considered worthy of their trust, Pico did not have any

After the gold rush, the Carrillo-Fitch elopement became one of the best-known events in early California history. This romantic, and inaccurate, 1875 painting by Charles Nahl illustrates the event's continuing power over the popular imagination. Courtesy of The Bancroft Library, University of California, Berkeley

trouble convincing me to accompany him. Together we rode on a fine horse to the place where Don Enrique Fitch was waiting for us with a sailboat manned by six sailors specifically chosen for that occasion.

Since it was already late, she only took from her home a small trunk containing a few petticoats and other items for daily use. She left her home and went to the place where Pío Pico was waiting for her. He helped her get on the horse first, then he got on and they rode as quickly as possible to the place where the boat sent by Captain Fitch was waiting for them. Once in the presence of her future husband, Don Pío Pico said, "Good-bye, cousin. May God bless you. And you, cousin Enrique, take care not to give Josefa reason to regret having joined her lot with yours." Captain Fitch answered that he promised, before God and man, that as long as he was alive, his wife would be happy. Doña Josefa Fitch says that he faithfully kept his promise. During the twenty years he lived by her side, he never caused her a moment's grief. Captain Fitch died on January 14, 1849. He was forty-nine years old, give or take a few months; Fitch was born on May

7, 1798. His wife was born in San Diego on December 29, 1810. The fruits of this marriage were: Enrique Eduardo, born June 23, 1830; Federico, born June 28, 1832; Guillermo, born November 7, 1834; José, born March 19, 1836; Josefa, born November 2, 1837; Juan, born April 6, 1839; Isabela, born August 24, 1840; Carlos, born September 1, 1842; Miguel, born March 13, 1844; María Antonia Natalia, born September 19, 1845; and Anita, born April 13, 1848.

Captain Fitch had barely arrived on board the *Buitre* when the mainsails were unfurled and the ship set sail. After seventy-four days at sea, the ship arrived safely at the port of Valparaíso, where Captain Fitch immediately ordered that preparations be made for the wedding. The marriage ceremony was celebrated by the parish priest of Valparaíso. The load of hides and tallow carried on the *Buitre* was sold in Valparaíso. Someone also offered to buy the *Buitre,* and the ship was sold in Valparaíso. Shortly afterward, Captain Fitch purchased the frigate *Leonora.* Loaded with bundles of food and other goods intended for the market in Alta California, the ship set sail for San Diego with a stop at the port of Callao. There, they loaded on board a large quantity of sugar and large jugs of *pisco de aguardiente de Ica.*[16] When the *Leonora* left the port of Valparaíso, the ship was flying the flag of North America, but Captain Fitch was planning to engage in coastal trading. He knew that at the ports in California every ship captain did what suited him best. He also knew that in the ports of the other states of the Union, only ships flying the Mexican flag could engage in coastal trading.

The Carrillo family house in San Diego. © *San Diego Historical Society, San Diego*

He therefore decided to enter the port of Acapulco to register his ship. He did so with little difficulty. From Acapulco he headed for San Diego. At that time, Don Juan Bandini was the customs administrator in San Diego. Bandini appraised part of the cargo and then sent the ship off to sail to ports along the coast.

While the cargo was being appraised, the *Leonora* remained anchored in the port of San Diego. Señora Fitch says that all the women who lived in the area came to pay her a visit and welcome her, including her mother and sisters. After exchanging greetings, Señora Fitch's mother told her that her father was very angry with her. He had vowed to kill her the moment he laid eyes on her again. When she heard this, she decided to go ashore without delay, because she preferred to risk death rather than live in anger with the man who had given her life. Once the decision had been made, she went ashore, accompanied by her female relatives and friends. She placed the young son she was carrying in her sister's arms and headed to her family home by herself. When she arrived at the threshold of her father's home, she pushed the half-open door. The first person she caught sight of was her father, who was seated near a small desk. He had a shotgun by his side. As soon as she saw him, she said, "Father, I have returned to San Diego to ask you to forgive me for leaving your home." Whether her father heard what she said or not, he kept silent. Seeing that a veritable storm was stirring within her father's soul, she threw herself down on her knees at the door of the room. In a humble tone, she again asked her father for forgiveness. She told him that if she had disobeyed him, she did it for the sole purpose of getting away from an odious tyranny that laws and customs condemned. She says that she spoke for a long time, but her father remained motionless and did not respond. Noticing that her father was no longer looking at the weapon, she crawled on her knees to the middle of the room. While she was moving, she continued to plead with her father. Finally, he was touched by her words. When she was but six *varas* away from where her father was seated, he got up, moved toward her, and took her in his arms. He picked her up and said, "Daughter, I forgive you because it is not your fault that our leaders are despots." After reconciling with her father, she returned to the door and motioned to her mother and friends to come and congratulate her. The home was immediately invaded by all the most highly respected women of San Diego, who were competing with one another to congratulate her on her happy return. The permission to marry prescribed by law was obtained from the proper authority, and that evening, a grand dance

Josefa Carrillo with members of her extended family in Healdsburg. She is seated in the middle row with her youngest daughter, Anita, and Anita's husband, John Grant. Also in the picture are some of Anita and John's children, other relatives, and friends. Courtesy of the Healdsburg Museum, Healdsburg, California

with lights was held at her home. That was a very pleasant way for this day to end, especially since it had been marked by signs of peril and storms.

Two days after the events I have described, the *Leonora* set sail for Monterey. The trip took seven days. After the visit by the proper authority, who made a pompous show of power, when we were preparing to go ashore, the assistant to His Excellency Governor Echeandía came back on board. He notified my husband and me that there was an order for our arrest. Even though Captain Fitch was surprised by such an order, he complied with it. Without causing any further delay, we went ashore. I was placed at the home of the wife of Captain Juan B. R. Cooper. Captain Enrique Fitch was taken to the harbormaster's office, which at that time was the responsibility of *Alférez* M. G. Vallejo. Our forced separation lasted three months. Then

His Excellency Governor Echeandía sent us to San Gabriel, the residence of Father José Sánchez, the president of the missions. Under his orders, the official documentation prescribed by Mother Church was drawn up. After the three months at San Gabriel were over, the many outlandish demands of the Catholic Church had been met, and they gave us permission to live as husband and wife.

I asked her what Captain Fitch did when he saw himself free from the persecutions of the friars and the governor. She said he began summary proceedings to demand payment for damages and losses he had suffered in his business interests. The Mexican authorities were more vicious than a water carrier's donkey. They put so many obstacles in the path of his legal proceedings that he was bored from wasting time and spending money and therefore put his demands aside. He also forgave his enemies for everything bad they had done to him. Just as her husband had forgiven his enemies, she forgave them as well.

I have read what Señor Cerruti has written down regarding what I told him and I find it consistent with the truth.

Josefa C. de Fitch

Catarina Avila

INTRODUCTION

On June 20, 1877, Savage's colleague Vicente Gómez interviewed Catarina Avila at her home in Santa Clara. Her life history represented two sides of the California experience. Her maternal grandparents had participated in one of the founding epics in California history, the second (1775) Anza expedition. Her husband had immigrated to California in the 1820s.

Catarina Avila's maternal grandparents, Ignacio Antonio Linares and María Gertrudis Rivas, were both natives of Sonora who had been recruited by Anza. They first served at the San Francisco presidio, and then they moved to San José in the mid-1780s. Their daughter María Antonia, their tenth child and the sixth born to them in Alta California, was born in the Pueblo de San José de Guadalupe in 1786. In 1805 María Antonia married soldier José Guadalupe Avila at Mission Santa Clara, and they settled in Monterey. There, in 1812, their fourth child and third daughter, Catarina, was born.[1]

It was in Monterey that Catarina Avila met Petronilo Ríos, a soldier who had arrived in Alta California in the mid-1820s. He had first served at San Francisco and was soon reassigned to the presidio at Monterey. In 1829 he was involved in the so-called Solís affair, when a number of the enlisted men at the presidio rebelled against their officers and the government. They locked some of the officers, including Mariano Guadalupe Vallejo, in the presidio jail for a time. The rebellion was put down after a brief series

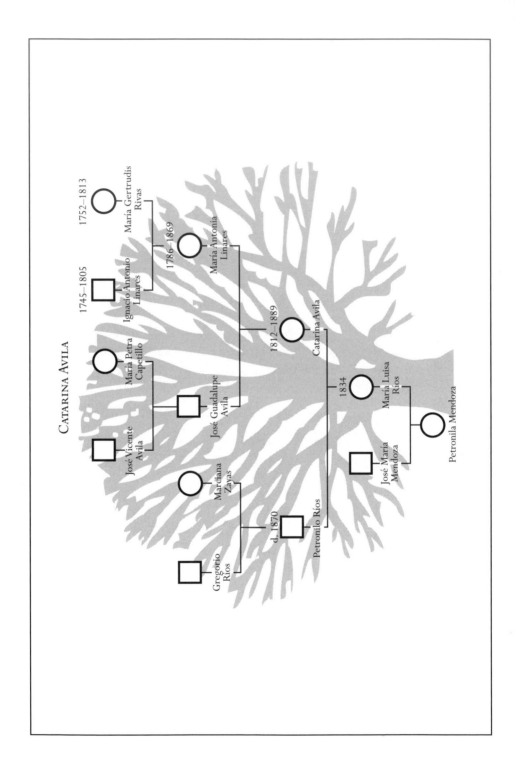

CATARINA AVILA

1752–1813 María Gertrudis Rivas

1745–1805 Ignacio Antonio Linares

1786–1869 María Antonia Linares

María Petra Capetillo

José Vicente Avila

José Guadalupe Avila

1812–1889 Catarina Avila

Marciana Zayas

Gregorio Ríos

d. 1870 Petronilo Ríos

1834 María Luisa Ríos

José María Mendoza

Petronila Mendoza

of skirmishes. In 1832 Petronilo Ríos and Catarina Avila were married at Monterey. By 1849 she had given birth to twelve children.[2]

Ríos spent most of the 1830s shuttling between Monterey, San Francisco, and Mission San Miguel, where he was a member of the guard. In 1839 he was promoted to the position of commander of artillery at Monterey.

Ríos retired from the military in 1840. Within two years he began to accumulate land. In 1842 he purchased the Rancho San Bernabé, between San Miguel and Monterey, from Jesús Molina. He took his family to live there and stocked it with about three hundred head of cattle. Manuel Castro later remembered seeing the entire Ríos family there, living in an adobe house, with ample cattle and horses and some land under cultivation.

In 1845, Ríos purchased Rancho Paso de Robles, just below San Miguel, from José Narváez. He moved his family there from San Bernabé, where they had been having trouble with Indian raids. Feliciano Soberanes, the husband of María Antonia Rodríguez, testified to the Land Commission that Ríos placed more than a thousand head of cattle there, cultivated the

Petronila Mendoza, granddaughter of Catarina Avila. Courtesy of Friends of the Adobes, San Miguel, California

land extensively, and occupied it until about 1851. In 1846, along with William Reed, an Englishman who had lived in the area for a number of years, he purchased the ex-Mission San Miguel.[3]

Ríos sold Paso de Robles in 1857, although he may have thought that he was leasing the land rather than selling it. The family moved to Santa Clara in the late 1860s, and he died in 1870. Catarina Avila lived with some of her children and then with her grandchildren. In 1886, one of her grand-daughters, Petronila Mendoza, was declared her legal guardian. Catarina died in 1889.[4]

The transcript of the interview apparently contains many of the actual words Catarina Avila used in her conversation with Gómez, although at one point Gómez did break in and refer to her in the third person. The interview itself was very focused. Gómez had clearly been instructed to take down her memories of a horrible event that had taken place at Mission San Miguel on the night of December 5, 1848. The day before, a group of six men, coming from the north, had passed through the mission. Two of the men had come to California with the U.S. military. One of them, named Peter Raymond, had been a member of Frémont's band, whose behavior Dorotea Valdez had so vigorously denounced. Raymond had recently escaped from jail, where he was being held for murder. At least two of the other three men were deserters from the U.S. naval vessel *Warren*. The sixth member was an Indian from the Soledad area named Juan.[5]

The group was welcomed at San Miguel by Reed, his pregnant wife, María Antonia Vallejo (an illegitimate daughter of Mariano Guadalupe Vallejo), their four-year-old son, and seven others, including a midwife, an African cook, an Indian sheepherder, and the sheepherder's grandson. During the course of the evening, Reed mentioned that he had just returned from the mines, where he had made a good amount of money by selling some sheep.

The travelers left the next morning but returned later that afternoon. That evening they systematically murdered everyone at the mission, robbed the place, and left. The bodies were discovered by the famed mountain man Jim Beckwourth, who at that time was carrying mail between Nipomo and Monterey. Beckwourth went to the nearest rancho and informed Catarina Avila and her husband of the murders.[6] He then continued on to Monterey to report the incident to the military authorities there. The next morning two ranchers who were heading to San Luis Obispo, John M. Price and Francis Z. Branch, also stumbled upon the scene. Word of the atrocity quickly spread throughout central California. A few days later, outside of Santa Bárbara, a posse headed by Cesáreo Lataillade (a brother-in-law of Teresa de la Guerra) caught up with the murderers. Juan had separated from the group, but the rest were all there. In the gunfight that ensued, Raymond and one other member of the gang were killed and the others were captured. A member of the posse, identified either as José Carrillo or Ramón Rodríguez, was also killed in the gun battle. The surviving members of the gang were found guilty by a special court and executed by a firing squad in Santa Bárbara on December 28.

Historical Recollections of California by Señora Doña Catarina Avila de Ríos, (Widow of Sergeant Petronilo Ríos)

This lady resides in Santa Clara; her husband served in the artillery in California many years and was at one time the chief commandant of his branch of the service.

I endeavored to get her husband's papers, but she assured me and Don Vicente P. Gómez that she had none.

She gave Gómez a full account of the wholesale murders committed in 1849 by tramps at the old mission of San Miguel. That account, furnished on 20 June 1877 at the lady's own house, appears in this book.

Tho.⁵ Savage
Santa Clara
June 20, 1877

Around December 1849, Mr. Guillermo Reed and his wife, María Antonia Vallejo, were living in old Mission San Miguel. He was from Great Britain and she was a native of Monterey. One of her brothers, José Ramón, was staying with them. They had a son who was about two or three years old and María was expecting another child at any moment. That is why the midwife, Josefa Olivera, was there with her fifteen- or sixteen-year-old daughter and her four-year-old grandson. An Indian who was about sixty or seventy years old was there as well, along with his four- or five-year-old grandson.

As has been said, this family lived peacefully at the mission. People frequently passed by the mission and the family was always generous with their hospitality. News of recently discovered gold prompted many people to head north, and at that time, it was necessary to travel along this road. It

Mission San Miguel. Courtesy of the California History Room, California State Library, Sacramento, California

still is necessary. The mission was granted to Señor Petronilo Ríos and to Mr. Reed by the last Mexican governor, Señor Pío Pico.

One afternoon in December, three or four Irishmen arrived at the mission accompanied by an Indian from Mission San Diego named José (or Loco). They asked Mr. Reed if they could stay at the mission and he let them stay. Mr. Reed provided them with everything they needed, both day and night. He treated them as if they were old friends and did not mistrust them at all. The men stayed at the mission for about five days. When they were about to leave, they asked if they could exchange some gold coins they had, so Mr. Reed had his brother-in-law bring him a canvas sack in which he kept stamped gold, silver, and placer gold, all mixed together. Mr. Reed had worked hard to obtain all of this. He exchanged the coins for them. Although it was already very late, the men left, but they only went as far as the area around Rancho de San Marcos. This rancho is probably half a league away, more or less. After nightfall, the men returned to the house at the mission and ate dinner in a room where there was a fireplace. They stoked the fire and engaged in conversation with Mr. Reed. His family had retired to other interior rooms. It was very late and the fire had died out, but one of the men decided to get up and go cut some pieces of firewood in the corridor. When he brought back the firewood, he also brought back the hatchet he had used to cut it. The women had not gone to bed yet. We know this because they met their death dressed in the clothes they were wearing during the day.

It is not known exactly when the men delivered the first blow to Mr. Reed's head. We know he was wearing his hat, because the hat was cut along the nape of the neck. The pool of blood that was there indicated that he died in that spot. The men then went to the rooms where the women were and began to kill them all. From what could be determined by the traces of blood on the floor and the victims' handprints on the walls, the killings took place in different areas. Two children were murdered. One was Señora Doña María Antonia's daughter and the other was her brother. They murdered the children with the hatchet while they were sleeping, for the pillows had been cut and were soaked in blood. After committing these murders, the men gathered up all the mutilated bodies and piled them up in the next room. From there they went to the kitchen and killed a black man who worked as a cook. He was not mentioned at the beginning of this account. The black man's body was just left there. Then they went to the room where the Indian sheepherder was sleeping. His little grandson was with him (he already has been mentioned). The men killed them and left both bodies there.

After committing all these atrocities, the men went to round up the horses that belonged to Mr. Reed, as well as other horses that travelers had left in his care. Then they gathered up all the money and jewels that belonged to the family. They had so much gall. They actually rifled through the family's clothing and picked out specific clothes they liked. When they finally finished all these activities, they went on their way. By dawn, they were eighteen miles away from San Miguel. They set up camp at the Río del Paso de Robles and built a fire there. It is known that they ate breakfast, because they left behind some tin containers, which some Indian servants from the Rancho del Paso de Robles found there. The Indians also found a new butcher's knife and a small box containing some gold earrings that had belonged to the deceased Doña María Antonia.

The woman who is relating this terrifying event does not remember who delivered the news to them at their Rancho del Paso de Robles. It could have been Mr. Juan Price, Señor Branch, or the mail carrier who would pass by there. But she does remember that one of these men gave Señor Ríos the empty bag in which Mr. Reed kept his silver money, stamped gold, and placer gold. She also remembers that at one point she did know how much money was in the bag, but now she cannot remember the amount.

It is believed that the mail carrier related the news about the murders as he traveled along his entire route. What is for certain is that the murderers were pursued and they were caught near Santa Bárbara. People had left Santa Bárbara to look for them. When the men were caught, a fight broke out between them and their pursuers. The thieves were able to fight with the firearms they had stolen from Mr. Reed at Mission San Miguel after they had committed the murders. She does not remember the outcome of this battle. She does remember that the judge from Santa Bárbara, Don Cesáreo Lataillade, wrote to Señor Ríos to ask if he wanted the murderers brought back to be hanged at the scene of the crime. Señor Ríos did not want that to happen. He said that the murderers should be punished there, and that is what happened. She also remembers that the leader of those murdering thieves threw himself into the ocean. His naked body was later found on the beaches of San Luis Obispo.

Because Señor Ríos was related by marriage to this unfortunate family, he went to San Miguel. After his first trip there, he returned again to bury the family. He had two graves prepared. After making sure that all the remains had been gathered, he buried all the victims.

The woman who is providing this account learned more about the details of this event from the evidence that was found in the house. Somebody also talked to her about it, but she does not remember who it was. She thinks it was Mr. Price. When he was at Rancho Paso de los Robles he said he did not know what had actually happened at San Miguel. He did say that the house was wide open and the sheep and cattle were penned up in

This adobe, a short distance from Mission San Miguel, is now known as the Ríos-Caledonia adobe. Constructed around 1835 under the general supervision of Petronilo Ríos, it was designed to serve as a residence for the mission administrator after secularization. Catarina Avila, Petronilo Ríos, and their family moved into the adobe around 1852. Reproduced by permission of The Huntington Library, San Marino, California, Pierce Collection #7778

the corrals and dying of hunger. Nobody was there. That is exactly what Señor Ríos discovered when he arrived there. The only door that was shut was the old door to the room where the bodies were piled up.

Señor Lataillade wrote to Señor Ríos and asked him to go and retrieve the stolen goods that had been recovered from the murdering thieves. However, Señor Ríos sent word by way of Don Pablo de la Guerra that everything should be given to José Carrillo's widow. Carrillo was a member of the party that left Santa Bárbara to pursue the thieves. The thieves killed him.

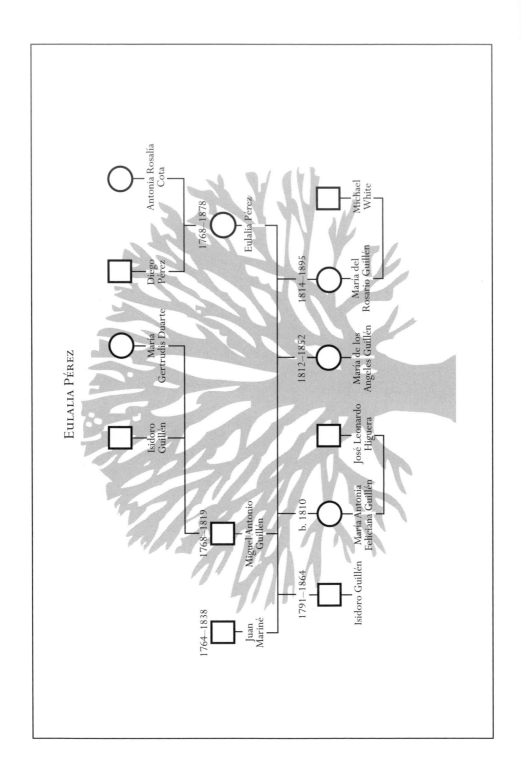

EULALIA PÉREZ

Antonia Rosalia Cota

Diego Pérez

1768–1878 Eulalia Pérez

Michael White

1814–1895 María del Rosario Guillén

María Gertrudis Duarte

1812–1852 María de los Ángeles Guillén

Isidoro Guillén

José Leonardo Higuera

1768–1819 Miguel Antonio Guillén

b. 1810 María Antonia Feliciana Guillén

Juan Mariné 1764–1838

1791–1864 Isidoro Guillén

Eulalia Pérez

INTRODUCTION

*E*ulalia Pérez was the first woman Thomas Savage interviewed. When he sat down with her in December 1877, she was already something of a tourist attraction in southern California: some local boosters were touting her advanced age as evidence of the wonderful effect of the salubrious climate of southern California. Some of her fervent advocates claimed that she was nearly one hundred and forty years old. The year before, one of her daughters had contracted to have her exhibited at San Francisco and at the Centennial Exposition in Philadelphia. Another daughter, María del Rosario Guillén de White, with whom she was living, had to go to court to prevent that from occurring. The fame of Eulalia Pérez, however, continued. For instance, on her trip to the West in 1877, Miriam Squire (Mrs. Frank Leslie) reported, "While in San Francisco we had been shown the photograph of Eulalia Pérez—the oldest woman in the world." Her age was actually given as one hundred and eleven in the 1870 census.[1]

Eulalia Pérez may, in fact, have been older than Spanish Alta California. Some modern authorities believe that she was born as early as 1768, the year before the Portolá expedition founded San Diego. As she reported in her testimonio, she was born in Baja California. Her parents were Diego Pérez and Rosalía Cota. She married a soldier of the Loreto company, Miguel Antonio Guillén, who was transferred to Alta California in 1802. They were stationed at San Diego until about 1810, and after that at San Gabriel. While married to Guillén, Eulalia Pérez gave birth twelve times. Seven of her children lived into adulthood.[2]

Eulalia Pérez, about one year before her death. She was erroneously reported to be 139 years old. Courtesy of the California Historical Society, FN-36278

After her husband died in 1819, the priests at San Gabriel took Eulalia Pérez in. After winning the cook-off that she describes in her testimonio, she was appointed *llavera,* "keeper of the keys," at the mission. She assumed a vast set of responsibilities at San Gabriel, which she proudly recounted to Savage.

In 1832 the priest at San Gabriel convinced her to marry Juan Mariné, a Spaniard who had come to Alta California as a soldier in 1795 and who had retired to Los Angeles in the early 1820s. Mariné stated that he had "the misfortune to lose by the floods of the year 1831 an orchard in the pueblo of Los Angeles," so he was in need of other sustenance. With secularization on the horizon, the missionaries at San Gabriel were seeking ways in which at least a portion of the mission lands might end up in the hands of those who were friendly to the mission system. Eulalia Pérez definitely fit that description. Her interview indicated that the priest wanted her to have the land and that Mariné was regarded as a kind of tool in the process. The

This Spanish colonial couple, possibly Ana María Bernal and Gabriel Moraga, were sketched by José Cardero in Monterey in 1791. Eulalia Pérez and her husband Miguel Antonio Guillén were attired in a similar fashion when they were stationed at the San Diego Presidio in 1802. Courtesy of the Museo de América, Madrid

missionaries most likely thought that Mariné's military past would justify giving the land to his wife.

After the marriage, Mariné was indeed granted a large rancho, San Pascual, in 1834. But neither the marriage nor the grant worked out. Eulalia and Mariné did not get along. Perhaps for this reason, Mariné never really developed the land or occupied it himself. When he died, his son sold off the grant to Juan Pérez and Enrique Sepúlveda. Both of them died in the early 1840s, and the rancho, which is now the site of the cities of Pasadena and Altadena, ended up owned by Mexican army lieutenant Manuel Garfias.[3]

Through all this, Eulalia Pérez remained in residence at San Gabriel. When Savage visited, she was living at San Isidro, near Mission San Gabriel, with her daughter María del Rosario, her daughter's husband, Michael White, and four of the couple's children. She died exactly six months after her interview with Savage, on June 11, 1878.

Her testimonio revealed Eulalia Pérez to be tremendously proud of the part she had played in the development of California. She recounted the series of responsibilities she had undertaken, from her indispensable role as midwife in San Diego through her important administrative posts at Mission San Gabriel. She described the nuts and bolts of mission life in considerable detail, no doubt because she herself had organized many of the processes for cooking and serving at the mission, feeding the native laborers in the fields, and keeping track of the comings and goings of the mission residents that she detailed. The mission was, in her telling, a place whose internal operations were largely directed by her and her daughters. And after half a century, she was still proud of her abilities as a singer and a dancer.

Through it all, she retained command of her memories. If she did not recall all the priests she met during her long stay at San Gabriel, she clearly said so. When she dealt with the controversial question of the amount of money at the missions, she reported what she had seen, but she refused to speculate about matters of which she had no direct experience. She knew how the priests with whom she had worked closely treated the Indians, but she would not be drawn into commenting about the behavior of other clergy.

Above all, she celebrated the Spanish and Mexican women of Alta California. They educated the children, they cured diseases, and at Mission San Gabriel, they administered the largest population center in the Los Angeles area. The mission had been her responsibility and her joy, and its decline was as painful for her as it had been for any of the clergy.

An Old Woman and Her Recollections, Dictated by Doña Eulalia Pérez, Who Lives at Mission San Gabriel at the Advanced Age of 139 Years, to D. Tomás Savage for the Bancroft Library, 1877

Eulalia Pérez, widow, first of Miguel Antonio Guillén, and next of Juan Mariné, lives in the San Isidro Ranch belonging to her son-in-law Michael C. White, who is upwards of seventy-five, and his wife, upwards of sixty-three years of age.

Whatever may be the real age of Madame Eulalia Pérez, she is certainly a very ancient person. There can be no doubt, from her personal appearance, that she is a centenarian. The accompanying photograph gives a very correct idea of her as I found her when I took from her lips the notes which appear on the annexd. thirty-three pages.

For a person of such an uncommon age, she is not entirely feeble or helpless, inasmuch as she can do some needlework and walk about the house unsupported even by a staff.

She sat by me upon a chair awhile yesterday; but her usual seat is on the floor, and when flies or mosquitoes annoy her, she slaps and kills them with her slipper on the floor. When wishing to rise, she places both palms of her hands on the ground before her and lifts herself first on four feet (so to speak) and then with a jerk puts herself on her two feet—for this she needs no assistance. After that she goes about the house without difficulty. She did it in my presence yesterday, and saying that she felt chilled, walked out and sat on the stoop to sun herself awhile, then came back and resumed her former seat.

I was assured that with support, and occasional rest on a chair taken with her, she walks to their granddaughter's house, a distance of five hundred yards or more.

Her memory is remarkably fresh on some things and much clouded on others, particularly on her age. She is at times flighty, but with patience and by asking her questions only when such matters as she could be conversant with, I found no great difficulty in obtaining intelligible answers. I had to resort to Mrs. White's assistance in asking the questions, because the centenarian lady is quite deaf, though not to the extent of needing to be addressed in an excessively loud tone.

I discontinued my questions as soon as I discovered that she was fatigued and have not returned to see her, because I had to leave Mission San Gabriel, near which the San Isidro ranch is, and visit this place.

*Thos. Savage
Spadra
December 11, 1877*

I, EULALIA PÉREZ, was born at the presidio of Loreto, in Baja California.

My father's name was Diego Pérez and he worked in the naval department at the presidio. My mother's name was Antonia Rosalía Cota.* They both were white people through and through.

I do not remember the date of my birth, but I do know that I was fifteen years old when I married Miguel Antonio Guillén, a soldier of the presidio company of Loreto. When I was living in Loreto, I had three sons and one daughter. Two of the boys died in Loreto at a young age and another boy,

*Savage's footnote here reads: "Michael White, her son-in-law, says Lucía Valenzuela."

Isidoro, came with us to Alta California. I had one girl, Petra, who was eleven years old, when we moved to San Diego.

I lived in San Diego for eight years with my husband. He continued his service as a soldier at the presidio of San Diego. I assisted the women who were in labor.

I had relatives who lived in the vicinity of Los Angeles and even farther north. I asked my husband many times if he would take me to see them, but he did not want to go with me. The presidio commander would not let me go either, because there was no other woman at the presidio who knew how to deliver babies.

Everyone in San Diego respected me very much. I was treated with much affection in the homes of the important people. Even though I had my own house, those families would have me stay at their homes all the time and they even provided for my children.

In 1812, while I was attending Mass at the church at San Juan Capistrano, there was a huge earthquake that knocked down the tower. I ran through the sacristy and was knocked to the ground in the doorway. I was pregnant and could not move, and people stepped on top of me. Soon after, I returned to San Diego and almost immediately gave birth to my daughter María Antonia, who still lives here in San Gabriel.*

After living in San Diego for eight years, we went to Mission San Gabriel, where my husband served in the guard. On October 1, 1814, my daughter María del Rosario was born. She is the wife of Miguel White. I am now living in their house.

About four years later, I returned to San Diego with my husband and family. My husband was sick and wanted permission to be discharged from the military. At first they refused his request, but in the end they granted it. About six months or perhaps one year later, we returned to San Gabriel. My husband was gravely ill and died in Los Angeles soon after. They sent me an escort to take me back to San Diego. Since my oldest son, Isidoro Guillén, was a soldier, they put him in charge of the escort. I returned to San Diego with my entire family and went to spend time at the home of Don Santiago Argüello, the commander of the presidio. Before Argüello became commander, Don Francisco María Ruiz had been the commander for many years. Before him, Don Manuel Rodríguez was commander, and before Rodríguez, some fellow named Don Antonio was the commander.[4]

When I first came to San Diego, there were no other houses at the presidio except for the commander's house and the soldiers' barracks.

---

*Footnote by Savage reads, "It must have been María de los Angeles."

There was no church. The missionary who would come from Mission San Diego would say Mass in a shelter made from some old walls covered with branches.

The first adobe house that was built in San Diego belonged to some fellow named Sánchez. He was the father of Don Vicente Sánchez, the *alcalde* of Los Angeles and delegate of the *diputación territorial*. The house was very small but everybody would go and see it as if it were a palace. That house was built about a year after I arrived in San Diego for the first time.

My last trip to San Diego was probably in 1818. My daughter María del Rosario was about four years old then. Something tells me that I was there when the insurgents came to California. I remember that they captured a foreigner and put shackles on him, but then they took them off.

About three years later I returned to San Gabriel. The reason for my return was that Father José Sánchez, the missionary at San Gabriel, had written to his cousin Father Fernando at San Diego. He asked him to speak with the commander of the San Diego presidio and beg him to give my son Isidoro Guillén an escort to bring me back to San Gabriel with my entire family. The commander granted the request.[5]

When we arrived here, Father José Sánchez provided me and my family with a small house where we could live temporarily until I found work. I lived there with my five young daughters. My son Isidoro Guillén was serving as a soldier in the mission escort.

At that time, Father Sánchez was between sixty and seventy years old. He was a Spaniard and a white man. He was of medium height and heavy set. He was a very good, loving, and charitable man. He, like his colleague Father José María de Zalvidea, treated the Indians very well. Both men were well loved by the *gente de razón* and the neophytes, as well as by the other Indians.

Father Zalvidea was quite old. He was very tall and a bit heavy. He was a white man. I heard it said that Zalvidea was sent to San Juan Capistrano because there was no missionary there. Later I found out that many years later, when Father Antonio Peyri fled San Luis Obispo, it was rumored that the Fathers were going to be killed. Father Zalvidea was very sick and, truth be told, he had not been in his right mind since they took him from San Gabriel. He did not want to leave that mission. I think the Father was scared. Two Indians from San Luis Rey went to San Juan Capistrano and placed him in a *carreta* used for hauling hides. They made him as comfortable as possible and took him to San Luis Rey, where he died soon after, due to the rough ride he had to tolerate.

Eulalia Pérez was living and working at Mission San Gabriel when Ferdinand Deppe painted this picture of the mission in 1832. Courtesy of the Santa Bárbara Mission Archive-Library

Father Zalvidea loved his "mission children" very much. This is what he called the Indians whom he personally had converted to Christianity. Sometimes he would go on horseback, and other times on foot, and cross the mountains until he reached the *rancherías* where the gentiles lived, so he could bring them to our religion.

Father Zalvidea introduced many improvements at Mission San Gabriel and helped it move forward in every way. He was not satisfied with feeding only the mission Indians an abundant amount of food. He also wanted the wild Indians to have something to eat. So he planted trees in the mountains and far from the mission so the other Indians would have food when they passed by those places.

The last time I came to San Gabriel, there were only two women in this whole part of California who really knew how to cook. One was María Luisa Cota, the wife of Claudio López, the *mayordomo* at the mission. The other woman was María Ignacia Amador, the wife of Francisco Javier Alvarado. She knew how to cook, sew, read, and write, and she could take care of the sick. She was a fine *curandera*. Her job was to sew and take care of the church garments. In her home, she taught some children how to read and write, but she did not have a formal school.

On important feast days, such as that of the patron saint and Easter, the two women would be called upon to prepare the large meal, the meat dishes, sweets, and other things.

The Fathers wanted to help me because I was a widow supporting a family. They looked for ways to give me work without upsetting the other women. Father Sánchez and Father Zalvidea discussed the matter and decided to see who was the best cook. One woman would cook first, followed by the next one, and I would be the last one to cook. The woman who surpassed the others would be assigned to teach the Indian cooks how to cook. The señores who would be deciding on the quality of the three meals were notified ahead of time. One of the men was Don Ignacio Tenorio, whom they called the "king's judge."[6] He came to live and die in the company of Father Sánchez. Senor Tenorio was a very old man. When he would go out, he would wrap himself up in a little shawl and walk very slowly, aided by his cane. His long walk amounted to going from the Father's house to the church.

In addition to the Fathers, the other judges who were asked to give their expert opinion were Don Ignacio Mancisidor, a merchant; Don Pedro Narváez, a naval officer; Sergeant José Antonio Pico, who later became a lieutenant and was the brother of Governor Pío Pico; Don Domingo Romero, who was my assistant when I was the *llavera* at the mission; and Claudio López, the *mayordomo* at the mission.

Whenever those men were at the mission, they would eat with the Fathers. They were present for the three meals on the designated days. I was not told anything about this until the day Father Sánchez called me over and said, "Look, Eulalia, tomorrow it is your turn to prepare the dinner, because María Ignacia and Luisa have already done so. Let's see what kind of dinner you will give us tomorrow."

The next day, I went to cook. I made several soups, a variety of meat dishes, and anything else that came to mind that I knew how to make. Tomás, the Indian cook, paid close attention to what I was doing, as the Father had told him to do.

The men I mentioned came at dinnertime. After they finished the meal, Father Sánchez asked them what they thought of the food, beginning with the oldest man, Don Ignacio Tenorio. This señor pondered for quite some time. He said that it had been many years since he had eaten as well as he had that day. He doubted that a person would eat better food at the king's table. The other men also praised the meal highly.

The Father then asked Tomás which of the three señoras he liked best and which one knew the most. He said it was me.

Based on this, I was given a job at the mission. First, two Indians were assigned to me so I could teach them how to cook. One was named Tomás and the other was "El Gentil." I taught them so well that I had the pleasure of seeing them turn out to be very fine cooks. They were, perhaps, the best cooks in this whole part of the country.

The Fathers were very happy and this helped me earn more of their respect. I spent about a year teaching those two Indians. I did not have to work; I just supervised them because they now had some basic knowledge of cooking.

The Fathers then talked among themselves and agreed to hand over the mission keys to me. This was in 1821, if I remember correctly. I remember that my daughter María Rosario was seven years old at the time and was gravely ill. Father José Sánchez administered the last rites to her. He attended to her with the greatest care and we were finally able to rejoice because we did not lose her. At that time, I was already the *llavera*.

The *llavera* had various responsibilities. First, she would distribute the daily rations for the *pozolera*. To do this, she had to count the number of single women and men, field workers, and vaqueros—those who rode with saddles and those who rode bareback. Besides that, she had to give daily rations to the people who were married. In short, she was in charge of the distribution of the rations for the Indians and she was also in charge of the Fathers' kitchen. She was in charge of the key to the clothing storehouse, from where material would be taken to make dresses for single and married women, as well as children. She also had to supervise the cutting of clothes for men.

She was also in charge of cutting and making clothes and other items, from head to toe, for the vaqueros who used saddles. Those who rode bareback received nothing more than their shirt, blanket, and loincloth. Those who rode with saddles received the same clothing as the *gente de razón*. They were given a shirt, a vest, pants, a hat, boots, shoes, and spurs. And they were given a saddle, a bridle, and a *reata* for their horse. Each vaquero would also receive a large kerchief made of silk or cotton, and a sash of Chinese silk[7] or red crepe cloth or whatever other material might be in the storehouse.

All work having to do with clothing was done by my daughters under my supervision. I would cut and arrange the pieces of material and my five daughters would do the sewing. When they could not keep up with the workload, I would let the Father know. He would then hire women from the pueblo of Los Angeles and pay them.

In addition, I had to supervise the area where soap was made, which was very large, and also the wine presses. I supervised and worked in the crushing of olives to make olive oil. Domingo Romero would drain off the liquid, but I would supervise him as he did this.

Luis, the soap maker, was in charge of the actual soap production, but I supervised everything.

I supervised the distribution of leather, calfskin, chamois, sheepskin, *tafilete*,[8] red cloth, tacks, thread, silk, etc.—everything related to the making of saddles and shoes, as well as everything that is needed in a saddle workshop and a shoe workshop.

I would distribute rations and supplies to the troops and the *gente de razón* servants every eight days. They would receive beans, corn, garbanzos,

This scene, Vaqueros Lassoing a Steer, *was painted by Spaniard Augusto Ferrán during his stay in California from 1849 to 1850. Courtesy of The Bancroft Library, University of California, Berkeley*

lentils, candles, soap, and lard. An Indian servant named Lucio, whom the Fathers trusted completely, was assigned to help me distribute everything.

When necessary, one of my daughters would do whatever I could not find time to complete. My daughter María del Rosario almost always worked by my side.

After all my daughters had married (the last one was Rita, who married in 1832 or 1833), Father Sánchez tried very hard to get me to marry First Lieutenant Juan Mariné, a Spaniard (Catalán) who had served in the artillery. He was a widower with a family. I did not want to get married, but Father Sánchez told me that Mariné was a very good man, which turned out to be the case. He also had quite a bit of money, but he never handed the box where he kept it over to me. I gave in to the Father's wishes. I did not have the heart to deny Father Sánchez anything because he had been like a father and a mother to me and to my entire family.

I was the *llavera* at the mission for twelve or fourteen years, until about two years after the death of Father José Sánchez. He died at this mission. In spite of his advanced age, Father Sánchez was strong and in good health until shortly before he died.

When Captain Barroso came and incited the Indians from all the missions by telling them that they no longer were neophytes but rather free men, Indians arrived from San Luis, San Juan, and other missions. They went into the teaching room with their weapons because it was raining very hard. The Indians placed guards outside the mission and they also had patrols. They had been taught to call out "Sentry—on guard!"*(centinela alerta)* and "He is on guard" *(alerta está),* but instead they would say, "Sentry—open!" *(centinela abierta)* and "He is open" *(abierta está).*

Father Sánchez was very distressed at seeing how the Indians had been led astray. He had to go to Los Angeles to say Mass, something he was in the habit of doing every eight or fifteen days, I cannot remember exactly. He told me, "Eulalia, I am leaving now. You know what the situation is. Keep your eyes open and take care of whatever you can. I do not want you or your daughters to leave here." My daughter María Antonia's husband, Leonardo Higuera, was in charge of the Rancho de los Cerritos, which belonged to the mission. María del Rosario's husband, Miguel White, was in San Blas.

Father Sánchez left to go to the pueblo, but right in front of the guard, the Indians went and cut the traces off his coach.[9] He jumped down from the coach and then the Indians took him by force to his room. He was filled with sorrow because of what the Indians had done. He stayed in his room for about eight days and would not come out. He became ill and never was the same again. His eardrums burst and he bled from his ears. His headache lasted until he died. After the incident with the Indians, he lived for little more than a month. He died in January. I think the year was 1833. There was a huge flood during that month. The river rose considerably and no one could cross it for more than fifteen days.

A person died at Los Nietos but could not be brought to the mission for burial for about fifteen days because of the flood. That same month, a few days after Father Sánchez had died, Claudio López also died. He had been the *mayordomo* at the mission for about thirty years.

There was a large number of neophytes at Mission San Gabriel. Those who were married lived at their *rancherías* with their young children.

The unmarried neophytes lived in two separate quarters. The one for the women was called the *monjerío* and there was another one for the men.

Young girls between the ages of seven and nine were brought to the *monjerío*. They would be raised there and would leave when they were to be married. An Indian mother would care for them in the *monjerío*. When I was at the mission, that mother's name was Polonia. They would call her *Madre Abadesa*.

The *alcalde* was in charge of the single men's quarters.

Every night the buildings were locked and the keys were turned over to me. Then I would hand the keys over to the Fathers.

A blind Indian named Andresillo would stand at the door to the *monjerío*. He would call out the name of each girl so that they would come in one by one. If any girl was missing when the girls were supposed to come inside, they would go out and look for her the next day. The girl would be brought back to the *monjerío*. If the girl had a mother, then she would be brought back as well and would be punished for keeping the girl away. The girl would be locked up for her carelessness in not returning to the *monjerío* on time.

The girls would be let out of the *monjerío* in the morning. First they would go to the Mass said by Father Zalvidea. He spoke the Indian language. Then they would go to the *pozolera* to eat breakfast. Sometimes the breakfast would be *champurrado* (chocolate mixed with *atole* made from corn). On feast days they would have bread and something sweet. On other days they would normally have *pozole* and meat. After breakfast, each girl would go to her assigned task, which might be weaving, unloading items from *carretas,* sewing, or something else.

When they were assigned to unload *carretas*, at eleven o'clock they would have to put one or two aside. These *carretas* were used to take drinks to the Indians who were working in the fields. The drinks were usually a mixture of water, vinegar, and sugar, but sometimes they were water, lemon, and sugar. I was the person who prepared and sent out those drinks so the Indians would not get sick. That is what the Fathers ordered done.

All work stopped at eleven. At noon, they would go to the *pozolera* for their meal of meat and vegetables. At one o'clock they would return to their jobs. The workday ended at sunset. Then they all would go to the *pozolera* to eat their dinner, which was *atole* with meat. Sometimes it was plain *atole*.

Each Indian man or woman would carry their own bowl which the *pozolero* would fill with their ration of food.

The Indian vaqueros or others who worked far away would eat at their homes if they were married. However, the majority of the Indians would go to the *pozolera*.

If the Indians showed a liking for a certain job, then that was the job they were taught. Otherwise, they would work in the field or care for the horses and cattle. Others had jobs as cart drivers or cowherds.

Coarse cloth, sarapes, and blankets were woven at the mission.

Saddles, bridles, boots, shoes, and other items of that nature were made. There was a place to make soap, as well as a large carpentry shop and a small one. The apprentice carpenters worked in the small carpentry shop until they had mastered enough to be sent to the larger shop.

Wine, olive oil, bricks, and adobes were made. Chocolate was made from cacao brought from abroad, and sweets were made. Father Sánchez sent many of the sweets that I made to Spain.

In each of the different work areas there was a teacher who was a Christian Indian. This person had received some formal instruction. A white man was in charge of the looms, but he stepped down when the Indians finally learned the skill.

My daughters and I would make chocolate, olive oil, sweets, lemonade, and other things. I made quite a bit of lemonade that was bottled and sent to Spain.

The Indians were also taught how to pray. Some of the more intelligent Indians were taught how to read and write. Father Zalvidea taught the Indians how to pray in their own language. A number of Indians learned music. They played instruments and sang at Mass.

The sacristans and pages who assisted at Mass were mission Indians.

The punishments that were imposed were the stocks and confinement to a cell. When the crime was serious, they would take the delinquent to the guardhouse. There, they would tie him to a cannon or to a post and whip him twenty-five times or more, depending on the crime. Sometimes they would put them in the stocks head first. Other times they would put a shotgun behind their knees and tie their hands to the gun. This punishment was called *Ley de Bayona*. It was very painful.

But Father Sánchez and Father Zalvidea always showed much concern for the Indians. I am not going to talk about what the others did, because I did not live at the mission.

As soon as the cattle had been fattened up, the slaughter would take place. The meat would be thrown out. Only hides, fat, loin, tongues, and horns would be kept. All of this, except for what was eaten at the mission itself, would be sold to ships.

The case brought against Don Enrique Fitch and his wife, Doña Josefa Carrillo, happened when I was at the mission. He had taken her to Chile on his ship and they were married there.

While the case was being decided, Fitch was held under arrest at the mission and was kept in the guest room. The ecclesiastical authority, Father Sánchez, who was also the president of the missions and the Vicar Forane, placed Doña Josefa at my house for a few days.[10]

I remember well when they brought the wounded Commander General Victoria to Mission San Gabriel in 1832. While he was here, I took care of him together with my daughters María Antonia, María de los Angeles, María del Rosario, and Rita. He had a wound under one of his eyes from a lance. I think it was the right eye. Father Sánchez had José Chapman come to the mission. Chapman was one of the insurgents who stayed in California. He was married to Guadalupe Ortega. They lived on the other side of the mission walls. He was a man who knew something about surgery. He stuck a probe in the wound, and it was about as deep as the length of a finger. José treated Victoria's wound and left him in my hands so that I could give him the medicines. Señor Victoria had no other injuries except that one and some bruises on his body.

Victoria was a tall man. He was very heavy and his skin was very dark. His hair was black and straight and uneven where it ended. He did not have much of a beard. When I saw him they had shaved it all off. While he was at the mission, he behaved very well and gave us no reason to complain. Everyone said he was a despot, but he did not appear that way when he was here. When he left he was practically cured.

This carreta, *photographed in Mexico around the turn of the twentieth century, was similar to the ones employed in Alta California. Courtesy of the California Historical Society. FN-36286*

Returning to something way in the past that happened about eighty years ago: when José María Pico, the father of Don Pío Pico, was corporal of the escort at San Gabriel, his wife, Eustaquia, was also at the mission. That is where she gave birth to Don Pío, and I was the midwife.[11]

The first time I came to Mission San Gabriel, the walls of the church (the same one that is here now) were about a *vara* in height. José Antonio was building the church. Everybody considered him to be one of the best bricklayers in California. He was a Spaniard by birth. That is why they called him *El Gachupín* after the change of flags.[12]

I remember that before Father Peyri left, there was a pile of leather sacks in a corner of Father Zalvidea's storeroom. The sacks were heavy, and some of them may have contained gold. We could often see the money through the seams in the bags. One day, when I was undoing packages to stock the shelves with supplies, my daughter María del Rosario came in. Besides the two of us, Father Sánchez, Domingo Romero, Claudio López, and Juan José Higuera were also there. After a while, my daughter left to do her chores. I stayed with Father Sánchez and the others. When my daughter returned, she said to Father Sánchez, "Look, Father, there is a very beautiful shawl over there and I would like to have it." The shawl was on the top shelf. I was not the least bit happy with what she had said, and I gave her a look of displeasure. Father Sánchez responded to my daughter, "Rosario, climb up and bring down that shawl you like." She did exactly that and then looked back at the shelf and suddenly said, "Look, Father, there is another shawl up there just like this one, and I am going to bring it down for Rita." Father Sánchez liked to see both girls dressed alike. She climbed up to get the shawl, and when she started to climb down, Domingo Romero said, "Rosario, do not come down that way," pointing to where she should not step. But she climbed down nevertheless. I told María del Rosario to go outside with the girls. I begged Father Sánchez not to give the girls everything they asked for. He responded, "They can have it because they have worked for it." María del Rosario left and walked past Father Zalvidea's room. From there she went past the reception room and the hall, and then she turned around. She had gotten it into her head to come back and find out why Romero had tried to stop her from climbing down a certain way when she was bringing the second shawl down from the shelf. She came back in, but Father Sánchez, Romero, López, and I were in the other storehouse putting things in order, so we did not see her come in. According to what she later told me, she went over to the spot where she was told not to step and saw a large piece of coarse cloth spread across the ground. She could not tell what was under the cloth, so she picked it up and then felt the ground with her hand to see what was there. There was fresh earth under the cloth. My daughters referred to Romero as "uncle." María del Rosario told him what she had seen, because I was going to punish her if she did not. She, as well as everyone else, had discovered the truth—all the money that was previously in the leather sacks had been buried there.

An old mission Indian once told me that when Father Antonio Peyri left Mission San Luis Rey to board ship, the only thing he took with him was a small bundle on his back. It was like a suitcase. The Indian saw him leave. Father Peyri took two young Indian boys with him. It was said that he wanted to take them to Rome.[13]

Around 1831 we heard people say that money was being taken from the mission on mules and in *carretas*. However, I did not see that. What I do know is that at one time there was a lot of money at the mission stored in boxes, sacks, and *guajes* (an Indian name for some big things that had small openings).[14]

Father Boscana was a small man but a bit plump. He had pale skin. When I met him, he was quite old. He would frequently come to San Gabriel to visit the Fathers and he would stay for quite a while. But I do not believe he was ever a permanent minister there. He was very fond of snuff. He was a very loving and good man, although it seemed to me that he was a bit crazy. When he would have an attack, nobody would talk to him, because he acted as if he were angry with everybody, including himself.

Father Nuez was tall, thin, and young when he baptized my daughter María del Rosario. He was very pale and had black hair. He was very kind to everybody.

I met many missionary Fathers when they were at San Gabriel, but I do not remember very much about their names or what they looked like to be able to describe them. I do remember Father Peyri. He was a good-sized man but very heavy and his skin was white. He was Catalán and a very friendly and loving person.

When Father Esténaga came to San Gabriel, he was already a sixty- or seventy-year-old man. He was somewhat tall, thin, very pale, and very intelligent when it came to managing the little that remained at the mission. He treated everybody with much affection, white people as well as Indians. If I remember correctly, he died and was buried here. I believe that Father Zalvidea was buried at San Luis Rey.

Father Blas Ordaz died here at the mission.

When I traveled, I met many Fathers. I would also meet them when Father Sánchez was president, because the other Fathers would come to his meetings.

One time, my daughter María del Rosario and I caught Father Sánchez and José Chapman burying a box in the Father's room. The box measured about a *vara* in length and was more than half a *vara* high. Of course the box contained money, because we saw José arranging and matching the coins in large quantities. Neither Father Sánchez nor José saw us.

In addition to supporting me and all my daughters until they married, Father Sánchez gave me two ranchos, that is, land for one rancho and land for an orchard. Before he gave them to me, he first had all the Indians gather together in the teaching room. Then Father Zalvidea, who spoke their language, asked them if they wanted to give me that land for an orchard and for a rancho, since I had always taken care of them and helped them. He said that those who agreed should raise their hand. All the Indians raised their hands and said they wanted me to have the land. When Father Sánchez turned over the land to me, I was already married to Juan Mariné. Later, Juan only gave me half the land and kept the other half for himself.

When I married him I was an older woman, but very strong and agile, and I hardly had any gray hair. However, I never had any children with him.

WHEN I CAME TO SAN DIEGO from Loreto, I was very fond of dancing, and I was considered the best dancer in the country. I was also a singer in the church at the presidio of Loreto. One time, Chepa Rodríguez and I danced together in Santa Bárbara. Chepa was famous for being a great dancer. We danced the *jarabe* and she got tired and had to sit down, but I kept on dancing. I also outlasted another famous dancer. There was a contest to see if anybody from San Diego to Monterey would come and compete with me in dancing, but nobody came. That was when the church at Santa Bárbara was blessed.

When I was young, I danced every type of dance: *sones*,[15] *jarabe*,[16] *pontorico*,[17] *medio-catorce*,[18] *fandango*,[19] *la zorrita*,[20] *las pollitas, el caballo*.[21] This last dance was done by women wearing hats. At a certain part in the verse, they would twirl their hats around in their hands.

With the *sones*, the *tecolero*[22] would go around tapping his feet to the rhythm of the music and then stop in front of the first woman in line. He would continue clapping his hands and then take her out of the line. Once the woman had finished dancing, she would sit down and the *tecolero* would take another woman from the line, until the last woman had danced. Let me see if I can remember a verse from each dance.

El caballo

Cuando el caballo
Entró en Cádiz
Entró por la barandilla
Lo salen a recibir
Caballo, jota y malilla
Anda, Caballo,
A la lavandera
Que paños lava
Como es chiquita
Ella se chiqueaba

The Horse

When the horse
Entered Cádiz
He entered through the banister
They go out to welcome him
Horse, jack and manille[23]
Go, Horse,
To the washerwoman
Who is washing her underwear
Since she is so tiny
She does nice little things for herself

La zorrita[24]

La zorrita se fue a la loma
Por andar de bureo, en bureo
Vino pelona

Y diciendo que se viene cayendo
Y que todo un dolor en el alma
Y porque ella es como la centella
Que corre, y se sube a la loma
Y al brinquito que da la zorrita
Ya está en el suelo

La zorrita se fue a Durango
Por andar de bureo, en bureo
Vino llorando

La zorrita, zorrita,
Se fue a la villa
Por andar de bureo, en bureo
Vino tordilla

The Little Fox

The little fox went to the hill
To have some fun, some fun
She came back hairless

And saying that she is on her way down
And that her soul is filled with sorrow
And because she is like a flash of lightning
That bolts, she climbs up the hill
And after the little fox takes a little leap
She finds herself on the ground

The little fox went to Durango
To have some fun, some fun
She came back crying

The little fox, little fox
Went to the village
To have some fun, some fun
She came back a dapple-gray horse

Las pollitas

He de casar mis gallinas
Con un gallo copetón
Para que salgan los pollos
Con chaqueta y pantalón
Que si se lleva la polla
Que no se la llevará
Que si la polla se lleva
Caramba! Yo voy allá

The Little Hens

I am going to marry off my young hens
To a rooster with a crest
So that they will produce chicks
With a jacket and pants
For if he takes her away
No, he won't take her away
For if he takes her away
Caramba! I'll follow her there

<table>
<tr><td>

El son

Una tiro y dos envío
Y en la mano traigo una
Un amor yo conocí
No quise conocer más

Cuando te estaba queriendo
Cuando te estaba adorando
Vino la muerte atrevida
Y me dejó suspirando

Tomasito, quien pudiera
Explicarte mi dolor
Para que caritativo
Me aliviaras con tu amor
Este es mi intento
Nunca ofenderte
Siempre tenerte
Ciega pasión
Con gran contento
Y en dulce calma
Rendiste el alma
Y el corazón

</td><td>

The Song

I throw one away and send off two
And hold one in my hand
I knew but one love
I refused to know any other

When I was loving you
When I was adoring you
Came death boldly
And left me sighing

Tomasito, if only someone could
Describe my sorrow to you
So that lovingly
You could ease my pain with your love
This is my intention
Never to offend you
To always have for you
Blind passion
With great happiness
And tender tranquility
You surrendered your soul
And your heart

</td></tr>
</table>

[Note in English by Thomas Savage:]
Señora Eulalia addressed this last verse to me as a farewell—first asking me for my given name. I told it to her in Spanish, Tomás, and she burst forth with the words while holding my hand in hers.)

Thos. Savage
Rancho de San Isidro
Near Mission San Gabriel
December 10, 1877

The information that appears on the preceding pages was dictated, in my presence, by my elderly mother, Doña Eulalia Pérez. I can corroborate the information dating from 1820–1822, because I was old enough at that time to understand what was happening around us. From the age of seven or eight, I was by my dear mother's side, helping her with all her work. I have heard her speak many times about what happened before 1820, but the stories vary so much that it is impossible to say that everything in her account is correct.

María del Rosario deWhite

Eulalia says that when a member of her family or somebody whom she loves very much bids her farewell, she responds in the following manner:

Adiós, y me voy llorando	*Good-bye, and I leave crying*
La pena y desdicha mía	*Sorrow and misfortune are mine*
Pero me voy acordando	*But I begin to remember*
Que te he de ver algún día	*That I will see you some day*
Aunque sea de cuando en cuando	*Even though it may only be from time to time*
A la luna y al sereno	*By a clear, moonlit sky*
Camina el hombre valiente	*The man walks with courage*
Y más si lleva en el cuerpo	*And even more so if in his body*
Un traguito de aguardiente	*He has a swig of aguardiente*

In June 1876, my sister María Antonia, the widow of Higuera, wanted to make some money, so she "sold" my mother for $5,000 for a period of six weeks, during which time she would be on exhibit in San Francisco at the Woodward Garden and then she would be taken to an exposition in Philadelphia. They had already secretly taken her as far as Los Angeles, but fortunately, *[manuscript stops here]*

[Information that Savage appended to the manuscript in English:]
In connection with the history of this centenarian:

1810 Nov. 23:
At the presidial church of San Diego, Father Pedro Panto christened María Antonia Feliciana Guillén, a daughter (born two days previously) of the private soldier of the *cuera* company of said presidio, Antonio Guillén, and of his wife, Eulalia Pérez. Godparents: Don Josef Antonio Carrillo, unmarried and a son of Capt. Raymundo Carrillo, deceased, and Doña María Antonia Carrillo, wife of Lieut. Josef de la Guerra y Noriega.

These pictures of Eulalia Pérez's daughter María Antonia and María Antonia's granddaughter were taken in connection with the efforts to have Eulalia Pérez exhibited at San Francisco and then at the Centennial Exposition in Philadelphia. Both courtesy of the California Historical Society. María Antonia: FN-36279. Granddaughter: FN-36280

1812 Oct. 4:

In church of same presidio Father Fernando Martín baptized María de los Angeles Guillén, an infant daughter of the above-named parents. God-parents: José Venegas, *mayordomo* of the mission, and Apolinaria Lorenzana.

(The above facts found in certif⁵ 1ˢᵗ Book of Baptisms of San Diego Mission existing 11 Jan 1878 in Catholic parish church of San Diego. Old town.)

1810 May 10:

Guillén and his wife, Eulalia, had their child Thomas buried by Father José Sánchez.

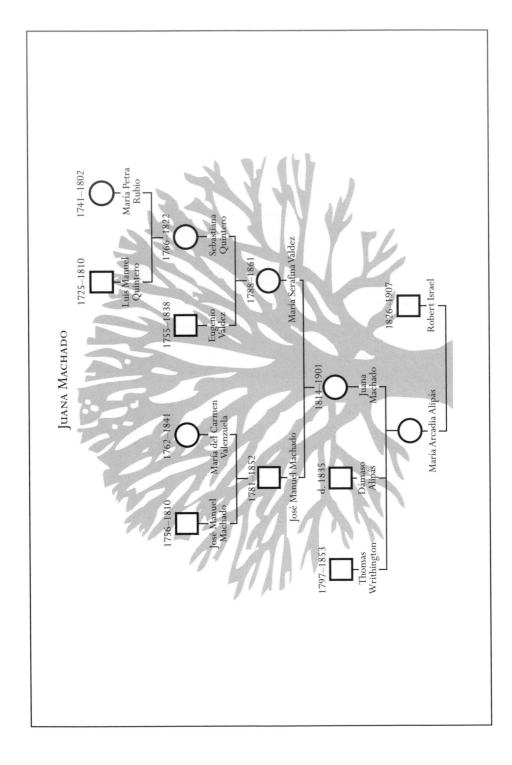

JUANA MACHADO

María Petra Rubio 1741–1802

Luis Manuel Quintero 1725–1810

Sebastiana Quintero 1766–1822

Eugenio Valdez 1755–1838

María Serafina Valdez 1788–1861

Robert Israel 1826–1907

María del Carmen Valenzuela 1762–1841

José Manuel Machado 1756–1810

José Manuel Machado 1781–1852

Juana Machado 1814–1901

Dámaso Alipás d. 1835

María Arcadia Alipás

Thomas Writhington 1797–1853

Juana Machado

INTRODUCTION

On January 7, 1877, Savage arrived at the church in Old Town in San Diego, hoping to copy mission records. The priest there introduced him to Juana Machado, a woman who had experienced a very eventful life and whose family history stretched back almost to the beginnings of Spanish Alta California. All four of her grandparents—Eugenio Valdez and Sebastiana Quintero on her mother's side, and Manuel Machado and María del Carmen Valenzuela on her father's side—had come to California as members of the 1781 Rivera expedition that brought in settlers for the new pueblo of Los Angeles. Juana Machado's maternal grandmother, Sebastiana Quintero, was a fifteen-year-old bride when she embarked. The rest of her family: her father, Luis Quintero, a tailor; her mother, María Petra Rubio; and their five children were members of the same expedition.[1]

Luis Quintero and his family went to Santa Bárbara a year after they arrived in Alta California and they settled there. Eugenio Valdez and María del Carmen Valenzuela settled in Los Angeles. Manuel Machado served as a soldier at the San Diego presidio. In 1805 José Manuel Machado, the son of Manuel and María del Carmen, married María Serafina Valdez, the daughter of Eugenio and Sebastiana Valdez, at Mission San Gabriel. In 1814 their third child, Juana, was born at San Diego.[2]

In 1829 Juana Machado married Dámaso Alipás, a soldier who was serving at the presidio. They had three daughters: Josefa, Ramona, and María Arcadia. Dámaso and his brother Gervasio were both involved in the 1831 movement against Governor Manuel Victoria that was centered at San

Diego. Both brothers came to violent ends. Dámaso was killed in Sonora around 1835 and Gervasio was killed by a vigilance committee in Los Angeles in 1836, after he and his lover, María del Rosario Villa, killed María's husband, Domingo Félix.[3]

Juana Machado remarried in the late 1830s. Her husband was Thomas Writhington, an American from Fall River, Massachusetts, who had jumped the hide ship *Ayachuco* in San Diego in 1833.[4] He set himself up in the port as a shoemaker. They too had three children: José, Luis, and Serafina. Writhington had become a Mexican citizen in 1833, and he served as *juez de paz* in 1844 and 1847. During the war against the United States, San Diego was a stronghold of pro-American feeling. After his defeat by the Californios at San Pascual, General Stephen Watts Kearny retreated to San Diego, where he had his wounded cared for at Juana and Thomas Writhington's house. Writhington, who identified himself as a "trader" in the 1850 census, died in 1853 after a fall from a horse.

Juana Machado remained in San Diego, raising her children. Her family remained active in public life. One of her sons-in-law, Robert Israel, for instance, commanded the firing squad that executed Antonio Garra. Juana Machado herself became closely involved with Father Ubach, the priest in Old Town San Diego, and would visit neighboring Indian *rancherías* with him in the 1860s and 1870s. This was undoubtedly the reason why the priest asked her to speak to Savage.

In the 1890s, Juana Machado left Old Town and moved in with her daughter María Arcadia and her husband, Robert Israel, who had retired after a long stint as a lighthouse keeper and had moved to Coronado Island. She died there in 1901.[5]

When Savage arrived in San Diego, he had probably never heard of Juana Machado, so he was rather unprepared to interview her. He apparently began by asking her about her father. She responded with a series of recollections about military life in the San Diego area and at the missions. Her initial comments were a good preview of the rest of the interview. She told the traditional military stories, but she insisted that women were an integral part of those stories as well. For instance, she told Savage how the mission guard was assigned and how many soldiers comprised it. But she also related how the women who were married to these soldiers had to arrange for the births of their children by returning to the presidios.

A mixing of the political and social worlds and, again, an emphasis on the active role of women marked Machado's other recollections as well. In

Juana Machado standing amid cactus plants at San Diego.© San Diego Historical Society

her treatment of early San Diego, she related that the women in the pueblo were heavily engaged in the domestic manufacturing on which Alta California depended during the 1810s, when supplies from the Mexican mainland were scarce. When she remembered the proclamation of Mexican independence in 1822, she recalled the conflicting emotions of women, fascinated by the new order symbolized by the Mexican emissary's colorful garb, yet sad at the loss of the longstanding traditions of dress and grooming which the new regime mandated.

Her treatment of the Indian attacks around San Diego in the late 1830s was marked by a similar focus on the importance of women. In her rendition of the Indian attack on the Pico ranch at Jamul, it occurred as it did because the male overseer refused to give credence to the warnings of both native and Californio women. Another attack in San Diego itself was forestalled because the men decided to listen to what the women were saying.

About halfway through the conversation, it appears that Savage steered Juana Machado toward the history of California's politics. He asked her if she remembered Governor Luis Antonio Argüello. She gave concise personal descriptions of Argüello and his successor, José de Echeandía. She interrupted the sequence of governors through which Savage was apparently guiding her to narrate the story of a military excursion into the interior of the state in which her first husband had participated. As she answered Savage's questions about the political turmoil of the 1830s, she was careful to distinguish between what she remembered from her own experiences and what she was relating from the community tradition of the San Diego region. But she always remained anxious to relate political events to the social world, as, for instance, when she related that Pío Pico was arrested during the performance of the *Pastorela,* a Christmas play, in his house.

Her memory of the American takeover was dominated by the killing of eleven Californios by Cahuillas in December 1846. Her *testimonio* ended with an incident which illustrated the complex choices made by some Californios during the turbulent period of the war in 1846/1847: after her mother's intervention, her brother served as a guide for a contingent of American forces. It was an appropriate conclusion, for the Mexican California that Juana Machado painted for Thomas Savage had always been a place in which women had actively participated in the pleasures, the pains, and the ambiguities that characterized frontier life.

Times Gone By in Alta California: Recollections of Señora Doña Juana Machado de Ridington, Bancroft Library, 1878

This lady is the widow of the late Thomas Ridington. Never had an opportunity to acquire an education—cannot read or write, but is able to speak English quite fluently. She is quite intelligent and conceals her age in the most extraordinary manner—is sixty-four years old and no one would take her to be much over forty-five—has hair as black as a raven's wing, without the slightest sign of gray.

She has one son and four daughters living—one son died—the four daughters are married to Americans. She also has two granddaughters married to American husbands, who have made her a great-grandmother.

She has now living twenty-four grandchildren and three great-grandchildren.

This lady likewise had a cousin named Catalina López, who married an American. They moved to Philadelphia—the wife died, leaving descendants there.

The old lady looks healthy and hearty and promises to live to see her great-great-grandchildren. She has assured me that she never knew what a serious illness was, and never had occasion to call a physician to attend on her, except when confined to bring her children into the world.

Tho.ˢ Savage
North San Diego
January 11, 1878

I, JUANA DE DIOS MACHADO, was born in the old presidio of San Diego. I do not remember the day, the month, or the year, but I believe I am about sixty-four years old.* My father, José Manuel Machado, was a corporal in the San Diego company. My mother, María Serafina Valdés, was born in Santa Bárbara. I believe that my father was born in Los Angeles, because his father was also a soldier. I knew my paternal grandmother.

I was married to Dámaso Alipás for five years. My marriage to Dámaso Alipás took place in the presidio on August 22, 1829. Father Antonio Menéndez married us.[6] I had been widowed for four or five years when I married Mr. Thomas Ridington, a native of Massachusetts.

Susana Machado de Bernard, a cousin of Juana Machado, with her children. Reproduced by permission of The Huntington Library, San Marino, California, Pierce Collection #8146

Footnote by Savage: "Examined the record of baptism and find she was born in San Diego, March 8, 1814, and christened on March 13, 1814."

Juana Machado at the far left of a group photographed by I. W. Taber in front of the American Hotel in San Diego. Courtesy of The Bancroft Library, University of California, Berkeley

My father was one of the founders of Pala, Las Flores, and Temécula.[7] He also served at San Luis Rey. When I was young, it was customary for the commander of San Diego to assign a sergeant, a corporal, and ten soldiers to Mission San Luis Rey each year. After those troops had served there for a year, they would be relieved by another similar group. After Lieutenant Colonel Echeandía came to govern the country, the mission guard at San Luis Rey was reduced to a corporal and five soldiers. That same number of troops maintained order at each of the missions from San Gabriel on down.

Later, during General Figueroa's administration, military headquarters were established at San Gabriel. Lieutenant Colonel Nicolás Gutiérrez was in command at San Gabriel. I was probably about eight or ten years old at that time and still at the old presidio.

When married soldiers like my father served in the mission guard, they would take their families with them. When my dear mother would be far along in a pregnancy and close to giving birth, she would give herself enough time to go to the presidio and stay at the home of *Alférez* Ignacio Martínez. He was married to Doña María Martina Arellanes. They were my godparents. I was baptized in the same old presidio, where one can still see the ruins of the buildings.

When I was eight or ten years old, my father left to command an expedition of twenty-five men. At that time, he was in charge of the Rancho de la Nación, which belonged to the presidio of San Diego. The purpose of the expedition was to go in pursuit of Indian horse thieves. At that time, three Indian criminals were famous for their offenses. Their names were Martín, Cartucho, and Agustín. Martín and Agustín were most likely runaway Christian Indians. I do not know about Cartucho. They all came by way of Jacum.[8]

The expedition went as far as the entrance to the Cañón de Jacum, which is a very narrow place. Indian allies of the runaways were on the two hills. However, only the three leaders had been involved in stealing the herd of horses from the Rancho de la Nación.[9] The soldiers managed to catch sight of the horses but were not able to recover them.

My father and his soldiers engaged in a very hard-fought battle with the Indians. Agustín grabbed hold of my father by his braided hair and pulled him down from his horse. Fortunately, one of the soldiers came to my father's aid. That soldier was José Antonio Silvas, better known as Pico Silvas.[10] My father was then able to take out his knife and bury it in the Indian's belly. He ripped out all his guts and left him for dead. My father also cut off his ears and scalped him, which was what they used to do then. When my father returned, he presented these items to the commander of San Diego. The other Indians fled to the mountains and the herd of horses was lost. The only horse they were able to bring back was the one Agustín was riding.

I remember well the expedition of insurgents commanded by Bouchard. After they were in Monterey, where they wreaked all kinds of havoc, they went to the Ortega rancho at El Refugio. There they caused all sorts of damage. From there, they went to Santa Bárbara, but they did not land. Later they went ashore at San Juan Capistrano and dumped out all the wine and olive oil that was in the storehouses. It was said that they stole silver ornaments and other items from the church. Although I remember those events well, I cannot speak with certainty about them because I was only six years old or perhaps a little older at that time.

From the gate of the presidio plaza we saw one of the frigates as it turned around in the false port so it could enter this port. The officers ordered the soldiers to take their families to Mission San Diego. But before taking us there, Serapio, one of the soldiers assigned to the *castillo,* came to report that the *castillo* had been taken by two officers and some soldiers who were brought to shore on a boat from the enemy ship. The insurgents did no damage to the *castillo,* but they did take Corporal Juan Osuna and a soldier who everyone called Dominguitos back to the ship. Corporal Osuna and the soldier were later put ashore in Ensenada, Baja California. They returned to San Diego by land.[11]

I heard it said back then that Bouchard's insurgents wreaked havoc at Cabo San Lucas and ransacked the church at Loreto. Several of the insurgents were killed there.[12]

Shortly before the expedition commanded by my father headed out, the one I spoke about before, I witnessed the changing of the flag. This was when the Spanish flag was lowered and the Mexican flag was raised in its place. Up until that time, for a number of years the soldiers and their families had suffered many hardships due to a lack of clothing and other things. Supplies from the king were not arriving because of the war of independence in Mexico. However, we did not lack food, because there was an abundance of cattle and other animals. It got to the point that we were used to eating only the finest and most succulent meat. The rest of the meat was thrown away or we would give it to the Indians if they were around. The women had their own shoe-making operation in their homes. They would make shoes out of scraps of cowhide and fabric. When the ships began to arrive, the hardships experienced because of the huge shortages of necessary goods and luxury items began to lessen. The ships would bring us chocolate, clothing, and other things. But this was very much toward the end.

The change of flags was in 1822.

I forgot to say that in 1819, the year after the insurgents paid us their untimely visit, Captain Don Pablo de la Portilla arrived in San Diego with a company of *mazatecos*. The troops were called the Active Militia Squadron from Mazatlán. They had traveled by land from Baja California. When they arrived from their journey they were in rather bad shape. The viceroy had sent them to reinforce the California garrison. When we found out they were on their way, the officers of this presidio sent them horses, but the majority of them came here on foot.

The officers of that squadron were Lieutenant Juan María Ibarra, a very dark, big, and ugly man; Lieutenant Narciso Fabregat, a Catalonian who was about thirty-eight or forty years old, fair-skinned, very handsome, thin, and about five feet eight or five feet nine inches tall; and *Alférez* Ignacio Delgado, young, fair-skinned, normal height, and a little fat. Delgado's wife, Doña Lugarda, was a native of Mazatlán, Sonora. She was an expert in all types of needlework and made artificial flowers and other fanciful crafts.

I would go to Doña Lugarda to learn how to do all these things. The young Pico girls and some other friends would go with me.

Around that same time I met a woman named Apolinaria Lorenzana. Everyone called her "La Beata." She never married. I know she is still living in Santa Bárbara at the home of Doña Trinidad Noriega. Doña Apolinaria arrived from Mexico with two other girls named Valenciana and Mariana. They were foundling children that the viceroy's government sent to California. Valenciana and Mariana married and had large families. Doña Apolinaria dedicated her life to serving the Church and taking care of the Fathers at Mission San Diego. At the mission, parents would ask her if she would please teach their daughters how to read and write. She did not have a formal school but would dedicate as much time as she could to teaching. She went by the name Doña Apolinaria la Cuna. She was the godmother to a large number of children, as much to children of *gente de razón* as to Indian children.

The change of flags in 1822 was as follows. A señor *canónigo* named Don Valentín Fernández de San Vicente arrived from the north. I do not remember if he came by land or by sea. This man had been sent here by the Mexican empire to establish the new order of things. He brought a chaplain or secretary with him; I am not sure what he was, because I do not remember ever seeing him dressed as a priest. I remember well that the *canónigo*'s attire was really very striking and colorful. His outfit was reddish in color. Whenever some woman or girl would be taken aback by the splendor and colors of his outfit, she would ask, "Who is that man?" Someone would answer, "the *canónigo*." Such a person had never been seen before in California. He and his companion stayed up at the home of the commander, Captain Francisco María Ruiz. He had been commander for many years.

The infantry, cavalry, and a few artillerymen were ordered to line up in formation in the presidio plaza. They placed the cannons outside the plaza, at the gate of the guardhouse, so that they would face the ocean. There was no flag pole. A corporal or a soldier held the Spanish flag in one hand and the Mexican flag in the other. Both of the flags were attached to little sticks. In the presence of Officer Don José María Estudillo, Commander Ruiz gave the cry "Long live the Mexican empire!" Then the Spanish flag was lowered and the Mexican flag was raised amidst salvos of artillery and fusillade. After this, the soldiers received nothing.

The next day, the soldiers were ordered to cut off their braids. This produced a very unfavorable reaction in everyone—men and women alike. The men were used to wearing their hair long and braided. At the tip of the braid there would be a ribbon or silk knot. On many men, the braid went past their waist. It was quite similar to the way the Chinese wore their hair. The only difference was that they did not shave any part of their head like the Chinese did.

The order was carried out. I remember when my father arrived home with his braid in his hand. He gave it to my mother. His face showed such sorrow. My mother's face was not any better. She would look at the braid and cry.

The way that men dressed when I was young, up until the arrival of Echeandía, was as follows: an undershirt made of cotton or another fabric, an unlined vest that went down to the waist. The vest could be of different colors but the soldiers wore blue ones. On top of the vest they would wear a *chupín*[13] that was like a frockcoat with lapels on both sides. The lapels had bright red stitching on all the edges and a red collar. That is what the soldiers and the native sons wore. There were few native sons. The retired soldiers wore more or less the same thing, the difference being their choice of color.

Men wore short trousers that went down to the knee with openings on the outer side of the leg. These openings had flaps that fell to each side and a row of six buttons. The soldiers wore cloth trousers. Others wore trousers made of cloth, nankeen, duck, or whatever material was on hand.[14]

Then came the chamois boots. They consisted of a piece of chamois, about three-quarters of a *vara* long. The chamois was wrapped around the leg and tied with ribbons or bands. The chamois was softened up by working it with iron. Underneath the chamois they wore socks and shoes.

On their heads, men would wear a hat made of felt, straw, vicuña, etc. They took special care of the fine hats that came from Spain. For everyday use they would wear hats the Indians made from palm fronds.

I remember something very sad that happened in California. I believe it was at the beginning of 1838.* Doña Eustaquia López (Pico's widow and the mother of Don José Antonio, Don Pío, and Don Andrés Pico) was at Rancho de Jamul with her unmarried daughters, Feliciana, Jacinta, and Isidora. Feliciana later married Ramón, the son of Captain Santiago Argüello. Jacinta later married her brother-in-law, José Antonio Carrillo, who had been Estefana's husband. Isidora is the wife of Mr. John Forster, the owner of Santa Margarita. One afternoon, an Indian woman named

---

*Note by Savage:"The affair at Jamul was related to me in conversation by Doña Isidora Pico (Mrs. John Forster), one of the young women who escaped with their mother, in almost the same terms, but Mrs. Forster could not remember the year."

Cesárea went over to the doorway that faced the street. This is where Doña Eustaquia was seated. In a loud voice, she asked her for some salt. Doña Eustaquia asked somebody to bring the Indian woman some salt, but the Indian woman used gestures to make Doña Eustaquia understand that she wanted Doña Eustaquia to bring her the salt. So, Doña Eustaquia got up and the Indian woman followed her. When they reached a place where they could speak privately, the Indian woman spoke to Doña Eustaquia in a language that she understood well. She told her that the Indians were going to revolt, kill the men, and take the women captive. Doña Eustaquia very cautiously went to the room where her daughters were sewing and told them to put down their sewing, pick up their *rebozos* (all women wore *rebozos* during that time), and go out to the edge of the cornfield. She would follow them shortly. She very discreetly summoned the *mayordomo*, Juan Leiva. He was a relative of hers. She told him what Cesárea had told her and added that for the last few days she had been noticing different things about the Indians that made her suspicious. However, it was nothing on a large scale. The *mayordomo* assured her that they were in no danger whatsoever and she should calm down. He said that he had men and twelve well-loaded

A fiesta at the Estudillo house in the late nineteenth century. José Antonio Estudillo lived here in 1838, when he was alcalde of San Diego and Jamul was attacked. Reproduced by permission of The Huntington Library, San Marino, California, Pierce Collection #7908

firearms. Doña Eustaquia again urged him to find a safe place for himself and his family. He felt confident about the situation and refused to do what she suggested. Then, Doña Eustaquia told him to have a *carreta* with oxen ready and waiting for her on the road to the cornfield. She headed out to meet up with her daughters. The *carreta* arrived and there was only one hide in it. She and her daughters arrived at Rancho de Jamachá at midnight. The rancho belonged to Doña Apolinaria, who had a *mayordomo* there. After informing the *mayordomo* at Jamachá and his family about the situation, they headed to the presidio of San Diego and informed *Alcalde* Don José Antonio Estudillo. He immediately sent people to the rancho to protect those who were there, but they arrived too late.

The Indians did not attack the rancho that night. The following night, they attacked the servants without warning. They killed *mayordomo* Juan Leiva, his son José Antonio, a young man named Molina, and another fellow from Baja California named Camacho. They killed everyone in the cornfield, except for Leiva, who raced off to the house to defend his family. As he headed for the room where the weapons were stored, an Indian woman who did the sweeping in the house had already locked the door to that room and put the key in her pocket. She taunted Leiva by dangling the key in front of him and told him he was out of luck if he wanted to get in the room. Leiva ran to the kitchen and defended himself for a while with hot coals. But in the end they killed him and threw his body into the main room of the house. Then they seized his wife, Doña María, their young son, named Claro, and their two daughters, Tomasa and Ramona. Tomasa was fifteen years old and Ramona was twelve years old. The Indians were going to kill Doña María and the boy, but Doña Tomasa's pleas made them stop. They completely stripped Doña María and the little boy of their clothes. Despite the shouting and wailing of the whole family, they took off with the two girls and headed for the Colorado River. Before leaving, they ransacked the rancho and took all the horses, cattle, and other items of value. They then burned down the buildings.

Poor Doña María covered her naked body with hay and arrived like that at Mission San Diego. Fathers Vicente Pascual Oliva and Fernando Martín were in charge of the mission.

All the efforts to recover the lost property, and the even greater efforts to rescue the kidnapped girls, were futile. To this day, nobody knows the fate of those poor children.

Sergeant Macedonio González, the famous Indian fighter, told us one time that he left Mission San Miguel in Baja California with a considerable force and headed for the mountain range of Jacum to see if they could rescue or save those girls. They were his nieces. When they arrived at the foot of the mountains, he saw many Indians, both men and women, eating beef from the cattle they had stolen. When the Indians saw him, they began to shout and threaten him, saying that they, too, were brave. They told him he could climb up to where they were located if he wanted to, because that is where he could find Tomasa and Ramona. In fact, he did see two girls who appeared to have white bodies. However, their faces and bodies were painted and their hair was cut short the way the Indians wore it. He was able to see their bodies because at that time the Indian women did not wear any clothing except for a covering made of rabbit skins over their private parts. They called this covering *pajales*. He did not dare shoot at the Indians for fear that, if those girls really were his nieces, the shots might kill them. The Indians then took the girls down from the rock where they had placed them and retreated. González was not able to climb up there with his horses. He spoke the Indian language well and he made them generous offers of cattle, horses, etc., in exchange for the girls, but the Indians did not accept any of his offers. A few years later, when peace was made with those Indians, they were again offered a ransom but their efforts were in vain. The leaders of that tragic affair were the Indians named Cartucho and Martín, whom I mentioned previously. Later, some other Indians said that Cartucho had taken Tomasa as his wife and Martín had taken Ramona as his wife.

When the Fathers were still at Mission San Diego, it was very common for the Indians to steal horses and cattle. The soldiers would go after the Indians and sometimes they would manage to recover the stolen property but other times they would not. Several times the ringleaders were caught and punished.

In 1838 or 1839, during or around Lent, it was discovered that the Indians were conspiring to steal property, kill the men, and take the women captive. The co-conspirators were Nario, a Christian from Baja California; José María, also from Baja California; an Indian named Carrancio from the Sierra de Cuyamaca who was married in San Diego; Juan Antonio, from San Diego; and Pedro Pablo. I believe that this last fellow was also from the Sierra de Cuyamaca.

Late one afternoon, at the home of Captain Henry D. Fitch, just as the family was about to dine, one of the servants told Doña Josefa Carrillo de Fitch that she should be on guard. The servant was a little Indian girl named Candelaria. Doña Josefa was the little girl's godmother. Candelaria had overheard the Indians in the kitchen say that they were going to kill the clerk at Fitch's store, an American named Lawrence Hatwell. They also planned to ransack the house and commit other crimes, such as burning down the house and kidnapping the women. Three of the Indians she named were servants at the Fitch home. Another one, José María, was a servant at the home of Don José Antonio Estudillo. I do not remember the other one very well.

The señora sent for *Alcalde* Juan María Marrón and told him what she had heard. Marrón and the clerk informed *Alférez* Macedonio González. I do not remember if González was here at that time or at Mission San Miguel in Baja California* and they had to send for him. What is for certain is that González rounded up the Indians very quietly and took their statements. Based on these statements, it was proven that the Indians had indeed hatched the plot that I spoke about previously. He then took them to a small canyon next to the present-day Protestant cemetery. Right then and there, without even giving the Indians the last rites, he had all five of them shot and buried on the spot. The execution took place around five o'clock in the afternoon the day after the Indians were taken prisoner. This was two days after Candelaria reported what she had heard. She also said that she heard the Indians mention they had *jaras* and clubs at the old presidio for when the other Indians came down from Cuyamaca. Then they would attack as they had planned.

The day after it was discovered that the Indians were planning to attack the pueblo, the decision was made to send the women to the drying sheds where the foreigners cured hides. These buildings were located on the same side and very close to the *castillo*. The pueblo found itself rather defenseless. The only men there were *Alcalde* Marrón, the elderly Don José Bandini, Captain Santiago Argüello, José Antonio Estudillo, a Spaniard named Don Rafael known as El Gachupín, and several others. We arrived there at sunset and spent the night. There were many of us—the Pico women and my family. About eight or ten foreigners protected us. The next morning, the foreigners went with us to the pueblo. They stayed on guard there for a week or so until after the Indian ringleaders were shot. Everything remained peaceful and we believed that we were out of danger, so the foreigners returned to their drying sheds. The man who led those workers and was their boss still lives here in San Diego. His name is John Steward

*Note by Savage:"Upon reflection and after asking other people, I [Juana Machado] can say positively that Macedonio González was here in San Diego. He was living in a house on the other side of the river that belonged to an old soldier named Herculano Olivas."

and he had a large family. According to what Steward remembers, he says this all happened in 1842, but I think it was in 1838 or 1839.

I should mention that during that time there was no military force here. The only authority here was Marrón, the *alcalde*.

The San Diego presidio company, or rather, the small part of it that remained in service at that time, was stationed at Mission San Luis Rey. *Alférez* Juan Salazar was in command. The presidio was no longer in existence. Nobody lived there. The people were living in what today is called North San Diego and at nearby ranchos.

I married for the first time in 1825. Lieutenant Colonel Don José María Echeandía, the first commander general appointed by Mexico, was already here. My husband, Dámaso Alipás, was a soldier in the San Diego company. I was about fifteen years old. The *madrina* at our wedding was Doña Isidora Pico. She was still single at that time. The *padrino* was my brother, Juan Machado. He never became a soldier.

Señor Echeandía and all the officers were present at the wedding and attended the dinner afterward. *Alférez* Romualdo Pacheco, *Alférez* Juan Rocha, Lieutenant Agustín V. Zamorano, and Captain Don Santiago Argüello were among the officers there.

After we left the church and returned home, around ten o'clock we had a breakfast that was followed by a dance. The dancing went on until two o'clock, when dinner was served. Señor Echeandía and the officers were at our house by then. When the meal was over, the dancing started again and went on all night. The commander general and the officers left at five o'clock in the afternoon and went back up to the presidio.

During that time, all weddings were usually celebrated like that.

I remember when Captain Don Luis Antonio Argüello, the acting governor and commander of arms of Alta California, came to San Diego in 1825 to turn over the command to his successor, Señor Echeandía. He stopped at the home of his brother, presidio commander Captain Don Santiago.

Don Luis Antonio Argüello was tall and heavy. His face was large and fat and he was fair-skinned. His eyes were black and his hair was even blacker. I never spoke with him but from what I heard and what I saw, he seemed to me to be a friendly and generous man. His brother Santiago was quite heavy and he was of normal height. He was very fair-skinned. His beard, hair, and eyes were black. He had a friendly nature. He was strict with the troops but never despotic. I never heard one single soldier complain about him all the years he was in command here.

Señor Echeandía was a very tall, thin man with a good physique. He was very fair-skinned. He had elegant manners and an extremely friendly nature. He loved dances, feasts, and other diversions.

During his command, he worked with the soldiers to build a mortar and stone dam in a canyon in front of the *castillo* buildings to supply the *castillo* with water. The dam lasted as long as Echeandía was here and for a bit longer after he was gone. After the soldiers were removed from the area, the dam was destroyed by the very water it contained. There are still some ruins of it left.

Señor Echeandía lived here in San Diego. He would take trips to Monterey and other military sites and also to the missions, but his residence was always in San Diego.

In 1829, a military revolt led by Joaquín Solís took place in Monterey. After they seized the plaza in Monterey and the one in San Francisco, the rebels headed for Santa Bárbara. Commander General Echeandía was waiting for them there with soldiers from different areas and settlers from Los Angeles and San Diego. If the rebels had managed to seize Santa Bárbara, they would have also attacked San Diego. That was their plan. The officers taken prisoner by the rebels in Monterey were Don Guadalupe Vallejo, Don José Fernández del Campo, *Sub-Comisario* Don Manuel Jimeno, and Don Juan Rocha. I do not remember if there was somebody else. They managed to escape from their cells and board a ship headed for San Diego. That is where I saw them. My husband, Dámaso Alipás, was one of the soldiers who accompanied Señor Echeandía to Santa Bárbara and took part in the fight against the rebels.

When Señor Echeandía arrived in California in 1825, he brought several officers and an infantry squad called the Fijo de Hidalgo. It was commanded by an *alférez* named Estrada.

I do not remember if it was in 1825 or in 1826, but very shortly after Señor Echeandía arrived, he went with *Alférez* Romualdo Pacheco and a cavalry squad to the Colorado River to establish a pueblo on the shores of a lake. They named the pueblo Laguna de Chapala. My husband went on that expedition. Nothing interesting happened. The Indians were not hostile. According to the way the Indians made themselves understood, they would be willing to help with the work, provided they received the daily salary that was promised. Once everything was arranged, Echeandía, Pacheco, and some of the troops returned. A small detachment was left behind. Very soon after, they received news that the Indians had revolted, so Don Romualdo Pacheco headed back with twenty-five men. Pacheco and his men joined the small detachment and together they attacked the Indians. My husband was also on the second expedition. The battles with the Indians were hard-fought and six of our men died. Several others were wounded by *jaras* and were brought back to the presidio. The plan to establish a pueblo was abandoned forever.

I remember well when Lieutenant Colonel Don Manuel Victoria arrived and got off the ship. He had come to succeed Señor Echeandía. I believe this was at the beginning of 1831. He did not find Echeandía in San Diego when he arrived, because Echeandía was farther north, busy with his plans to secularize the missions—one of Echeandía's last acts was to send out a decree for the secularization of the missions. However, everything came to a stop when Victoria arrived. It seems that he had brought different orders from the supreme government. I remember one day when my father went to Mission San Diego. When he returned, he told my mother that the missionary Fathers had told him that Victoria had promised them that everything would be as it was before. That is to say, the missions and the Indians would remain under the care of the Fathers. This made them very happy. We all rejoiced when we heard that news, because at that time, we believed the Fathers to be holy men. To prevent the Fathers from managing the temporalities of the missions would be a huge theft against the Church and an injustice to the Fathers.

Victoria finally took over the command. Echeandía returned to San Diego to live as a private citizen at the home of the Estudillo family. They provided him with some rooms and food and helped him in other ways.

Señor Victoria remained in command for the rest of the year 1831. He maintained his residence in Monterey. While he was in command, I do not remember him returning to San Diego until the beginning of 1832, which is when he set sail for Mexico.

Victoria was tall, overweight, and olive-skinned. Here they gave him the nickname "Negro of Acapulco" but I do not believe he had any black ancestors. He appeared to be quite jovial. Since he was not here for very long, I did not have the opportunity to know how he treated people. I never spoke with him. The officers' behavior toward the soldiers was not what it used to be. Now the officers would put on airs. They looked down on the soldiers and would not visit the soldiers' families. It used to be that these types of distinctions were not made. The families of officers and soldiers would treat each other as equals. I am speaking, of course, of the honorable families who could not be denounced for any reason.

Later, there was much negative talk about Victoria. He was accused of being a despot. Everybody was angry with him.

Finally, during the last days of November 1831, Don Juan Bandini, Don Pío Pico, and others outlined a plan of revolution against Victoria. And if I remember correctly, on November 30 they attacked the guard, seized the barracks, and then arrested Captain Portilla and Captain Argüello. Portilla and Argüello soon realized that they and their soldiers had no other option than to join the rebels.

Once everything had been arranged in San Diego, soldiers headed for Los Angeles under the command of Captain Portilla. They seized the pueblo and put *Alcalde* Vicente Sánchez in shackles—Sánchez and Victoria were friends. One of Sánchez's brothers managed to leave the pueblo and headed to where Victoria was located. Victoria had already heard rumors about the revolt that had taken place here. He and twenty to twenty-five men were on their way on a forced march. Officer Don Romualdo Pacheco was also a member of the company.

At Arroyo Seco, near Los Angeles, the opposing forces met, but they did not engage in a battle, because Portilla's men retreated. There was a personal fight between Don José María Avila and Don Romualdo Pacheco. Pacheco died and Avila was wounded by Victoria. Avila was finally killed by one of Victoria's soldiers but not before wounding Victoria with his lance.

Victoria did not continue on to Los Angeles because he did not have very many soldiers. Instead, he went to San Gabriel to recover from his injury. I heard it said that Victoria's soldiers later rebelled against him and joined his adversaries.

The rebels called upon Señor Echeandía to assume the command he previously had, and he agreed.

The *diputación territorial* called upon its senior member, Don Pío Pico, to assume the position of *jefe político,* but the *ayuntamiento* and the pueblo of Los Angeles were opposed. They preferred to have Echeandía assume both commands and that is how it remained. Pico never even got to pretend to be *jefe político.*

Señor Victoria found himself abandoned by his troops and with no authority or means whatsoever of regaining his power. He therefore decided to surrender, which meant he was forced to leave California. As soon as he recovered from his injury, the rebels put him aboard an American frigate that was here in San Diego. I think it was called the *California.*

That is how California was freed from a leader who had made himself hated by his despotic actions and by his opposition to the Californios' desires.

I can hardly remember anything about Señor Echeandía's second term in office. I was too young to be concerned about governmental matters.

At the beginning of 1833, General José Figueroa assumed the command. I saw him once, here in San Diego. He was on his way to church from the military headquarters. I do not remember enough about him to be able to describe him.

In 1834 Señor Juan Bandini arrived at this port on the Mexican brig *Natalia*. He had been the delegate from California to the Mexican congress. Don José María Híjar arrived with Bandini, along with part of the colony that was sent to settle here.

When the colonists landed, they first went to the drying sheds the foreigners had at the port. From there they came toward the pueblo but stopped at a place next to the river called Huisache. This place was named after the little tree that was and still is there. The presidio commander received word that some of the colonists had the measles. The commander sent word to the mission to send food to the sick and to also send Doña Apolinaria Lorenzana, who was a healer. She came and attended to them in every way, making sure that they were given the proper food. A kitchen was set up right there at Huisache.

The men, women, and children who were healthy continued traveling north. As soon as the sick had recovered, they also headed north. Some of them died. A few were buried at the presidio, but most of them were buried at Mission San Diego because it was feared that if the bodies were brought here, the disease would come with them.

I did not see Señor Híjar. Here, people talked about the colony as if it were Bandini's idea. It was called the Colonia de Bandini.

A few months later, I saw some of those colonists at San Luis Rey. Some of them were sick and others were recuperating, but they all kept saying that they needed to continue traveling north.

When General Figueroa died in 1834, Lieutenant Colonel Gutiérrez succeeded him as acting governor. I saw Gutiérrez once at San Gabriel. He was on horseback and was about ready to leave for Los Angeles. It seemed to me that he was a fat man. I did not have the opportunity to get a good look at his face. They told me that he was very handsome.

Soon after, Colonel Mariano Chico arrived as commander general and *jefe político*. I never saw him. He was not in California for very long. We heard it said that he had serious disputes with the *ayuntamiento* of Monterey and the *diputación territorial* because the people of the north thought little of Chico's authority. He was an outlandish and contentious man and he was immoral. He was ready to impose his authority in a despotic fashion. But when he saw that the people did not fear him and paid little attention to him, he became enraged and headed back to Mexico. His plans were to return with a considerable force that would show the Californios how to respect his authority. Everyone here was very frightened for quite some time because we believed that Chico could make good on his threats. Fortunately, nothing happened, and Señor Chico did not return.

When Chico went back to Mexico, he left Lieutenant Colonel Gutiérrez in charge of the civil and military commands. Shortly after, the people of Monterey revolted against Gutiérrez and forced him and his supporters to get on a ship and head back to Mexico.

The rebels called upon Don Juan Bautista Alvarado to be governor of what they called the "Free and Sovereign State of California." The people of Los Angeles and San Diego did not recognize this regime. Troops left San Diego to join those from Los Angeles to oppose the plans of Señor Alvarado and his supporters from Monterey. I was not able to learn very much about that situation because at the time I was at our rancho, which is ten leagues from San Diego. No one in my family took part in those wars and disputes, nor in those that came later between Alvarado and Don Carlos Antonio Carrillo, who both laid claim to the title of governor.

I know that our people in the south suffered defeats at San Buenaventura and later at Las Flores. Carrillo and his son Pedro, Don Andrés Pico, Don

Pío Pico with his wife, María Ignacia Alvarado. They are flanked by two of their nieces.
© *San Diego Historical Society*

Gil Ibarra, who was the *alcalde* of Los Angeles, Don José Antonio Carrillo, and several others were taken prisoner and sent to Santa Bárbara. A few of them were sent as prisoners to Sonoma. That is where Commander General Don Mariano G. Vallejo lived.

On the night of December 24, 1837 (if I remember the year correctly), all of the San Diego families were at the home of Don Pío Pico. He had the role of the devil in the *Pastorela*. This was a type of religious play in which various characters appeared, such as an angel, the devil, a hermit, a fellow named Bártolo, and six girls dressed in white with little red capes who would stand on each side. During the performance, women would sing songs about the adoration of the Christ child. I remember that Doña Isidora Pico and Doña Guadalupe Estudillo, who were young and single, took part in the performance. I think that Doña Felipa Osuna de Marrón also took part.

While we were all engrossed in the performance, a man came and knocked on the door. This man was none other than Don José Castro, commander of the Monterey forces. He had positioned his people all around the house and had us completely surrounded. He arrested Don Pío Pico right there at the door. Others were arrested as well. Don Joaquín Ortega was one of them, but because of his wife's pleas, they set Ortega free on the road.

The play ended abruptly and the families returned to their homes, distressed by the fate of our countrymen who had been arrested.

Castro did not take the prisoners from the house that night. He stayed there with them instead. The house was guarded on all sides. At dawn, they headed off to the north.

I believe that the sad events at Pico's Rancho de Jamul happened while he was detained in Santa Bárbara.

The uproar between Alvarado and Carrillo finally ended because the Mexican government appointed Alvarado governor. Señor Alvarado completed the secularization of the missions. He was governor until the end of 1842, when General Micheltorena arrived as governor and commander general of this department. Micheltorena brought with him a large retinue of officers and an infantry battalion that our people called *cholos*. The battalion was called the Batallón Permanente Fijo de Californias. It was made up of thieves and criminals taken from the prisons in Mexico as well as prisoners from Chapala. That is what was said about them. They could not do any harm here in San Diego. We were so afraid of them that we hid everything. There were some good men among them and the officers behaved well. General Micheltorena endeared himself very much to the people and we never complained about him. And if one of his soldiers committed some offense, he would have that soldier punished immediately.

They were here for quite some time. While they were here, the general had the troops learn how to handle weapons. Then they left for Los Angeles. I do not remember if they went directly there on land or if they sailed to San Pedro and then went to Los Angeles.

Señor Micheltorena governed until the end of 1844, when they revolted against him in Monterey. We heard little or nothing about the governor's actions, but there was no shortage of rumors about his troops' bad behavior.

The result of that revolt was that at the beginning of 1845, the troops sent by General Micheltorena and those sent by Don José Castro, the leader of the rebels, met at Cahuenga. An agreement was reached in which Micheltorena was ordered to leave California with his officers and his troops. A few officers and perhaps a few soldiers stayed behind. There was no reason to dislike them.

Micheltorena and his men boarded a ship in San Pedro and left California. Then, Don Pío Pico, the first member of the assembly, became the acting governor. I believe that his official appointment came later from Mexico. Don José Castro became commander general.

From time to time we would hear rumors about bad blood between Pico and Castro, but I do not dare speak about those matters, because I do not have the necessary knowledge to describe them in detail or to give an opinion.

The Americans took over this country in 1846 while Pico was governor.

Frémont was here with his people for two or three days and then went to Los Angeles. In that same year, 1846, things happened in Los Angeles. Commodore Stockton arrived from San Pedro with his forces and took the plaza with no opposition. He remained there a few days and left behind a garrison under the command of Gillespie, much like the garrison that was left in Santa Bárbara and the one that was here in San Diego. The Californios forced Gillespie to abandon Los Angeles and retreat to San Pedro, where he boarded ship.

Captain Mervine attempted to march to Los Angeles from San Pedro with some seamen and sailors, but Don José Antonio Carrillo and his troops forced him to return to his ship with some casualties.

Gillespie came to San Diego, and from here, Commodore Stockton dispatched him with thirty-five or forty men to go and meet up with General Kearny. They received word that Kearny was with a small force at San Felipe, near Agua Caliente. This information came to them from a man who had obtained it from the Indians. Gillespie reunited with Kearny at Santa

María Arcadia Alipás was the youngest child of Juana Machado and Dámaso Alipás. She married Robert Israel, an American. Juana Machado died at the couple's home at Coronado in 1901.© San Diego Historical Society

María (Rancho de los Stokes) and from there they went down to San Pascual. There they met up with a small force of Californio soldiers led by Don Andrés Pico. Kearny was beaten. He and Gillespie were injured. Two captains and many soldiers were killed. Since many others were injured, they had to retreat to the Cerro de las Piedras (Rock Hill) on this side of San Pascual. There, the Californios tried to surround him. Kearny and his men continued fighting, while retreating, until they arrived at Los Peñasquitos. His troops were not bothered by the enemy there. It was said at that time that during those days of combat, Kearny and his people had to eat mule meat. This is quite possible, because the Californio cavalry had cut off their supplies. Nevertheless, they managed to communicate with the port of San Diego and they were sent reinforcements. They retreated to San Diego with the reinforcements without difficulty.

A few days before the battle at San Pascual, eleven Californios were murdered by Indians at the Arroyo de los Alamos, which is on this side of Agua Caliente. They had retreated to that spot with their few belongings so as not to take part in the war between the Americans and the Californios. I believe this happened in November.

The Indians captured twelve people at the house at Rancho de Pauma, which belonged to José Antonio Serrano. They took the people to the Valle de San José. The place where they murdered eleven of the people is near there. They spared the life of the other person because he was one of their

Andrés Pico was a leader in the Californio resistance to the American invasion. He led the troops that defeated Kearny at San Pascual and later negotiated the Californio capitulation to Frémont. Courtesy of The Bancroft Library, University of California, Berkeley

Indians. The name of the Pauma Indian chief who captured them was Manuel. He turned them over to Antonio Berras, another Indian chief. Berras was the chief at Agua Caliente.

A fellow named Juan Garras and another man named Bill Marshall had sided with the Indians and advised them to kill those prisoners. The Indians complained that the *gente de razón* would come and rob them. Garras and Marshall told them that General Kearny had authorized the Indians to kill whoever came. This was a lie, because General Kearny gave no such authorization and did not approve of the conduct of those Indians. Juan Garras and Bill Marshall were hanged a few years later here in San Diego for that crime and others they had committed.

The names of the Californios who perished in that massacre were Francisco Basualdo (artillery sergeant), Ramón Aguilar, Santos Alipaz, Domínguez (the one called Dominguitos, who was now an old man), Santiago Osuna, José María Alvarado, José López, Manuel Serrano, Eustaquio Ruiz, Juan de la Cruz (from Baja California), and one more whose name I cannot remember.[15]

At the end of December, Commodore Stockton and General Kearny left San Diego and headed for Los Angeles with about six hundred men.

Juana Machado on the porch of her house in Old Town San Diego, on a corner of the town plaza. After the battle of San Pascual (December 6 and 7, 1846), some of General Stephen Watts Kearny's wounded were treated at this house. © San Diego Historical Society

At the Paso de Bártolo and at La Mesa (on January 8 and 9, 1847) they engaged in battles with the Californios, and the Americans were triumphant. On January 10 they entered Los Angeles without further resistance, and a few days later, Don Andrés Pico surrendered to Colonel Frémont at San Fernando. Since then, this country has been under the flag of the United States.

One of my brothers, Rafael Machado, was also at Pauma for a short time, along with many others who managed to escape from the Indians (except for the twelve people I spoke about previously). My brother managed to arrive here a few days before Kearny's entrance. When my brother appeared, our mother went to see the commodore to obtain a safe-conduct pass for him. He was granted the pass without difficulty. When Gillespie left to meet up with Kearny, my brother went as a guide and took Gillespie and his troops to Santa María. He then continued on with the American forces until they arrived in San Diego, but he did not take part in the fighting.[16]

Tho.[S] Savage
North San Diego
January 11, 1878

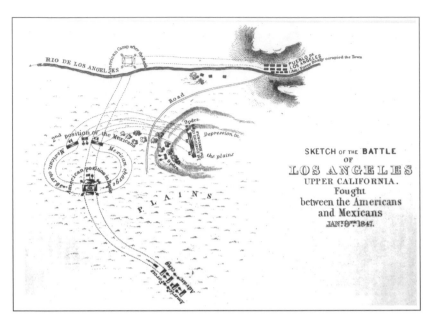

This map of the battle of La Mesa (January 9, 1847), which the Americans termed the battle of Los Angeles, was drawn by Lieutenant William H. Emory, an American participant. Courtesy of The Bancroft Library, University of California, Berkeley

[Note in English by Savage:] José Antonio Serrano told me the ten names mentioned in Mrs. Ridington's statement. He, also, failed to remember the eleventh name, though his wife of that epoch was present and was in some difficulty. He told me that they had assembled there with their property with the intention of moving into Lower California, as they expected to get the privilege through Santiago E. Argüello, Pedrorena, and others, who were with the Americans, and were their personal friends who would not impugn them, knowing that they wished not to take any part in the war on one side or the other. They didn't know that the Indians had been won over to the Americans. Still, they had no reason to apprehend danger from any quarter where they were. The Indians were ordered to watch the frontier and were authorized to protect themselves from white raiders, but they had not been authorized to kill peaceful people. They were put to it by villains to take advantage of the troubles and confusion the country was in.

Tho.^S Savage
North San Diego
January 26, 1878

Felipa Osuna

INTRODUCTION

After speaking with Juana Machado, Savage interviewed Felipa Osuna. Her ancestry symbolized the close-knit and interrelated nature of many members of the Californio community. Her maternal grandmother was María Feliciana de Arballo, the widow whose behavior on the second Anza expedition had so upset Father Pedro Font. María Feliciana was also the maternal grandparent of Josefa Carrillo, whom Henry Cerruti had interviewed more than two years previously. Felipa Osuna's paternal grandparents were Juan Ismerio de Osuna and María Ignacia Alvarado. They were also the paternal grandparents of Miguel Avila, whose widow, María Inocenta Pico, Savage himself would interview in less than three months' time.

Juan Ismerio de Osuna had been a member of the presidio company at Loreto, in Baja California, and was a member of the Portolá expedition in 1769. After the expedition he returned to Baja California, where he continued in the military. In 1774, Governor Felipe de Barri sent him as a special courier with some important reports he wished to send to Mexico City. He went to Alta California in the 1770s and served at the San Diego presidio and with the mission guard at San Gabriel. He died at that mission in 1790.[1]

In 1806 Juan María Osuna, son of Juan Ismerio de Osuna and María Ignacia Alvarado, married Juliana Josefa López, daughter of Francisco López and María Feliciana de Arballo, at Mission San Diego. Their second child, María Felipa de Jesús Catarina Osuna, was born in 1809.

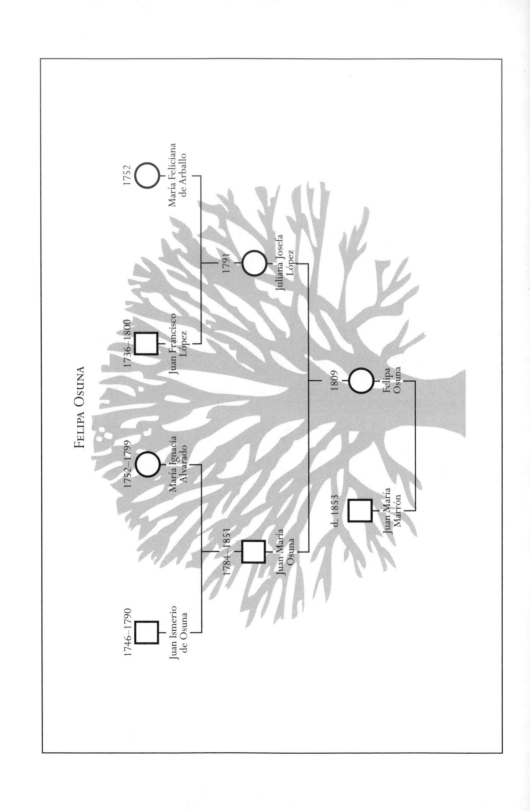

FELIPA OSUNA

1746–1790 Juan Ismerio de Osuna

1752–1799 María Ignacia Alvarado

1784–1851 Juan María Osuna

1736–1800 Juan Francisco López

1752 María Feliciana de Arballo

1791 Juliana Josefa López

1809 Felipa Osuna

d. 1853 Juan María Marrón

The Sylvestre Marrón adobe at Rancho Agua Hedionda. Felipa Osuna visited this rancho frequently in the 1850s. © San Diego Historical Society

In 1834, Felipa Osuna married Juan María Marrón, a seaman and trader who had settled in San Diego around 1821. At least three children survived into adulthood.[2]

Felipa Osuna's husband and father were both very involved in public life in the San Diego area. They were both involved in the movement against Governor Victoria in 1831. Her father received Rancho San Dieguito in the early 1830s. Her husband served as *regidor, elector,* and *juez suplente* before 1845, when he was made administrator of the former mission of San Luis Rey. He was chosen *alcalde* of San Diego in 1846.[3]

Juan María Marrón was granted Rancho Agua Hedionda, just south and east of present-day Carlsbad, in the 1830s. Marrón began living there in 1839 or 1840. J. J. Warner testified that the rancho "had an adobe house, corrals, cultivated fields, and a respectable stock of cattle and horses."[4] His family normally stayed there for the summer and fall and returned to San Diego in the winter. Marrón died on September 11, 1853. After the death of her husband, Felipa Osuna continued to live both at the rancho and in the city. She made frequent trips to Agua Hedionda throughout the 1850s. In the 1870s, Judge Benjamin Hayes called her the oldest resident of Old Town.[5]

When Savage began his interview with Felipa Osuna, he seemed to want her to talk about her father and her husband. She gave him very brief

San Diego in 1850. Lithograph by G. C. Conts. Courtesy of The Bancroft Library, University of California, Berkeley

descriptions of their careers. But as she was describing her husband's tenure as administrator of the ex-mission of San Luis Rey, she began to defend his reputation against those who claimed that he was one of those who had despoiled the mission property for personal gain. She even cited a source—the mission inventory—as evidence for her judgment. Then she spent a great deal of time describing the final years of Father José María Zalvidea, who had spent forty years as a missionary in California. More than thirty years after his death, she was still very protective of him; she tended to attribute his more bizarre behavior to exhaustion resulting from his constant penances and his years of selfless dedication.

Felipa Osuna's remembrance of Father Zalvidea's death at San Luis Rey led her into a set of reminiscences about the war, since American troops had occupied the former mission in early 1847. Many Californios found themselves quite conflicted about how to react to the American invasion, and Felipa Osuna's testimonio offered a sharp illustration of the cross-currents that affected portions of the Californio community. On the one hand, she proudly remembered how she had hidden José Matías Moreno, Pío Pico's secretary, from the Americans. Yet she was also bitter about the way in which the Californio forces had appropriated the one hundred head of cattle that Father Zalvidea had given her. She and her husband were accused by some of being on the side of the invaders, and her account of those tension-filled months of late 1846 and early 1847 vividly captures the divisions within the community as the Americans were assuming control of the land.

As Felipa Osuna described the condition of her house during the war, she was reminded of her role in thwarting the Indian attack in San Diego, of which Juana Machado had earlier spoken to Savage. Felipa Osuna's memories of the episode were mixed. While she was gratified that the attack had been prevented, she was greatly troubled by the violent retribution which some soldiers exacted against Indians living in the pueblo. Since she had been one of the informants against the Indians, she felt personally responsible for the summary executions of some Indians that had taken place then.

In his introduction to his interview with Felipa Osuna, Savage wrote, "Her memory is at fault upon many events that occurred in her earlier years. For that reason I gave up the hope I had entertained of getting much information from her on local matters." That judgment was too harsh, and it indicated that Savage could be too focused on politics and battles to appreciate what he was hearing from the women he interviewed. Felipa Osuna's testimonio was extremely valuable, recalling in a unique fashion the tensions, conflicts, and uncertainties that were so prominent a part of life in Mexican California in the 1830s and 1840s. California was economically opening to the world in that period, but indigenous peoples hostile to the Mexican presence were regaining ever more control of the southern boundaries. Relations between the peripheral territory of Alta California and the metropolis of Mexico City were strained. Some Californians wanted to strengthen ties to the Mexican Republic, of which California was a part, while others desired to emulate Texas and become independent of Mexico. Still others believed that a viable future demanded some sort of affiliation with a European power or with the United States. Felipa Osuna's testimonio captured California life in all of that tension and uncertainty.

Recollections of Doña Felipa Osuna de Marrón, Native of San Diego, Where She Currently Lives, with Various Original Documents from the Private Files of This Same Señora, Who Gave Them to the Bancroft Library, 1878

This lady has been a widow 25 years, resides in San Diego, and is connected with most of the old families of the place, either by blood or marriage.

She seems quite intelligent, but is entirely unable to remember dates, and her memory is at fault upon many events that occurred in her earlier years. For that reason I gave up the hope I had entertained of getting much information from her on local matters.

She was very happy to learn that Mr. Bancroft was engaged upon a history of her native country from its earliest days and desired me to express to him her best wishes for his success.

> *Tho.ˢ Savage*
> *North San Diego (old town)*
> *January 26, 1878*

Madame Marrón told me that all her husband's papers on public matters were burnt, that she had only such as relating to their real estate.

I, Felipa Osuna de Marrón, was born at the old presidio of San Diego on May 1, 1809. My father was Juan María Osuna and my mother was Juliana López. My father was a soldier and a corporal of the San Diego company and served for many years. After his retirement, he established his residence in San Diego. Over a period of years he held the posts of *regidor, síndico, alcalde,* and justice of the peace. He had the satisfaction of earning the high regard of his peers. He died when he was about sixty years old.

When I was about twenty years old, I married Juan María Marrón, a rancher. He also held positions in public office in San Diego and was the district elector. Finally, the government appointed him administrator of Mission San Luis Rey. Unfortunately, when he took over the mission, it was already in very bad shape. There were barely any agricultural fields left at the mission and there was very little in the storehouses. This was clear from the inventory that Don José Joaquín Ortega gave Marrón. Ortega was Marrón's predecessor. The sad truth is that when Marrón was the mission administrator he did not receive any wages, yet he personally had to maintain the mission and the missionary, Father José María Zalvidea. For this reason, Father Zalvidea was so grateful to me and my husband. The Father had seen how José Joaquín Ortega was embezzling, and he continually reprimanded him for that in no uncertain terms. He even said that Señor Ortega had taken tables, planks, benches, and everything else that was in the storehouses.

Because of statements like this, Señor Ortega and others were in the habit of saying that Father Zalvidea was crazy. In fact, whenever somebody came to visit, and even when he was by himself, Father Zalvidea would burst forth with those denunciations of Ortega.

Father Zalvidea would have moments of spiritual intensity. He could be heard speaking with the devil. He would then stamp his foot heavily on the ground and shout, "Go away, Satan. You are not going to upset me. You cannot have power over me." This went on continuously, day and night, in the mission plaza, in the corridors, or in his own room.

Once when he was walking and reading his book near the place where the animals were slaughtered, a young bull headed toward him. Everybody was yelling at the Father to flee, but all he did was kneel down and say in a tone of great satisfaction, "Come on now, yes sir, don't worry, don't worry." The young bull walked right by him without touching him. He experienced a number of risky situations like this but it seemed as if the raging bulls respected him.

The way he ate was strange. He would put all the food that was served to him, whether salty or sweet, on one plate, and he would eat everything. The only things he left behind were the bones from the meat or fish. The same thing happened with beverages, so it was necessary to serve him in moderation. We had to keep the food and drink under lock and key because he wanted to eat all the time. There were times he would get hold of large pieces of butter and eat them with his bare hands. Although he demonstrated good common sense in his conversations, he behaved like a child with regard to some things.

No one ever saw Father Zalvidea touch money. When he was in charge of the mission, he instinctually knew when something had been stolen or pilfered. He did not have to look into the matter, he just knew. People eventually claimed that he had a gift for performing miracles. There were those who tried to brand him insane, but they had no basis in fact. They were just reacting to the Father's habit of telling them the bitter truth about their abuses and disorderliness.

Father Zalvidea's whole body was scarred by the *silicio* because he constantly whipped himself while shouting at Satan, to scare him off. His feet were in miserable condition because he had buried nails in them. He only wore sandals.

The hour when he was to hand over his virtuous soul to the Creator finally came. He became ill and was bedridden. He could no longer move. I was living at the mission, so I took on the responsibility of caring for him with the assistance of Guadalupe Hernández, a native of Mazatlán. I removed huge nails from his body and his feet. He no longer had any toes and another part of his foot was gone as well. When I treated him, he could see that I was horrified by his condition. He would say, "Come on now, Señora. Come on now, that's nothing." Our rancho, which was called San Francisco or Agua Hedionda, provided everything that was needed to care for and feed Father Zalvidea. The rancho was right next to the mission.

Father Zalvidea was always saying, "Come on, come on, this señora has so many children, and it is very hard for her to take care of me and feed me. This is Señor Ortega's fault because he took everything with him." In San Dieguito, Father Zalvidea had given my father half-ownership of one hundred cows that belonged to him. When the Father became gravely ill, he told me, in front of my husband, that he was going to write to my father and have him send him the one hundred cows. I asked him why and he said it was because it bothered him to see me have to make sacrifices in order to take care of him. If a doctor were caring for him, the one hundred cows would already be gone. He said he wanted me to have them. I refused to accept them, but he insisted that it was the right thing to do.

Father Zalvidea never allowed anyone to watch over him at night, nor could anyone sleep in his room, not even when he was gravely ill. He spent day and night on his back without being able to move. From a lying position, he would baptize, hear confessions, and perform marriages. And he was always reading. He would tell Father Vicente P. Oliva that he was dying like a good soldier, at his post.

One morning, the page informed me that when he entered Father Zalvidea's room, he found that the mattress, blankets, and pillows were burned. I ran to the room and sure enough, everything was burned, except for the place where his body had been.

I frequently hid the disciplines far away from his room. But somehow, and I was never able to figure it out, the next morning I would find them on his bed covered in blood. How he was able to find them and whip himself with them was incomprehensible to me. To this day, I still cannot explain it.

During the final moments of Father Zalvidea's life, Father Vicente Pascual Oliva, Doña Isidora Pico, Don Juan Avila, Doña Apolinaria Lorenzana, and many others came to the mission to take Father Zalvidea to Mission San Juan Capistrano in a *carreta* that was very well-lined. When he found out that they were coming for him, he said, "Come on now, come on now. Yes, Lord, they are coming for me, but I cannot go because I am dying like a good soldier. I hear confessions and baptize here. What will this place be like without a Father?" Father Oliva and Doña Apolinaria told him that it was not possible for him to stay there. He was reluctant, but in the end, they decided that they would take him against his will the next morning. They paid no attention to what he was saying. He told them that I was taking very good care of him and that I had been like a mother to him. There was nothing he lacked. He said he did not want them to move him from there. He also said that everything he had in his trunks would be mine when he died. He had a little bit of money and a silver shell. They did not give me anything that was in the trunks. But before he died, he had given me the cows. When the American forces came, Californio troops ate all the cows. They did not leave me a single one.

Doña Apolinaria and I discussed the situation and I told her that Father Zalvidea was very weak and would not endure the trip. But since they were determined to take him the following morning, it would be wise to give him the last rites that evening, just in case. I said the same thing to Father Oliva, and they gave him the last rites.

That night, Father Zalvidea sent everybody out of his room. Doña Apolinaria thought that he would be able to travel, because he seemed so happy. His eyes were lively and he did not look like a man who was about to die. In the early morning the page came and informed us that he had just gone in to see Father Zalvidea and found him dead. That is what really happened.

Father Zalvidea was so revered by everyone. Before he was buried, everybody cut off a little piece of his habit or his cord. He was practically left without any habit at all.

He had given me a large crucifix and another small one, and an image of the Virgen del Pilar. I still have these items. He also gave me a gold reliquary that he kept at the head of his bed. I left it there and somebody stole it from me.

He was buried the next day after Mass on the left-hand side of the altar. His predecessor, Father Francisco, was buried on the other side.[6]

After the burial, people came on behalf of the Fathers and demanded that I turn over the one hundred cows, but the Californio soldiers had already eaten them. Even if I had them, I would not have turned them over.

Mission San Luis Rey, drawn by Frenchman Auguste Duhaut-Cilly, who visited the mission in 1827. Courtesy of The Bancroft Library, University of California, Berkeley

Mission San Luis Rey was sold by Governor Pico to José Antonio Pico and José Antonio Cota. In 1846, José Antonio Pico came and told my husband that he was now the administrator and that the mission was his. My husband told him, "Well, I will hand over the mission to you just as I received it." Pico did not take it and left for Pala. Later, Don Juan Forster came to take possession of the mission in the name of the buyers, right when Frémont's troops were approaching. Forster left my husband in charge of the mission so he could manage it for the owners.

Magdalena Baca, the wife of Lieutenant José Antonio Pico, would tell me, "This mission is now mine." I answered her, "Mi——a——u (meow) says the cat.[7] The people who are going to own the mission are already coming from over there." Frémont entered the mission with troops at about one or two o'clock in the afternoon and left the following morning. My husband was at his rancho, Agua Hedionda, so the Americans decided to wait for him. I was so frightened, but they were not disrespectful to me at all. They did not ask me for anything. After my husband arrived, the Americans did a thorough check of the mission and then left to set up camp by El Chorro.

When those troops arrived, Don José Matías Moreno was having an afternoon snack with me. Don José was the secretary for the governor's office. Moreno had told me that my cousin, Pío Pico, was fleeing and was hiding at Santa Margarita.

I left Don Matías seated in the *sala* and casually went over to the door.
All of a sudden I saw the entire mission surrounded and the corridor filled
with armed foreigners. Very agitated, I shouted, "My dear Don Matías, the
entire place is filled with armed men. They surely are coming for you." He
said he did indeed think they were coming for him. He was very frightened
and said, "God help me. Where can I hide?" He wanted to hide in one of the
large cupboards in the last room, but I told him not to, because they would
easily find him there. The situation was very tense and there was no time to
ponder. Don Juan Rowland was on his way with the troops. I did not want
to leave until Don Matías was well hidden. I came up with an idea. He
could pretend to be sick. First he would have to get undressed, tie a rag
around his head, and then climb into bed in a nearby room. When Don Juan
Rowland asked me about the administrator, I said that he had gone to our
rancho and would return shortly. Rowland saw that I was shaking, so he
approached me and told me not to be afraid, nothing was going to happen
to me. He then told me that they had come to the mission in search of the
governor and his secretary. I told them they could not enter the mission
without my husband being there. Rowland told me that they had no intention of showing any disrespect and would not enter. Then I said, "Well, if
you want to come in, you can search the whole house. You will only find a
nephew of mine who is sick in bed," and I pointed to the room. The bed was
at the entrance to the room. After my husband arrived and had taken off his
spurs, they searched the house. Very quickly and in a low voice I told my
husband what I had said to Rowland about my "nephew" so that he would
be forewarned. They went in, walked around the room, and looked at the
"sick person." They did not suspect him to be the secretary. Aside from that
search, they did not do anything else.

If Don Matías Moreno had hidden himself where he had suggested, they
would have caught him the minute they searched the cupboards. When
they were unable to open the door of an upstairs storage area, because the
key was lost, they knocked down the door. They thought that the secretary
was in there, but they realized they had made a mistake. That night they
camped by El Chorro.

After the men who had conducted the search left, Don Matías got up
and sent for Don Santiago Emilio Argüello, who was with the Americans.
Argüello was a friend of his. I could not understand why he did something
so crazy. As soon as I discovered that he had sent that message, I became
very angry and told him to saddle up and leave immediately. And he did just
that. He left on a magnificent horse that my husband had. He mounted the

horse and had barely gotten through the back gate of the mission when a party arrived with Santiago Emilio Argüello and Captain Gillespie in the lead. They wanted to see Moreno, but we said that he had already left. Gillespie became very angry with my husband and made him leave the mission. They sent search parties out in all directions but they were not able to catch Don Matías. He later told me that he watched his pursuers from a vantage point where he could not be detected. He knew that Pío Pico was hiding at Santa Margarita and went there to meet up with him. Later, they were able to go to Baja California.

I never suspected that the Americans would have been looking for Don Matías Moreno or we would not have been so careless. He was within an inch of being caught.

Very shortly after, my husband and I went back to our rancho.

My husband never got involved in the intrigues of those times.

When the Americans took San Diego, my husband brought me here. When the Californio forces under the command of Leonardo Cota and José Alipaz were around these parts, my husband went to the rancho and left me behind here. The Californios seized him and wanted to make him go with them to fight against the Americans. San Diego was full of Americans. Don Miguel Pedrorena, Don Santiago Emilio Argüello, Don Pedro C. Carrillo, and others had sided with the Americans. We, the women, all left our homes and gathered together at the Estudillo home. The Californios were coming down from the small fort they had erected on the hill. I wanted to go and be with my husband, but he had to obtain permission from Alipaz and Cota to come and take me away from there. That is why we raised a white flag at the house. Alipaz and Cota told Marrón that he would not be seized by the Americans because he was on good terms with Pedrorena, Argüello, and Carrillo. Those at the Estudillo home allowed him to enter because the Californios saw me waving a white flag. After he entered, I felt bad because Pedrorena and a party of Americans went out to receive him. They seized his horse and weapons and took him to the barracks. Since he was delayed here for a number of days and had not returned to the Californios' camp with me, they believed he had gone over to the American side and became very angry with him. The delay was because he had not been able to obtain the safe-conduct pass from the commodore.

We were very anxious to go and reunite with our countrymen. I was very afraid of the Americans because they were undisciplined troops. We finally managed to leave under our word of honor that we would not take up arms against the United States. They gave us a safe-conduct pass and wherever we met up with American troops, we showed them the paper and they let us pass. My husband, our children, and I traveled on foot. We thought that we would be welcomed at the mission by our countrymen but discovered that they were furious with Marrón and even wanted to shoot him. The Californios had taken all of the horses from our rancho. They made us go on foot to Agua Hedionda. I stayed there. They took my husband and all of the non-Indian servants with them. They accused my husband of sending messages to the Americans, which is something that had never occurred to him. He was in great danger of being killed by them.

In the end, my husband pretended to be very ill, so they allowed him to go back to the rancho to recover. All of the Californio forces in the area would come early in the morning and take our cattle. That is how we lost a large part of our cattle and the cattle that Father Zalvidea had given me.

During the time they kept my husband prisoner, the Indians helped me gather a good deal of corn, beans, and a large amount of grain, and we hid everything in *chamizales*. That is how we were able to have food to eat when the war ended.

The accusations that Marrón and I were allied with the Americans did not cease. My husband was upset that his countrymen would treat him this way and that they were making off with all his possessions. So, soon after

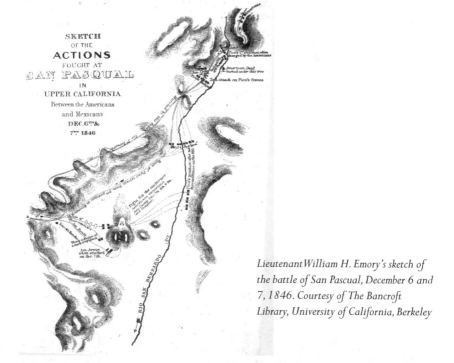

Lieutenant William H. Emory's sketch of the battle of San Pascual, December 6 and 7, 1846. Courtesy of The Bancroft Library, University of California, Berkeley

Battle of San Pascual *by William L. Meyers. Courtesy of the Franklin Delano Roosevelt Library, Hyde Park, New York*

the battle of San Pascual, my husband wrote a letter to the commodore and asked him if he could return to San Diego. The commodore responded and told him he could come back and so could anyone else for that matter. Everyone would be welcomed and no one would be harmed.

My children went about recovering what few cattle remained. The Californios thought my children were doing this for them! One day, around three or four o'clock in the afternoon, we left the rancho with two *carretas* loaded with birds and anything else we could gather up. We also had a flock of lambs and some cattle that we were trying to hurry along. We traveled on foot, while others went on horseback or in *carretas*. We traveled all night along the beach and arrived at Tecolote at dawn as the cornet was sounding reveille in the plaza. My husband waved a white flag and they immediately came to receive us and allowed us to enter. The flock of lambs and the cattle stayed behind. The commodore provided my husband with some men to help him bring the animals in. Commodore Stockton always showed my husband great kindness.

The Americans were stunned when they saw the lances carried by some of the men who came with my husband. These were men who had fought in the battle of San Pascual. Among them were Jesús Machado and my brother, Leandro Osuna.[8] My brother was the person who killed Captain Antonio, the man who attacked Andrés Pico.[9] The bandolier of my brother's lance was bloodstained. I saw that the Americans appeared to be angry with him and were making hostile gestures. I feared that we were going to have trouble, but they did not do anything to us. Two days later, the

Andrés Pico at the former mission of San Fernando, by EdwardVischer, 1865. Courtesy of The Bancroft Library, University of California, Berkeley

cattle arrived and the Americans were very happy. My countrymen were in for a huge disappointment the day after we left the rancho. When they came for cattle, as usual, there was not a single soul at the rancho except for the Indians. The doors were closed, so they knocked them down and did other damage. They took whatever they could find of value, but they did not dare follow us, because they believed that the commodore had sent an escort to accompany Marrón to San Diego. Some of the Californios would come as far as the little hill, but they were not bold enough to go any farther than that.

The Californios always went to the little hill to shout shameless remarks and spew threats. Frequently, some of them would enter San Diego at night. One day, they fired a shot from the small fort. Pedrorena and I were headed to my home and the shot just missed Pedrorena's leg as it flew. He reacted by taking off his hat and bowing to the Californios.

The Americans had the house in which I am currently living completely surrounded by trenches and embrasures. Some of Frémont's men were mercenaries, and one day they robbed our home. Robberies became almost commonplace until the commodore arrived to begin his march to Los Angeles. We were then well protected and received daily rations.

*Anita Pico, daughter of Andrés Pico, is on the right. She is sitting with Catarina Moreno.
Courtesy of the Seaver Center for Western History Research, Natural History Museum of
Los Angeles County, Los Angeles, California*

On December 29, 1846, Commodore Stockton, General Kearny, and a
respectable force left San Diego for Los Angeles. There were no longer any
Californio troops in these parts. We stayed in San Diego and divided our
time between here and the rancho.

The commodore bought all the cattle, sheep (about one thousand), and
other things that we had brought from the rancho. He paid for everything
in cash. The only things they still owed us for were the twenty-five good
horses that Gillespie took and a few other items my husband forgot to list
on his claim. After I was widowed, I received a payment order from the
government for the twenty-five horses. A man took it from me to collect
the money and never brought the money back to me.

One day, when I was in this same house, I saw that some Indians were
talking to my gardener, a Diegueño Indian named Juan. I already had been
noticing that every afternoon other Indians would come and speak with
him. Since I understood the Indian language, I took great care to find out
what they were talking about on that particular day. They did not have the
slightest idea that I could understand them, so they spoke frankly. They

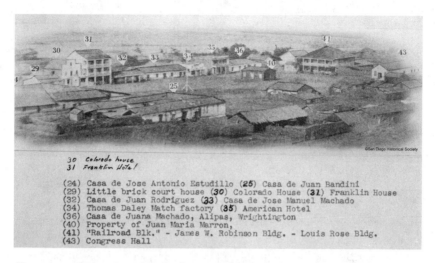

30 Colorado house
31 Franklin Hotel!

(24) Casa de Jose Antonio Estudillo (25) Casa de Juan Bandini
(29) Little brick court house (30) Colorado House (31) Franklin House
(32) Casa de Juan Rodriguez (33) Casa de Jose Manuel Machado
(34) Thomas Daley Match factory (35) American Hotel
(36) Casa de Juana Machado, Alipas, Wrightington
(40) Property of Juan Maria Marron,
(41) "Railroad Blk." - James W. Robinson Bldg. - Louis Rose Bldg.
(43) Congress Hall

The property of Felipa Osuna's husband, Juan María Marrón, is marked "40" in this annotated rendering of old San Diego. © *San Diego Historical Society*

began by saying that they had formulated a plan to rob Captain Fitch's store and kill Lawrence Hatwell. Then they planned to take Fitch's wife and me with them. Captain Fitch was away on a trip and he had asked my husband and me to spend the nights at his house during that time. The Indians who were engaged in that conversation with my gardener were two Indians from the Fitch home and a fellow named Juan Antonio who was a cook at the Estudillo home. From their various conversations, I discovered that they had *jaras* prepared at the old presidio. After they finally had said when they would put their plan into action, I thought I should warn my husband and alert Señora Fitch. The plan was for the Indians to enter the Fitch home in the evening when she was kneading bread. They would kill Hatwell, rob the store, and take both of us out through the back door to the horses they would have ready and waiting.

After I warned my husband, he notified Hatwell but told him that he did not know if it was true or not. At nightfall, I went to the Fitch home. It was already dark when Josefa Carrillo de Fitch began to knead bread in the dining room. Two tall, strong Indians came and stood right in the doorway as if to block the path. Hatwell and my husband were prepared and they went and grabbed them. The Indians did not put up a fight.

Very early the next morning, *Alférez* Macedonio González arrived in the pueblo with some armed men. One of the men was José María Soto. They set out to look for the Indians but as soon as the Indians began to get suspicious, they realized that they had no place to hide. González seized the two Indians from the Fitch home and Juan Antonio, the Indian from the Estudillo home. My Indian had left very early to look for firewood, and he was never seen again. There was another Indian, named Carrancio, and I believe a few others. I do not know exactly how many were shot. I only know about the three main players. They were taken to the *juzgado*. From what they said in their statements, they appeared to be guilty. Macedonio González ordered that they be shot right then and there. This was the same place where Kearny's dragoons who died at San Pascual were later buried. Many more were captured, but not all were sentenced to death. I know that one Indian from the Bandini home was set free, but he suffered for the rest of his life until he died.

When I saw how much the Indians suffered, it caused me great sorrow knowing that I had informed against them. It distressed me greatly. The judge, Don José Antonio Estudillo, did not approve of the violent methods Macedonio used with the Indians. However, I must confess that the punishment produced a very beneficial effect, because after that, there were no more robberies by Indians in San Diego. Before that, we were on constant alert because there were always rumors that the Indians were coming to attack us.

One night the Indians attacked Pío Pico's Rancho Jamul. His family had come to San Diego. The Indians killed the *mayordomo,* Juan Leiva, and other *gente de razón*. They took two young girls with them, Tomasa and Ramona, and nothing has ever been learned about their fate. Their mother appeared in San Diego, naked, with her little son Claro.

I do not remember when those events happened.

Felipa Osuna de Marrón
by Thomas Savage
North San Diego
January 26, 1878

[from a loose page:] It was painful to see Macedonio's people running after the Indians like a pack of hunting dogs. Some of the Indians were pulled out of their homes, others were lassoed as they tried to run away, terrified. One of the Indians came into my house and begged me to hide him, but his pursuers saw him go in and he was caught. I was so sorry that I had informed on the conspirators. The other women also felt sorry for the Indians and accused me of causing the whole thing. How could I have concealed a conspiracy against the lives, liberty, and possessions of so many people? They would have died. What would have been the fate of the women of San Diego if the Indians had seized them? It was confirmed that the Indians who were shot had been conspiring with the hostile Indians from the outside. They may have confessed to this, but I did not hear them say anything about it when they were talking in our garden.

Apolinaria Lorenzana

INTRODUCTION

*S*avage arrived in Santa Bárbara on March 1, 1878. His major aim was to obtain as much information as he could on the de la Guerra family, whose patriarch, José de la Guerra y Noriega, had been the most prominent figure in central California during the Mexican period. He immediately presented various letters of introduction to members of the family but found that the family was preoccupied with the illness of one of its oldest members, Miguel de la Guerra. Savage took up residence with Edward F. Murray, who had already worked for Bancroft at the task of transcribing some of the Santa Bárbara Mission records. Murray had recently been given permission by Thomas Dibblee, executor of the de la Guerra estate, to make extracts from some of de la Guerra's personal and business papers. Savage and Murray roomed together at Cook's building, on the corner of State and Carrillo Streets, a few blocks from the old de la Guerra house.

One of the de la Guerra sisters, Angustias, told Savage that she would be unable to talk to him immediately due to her brother's critical condition. But she recommended that he interview Apolinaria Lorenzana, who also lived in Santa Bárbara. Savage took her advice.

In our introduction we have already summarized Apolinaria Lorenzana's life up to the time she was placed in the house of Raymundo Carrillo. After spending time there, she went on to San Diego, where she was placed with a newly married couple, Sergeant Mariano Mercado and Josefa Sal, daughter of one of the most important Spanish officers in eighteenth-century

An anonymous eighteenth-century painting of Francisco Antonio de Lorenzana y Butrón, who
served as Archbishop of Mexico from 1766 to 1772 and founded the orphanage where
Apolinaria Lorenzana and countless others were given his surname. The painting is at the
Metropolitan Cathedral, Mexico City. Courtesy of CONACULTA

Spanish California, Hermenegildo Sal. We have already met Josefa Sal: she
was the woman who named Josefa Carrillo.

Apolinaria Lorenzana, who had learned to read at the Real Casa de Expósitos, served as an instructor in Sal's school. She also spent a great deal of
time at the mission, where she took on a greater and greater set of responsibilities. According to Franciscan historian Zephyrin Engelhardt, who
engaged in an extensive study of the mission records, she may have served
as godmother at more baptisms than any other individual in Alta California. For instance, she was godmother to one of Eulalia Pérez's daughters.[1]

She also became a ranchera. As we have seen in the case of Eulalia Pérez,
in the early 1830s, as secularization loomed on the horizon, some missionaries tried to ensure that at least part of the mission lands would go to
those who had been active supporters of the mission system. Apolinaria

Lorenzana was one such individual. In 1831 she began to occupy the Jamachá Valley, which was part of the Mission San Diego holdings. In 1834 Father Fernando Martín formally certified that the mission had not occupied and did not need the land she was developing. This cleared the way for her to seek a formal grant of the rancho, which she finally obtained in 1840. She did not usually live on the land. Rather she hired a *mayordomo* to attend to its affairs as she continued to live close to the church. As Santiago Argüello testified, "she built a house there and had a *mayordomo* living in it...she lived in it a part of the time herself." In 1843 she received another grant, Cañada de los Coches. Argüello described her activity there: "She has constructed two dams to obtain water for irrigation and has been raising wheat and barley."[2]

The end of the Mexican era was a turbulent time for Apolinaria Lorenzana. In 1846 she cared for the dying Father Zalvidea at San Luis Rey. As Felipa Osuna related, she had arranged to transport him to San Juan Capistrano, but he died the night before the trip was to occur. Later in 1846, Father Vicente Oliva left the former mission of San Diego and sought refuge at San Juan Capistrano. When the Mormon battalion occupied the site of the mission in January 1847, Apolinaria Lorenzana herself left San Diego. Taking as many of her cattle as she could, she headed for San Juan.[3] She appointed John Forster as her agent for Jamachá, and he allowed the U.S. army to use it for grazing livestock.

In February 1847, Father Oliva asked her to undertake a dangerous mission: to go to San Luis Rey and try to recover a chalice which had been hidden in an arroyo and also to try to secure as many of the mission registers as she could. She agreed to try. She went to San Luis Rey, recovered the books and some other items, and left them at the Pico rancho at Santa Margarita. After Oliva died in January 1848, she offered to go back to San Diego and see what she could rescue there.[4]

After the war, Apolinaria Lorenzana gradually lost her land through a series of legal maneuvers which she probably did not understand clearly. She petitioned for her grants before the U.S. Land Commission in 1852. However, the very next year, she signed a document which in effect sold Jamachá to Colonel John Bankhead Magruder for the sum of $2,500. As her testimonio indicates, she believed that she was signing a document acknowledging that Magruder was paying her for having used her land to graze his cattle. In this document, she did retain some residual rights through a mortgage, but in 1860 she signed another document which had the effect of transferring that mortgage to someone else. It is not apparent what she thought that document actually was. It is difficult to escape the conclusion that she was taken advantage of and that the land was basically stolen from her. She clearly thought that she still held the legal rights to her property. In 1877 she sold those rights to Reginald del Valle, and in the very next year she deeded her ranchos to Mónica Romero de Ruiz. Landless and without a family, she lived her last years on the charity of friends. Blind and enfeebled, she died in April 1884.[5]

Apolinaria Lorenzana began by telling Savage about her earlier life, the journey to Alta California, and her stays with various presidio families. As we have seen with other women, she emphasized that military life in California could not be conceived of as having been an entirely masculine affair. She was extremely proud of the fact that she taught herself to write while living with soldiers and their families. What the men would toss away, such as cigarette papers or other scraps, became her learning tools. And she found in herself a passion to spread the knowledge she had so painstakingly attained. She became a teacher of other girls. Mothers sought her out so that she could teach their daughters to read and recite the catechism. She also taught sewing and embroidery to support herself.

Apolinaria Lorenzana's testimonio makes it clear that she found a home at the mission. Starting as a nurse, she gained ever greater responsibilities, which she listed for Savage. Like Eulalia Pérez, she provided a close and full account of many aspects of the mission routine. She told how she supervised purchases of grain and negotiated with ship captains and supercargoes.

Her account of the war period complemented what Savage had already heard from Felipa Osuna. Both women looked after Father Zalvidea, and Apolinaria Lorenzana interacted with Felipa Osuna and her family around San Luis Rey. In the midst of the instability that prevailed in the area during the invasion and its aftermath, she strove to keep her mission supplied. She stayed behind even after the last resident priest departed. She was not happy with the outcome of the American takeover. She was still angry as she related her inability to prevent the loss of her land to the newcomers. She vigorously insisted that she had never sold them her ranchos. She ended her narrative by drawing a sharp contrast between her past accomplishments and her present poverty.

Savage then asked her about the attack on Jamul. She was able to add important details to what he had already learned. Apolinaria Lorenzana was at her own nearby rancho at the time, and she was the first person to whom the survivors told their tales. Like Felipa Osuna, she was troubled by the retaliation in San Diego against the Indians there. She placed the planned attack on the Fitch store in the context of that retaliation. She argued that it was designed as revenge for the violence which had been visited on the Indians by Macedonio González and his men.

After this discussion, Savage apparently asked her some questions about social life in San Diego. He asked her why she had never married. Then he inquired about the *Pastorela*, about which he had heard from Juana Machado. He ended by asking her how old she thought Eulalia Pérez really was. Then he asked her to sign the paper on which he had been taking notes. She realized that he was ending the interview, so she hastily added a few sentences about her experiences taking the sick for treatment at the hot springs east of San Diego. She seemed to be telling him, "I want you to remember me, above all, as a woman who nursed the sick."

Recollections of Doña Apolinaria Lorenzana, "The Pious Woman," an Old Woman about Seventy-Five Years of Age. Dictated by Her in Santa Bárbara in March 1878 to Tomás Savage, Bancroft Library, 1878

This old lady residing in Santa Bárbara was one of the foundling children sent to California by the viceroy of Mexico in the early part of this century. She does not know her age but calculates that she may be from seventy-five to seventy-eight years old. She never married, preferring to devote herself to the care of the church and missionaries at San Diego, in addition to her other duties. On my visit to San Diego this year, many of the native Californians there of both sexes spoke of her in the highest terms of praise. She was known by many as Apolinaria la Cuna (the foundling), and by most as La Beata (the pious). She appears to be a good old soul—cheerful and resigned to her sad fate, for in her old age, and stone blind, she is a charge on the county and on her friends, having by some means or other lost all her property. She was loath to speak on this subject, assuring me that she didn't want even to think of it. Considering her advanced age and feeble condition, her memory is quite fresh. But it is evident that she passed her life in the mission, and had but little opportunity of ascertaining what happened of a political nature around her.

The annexed pages were dictated by her, upon the recommendation of Mrs. Angustias de la Guerra Ord.

Tho.⁵ Savage
March 14, 1878
Santa Bárbara

I, APOLINARIA LORENZANA, was born in Mexico. When I was very young, barely seven years old, the government of Mexico (which at that time was a part of Spain) sent me and a large number of families and children of both sexes to Alta California. We left Mexico City and headed to San Blas. There they put us on one of the king's ships, *La Concepción*. Our destination was Monterey, which was the main port. When we arrived in Monterey, the government distributed some of the children, as if they were puppy dogs, to the families there. Some children were left here in Santa Bárbara, while others went to San Diego. I stayed with my mother and several other women in Monterey.⁶ Francisca and Pascuala came here as adults. They both married right away. Francisca married Juan Hernández and Pascuala married Joaquín Juárez. It is possible that another woman named Inés stayed as well. My mother married an artilleryman, but when the relief artillerymen arrived, it was my stepfather's turn to return to Mexico, and he took my mother with him. That is how I became separated from my mother. I never saw her again. Shortly after she arrived in San Blas my mother died, perhaps from a broken heart because she had to leave me behind. My mother came with me on the ship up to Santa Bárbara. At that time Lieutenant Don Raymundo Carrillo came to relieve Captain Don Felipe Goicoechea and take charge of the command here. Goicoechea was headed back to Mexico with the position of *habilitado general* of these presidios.

I stayed with my mother until she was ready to leave for San Blas. Then she turned me over to Don Raymundo. I lived with his family for many years.

During that time, Colonel Don José Joaquín de Arrillaga was the governor of the Californias. When the number of soldiers at the presidio companies was increased, the lieutenants at Santa Bárbara, San Francisco, and San Diego were promoted to captain. Don Raymundo Carrillo was promoted to captain and commander of the San Diego presidio company. Don José

Darío Argüello, who was a lieutenant but was commissioned as a brevet captain, was promoted to captain and commander of the Santa Bárbara presidio.

Captain Carrillo relieved Don Manuel Rodríguez of the command in San Diego. Carrillo, who was married to Doña Tomasa Lugo, took me to San Diego with his family. I was probably about twelve or thirteen years old. I remained with that family for a number of years. Later, when it was time for me to leave, I moved to the home of Sergeant Mercado. He was married to Doña Josefa Sal. She was the daughter of Lieutenant Don Hermenegildo Sal, who died in Monterey. Lieutenant Sal had another daughter, Doña Rafaela. She was Don Luis Antonio Argüello's first wife.

I was at Sergeant Mercado's home for only a short time because I became very ill. Then the Fathers took me to the mission. I stayed at the mission until I had recovered sufficiently. I then returned to the home of Doña Chepita Sal. Before I left for the mission, she became a widow. I stayed a bit longer in Doña Sal's home. The Fathers wanted to help me, so they took me back to the mission to become a nurse. The Fathers had spent quite some time building two hospitals, one for men and the other for women. When these hospitals were finished and the sick were placed in them, Father José Sánchez came to the presidio to say Mass. He told me to get ready to return to the mission because he was going to make me the nurse for the women's hospital. His reason for giving me that job was an act of charity, because I was still quite ill and could do very little work.

During the time I was at the presidio, nothing happened to me that is worth telling. Before coming here from Mexico, when I was very young, I was taught how to read, and I was taught the catechism. Then, when I was older and already in California, I taught myself how to write. Using whatever books I could find, I would copy the letters onto any sort of paper I could obtain, such as empty cigarette papers or a blank piece of paper that somebody had thrown out. That is how I managed to learn enough to make myself understood in writing whenever I needed something.

By the time I was living at Doña Tomasa Lugo's home, I had already begun to teach a few girls how to read, and I taught them the catechism. Later, I did the same thing at Doña Josefa Sal's home. After she became a widow, Doña Josefa started a school to teach girls how to read, pray, and sew. Since she had a large garden that kept her very busy, I was in charge of the school almost exclusively. Some parents entrusted their daughters to me specifically and I also taught them.

I taught the three daughters that *Alférez* Don Ignacio Martínez had at that time—María Antonia, Juana, and Encarnación. Their mother was Doña Martina Arellanes. I also taught one of Doña Tomasa Lugo's nieces. Her name was Bernarda Ruiz and she is still living here in Santa Bárbara. Many other girls learned how to read and how to sew with me.

When I was at the mission I was very ill. Father Sánchez took me in as an act of charity because I could not work. My left hand was so paralyzed that it looked like it was dead. I could not move my hand at all for about two years and eight months. Then over a period of about four months my hand began to recover very slowly.

I supported myself by working with my hands—for example, by sewing. I made meticulously finished embroidered shirts. I also sewed shirts however people wanted them made. I embroidered sashes and vests and decorated the silk garters for the soldiers' and the civilians' suede boots. The tips of those silk garters were embroidered and decorated with sequins, rough silk, and other things that were difficult to work with.

The men wore neckerchiefs with tips that were embroidered or decorated with fillets that resembled lace.[7] I would make them.

During the three years that my hand was paralyzed, I could not work. Instead, I took care of the sick in the mission hospital, even though Father Sánchez told me not to do this all by myself. He said I should teach others how to care for the sick and be present to supervise them and make sure they did the job well. But I was always involved in caring for the sick women.

In addition to common illnesses such as headaches and mild fevers, the Indian women suffered from syphilis and sores. The married women who lived at the *rancherías* and would leave the *rancherías* to go to work would get these diseases. This happened despite the many efforts of the Fathers and the *mayordomos* to keep the women from engaging in bad behavior or from dealing with people from outside the mission.

The single women would sleep in separate quarters commonly called the *monjerío*. In that same place there was a large patio with a corridor where the women would weave wool or card and weave cotton. Much cotton was grown at the mission. One of the places that was given to me later was the little valley called San Jorge where much cotton was produced. Every week from June to October, an Indian would come with a mule loaded down with a sack filled with cotton. The sack would practically drag on the ground. All the tablecloths, napkins, towels, and many other types of cloths used at the mission were woven by the neophyte women with

An Indian woman grinding corn in a stone mortar in southern California in the late nineteenth century. Reproduced by permission of The Huntington Library, San Marino, California, Pierce Collection #1768

cotton grown at the mission. The girls did the weaving. All the candlewicks used at the mission were made from the cotton grown and prepared there.

The single young men also had their own quarters. During the day they would leave their quarters to go to work. The single men and the single women slept in locked quarters. The *alcaldes* would gather up all the men and lock them in their quarters at night. Then the *alcaldes* would leave the key at the Father's house.

The single women were under the care of an older Indian woman who was like the matron. This woman kept a close watch over them. She would go with the young women when they bathed and never took her eyes off them. In the evening after dinner, she would lock the young women up in the *monjerío* and take the key to the Father.

The Indians would get up very early. Right at dawn the bell would ring for Mass. While the Father was saying this first Mass, all the Indians would be reciting prayers, with the exception of the Indians who were ill. After the first Mass, the other Father would say a second one, but by then all the Indians had left after breakfast to go to work.

Before the bell rang at dawn, all the Indians who lived at the *rancherías* would come to the *pozolera* to eat their breakfast of *atole*. The *atole* was made from finely ground and toasted barley. The Indian women sifted the barley so carefully through wicker frames that it seemed like the barley had been passed through a sieve. The pregnant Indians and those who had recently given birth had the job of toasting and preparing the *pinole*. The *llavero* would then store the grain and distribute what was needed each day to the *pozolero*.

The single men and single women ate breakfast after Mass. The single women were required to attend Mass each day.

There were prayer leaders who directed the prayers. Normally, the prayer leaders taught the *gentiles* who wanted to be baptized how to pray. The job of prayer leader was generally given to blind men or blind women.

Planting wheat, corn, and vegetables were some of the jobs at the mission. Other jobs involved cutting and carrying firewood. The mission had carpenters, blacksmiths, cartwrights, saddle makers, and other types of jobs. Some men were in charge of the droves, while others were vaqueros. The vaqueros were always supervised by a *mayordomo* who was a *gente de razón*. San Diego always had three *mayordomos*. One was in charge of planting at El Cajón and another was in charge of planting at Santa Isabel, which is where the best wheat and corn came from. There was always water at Santa Isabel for irrigation, whether it be rainwater or water brought from the watering place. The *mayordomo* at the mission was in charge of the cattle and the herds of horses.

There was a *llavero* who took care of the granaries. After I regained the use of my hand, I began to do a lot of work at the mission. When somebody came to buy a *fanega* of wheat or corn or something else, I was the person who went and witnessed the handing over of the grain by the *llavero*. On Saturdays, when the soldiers of the escort (a corporal and four soldiers) were given their rations, I had to be present for the distribution of the food.

I taught the Indian women how to sew. I had them working continuously on the sewing projects for the church or for the Fathers. Everything was done under my direction and care. I was in charge of the church garments, both the sewing and the washing of them. I had Indian *lavanderas* for this purpose.

I was, of course, in charge of taking care of the sick women in the hospital.

When ships arrived at the port, the supercargoes would alert the Fathers, who would select from the invoices the goods needed at the mission. Then they would make up their lists. Later, when I had enough time, I would board the ship with some servants to receive the goods. I always

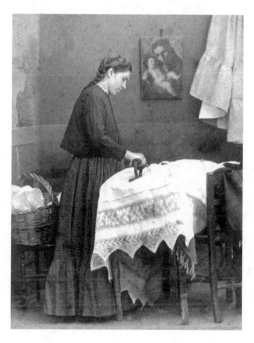

This late-nineteenth-century domestic scene shows a woman at tasks similar to those described by Apolinaria Lorenzana. Courtesy of The Bancroft Library, University of California, Berkeley

was authorized to take any goods I thought might be useful for the mission, even if they were not written down on the list prepared by the Fathers.

The Indians' second meal was at eleven o'clock. Between eleven and twelve o'clock, the married Indians ate at their *rancherías*. The single men would return to the *pozolera* to pick up their rations and then leave. If a person was busy or not close by, one of their relatives would pick up their rations for them. Or the *pozolero* would keep the rations for them. He was very careful to make sure that nobody went without food.

The single women would go with their *matrona* to get their rations.

The workday ended at five o'clock. The bell would ring to signal that it was time for prayers. Everyone was required to go and pray, except for those who were working away from the missions. After prayers, they would go to the *pozolera* for their evening meal of *atole*. Then everyone would leave.

Mission San Diego was a poor mission. It did not have an abundance of cattle like the other missions. That is why cattle were killed only every fifteen days and only when the sheep were being sheared. Raw beef was given to the Indians. Lamb, however, was put in the *pozolera* and stewed. The Indians ate this at the midday meal.

Indian men had a cotton shirt and a loincloth. The women had a coarse woolen skirt and a blouse. Both men and women received one blanket each year. All woolen goods were made at the mission.

Vaqueros were given hats, pants, boots, and saddles with ropes.

Indians who did not fulfill their obligations or were somehow delinquent were punished by the *alcaldes,* who received orders from the Father. Punishments were based on the seriousness of the offense and included being locked up in a cell, with or without shackles, or being placed in stocks. If the offense was somewhat serious, the person would be whipped. Rarely did the whippings exceed twenty-five. On many occasions the number of whippings was fewer than that. But if the crime was significant, the delinquent would be turned over to the corporal of the guard, who would proceed according to the instructions he was given. The corporal would carefully verify the details of the case and locate witnesses who could testify. Then, with this information, he would prepare a report for the presidio commander. If the offense was serious enough to warrant an indictment against the prisoner, a corporal and a soldier would come on horseback and take the prisoner back to the presidio. An indictment would then be drawn up by a prosecutor appointed by the commander.

I worked at the mission for many years, even after it was secularized and there were no longer any neophytes there. During the final years, the Indians were somewhat free. I stayed on at the mission to take care of the

An Indian ranchería *east of San Diego, photographed by I. W. Taber. Courtesy of the California Historical Society, FN-36287*

Isidora Pico, wife of John Forster. Courtesy of the Seaver Center for Western History Research, Natural History Museum of Los Angeles County, Los Angeles, California

church and Father Vicente Pascual Oliva. He was the last missionary at San Diego. He stayed until 1846.

Father Oliva left Mission San Diego when Father José María Zalvidea, who was at Mission San Luis Rey, sent for him. I went with Father Oliva. At San Luis Rey, we found Father Zalvidea bedridden. He and Father Oliva heard one another's confession. When we arrived at the mission, the mission administrator, Don Juan María Marrón, and his wife, Doña Felipa Osuna, were not there. One of Doña Felipa's sisters was taking care of the Father. We had been at the mission for two days when they returned. After we had been at the mission for about four days, Doña Isidora Pico de Forster arrived with twenty people from San Juan Capistrano. They had come to take Father Zalvidea back to that mission. In order to do this, they obtained permission from Father Narciso Durán, the president and prefect of the missions. Doña Isidora brought a *carreta* to transport Father Zalvidea. She asked me to go with them so I could take care of the Father.

John Forster. Courtesy of the San Juan Capistrano Historical Society

Two days after Doña Isidora arrived, on the morning that we were supposed to leave, we found Father Zalvidea dead. Nobody saw him die. The
Indian, Santiago, who was the sacristan and cook, was the only person in
the Father's room, but he was probably asleep when Father Zalvidea took
his last breath. Father Zalvidea's remains were buried the following day in
the mission church on the left side of the altar. Another Father who died a
few years before was buried on the other side of the altar. If I remember
correctly, his name was Father Francisco González Ibarra.

Father Zalvidea had two trunks. One was for clothing and the other was
for books. Before Doña Felipa Osuna returned, Father Zalvidea asked
Doña Isidora Pico to pack up the two trunks so he could take them with
him. The truth is that he had very little clothing of his own in the trunk designated for clothes. Most of the contents in that trunk were printed cotton,
common cloth, and small cloths that Father Zalvidea kept to give to the
Indians who were of assistance to him.

When Father Zalvidea died, Doña Felipa Osuna went to see Doña
Isidora and insisted that she give her the keys to the trunks. At first, Doña
Isidora did not want to turn them over, but Doña Felipa said that since she

had taken care of the Father, it was also her responsibility to take care of the trunks. Doña Isidora handed the keys over to her.

Doña Isidora and the rest of the people who came with her returned to San Juan Capistrano. Father Vicente Oliva and I returned to San Diego. When it was time to say good-bye, Señor Marrón asked Father Oliva to come back to the mission to celebrate the feast day of San Luis on August 25. Father Oliva said that he would and then we left. But on August 25, Juan María Marrón was no longer at the mission, because Frémont and his people had thrown him out. We knew nothing about this. When we passed by Agua Hedionda, Juan María Marrón's rancho, we saw that the whole family was there. Father Oliva then said to me, "Something must have happened, because it looks like the Marrón family is at the rancho." Marrón saw us, too, and sent a boy out to tell us to come to his house instead of going to San Luis Rey. And that is what we did. Juan Marrón and his wife told us that Frémont had removed Marrón from his position as administrator because the Indians had gone to Frémont and had told him they no longer wanted Marrón there. They asked Frémont to remove him because they wanted Americans to manage the mission instead. Frémont, who spoke Spanish quite well, told Marrón that it bothered him that he had to make him leave. He said it was necessary to do this to appease the Indians and prevent them from harming Marrón's family. In light of that, Marrón sent his family to the rancho, and he stayed at the mission to complete the transition.

We had been at Agua Hedionda for about three hours when an Indian *alcalde* arrived with another message from the American who had been left in charge of the mission. I do not remember his name but do know that he spoke Spanish well and was married to a woman from the Coronel family.*

The Indians told the administrator that Father Oliva was going to be there to celebrate the feast day of San Luis. When the administrator found out that Father Oliva was at Agua Hedionda, he sent the *alcalde* to invite him to come to the mission. He had nothing to fear, because they promised not to harm him. He would be treated with the utmost consideration and respect. Father Oliva did not want to leave right away and sent word that he would go to the mission the following morning. The *alcalde* brought a second message saying that Father Oliva should go to the mission that very day and that he had nothing to fear. His room had been prepared for him. We then left for the mission in a *carreta*. When we arrived, Godey welcomed us

*A footnote in the manuscript reads, "After I wrote this down, she remembered that Godey was the man's name. Godey stayed at the mission with four other Americans."

warmly. Señor Godey was a very good and tranquil man. However, Godey did not give Father Oliva one of the interior rooms. Instead, he gave him one of the rooms on the outside, right next to the Fathers' former room. His room was clean and furnished. We would always bring bed linens with us when we traveled. Two or three days later, Father Oliva celebrated the feast day of the patron saint.

After the festivities ended, I told Father Oliva that I wanted to go to San Juan Capistrano where the Forster family was. I was very sad because of the American takeover of the country and did not want to return to San Diego. Then Father Oliva said, "Well, if you are going to San Juan, then I am going there, too. What would I do all by myself in San Diego?" First we went to Santa Margarita and stayed there for several days. I told Father Oliva to stay at Santa Margarita and I would go on to San Juan Capistrano. I was furious about the situation with the Americans. I thought, "If I leave, then the Americans will leave, too." What was I thinking? Father Oliva decided to go to San Juan with me.

Our main reason for going there was to obtain seeds and other food that we could bring back to San Diego, because it was a very poor mission. There was nobody at San Diego to do the planting, or for that matter anything else.

It should be noted that after the missions were taken away from the Fathers, a commission came to the mission. It was made up of Don Guillermo Hartnell and some man named Castro. They put Father Oliva in charge of the mission. It seems that this commission had orders from the government which stated that every mission that was in ruins should be turned over to the missionary. Any mission that still had some assets would be assigned an administrator. In general, the majority of the missions did have some assets and *mayordomos* or administrators were assigned to them. The exception was San Diego because it was destroyed. I found it very hard to provide Father Oliva with food.

When Father Oliva and I were on our way back to San Diego with seeds, corn, chile, and other things, we stopped at Santa Margarita. We were already there when Señor Don José Joaquín Ortega arrived. He was headed to Los Angeles. He ate with us and then left. Ortega got only as far as Los Alisos, which is located between San Luis Rey and San Juan Capistrano. It is actually closer to San Luis Rey than to San Juan Capistrano. When Ortega got to Los Alisos, he spoke with somebody from Los Angeles who told him that a war was about to break out. He therefore turned around and came back to Santa Margarita. Many people in Los Angeles were uniting to see if they could throw the Americans out of California. Señor Ortega continued on to San Diego. The next day, we arrived at San Luis Rey and found that Godey was no longer there. Another man, with four Americans, was there. We had already decided to continue on to San Diego when the American in charge of the mission began to insist to Father Oliva that we should definitely leave for San Diego as soon as possible. He also had heard about the uprising of the Californios against the Americans. After dinner, the man in charge told Father Oliva that he needed to speak with him. I went to another room to wait for the Father. When Father Oliva returned, he sat down on the bench. I asked him if we would be leaving the next day. He told me that he did not know what to say, but I finally dragged it out of him. The man in charge had asked him to stay for three days because he was going to race off to San Diego to find out what was going on. He said he would be back when three days were up. The other four Americans left the mission that very night.

Exterior and interior views of the chapel at Pala. Reproduced by permission of The Huntington Library, San Marino, California, Pierce Collection #2981 and #2987

Indian houses at Pala. Reproduced by permission of The Huntington Library, San Marino, California, Pierce Collection #1714

That same night, as soon as the man in charge was able to yank an agreement out of Father Oliva, he took to the road. To this day, I have not seen that man again. Father Oliva and I stayed at the mission for about two months or more. Nothing of importance happened. However, we always had a sense of impending danger. All the Indians at Pala supported the Americans. Pala was a large and prosperous rancho. It had a large orchard with many fruit trees and an abundance of grapes. They made a lot of good wine there—muscatel, red wine, and other types.

We were at the mission when Doña Juana Moreno's family arrived. They were headed to Santa Ana or Los Angeles because they had relatives there. They told us that all the families were abandoning San Diego. Doña Juana asked Father Oliva for a room where they could spend the night, and he gave her a room right next to his and to mine. The Indians' threats were increasing. Two days before, six or seven Indians arrived at the mission on horseback. They were carrying little sticks with red flags attached. This was a bad sign. They did not go and see Father Oliva but went instead to the wall that had the streams of water. One Indian came over and started to race up and down the corridor, trying to provoke somebody to fight him for the water. But since Father Oliva and I, and one other person who was sick, were the only ones there, nobody said anything to the Indian. Then they all left.

While Doña Juana Moreno and her family were at the mission, an armed Indian arrived during the afternoon. He wanted a bottle of wine for his chief. Father Oliva said to give it to him and asked the Indian where his chief and his people were. The Indian said they were in Guajomita, a place very close to the mission. The Indians had come with the intention of attacking the mission. Everything seemed very suspicious. In the evening, when we were eating dinner, Doña Juana Moreno knocked on the door. We opened it and there she was, half-naked and very frightened. She told us that a little Indian boy, who was her son's friend, told her they should leave because the Indians were going to attack the mission and kill all the white people there. Right after Doña Juana came in, the Indian who had taken the wine came in as well. His quiver was filled with arrows. He said that his chief wanted more wine. Father Oliva reprimanded the Indian for coming to his house armed as he was. He then ordered him to leave and not come back. He did, however, give the Indian another bottle of wine. The Indian left without saying a word.

We went out to another room. Then, Señora Juana Moreno's son, accompanied by our Indian cook, named Santiago, and the little Indian boy I spoke about previously, went to get the horses from the corral so they could go to Santa Margarita. That is where Sérvulo Varelas and thirty men were. Varelas and his men had been at the mission that morning, probably around twelve o'clock, and I gave them some food to eat. The men and the horses were very tired. They needed to rest and change horses. Then they left for Santa Margarita, where they spent the night. Sérvulo Varelas, who later became my *compadre,* led the group. He was determined to fight in the war against the Americans. Father Oliva sent him a message to come back right away because the Indians nearby were rising against the *gente del país* and were threatening to kill us.

Varelas arrived at the mission at dawn with ten men. Varelas behaved very well. As you can well imagine, we did not sleep at all that night. Father Oliva sat on a bench all night. When morning came, he was still on that bench. That night there was so much light, it almost seemed like day. I went to the *pozolera* alone to see if I could hear any rumblings or commotion, but I did not hear or see anything suspicious. I returned and tried to convince Father Oliva to at least lie down, but he refused. As dawn was breaking, messengers arrived and brought the welcome news that Sérvulo Varelas and his men were approaching. Varelas sent two or three men to Guajomita to find out if the Indians were there, and that is exactly where they found them. Varelas sent for the Indians the next day, but they had already headed back to Pala. Their chief, or man in charge, left with quite a few Indians. The night before, Varelas had taken all the necessary precautions. When the

Indians arrived, Varelas harangued and reprimanded them for their hostility toward the *gente del país*. He told them that their attitude made no sense at all, because they and the *gente del país* were one. The Indians promised to do what he advised. They were treated to food and wine and then they left.

The next day, Father Oliva left for San Juan Capistrano with an escort. Varelas recommended this person to be the escort because he would take good care of the Father. I stayed behind to clean up everything. When I finished, I went to Santa Margarita to sleep. The next day I left for San Juan Capistrano in a *carreta*.

We stayed in San Juan Capistrano until Father Oliva died. That was January 1, 1847. I was in San Juan when Commodore Stockton and General Kearny passed through there with their artillery on their way to Los Angeles. Nothing happened worthy of mention. I remained in San Juan for a while longer, then I went to Los Angeles. From there, I went to Santa Inés to inform Father José Joaquín Jimeno about what had happened and everything relating to Father Oliva. I stayed in Santa Inés only a short time. On November 30, 1847, I slept in Cahuenga and arrived in Los Angeles the following day.

I lived in Los Angeles for about a year and then returned to San Juan Capistrano because that is where I had all my things. I lived there for quite some time. During that time, I still had all three of my ranchos. I bought one of the ranchos. It was called Capistrano de Secuá and was located halfway between my other two ranchos. My *compadre* Juan López sold it to me. The government gave me the other two ranchos years ago. One of them was Santa Clara de Jamachá, located near Mission San Diego, and the other one, called Buena Esperanza de los Coches, was even closer. Whenever I acquired land, I had it blessed and named it in honor of a saint. I have always had faith in the power of the saints, and above all, faith in the one who surpasses them all—God himself.

Since I did not return to San Diego, I put a man in charge of the ranchos. I should say Don Juan Forster was the person who put the man in charge.

In 1850 or 1851, when the American forces came to California by way of the Colorado River, Captain Magruder arrived with them. Magruder wanted to know who owned Rancho de Jamachá and he asked Señor Forster. Forster told him the rancho belonged to me and that he was in charge of it. Magruder asked if he could use the land to keep the horses there. I had placed my trust in Señor Forster and he violated that trust by letting others use the rancho. I never saw my rancho again. And I never heard from Don Juan Forster again either, because he went to a rancho he owned. Nine years later, Señor Magruder came to San Juan Capistrano, where I was living, and spoke to me about the rancho. He wanted me to let him use it again. The truth is that I never received anything in return for the use of my rancho. Ultimately, somebody took possession of it, probably Señor Magruder himself. The second time Magruder tried to get me to let him use the rancho, he was very insistent that I sell it to him. I refused. It is a long story and I do not want to talk about it. Somehow, my other two ranchos were also taken away from me. So, after working for so many years and after owning property, which I did not sell or give up by any other means, I find myself living in dire poverty. I live by the grace of God and by the charity of those who give me a bite to eat.

I remember the sad events at Rancho Jamul, which belonged to Don Pío Pico. I think the events took place in 1838. Don Pío rarely went to that rancho, and neither he nor any of his brothers was there during that time. It seems to me that Don Pío Pico no longer was employed by the government then. I base the date of the events on that set of circumstances.

Don Pío's mother, Doña Eustaquia López, says that she was at the rancho with her three unmarried daughters, Isidora, Jacinta, and Feliciana. I do not remember if they were there or not, but I am inclined to believe that they were. The events at Jamul happened two days after I arrived at Rancho Jamachá. I had hired a *compadre* of mine, Valentín Ríos, as *mayordomo.* He had a wife and young children. Cayetano, the previous *mayordomo,* had left. He was Mexican.

I am going to relate what Doña María de los Angeles, Don Anastasio Leiva's wife, told me. Leiva was the *mayordomo* at Rancho de Jamul. The day before, Leiva had sent word to Camacho, a servant at my rancho. Leiva told him that he was planning on going to the Rancho de la Nación for the roundup. He invited Camacho to go with him to see if they could find any of my cattle there. Camacho went straight to the Rancho de la Nación to meet up with Leiva. When I arrived at my rancho, I asked where Camacho was. They told me he had gone to the roundup. After the roundup ended, Leiva asked Camacho to help him take the cattle back to Jamul. Camacho had found six of my cattle and he took them back to Jamul with the other cattle. Leiva also insisted that Camacho stay overnight at Jamul. He said that the next morning they could separate my cattle from the rest and he would help Camacho lead them down from the rancho. Camacho decided to stay. It was still early. Doña María de los Angeles said to her husband, "Let me at least go to Señora Apolinaria's rancho, because I am really frightened." Her husband asked her who she was afraid of, since he was the only one there. She then told him that an old Indian woman had come to the *rancho* and had told her that they should leave because the Indians were going to attack and kill everyone there. Leiva responded in a joking manner that there were no such Indians around. He said that if they did come, he would put the family in a room filled with cowhides. Obviously, the Indian woman's warning had no effect on him.

Early the next morning, María de los Angeles was making breakfast for the men and for her family. After Leiva, Camacho, and the other men had finished breakfast, Leiva and Camacho got up to go. They had already sad-dled their horses so they could go to the corral and separate the cattle. Leiva went back in the house to get a half-burnt stick to light his cigar. At that moment they heard the war cry of the hostile Indians. These Indians were *gentiles* and Christians. The worst ones of the bunch were the Indians from the house who had incited the others to come. Doña María de los Ange-les was very alarmed and said, "Oh, Anastasio, the Indians are coming to kill us!" Anastasio Molina, one of Don Joaquín Ortega's servants, was there, too. That fellow Molina was about to marry Tomasa, one of the Leiva daughters. He had gone to their house to ask Leiva to take Tomasa to the mission so they could become officially engaged and publish the marriage banns.

Camacho had gone to the corral to wait for Leiva so they could separate my cattle from the rest. A servant who was in charge of the planting had taken a piece of meat out to the cornfield to eat it there. The kitchen was separated somewhat from the main house. Leiva and Molina were headed back to the house to get their weapons. An Indian woman went in ahead of them and shut the door to the room where the firearms were kept, so now they had no access to their weapons. The Indians, who first killed the ser-vant in the cornfield and then killed Camacho in the corral, attacked the house. María de los Angeles ran to hide in the orchard with her two daughters and two sons. The Indians killed Leiva and Molina beneath the corridor. Then they went searching for the family. When they found them in the orchard, they grabbed the two girls and took them. Tomasa was about eighteen or nineteen years old and Ramona was about eleven or twelve years old. The Indians stripped the mother of her *rebozo,* leaving her with only her skirt. They told her to leave with her sons because they did not want to kill them. If they did not leave right away, they would kill the boys as well. José Antonio, the oldest boy, was about twelve years old. The other boy's name was Claro and he was about six years old. The girls were screaming and the youngest one was hanging on to her mother's skirt, trying not to let go. But the Indians tore her away from her mother. With repeated threats, they forced the mother to leave with her two sons.

The Indians set fire to the buildings at the rancho and the bodies were burned in the house. That is why, when help later arrived, the victims' features were no longer recognizable. The charred bodies were carried out on a piece of cattle hide and they were buried near the house.

That is what Doña María de los Angeles told me when she arrived at my rancho. The first person to arrive at the house was José Antonio. His mother stayed back near the oven where we would burn lime. The *mayordomo*'s wife, Nieves, who was my *comadre,* was with me, and an Indian. We were cleaning out a watering trough. The other Indians were working with the *mayordomo.* José Antonio spoke to Nieves and asked her, on his mother's behalf, to send her something so she could cover herself up. Nieves ran back to the house to look for whatever she could find. Along the way, José Antonio told her where his mother was and everything that had happened at Jamul. I believe that Nieves gave him a bedspread. When she returned, she told me the whole tragic tale. I told the Indian to stop working and go get the *mayordomo* and all his people. They came right away because the Indian told them what had happened at Jamul. The poor mother could neither speak nor cry. She was overwhelmed by sorrow. I tried to console her and to get her to eat something but she was sad beyond comforting. I could not get her to eat anything. That same afternoon, I sent her to San Diego in my *carreta* because this was what she wanted to do.

When my *mayordomo,* Valentín, arrived at the house with the Indians, I told one of the Indians to get a horse and ride as fast as he could to the Indian *ranchería* of Secuá and have the Indians come right away with their weapons. Although these Indians were gentiles, they were very gentle and very good people. Three of my Indian servants were from Mission San Diego and almost all the rest were from Secuá. Some other Indians who were of a peaceful nature also came from much farther away to help us.

Eight or ten Indians from Secuá came, in addition to those who were already here. They all were well-armed with bows and arrows and ready to defend us if the hostile Indians attacked.

I wrote two letters and sent them off. One was sent to El Cajón, to my *compadre* Rosario Aguilar, who was the *mayordomo* there. The other was sent to Don Joaquín Ortega at the mission. I told him everything that had happened at Jamul so he could alert the authorities in San Diego.

I sent word to a *comadre* of mine who used to live with me in my house at the mission. I told her where I kept the gunpowder and bullets and asked her to send me that ammunition. I asked Father Vicente Oliva and Father Fernando Martín to send me paper so we could make cartridges.

Everything arrived without delay. I did not leave the rancho until the next day. That is when they brought back the bodies of Molina and the servant who had been killed in the cornfield at Jamul. I had Valentín Ríos go to Jamul with a group of Indians from Secuá and a servant *de razón* to see how the situation was there. They were instructed not to touch the bodies until a judge arrived to start an official investigation.

During that time, Don José Antonio Estudillo was the judge for San Diego. His son Salvador was my godchild, and I was the confirmation sponsor for one of his daughters. Estudillo went to examine the bodies and draw up an indictment. After completing these necessary steps, he came to my rancho and authorized the burial of the bodies. The bodies of Camacho and the other servant were taken to the mission and buried in the mission cemetery. I think that took place in April or May 1838. I remember that the servant who was killed had been taking care of the wheat fields because the corn had not yet been planted.

Sergeant Macedonio González was sent for and he came with some soldiers from Baja California. Some settlers from San Diego joined him and his troops. Together they all went to the mountains to try and rescue Leiva's daughters. When they arrived, they saw the two young girls seated on some large rocks, with Indians guarding them. The girls were crying out to the men to climb up and rescue them, but the Indians kept covering their mouths. The soldiers and settlers killed several Indians, but they were unable to reach the girls because of the rugged terrain and the large number of Indians there. In addition, there were many caves and caverns in the area and Indians lived there. It was impossible to fight them. Finally, after many futile attempts, Macedonio González had to retreat with his people. I heard that the Indians went to the Colorado River area and sold the girls.

A few years later, a fellow named Muñoz, who had worked for me and whose child I had baptized, got it into his head to go to Sonora. He lived there for quite some time. But when his wife died and possibly his son as well, he returned to California. He brought me a few little gifts. He gave them to me at my Rancho de Jamachá. He told me that on his return trip he saw the youngest Leiva daughter seated behind a house. He said that he went up to her and greeted her. When he realized that the girl spoke excellent Spanish, he asked her who she was. She said she was from San Diego and she had been abducted by the Indians. In the end, she told him about the tragedy and begged him to take her with him, but he did not dare do that because he only had one horse. That horse was already quite tired, and if he took the girl with him, the horse would tire even more and the Indians would be able to catch up with them and kill them both.

I do not know if anything else was done to rescue those girls from the clutches of the Indians.

It was my understanding that the Indians who committed those hostile acts were from Tecate, the Colorado River, and other well-known places. It has been said that Chiefs Cartucho, Martín, and Pablo took part in the attacks. I doubt this very much because Sergeant Macedonio González knew them well and he never mentioned them as being the leaders. The real leaders were the Indians from the rancho who encouraged the other Indians to participate.

At Rancho Tijuana, Captain Santiago Argüello took precautions in case the Indians headed that way. But the Indians withdrew completely after ransacking, burning, and committing other crimes at Jamul. They did not go to any other rancho. They could have come to mine, because it was very close. This is what I feared, but they did not come.

Doña María de los Angeles's spirit was shattered and she suffered the rest of her life. She never recovered from the tragedy and finally succumbed to the burden of her sorrows.

After those events, a gentile Indian named Janajachil who was one of my servants asked me for permission to go to the mountains to bring his wife back to the rancho. He was a very hard-working man. He was of a peaceful nature and obedient. It was feared that the hostile Indians would attack his

Residence and outdoor oven at Rancho Tijuana. Reproduced by permission of The Huntington Library, San Marino, California, Pierce Collection #7923

Santiago Argüello, owner of Rancho Tijuana, testified on behalf of many Californios in the land cases of the 1850s. Courtesy of The Bancroft Library, University of California, Berkeley

ranchería, and that is why he was so anxious to bring his wife back to the rancho. He promised me that he would return in three days, so I gave him permission to go. After Janajachil had returned with his wife and was back working, Sergeant Macedonio appeared one day at my rancho. Without warning, he killed Janajachil. I was at the mission when it happened. Perhaps he had suspicions about the poor man, but I am convinced that this poor Indian was innocent.

I remember when Macedonio González showed up one day in San Diego with armed men and shot several Indians who were servants in various homes. One of the victims, named Juan Antonio, seemed quite Spanish. He was a good cook and was employed in the home of Don José Antonio Estudillo. Juan Antonio had conspired to kill the white men as revenge for their having killed his brother Janajachil for no apparent reason.

I was at the mission that day and did not see what happened. But I do know that Macedonio González shot and killed several Indians in the pueblo who had been accused of plotting to kill the white people. They were also accused of robbing houses and stores, of kidnapping any woman they wanted, and of being allied with gentile Indians and Christian Indians from the outside. Macedonio González proceeded with much force and harshness.

During that time, most of the Indians who rebelled were gentiles. However, there were some Christians among them. Sometimes those same Indians would tire of their own foolishness and would go to Los Angeles. There they would find work as servants in homes and they would behave well. One of those Indians was working in an orchard in Los Angeles and was behaving himself well. Macedonio González knew that he had a criminal record so he had him taken from the orchard and shot.

Horses were constantly being stolen. The horse thieves were generally the same mission Indians who had encouraged the gentiles to help them. In the Valle del Cajón (between the mission and El Cajón), the Fathers had a milking place where they made cheese. One day, I think it was in 1836, the Indians killed the vaquero and a boy who helped him. They also attacked an Indian sheepherder who took care of the sheep ranch and had gone there to bury another boy. The sheepherder managed to escape and went to warn his wife. The Indians killed the cattle and took all the meat. They also took the vaquero's wife, who was an Indian, and all the horses. They let the woman go after about fifteen days.

During the years I was at the mission, parents would ask me to teach their boys and girls how to read. I would do this when I had some free time from my work. I always had several girls under my care. Many of them were my goddaughters. One girl in particular was under my care from the age of two or three. The little girl's mother was my goddaughter, and I had stood up for her at her wedding. I was later godmother to three of her sons. The little girl was her first child. I taught her how to read, pray, sew, and other things. When the time was right, she married, and today she is the mother of a family.

I have no idea how many godchildren I have, nor do I know the number of girls for whom I have been godmother at their confirmation. I am talking about *gente de razón* as well as Indian children. It is probably more than one hundred children, and it would not surprise me if it were close to two hundred. I had the satisfaction of being well loved by young and old and rich and poor. Maybe it was because I was good-natured and would do whatever I could to help people. I imagine that if I went to San Diego, I would be well received. But I live far away and I am blind, and those people are not in a very good position to help me. So here I am, poor, weak, and in failing health. I will manage like this until God calls me to his bosom.

When I was a girl, there was a young man who tried very hard to get me to marry him. I was not drawn to the state of matrimony, even though I was aware of the importance of such a sacred institution. I refused his offer. He then told me that since I did not want to marry him, he would leave for

Mexico. And that is exactly what he did. However, he did come back two years later. He was married but did not bring his wife with him. Shortly after, he returned to Mexico.

When they wanted to perform the *Pastorela* in San Diego, they would call upon me to look for people to play the various roles, especially the role of the angel. I would also organize everything. I was the person who had to put together the angel's costume. Consequently, I was always at those fiestas. They were the only festivities I would attend. The *Pastorelas* were performed in the pueblo on Christmas Eve. Eight days later they would be performed again at the mission and then at private homes. I had to accompany the angel, Gila, and the girls who had the roles of *pastoras*. I took care of them. Some of the older girls who had roles in the *Pastorela* were entrusted to me by their mothers. Since I had no daughters of my own, I took care of everybody's daughters.

The patron saint of the soldiers at San Diego was La Purísima Concepción. In Monterey and Santa Bárbara it was La Virgen de Guadalupe. I do not know the patron saint of San Francisco.

I met Eulalia Pérez in San Diego when I went there with Captain Raymundo Carrillo's family. She was Guillén's wife. At that time, her daughter Petra was already old enough to marry and her son Isidoro was already a young man. Around that time, Petra married Santiago Rubio, who was a soldier of the San Diego company. I was godmother to two of Eulalia's daughters, María de los Angeles and Rita. I was also godmother to one of her sons, Tomás, who was very frail and died.

When I first met Eulalia, she was already a mature woman. I figure she was probably about thirty years old, more or less. It is possible that she was older. That was probably around the year 1808.

Santa Bárbara
March 14, 1878

(Above is an attempt of the old lady to make her rubric—Savage)

I forgot to say that many times each year I would take the sick women and even the sick men from the mission to Agua Caliente, which was in the Sierra de Santa Isabel, twenty-four leagues from the mission. I would stay there with them for two months. I would bathe them and take care of them.

Augustias de la Guerra

INTRODUCTION

*S*avage's attempts to interview members of the de la Guerra family in Santa Bárbara met with mixed results. One son, Miguel, was critically ill during the time Savage spent in the city. He died a few weeks after Savage departed. His illness had hindered the family's willingness to be interviewed. Another son, fifty-two-year-old Antonio María, had, according to Savage, "lost a part of the roof of his mouth and was blind. He declined making any statement, alleging ignorance of events in his youth, many years of which he had spent in Chile."

However, after interviewing Apolinaria Lorenzana, Savage did manage to interview Angustias de la Guerra, the second daughter. The fact that Cerruti had interviewed her sister Teresa at Rancho Alisal some three years earlier may well have induced her to make time for Savage. He obtained a very full testimonio from her.

Angustias de la Guerra was born in San Diego on June 11, 1815, two years after her sister Teresa. As the child of one of the leading men in Spanish and Mexican California, she began to assume various responsibilities at an early age. When she was barely ten years old, for instance, she stood as a godmother for an infant child, José Guadalupe Valdez, whose father was a soldier at the presidio. At the age of fifteen, she performed the same role at the baptism of an Indian child. In all, she served in this capacity more than any other member of her family—over twenty times. One of the people for whom she was godmother was Romualdo Pacheco, whose father had

ANGUSTIAS DE LA GUERRA

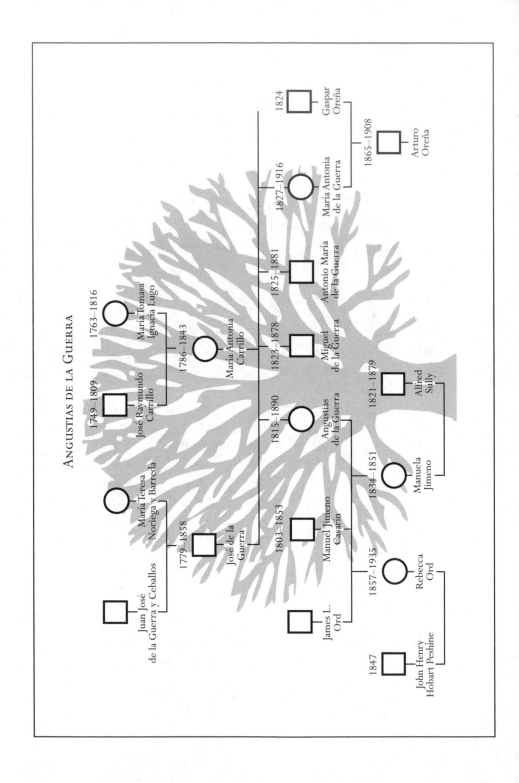

Angustias de la Guerra. Courtesy of the California Historical Society, FN-36284

been killed in battle in 1831 before he was born. In 1875, Pacheco became the only Latino governor of California since the U.S. conquest.[1]

As we have seen in the case of the marriage of Teresa de la Guerra to William Hartnell, in the heavily patriarchal society of Mexican California, José de la Guerra used his daughters as a means of establishing commercial or political alliances. In the early 1830s, de la Guerra formally presented Angustias to Governor Manuel Victoria. According to the closest modern student of the de la Guerra family, with this gesture he may well have been signaling his approval of a possible alliance with the governor. However, this did not occur—a stroke of good fortune for de la Guerra, for the governor was expelled from California after a rule of less than two years.[2]

In 1833, however, Angustias de la Guerra did enter into a marriage that had great strategic possibilities for the family. She wed Manuel Jimeno Casarín, one of three brothers who had come to Alta California from Mexico in the late 1820s. Manuel was on his way up the political ladder. He had

The de la Guerra house in Santa Bárbara, as it appeared three years before Savage's 1878 visit.
Courtesy of The Bancroft Library, University of California, Berkeley

already served at the Monterey customs house and on the *ayuntamiento* there. His two brothers were both Franciscan priests. Antonio had been serving at Mission Santa Bárbara since 1829, while José Joaquín, after three years at Mission Santa Cruz, had just been placed in charge of nearby Mission Santa Inés. The marriage of Angustias de la Guerra to the thirty-year-old Manuel thus placed the de la Guerra family close to both church and state at a time when relations between the two were confused and the ultimate outcome of the incipient struggle over secularization was still unknown.[3]

The recently married couple soon moved to Monterey, where her sister Teresa and her husband William Hartnell were already living. Angustias de la Guerra and her husband had thirteen children. Three girls were born within the first four years. The last births were of twins, in early 1853. Manuel Jimeno Casarín advanced through the ranks and served in a variety of offices, including as secretary to both Juan Bautista Alvarado and Manuel Micheltorena when they were governors. And she got a bit involved in public life herself: she once helped her cousin Gaspar Oreña smuggle about five thousand dollars' worth of goods he had brought to Monterey from Lima past the customs inspectors.

Manuel Jimeno Casarín received a number of land grants, including Salsipuedes in Santa Cruz, Santa Paula y Saticoy in the Santa Bárbara area, and another grant in what is now Colusa County. But it does not appear that he spent much time or energy developing most of them.[4]

During and after the war, Angustias de la Guerra lived in the Monterey area. This community, as the old Mexican capital and the headquarters for

The parlor of the de la Guerra residence in 1874. Courtesy of The Bancroft Library, University of California, Berkeley

the U.S. military rulers of California, became something of a meeting place for U.S. officers and former Mexican officials. As the spouse of such an official, Angustias de la Guerra had occasion to interact with many of the conquering officers. She became well known among them as a woman who outspokenly opposed their conquest of her country and yet was willing to socialize with them and assist those among them who were sick. When Joseph Sadoc Alemany arrived to take up the office of bishop, she and her husband offered to sell him their house in Monterey so that he could use it as an official residence.[5]

At the same time, she continued to attend to family affairs. Her oldest daughter, Manuela, married Alfred Sully, an American, in about 1850. The Santa Bárbara branch of the family objected to the marriage, although Angustias de la Guerra apparently supported her daughter.

Manuela died giving birth to her first child, in 1851. Angustias de la Guerra then took over and nursed her own grandchild, but the child died. Sully wrote to his sister that his mother-in-law had accidentally strangled the baby in her sleep, although the attending doctor, James L. Ord, assured her that the baby had died of a convulsion.[6]

Angustias de la Guerra and Manuel Jimeno Casarín separated in 1853 and he went to Mexico, where he died in that same year. She decided to go to Mexico, apparently to try to recover some of the property he may have had. Armed with a letter of introduction from Bishop Alemany, she left toward the end of 1854, but her time in Mexico was very difficult. The fourteen-day trip on a steamer from San Francisco to Mazatlán left her seasick, and when she got to Mazatlán, she was robbed inside a church. Nevertheless, she remained in Mexico for over a year. Eventually, after becoming bitter over the ways in which her late husband's relatives had been able to allocate his financial interests among themselves and exclude her, she returned to California in early 1856.[7]

In October 1856, Angustias de la Guerra married the same Dr. James L. Ord mentioned above. He had come to California as an army assistant surgeon with his brother, Lt. Edward O. Ord. They had one daughter, Rebeca, named after Ord's mother. They took up residence in Santa Bárbara and became involved in a series of financial controversies with her family. When her father died in 1858, he left most of his property to his sons. Of his daughters, he wrote, "Although it might be my strongest desire to leave them more prosperous, my estate is not sufficient to enable me to comply with such desires." Angustias de la Guerra bitterly complained about the will, and four of her brothers sent her an angry note on July 8, 1858, in which they told her that they had decided to sever all relations with her, fraternal and otherwise, "forever." Matters remained tense, evidenced by bills her husband sent the family for medical treatment. Things got so difficult within the family that when her youngest sister, María Antonia, became ill in 1866, her husband, Gaspar Oreña (whom Angustias had assisted in Monterey in the 1840s), refused even to consult Ord.[8]

In 1875, Angustias de la Guerra and James Ord were divorced. The reason was apparently his infidelity. Angustias de la Guerra died in San Francisco on June 21, 1890, and was buried in Holy Cross Cemetery in Colma. The ten-dollar cost for her Colma grave was paid by Arturo Oreña, a San Francisco druggist. Arturo was the son of her sister María Antonia. In 1919 the remains of Angustias de la Guerra were moved from Colma back to Santa Bárbara, at the request of her daughter Rebeca.

In 1887 Rebeca had married John Henry Hobart Peshine, who had a long army career which included a stint as military attaché to Spain. Peshine died in the 1920s, and Rebeca died in Santa Bárbara in 1935, one hundred and twenty years after her mother had been born in San Diego.[9]

When Savage talked to Angustias de la Guerra, he was speaking to someone who had been one of the most well-connected people in Mexican California. Her testimonio indicated that she was very well aware of her position. For example, at one point in the interview she remarked that she doubted that a certain event had actually occurred. If it had happened, she was extremely confident that "I surely would have known."

Savage focused most of his attention on political and military events. He started with the Bouchard raid, and he took her systematically through the major public events in the territory's history. Since Angustias de la Guerra's father had been close to the missionaries, Savage sought any knowledge she might have about them. At one point in the conversation he ran through a list of them and asked her what memories she had about each individual. Her interview ended with her recollections of events in Monterey during the American invasion. Savage pronounced himself highly satisfied with the information he had obtained from her, and he expressed regret that he had been unable to follow up with another interview on "the manners and customs of the Californias."

During the interview, Angustias de la Guerra seems to have bristled when Savage focused his questions on the deeds of various men. She insisted that she and other women had been active participants in the history of their land. At various points in the narrative, she broke the flow of Savage's questioning to insert an event in which she had been a significant agent. As Savage was asking her, for instance, about the ultimate fate of some officers who had participated in the Solís revolt of 1829, she interrupted him to relate a story about the imprisonment of one priest implicated in the affair. "Returning to Father Martínez," she broke in, and then recalled how she had served as an intermediary, delivering secret messages to Martínez from her father. She also related how in 1836 she had volunteered to go to Mission Santa Bárbara and personally warn Father Narciso Durán that people were coming to arrest him. She also remembered how she had peremptorily refused to hand over the keys of the Customs House to the Americans in 1842 during the short-lived capture of Monterey by Thomas ap Catesby Jones. She ended her testimonio with a story about the way in which she successfully hid José Antonio Chávez in her house, out of sight of the American forces who were seeking to capture him. She was able to accomplish this even though she was recovering from the birth of a child just a few days earlier. In this, as in virtually everything else she did, she was very confident of her ability to participate in the worlds of war and politics. When her brother suggested that hiding Chávez might prove too dangerous for her, she snapped at him: "I angrily asked him if he really believed the Yankees could find someone I had hidden."

Her focus in the testimonio was not only on herself; she insisted that other women played public roles. She gleefully described, for instance, the fashion in which Santa Bárbara's women blocked the government's attempt to seize Father Durán and transport him to Monterey.

Angustias de la Guerra took her role as a custodian of California's past very seriously. Her testimonio indicated that she consulted with her brothers when Savage was interviewing her. She did this to ensure that she was as accurate as she could be. She also revealed that she was very aware of what was then being commonly said about events of the past. If she disagreed with the conventional wisdom, as she did for instance about Juan Bautista Alvarado, she attempted to set the record straight. And she did not hesitate to criticize. She lambasted José Castro for his disloyalty to Manuel Micheltorena after Micheltorena had protected him in Mexico.

All in all, Angustias de la Guerra's own past had enabled her to see and experience many sides of California. The extraordinary value of her testimonio lay in its presentation of California as a multifaceted place and in her own conscious ambivalence about that. Yes, she said, she and the women she knew hated the American conquest. She also hated the way the invaders had treated her family. But on the other hand, before the invaders ever came, "California was on the road to utter ruin." Yes, she would gladly aid a Californio soldier who had fought against the Americans. But her last words to him were, "What I did for you today, I would do for an American tomorrow if you were to unjustly do him harm." Her father a Spaniard, her mother a Californio, her first husband a Mexican, her second husband an American—Angustias de la Guerra encountered many worlds. Her testimonio revealed that she saw the light and the darkness in all of them.

Note: The de la Guerra papers at the Santa Bárbara Mission Archive-Library contain correspondence between Angustias de la Guerra and members of her family. They also contain two more extensive pieces, which we have included immediately following the testimonio itself. The first contains part of a journal that she kept from 1846 to 1847. Her daughter Rebeca found it in her father's desk in 1901. The second item is a set of reminiscences—recuerdos—that Angustias de la Guerra told to Rebeca in 1890. This material is mainly focused on social life in California, and it nicely supplements what she had said to Savage in her testimonio.

Occurrences in California as Told to Thomas Savage in Santa Bárbara by Mrs. Ord (Doña Angustias de la Guerra), 1878

The accompanying pages were dictated to me by Mrs. Ord at a time when her mind was very uneasy, owing to the serious illness which threatens to remove one of her brothers from among the living. For all that, she manifested a disposition to contribute her share toward the success of Mr. Bancroft's labors in procuring complete data for his History of California *and at the same time comply with the duties imposed on her by the strong recommendation given me by her sister Mrs. Hartnell of Salinas City. She therefore cheerfully devoted several hours to the task.*

Mrs. Ord (nee Angustias de la Guerra, and whose first husband was Don Manuel Jimeno Casarín, Secretary of State, Senior Member of the Assembly, and several times Governor pro tem of California) is well known as a lady of intelligence who, from her connections and position, was enabled to inform herself upon governmental affairs prior to the transfer of this country to the United States. She also bears a good name for veracity.

I had hoped to obtain from her much information on manners and customs of the Californias, which would, no doubt, have been interesting and reliable, as proceeding from a lady of her intellectual and social standing, but a regard for her distressed condition of mind deterred me from occupying her attention any longer.

Thos Savage
April 1, 1878
Santa Bárbara

I, María de las Angustias de la Guerra, was born in San Diego on June 11, 1815. My parents were Lieutenant (later Captain) Don José de la Guerra y Noriega, who was serving there at that time, and Doña María Antonia Carrillo, daughter of Captain Don Raymundo Carrillo and Doña Tomasa de Lugo.

I was probably about forty days old when my parents moved to Santa Bárbara, taking me with them. My father was going there to take command of the presidio because Captain Don José Argüello either had left or was about to leave for Baja California to occupy the post of governor.

Toward the end of October 1818, an American ship under the command of someone named Don Enrique arrived in Santa Bárbara. He informed my father that an expedition of privateers in the Sandwich Islands was arming itself to come and attack California, which was still under the authority of the king of Spain.[10]

This Don Enrique had previously been detained by the government for a period of time. I do not know if it was for smuggling or for hunting otters along the coast, which foreigners were prohibited from doing. While he was detained, he lived in my father's home and was treated very well. This is why Don Enrique was so fond of him. So when he learned of what was being planned in the Sandwich Islands, he wasted no time in coming to California to give my father, whom he considered his best friend, advance warning so that preparations could be made to face the invaders.

My father immediately notified Governor Don Pablo Vicente de Solá (my godfather). This señor then gave orders for the defense of the country and the protection of the interests of the missions. But since it took longer than a month or more for ships to arrive, Señor Sola wrote a very insulting letter to my father, accusing him of being influenced by cock-and-bull stories. After the courier who brought that letter for my father left Monterey, the two insurgent frigates arrived in Monterey under the command of Hipólito Bouchard. They were flying the flag of Buenos Aires.

There was considerable exchange of fire. José de Jesús Vallejo, corporal of the militia artillery, was manning a cannon and was lucky enough to cause some damage to the large frigate, according to what I found out later. But the outcome of it all was that Bouchard sent a formidable force ashore. They burned down the pueblo after seizing everything that could be of use to them. The governor, all the troops, and the families had left. Most of them fled on foot to the mountains or sought refuge at the missions.

I heard it said that the governor feared the invaders would go to Mission Santa Cruz. He therefore ordered the ministers and neophytes to leave the mission and take all the supplies with them so the invaders would not be able to seize anything. But the insurgents did not go there and the mission was ransacked considerably, by Indians and others who were not Indians.

Bouchard's ships remained in Monterey for a few days and then they weighed anchor. When they passed by El Refugio (the ranch belonging to the Ortega family), they sent men ashore. They ransacked the warehouses, burned the buildings, and then boarded ship again. Some soldiers left from here, under the command of my uncle, the distinguished Sergeant Don Carlos Antonio Carrillo. He managed to arrest an officer, some fellow

Left. José de la Guerra y Noriega. Courtesy of the California History Room, California State Library, Sacramento, California. Right: Hipólito Bouchard. Courtesy of the City of Monterey, Colton Hall Museum Collection, Monterey, California

named Joseph Chapman, and perhaps a few more. I do not remember for certain how many were caught.

After committing those acts of piracy against a defenseless pueblo, the insurgents left. The prisoners were taken to Santa Bárbara, where the officer was handed over to Bouchard in exchange for a fellow named Molina.

When my father, Captain de la Guerra, learned of the arrival of the insurgents in Monterey, he made all the families at the presidio leave so they would be out of harm's way. Many families, including the de la Guerra family, had left when they received the first warning. My father remained behind with the troops at the presidio. All the families, and perhaps some elderly or ill *gente de razón,* left under the protection of the mission Indians (the vaqueros). A number of families left on foot. I remember that Fray Antonio Ripoll, minister of Mission Santa Bárbara, left on horseback but got off his horse to give it to a woman who was ill. Some of the families headed for San Buenaventura. The majority of them headed for Santa Inés, some by way of El Refugio, the Ortega family rancho, and others by way of San Marcos. Our family went by way of this last route. I remember it was raining very hard the day we left and they took me in a buggy. The rain entered the buggy from all sides.

Mission San Buenaventura. Courtesy of the California History Room, California State Library, Sacramento, California

The insurgents did not commit any atrocities in Santa Bárbara. A boat arrived bearing a white flag and a man leaped from it onto the beach. He left a piece of paper there and then immediately departed. I do not know what was written on that paper, but I do have an idea that Bouchard proposed an exchange of prisoners. I know that a fellow named Molina, a Peruvian they captured in Monterey, was put ashore. Many years later, Molina was my father's servant and he died in that role. He was a man who would give himself over to drink. It seems that he got involved with the insurgents when he was drunk and they took him aboard ship.

My family went as far as Santa Inés. We remained there for some time, until there was no longer any danger of the enemy returning. The enemy went from Santa Bárbara to San Juan Capistrano, where they also caused much damage, such as pouring out all the wine they did not drink. They took olive oil and other things with them. Some of the insurgents who did not want to continue on surrendered to our troops with their weapons.

When the ships were spotted here in Santa Bárbara, my father had his troops and some settlers from here and from Los Angeles position themselves at the edge of the beach in a grove of willow trees that was there at the time. The total number of men, not counting the Indians, probably did not exceed more than fifty. I was familiar with that willow grove but it no longer exists. There he had his men carry out evolutions so the enemy would think that he had a large force. But I already mentioned that the enemy did not go ashore.

I learned that the insurgents went from Capistrano to San Diego, where they wreaked havoc. Then they headed for Loreto, in Baja California, and looted the church. They stole the magnificent garments with exquisite pearls that covered the image of the Virgin of Loreto.

IN 1824, WHEN I WAS ABOUT NINE YEARS OLD, an Indian uprising took place at Missions La Purísima, Santa Inés, and Santa Bárbara. Captain Don Luis Antonio Argüello was the acting governor of California, which was already under the Mexican flag. A soldier who was fleeing from one of the missions arrived to warn my father that the Indians were rebelling and were threatening to kill the *gente de razón* families. At that time, my father was the commander of the Santa Bárbara presidio. This was on Saturday, between twelve noon and two o'clock in the afternoon. My father immediately ordered my uncle, Don Anastasio Carrillo, to go with fifteen men to help the missions and the families. That night, my uncle prepared to head out with a slightly larger force the following day. Since it was Sunday, one of the Fathers from the mission, Fray Antonio Ripoll, was coming to say Mass for us.

The troops were ready to head out, so my father decided that Mass should be said right away. That way they could leave immediately after Mass was finished. The Father sat down. He was very sad and my father asked him what was wrong. He said the Indians did not want to go to Mass. Then my father asked him if anything had changed. The Father said the Indians were frightened because troops had left for Santa Inés and La Purísima. Then my father asked him to be honest with him and tell him if the Indians were rebelling. Father Ripoll answered that they were. My father then decided that the missionary should not say Mass and that the troops should remain at the presidio so that he could go with them to Santa Bárbara and attack the Indians.

Father Ripoll stood up, crying like a woman, and said, "My God! Do not kill my children. I will go see them first. Do not let the troops go." My father did not want him to go, fearing that the Indians would kill him, but he went anyway. When the Indians saw Father Ripoll, they told him that they had been planning to kill him but some of the Indians were against it. They advised him to return to the presidio, because they had no intention of refraining from killing as many *gente de razón* as they could. After that, they would retreat to the mountains. This information about killing *gente de razón* was not told to us by Father Ripoll but rather by the Indian who accompanied him and who remained with him at the house.

Father Ripoll's colleague at the mission was Fray Antonio Jayme, a man of advanced age who walked with difficulty. When the Indians were returning Father Ripoll to the presidio, he asked Father Jayme to come with him,

Mission Santa Inés. Courtesy of the California History Room, California State Library, Sacramento, California

but the Indians refused to let him go. They did, however, reassure Father Ripoll that they would not harm Father Jayme.

When Father Ripoll arrived at my father's home, my father asked him what the Indians had decided to do. He responded, weeping, that they would not do anything to Father Jayme. My father immediately went to the mission with the troops. No other Indians could be seen except for those who were in the corridor. They had positioned Father Jayme as a parapet and were firing their arrows from behind him.

There was a Russian at the mission named José, who was a servant there. He was with the Indians and was firing with a gun. The troops from here killed a few Indians who made themselves visible when they came out from behind the rocks to shoot their arrows. A few of the Indians kept the troops busy while the majority of them left the mission and headed toward the mountains. The Indian women and small children had already left for the *tular* the previous afternoon and evening. The troops remained from eight in the morning until one in the afternoon to see what they could do by attacking the Indians.

At around one o'clock, there were almost no Indians at the mission, but the troops did not know that yet. At that hour they went back to the presidio to have some food and they took two injured comrades with them. All that time, Father Ripoll had been in a room with a window that faced the mission, with nothing to eat. My mother sent him a bit of broth. I went in with the servant and told Father Ripoll, "They killed some Indians." He began to cry and did not taste a single drop of broth. I left feeling heartbroken for having given him news that saddened him so much.

Shortly after, the Indian sacristan arrived from the mission with the keys to the church. He told the Father that the *alcaldes* said they were going to take everything at the mission, because it all belonged to them. However, they were not going to take anything from the church, because it all belonged to God. They also said that the Indians who had revolted had gone off to the *tular*.

Father Ripoll loved his neophytes like a loving mother. His sorrow was so great that he became ill, but not seriously ill.

That same afternoon, two Indians came to my father's home and brought Father Antonio Jayme with them. Even though the Indians kept him at the mission all day, they did not forget to give him food. The priests remained at our home. This turmoil happened on February 22, 1824.

When my uncle, Don Anastasio Carrillo, arrived at Santa Inés, the Indians had already set fire to the mission. The priest in charge of that mission was Fray Francisco Uría. He was Basque and a first-rate farmer.

When the Indians began to set fire along one side of the mission, six or seven *gente de razón* families and the men who were there, including the missionary and the guard, had already taken refuge in the Father's quarters. From there they fired on the Indians until nightfall because the Indians had sworn they would kill them. At dawn, after a brief battle, my uncle seized

How the California Indians Fight, *by Tomás de Suría, 1791. Suría did the drawing in Monterey while visiting there with a Spanish scientific expedition. Courtesy of the Museo Naval, Madrid, Spain (MS 1726-47)*

the ringleaders. The rebel Indians lost some lives in that combat and also in the fire they had set the previous day. Father Uría came to live at my father's home and the families were relocated to the presidio.

The Indians at La Purísima seized all the *gente de razón* families but they did not harm them. They sent word that if troops were sent to fight against them, they would kill those families. But if they did not send troops, then the Indians themselves would bring the families back. I know they fulfilled their promise. They brought the families to Santa Bárbara without having harmed them.

The day that the Indians at La Purísima rebelled, two residents from Los Angeles were passing by there on their way back from Monterey and were killed. One of the victims was named Dolores Sepúlveda. The murderers of those people were caught, except for one. They were tried by a council of military officers and sentenced to death. They were shot right then and there. Troops from Monterey, under the command of Don José Estrada, went there. I forgot to say that the Indians from Santa Bárbara killed two white people at the rancho called San Emigdio. One was an American named Daniel (I do not remember his last name) and the other was a Californio named José Antonio Félix. They both were very fine men. About four or five years earlier, Señor Félix was attacked by an Indian. He slapped the Indian so hard that he knocked him down dead. At first, he believed the Indian had just lost consciousness as a result of the blow, but he soon realized he had killed him.

When the Indians got hold of Señor Félix, first they cut off his right hand so they could dance with it, and then they killed him.

Later, troops went in pursuit of the Indians who had gone off to the *tular*. The troops from Santa Bárbara were commanded by Lieutenant Don Narciso Fabregat, a Catalonian, and my uncle Carlos Antonio Carrillo. I believe the troops from Monterey were commanded by Don José Estrada. The expedition was not successful. The Indians engaged in some skirmishes and then hid. The troops returned. A short time after, the troops returned to where the Indians were located, but this time Father Vicente Francisco de Sarría, the prefect of the missions, and Father Antonio Ripoll, the minister of Santa Bárbara, went as well. The efforts of those missionaries resulted in a most successful outcome. They had been authorized by the government to offer the rebel Indians a pardon for their past actions. The Indians listened to the Fathers and returned to their respective missions. That is how the revolt ended, a revolt that threatened to destroy all the progress that had been made for the sake of religion.

Mission La Purísima. Courtesy of the California History Room, California State Library, Sacramento, California

Fortunately, hostility existed between those Indians and the Indians at San Buenaventura. If that had not been the case, the Indians from San Buenaventura would have rebelled and the Indians from San Fernando, San Gabriel, and other missions would have followed suit.

AROUND THE YEAR 1822, *Canónigo* Don Agustín Fernández de San Vicente came to California from Durango. He had been commissioned by the Mexican empire to raise the flag of independence in place of the Spanish flag. I remember when they swore allegiance to independence in Santa Bárbara. My dear father was not here. He was at some rancho. The soldiers swore allegiance in the plaza, but the officers who were in the plaza left.

Later, the *diputación* that had been elected and had convened met in Monterey and elected Señor Solá delegate to the Mexican congress. Up until then, he had served as governor of the territory under the new regime. In Solá's absence, the command became the responsibility of my father, who was the captain who had the most seniority, according to what I heard said. But there was opposition by the *diputación*. I believe it was mostly because my father was a native of Spain. Despite the fact that the majority of the officers voted for my father, Don Luis Antonio Argüello, captain of the San Francisco presidio, was called upon to be governor of the country on an interim basis.

This Argüello was the son of Captain Don José Argüello, who had served for many years in Alta California at various ranks in the militia, up to the rank of captain. He was even interim governor of Alta California for a few months when Governor Don José Joaquín de Arrillaga died in 1814 at Mission Soledad. Don José Argüello was the commander of the Santa Bárbara presidio and interim governor of California at the time he was appointed governor of Baja California. In 1815, he went from Santa Bárbara to San Diego, and from there he headed to Loreto. Don Pablo Vicente de Solá remained here as governor. I was told that I had just been born when my father received orders in San Diego to go and assume the post of commander that Señor Argüello had relinquished. Don José continued as governor until shortly before the change of flags. I believe he died in Guadalajara. I know that he and his wife, Doña Ignacia Moraga de Argüello, moved to Guadalajara to live with their son, Don Gervasio Argüello. He was the *habilitado general* of Las Californias and was married to one of the Bernal women.

In 1828, Argüello's widow and some members of her family were in Guadalajara. That is where my father saw her. She wanted to return to California with my father, but this was not possible because, by virtue of the decree expelling the Spaniards, my father had to return to California on the sly by way of Acapulco. Moreover, the widow was too old and in poor health to undertake such a long journey. My father was sure that as soon as he returned, nobody would touch him, because the Californios at that time were a people who were very Spanish, except for a few who were supporters of independence.

Señor Don Luis Antonio Argüello and my father were close friends. During the time that Argüello was governor, my father was always commander of the Santa Bárbara presidio. He held this post until he departed for Mexico in 1828 to serve as a delegate in congress. My father was dismissed from his post because of an order from the Mexican government in 1827 that dismissed all Spanish officers from their posts. Lieutenant Gabriel Moraga had already died and, if I remember correctly, first lieutenant of the Mazatlán squadron Don Juan María Ibarra was named commander of the Santa Bárbara presidio.

In 1825, my sister Teresa married Don Guillermo Eduardo P. Hartnell at the presidio chapel. Father Ripoll officiated. On that same day, the Spanish war brigantine *Aquiles* entered the harbor. There had been a mutiny aboard and the chief officers had been thrown off the ship on some islands. The officer, who was acting as commander, and another man came ashore and headed toward our home, which was the military headquarters. When they came in the house they were surprised to see so many people gathered together. Their surprise was obvious because they turned pale, undoubtedly because of the crime they had committed. But it also might have been because they believed they had arrived at the office of the military head-quarters and instead they stumbled upon a wedding feast. After speaking with my father privately, they were invited to dine and accepted the invitation. Hartnell and others were trying to find out why that ship had come, so they made the men drink lots of wine and liquor. I believe they got some information out of them. This ship did not surrender as the *Asia* had done in Monterey. Instead, after loading water and some provisions, it put to sea. It must have been anchored there a few days because at that time, in order to load water, you had to bring barrels to shore in a boat and then take the barrels to a stream near the beach. That stream gave little water. This was a long and trying process.

In 1825 the first *jefe político* and *comandante general* appointed by the government of the Republic arrived. He was Lieutenant Colonel of Engineers Don José María Echeandía. He was tall, very thin, and light-skinned. He had rather small eyes, light chestnut-colored hair, and was between forty and fifty years old. Echeandía was a very friendly man with fine manners. He seemed like a man incapable of harming anybody. *Alférez* Agustín V. Zamorano, a native of Florida, and *Alférez* Romualdo Pacheco, a native of Guanajuato, came with him. Both men were engineers. Don José María Ramírez, of the cavalry, Don Juan Rocha, first sergeant of the artillery, and *Subcomisario* Don José María Herrera also came.

Very shortly after, Echeandía and Herrera were at odds with one another, perhaps because Herrera was very good friends with the captain of the artillery, Miguel González, who had had serious disagreements with the *jefe*. Herrera was accused of embezzling public funds. He had been given money in Mexico to pay the California troops, but instead he invested a portion of that money in trade goods for personal speculation. My father and other officers had to testify in the case. Echeandía and Herrera's disagreements reached such a point that Herrera resigned from the *comisaría* and was preparing to leave for Mexico. This was because Echeandía removed Herrera from various branches of the treasury for which Herrera had personally assumed responsibility. And also because Echeandía insisted that those responsibilities were the job of the *habilitado* of Monterey. Echeandía denied Herrera a passport until it had been determined whether he truly was an embezzler of government funds.

Even though Señor Echeandía lived in San Diego almost the entire time he was governor, I do know that he was at the other presidios. I saw him in Santa Bárbara when he stayed at my father's home. The reason he lived in San Diego was because his health was very delicate. I remember hearing that one time he tried to swim in the ocean in San Diego and they had to pull him out of the water because he was stiff from the cold. I do not remember any event in 1826 and 1827 worthy of mention. Señor Echeandía went up to Monterey and then returned to San Diego.

At the end of 1827 or the beginning of 1828, my father boarded one of Don Enrique Virmond's ships in San Diego and went to Mexico to occupy the post of delegate for California in the national congress. Virmond was the tallest man I have ever seen. I am not quite sure if my father was not permitted to take a seat in the congress, but I believe that to be so. What is for certain is that he had to flee Mexico and return to California. His only crime was that he was born in Spain, despite the fact that he had come to Mexico when he was eight or nine years old.

I believe my father was still in San Diego, on his way to Mexico with my brothers Pablo and Francisco to enroll them in a school, when my mother wrote to him from Santa Bárbara to inform him that Father José Altimira and Father Antonio Ripoll had fled. They boarded an American ship as if they were going to buy some goods, but they never returned to shore. The ship was owned by Joseph Steele. They left a letter on the beach addressed to my father, bidding him farewell. My mother picked up the letter and sent it to my father.

The Fathers left because they saw the way the Mexican government was treating the Spaniards. They figured that it would not be long before Mexican missionaries would arrive to replace them and they might be expelled without any consideration. Steele took them on his boat to board the ship. When the Fathers boarded, they bid farewell to the Indians who had gone with them, but they did not say they would not be returning. Father Ripoll cried as he said good-bye, but Father Altimira did not say a word. The Indians arrived at my father's home with the farewell letters the Fathers had written and told him that the Fathers were gone. They did not take any money with them, only a few provisions for the journey. All the money that belonged to the mission remained there.

Altimira had been in Santa Bárbara for several months because he was ill. Father Ripoll's missionary colleague was a blind man named Francisco Suñer. He was Catalonian. Those Fathers, like all the other Spanish missionaries, had refused to swear allegiance to the Mexican constitution. I know that is why Señor Echeandía had Father Prefect Vicente Francisco de Sarría arrested, even though Father Sarría had given his subordinates the freedom to follow their conscience on this matter. The arrest of Father Sarría was an injustice that Echeandía committed but it was undoubtedly sparked by those around him, because he was a very good-hearted man. Such a dishonorable act would not have been his idea.

In 1828 the presidio soldiers in Monterey revolted because they were not being paid. The uprising was easily suppressed without any serious consequences. In November 1829, there was another revolt, mainly by the presidio soldiers of Monterey and San Francisco, but this time, ramifications were felt here and in San Diego.

But before beginning the account of that event, I will say that in the year 1829, if I remember correctly, a ship from Mexico arrived in Santa Bárbara with two hundred or more men. All of them were convicts and the majority of them had committed very serious crimes. Don Romualdo Pacheco was here as commander and was already married to one of the Carrillo women who was a second cousin of mine. The convicts went ashore. Most of them were naked. My father begged Pacheco not to allow the convicts to come to the pueblo until they had bathed and dressed. My father sent them shirts, pants, and his own blankets. Those poor men begged to be allowed to go and thank the person who had acted on their behalf. I saw them when they gathered together in groups in front of our house (the same house that is still standing on Calle de la Guerra, at the corner of State Street). My father went out to receive them and addressed them forcefully. He hoped that if they had broken the law in the past, perhaps it was because they had been motivated out of necessity. However, here in California they would have the means to earn an honest living and everyone in California would cooperate gladly toward that end. He assured them that he would be like a father to all who behaved well. If anybody found himself in need, that person was to come to my father for help. This may seem as if I am singing my father's praises, but besides being the truth, my reason for relating this episode is my desire to firmly impress upon people that those unfortunate Mexicans never gave any reason for complaints. They all behaved well after that.

Don Romualdo Pacheco was planning on sending the convicts to one of the islands.[11] That is what he did with most of them, but first he provided them with seeds to sow and some animals, such as cows and a few horses. Those who remained here were assigned to various families to be servants. My father assigned eight or ten convicts to work at his home and his rancho.

After living for some time on the island, the convicts who were there lost everything they had in a fire. We saw the blaze from here. Much time passed before any aid was sent to them. Perhaps it was because the schooner that was used to transport provisions between here and the islands had not arrived. The convicts made some rafts and some of them came back this way on the rafts. They landed near Carpintería or El Rincón and were seized and imprisoned at the guardhouse. Orders were given that the convicts receive corporal punishment—whippings or beatings. Two or three of the convicts were left in very bad shape. Later, the commander sent for the rest of them. They all came to Santa Bárbara and there were never any complaints about them. Some of the convicts were sent to Monterey.

Before that expedition of convicts came, another one from Mexico had arrived in Monterey. Included in that group were Francisco Badillo and others whose names I will not mention because they have left behind descendants or respectable connections whom I should not denigrate. I cannot give details about that group because I was a very young girl during that time, and it was customary for the adult Californios to refrain from talking about bad things in front of the children. Instead, they would speak in general terms and never refer to specific people. They did this so that we would not be on the lookout for these people. Thus we could never, at any time, point out a family that had the misfortune of being related to a person who had been a criminal.

In November 1829, the troops in Monterey revolted because they were not being paid. That is the reason they gave. They arrested and locked up the officers, *Alférez* Mariano G. Vallejo, *Subcomisario* Don Manuel Jimeno, and artillery officers Don José Fernández del Campo and Don Juan Rocha.

Then they formed their plan of insurrection, which was said to have been drawn up by ex-*Subcomisario* Don José María Herrera. They sent for Don Joaquín Solís, a convict whom I believe was here for political reasons. Solís was at his rancho near San Juan Bautista. He came and placed himself in command of the force that was organized. They left a garrison behind in Monterey and the officers remained imprisoned. Then they headed for San Francisco, where they encountered no difficulty at all in getting Lieutenant Commander Ignacio Martínez to surrender the post, since Martínez's soldiers, as well as the small artillery detachment, were already in cahoots with the others.

From here, they headed out to take control of Santa Bárbara. On December 4, 1829, or rather on the night of December 3, the few artillery soldiers in Santa Bárbara revolted, with the exception of their commander, Corporal Basualdo. They say that he ran to hide at the home of the presidio commander, Lieutenant Romualdo Pacheco.

Their uprising lasted no more than a few hours, after which they were caught and imprisoned. After this, Solís and his people came. It was known

The soldiers' barracks in Monterey, photographed in the late nineteenth century. Courtesy of the California History Room, California State Library, Sacramento, California

in advance that they would come back this way, so Señor Pacheco positioned soldiers at the foot of the hill. But one night, when they least expected it, the enemy arrived and our soldiers had to retreat to Santa Bárbara, leaving their provisions and some ammunition behind because they did not have time to recover them.

Commander General Echeandía was already in Santa Bárbara when he learned that Solís and his people were approaching. He ordered the families who lived in quarters outside of the presidio quadrangle to remain within the quadrangle during the night. A small reinforcement of settlers from Los Angeles had also come to serve under the military authority here.

The few foreigners (men) who were here in Santa Bárbara created a makeshift barracks at my father's home where they stored their valuables. They themselves kept watch at night.

Solís and his people did not go beyond the mountains and headed back to Monterey. Solís's people, with the exception of the most committed ringleaders, began to abandon him and turned themselves in to the authorities. When Solís arrived in Monterey, he discovered that the garrison he had left there had turned against him. Also, the officers who had been imprisoned were already free.

In the judicial investigations that were later made to determine the causes of the revolt, it appeared that the rebels and Father Luis Martínez of Mission San Luis Obispo had conspired to raise the Spanish flag again in this territory. The Mexican artillerymen Joaquín and Lázaro Piña testified that this had been the plan and that Father Martínez had said something to them about that. This was ridiculous, because Father Martínez was not some uncultured man who would get involved in conspiracies of that sort. They could not fool him. This was a crazy plan that only a child would participate in, not a friar as intelligent as he was. Father Martínez was a staunch royalist, but he was no fool. Solís retreated to his rancho, where he was later apprehended, along with his companions Raimundo de la Torre, Pablo Véjar, Corporal Peguesos of the artillery, and a number of others from the leatherjacket company of Monterey and from the artillery company.

After the investigations were concluded, it seemed that, up to a certain point, it was proven that ex-*Comisario* Herrera was the author of the plan. He and the rest who were involved were sent off to Mexico to be dealt with by the government and tried for the crime of high treason.

But it seems that they were able to put together their plan in such a way that there was no mention of returning California to Spanish control. They were released from prison, but the soldiers were assigned to serve in Mexico. Two or three of the Californios returned to California years later. *Subcomisario* Herrera also returned, during the time of General Figueroa, and was reinstated in the position that rightfully belonged to him, a position that had only been provisional.

But returning to Father Martínez, he was accused before Echeandía as an accomplice in the supposed conspiracy to return this country to the Spanish crown. Martínez alleged that he knew many of the rebels who came to Mission San Luis Obispo. He treated them very well, since he could do no less. If he had not done so, they might have looted the mission or committed other offenses. This is how the idea was born that Father Martínez was supposedly involved in the revolution. Señor Echeandía ordered that Martínez be arrested and brought to Santa Bárbara. He was treated without any respect or consideration. In fact, he was not even given enough time to pick up a handkerchief. Father José Joaquín Jimeno was left in charge of the mission. He was the brother of the man who later became my husband. My husband told me about that event.

Father Martínez was placed in a room of the military headquarters. Commander General Echeandía and Commander Pacheco were there. He was kept incommunicado. The only person he managed to speak a few words with was Ramona Carrillo, the wife of Pacheco himself. She personally looked after the needs of the Father.

My father was a countryman and close friend of Father Martínez. He was prevented from seeing him because of the strict measures that were in place and because he was a Spaniard. So one day, my father said that he wanted to write Father Martínez a note (since he was not permitted to speak to him) and send him some clothing and other things for his comfort. I told my father that I would go and see Father Martínez and make sure that he was given the note. My father agreed and gave me the note. I was probably about fifteen years old when I undertook that task. A boy went with me and carried the clothing. I took a handkerchief to Father Martínez. It was a gift from me. I ran into the officer of the guard, *Alférez* Don Miguel Lobato, and I asked him how Father Martínez was doing. He said that he was fine. I then asked him if he would allow me to say hello to the Father, because I had always been very fond of him. He said that I could. I told him that I wanted to give Father Martínez a small handkerchief, and I showed it to him. When I gave Father Martínez the handkerchief, I touched his hand with my finger and slipped him the note. He was shrewd and took the note and slipped it into the sleeve of his habit.

This happened in the presence of the same officer who had gone in with me, but he did not notice a thing. After this, whenever Father Martínez needed something, they let him request it of my father on a piece of paper that was sent unsealed with the officer. Lobato was the officer who was hardest on Father Martínez. I do not remember how long the Father was locked up. What is certain is that they never allowed him to go free for even a few hours. He was taken directly from the room in which he was incommunicado to the frigate commanded by Captain Wilson. This is the same man who a year later married Ramona Carrillo, the widow of Captain Romualdo Pacheco.

Father Martínez was taken from his prison in a small buggy that belonged to my father. My father went out to say his final good-bye to Father Martínez and made them stop the buggy. He stood on the step of the buggy and bid Martínez farewell. The Father then said, "*Paisano,* Don Miguel Lobato is staying behind in my place. Treat him as you would treat me." Lobato was in the buggy. This statement was Father Martínez's revenge against Lobato, who had treated him so harshly. Then my father said to Lobato, "You have heard what my fellow countryman has instructed me to do. From this moment on, I am at your service to help you in any way I can."

Father Martínez set sail on the same ship on which Don José Antonio Cot (a Catalonian) was being held under arrest.*

The only reason he was arrested was for being a Spaniard. Cot was not allowed to go ashore, but since his wife was a native of Lima and his three children were at my father's home, he would sneak off the ship between eight and ten o'clock at night and go ashore to be with his family. He would then return to the ship at dawn. Commander Pacheco had an inkling about this because he would visit my father's home almost every night. One day, however, around six o'clock in the morning, *Alférez* Don Mariano G. Vallejo appeared at the house to take Cot back to the ship. Cot barely had time to get dressed.

Around that time, another prominent Spaniard was in California. His name was Mancisidor and he had conducted business in California for many years. Cot came to California because he had been persecuted in Peru for being a Spaniard. After he had been here for some time, his wife came with the children. Mancisidor was never prohibited from coming ashore, undoubtedly so he could finish up his business and leave. The two men left. Mancisidor, who was Basque, returned to his country and was married there. He wrote to us. Cot returned several years later—the first time as a merchant on the frigate *La Rosa*. Later he settled in Los Angeles. Finally he died at my father's home, probably around 1860, a year after my father died.

At the beginning of 1831, Lieutenant Colonel Don Manuel Victoria arrived in San Diego. Señor Echeandía was neither in San Diego nor in the north. I believe he had gone to visit some of the missions of Baja California. Days went by without Echeandía turning over the command. This resulted in some bitter correspondence between the two men. However, Victoria had begun to give orders long before being in command. One of his orders

---

*An asterisk in the original manuscript identifies this material that was written on a loose page in the manuscript: "Father Martínez was a man of medium height and he was quite heavy. His skin color was somewhat brown. He had a very large nose that was quite crooked from a blow he had received a while ago. This happened when he was riding in a buggy with my father and the buggy tipped over as they crossed either the Nacimiento River or the Arroyo Seco. I do not remember which one. His character was very rough. His manners were brusque but he had a warm heart. He would gladly help any poor Californio who asked him for a favor. He was a generous man. His table was praised for its neatness and good service. His attire was that of a poor Franciscan and he always faithfully fulfilled his priestly duties. But he was a bit vain when it came to showing off his vaqueros and their mules. He did not want anybody to surpass Mission San Luisito (as he called Mission San Luis Obispo) with regard to vaqueros or mules. At this mission, cotton was woven with a good deal of perfection. They made rebozos, blankets, and other articles with that material."

was to counteract the measures that Echeandía had taken for the secular-ization of the missions.

It has been said that the missionary Fathers won over Señor Victoria. I believe that is wrong, because Victoria, when he first arrived, seemed more like a friar than the friars themselves. When the governors and command-ers general would arrive at a presidio, it was the custom that they would stay at the military headquarters. Victoria would not do that. Instead, he would immediately head to the closest mission. This demonstrated the great bond he had with the Fathers in all things that did not interfere with governmental matters.

Victoria was a very simple man but very despotic in his governing. When he arrived in Santa Bárbara, he headed, of course, to the mission, accompanied by only one or two soldiers. He did not give the missionaries any advance warning that he was coming, undoubtedly to keep them from welcoming him with the honors his position merited.

Whenever the governor or *jefe político* would appear, all the mission bells would begin to ring from the moment they caught sight of him. The Reverend Father, wearing his vestments, would come out through the church door with processional candlesticks to welcome the *jefe,* whom they would lead inside. Then the Te Deum would be sung. This was only done the first time the high official visited a mission. On other visits that he would later make, I believe the honors were limited to the ringing of the bells.

Victoria appeared at Mission Santa Bárbara unexpectedly and there was no time to welcome him with honors. My father and all the officers went to the mission to greet Victoria, who received them warmly. I was not there to see that.

The next day, we went to Mass at the mission instead of the presidio church, because it was damaged. The presidio church had been poorly con-structed and also had been damaged by the strong earthquakes of 1812. While I was in the mission corridor with some girlfriends, it occurred to me to say to one of them, "Since he is here, let's go see if we can meet the commander general to see what he is like. My father came to greet him and I want to meet him." At that moment we saw a rather dark-complected man who was leaning on the railing. He was wearing a red flannel shirt with a jacket over it. We took him for a soldier but he turned out to be Señor Victoria. Father Jimeno, the minister at that time, entered the room. My father came out shortly after and called me into the room and introduced me to Señor Victoria. I noticed that he had very beautiful eyes. His manners were brusque for a man of his standing, but it was said that he had been a fine soldier in the Mexican War of Independence.

When I went to Mexico in 1871, Father Antonio Jimeno was alive. He was a missionary in Alta California and also my first husband's brother. He was blind. He told me that Don Manuel Victoria had recently died. I believe Victoria died around 1868 or 1869 in Mexico City.

Don José María de Echeandía visited me several times in Mexico City in 1855. I returned here in 1856. When I left, he was alive and well. I did not notice any change in his appearance from the way he had been in 1830, which was the last time I saw him in California. When I returned to Mexico in 1871, they told me that he and his two stepdaughters, who lived with him and took care of him, had died.

When I saw Echeandía in 1855, on one of my visits to see his daughters, he told me that before he came to California he had made arrangements in Mexico for his wife to receive half of his salary. He was an engineer and had been the director of the College of Military Engineers of Mexico. When he returned from California in 1833, he found that the government still owed his wife all of the salary that she was supposed to receive. He could not get the government to pay her any of it. He owned some olive oil mills and other small properties. He and his family had lived on a shoestring off this property, and they suffered. However, he said, "Divine Providence wanted to offer me the opportunity to live quite comfortably, because in the year 1835 (I think he said it was that year) there was a 'blessed earthquake' (he said these words with much laughter) that damaged some convents and some homes that belonged to rich people. And, since I was an engineer, I was called upon many times to repair those damages. Consequently, as you can see, I am living very well here." When I arrived in Mexico in 1855, Señor Echeandía was under arrest by order of President Santa Anna because of something Echeandía had said to Santa Anna regarding his failure to fulfill his political obligations. But after a few days he was set free.

From Santa Bárbara, Señor Victoria continued on to Monterey and established his residence there. Among Señor Victoria's despotic acts was his order to arrest my uncle Don José Antonio Carrillo. My uncle demanded to know the reason for his arrest and the only answer he received was a peremptory order to leave for Baja California.

From the beginning of his governorship, Señor Victoria showed himself to be despotic. Unfortunately, he suffered from the shortcoming of allowing himself to be taken in by the stories of certain protégés that surrounded him. One of his sycophants and blind instruments of despotism was Lieutenant Rodrigo del Pliego, one of the most cowardly men known in this country. Victoria wanted to govern everything in a military fashion. And in the administration of justice, he demonstrated an unusual inflexibility that scandalized the inhabitants. For example, he ordered a number of people shot for petty thievery. In this he received much cooperation from the assessor of the territory, Don Rafael Gómez. Nevertheless, there was one occasion in which Gómez had to clip Señor Victoria's wings. That was when Victoria wanted to militarily prosecute the *alcalde* of San José, who was accused of embezzling the municipal funds. This persecution originated because the *alcalde* of San José had worked with the *alcalde* of Monterey to jointly ask Victoria to convene the *diputación territorial,* because the time for its convening had passed.

In his legal report, *Licenciado* Gómez denied Victoria the authority to institute judicial proceedings, much less military ones, against anyone on those charges. Señor Victoria had his own reasons for refusing to convene the *diputación.* He did not want any interference from that body or anything that would hinder his actions.

However, I should say on his behalf that he always was insistent that matters regarding the treasury be carried out in an orderly fashion. The soldiers were paid and furnished with supplies on a fairly regular basis, which had not happened during Señor Echeandía's time.

Abel Stearns and his wife, Arcadia Bandini. Courtesy of the California History Room, California State Library, Sacramento, California

A number of influential people were demanding that the *diputación* be convened, including some members of the *diputación* itself. Señor Victoria reacted by letting loose with violent and threatening language against some of these people, even against the *diputados*. Some of the *diputados* sent complaints directly to the supreme government in Mexico.

Victoria ordered my uncle Don José Antonio Carrillo and Don Abel Stearns to leave the territory. And I believe he ordered *Ayudante Inspector* Lieutenant Colonel José María Padrés to leave the territory as well.

This Padrés was a man whose ideas were so liberal that they could be termed extreme. He was the first to instruct our young Californios, such as Vallejo, Alvarado, and many others, in the principles of the federal system that prevailed in Mexico. He instilled in them political ideas previously unknown in California. Padrés left for Mexico and Don José Antonio Carrillo went to Baja California. Don Abel Stearns was in San Diego preparing to leave when, at the end of November 1831, Pío Pico, Juan Bandini, Andrés Pico, and others forged the plan to overthrow Victoria. As a matter of fact, they had Don José Antonio Carrillo come back. Don Abel Stearns also took part in the conspiracy.

The *alcalde* of Los Angeles, Don Vicente Sánchez, was a supporter of Victoria. He noticed telltale signs of upheaval in Los Angeles, so he ordered that various prominent young men be imprisoned, among them Andrés Pico and others. They were put in shackles. It should be known that the first thing done to any man arrested for a serious offense was to clamp shackles on his legs.

The San Diego conspirators attacked the guard and took control. Then they arrested Captain Santiago Argüello, commander of that place, and Captain Pablo de la Portilla, commander of the Mazatlán squadron. The next day, the troops joined them and they immediately marched on Los Angeles and captured it without difficulty. Then they set the political prisoners free and placed a pair of shackles on *Alcalde* Vicente Sánchez.

By this time, Victoria had already received news of the revolutionary activity in the south. He hurried from Monterey to Santa Bárbara (probably on December 2) with a handful of men and ordered Captain Romualdo Pacheco, commander of the Santa Bárbara presidio, to follow him with some *mazatecos* who were garrisoned here.

Before leaving, Pacheco went to say good-bye to my father. He told my father that he was entrusting his family to him, because his wife had given birth to a son just a month ago. This son was Romualdo Pacheco, who later became governor of the state of California. Victoria did not believe that he

José Antonio Carrillo. Courtesy of the California History Room, California State Library, Sacramento, California

would engage in battle with the rebels of the south. He thought they would disband as soon as they saw him with his handful of men. I doubt very much that he had more than thirty men with him. I remember that my father asked Pacheco how many men were going, and when Pacheco told him, my father thought it was a crazy idea. But Pacheco said that he had already told this to Victoria, who said he did not need any more people than that. Then my father told Pacheco, "Be careful, those men are stubborn—José Antonio Carrillo is there."

So they left. When they arrived in Los Angeles, Pacheco saw that the enemy forces were far superior in number, and he reported this to Commander General Victoria. With an insulting tone, Victoria responded that if Pacheco was somebody who allowed himself to be ordered around by women, then he should retreat, because he (Victoria) did not allow women to control him, or words to that effect. Pacheco, who was not cowardly at all, spurred his horse and headed straight for the rebels. He was killed immediately. From what people say, Pacheco wounded José María Avila,

A self-portrait of Agustín Vicente Zamorano. Courtesy of the California History Room, California State Library, Sacramento, California

who in turn wounded Victoria. Then Pacheco was killed by a *mazateco* named Isidro Ibarra. That is what people here said.

The rebels began to withdraw and the battlefield was left to Victoria, who was quite badly wounded. His soldiers did not abandon him, but for very obvious reasons he did not dare enter Los Angeles. Instead he retreated to San Gabriel. There he finally understood that he was on his own, because the country was armed against him. For this reason, as soon as he had recovered somewhat, he decided to leave for Mexico. In order to do this, he began to negotiate a surrender with the rebels. From San Gabriel, he went to San Luis Rey for a short time. When he had recovered sufficiently from his wounds, he was put on a ship in San Diego.

The rebels placed ex–Commander General Echeandía, who had not gone to Mexico, in command. The members of the *diputación* who had convened in Los Angeles appointed Don Pío Pico to the post of *jefe político*, since he was the senior delegate. But the *ayuntamiento* and the pueblo of Los Angeles did not believe he had the necessary qualifications and refused to recognize him as *jefe político*. They preferred to have a knowledgeable man

with experience in charge of public affairs, somebody like Señor Echeandía. Therefore, the action of the *junta territorial* had no effect, in spite of
the steps it took in favor of Pico.

But soon after, there was a counter-declaration in favor of what was
called "legitimacy." Don Agustín V. Zamorano, captain and commander of
Monterey, placed himself at the head of this. He called himself Commander
General. Two auxiliary militia companies were organized to defend Monterey in case of an attack and also because Captain Zamorano would be
heading south with the experienced soldiers. Santa Bárbara and its garrison
were in favor of Zamorano.

The opposing forces did not fight. The leaders had the good sense not to
push matters to the point of bloodshed. An agreement between them was
reached which left California divided into two districts: the north, which
comprised the area down to and including Mission San Fernando, and the
south, which was everything else, including the Baja California frontier.

That is how things remained. Nothing worth noting occurred until the
beginning of 1833, when Brigadier General Don José Figueroa arrived in
Monterey in the roles of *jefe político* and commander general.

Regarding Señor Echeandía, I forgot to say that when he arrived in California in 1825 he talked about republican and liberal principles that were
stirring in the minds of the Mexicans of that time. He was a man of
advanced ideas and an enthusiast and lover of republican liberty. He was
sent to California to introduce the new regime and he certainly put these
ideas into practice. For until then, the governmental regime during
Argüello's administration was basically the same one that existed during
the time of Spanish rule. The only difference was that now there were a
constitution, a *diputación*, and an *ayuntamiento*.

Echeandía led the Indians to believe that they too were free men and
citizens. This produced a harmful effect on the Indians' minds, for they
began to demand that those rights be put into practice. Of course an eas-
ing of discipline was noticed. The Indians were no longer passively obeying their missionaries. Before that, the Indians would obey their minister
like a child obeys his father—that is to say, the way children respected
and obeyed their parents during that time. Paternal authority had no
limits, and it continued even after children married and had children of
their own.

My father and Echeandía were on very friendly terms. A number of
times they spoke about the effects of having instilled the ideas of citizenship
and liberty in the neophytes. My father advised Echeandía to temper his

enthusiasm and try to keep the Indians in check, because many of them were traitors. He said that on any given day the Indians could revolt and kill the white people, including Echeandía himself, the man who was giving them so much encouragement.

Señor Figueroa was immediately recognized as *jefe superior, político, y militar.* One of his first acts was to announce that those who had pronounced against Victoria would be pardoned. And, the rebel officers would be called back on duty.

He immediately convened the *diputación,* and until the day he died he maintained a good relationship with that body.

When Figueroa arrived, I was not in Monterey but in Santa Bárbara. I met him in June 1833 at the Rancho de Santa Margarita, which at that time belonged to San Luis Obispo. Whenever he visited different places in the territory, he would always travel with an entourage of officers and some soldiers.

In January of that same year, I married Don Manuel Jimeno Casarín. We stayed in Santa Bárbara until June and then we left for Monterey. My husband stayed so long in Santa Bárbara because of his brothers. Fray José Joaquín Jimeno was at Santa Inés and Fray Antonio Jimeno was at Santa Bárbara. During that same time, Fray Narciso Durán, the prelate of the missionaries from the Colegio de San Fernando, was at Santa Bárbara. These missionaries had already turned over the missions of the north to the missionaries who came with Father Vice-Prefect Francisco García Diego from the Colegio de Guadalupe de Zacatecas. The Fernandinos were left in charge of the missions of the south—that is, from and including San Luis Obispo on down.[12] Nevertheless, when I went up north in 1833, I still found that the Fernandinos were in charge of a number of the missions. For example, Father Luis Gil Taboada (a Mexican by birth, although his sentiments were very Spanish) was in charge of San Luis Obispo; Father Juan Cabot (a Mallorcan) was in charge of San Miguel; and Father Pedro Cabot, his brother, was in charge of San Antonio. Of the two Cabot brothers, Pedro was very handsome and elegant, and had fine manners. The other one was very friendly and loving but extremely ugly. Father Vicente Francisco Sarría, an eminently virtuous priest, was in charge of Soledad. One night I dined at his mission. That was a day of fasting for him. The only nourishment he had was a little water and a borage leaf dipped in flour and then fried.[13]

Speaking of Father Luis Gil Taboada, he told me that when he was in Santa Bárbara in 1812, the earthquakes were very strong. On December 8, while he was at the presidio of Santa Bárbara, there was such a strong earthquake that the sea withdrew and turned into what appeared to be a tall hill.[14] He and all of the people from the presidio took off running toward the mission, singing litanies to the Virgin. I jokingly asked him why he had not gone to see what was at the foot of that hill. He told me that they drove a pole with a ball tied to it into the ground at a place where the wind did not blow. But the ball moved continuously for eight days. It stopped moving for two or three hours and then it began to move again. This lasted for about fifteen days.

After we bid farewell to Señor Figueroa at Santa Margarita, we continued on to Monterey and he went on south.

When we arrived in Monterey, we found that a Father from Zacatecas named Moreno was already there. I do not remember his first name. A few months after I arrived in Monterey, this Father gave my brother Juan a drawing that was in the *sala* of the mission.* This drawing was about a foot high and depicted the official reception of the Count of La Pérouse at the door of the mission church when La Pérouse was there.[15] The three Fathers present were dressed in their ecclesiastical robes and one of them wore a cope. Father Juan Amorós and Father Noriega were two of those Fathers. I believe the other one was a portrayal of Father Junípero Serra but I have some doubts about it. And I am not that certain about the portrayal of Father Amorós. However, I am sure that one of the Fathers was Father Noriega. He was the missionary at Carmel. The drawing also depicted some mission Indians ringing the bells. Some of the Indians who were witnessing the event were completely naked. On the other side there was a person who was supposed to be La Pérouse. He was accompanied by various officers from his entourage. One of those officers was the person who created the drawing. Although it had been damaged over time, the drawing appeared to be a very artistic work.

The count was depicted as a tall, slim man with long gray hair braided in the back to form a queue. He was wearing a long frock coat that practically touched his heels. He had his hat in his right hand and his head was turned slightly toward the priests.

The following footnote about her brother Juan appears in small print at the bottom of the page in the manuscript:"He had been educated in England and was there for nine years. During the time of which I speak, he was in Monterey completing his study of mathematics with Father Patricio Short (an Irishman of the Society of the Heart of Jesus and Mary [Picpus Order] who was living with Father Moreno at Mission San Carlos. Father Short and his prelate, Alejo Bachelot, had been expelled from the Sandwich Islands and thrown"[the rest is cut off the page]

26

This drawing, made in 1791 by José Cardero, is a copy of an original made in 1786 by Gaspar Duche de Vancy. Angustias de la Guerra had seen the original and described it in her testimonio. Courtesy of the Museo Naval, Madrid, Spain (MS 1723-1)

When my brother Juan was debilitated by the illness from which he died, he gave me this drawing. I kept it in a trunk until the year 1838 or 1839. That is when somebody took it out of the trunk. I never saw it again, despite all my efforts to find it.

Father Ramón Abella, who preceded Father Moreno and perhaps another person at San Carlos, was good friends with Don Manuel Jimeno. He gave Jimeno a map of Alta California that had Father Salvatierra's signature at the bottom, which indicated that Salvatierra had drawn the map. We saved it and put it away since it was unusual. One day, after the Americans took over this country, my husband, Jimeno, brought out the map to show it to several American officers who were talking about California.

Lieutenant (now General) Edward Ord asked us for it so he could make a copy. Two days later he returned somewhat distressed. He said that the secretary of state, Lieutenant Henry W. Halleck, had taken the map from his room. Ord had gone looking for Halleck so that he could return the map to him. My husband told Ord not to worry about it and to do him the

Mission San Carlos *(1827)* by Richard Brydges Beechey. Courtesy of The Bancroft Library, University of California, Berkeley

favor of keeping his mouth shut. Later, Señor Halleck told my husband that he had taken the map because it belonged in the government archives. Señor Jimeno assured him that the map had belonged to Mission San Carlos, which had given it to him, but if the government wanted the map, it could keep it. I assume it must be in some archive of the general government. On that map there were small pieces of agate indicating the location of mineral-laden hills. Many years later, placer gold was discovered in those spots.

During Figueroa's administration, an order to secularize the missions came by land from the supreme government. Figueroa enforced the decree and always worked in accordance with the *diputación*.

Señor Figueroa brought a number of officers from Mexico who would later play a role in the events in California. These men were Captain (later Lieutenant Colonel) Nicolás Gutiérrez, Lieutenant Bernardo Navarrete, cadet Francisco Araujo, surgeon Manuel de Alba, and Lieutenant Rafael González, who was customs administrator and interim *subcomisario*.

Señor Figueroa was sent to California as a form of honorable exile because he had liberal tendencies and because he supported President Guerrero. Figueroa was not in good health and had asked to be relieved of the political command.

At that time, there was a person named de la Mota here in California. He was a convict who had rendered great service to the Mexican independence movement and had attained the rank of colonel. After the Morelos revolutionary movement was put down, Mota, along with Figueroa,

Nicolás Gutiérrez, and others, refused to accept the pardon offered to them by the viceroy and stayed in the mountains with General Guerrero. When Mota was the *mayordomo* at my Rancho del Pájaro, he told me that his wife had taken care of me when I was very little. He also told me that he had remained faithful to Guerrero's cause. When Guerrero was ousted from office and killed, bands of guerrillas still remained. They committed hostile acts and even robbed friends and enemies alike. Mota was the leader of one of those bands. He was apprehended (I do not remember the name of the place he mentioned) and sentenced to exile in California.

Mota was an excellent man. Figueroa respected him. During the War of Independence they had been comrades in arms and close friends. As soon as Figueroa arrived in California he sent Mota a very warm letter in which he asked him to come. Figueroa always treated Mota with great kindness. At the time that placer gold was discovered, Mota was living at our Rancho del Pájaro. He sold the gold he had for about $20,000 and headed back to Mexico. He was there when I went to that capital in 1855, but everything had been stolen from him, he was living in dire poverty, and his wife had died. When I returned to California in 1856, I brought him and his two sons back with me. They went and settled in San Juan. I think Mota has probably died.

While I was in Mexico, the elder Mota came to see me and he was very distressed. He said they had taken his oldest son and made him a soldier. I went to see General Gadsden, who was minister of the United States. Both of Mota's sons were born in California and they and their father had acquired American citizenship because of the Treaty of Guadalupe Hidalgo. So I told Gadsden that an American citizen had been forced to become a soldier. Gadsden demanded the boy's release and he was set free immediately.

When General Figueroa resigned as *jefe político* of California, the Mexican government appointed Don José María Híjar to that position. Híjar was also the director of a large colony that was formed under the auspices of the Mexican government to colonize California. The Mexican government was led at that time by Vice President Gómez Farías. The colonization effort was strongly supported by *Ayudante Inspector* José María Padrés and Don Juan Bandini, the California delegate to the Mexican congress.

The colonists arrived on two ships at the beginning of 1834. One of the ships, the brig *Eulalia,* arrived in San Diego. On board were Señor Híjar, Don Juan Bandini, naval officer Don Buenaventura Araujo, Don Florencio Serrano, and many others.

The other members of the expedition were on the corvette *Morelos,* and they landed in Monterey. Don José María Padrés, the vice-director of the colony, Captain Gumersindo Flores, Don José Abrego, and others came aboard this ship. I was on the beach at Monterey when they landed.

Señor Híjar and Buenaventura Araujo were with the group of colonists who landed in San Diego. As the colonists were heading north, a messenger with an urgent dispatch passed them on the road. He had come from Mexico to deliver documents to General Figueroa that ordered him not to surrender the political command to Señor Híjar or allow him to interfere with the affairs or financial interests of the missions. It seems, or at least it was said, that Señor Híjar came with authorization to dispose of the mission property.

In light of this peremptory order, Señor Figueroa did not surrender the political command. After several bitter exchanges between Figueroa and Señor Híjar, the *diputación* decided that Híjar would have no involvement whatsoever with the missions, but the *diputación* did acknowledge his position as director of colonization. He would receive the same four-thousand-peso annual salary that the supreme government had allotted him when it appointed him to the two posts.

The majority of the colonists and the colony's directors settled in the Sonoma Valley. The colonists were given land. Señor Figueroa provided all the resources he could obtain as well as those the missions could provide to help the colonists get established. Thus, he followed the orders he received from the supreme government of Mexico. Figueroa even went to the Sonoma Valley to found a new settlement that would bear the long name Santa Anna y Farías. He was occupied in that endeavor when he received news that there had been a revolt in Los Angeles by people from Sonora and other natives of Mexico. They did not recognize Figueroa's authority and declared him a traitor who disobeyed government orders. That uprising lasted no more than a few hours, because Juan Gallardo and the rest of the rebels did not have the nerve to wreak havoc or harm the people. They tried to get the authorities, that is, the *alcalde* and the *ayuntamiento,* to support them. When they saw that these authorities rejected the plan, they listened to the voice of reason and went back to their homes. But before doing so, they turned over the instigators of the rebellion—a doctor named Torres, a Spaniard named Apalátegui, and I do not know if there was somebody else.[16]

Figueroa soon received news that the colonists in Sonoma were hatching a plot against him. The general acted quickly. He had *Alférez* Don Mariano

Guadalupe Vallejo, who was already at the military post in Sonoma, arrest the leaders and gather up all the colonists' weapons and ammunition. Híjar, Padrés, and the other leaders were sent out of the country. That is how the proposed rebellion was squelched. At the same time, the colony fell apart and the colonization project of the Cosmopolitan Company was completely abandoned. A large number of colonists returned to Mexico but many remained scattered throughout California. They engaged in different types of work and were viewed very favorably by the government and inhabitants of California.

Some of the colonists came with the intent of establishing schools in various places throughout the territory. Among them were Don Mariano Bonilla, Don Florencio Serrano, Don Víctor Prudón, Don Ignacio Coronel, and others. They all stayed here and later obtained honorable positions in the country.

However, the person who dedicated himself with utmost zeal to the education of young people was Don Ignacio Coronel of Los Angeles. Don Agustín Janssens was another person who came with the colony. Years later, Janssens owned ranchos and was the administrator of San Juan Capistrano. He presently lives here in Santa Bárbara.

Governor Figueroa had earned wide respect and continued governing the country with great skill. As I said before, he always maintained good relations with the *diputación* and other civil authorities. His health was declining with each passing day and he yearned for someone to relieve him of his responsibilities, but that person did not come. In the end, he died from a cerebral attack in August 1835. His death was deeply felt by all. Although I was living in Monterey at that time, I had gone to Santa Bárbara to see my parents and I was there when Figueroa passed away.

The body was embalmed and his remains were sent to Monterey. There he received the appropriate honors that a man of his rank and standing deserved. Before he died, he had arranged for his body to be buried at Mission Santa Bárbara, and his wishes were honored. Captain Muñoz, who represented the military, and my husband, Jimeno, who represented the *ayuntamiento,* accompanied the body on a ship from Monterey to Santa Bárbara. I do not remember if a representative from the *diputación* went along. Fathers Narciso Durán and Antonio Jimeno, who were the ministers at Mission Santa Bárbara, had Figueroa placed in a niche in the mission crypt. I believe that the mission was already secularized but it still had all of its wealth. The situation was not the same at San Miguel, which was a very rich mission in 1833. Father Juan Cabot showed me all the storehouses at San

El Funeral del Gobernador José Figueroa, *a large painted mural of the early twentieth century by Dutch painter Theodore Van Cina (1865–1940). Van Cina came to California in 1924 and was active in Hollywood and Santa Bárbara until 1933, when he moved to NewYork City. Used by permission of the Santa Bárbara Courthouse Legacy Foundation*

Miguel. They were filled with goods, grains, etc. And there was also a good amount of money that belonged to the mission. However, when I returned to San Miguel in 1835, I could not even find a glass so I could drink some water. I had to drink water from a little cup that I had brought with me. Everything that belonged to the mission, including the cattle, had disappeared.

Some people have stated that when the missionary Fathers sensed that the secularization of the missions was imminent, they decided to sell off as much of the cattle as they could before the secularization actually happened. But in order to do this, they had to slaughter huge numbers of cattle. So the missionaries contracted with private individuals and agreed to split the profits in half. Thousands of cattle were killed and only the hides were used. The slaughter was so massive that the authorities feared the country would be left without any cattle at all if they did not put a stop to it. In fact, the *jefe político* took steps to stop that destruction of animals.

My father had been the *síndico* for the missionaries for many years. The Colegio de San Fernando appointed him to manage the Fathers' finances. Later, when the missions of the north were turned over to the Guadalupanos, he stayed on as *síndico* for the Fernandinos until he died. All the Fathers would come to him for their funds. They never took any money, not one cent, not even for alms, without seeking my father's permission and advice. Each Father was allotted a certain amount of money each year and they would use the majority of this money for alms. They all considered my father

This 1851 document is headed by a drawing of a steer conspicuously branded with a large "Y." Courtesy of the Seaver Center for Western History Research, Natural History Museum of Los Angeles County, Los Angeles, California

their best friend and they loved him like a brother. As for me, I had two brothers-in-law who were missionaries. They loved me as if they were my own brothers.

If there really had been such a huge slaughter of cattle in order to amass money before the missions were secularized, I would have known about it. My father would have been informed. I do not waver in my belief that the story is false, like many other stories that have been told to tarnish the good name of these Fathers. They were living examples of virtue and devoted their lives to the well-being of their neophytes.

It is true that at certain times of the year the missions conducted a large-scale slaughter of cattle for the hides and tallow. They would use the hide and tallow to purchase items from ships, such as material to clothe their neophytes. The meat was also used to make jerky to feed those same Indians during the winter.

It was said that Mission San Gabriel had about one hundred thousand head of cattle. I have heard that the mission contracted with some settlers from Los Angeles and perhaps some from San Diego to kill a large number of cattle and split the profits. It was said that the cattle from Mission San Gabriel extended from there to San Diego, since there was not enough mission land to accommodate the cattle. The men who killed the cattle were supposed to keep half of the hides from the cattle they slaughtered and turn over the other half to the mission. I do not know if these contracts were made before the death of Father José Sánchez or if the slaughter began before he died, but the destruction happened after his death. I heard it said that more than thirty thousand head of cattle were killed at Mission San Gabriel. It was feared that there would be an outbreak of cholera or some other epidemic as a result of so much spoiled meat strewn throughout the fields.

They may have done the same thing at San Luis Rey, since it too was a mission that had abundant cattle. I do not believe that any other mission had such large-scale slaughters of cattle other than the yearly slaughter. If there had been such slaughters, I surely would have known about them.

Much has been said about the missions possessing large amounts of money. San Gabriel, in particular, has been mentioned as having large stores of money. I do not know how the mission could have obtained such large amounts of money, since their business dealings with merchants involved an exchange of goods. There was little currency in the country. The ships barely brought enough currency to pay their import duty. Many of them borrowed money here to pay the fees. I am sure that the missions must have had some money, but it was probably a modest amount. It is possible that some of the missions in the north that were trading with the Russians might have had more opportunity to obtain some hard cash. But even there, I doubt they would have obtained very much, because when the Russians bought wheat, they would pay for it with a combination of cash and goods.

Almost all the missionary Fathers whom I knew in my time died here. The only ones who left the country in my time were Ripoll and Altimira. According to what they themselves wrote, they took enough money with them to pay for their passage. Father Luis Martínez was thrown out and all the money he took with him came from my father's house. I suppose that these were his *sínodos*.

Father José Viader took his funds from my father's house so he could leave.

Father Antonio Peyri, who founded Mission San Luis Rey and managed it until he left, took the three thousand pesos that had been allotted to him. Peyri wrote the commanding general and told him about this. He, in turn, transcribed the paragraph for my father. Peyri also took two or three Indian boys with him to Rome so they could be trained for the priesthood. Naturally, he paid for his companions' travel expenses out of the three thousand pesos.

Those who died in California in my time were:

Father José Señán, at San Buenaventura. I was very young.

Father Antonio Jayme, at Santa Bárbara.

Father Uría, at my father's home. He was a very generous man. That is why he probably did not have any money left when he died.

Father Buenaventura Fortuny, at the home of Don José Antonio Aguirre in Santa Bárbara. He had no money left when he died, because whenever he had one peso from the *sínodos* he would ask the *síndico* for permission to give the money to the poor.

Father Vicente Francisco de Sarría was found almost dead at Mission San Antonio in 1835. I heard it said that he starved to death because he had no food to eat. Out of ignorance or for some other reason, the administrator did not supply him with provisions. Father Sarría was buried in the mission.

Father Luis Gil y Taboada died at San Luis Obispo before the mission was secularized.

Father Ramón Abella died at Mission Santa Inés in 1842. Since he was quite elderly, my father would send him, from here, everything that he needed and would pay for it out of his *sínodos*. I believe he had no money left when he died.

Father Marcos Antonio de Vitoria was an angel. He really was like a child. He died at Santa Inés. He was very giving, which is why I doubt that he had anything left when he died.

Father Juan Moreno, I believe he died at Santa Inés. I was not here, nor did I find out if he had anything left.

Father Pedro Cabot died at San Fernando. His *sínodos* were given to his nephew, who came from Spain. He was the son of one of his brothers.

Father Blas Ordaz, at San Gabriel. I believe he left nothing.

Father Barona died at San Juan Capistrano. I never knew him.

Father Gerónimo Boscana: I saw him once in Santa Bárbara, at my father's house. He was quite elderly at that time. He was a man of medium height but somewhat bent over, undoubtedly because of his age. He was not heavy. I believe he died at San Gabriel in 1831. I was very young at that time and my memories of the Father are very vague.

Father Antonio Rodríguez: I met him at my father's house when I was barely eight years old. He was a Fernandino but he was a native of Zacatecas. I believe that he died at the end of 1824 at San Luis Obispo. I can picture him as if I had just seen him. He was a man of normal height, but he was very heavy. He had a very large face and big, bulging eyes. In spite of all this, he was extremely friendly and he had very fine manners.

Father Tomás Esténaga: I never knew him.

Father Zalvidea: I never had the pleasure of meeting this very virtuous and wise Father, who was also so energetic and hardworking. He died at San Luis Rey.

Father Francisco González Ibarra, from Mission San Fernando: I met him when he came to Santa Bárbara. He was known by the name "Padre Napoleón." Everyone in town, including my father, called him that. I do not know why he was called that. My father joked with him quite a bit, because the Father was funny and was fond of joking. I believe he died at San Fernando around 1831 or 1832. I know that it was shortly before the secularization of the missions.

Father José Sánchez died at San Gabriel in 1833, the year I got married. I met him in Santa Bárbara. I was very young and I do not remember what he looked like.

Father Juan Amorós: I never met him.

Father Magín Catalá: I heard people speak a great deal about this missionary, but I did not know him. I heard it said that many years before the Americans came to take over the country, this Father would speak in church and in public about the abundant riches of gold that could be found in Alta California. But he said it would be better not to discover the gold, because it would cause very serious problems for the Californios. The people considered Catalá a saint. For many years there was talk about his prophecies, some of which have been fulfilled.

Father Felipe Arroyo de la Cuesta. He died at Santa Inés in 1840. I knew him well. It was said that he was a highly educated man. I believe he was a Spaniard from Old Spain. He was a man of normal build, but when I met him around 1833 or 1834, his legs were crippled and his hands were somewhat that way, too. He could write, but with effort. He had a pleasant appearance and good coloring. At that time, he was probably about fifty years old. He did not look like an old man.

Father Fernando Martín, from San Diego: I did not know him, but he was the one who baptized me.

Father Juan Moreno, the Fernandino, died in 1845. He came to California with my brother-in-law, Father Antonio Jimeno. I believe it was in 1824. Father Moreno was of normal build, but more on the thin side. He had a very nice face. He was young when he came and somewhat innocent in nature. I had many dealings with him but never saw him ill at ease.

Father Juan Martín, from San Miguel: I did not know him. He died when I was a girl.

Father Nuez died when I was very young.

Father Mariano Payeras was the prefect of the missions. I met him when I was a little girl. I remember that he had very good coloring and a very kind face. I have heard my parents, as well as other people, speak at great lengths about this missionary's virtues, good qualities, talent, and hard work. It fell upon him to be the prelate of the missions during the most difficult period of life in California. His good administration of the other missionaries, as well as his influence on them, helped sustain the troops during the Mexican War of Independence, a time when nothing would arrive from Mexico. The requisitions from the king did not come for many years. The troops suffered great shortages of clothing, shoes, and other items, but not shortages of food, because there was an abundance of meat and other types of food. Grain and everything else produced by the missions were purchased on credit because the government did not have the resources to pay for them. Even though I witnessed these things, I do not remember any of it because I was very young at the time. However, I did hear my parents and the older people talk at great length about how the officers and soldiers suffered during those years.

Father Juan Bautista Sancho, the minister at San Antonio, died at that mission around 1830. I never knew him, nor did I find out anything about him.

Father Francisco Suñer died at San Buenaventura in 1831. I met him in Santa Bárbara. He was one of Father Ripoll's fellow Franciscan colleagues. He was a man with a violent character and a very bad temper. He was thin and fairly tall, but actually more on the short side than tall. He had somewhat broad shoulders. He was an older man. His manners were very brusque. I remember that we children did not like him at all.

Father Ulibarrí: I did not know him. He died at San Gabriel when I was very young. I do not remember any of the other old Fernandinos except for my brother-in-law Father José Joaquín Jimeno, who died here. Father Antonio Jimeno went back to Mexico. When I was in Mexico, I was saddened to see that he was blind and very poor. He was living, as they say, on charity.

Before my time, there was a missionary Father named Viñals who was a great friend of my father's. I have heard my father say that Viñals played the *vihuela* and sang very well.[17] He was a very pleasant and entertaining man. One day, when he was playing the *vihuela,* he set the instrument aside and said to my father, "*Paisano,* this is not suitable for a friar. I am going to enter a Carthusian monastery." My father thought he was joking, but it did not turn out that way. After Father Viñals returned to Mexico, he went to the Carthusian convent in France or some other place in Europe. The very day he entered that convent, he wrote my father a letter telling him that his goal was being realized. He stated the hour that he entered the order and bid my father farewell forever.

I forgot to speak about Father Narciso Durán, a great friend of my parents and of everybody here in Santa Bárbara. He came to settle here in 1833. He very quickly won over all of the inhabitants, to the point that everybody was willing to do anything for him. He worked very hard during his long life, especially after the political upheavals in this country began. He tried to reconcile opposing parties and prevent bloodshed. He did not always manage to calm the storms, but I believe that his good advice and influence at least contributed to making those disturbances less deplorable. Fortunately, he had an effect on unpretentious people who were not at all bloodthirsty. I must confess that the Californios never gave signs of favoring human bloodshed like their compatriots in other parts of Mexico.

In 1833, Father Durán looked like a fifty-eight or sixty-year-old man. He was Catalonian, of normal height, somewhat heavy, pale, and he had blue eyes. He did not wear sandals like the other friars, because he had rheumatism in his feet. Rheumatism is what ended his life, in 1846 at Mission Santa Bárbara.

Fray Francisco García Diego was the first Bishop of California. Believing that his death was imminent, Father García Diego appointed Father Durán and Father González "governors of the mitre."[18] Durán was appointed prefect of the Fernandino Fathers and González was appointed prefect of the Guadalupano Fathers. Father Durán died about a month after the bishop died. This left Father José María de Jesús González Rubio the sole "governor of the mitre" until Señor Alemany was appointed bishop of Monterey. Alemany is the present archbishop of San Francisco. Father Durán always had a kind word or deed for everyone, so his death was deeply felt by everyone—natives and foreigners alike.

Mission Santa Bárbara. Courtesy of the California History Room, California State Library, Sacramento, California

When General Figueroa sensed that death was near, he summoned Don José Castro, the senior member of the *diputación,* and authorized him to take charge of the political command when he died. He had already summoned Lieutenant Colonel Don Nicolás Gutiérrez, who was at San Gabriel, to come and take charge of the military command.

Actually, after Figueroa died, Castro was the *jefe político* for a few months, from August 1835 until January 1836. I do not know if it was because of orders from the supreme government or for some other reason, but Señor Gutiérrez demanded that Castro turn over the political command to him. Castro complied. Señor Gutiérrez continued governing in civil and military matters until April 1836, when Colonel Don Mariano Chico appeared. Chico had been appointed *jefe superior político* and commander general. I do not remember where Señor Chico landed, because at that time I was confined to my bed due to an attack of typhoid fever that put my life in danger.

I remember an incident that a number of people told me about, especially my brother-in-law, Father Antonio Jimeno. Señor Chico was in Santa Bárbara on his way to Monterey to assume the command. Father Jimeno ordered that food be prepared at the place called Tecolote. An Indian neophyte lived there. He was about sixty years old and was quite lively. He was very funny when he spoke Spanish. Father Jimeno sent word to the Indian ahead of time so that he would be on hand at the meal. He had spoken to

Chico at length about the Indian's sense of humor. When they arrived at Tecolote the Father asked to see the Indian. The Indian's son went to find him and when he returned he said that he had not been able to find his father.

And so, Señor Chico did not see the Indian Cristóbal Manojo. After the meal, Chico continued on his way but Father Jimeno stayed behind so he could return to Santa Bárbara later. Then Manojo appeared. When Jimeno asked him where he had been and why he had not come to greet the *jefe,* Manojo answered: "Oh, Father, it doesn't sit well with me to be around a bad man. This fellow is crafty. Don't you see it, boy? He wears glasses. I saw him when he arrived and I looked at his eyes. They were peering out from under the glasses. I'm afraid of him." Father Jimeno told Manojo, "He is a good man. He is our general." And the Indian responded, "You just wait awhile and you will see how he does things. You can tell me later if he is good or bad. We'll see who wins, you or me." When Father Jimeno got back to Santa Bárbara he told us the story about the Indian.

When Señor Chico arrived in Monterey he assumed the political and military commands.

In 1836, around June 6 or 7, I went to Santa Inés with my husband. Fray José Joaquín Jimeno and Fray Marcos Antonio de Vitoria were the ministers there. The purpose of my trip was to see if a change of weather would help my convalescence. I was already almost completely recovered. My other brother-in-law, Father Antonio Jimeno, went to Santa Inés after I did so he could be present at my birthday celebration, which was on June 11.

When we sat down at the table that day, an Indian arrived and told Father José Joaquín: "Here comes the general." My husband had left for San Luis Obispo and I was the only woman there, so I told my brothers-in-law that I was going immediately to the home of *mayordomo* Don Francisco Cota. He was my mother's cousin. Cota had five young daughters who, in addition to being my relatives, were very good friends of mine. Two of them went with me to a room off the *sala.* From there we saw the commander general arrive and get down from his carriage. The three Fathers went out. One of them opened the carriage door and the other took Chico's hand—those two men were the Jimeno brothers. Father José Joaquín said to Chico, "I have not welcomed you, Sir, as I should, because I did not know ahead of time that Your Lordship was coming." As the Father was saying that, the bells were now ringing. There had not been enough time to do anything else. Señor Chico stood at the door of the *sala,* accompanied by the Fathers. Father José Joaquín invited him to come in and eat, because the table was set. Señor Chico's response was, "Is Señor Jimeno's wife here?" The Father answered, "Yes, she went to her relatives' home." Chico turned to his officers, Domingo Carrillo and Raymundo Carrillo, who were relatives of mine. I do not know if there was another officer there whom I did not see. He told them to hitch fresh horses to his carriage and then left the room. Father José Joaquín Jimeno and Father Vitoria followed him. The food was on the table and they invited Chico to have something to eat, or at least have some wine. Señor Chico refused to accept anything. He climbed into the carriage and went to the place called Huejote. It is near Santa Inés, before you go up the hill.

Father José Joaquín Jimeno was so distressed. He spoke to me and said that we should send food to the commander general. I did not want to do it, but the Father insisted. We then put together an abundant supply of chicken, turkey, and various other things. Don Francisco Cota, who was the *mayordomo,* or administrator, and some Indians delivered the food.* Cota informed Chico that the Fathers had sent him that food. Chico responded in a serious tone, "Sir, take that food back to those friars because I do not want anything from them, nor do I want to have any dealings with them. Bring me some horses and other things I need." Cota returned with Chico's response and I was present when he gave it to the Fathers.

I should point out that when Señor Chico arrived in Santa Bárbara from the south, I was in bed with typhoid fever. He stopped at my uncle Don Carlos Antonio Carrillo's home. Chico met him in Mexico when Carrillo was there as a California delegate to the Mexican congress in 1830 or 1831.

When Chico stopped by to visit my father, he found out that I was seriously ill. He asked my father for permission to see me. I was not in my right mind. I do not remember seeing him, even though he told me that he came into my room and had seen me in bed. According to Chico, I had told him, in my dazed state, that if he wanted to see me so badly, he could. I do not remember any of this. Somebody told me about it afterward.

After the incident at Santa Inés, Chico arrived in Santa Bárbara. The Fathers had already sent an urgent message to Father Prefect Durán explaining what had happened with Chico. In my father's presence, Chico complained to Father Narciso Durán about the two Jimeno brothers and Father Vitoria. He accused them of welcoming him at Santa Inés as if he were an

---

*A footnote here in the original interview reads, "I think that the mission was not yet secularized. Cota had been the mayordomo there for many years while the missionaries were in charge. Later, based on a recommendation from my husband and his brothers, he was the administrator for the government. Under his management, the mission remained in good condition for many years."

Indian and of sticking him in the scullery. Father Narciso asked him if he had sent word ahead of time that he was going to Santa Inés. Chico said that he had not done so, but he thought it was odd that they would not have known he was coming. Father Durán pointed out that those Fathers did not know that Chico was coming to their mission. "What? You want to defend them? I wanted to see Jimeno's wife because the last time I saw her she was seriously ill. I asked if she was there and they said no, that she was at the home of some relatives. However, I do not believe that the Señora has Indian relatives." My father did not like hearing Señor Chico express himself in that manner and reminded Chico that Jimeno's wife was his daughter. He also informed him that Don Francisco Cota was his wife's (my mother's) first cousin. Chico said, "I don't know. I don't believe it. What I do want is for you (speaking directly to Father Durán) to summon those friars and punish them." Father Durán told him that he would have the Fathers come and he would look into the matter, but he would never believe that they were at fault.

This issue gave rise to serious incidents which I will relate at the right moment.

Señor Chico continued traveling south to Los Angeles. I honestly do not remember where he ended up.

After my convalescence, I returned to Santa Bárbara. The Father President had Father José Jimeno come and explain what had happened at Santa Inés with Chico. Father Vitoria, whose word nobody ever doubted, documented the details of the case for his prelate.

I suppose that Father Durán wrote to Chico and showed him that there was no reason to impose any punishment whatsoever on the Fathers at Santa Inés.

When the *diputación* convened in Monterey, Señor *Jefe Político* Chico appeared before it and made accusations against Father Durán. I do not know what the charges were. Chico had no friends in the *diputación* because he had made himself hated for a variety of reasons. For example, he had hurled insults at *Alcalde* Don José Ramón Estrada and at the *ayuntamiento* of Monterey. The people in Monterey believed that it was quite probable that Chico would have Father Durán exiled, so the members of the *diputación*, which included my brother Don José Antonio de la Guerra, said that it was important for Father Durán to appear before the *diputación* and send him into exile. The *diputación* had an ulterior motive for doing this. It was well known that Father Durán was loved by the Barbareños without exception. And since the people of Santa Bárbara had never rebelled against the government before, they wanted to goad them into rebelling against Chico.

Chico fell into the trap and the *diputación* sent Don José Antonio Carrillo and Don Joaquín Ortega (both members of the *diputación*) to go with some soldiers to Santa Bárbara and arrest Father Durán. It was rumored that an order had been received stating that Father Durán was to be put in shackles. Then he was to be placed aboard one of Don José Antonio Aguirre's ships that was in Santa Bárbara and sent to Monterey. My uncle Don José Antonio Carrillo arrived at his brother Don Domingo's home at about two o'clock in the morning (I think this was in July). He very discreetly told my uncle Domingo why he had come. When Don Domingo saw that his brother was finally asleep, he slipped out through a window, went and warned my father, and then returned to his home. When my father got up (he was now in the habit of getting up late), I sensed movement in his room. It seemed like he was pacing. I was frightened. I got up and asked my mother, who was also up, if my father was sick. She told me that he was not sick, he was sad. I then went into my father's room and asked him what was wrong. He told me that my uncle Domingo said that they had come to arrest Father Narciso and that he deeply regretted that they were going to catch him by surprise at the mission. My uncle also said that he did not know how to warn him for fear of arousing suspicion. I told my father that I would go and warn him. If anybody asked me why I was going to the mission, I would answer that my brother-in-law Father José Antonio Jimeno, had invited me to have lunch. My father said that he would be very grateful if I did that. I went to the mission, accompanied by my brother Francisco. He was young at that time, about fourteen or fifteen years old. When we arrived at the mission, I found Father Durán in the corridor. On behalf of my father, I gave him the bad news. He responded laughing: "Tell the patriarch that blessed are those who suffer persecution for justice's sake, for theirs is the Kingdom of Heaven. He should not worry about that."

The members of the *diputación* went to the mission and informed Father Durán that he had to board ship and should prepare to do so immediately. They did not touch him; they just had a guard stand watch over him. A few days later they ordered Father Durán to board ship and took him to the beach in his small carriage. When they arrived at the beach, all the women from the pueblo were already there, except for the women from the more important families. It was a well-orchestrated plan. I do not know how the entire pueblo found out about it, but what is for certain is that everybody agreed that Father Durán should not leave. When Father Durán arrived at the beach, Don José Antonio Aguirre, who owned the ship and was of course a good friend of Father Duran's, asked him to please step down from the carriage and get into the boat that was waiting for them. Then all the women rushed over to the carriage, crying out that the Father should not leave.

Señor Aguirre acted as if he were angry and ordered them to step back. One woman grabbed a stick so she could hit Aguirre with it. All the women began to cry and scream. The fathers, husbands, and brothers, who were hiding in a nearby willow grove, as well as other people from the pueblo who ran to the beach responded to the women's cries. They said that the women's wishes should be honored and they would see to it that they were, no matter what the cost. They informed Aguirre that if he insisted on putting the Father aboardship, they would arrest him. The people sent Father Durán back to the mission in his carriage and everyone accompanied him there. Several men stayed at the mission to guard him until the commissioners and their troops had left.

Well, we finally see the pueblo of Santa Bárbara openly rebelling against Chico's authority.

I was not in Monterey at that time, so I cannot give a detailed account of what happened there with Chico. I do know that Señor Chico believed that his authority was not respected and that he did not have enough soldiers to force the people to respect him. Therefore, he decided to leave for Mexico to ask the government to provide him with the necessary forces, and then he would return. I believe he made this decision in accordance with the *diputación,* which wanted to be rid of him by any means possible.

Chico appointed Lieutenant Colonel Don Nicolás Gutiérrez to take charge of the civil and military commands. Chico left but threatened to return soon to punish the disobedient Californios. I do not know if the government heeded his requests or not, but what is certain is that he never returned again.

Señor Gutiérrez did not have any friends either.

Chico had insisted on allegiance to the principles of the new centralist government that had been introduced in Mexico. This type of government was not to the liking of the Californios who had come to terms with the federalist system of 1824. On the other hand, for a long time they had been anxious to be governed by native sons of the territory.

They took advantage of the allegation that Gutiérrez was misappropriating public funds. In addition, his personal conduct was extremely immoral. On November 7, 1836, the people of Monterey rose up against him.

I REMEMBER THAT MY BROTHER José Antonio and Ramón Estrada, together with various other important men from Monterey, were in Santa Cruz and other places in the north. They probably were gearing people up for the revolt that broke out.

The Californio troops were joined by a unit of foreign riflemen under the command of Isaac Graham. After they took control of the *castillo* and laid seige to the presidio, they fired a cannonball that directly hit the military headquarters. Señor Gutiérrez suspected that many more cannonballs would soon follow, and since he and his officers had limited forces, they surrendered. Gutiérrez had been overthrown. A few days later the commander general and a number of the officers were shipped off to the interior of Mexico.

Even though the district judge, Don Luis del Castillo Negrete, had not been ordered to leave California, he did so on his own. His brother, Don Francisco, had been government secretary under Chico and Gutiérrez. He also left.

The masterminds of that uprising were Don Juan Bautista Alvarado, Don José Castro, Don Angel Ramírez (customs administrator), *Licenciado* Cosme Peña, Don Ramón Estrada *(asesor),* and others. Among those who supported the movement with their influence and their military might were the three Vallejo brothers (Mariano G., José de Jesús, and Salvador), Captain Hinckley (an American who commanded one of the ships that engaged in coastal trading), and my brother José Antonio. My father was not at all pleased to see my brother mixed up in revolts, but he could do nothing about it.

After Monterey was captured by the rebels, Juan Bautista Alvarado and José Castro came to Santa Bárbara with soldiers. While they were here, there was a counter-revolt in Monterey by natives of Mexico. It was led by Don Francisco Figueroa, Don Cosme Peña, and others. They took control of the *castillo* and the presidio but did not capture the small garrison or its commander, Don José de Jesús Pico. That revolt was short-lived. It was squelched by a small force of Californios led by José María Villavicencio and a host of foreign riflemen led by Captain Graham. Some of the people involved left for Mexico and others remained in the country.

The garrison and the pueblo of Santa Bárbara supported the revolt led by Don Juan Bautista Alvarado in the role of governor. The purpose of the revolt was to make California independent. The fact is that a congress was convened that declared California a free and sovereign state.

From here, Alvarado and Castro headed south to enlist support for the plan from the people there, because rumblings of opposition had been detected in that region.

I do not remember what happened in the south except that in the end, Señor Alvarado was recognized as governor. During that time, the man who had been appointed commander general by the revolution was here. He was my mother's cousin Don Mariano Guadalupe Vallejo, lieutenant of the San Francisco company. Señor Vallejo had been informed by the people of Santa Bárbara that my father was the only military commander they wanted here, so Vallejo appointed him commander of arms. Santa Bárbara was no longer a presidio but a pueblo.*Alvarado and his associate, Castro, withdrew with the troops that were escorting them. They arrived at the pueblo called Tecolote, where Cristóbal Manojo was living. He is the Indian I spoke about previously. When Manojo saw them approaching he shouted to them, "Long live free California. Take any part of it." They responded: "What do you mean, 'Take any part of it'?" Manojo answered, "Well, you steal everything from it anyway." They all burst out laughing and did not say anything to him.

Commander Vallejo also retreated to the north. The small force that remained as the garrison in Santa Bárbara lasted no more than about six or eight months. The government had stopped paying the soldiers on a regular basis, so when they left, my father paid them a portion of the salary they were owed out of his own pocket. He did not want to take anything from the missions for that purpose without paying for it.

The missions were secularized. My father had been an officer in the past, and many times he had asked the missions to provide food and other goods to sustain the troops. The Fathers always gave everything they could, because they trusted the government to reimburse them. However, since the missions were now secularized, the situation was as Manojo had described it: "Take any part of it." That is to say, the process of taking everything that

---

*Savage placed an asterisk after the word "pueblo" to signal an added page: "After reflecting on this point and asking my brothers about it, I see that I have made a mistake. My father did not remain as commander of Santa Bárbara until after Señor Alvarado was appointed governor of California by the supreme government of Mexico. My father was not a man who got involved in revolutions. He always recognized and obeyed the government in power. It is true that he was very happy when the people did not allow Father Durán to be taken away, but my father did not take part in the movement.

"The person who was commander in Santa Bárbara during the time of the revolt was Don José María Villavicencio, generally known by the name Villa. He was half Indian. My uncle Don Carlos A. Carrillo and my mother were his godparents. He was a man who had a very good heart. He was called 'captain' because Alvarado and his close associates had made him a captain.

"I also said that my father disbanded the troops when he was the commander of arms. My father had been maintaining the troops with his own money. He was going to disband the troops for lack of resources, but a small ship arrived with some resources for the troops. And then Brevet Lieutenant Colonel Gumersindo Flores relieved my father and he turned over the command to him."

was needed from the missions, without paying for a thing, had begun. My dear father found this to be highly repugnant.

In 1836, before the revolt against Gutiérrez, my uncle Don José Antonio Carrillo had gone to Mexico as a California delegate to the Mexican congress.

The government under Alvarado tried to make peace with the general government when it found out that the general government was very angry with the Californios for having separated from the rest of the republic. But the overtures that were made were unsuccessful because they fell on deaf ears.

The supreme government was determined to make the Californios feel the weight of its anger, and it was preparing to send a formidable expedition to this country. It was said that the expedition consisted of twelve hundred men. These men were so well equipped that they were going to force the Californios to respect the authority of the republic, and they would punish those who had the audacity to ignore it.

My uncle Don José Antonio Carrillo made his voice heard by making use of the influence that he and his brother Don Carlos Antonio had acquired during the time he was a delegate from California. He showed the supreme government how unnecessary it was to send such an expedition, because it would jeopardize the public treasury and the resources of California. In fact, all Californios were loyal to the republic and to its government. However, it had been their misfortune to be governed by recently appointed leaders who were noted for their despotic and absurd qualities. Therefore, they held fast to their idea of having native sons of California govern them, because these men knew their countrymen and they also were aware of the needs of California. This was the only way they could hope for a future marked by progress and well-being.

When my uncle was able to get them to listen calmly to reason, he told them that his brother Don Carlos Antonio Carrillo, who was already known in Mexico, was a man of honor and was well respected. If he were appointed governor, everything would be resolved and California would again heed the national government without difficulty.

Whether the government regretted its intended plan to send the expedition, which would have incurred large expenses, or whether it believed the Californio delegate's reasons to be sound, the fact is that it drew up the appoinment of Don Carlos Antonio Carrillo as interim governor. And since the true state of affairs here was not known, the government authorized Carrillo to set up his government wherever existing conditions would allow.

I should mention that the national congress had long since granted Los Angeles the title of "city," declaring it also the capital of this department. California was now considered a department, like the states had been under the prevailing centralist system.

Don José Antonio Carrillo returned to California at the end of 1837. He brought with him the title of "city" and "capital" for Los Angeles and his brother's appointment as interim governor.

Don Carlos Antonio Carrillo lived in Santa Bárbara but went to Los Angeles when his brother contacted him. As soon as he saw his appointment, he summoned the *alcaldes* so they could convene the *ayuntamiento.* He presented his appointment to the *ayuntamiento,* which, of course, approved it. He took the oath of office on December 6, 1837.

The pueblos to the south of Los Angeles, down to the border of Baja California, also regarded him as their governor.

Governor Carrillo began to correspond with Don Juan Bautista Alvarado and demanded that he turn over the government archives and other property.

Alvarado was playing hard to get for a while. He had different excuses at different times for not complying with Carrillo's demands. Finally, Alvarado said that he had submitted several reports to the supreme government and he had yet to receive a response. Carrillo was putting pressure on him, but Alvarado would not turn over the command until he received a response telling him directly about Carrillo's appointment. Much correspondence went back and forth between the two of them, as well as between Don Mariano G. Vallejo on one side, and Alvarado, the two Carrillos, and José Castro on the other side. But I have already described how this turned out. Alvarado did not turn over the command. In fact, he had sent the government his reasons for not turning over the command. The government probably refused to honor Alvarado with a formal reply because at that time it was seeking to work out an arrangement with him. That is why the government did not inform him that it had appointed Carrillo governor.

It is true that the announcement did not bear the seal of the president of the republic and the countersignature of the minister of relations. Alvarado used this as a reason to declare the appointment a sham. But the appointment was simply a ploy. It was only intended as a means of taking care of immediate needs until the situation calmed down in the country and the *diputación* could send the list of three candidates for the position. This was required by the constitution already in existence. The legitimate governor would be selected from this list. From what I was told, I believe only the signature of Minister Peña y Peña was needed for the appointment to be valid.

In light of Señor Alvarado's unwillingness to turn over the command, Governor Carrillo organized a good number of troops under the command of Captain Juan Castañeda. They arrived in Santa Bárbara with orders to take the pueblo before reinforcements could come from Monterey and other points north.

As I have said, the pueblo was under the command of Captain Villavicencio, or Villa. He had about twenty or twenty-five men. When it was learned that Castañeda was bearing down on us with one hundred men or more, the men of the pueblo joined forces with the garrison to defend Santa Bárbara. Together they comprised a force of about one hundred men.

Castañeda got to within three or four leagues of Santa Bárbara, around La Carpintería. I do not remember if he demanded a surrender or not. What I do know is that Father Durán and my father went to meet with him to avoid a skirmish and bloodshed.

Some people have assumed that my father and Father Durán were supporters of Alvarado and his followers in the revolt. That assertion is groundless. Neither man could be a supporter of an array of issues that were destroying the missions. Besides, as far as my father was concerned, he knew very well that Don Carlos A. Carrillo was the legitimate governor of California, appointed by the supreme government of Mexico. Therefore, he should be respected and obeyed as such. It should be added that Carrillo was my father's brother-in-law and a man he had been very fond of ever since childhood. All of this, in addition to my father's great repugnance for revolts, shows that he could not be hostile to his brother-in-law's aspirations, nor could he favor his rival. I repeat, the meetings between my father, the Father President, and the "Carrillista" commander were for no other reason than to avoid a violent clash. They wanted to give it time to see if the problems could be resolved peacefully. They managed to persuade Captain Castañeda to withdraw with his troops to San Buenaventura, whereupon José Castro arrived with his troops. Castro came, as is commonly said, at breakneck speed. He picked up more men here in Santa Bárbara and headed straight for San Buenaventura. They were caught by surprise, since they were not expecting him there. After seizing the enemies' horses, Castro and his troops surrounded the mission. All day long there was a spirited exchange of gunfire between the two sides. We could hear it from Santa Bárbara. It turned into a huge thunder of artillery but only one man died. His name was Juan Cordero. He was from Santa Bárbara.

That same night, those who had seized the mission abandoned it. Almost all of them were then arrested.

Don Andrés Pico, Don Luis Arenas, and another person who had stayed hidden in the mission appeared before Castro when he seized the mission. I believe they locked them up at Santa Inés.

Governor Carrillo was in Los Angeles. When he learned of the defeat at San Buenaventura, he immediately headed to San Diego. Thus the city of Los Angeles was left unprotected and at the disposal of Don José Castro. Consequently, Los Angeles rose up against Carrillo, but this did not keep a number of the city's inhabitants from remaining faithful to Carrillo.

In San Diego, Carrillo immediately began to assemble troops to defend his rights. His brother Don José Antonio, a talented man with a will of iron, cooperated in every way.

Once the troops had been assembled, Captain Tovar was chosen to lead them. He had recently arrived from Sonora. The men left to attack Castro's troops. They arrived at Las Flores. Knowing that Castro was on his way with his men, they prepared themselves for battle. I believe that Castro arrived with Señor Alvarado. There was no fighting except for a gunshot here and there. It is said that Carrillo prohibited all hostile acts without his express orders. Instead of coming to blows, Carrillo and Alvarado entered into negotiations. In the end, they signed some preliminary agreements which formed the basis of the peace treaty that would be completed at San Fernando.

While they were in the process of negotiating, there was some artillery fire from Carrillo's camp. This angered him greatly and he prohibited any repetition of this type of action. It is necessary to understand that Don Carlos Antonio Carrillo always was a timid man. Despite the fact that he had been a soldier from a young age and rose to the rank of distinguished sergeant, he never was inclined to cause harm. He was incapable of even harming an insect. Everything he did to defend his rights as governor was because his brother José Antonio (who was not timid at all) and others had pushed him to do it.

Tovar and the troops were angered by the apparent cowardliness of the governor and decided to leave him to fend for himself. Tovar headed for Sonora. Many of the Diegueños returned to their homes, and the Angelinos did the same. Carrillo, therefore, was left without troops to defend him. As a result, clever Alvarado and his colleague Castro were able to

Mission San Buenaventura, 1876. Courtesy of the California History Room, California State Library, Sacramento, California

treat Carrillo like a puppet. He acted more like a prisoner than a negotiator or the *jefe político* of the department.

In the end, Señor Alvarado got his own way. He relegated Señor Carrillo to his home in Santa Bárbara since no one there would heed his authority as governor. They would view him more like a prisoner. I remember my father telling him, "Carlos, it seems to me that you are the governor of the island," referring to when Sancho Panza was the governor of Barataria. Of course my mother did not like those jokes at her brother's expense. But my father did this because of the great friendship, affection, and trust that existed between him and my uncle Carlos.

The situation continued like that for the rest of the year 1838.

In 1838, Don José María Covarrubias (the same man who would later play a role in Governor Pico's administration) married a cousin of mine named María Carrillo. A few days after the marriage had taken place, Don Carlos Antonio Carrillo and Señor Covarrubias fled Santa Bárbara. Covarrubias was a Frenchman by birth but was raised in Mexico and came to California with the Híjar colony in 1834. Carrillo and Covarrubias took Don Carlos's son Pedro C. with them. He was very young at that time. No one here knew anything about this until the next day when it was noticed that the three of them were missing. They sailed off in a boat. However, the weather was bad so they went ashore and stopped at a ranchito called Máligo. I think it is near San Fernando. Then they went on to San Diego and stayed there because they thought it would be safe. It was safe until

Christmas Eve, which is when Don José Castro appeared with his troops, surrounded the area, and captured Don Carlos A. Carrillo, Don Pío Pico, and Don José Joaquín Ortega. They set Ortega free soon after. I heard it said that Castro also tried to capture José Antonio Estudillo but he could not find him. The prisoners were taken away and then turned over to Captain Villavicencio, who was responsible for taking them all back to Santa Bárbara. I remember when the captain arrived here with my uncle Don Carlos. My mother asked him, "José María, how can it be that you have brought your second father back as a prisoner?" He answered, "Godmother, they give me orders and I have to obey, but throughout the trip I took care of him as if he were my own father." And that was the truth, because during the trip he treated my uncle as if he were his servant instead of the officer who had him in custody.

I remember that the arrest took place on Christmas Eve 1838, because I am sure that shortly after, in April 1839, my cousin, Covarrubias's wife, had her first son here in Santa Bárbara. That boy was Nicolás Covarrubias, who is currently the county sheriff. I had also given birth to a son here in Santa Bárbara, but it was in February of that same year.

Shortly before I gave birth, Alvarado offered my husband Jimeno the position of secretary of the government. He accepted with the condition that he would not have to go to Monterey until I recovered from having given birth. He waited for a few days, but seeing that the baby's delivery was not imminent, he left. I gave birth on February 25, two or three days after his departure. He left on February 21 or 22.

Shortly after the incident at Las Flores, a number of prominent people, such as Don José Antonio Carrillo, Don Pío Pico, Don Gil Ibarra, and Don Narciso Botello, were arrested in Los Angeles and other places. They were then brought to Santa Bárbara. There were some others in Santa Bárbara, among them Don Ignacio del Valle, Don Andrés Pico, Don Roberto Pardo, and I do not remember who else. Don Pío Pico was very ill, but he was able to obtain permission to remain in Santa Bárbara as a prisoner because friends interceded on his behalf, whereas the rest of them were sent to Sonoma, where they were imprisoned under the command of Commander General Vallejo. They remained there for several months. According to what they said, they were not treated very well. At that time, there was a smallpox epidemic in Sonoma and two of them came down with it. One of the men almost died. They were finally set free around the end of 1839.

I am a bit confused with regard to the dates of the two arrests that I described above, but I do remember well that at the end of January or the beginning of February 1839, Alvarado returned to Monterey. My husband followed him about twenty days later. I also remember that during that same year, at the beginning of October, I arrived in Monterey accompanied by my sisters. My husband had wanted to go and get me, but Señor Alvarado was sick and would not allow it. He turned over the government to my husband on an interim basis. Señor Jimeno had already been elected first member of the departmental assembly. If I remember correctly, Señor Alvarado was still the interim governor. I do not have this clear in my mind. I know that the assembly selected three candidates and Señor Alvarado was at the top of the list. The list was sent to the supreme government, which quickly issued the appointment of the legitimate governor. Señor Vallejo was also recognized as commander general.

When I arrived in Monterey, Governor Alvarado was already married.

Alvarado's administration ended up destroying the missions, but he did not profit from it personally. When there were revolts or other difficult situations, the government would make use of the missions' assets but would not pay for them. Because the government believed it owned the missions, it granted mission lands to others and loaned cattle to many government supporters so they could establish their own ranchos. These loans were never repaid.

Some of the mission administrators were incompetent, while others had no morals. There were some, that is, very few, honest men who did everything possible to protect those mission assets. However, their efforts were dashed by governmental orders that came continuously, instructing them to turn over those assets. Of course many of the mission administrators took advantage of the opportunity at hand to get rich and would steal at will. It reached such a point that they even stole dishes, pots, doors, roof tiles, and other things from various missions.

At first, Señor Alvarado established a set of regulations and appointed my brother-in-law, Don Guillermo E. P. Hartnell, visitor general.

Hartnell tried to enforce the regulations. He visited all the missions and made every effort to ensure that there was order and an efficient use of resources. But he soon was convinced that all his work was in vain. He had had enough and resigned.

Alvarado could not stop the excesses and the squandering, because he had to keep his supporters happy, especially Don José Castro. He had even more reason to do so after the disagreements erupted with his uncle Señor Vallejo, who had established himself in Sonoma. He had practically set up a fortress there. It reached the point that Vallejo was given the nickname "little King." Vallejo complained that the government was squandering funds without bothering to maintain the troops. He was constantly battling with the treasurer, Don José Abrego, so that he would provide him with means to support his soldiers. On the other hand, it was said that Señor Vallejo was angry because the government would not grant him all the authority he wanted to exert from behind his parapets in Sonoma. It was well known that during the revolts and campaigns, he never put himself at risk the way that Alvarado, Castro, and others had done.

I remember one time when Señor Vallejo came to Monterey with his honor guard. He stayed at his sister's home, Señora Cooper. Señor Alvarado, who was and is their nephew, did not go and visit Vallejo. Señora Cooper told Vallejo that Alvarado was somewhat ill. I saw Vallejo walking back and forth in front of the door to Alvarado's house. I went by the house and greeted him and asked him what he was doing there. He told me that he was going to see Alvarado and was waiting for someone to say he could go in.

Vallejo was angry, because when he arrived at the door and asked to go in, Alvarado's assistant told him that he would go and let the governor know that he was there. The assistant did not return for a long time; thus Señor Vallejo was not treated with the respect and decorum he deserved due to his familial ties with Alvarado as well as his official position.

Much has been said about Alvarado and those in his inner circle squandering public funds on banquets, huge parties, and dances. But this is not for certain. During his entire tenure, Señor Alvarado probably hosted three or four dances to celebrate some event, just like everybody else did. The government also had some modest celebrations to honor the national holiday or to welcome foreign officials. Everything was done properly. The family parties he gave were certainly paid for out of his salary. Back then, it did not cost very much to host a dance or a banquet. In Monterey, dances were held constantly, as were excursions out into the country, but those were given by us, the señoras (not by Alvarado's wife), and they cost little or nothing.

The person who did squander a lot of money was José Castro. He lived in San Juan Bautista or San Juan de Castro (as it was later called), and he finished off all of that mission's assets. It is true that his father, Don José Tiburcio Castro, had a rancho, but it was not anything to speak of.

In 1840, when I was in Monterey, a large number of foreigners were brought to Monterey as prisoners. They were accused of wanting to start a revolt. On the same day the first prisoners were brought, a person named

Diego Féliz brutally murdered his pregnant wife at around seven or eight o'clock in the morning. Féliz was arrested, tried, and sentenced to death on that very day. Between seven and eight o'clock that night he was executed.

For a number of days they kept bringing foreigners in from everywhere. They were either foreigners whose residence in the country was not legally documented, or foreigners accused of being involved in planning the revolution to take over the country.

One of the conspirators told Father José María del Real about the plans and he, in turn, informed my husband and probably Señor Alvarado as well. I found out about the planned takeover from my husband, before the accused were arrested. The informant was very sick and believed to be at death's door, so he asked to see Father Real so he could give him that information before he died.

All of those foreigners were placed aboard a frigate and taken to San Blas, under the command of Captain Don José Castro, Lieutenant Joaquín de la Torre, and a guard. All those prisoners continued to deny that such a conspiracy existed. And even today, those who are still alive say the same thing.

Isaac Graham was one of the prisoners. He was the person who had helped Alvarado obtain the position of governor. He returned later with a large sum of money he had received from the Mexican government as compensation for damages and liabilities. It should be known that the supreme government set all the prisoners free and had to yield to the demands of the American and British ministers. The government was required to pay a considerable amount of money to compensate the prisoners for the damages and suffering they endured.

Don José Castro was arrested and handed over to the war council. According to what was said, he was absolved, thanks to the defense he received from General Don Manuel Micheltorena.

By 1842, the Mexican government was already tired of the mutual accusations and recriminations from Alvarado and Vallejo, so it decided to relieve them both of their commands and send a *jefe superior,* known for his skills, to take over the political and military commands of California. He also would have additional authority to resolve issues facing the country in a manner that would be satisfactory to the inhabitants. Unfortunately, many bad officers (among the few that were sent) and a battalion of thieves and pickpockets taken from the jails were placed under his command. Brigadier General Don Manuel Micheltorena landed in San Diego toward the end of 1842 with those troops. After marshalling his battalion and disciplining them to a point, he took the troops with him to Los Angeles.

Commander General Vallejo quickly surrendered the military command to Micheltorena and placed himself under Micheltorena's command. Vallejo was appointed commander of the northern region, which extended from Santa Inés up to Sonoma.

When Alvarado learned of Micheltorena's arrival in Los Angeles, he turned over the political command to my husband. He then traveled to Los Angeles with Don José María Castañares, the *fiscal* of the superior court, and Don Francisco Arce, chief officer of the *secretaría,* and surrendered the command to Señor Micheltorena. It was understood that Micheltorena would begin to serve on January 1, 1843.

However, there was an unwelcome incident before my husband left for Los Angeles to surrender the command to Micheltorena on behalf of Alvarado. One day, Commodore Jones of the U.S. navy turned up in Monterey, claiming that war had been declared between his country and Mexico. He ordered Governor Alvarado to surrender the plaza and everything that was there.

That night, Alvarado held a meeting of civil and military officials. Some private citizens also attended. The governor flatly refused to comply with the surrender that was being demanded, yet he wanted to take his family away from Monterey. The others at the meeting knew that it would be futile to resist, so they decided that the plaza should be surrendered. Alvarado, however, stuck to his guns. The others knew that Alvarado intended to leave Monterey, but they made him understand that neither he nor his family should leave Monterey, nor should anybody else.

In order to keep Alvarado from leaving, he was not left alone. They quarreled for almost the entire night, but Alvarado finally agreed to surrender. The next morning, a delegation boarded Commodore Jones's flagship and said that Commodore Jones could do as he pleased. He would encounter no resistance, because they did not have the means to do so.

That morning, the American troops landed and occupied the government headquarters, the barracks, and the *castillo.* The few garrison soldiers who were there were removed.*

---

*The following passage is noted with an asterisk in the original text and is on a separate page: "At that time, my brother Pablo de la Guerra was the interim customs administrator, due to the absence of Don Manuel Castañares, who was the actual customs administrator. Castañares had gone to Mexico as a delegate to the Mexican congress. My brother was in Monterey when Commodore Jones demanded the surrender of the plaza. As soon as Governor Alvarado agreed to the surrender, my brother Pablo, Rafael Pinto, and several others came back to Santa Bárbara. The commodore's secretary, Henry de la Rentería, appeared

Señor Alvarado headed off to Alisal with his family, but no other families left. A communiqué was sent to General Micheltorena. When the courier found him at San Fernando, Micheltorena was already on his way to Monterey. When he received the news about the occupation of Monterey, he returned to Los Angeles with his battallion to prepare to defend the country.

The American troops remained on shore for thirty to forty hours. Then Commodore Jones summoned Artillery Captain Silva. Jones informed Silva that he had been mistaken when he committed those acts of hostility, for he had believed that his country and Mexico were at war. Now that he was convinced of his mistake, he wanted to return the plaza and everything else that had been seized and raise the Mexican flag again in order to honor it with a salute. In addition, he promised to head south to meet with the commander general and make reparations. The American troops returned to their ship and our soldiers returned to their posts. The American flag was lowered, and the Mexican flag was raised and honored by the commodore with a twenty-one-cannon salute.

In accordance with his promise, Señor Jones went to San Pedro. From there he headed to Los Angeles, where he and his staff visited General Micheltorena and settled their differences amicably. According to what was said, General Micheltorena, his officers, and the families from Los Angeles held a dance and a banquet in Los Angeles and San Pedro in honor of Señor Jones and his officers.* I forgot to say that before Micheltorena arrived in California, Monsieur Duflot de Mofras was here on assignment. He was an attaché of the French diplomatic corps in Mexico. He visited Monterey and received attention and gifts from the government as well as from members of society.

When Micheltorena came to California, Señor Alvarado did not show any signs of surrendering the command to him at first. The commander did

---

*The following passage is noted with an asterisk in the original text and appears on a separate page:
"Some people have said that a dance was held in Monterey for Commodore Jones and his officers after he returned the plaza. If such a dance was given, I did not know about it, which would have been impossible because of my standing in Monterey, in addition to Monterey being such a small place. The fact is that no such dance was held. They probably have the events confused.

"A grand ball was held at the customs house in honor of Commodore Armstrong (Jones's successor) and his officers. The elite of Monterey attended this ball. If I remember correctly, this ball was held to reciprocate for the dance they held for us aboard the Savannah. Be that as it were, they bestowed that honor upon us. They were a striking group of officers."

[continued from page 257] at my home (where my brother was living) and asked me for the key to the customs house. Rentería claimed that they knew the key was in my home, but I did not hand it over. I told him I no longer had the key. Rentería threatened to break down the customs house door, and I told him to do whatever he wanted to do."

not specifically say that he would not surrender the command, but he did not really want to do it. After Jones seized Monterey, he no longer objected to having the weight of responsibility lifted from him. He was actually rather happy about it.

Señor Micheltorena stayed in Los Angeles for almost all of 1843. By the end of that year, I was already in Monterey. I remember that my husband, who was first delegate and president of the *diputación,* swore him in at the customs house.

Micheltorena was a tall, slim man. He was very fair-skinned, had very smooth, chestnut-brown hair, and his eyes were somewhat dark. He was a very handsome man. His manners were excellent. He was extremely refined and good-natured and incapable of causing harm to anyone. However, he was ill-suited for the position of *jefe* because of that generosity of spirit which guided him. He died in Mexico at the end of 1852. His wife's name was Josefa. Micheltorena's shortcoming was his laziness. He would not get up until noon and would not attend to business.

The soldiers of the Permanent Battalion that he brought with him were unbearable. The officers were no good at all, with the exception of five or six of them. The soldiers were consummate thieves who committed all sorts of crimes every day. One night at about seven o'clock, a band of these men stabbed a French sailor on guard duty merely because he refused to give them the two *reales* they demanded from him. The poor wounded man was brought to my house and was cared for there. Although he escaped with his life, he was permanently crippled.

A captain named Noriega, the same as my name (thank God, however, that he was not a relative of mine) committed a robbery with two other men in my home. One of the men was named Segura, but I do not remember the name of the other man.

That fellow Segura had been sent to work in the office of my husband, the government secretary. The secretary's headquarters were under construction and part of the archives were at our house. The secretary's business was conducted in one room of the house where there was a writing desk and a box of knives that belonged to my brother Pablo.

One morning, Segura was talking to me in my sitting room when Pablo came in and handed me fifty coins. He told me to put them in his writing desk. I kept the coins in my hand and after Pablo had left, a servant came in wanting to speak with me. Then Segura left.

Because I was lazy, I did not put the money in Pablo's writing desk. I put it in a trunk instead. During the night somebody broke the window glass in the government secretary's room. My husband and I were asleep in the next room and we did not hear any noise.

The next day when I walked by the room, I saw the open window and noticed that they had taken the writing desk, the case, and several other things. I immediately informed Pablo and Jimeno. They went and reported the incident to Micheltorena to see if the thieves could be found.

After my husband and Pablo left, the first person to appear at my home was Segura. He asked me, "So you've been robbed?" I told him yes, that they had stolen the writing desk and other things. And I added, "Do you remember those coins my brother gave me yesterday? The ones he wanted me to put in the writing desk? They are over there in that trunk." Segura's response was that there probably was money in the writing desk. I told him no, that there was no money, just some blank signatures of Don José Antonio Aguirre, and he would let us know, with plenty of time to spare, when to invalidate those signatures. Later, it was discovered that those individuals were the thieves. Nothing happened to them because the matter was covered up. I believe they found the broken boxes strewn on the beach three days later. Segura did not return to the office of the government secretary nor did he enter my home ever again. He figured that I suspected him.

One night the *cholos* broke into my kitchen and made off with the pots that contained our dinner. When the cook went to bring out the dinner, he could not find it. I did not complain about this to the governor but I did bring it up in conversation one day when he came to our home to pay us a visit.

The soldiers who were committing those crimes were punished. The truth of the matter was that the officers were worse than the soldiers. The majority of the officers were vicious and corrupt.

At the end of 1844 there was a revolt against Micheltorena in Monterey. The intent was to make him send the troops back to Mexico. The rebels made it known that they were in agreement that Micheltorena should continue to govern the country and they would support him. Micheltorena responded that he could not release the troops from their service in California because the supreme government had assigned them here. The rebels seized all of Micheltorena's horses and then came back to the Cañada of San Miguel. I was in Monterey when that revolt broke out. I then came back to Santa Bárbara, so I did not see what happened in the north.

Around the end of January 1845, the rebels arrived in Santa Bárbara. José Castro and Juan Bautista Alvarado were their leaders. Nobody from Santa Bárbara joined them, and everything remained peaceful. General

Micheltorena appointed Don Andrés Pico squadron commander and sent him from Monterey to Los Angeles with weapons. In Los Angeles he would be able to form a militia. Pico later rebelled against Micheltorena.

Micheltorena went in pursuit of the rebels and arrived here in the early days of February. He camped at El Rincón and later at Mission San Buenaventura. Castro's rebels, who had been joined by reinforcements from Los Angeles, went to the mission to attack him. Micheltorena fired some cannons but the shots passed high above the rebels. No one was harmed and the rebels retreated. Micheltorena continued on with his march. The forces met up with one another in Cahuenga, but the only exchange of fire was a few cannon shots from one side and the other. No harm was caused.

Micheltorena realized that things would not go well for him in California and he decided to leave. In order to do this, he entered into discussions with Castro which resulted in Micheltorena's heading off with his troops to San Pedro, where they would set sail for a port in Mexico. He stopped in Monterey to pick up the rest of the officers and soldiers he had left there, as well as his wife, other family members, and his baggage, and he then continued on to Mazatlán.

Don Pío Pico remained as governor. Don José Castro, who was already a lieutenant colonel, remained as commander. Micheltorena brought the communiqué to Castro himself and placed the insignias on him with his own hands. Castro owed Micheltorena many favors, and he paid him back by rebelling against him.

Pico and Castro did not get along well with each other. Castro made various attempts to overthrow Pico or render him powerless until finally, around June 1846, Pico came with a force that was organized in Los Angeles to attack Castro and force him to respect Pico's authority. Pico was under the impression that Castro was planning on heading south with a well-organized force to capture him. Here in Santa Bárbara, Pico found out that the foreigners who were fighting under the banner of the bear flag had taken Sonoma and had seized all of Lieutenant Don Francisco Arce's horses. He also learned of the battle between Captain Joaquín de la Torre and his troops and the men who had taken Sonoma. Pico issued a furious proclamation against the invaders and called all Californios to arms. However, it was clear to him that little or nothing would be achieved as long as he and Castro remained on bad terms. Since he did not count on reaching any satisfactory agreement whatsoever with his rival, he decided to continue on to the north and punish the commander general for his impudence.

As soon as he arrived at Rancho Santa Margarita, Pico received news that the Americans, under the command of Commodore Sloat, had taken Monterey. In light of the critical circumstances in which California found itself, with the assistance of some friends, Castro and Pico made peace with one another because it was necessary to gather all the troops and individuals who were available to defend California, and there were not many of them.

But returning to events that came before that, I believe that Captain Frémont of the American army arrived in Monterey in December 1845 or January 1846. He was accompanied only by a servant. He had a force of about seventy men, but he had left them in the area around San Juan de Castro. Frémont had a meeting with Commander General Castro to discuss obtaining permission to conduct scientific expeditions throughout the country, but this was merely a pretext. The real objective of his visit was to be in league with Consul Larkin. Castro denied him the permission and ordered him and his troops to immediately withdraw from Mexican territory. Frémont left very angry. A few days later, news arrived that Frémont and his people had barricaded themselves in the Gavilán hills, where they raised the flag with the stars.

This news produced an intense reaction because the taking of Monterey in 1842 by Commodore Jones was still fresh in people's minds. As the popular saying goes, "It never rains but it pours." A respectable force was immediately organized and headed out for San Juan to teach that impudent Frémont a lesson. He had insulted the Mexican nation by raising his flag in our territory.

The opposing forces did not meet because Frémont did not expect them to attack him. However, according to what was said, there was more than a glimmer of truth to the fact that Castro was not very anxious to attack. It did not matter how much Alvarado and the others who were with him urged him to do so. Castro was not keen on placing his valuable self in the line of fire. He preferred to come to a friendly agreement, either by scheming or some other means, as long as he protected his own hide.

Frémont went to Sacramento and soon after, on June 11, some foreigners who were living near Sonoma took possession of this military post by surprise. They captured the two Vallejo brothers, their brother-in-law Leese, and Víctor Prudón, and took them as prisoners to Sutter's Fort. They were imprisoned there for about two months until Commodore Stockton had them set free on their word of honor.

I should point out that three or four days after Frémont left Gavilán, Señor Gillespie appeared in Monterey. He had traveled from San Francisco

The Taking of Monterey, 1842, *by American soldier William H. Myers. Courtesy of The Bancroft Library, University of California, Berkeley*

to Monterey by land. Larkin, the American consul, introduced Gillespie to the upper crust of Monterey society at a dance he hosted in his home. He told us that Señor Gillespie was an ill man who had come to travel through California to see if his health might improve. He arrived in San Francisco on an American warship. I must confess that neither I nor Señora Spence was deceived by that so-called introduction. We found it difficult to understand why the U.S. government would send an entire warship just to bring an ill young man to California. I must point out that nothing was mentioned about Gillespie being an officer on that ship. We brought this to Castro's attention and suggested that perhaps Gillespie was an emissary who was up to no good and should be arrested and sent off to Mexico. But Castro told us that we were thinking badly of a man who was ill. He accused us, and all women in general, of thinking badly of others, which according to Castro was something women did much more than men. Our response to Castro was that women almost always hit the nail on the head—more often than men do.

I figured that Larkin hosted that dance specifically to honor Gillespie and to put him in contact with the people of Monterey. All the families attended because we had been told that a refined and well-bred young man would be at the dance. There was nothing to suggest that he was a U.S. officer. Gillespie stayed in Monterey for only a short time and then left to

Thomas O. Larkin constructed this two-story adobe and brick home in Monterey. Courtesy of the California History Room, California State Library, Sacramento, California

meet up with Frémont. People in Monterey commented on this later. The taking of Sonoma happened right after that.

A few years back, the feast day of Nuestra Señora del Refugio was celebrated on July 4. She was the patron saint of the bishopric of the Californias. Nobody would work on that day. Instead, there would be a solemn religious ceremony at church. Since the feast day coincided with the American holiday, there usually were salvos, a dance, and other things. It was a day of grand celebration. If I remember correctly, there were one or two American warships in the port on July 4, 1846. A few days earlier, there already was talk that those ships were going to take the plaza on July 4. So with that in mind, the priest was told to finish the afternoon prayer very early. The people of the town believed so firmly that the plaza would be taken that during prayer, at around five-thirty or six o'clock, a rumor spread through the church that the Americans were landing. The people left the church in a mad rush and one poor woman was somewhat injured.

When the news of the taking of Sonoma was received, the superior officer of the American ships was informed. The ships had either entered the port after the event or were already here. The superior officer said that the incident had no connection with him or his authority.

July 7, that unforgettable day, finally arrived. If I recall correctly, there were three warships in the port of Monterey that morning. One of them was flying the insignia of Commodore Sloat. In the morning, we could also see that they were readying the ships. There were many armed boats filled

José Castro. Courtesy of the California History Room, California State Library, Sacramento, California

with people who came ashore. They took possession without any resistance, since there was no garrison whatsoever. I believe that Captain Mariano Silva was the only Mexican officer here, and he was an old man.

The taking of California was not at all to the liking of the Californios, and least of all to the women. But I must confess, California was on the road to utter ruin. On the one hand, the Indians were out of control, committing robberies and other crimes at the ranchos. Little or nothing was being done to curb their pillaging. On the other hand, there was discord between the people of the north and the south. In addition, both north and south were against the Mexicans from the mainland. But the worst cancer of all was the widespread thievery. There was such squandering of government resources that the funds in the treasury office had bottomed out.

Commander General Castro kept a roster of officers that was large enough to staff an army of three thousand men. Somehow they all received a salary. These officers had no other use for the money than to grease the palms of their supporters who would help them achieve their personal goals. Few of those officers served their country when the time came to defend it against the foreign invasion. The majority of them did about as much work as a figurehead on a ship.

The Americans took the entire country. They occupied the ports and the pueblos and even the city of Los Angeles. When Commodore Stockton withdrew from Los Angeles, he left a small garrison there under the command of Señor Gillespie. I spoke about him before.

The Californios from that area, and many from the north who had headed south with Castro, raised the banner of revolution and forced Gillespie and his troops to head to San Pedro and board ship there. The Californios retook control of Los Angeles, where they began to make the necessary preparations for a strong defense. Captain José María Flores was in charge as governor and commander general, and my uncle Don José Antonio Carrillo was major general. And Don Andrés Pico, the commander of the squadron, led the troops that went to harass the enemy who had occupied San Diego.

After the reoccupation of Los Angeles, certain individuals from the north who were in the southern ranks formulated a plan to create a diversion in the north that would undermine the enemy. Those individuals were Manuel Castro, prefect from the second district; Francisco Rico, captain of the militia; José de Jesús Pico, captain of the militia; Lieutenant José Antonio Chávez; Juan Ignacio Cantúa; Vicente P. Gómez; and others. Since there would be no advance warning of their presence in the north, their plan was to descend upon the enemy at San Juan de Castro and take all of Frémont's horses as well as those belonging to the rest of the American leaders. Thus the Americans would be left to travel on foot and it would be impossible for them to move quickly.

Those individuals from the south did, in fact, come. When they arrived in the area near Rancho de los Vergeles, they received news that Larkin, the American consul, was spending the night at the rancho. They believed that apprehending Larkin would be a master stroke on their part, so they decided to capture him. With that as their goal, José Antonio Chávez and some others appeared at the rancho during the night and forced Larkin to get up and go with them.

Unfortunately, Larkin's servant saw them and hurried to San Juan to inform the American forces. The Americans detached an unspecified number of soldiers who met up with the Californios at the place called La Natividad. A rather hard-fought battle took place in which two American officers and some other men died. Several others were injured.

On the Californio side, two men died (one Chilean and another man). Several men were injured, among them José Antonio Chávez and the standard bearer, *Alférez* Juan Ignacio Cantúa.

From what I understood, the two opposing forces retreated because each side ran out of ammunition. The Americans headed back to San Juan and the Californios hurried off to the south, taking Larkin with them as their prisoner.

Cantúa was taken to the home of the Moreno family in El Sauzal. He was cared for there until his mother came later and took him back to Monterey.

After the battle, Chávez was hidden in the home of some Indians who lived in those parts. He told us it was a temescal. From there Chávez went to Monterey to the home of Francisco Day, an American. Day was married to a Californio woman. She was loyal to the Californio cause but her husband was a bitter enemy of the Californios. At that time, however, Day was at his rancho near Tehama.* They said that Chávez was in that house to spy on the actions of the Americans who visited there often.

One night, when the owner of the house arrived, Chávez was there and Day knew it. Because he was such an enemy of the Californios, Day tried to catch Chávez by surprise, but he was not able to. Instead of entering through the door, Day jumped over the adobe wall. Chávez found out in the nick of time that Day had returned and jumped over the wall to another house. Day fired his pistol at him but missed. Chávez fell into the yard of the other house and dislocated his foot. This little house belonged to an old Mexican soldier. The house consisted of two very small rooms where the family lived. The soldier had several children. The soldier did not know what to do with Chávez, so he wrapped him up in a blanket and stuck him under a bed. He told Chávez that he could not keep him in his house because his children might let on that he was there.

Chávez thought it over and remembered that of all the people he knew, I was the one who lived the closest. He told the soldier to go and speak with me.

I was in bed because I had just given birth to a daughter a few days before. I was very surprised that the old soldier was so determined to speak with me in private. He told me what had happened to Chávez. He asked me, for the love of God, to come and take Chávez and hide him in my house. The words "for the love of God" have a tremendous impact and they forced me to stop and think. My husband was away at our Rancho del Pájaro.

---

*This footnote appears in the transcript: "Chávez was a native of Mexico. General Figueroa brought him to California when he was ten or twelve years old. He was the son of one of Sergeant Major Eugenio Montenegro's sisters. General Figueroa was very fond of Montenegro. There were those who said that Chávez was actually Figueroa's illegitimate son."

Even though it was raining hard, I decided to get dressed and go see my brothers Pablo and Miguel, who were prisoners. I wanted their opinion as to what I should do, since I could not consult with my husband, because he was not there.

Pablo told me that the first thing I should consider was that the American authorities probably knew where Chávez was and they would come after him. But if I believed that I could bring him back and hide him so he could not be found, then it would be an act of charity to do so.

I was so angry with the Americans for mistreating my brothers and keeping them imprisoned for no rhyme nor reason. I angrily asked my brother if he really believed the Yankees could find someone I had hidden.

In short, I personally went to the soldier's house. Chávez and I talked about ways to take him to my home, since he was not able to walk because of his dislocated foot. The soldier's son-in-law was a short Portuguese man and Chávez was also short. So, if the two of them were put together they would form a man of normal height. The Portuguese man carried Chávez on his back. Chávez had a Spanish cape wrapped around him and was wearing a top hat which I had provided him with. That is how they got by my "señores Yankees" and by the guards and arrived at my home without being discovered. I had already returned home and had gotten back in bed, but before getting into bed I mentioned that I had gotten a chill from the dampness and needed two more narrow, lightweight blankets so that my bed would feel warmer. The space left without a blanket could be filled with more blankets. I did not tell anybody about my plan and nobody suspected a thing.

While my husband was away, Captain Mariano Silva and his wife, María de la Torre, were living in my home. I told them about the situation with Chávez. When Chávez arrived, he was locked in a room. No one saw him except myself, Captain Silva, and his wife, and my daughter Manuela. She later became the wife of Corporal Sully, and she has since died. After being there for two days, Chávez told me that he wanted someone to bring him a horse so he could go down to Santa Bárbara. I told him that I did not trust anybody, but if he did, he should tell me the person's name. He mentioned Francisco Pico, and Chávez's request was sent to him. Pico responded that he would bring a horse the following day.

There was a full moon and during the night I heard a noise in the little garden. Some sheep I owned had wandered in. I ordered a young Indian girl to go and tell the cook to remove those sheep. She had no more than opened the door when she saw armed soldiers. She immediately closed the door and came to warn me.

Then I spoke to Silva. I told him I believed that the Americans had surrounded my home. And then we heard a knock at the door. I told Silva to go and see what they wanted. I then told my servants that Chávez was hidden in my room because the Americans wanted to kill him. Silva's wife went to get him out of the room. In the meantime, the Indian girls took out the blankets that had been used to fill the opening in my bed. We put Chávez inside that opening, with his face toward the wall so he could breathe easily. And since he was so very thin, the empty space around him was filled with blankets so that it would all look even. We placed my baby, Carolina, on top of the bed. Silva's wife laid down with me on the bed.* There was another bed in my room that my daughter Manuela used. Without saying why, I asked a lady who helped me if she would sleep with my daughter.

I should explain that there were powerful reasons to fear that Chávez would be killed if the Americans caught him. He was accused of being a spy. Although it would be necessary for them to first prove that he was a spy in order to impose the death penalty, the incident in Santa Bárbara with a young man named Ruiz was still fresh in people's minds. Ruiz was one of McKinley's servants and he was taken prisoner along with McKinley. Maddox, the commander of Monterey, asked Ruiz if he had seen any armed Californio troops on the road. Ruiz said no, but Maddox threatened to hang him if he did not tell him the truth. Ruiz kept saying no, that he had not seen any armed Californios on the road. To frighten him, Maddox had Ruiz hoisted up by a rope around his neck. Ruiz fell to the ground, semiconscious. That way of treating people did not inspire confidence, especially when it was carried out by a naval officer, as was the case with Maddox.

Besides, if the troops stationed in Monterey had been the regular, disciplined troops, perhaps there would not have been any reason for so much fear. But the garrison was comprised of people from every class, picked up from here and there, from land and sea. They were almost all adventurers who lacked discipline and a sense of responsibility. These were the people, fifty in number, who came to my home under the command of Lieutenant Baldwin. I had already told the lady who was sleeping with my daughter Manuela to go lie on the bed that Chávez had used so that the Americans would not discover that it was warm.

Silva opened the door and said that he was not the owner of the home and that the lady of the house had retired to her bed. Lieutenant Baldwin

---

*This footnote by Savage appears in the transcript:"Esteban de la Torre, in conversation in Monterey, related this affair in the same terms in his remembrances in 1877."

said that it did not matter to him. They searched all the rooms and left a soldier on guard in each one.

Poor Silva, when he entered the room where Chávez had been hiding (he did not know about the change that was made) and saw the body on the bed, he was flabbergasted.

The lieutenant and his people finally came into my bedroom without uttering a single word. Baldwin had a pistol in one hand and a candle in the other. He searched underneath my bed and did not find a thing. Then he came close to where I was and put the candle and the pistol to my face.* He told me that he had come looking for a man that was said to be hiding in my home. I asked him if he had found him and he said no. I told him that I was very pleased because I never had planned on lying to them. Then he said that he was rather tired and was very sorry that he had come and bothered me. He figured that I was probably somewhat scared and he wanted to grab a chair and sit down. I replied that nothing frightened me and he could go and rest in his own home, because only my family and friends were allowed to rest in my room. He said good night, but we did not respond in kind. The Americans left and Captain Silva accompanied them until they were out the door. Some of those men spoke Spanish.

That search and military occupation of my home lasted from ten o'clock at night until about two or three o'clock in the morning.

Chávez then came out from his hiding place and Silva's wife treated his injured foot. He told me, "Señora, I am alive today because of you." To which I replied, "What I did for you today, I would do for an American tomorrow if you were to unjustly do him harm."

Chávez left my home two days later dressed as a woman. Around the Point of Pines, he got on a horse and then headed for Santa Bárbara.

A. de Ord
Santa Bárbara
April 1, 1878

Partial footnote appears in transcript:"Later, this action made him blush because"

Angustias de la Guerra Ord Journal, 1846–1847

There were many papers that belonged to my mother in my father's writing desk, which was at my Aunt Georgiana's home.

In 1901, when I was headed to Manila with Enrique, Burke Holladay brought the writing desk to me at the Palace Hotel. Inside the desk I found letters that my grandfather had written to my father, which I still have, as well as letters that his brothers who lived in the East had written him. I still have some of those letters.

1.Letters that Don José Puig wrote to my mother. I sent those letters to my brother Santiago Jimeno because they all dealt with the property and the will of his deceased father.

2.A pen that was used to sign the California constitution. My mother had told me about that pen. Those who signed the constitution had given it to her.

3.A letter from Colonel Mason, thanking her for taking care of Lieutenant Minor, who died in her home.

4.Notes about things that happened in Monterey at the beginning of 1846 and during the years 1847 to 1848. Everything is very interesting. I have copied these notes here, just as I found them.

Rebeca

January 6, 1846

Don Guillermo Hartnell was here and again we spoke about Fr. Patricio and what he told the commander of the English ship *Collingwood*. These Englishmen are somewhat like gauchos. They are so cold, but when they begin to warm up they manage to tangle us up. Sometimes I think that Don Quixote has found his way into the core of our being. Either we inherited this quality or it is because we have read the novel with such pleasure. I can see the "ingenious gentleman" right here in my *compadre* Jacinto. At other times, I see him in Pablo and in Abrego! But if we are talking about appearances, my English brother-in-law is the one who looks most like the "knight of the sorrowful face." Poor Don Guillermo. He is such a good man and I am making fun of him.

May 14, 1846

Last night, all of our important friends were here to resume the discussion and see what resulted from the last meeting. Fr. Patricio was also here with us. Admiral Seymour has offered to put the Californios under the

Rebeca Ord, daughter of Angustias de la Guerra and James L. Ord. Courtesy of Special Collections, Georgetown University Library, Washington, D.C.

protection of England. But my brother-in-law Don Guillermo said, "I am English and loyal to my country but not one of you has left here. My children are natives of California and it is very natural for me to want them to have everything that California can give them. Now, if you request the protection of England, you will always be subjects and California will be an overseas colony. But if California belongs to the United States, then everyone will have the same rights and our children will be able to attain the highest positions if they so desire."

"Don Guillermo is right," I said. I was listening to everything along with the others. "I do not know what will happen. Like the blind man says, 'We shall see.'"

July 1846
If the Americans are going to come, let them come, just as long as they send decent people who know how to treat us more reasonably than Frémont did. He arrived wanting to give us orders. He did not even pay attention to

Don Tomás Larkin, who was the American consul. That arrogant Yankee then threatened Don Manuel Castro, who was the *alcalde* of San José at that time. Frémont had the gall to tell Castro that he should thank God they did not rope him with a *reata* and throw him out of American territory. Once the government finds out and they look into the matter regarding the horses, we shall see how things go for him.

Don Alfredo Robinson (my brother-in-law), Don Daniel Hill (Rafaela's husband), Don Tomás Larkin, Don Abel Stearns, and Don Luis Leese, who are all good Yankees, tell us on the sly that we are not going to regret it if we belong to the United States government.

July 20

A messenger has just arrived from Santa Bárbara with the news that "la Pantolla" (María Antonia) has given birth to a little girl. Don Cesario must be so happy! The baby was born on July 5.

The American flag is already flying in Monterey, but how long will that last! We should not be blind to this. Even though they look like rancheros and have rough-hewn hands, they are such good people. We should judge them based on those who came in the past and married native Californio women. When one thinks about everything that has been done by the Americans who came here before, who knows—with time, California may be the envy of the world. Judging by what Don Jorge Seymour said, when the English see us so happy it makes their mouths water, because there is no doubt that they want California.

After Sloat raised the flag, the sailors immediately put up a small building to act as a fort. But their carpenters are just like ours here—they shatter the wood. But what can you expect from some poor sailors?

August 1846

If we could only see what will happen later! If we could have the power to imagine it! With the new government!

Currently, our family owns so much land—and that is just counting the ranchos we have in Santa Bárbara County. San Julián and a portion of Salsipuedes and Jalama belong to my dear father. Zaca, Cuyama number one, and Cuyama number two belong to my sister María Antonia, the wife of Don Cesáreo Lataillade. Los Alamos and Las Flores belong to my brother "Toño" (José Antonio de la Guerra.)

Todos Santos belongs to my sister Teyá (María Teresa de la Guerra), the wife of Don Guillermo Hartnell. Simi and Las Pozas belong to my brother

"Cuchichilo" (Don Francisco de la Guerra) and comprise twenty-two leagues.

El Conejo comprises seven leagues and belongs to my father. He is planning on giving it to my brother Joaquín, when he settles down a bit. He is too young now.

The ranchos in Monterey County and San Luis Obispo County that belong to my siblings are: El Alisal, which belongs to Teyá, the wife of Don Guillermo Hartnell, and El Pájaro, which belongs to my husband, Don Manuel. Because my husband was Mexican, the rancho and the title to it were given to him!

When foreigners married native Californio women, the property was granted to the women, who were Mexican or Spanish.

Los Cosumes in San Luis Obispo County also belongs to Teyá.

September 3

I think what the English are going to like most is that we do not live all crowded together like those poor people do in thousands of towns. Their island is so small that only a small piece of California would fit on it. Of course, the Americans are not in the same boat. They already have half of the world. They will say that California is neither Liverpool nor Boston! How could it be? In the first place, we do not have those large communities of people because there are not that many people here. And we are very happy by ourselves. Second, the communities that form the large towns are centered around industries and factories. They make the products in Boston and we enjoy them here! The other day a box arrived with items from Liverpool. Among the items were some dresses for Teyá. My brother-in-law Don Guillermo gave me a very colorful dress. It was a beautiful Scottish plaid. It looked more like a flock of hummingbirds that had burst into flight than a fabric used by the Scots to make tartans and dress coats. I wore the dress for the first time when I went to a small dance at the Malarín home. When Don David Spence saw me, he came right over to dance with me. Poor Don David became filled with that love that you only feel for your native land. I wonder how the people who come from those big cities feel when they see us scattered about and each person in the possession of leagues of land. But I think that is why we are the way we are. There are those who believe that "the character of the land corresponds to the nature of its inhabitants."

The girls from San Diego
Are like cold atole

The ruffled shoe
And the empty stomach!
Look, you conquerors
At the girls from Santa Bárbara
And you will see that the country's poets
Have depicted them well.
The girls from Santa Bárbara
Are few but pretty
But they are more persistent
Than the souls in Purgatory.

September 17, 1846
Yesterday, September 16, I refused to write, because I am more Spanish than Mexican. Although I am that way, based on the news we receive, I cannot help but feel that we do not know what will happen to the poor flag! This can all be blamed on the distance between the center of government and the inability to get to Mexico quickly! Who can arrive in Mexico in less than a few months' time? Only those who are lucky enough to travel by steamship. But everything has been like that and I am going to be loyal. I will attribute whatever may happen to "Destiny!" And that is such a pretty song. There is so much truth in the verse "I find myself a foreigner in this world!" Ay! Ay! Dear God, just thinking about that song gives me a chill. It is probably because I am pregnant. I am already six months along and will give birth at the beginning of December. Ay! Ay! As the song goes, "With the seal of misfortune!"[19]

September 20, 1846
Ah! What I would not give to be able to think like the last time that I wrote. I have so much. And I can get anything else I want from my cousin Juan Alvarado, who still has so much power. But everything is changing. It is like trying to catch a shadow that keeps moving farther away as it takes our cherished times with it. It must be God's will. I should not be sad. It must be the withering leaves or the lack of fog that makes us sad. But Destiny is not merciless! Things are going to change!

September 28
For days I have been thinking about that nice fellow Duflot de Mofras. Whenever he wanted to be on good terms with me he would tell me that my eyes were like liquid emeralds. But I do not think they are like that. When I look at myself in the mirror (which is made of fine crystal) my eyes

appear to be green like the ocean here in Monterey. This green is darker and not common like bottle glass! To me, my eyes resemble the ocean when it is beginning to grow rough. Poor de Mofras!

October 3, 1846

The autumn storm is about to hit. Now, my eyes will surely look like the ocean waters of October! My body is slender and I am constant in my affections like the waves in the ocean. But there is something tragic about the sadness that I have been feeling. It seems like the sorrowful death of an era!

November 4, 1846

Just a few days ago, people were keeping me entertained with conversation since I am not able to go out very much. I am expecting and do not want to be out dancing the day before giving birth! They told me about my uncle Don Antonio María Lugo's visit to San Francisco and Sonoma. He is my grandmother Tomasa's brother. My uncle went to visit Vallejo, who is the son of his sister María Antonia Lugo. The day after my uncle arrived in Sonoma, Vallejo told him, "Uncle, here are one thousand pesos for your daily expenses." My uncle Antonio María boasted, in typical Lugo fashion, "No, I am not here to beg for alms. José del Carmen has around forty thousand pesos on him, enough for fifteen days." Another day, my uncle Guadalupe Vallejo told my uncle Antonio María Lugo, "I had them saddle up my dappled horse for you." My uncle responded, "I have not come here to tame colts. I have my own dark brown saddle horse that my nephew Anastasio Carrillo gave me." Then they went to a roundup and my uncle Antonio María observed, "Ah, I see you have your little herd of cattle! At the roundup at Agua Caliente in San Bernardino, José del Carmen herded thirty thousand head of cattle!"

If a person were to read this, they would think that this is a tale from the *Thousand and One Nights,* but in his time, my uncle Antonio María Lugo was one of the wealthiest men in California.

November 5, 1846

Yesterday, late in the afternoon, while Teresa, my cousin Josefa de Abrego, and I were seated in the corridor watching the sunset after drinking some chocolate, Fr. Antonio's trusted Indian arrived. He had a letter for me from my brother. What he said was hard to believe because it was such a coincidence. I am going to write it down word for word to see if it comes true:

Santa Bárbara

St. Teresa's feast day

My dearest sister, who deserves my utmost respect and consideration,

I do not know when you will read this letter but I do know that it will be
when you least expect it. Justo has to deliver letters to Mission San Antonio
and perhaps Mission San Miguel, and Mission San Carlos is not far from
there. I am sending you turrón, biznaga candy, and some olives because it is
necessary to lavish attention on women who are expecting.[20] Even though I
have worn the Franciscan habit all these years, I have not forgotten the poems
about the angels who envy the woman who is about to become a mother. I do
not know why, but I have the feeling that you are going to give birth to a
girl. If that turns out to be the case, I ask that you honor the founder of our
order by naming her Carolina or Carlota. Those names derive from the name
of the patron saint of the second mission, San Carlos, which was founded by
the blessed Fr. Junípero. Who knows if [page cut off]

They say that troops have left the port of New York and are headed to
California. And the English fleet is sailing along the coast of Mexico, show-
ing itself off like a peacock! It is possible that we will lose our beautiful Cali-
fornia after such a heroic effort!

"He picked up the pieces of his King's scepter
from the bloody floor
and held a new throne in his strong arms..."

Sister, I cannot write more.

Good-bye,

Antonio Fr. + S.F.[21]

January 1847

I started these notes a year ago. What a difference a year makes! I sit in my
corridor at the hour when the sun is disappearing into the deep sea and the
sky is full of colorful clouds—some are pink like the dresses you see on
girls who are making their entrance at a dance. At other times the clouds
are violet, like a rainbow that is fading away, or dark like the color of iron.
You can hear the cannon blasts from the little American fort! But the beach
at Monterey is brimming with life. Amidst the women who are out for a
stroll wearing their embroidered shawls, you can see the officers in their
uniforms. Some of them are very handsome. There is one officer who looks
like a carrot. To tell the truth, his dark blue uniform looks good on him,
except for the red fringe on his pants and on his shoulders which clashes
with his hair. Another officer, "the handsome one," looks like one of us. He is

very charming and dances divinely. His skin is somewhat dark and he has dark blue eyes. He is very nice. He is tall and slim. It is Don Eduardo! Putting the laughter and dancing aside, we are all ill at ease because we do not know how we, the owners of all of this, will end up! May God be with us!

February 2, 1847
We did go to Mass. When we arrived, we heard that the officers were going to host a dance on the deck of the steamship. All the women were excited and anxious to attend because Lent was approaching and then we would have to do penance. The American officers are very nice. Most of them are ugly, but they do have a certain air about them. Their uniforms are very different from those of the officers on the French corvette *Danaïde* that came here three years ago. That ship brought the charming Duflot de Mofras, among others. When I think about how he tried to woo me, I get a nervous shudder and almost start to get the chills. Fortunately, we had a candlelight procession this morning, because who knows how many love affairs will result from this officers' dance.

February 14
The American flag is here for good. American...but with the way the Americans speak Spanish, especially those two handsome men, we will console ourselves. These are difficult times, and if I dared to write down everything in this diary...but no. This morning, Don Eduardo told me that from time to time I should write down what is happening. What for?! But we have no reason to complain, because the Americans did not come here with cannons blazing. The first people they conquered were the women, and that is why it worked out so beautifully for them. There were lots of unhappy people, including many of my relatives. But they have always wanted to give orders, and it is going poorly for them. That is what is happening now.

February 16, 1847
The dance last night was marvelous! I remember the names of some of the people who were there, but not everybody—Don Eduardo Ord, Don Guillermo Sherman, Don Santiago Ord (the doctor of the dictionary), and Señor Engineer Don Guillermo Halleck. Halleck has very dark skin and beautiful hair. But he has beady black eyes that look like they belong to a rat. I hope he did not eat all the cheese! Minor is also very nice. There was another fellow named Loeser who is quite fond of drink, and he kept a

James L. Ord in 1856, the year he married Angustias de la Guerra. Courtesy of Special Collections, Georgetown University Library, Washington, D.C.

close eye on the wine and *aguardiente*. Although we do not have much contact with him, Loeser is a good dancer.

We were all there together—Teyá, my cousin Josefa de Abrego, Teresita, my daughter Manuelita, and I. After Lent is over, we are going to host a dance for the Americans. The best thing about last night's dance was the trick I played on Colonel Mason. I broke an eggshell on him. It was filled with small pieces of tinsel and it looked like powdered gold! I was carrying two eggshells and since I am left-handed, I had one of them hidden. Don Eduardo took me aside and told me that he could handle a fencing foil with great skill and that it would be impossible for me to break an eggshell on his head. I told him that I was going to break an eggshell on him and he told me to go ahead and try. He then began to defend himself. After I went round and round his head with my right hand and acted like I was going to break the eggshell, he grabbed hold of my hand. Then, with my little left hand, I cracked the eggshell on his head. Ah, ah, what pleasure!

August 21, 1847

This afternoon I received a letter written in English. It was in Sherman's handwriting but was signed by Colonel Don Roberto Mason. The letter was also translated into Spanish and this is what it says:

> *At a meeting of the officers of the U.S. military forces that are stationed here, a resolution was passed that grants me the privilege of sending you this letter. The officers want me to express to you their sincere gratitude for the kindness you showed our dear departed comrade, Lieutenant Coleville J. Minor, as he suffered from his long and fatal illness. He was a foreigner in a strange land but you sought him out and brought him to your home. You took great pains to give him the best of care, both day and night. You attended to his every need with unending generosity. Neither a mother's care nor a sister's attentiveness could have done more than your generous affection.*
>
> *If the most diligent care had been enough to save that young officer, he would still be alive to grace our ranks. The unfortunate news of his death will bring sadness to a wide circle of friends. However, the kindness you showed him will bring them much consolation, and the memory of what you did will remain in our hearts for a long time. When we return to our families and friends, we will tell them about the generous, kind, and virtuous Doña Angustias.*
>
> *With the utmost respect and appreciation, I remain, your faithful servant,*
> *(Signature) R. B. Mason*
> *Governor of California*
> *Señora Doña María de las Angustias de la Guerra y Carrillo de Jimeno*

I have copied the letter here because I do not want it to get lost. One sees so many things that even the saints end up without capes, just like San Martín. I would not be surprised at all if somebody stole this letter from me. Although it pains me to say this, I do not receive the loyalty that I deserve from members of my own family. It is hard to believe that such envy and jealousy can exist in people who were brought forth into this world from the same mother's womb. But for the grace of God! Ah! Ah!

Recuerdos

(Following are further reminiscences of Angustias de la Guerra, dictated to her daughter Rebeca. The first seven paragraphs, presented verbatim here, were written in English.)

Indians

When an Indian maiden wanted to get married, she would come to the Priest house accompanied by an Indian matron, but more generally by an alcalde (chief) who would act as interpreter, and ask the Priest for a husband. I was once at the Mission of Santa Barbara where I witness the following proceedings:— An alcalde came in with an Indian girl and told the priest that the maid wanted to speak a few words with him. "What do you want" said the Priest. "I want to marry such a one" answered the girl. "And does he know that you want to get married to him." continued the Priest; to which the girl answered that he did not know anything about it. Then the Priest ordered the alcalde to summon the man in question to his presence and addressed him saying— "This girl likes you very much and wants you for her husband" The indian remained silent and after looking at the girl from head to foot, said:- "I do not like her" Then the man finding he was needed no longer left and went about his business. Turning towards the disappointed maid the Priest told her to look for another because the one she liked did not care to have her. This happened at every mission when there was an Indian settlement.

Once I went to awaken an Indian Servant; (she and her husband were of the Papuma Tribe who lived in the Island of Santa Cruz. This tribe were very friendly with one another.) On my entering the room I found her lying between two men. "Why are you there between those two men" Then the husband (who was one of them) answered me saying:— "This man is my countryman he came from the Island he has no wife and I lent him mine." This is one of the many proofs that the Indians in their simplicity were faithful to nature's laws.

Native Californians
Their food, their dress and their mode of living
The majority of the Californians lived on very plain but substantial food.

For breakfast the[y] had a kind of gruel made of corn which the[y] called "atole" (the indian name for gruel) and milk. Their dinner and supper consisted of beef generally broiled or stewed; with frijoles and baked pumpkin and tortillas. The beans or frijoles were stewed and eaten with curdled milk made into little rolls;

They did not raise many vegetables. There was no tea except at my father's house, and in case of sickness they would come and ask for some there.

The women's dress consisted of a dress or woolen skirt:— and the dress which was made of calico; they wore no jacket or bodice of any kind. This was the case with everybody excepting four or five families who wore jackets at all. The babies had only a little shirt which they would roll it around their little bodies and then tie in a knot behind to preserve from getting soiled when they were creeping. People had shoes but no stockings, as a general thing, and if they had the[y] would keep them for Sundays when they would dress up with their best garments and stockings and a narrow shawl, to go to church.

When ladies traveled they wore a "Paño de Sol" (Sun Handkerchief) on their heads, this was pinned under the chin and on the back it reached as far as the waist. Everybody wore these but those who had the means had them of linen very fancily embroidered with colored silks and scalloped all around over this Paño they would put their hats. The object of the paño can be readily known from the name, to protect from the sun.

When I was very young the men wore a kind of knee-breeches, buttoned above the knee with three fancy buttons, some men had them made of silver. They tied their breeches with fancy silk or china crape sashes of the width of the material embroidered in bright colors and some with silk other with bullion fringe.[22] The poorer class did not wear such extravagant ones; and although for the same purpose the[y] were narrow ones brought from Mexico ready made. Something resembling striped sash ribbons of now-a-days. Vests were usually of silk or of a species of marseilles cloth. Neckties were of cotton or of linen and generally a handkerchief folded bias would make two neckties; these were trimmed with lace and an orange blossom made out of thread finished off the point.

[The *Recuerdos* continue in Spanish from this point.]

Most people have very small houses. None of the houses had actual floors but the ground was always kept clean. The roof was made of tile or tule. A house consisted of two rooms, one window, and a door. The window was small and placed rather high so that the young girls would not be able to chat with their boyfriends, who were very jealous. The window had wooden bars on it instead of glass. Some of the small houses I saw had doors made of cowhide. The furniture consisted of a table, some benches made from whale bone, and some *cacastles,* which are small boxes made from willow branches.[23] Some houses had one bench. In 1824, the total number of houses in Santa Bárbara, including huts, was no more than forty.

People traveled on horseback and transported their provisions, blankets, and clothing on mules. Whenever we would arrive at a pretty spot, we would take a siesta. If we were far from our own beds, we would light fires to keep the bears away. People would travel with many horses and would send them ahead so they could get fresh horses when needed. If you saw cattle on your journey, you could freely take a calf to have fresh meat to eat, no matter who the animal belonged to. This was not considered stealing. At some point, however, you were expected to let the owner know what you had done. This was how we all shared what we had with one another.

When a traveler would arrive at the missions, which were occupied and managed by the Franciscan friars, the friars would welcome the person like a friend. Travelers could stay at the missions and the friars would provide them with anything they needed. When it was time for the person to leave, the friars would give them a horse and everything they might need for their journey until they arrived at the next mission. There they would receive the same form of hospitality. This was done from mission to mission, from San Diego to San Francisco.

In 1824, the Indians of Missions La Purísima, Santa Inés, and Santa Bárbara revolted. A man named Francisco Bermúdez was able to escape and come and warn my father, who was the commander. My father sent Don Anastasio Carrillo with a squad of fifteen or twenty men to calm things down. There were about three thousand Indians.

In the past, whenever a leader arrived at a mission, he would be received with great formality. The prelate and his assistants would come out carrying processional candlesticks and the bells would ring as a sign of celebration. If they had a cannon, they would fire it in salute.

When I was very young, perhaps about three or four years old, some insurgents came to the coast of California intent on stripping the people of everything they could lay their hands on. They did not achieve their goal because an American named Don Enrique traveled here from the Sandwich Islands to alert my father to what he had learned. It seems that this man had been a guest in my father's home in the past. Because the man was grateful, he came and told my father, "I am your friend and I have come to warn you so that you will be prepared." My father immediately had a message sent to Governor Don Pablo Vicente de Solá, who was living in Monterey, the capital during the Mexican period. My father then ordered all the soldiers' families to leave. As the time approached when the insurgents were supposed to arrive, there were no insurgents in sight, so Governor Solá sent my father a very harsh letter. My parents told me about this letter when I was much older. The letter said, "You believe any story you are told. Without my orders you have no right to tell the families to leave the pueblo. Make them return!"

Two days after that letter arrived, the insurgents arrived in Monterey. After they robbed the families, they burned down the pueblo. They came to Santa Bárbara but found that the soldiers were ready to receive them. Perhaps the insurgents were afraid, because they did not do anything here. They left and landed at the Rancho del Refugio. This was one of the best and most prosperous ranchos in the Santa Bárbara area. It belonged to the Ortega family. At the Rancho del Refugio, the insurgents committed thefts and burned the houses.

During this time, when we were still under Spanish rule, there was a school that was funded by the government. There we learned to read and write and some arithmetic. We would read from a primer or from the catechism.

In 1824, we went to another school that was funded by the government. The teacher's name was Bernardina Alvarez. We were taught the same things at this school. Every day at twelve o'clock, our lunch would be brought to us on a silver serving dish with handles. Since I was a bit mischievous, I would say to the other girls, "Look, girls, this dish will not break no matter how much you throw it down." Then I would throw down the dish and they would see that it did not break like the other dishes. One time at school, I saw the teacher's family eating and I was anxious to try their food. I asked if I could and the teacher responded, "Child, I would give you and your siblings some of our food but you are not used to it and it might harm you to eat this." When I returned home, I told my mother what the teacher had said. My mother replied, "Tell your teacher that you children are just the same as the other children." After that, we always ate some of their food and we would give them some of what was brought to us. The main thing that the teacher's family ate were beans with *cuajada*.[24] I liked this dish so much that years later, when I visited Santa Bárbara, my teacher Bernardina invited me to have a bite to eat at her house and she surprised me with my favorite dish. Francisco, Pablo, and I attended that school and we have reminisced so many times about the happy days that we spent there.

Jefes in Alta California

Don Pablo Vicente de Solá was the last leader under Spanish rule. He was a small man and somewhat of a coward. Don José María Echeandía was a Mexican. He was tall, white, and very well educated. He behaved very well in California. His courage was not tested because there were no revolutions during his tenure.

Don Manuel Victoria was tall, had light-brown skin, and was very brave. During his tenure, the people of Los Angeles revolted and he went there with fifteen or twenty men. Don Romualdo Pacheco was one of those men. As they were approaching Los Angeles, Pacheco saw that they were outnumbered by the opposition and said to Victoria, "Señor, there are many men bearing down on us. We are much fewer in number than they are." The general responded, "Maybe you allow people in skirts to order you around, but I don't." Pacheco then spurred his horse and headed straight into battle, and they immediately killed him. Victoria was mortally wounded and his soldiers took care of him. They took him to San Diego and put him on a ship headed for Mexico. General Victoria wanted to marry me but I did not marry him because he was Mexican and was very anti-Spanish. Ironically, I later ended up marrying a Mexican.

The order to secularize the missions arrived when General José Figueroa was here. This order stripped the friars of their control over the missions and put the missions in the hands of administrators. Some of these administrators were bad and others were good, but most of them did not know how to manage the Indians. The friars treated the Indians as if they were their actual parents.

I got married in 1833, during the time Figueroa was in office. I was seventeen years old. After I got married, I was in Monterey. That is when General Micheltorena came.

When they killed Don Romualdo Pacheco, his wife, Ramona, was at my father's house. That is where Pacheco's son, Romualdo, was born. The year was 1831. I baptized him. Ramona was my cousin and she loved me very much. She was my father's goddaughter. The baby was born in my room. That is the room at my father's house where I would sleep when you were a little girl, Rebeca. Since Pacheco was my godchild, sometimes he would call me "mamá." Several years later, my cousin Ramona married Don Juan Wilson. They had three children—Negra Wilson, Juanito, and Ramoncita.

Left: Ramona Carrillo, a younger sister of Josefa Carrillo, married Romualdo Pacheco, who was killed in the battle of Cahuenga in 1831. Right: Romualdo Pacheco, son of Romualdo Pacheco and Ramona Carrillo, served as governor of California in 1875. Angustias de la Guerra was his godmother. He is pictured with his wife, Mary Catherine McIntire. Both images courtesy of The Bancroft Library, University of California, Berkeley

Pacheco had another brother named Mariano. He married Pancha Ortega, the sister of Manuelita Carrillo and Vicente (el Mudo) Ortega.[25]

My Marriage

When I got married, the ceremony took place at the mission. My father would always host a huge feast for the whole pueblo whenever one of his sons or daughters got married. A long table that extended from one end of the corridor to the other would be set up. That is where the pueblo of Santa Bárbara sat to celebrate the wedding of the commander's daughter. My brother-in-law Fray José Jimeno, who was the Franciscan prelate, hosted this feast, not my father.[26] My father later did the same thing at his home. All of the important people of Santa Bárbara ate in the *sala grande*. The rest of the people ate at tables that were set in the interior patio of the house. Later, some good food would be sent to the prisoners.

In the past, the marriage ceremonies here were different. The couple would join hands at night, in the presence of their *padrinos*. The next day there would be a Mass and a nuptial blessing. During Mass, the bride and groom and their *padrinos* would kneel in the sanctuary while holding a lit candle in their hands. The couple would receive Communion and then the priest would perform the nuptial blessing. After this ceremony, there would be a blessing at the tower, which is on the right side as you enter the

church. My husband and I also served as *padrinos*. The church is still standing and anybody can see the tower.

The food for the fiestas generally consisted of *olla podrida,* roasted pork,
stuffed hens, roasted lamb, and a stew made with lamb chops and wine.[27]
The desserts were sweet pumpkin, rice pudding, and bread pudding. We
also had olives and raisins.

The missions between Santa Bárbara and Monterey were Santa Inés, La
Purísima, San Luis Obispo, San Miguel, San Antonio, and Soledad. Today, in
1881, there are pueblos at almost all of these places.

Marriage

When a poor woman was to get married, her relatives would go with a soldier or with their son to ask the wealthy people to help dress the bride. My
father was the commander of the pueblo of Santa Bárbara for a number of
years. When the command was taken away from him because of Mexico's
independence from Spain, he was still considered a figure of authority.
Even up until recently, there were people who would refer to him as "my
captain" when they would speak about him. For this reason, many poor
people would come to my father's home and would receive courteous
attention from him.

Very early in the morning on the day that a girl was to be married, the
bride and groom's parents would arrive at my father's home. They would
bring "their captain" a gift of small breads and sweets for his breakfast. After
the wedding ceremony in the church, the couple would go and visit my
father and drink chocolate with him. Then they would invite the family to
the wedding banquet.

Soldiers

The soldiers in Santa Bárbara were known as *soldados de cuera* (leatherjacket
soldiers). A *cuera* was a jacket made of two thicknesses of sheepskin which
was used to keep the Indians' arrows from getting through to the soldiers'
bodies. When the soldiers were on horseback, the *cuera* went down as far as
their saddle. They also carried a shield made of rawhide. During the Spanish period, the shields bore the coat of arms of the king. The soldiers' wives
made the buttons for the men's shirts out of thread. Once, when I was
about ten years old, I went to a soldier's house. All the soldiers lived in
what was called the presidio quadrangle. There I saw a man making little
circles out of gourds. I asked him what he was doing and he told me he was
making buttons for his children's clothes. The men had silver buttons on

This picture of a fully outfitted Spanish colonial soldier on the northern frontier of New Spain is from 1803. Most colonial and Mexican soldiers in Alta and Baja California had considerably less equipment. Courtesy of the Ministerio de Educación, Cultura y Deporte. Archivo General de Indias. MP. Uniformes 81. Soldado de Cuera

their pants but they only fastened three of the buttons. The largest button was called the *atracador* because it would hold up everything.

Food and Utensils

People had spoons made from horns and those who could also had forks. They would drink water from gourds or in glasses made from horns, but gourds were normally used. They usually ate beef that was roasted. Cattle were the people's mainstay and supplied them with milk, meat, lard, tallow for candles, *reatas,* horns, bones to obtain lime, and hides. They would exchange hides for clothing and other things they needed that were brought on merchant ships.

The Monjerío for Indian Women

The place where the young, unmarried Indian women lived was called the *monjerío*. The girls were watched over by older women who had high moral qualities. The *monjerío* was a type of convent. The older women were like mothers to the girls. They would take them out for strolls and would teach them how to do things that would be useful to them, such as sewing. The *monjerío* had three different locks with corresponding keys. The prelate of the convent had one key, the *alcalde* had another, and the corporal of the guard had the third key. That way it was impossible to enter the *monjerío* without the consent of all three people. Whenever the girls needed anything, they would pull on a rope that would ring a bell in the Father's room. When the young Indian girls wanted to get married, they would ask the Father for a husband and then would leave the *monjerío*.

Entertainment

On certain days there would be a general celebration for everybody. The feast day of Santa Bárbara was the most important. The celebration would begin with a sung Mass. Then the Indians would set up what looked like little houses filled with good things to eat. After Mass, the Father would visit the Indians at these little houses. As he passed by, somebody would play a musical instrument and then they would toss out chestnuts, pine nuts, and *islay* (a fruit like coffee).[28] Indians from San Buenaventura, Las Cieneguitas, and Santa Inés would be invited to come. They would arrive dancing and the Indians would toss grains of corn, chestnuts, and other seeds at them.

Sometimes an Indian man would perform the snake dance at fiestas. In this dance, he would call out to the snake and try to make it come close to him. The furious snake would do it, but if it attacked, the Indian would not get hurt because he had put something on his body to counteract the venom from the bite. To keep the snake within a specific area, they would place pieces of cactus around to form a little corral.

Harvests

When the Indians finished their work for the Fathers, they would ask permission to go and gather pine nuts, chestnuts, *islay, cacomites* (it has a root like an onion but tastes like a potato), and other things.[29] They would gather this food and save it for the winter.

Land Titles

My husband was the government secretary and for a time he held the position of provisional governor of Alta California. Before the government headquarters were built, a room in my house served as an office. The archives were kept there. Actually, all important papers that needed to be saved were kept at my house. We also had stamped paper that was used for documents, etc. Petitions for the granting of ranchos were made on stamped paper. The petition would be presented and then the commander general would write on the petition, "Have the secretary look into this." Since the secretary had access to the archives, he knew if there would be any problem in granting title to the land. The commander general would determine whether to grant the title, based on the information provided by the secretary. The paper used for the land titles was called "first seal" and was worth eight pesos. The commander general would sign blank sheets of this stamped paper and it would be kept in the office at my home. After the taking of California by the Americans, there were still things in my house that belonged to the government. I found two pieces of "first seal" stamped paper among the items. I gave one sheet to Don Andrés Pico, the brother of Pío Pico, who was the last governor of California during the Mexican period. I gave the other sheet to Don James Forbes. Don Andrés Pico chose the land he wanted and he was granted title to that land on the stamped paper. Señor Forbes was granted title to land that had previously belonged to him, land that he had asked the government to exchange for other land. Since I believed that everything would eventually be lost, I told them, "I am going to give these to you, because in the end the Moor will take what the Christian took."

The Arrival of the French before the Taking by the Americans, 1842
While I was at my sister's Rancho Alisal, I received a letter from my husband telling me that the French corvette *Danaïde* had arrived with a number of French gentlemen who had come on a pleasure trip. These gentlemen wanted to go to a rancho to see cattle. They arrived at Alisal and the next day a rodeo was put on for them.

We all went on horseback to see the cattle. They were a bit afraid to get too close, but my sister and I went over to the cattle so the men could see that there was no danger. They wanted to see how a bull was roped. I then approached a very brave Californio and told him what a certain gentleman wanted to see. The Californio then picked up a *reata,* lassoed the bull, and threw it down. He got off his horse and tied up the bull. The French gentlemen admitted how quickly and skillfully this was done. One of the men took out a pencil and paper and made a sketch of what he had seen.

After the employees arrived in Monterey, a dance was held. Dances and picnics in the country were the main diversions. Everyone was dressed elegantly; that is, with a frock coat, etc. We, the women, were all dressed up for the dance. De Mofras was among the employees. He was the illegitimate son of Luis Felipe. At the present time, de Mofras was a member of the French delegation in Mexico. It so happened that an American warship was in the port of Monterey at this time. The ship was commanded by Commodore Jones. An invitation to the dance was extended to the officers of the ship. Everyone was already at the dance when the commodore

Thomas O. Larkin and his wife, Rachel Hobson Holmes Larkin. Courtesy of the California History Room, California State Library, Sacramento, California

appeared, wearing short pants and a jacket. He was not the least bit charming and his outfit did not fit him properly. He strolled around the room, looking for a woman to his liking to dance with him. None of us wanted to be the chosen one. We finally saw that his taste in women was the wife of the American consul, Thomas O. Larkin. She was the only American woman at the dance. They wanted to waltz, but they were not very successful. Even though they practically had the dance floor all to themselves, they decided that it would be better if they sat down, because neither one of them knew how to dance.

Contraband

When my brother was the customs administrator, he lived at my house. A friend of mine named Gaspar Oreña had gone to Lima, Peru, on a merchant ship. When he returned, he brought back three trunks with very elegant goods to sell. Oreña was poor. He wanted to take the trunks off the ship without having to pay duty. He therefore came to me and said, "Doña Angustias, I am in a bind. I have brought back some goods and if I could just take them off the ship without having to pay customs duty, I would earn quite a bit of money. But I am afraid of the administrator because he keeps such a close watch on everything." We formulated a plan. Oreña and I went to the beach because my house is close by. Shortly after, he told me,

The Monterey Customs House. Courtesy of the California History Room, California State Library, Sacramento, California

"Señora, I am sorry to leave you here, but I have to board ship." I responded, "It does not matter. One of the guards will walk me back home." The guards were four decent young men. Then I said to the guards, "Why don't you four come with me to my house for some tea. I had some tasty tortillas made for this afternoon." They were afraid that the administrator would come, so we had a little Indian girl be our lookout. She was to tell us if my brother was coming. Some of the men were still afraid and I told them that they were cowards. I said this to see if I could hurt their self-respect. They decided to come with me. As soon as Gaspar Oreña saw that I had managed to take the guards with me, he unloaded his trunks at a spot called La Playita. This is the place where the Spaniards landed the first time they were in Monterey, and it is the spot where the friars placed their cross. As soon as I arrived, I sent out a servant, who had prepared a small *carreta* ahead of time to bring the trunks to the house. When he came back, the only thing he was supposed to say to me was "Señora, I am already back." He was supposed to enter through a back door while I entertained the guards. After tea, I kept talking so much to the guards that they did not have a chance to say "let's go." When the servant arrived, I was no longer interested in detaining the guards. They could leave when they wanted to. I thought it best to put the trunks under my bed. Oreña sold everything for a good price and even Pablo, the customs administrator, bought some goods.

Eggshells

As many people know, at a certain time of the year, many countries celebrate "carnaval" with different types of games, usually a day or two before Ash Wednesday. This is the time when the women would have dances and break *"cascarones."Cascarones* are whole eggshells that have been cleaned out by means of a tiny opening at one end. The eggshell is normally filled with tinsel or colored paper and silver paper that has been cut into very fine pieces, almost like dust. A certain colonel was at one of these dances. He had distinguished himself by his skill in removing arrows from his body from fighting the Indians. I found out about this from the American officers and I set out to see if I could break an eggshell on him. This colonel never went to dances because he did not know how to dance. However, he attended this dance because it was held on February 22, Washington's birthday. The dance was hosted by the American officers. All of us women went to this dance. It was the first time that we attended a dance after discovering that Mexico had sold California. We now considered ourselves American citizens.

My husband was away from Monterey and I attended the dance with an American lieutenant who lately has distinguished himself greatly. His name was Sherman. After arriving and dancing with my companion, I danced

Monterey, California, *1849, by Alfred Sully. Sully came to Monterey in 1848 with U.S. army forces. In 1850 he married Manuela Jimeno, the oldest daughter of Angustias de la Guerra and Manuel Jimeno. Manuela Jimeno Sully died in 1851 from complications arising from the birth of the couple's first child. Courtesy of the Thomas Gilcrease Institute of American History and Art, Tulsa, Oklahoma*

Angustias de la Guerra with two unidentified young men. Courtesy of The Bancroft Library, University of California, Berkeley

with another lieutenant, by the name of Ord. The Señoras all were carrying many eggshells but I only had one that was specially filled with small one-peso coins and gold and silver sequins. While I was dancing with Lieutenant Ord, I saw Colonel R. B. Mason and was surprised, yet at the same time I assumed that he had come because it was February 22, 1847.

I asked my companion to take me over to the colonel so I could break an eggshell on him. After I greeted Mason, I told him what I was planning on doing. I said that I knew he was very brave and that he had defended himself from the Indians, etc.

Then I told him, "Let's see if you are capable of defending yourself from me." He was very tall, so I naturally asked him to sit down. "I have here an eggshell that I can break on you. Where would you like me to break it?" He smiled jokingly and responded, full of pride, "on my forehead" and pointed to it with his finger. I moved closer to him and threatened him three times. The last time I said, "Defend yourself!" I pretended that this was my last try and I started to bring my arm down toward his arm and showed him the egg I had in my right hand. He raised his arm quite a bit to resist my effort, but I stuck my left hand underneath his arm and broke the eggshell where he had said to do it. I am left-handed and can use both hands equally well. I told him, "You were able to escape from the Indians but not from a clever woman!" While we were engaged in this "conflict," everyone drew closer to see who would triumph. There was much applause. My pride had been satisfied. Many of the people who were in attendance, such as Halleck, Sully, Sherman, Ord, and Mason, would later be important figures in the United States.

Spanish Generosity and American Stinginess
Ajuria and Don Eduardo
One time, when a Spaniard named Don Gregorio Ajuria was in my living room engaged in conversation, he had something in his pocket that appeared to be bothering him. He stuck his hand in his pocket and pulled out two pieces of gold. He gave them to my daughter Carolina to play with. Shortly after, I went into the dining room and found my American friend Don Eduardo Ord weighing gold on a small scale. Every time he emptied the scale he would clean it so that none of the precious gold dust would be left behind. When it was time to eat, I told the two of them and several other friends that I had seen an interesting contrast in the morning. On the one hand, we see a Spaniard throwing gold around because it is bothering him, and on the other hand we have a Yankee who cleans the plate on his scale with the same care that a priest cleans the paten.

I would let all friends and decent people eat at my house because of friendship. At that time, it was not customary to charge for anything. People were very hospitable and that did not change until they were reduced to poverty. They would freely give to anybody. There were times when I would spend five hundred pesos in one week, especially during the gold rush, because everything was so expensive then.

Angustias de la Guerra,
dictated to her daughter
Rebeca

Angustias de la Guerra and her daughter Rebeca Ord in 1885. Courtesy of Special Collections, Georgetown University Library, Washington, D.C.

These are the recollections my mother related to me in the house in Mission Canyon where we used to live. The house was later bought by Mr. George Steward and [illegible], who still live there. I started to write some things in English. However, I found that I was not able to portray things exactly as she said them. Since I wanted to give an accurate account, I wrote down her words exactly as she said them to me.

Rebeca R. Ord-Peshine
December 31, 1880
Santa Bárbara, California
Foster Cottage—Mission Canyon

María Inocenta Pico

INTRODUCTION

*T*he last woman to be interviewed by the Bancroft staff was María Inocenta Pico. When Savage sat down to interview her in April 1878, he was facing a woman whose family dramatically embodied the difficulty and fragility of frontier life in Alta California. Both her parents, José Dolores Pico and María Isabel Ascención Cota, had personally experienced the losses that characterized family life in that corner of the Spanish empire.

Her father's first marriage was to María Gertrudis Amezquita, in June 1791. This was María Gertrudis's second marriage. She had first married José Antonio Altamirano in 1787, but he died less than two years later. The daughter that she had with him, three months old at the time of José Antonio's death, died just a few weeks later. María Gertrudis died in 1800. María Isabel Ascención Cota had been married once before, to José Manuel Féliz in 1798.[1] She and José Dolores Pico were married in 1801.

María Inocenta Pico, like many of the women in this volume, was connected to the founding events of Alta California. Her paternal grandparents, Felipe Santiago de la Cruz Pico and María Jacinta de la Bastida, were on the second Anza expedition, along with her father, who was six years old at the time. We have already met her husband's maternal grandfather, Juan Ismerio Osuna, a veteran of the Portolá expedition. He was Felipa Osuna's paternal grandfather.[2]

María Inocenta Pico's parents, José Dolores Pico and María Isabel Ascención Cota, were married at Mission Santa Bárbara in 1801. María Inocenta, the fourth of ten children, was born in 1810. By that time, her father had

MARÍA INOCENTA PICO

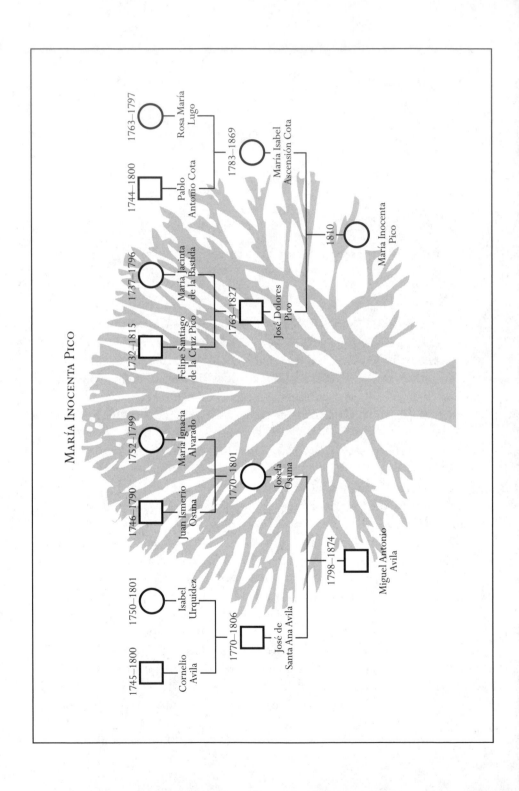

1745–1800
Cornelio
Avila

1750–1801
Isabel
Urquidez

1746–1790
Juan Ismerio
Osuna

1752–1799
María Ignacia
Alvarado

1732–1815
Felipe Santiago
de la Cruz Pico

1737–1796
María Jacinta
de la Bastida

1744–1800
Pablo
Antonio Cota

1763–1797
Rosa María
Lugo

1770–1806
José de
Santa Ana Avila

1770–1801
Josefa
Osuna

1763–1827
José Dolores
Pico

1783–1869
María Isabel
Ascensión Cota

1798–1874
Miguel Antonio
Avila

1810
María Inocenta
Pico

been transferred to Monterey after periods of service at a number of places, including Santa Bárbara and Santa Cruz. In 1826 she married Miguel Avila, a soldier of the presidio company there.[3]

Miguel Avila was born to José de Santa Ana Avila and Josefa Osuna in 1798. His family also had its share of early deaths. His mother's first husband, José Gabriel Espinosa, died very shortly after their wedding. Miguel Avila was sent to San Francisco and later to Monterey for schooling, and served for a time as a copyist there. His service in the military took him to San Luis Obispo as a member of the mission guard. He had a very stormy relationship with the resident priest, Father Luis Antonio Martínez. After a series of confrontations in 1824, he was reassigned to Monterey. He and María Inocenta Pico were married there in 1826. She had ten children, at least two of whom died before they reached the age of six.[4]

Miguel Avila received a grant of the San Miguelito rancho, along the coast south of San Luis Obispo, in 1839. He built an adobe house about a mile inland from the shore, near the mouth of San Luis Creek. He also constructed two pens for cattle, one near the house and the other near the coast, where he also built a rough shelter for the vaqueros who tended the cattle. He had about five hundred head of cattle on the rancho and he may have been one of the first Californios to engage in systematic dairy operations. He became a man of some local renown and he served as *alcalde* at San Luis Obispo in 1849.[5]

Like many Californios, Avila struggled to protect his lands from the newly arrived Americans. In the late 1850s, he wrote a series of letters requesting the assistance of Pablo de la Guerra, who was serving in the state legislature, because the town of San Luis Obispo and some of its leading citizens were trying to seize parts of his rancho.

His ranching operations suffered from a drought in the early 1860s, and he and the family sold some parcels of land near the beach to local settlers. This area became the nucleus of the present town of Avila Beach.[6]

Miguel Avila died in 1874. His body was discovered near a creek on his rancho where he had gone to bathe. The local paper chided him for not assimilating more into the new order of things: "He was a man of more than ordinary education in his own language, but failed to acquaint himself with the language or the ideas of the race which succeeded his own in the occupation of the country." María Inocenta Pico continued to live at the rancho and in town. Two years after she talked with Savage, she was recorded in the 1880 census as residing with two of her children.[7]

Savage began the interview by asking María Inocenta Pico about her husband and his family. That led her into a description of her husband's involvement in the revolts against two governors, Nicolás Gutiérrez in 1836 and Manuel Micheltorena in 1844 and 1845. Both narratives evolved into tales in which the dangers her husband faced drew María Inocenta Pico herself into active participation.

She spent most of her time discussing the movement against Gutiérrez. She attributed her husband's involvement to a personal dispute between him and Captain Juan Antonio Muñoz over the alleged contamination of the town's well by Manuela Cruz, Muñoz's wife, and two other women, including Prudencia Amesti, the sister of Mariano Guadalupe Vallejo. María Inocenta Pico's description of her role in outfitting the rebel force and in urging on its soldiers provides an inside look at the process by which many of the forces that marched through California in the mid-1830s and mid-1840s were equipped. Her narrative offers a glance at a side of California's military operations which rarely made its way into the official reports.

Savage then asked her the standard questions about specific episodes in California's past. María Inocenta Pico provided a vivid account of the 1818 evacuation of Monterey from the perspective of a young and frightened child. She also remembered details about the type of education—both secular and religious—given to girls. In the course of discussing secularization, she offered some astute observations on the rivalries that existed between the administrators of the former missions and the families who were seeking to set themselves up as rancheros. Her remarks on the Solís revolt of 1829 and on the movement against Governor Victoria in 1831 combined personal reminiscences with the sadness and loss her extended family experienced over the death of her husband's uncle. In sum, her testimonio provided a unique perspective, demonstrating how the public events that rocked Mexican California affected—and were affected by—one woman and her family.

Things about California as told to Thomas Savage in Avila and San Luis Obispo by Doña María Inocenta Pico, widow of Don Miguel Avila, 1878, Bancroft Library

Doña María Inocenta Pico is the widow of Don Miguel Avila. She is also the owner and resident of a fine rancho that consists of about eight hundred acres. The rancho is located nine and one-half miles from San Luis Obispo, along the coast. The train from San Luis to Port Harford passes in front of the rancho. Doña María Inocenta is sixty-seven years old. She is a very active and intelligent woman. She appears to be blessed with a very good memory and good judgment when it comes to managing her large family and her considerable amount of property. Her father, Sergeant José Dolores Pico, served as a soldier for many years. In addition, he gave California many children, some of whom took part in the events which are part of California's history before the United States occupation. One of the children, Antonio María Pico, later held a number of important posts.

Upon the recommendation of her brother Captain Don José de Jesús Pico, this señora kindly gave the Bancroft Library the only documents that have remained from the vast collection her husband had compiled. The majority of the documents were destroyed by fire. She personally destroyed other documents so that the families of various people who had been cast in a bad light in these documents would not suffer negative consequences.

She also was kind enough to dictate to me a few pages of personal recollections both at her rancho and in San Luis Obispo. They appear as follows.

Thos. Savage
San Luis Obispo
April 19, 1878

DON MIGUEL AVILA WAS BORN on February 9, 1796, in Santa Bárbara. His father was Santa Ana Avila, a native of Sinaloa, and his mother was Josefa Osuna. His father had a number of brothers in California: Francisco, Antonio Ignacio, José María, Bruno, and Anastasio. None of these men were ever soldiers yet they all lived quite comfortably in Los Angeles.

Don Antonio Ignacio Avila was the father of Don Juan Avila of San Juan Capistrano. Don Antonio was a very useful man in California. Don Juan was recognized for his public service, his noble qualities, and his honesty.

José María Avila was the man who killed officer Don Romualdo Pacheco in battle. He wounded Commander General Don Manuel Victoria and others, but died in the skirmish.

In San Francisco my husband, Miguel Avila, learned how to read and write from an artilleryman named José Antonio Peña. He also learned some principles of arithmetic. He was in San Francisco for twelve years. When their father died, Miguel and his brothers were placed in the care of their uncle and godfather, Francisco Avila. He was the person who sent Miguel to San Francisco to be educated. He paid for his room and board and other expenses.

When Don Francisco finally believed that Miguel was capable of helping him with his business affairs, he sent for him to do bookkeeping. He soon discovered that Miguel was lacking considerable preparation in the area of accounting. So he sent him to Monterey to learn whatever they could teach him there. He was taken on at the office of Don Manuel Gómez, who was the commander of the artillery company. But instead of allowing him to continue his education, they forced him to become a soldier in the leather-jacket company. I believe he joined in 1816 and obtained his discharge in 1827. In 1826, I was between fifteen and sixteen years old and we were already married.

After his discharge, my husband stayed in Monterey as a businessman, buying and selling at his store. He was also constantly busy at the government offices.

The fruits of our marriage were eight sons and seven daughters. Five of the children have died.

When he was the *síndico* and treasurer of the community funds of Monterey, he found himself in serious danger of losing his life. This was due to the hostility of Captain Antonio Muñoz and the despotism of the interim commander general, Lieutenant Colonel Nicolás Gutiérrez.

The actions Gutiérrez leveled against Miguel forced him to throw himself headlong into the revolt led by Juan Bautista Alvarado, José Castro, my brother José de Jesús Pico, and others. I will speak in more detail about those circumstances later. At the onset of the revolt, Governor Alvarado appointed my husband *alférez* of the civil artillery militia.*

---

*The following footnote appears in the interview:"I cannot forget to mention something unusual about my husband's commission to the rank of alférez back then. It was issued on December 12, 1836, by Alvarado in his role as 'Governor of the Free and Sovereign State of California.' California had only been independent of Mexico for a few days. A seal of the Mexican Republic was stamped on the paper but it had not been franked."

When the revolts and wars in California ended, Avila spent time on his business dealings and also at his rancho. Avila found himself in grave danger again, as I will now explain.

When General Micheltorena was in command, he sent Captain Don Juan Cooper to Mazatlán to bring back funds that were supposed to have been collected there for the maintenance of the California troops. There was talk that those funds should be taken off ship at the bay in San Luis Obispo. Don José Mariano Bonilla informed Micheltorena that Avila and others had formulated a plan to get hold of those funds and use them for the current revolt against the general. An officer and thirty armed men arrived at Avila's rancho (San Miguelito) at about twelve a.m. to take him to San Luis Obispo. They took Avila to where Micheltorena and his troops were located. At that time, Micheltorena and his men were in pursuit of the rebel forces. Until they arrived at Santa Inés, Avila was in constant danger of being killed by those men. At least that is what they led me to believe. And as you can well imagine, I was in a terrible state of anguish. Be that as it may, it seemed certain that they were going to execute my husband at the place called El Pismo, which is a league and a half from Rancho San Miguelito. I had no other recourse than to reconcile with the general. I have to say that he did listen to my pleas and I was able to appease him.

I have already mentioned that they took Avila away at midnight. At dawn, I had someone go and find out what was happening. A man named Araujo sent word to me in a letter that nothing had been resolved and that my husband would be judged at El Pismo.

I then quickly had a wide variety of provisions put together for the general and his officers. These included chickens, mutton, cakes, cheese enchiladas, good wine, whiskey, and more. Everything was arranged in an elegant fashion with fine napkins, etc., and sent off on two mules that were loaded down. I also separately sent supplies for my husband. The general wrote me a letter and sent it back to me with the same man who had transported the provisions. He told me not to fear for my husband. He would send him back to me from Santa Inés. In light of this, I decided to continue supplying the general with provisions until they reached Santa Inés. Micheltorena kept his word. He set my husband free at Santa Inés and returned all the horses they had taken from us. However, all the horses came back without ears or tails, but this did not matter to me at all. My husband was free and they had not indicted him. On the contrary, they treated him very well. The general thanked me for the provisions and said they had made good use of them. Because of those provisions, beginning at

El Pismo, my husband was no longer watched over by a guard and was allowed to billet with the officers. It is true that there was no reason for the arrest. Bonilla's accusation was false and he was very embarrassed when he saw my husband come back.

My husband did not take part in the war against Micheltorena. When the United States occupied the country, he did take part in that war of occupation when it began. My husband participated in the battle of La Natividad (1846) and carried out his duty with courage and vigor. Avila was a strong man with much character. At the same time, he also cherished freedom and public education (as do I) and he was a preserver of documents. Unfortunately, the great majority of these documents have been destroyed.

After this country was turned over to the United States, my husband regarded himself as a citizen of that republic. He tried (as far as his influence could extend) to get his Californio countrymen to take advantage of the benefits the new regime offered for progress.

In 1849, my husband was first *alcalde* of San Luis Obispo. General Riley, who at that time was the military governor of California, appointed him *juez de primera instancia* of that district. He held that post for some time. Later, because of his ailments and advanced age, he refused to let anything interfere with his private life.

Avila was very partial to taking very long, cold baths. He would do this for hours at a time. He never gave up this habit, not even in his last years, no matter how much he was advised to do so. On February 22, 1874 (when he was more than seventy-seven years old), he went to bathe in the river. While he was getting dressed, he died by the edge of the pool of water where he had been bathing. It seems that his body got too cold. His half-dressed body was found about nine hours later. Avila was buried in the San Luis Obispo cemetery on February 25.

In 1836 Avila was the *síndico* of Monterey. One time when he was passing through the Cañada del Blanco, he saw three women bathing in the well from which the pueblo took its water. They had filled the well with soap. They were the wives of Artillery Captain Muñoz, Don Teodoro González, and Amesti (his wife was Doña Prudencia Vallejo). Avila reprimanded the women for what they had done and they took offense. Captain Muñoz urged them to go before the judge and start legal proceedings against Avila and they did. After a few days, once the formalities of the case had been carried out, the complaint was dismissed. Captain Don Antonio Muñoz (an extremely despotic man) then appealed to Commander General Don Nicolás Gutiérrez, the military authority, to avenge the offense he believed had been committed against his wife. Because my husband was a member of the militia, Gutiérrez said that he fell under his jurisdiction. He had him arrested and put in a jail cell in the guard house, incommunicado. They then began to draw up a military indictment against him. It was raining heavily and barely fifteen days had gone by since I had given birth to a girl (Josefa). But as soon as I found out about my husband's arrest, I had my brother-in-law Louis Pombert take me to the government headquarters that same afternoon. My brother-in-law is the man who later became sergeant of the company of foreign riflemen led by Graham. At the government headquarters, I spoke with Don José Castro about the matter. He held some important political post.

First, I should point out that when they arrested my husband, I sent my brother Francisco Pico to see Don Salvador Espinosa. He was the judge of Monterey. Espinosa was at his rancho in the Salinas Valley, located right before you get to the Cañada de San Miguel. I figured that it would take my brother a long time to return, so I sent off another letter with a Mexican named Barretes.[8]

The *ayuntamiento* of Monterey immediately convened. Together with the pueblo, they began to take steps to release my husband from jail, by force if necessary. The revolt against Gutiérrez was triggered a few days after the arrest, which was one of the main reasons for the revolt.

During this time, Don Juan Bautista Alvarado, the first *vocal* of the assembly, had already left Monterey. Alvarado had been accused of putting up a satirical poster against the commander general, who had insulted Alvarado and possibly threatened him. Alvarado was somewhere around the ranchos near San José.

Returning to my topic, when I appeared before Castro, he told me to go and see Señor Gutiérrez to find out if he could arrange to have my husband set free without further legal proceedings. The following morning, I went to see Gutiérrez, accompanied by my little four-year-old boy, Francisco. I was on friendly terms with Gutiérrez because he had visited my home a number of times. Señor Gutiérrez asked me if I preferred to have them shoot my husband five times or have him exiled to Guadalajara for many years. I do not remember the number of years of exile but it was many. I was seething as I listened to such vicious remarks. I responded that if he thought it was fair, then he should shoot my husband five times, because there probably would be justice on earth as surely as there was justice in Heaven. I was determined that he would not see one bit of cowardice in me.

From there I returned to José Castro's office. I told him what had happened to me with Gutiérrez. I then went to the commander general's office to deal with him about my situation. While I was there, the *alguacil* of the *ayuntamiento,* Antonio Lara, arrived with an official letter for the commander general demanding the release of my husband because he was a *síndico* and treasurer. Castro grabbed that letter and stuck it in his pocket before Gutiérrez could see it. He was afraid that Gutiérrez would fly into a rage because of the *ayuntamiento*'s demand, in which they also made threats against him. And then he would issue some violent order that would have to be carried out against my husband. Castro was right about that. We found out later that the guard had orders to shoot my husband right there in his cell, without further legal proceedings or considerations, if the pueblo tried to take him out of jail.

Shortly after Castro returned to his office, Captain Muñoz came there to see me. He took my son in his arms and told him, "As soon as you arrive at your house, you will find your father free because you are his liberator." I do not know if those were the exact words he used, but that was their meaning. The truth of the matter was that Muñoz and his superior saw that the pueblo was determined to set my husband free and they were afraid that their acts of violence could have negative consequences. I returned to my home and found my husband free.

But the *ayuntamiento* remained in permanent session, with the pueblo armed and ready to defend itself. The commander general did not have enough military might to ride out the threatening storm. That group of people was very upset that pleas were successful in obtaining Avila's freedom, because they had wanted to force the commander general to turn him over.

After that event, Don José Castro went to San Juan, the place where his father, José Tiburcio Castro, was living. The younger Castro used to go there for periods of time and would trust me to take care of his home and his other belongings while he was away. When he was in Monterey, he would eat at my home, because there were no hotels or public lodging houses during those times. Castro, Alvarado, and the Vallejo family were my relatives and were all regular visitors to my home when they were in Monterey.

In the beginning of November, a few days after my husband's release, the revolt against Gutiérrez broke out. One morning, at daybreak, a throng of inhabitants from Monterey and from points north surrounded the plaza because there were troops at the *castillo* and at the presidio. The

Mission San Juan Bautista. Courtesy of the California History Room, California State Library, Sacramento, California

inhabitants' commanders were José Castro and Juan B. Alvarado. I was naturally furious because of Gutiérrez's despicable behavior against my husband, so I sent word to José Castro and offered him gunpowder, saddles, and other supplies for the campaign. In fact, I sent him everything I had: about twenty saddles, twelve flasks of gunpowder, fifteen saddle horses, ropes, many bottles of *aguardiente*, provisions, etc. Everything was sent to *La Huerta Vieja*.

Gutiérrez found out from my Indian cook that I had sent those shipments to the rebels, or at least that is what he assumed. My cook was taken prisoner after the lookouts in the church tower saw people on horseback leaving my home. Gutiérrez ordered that if the plaza was attacked, my home was to be riddled with gunfire, since it was right in front of the *castillo.* I was terrified, so they moved me and my whole family to Doña Hilaria Buelna's home. They did not attack my house, because the rebels were one step ahead of them and had seized the *castillo* and soon after that the presidio. Gutiérrez then surrendered with his minion Captain Muñoz, the rest of the officers, and the few troops.

Castro and Alvarado entered triumphantly. I was very satisfied with that outcome, since I had contributed greatly with my resources, my influence, and even with my own hard work. Many times my hands were the ones that put the bridles on the horses. And many of those bridles were made with pieces of my clotheslines.

The presidio of Monterey (1826–1827), by Richard Brydges Beechey. Courtesy of The Bancroft Library, University of California, Berkeley

Gutiérrez and various officers such as Muñoz, Navarrete, Nicanor Estrada, and others were later shipped off to Mexico. Some other officers and government employees who disapproved of what was done, such as District Judge Don Luis del Castillo Negrete and Captain Zamorano, also left.

On the day our people were prepared to attack the plaza, close to twenty-five men passed by my house about a half hour before the surrender of the plaza. I called out to them and gave each of them a glass of *aguardiente* to warm their hearts and blood so they would not give up. I urged them to enter bravely into battle, knowing that some might die.

My husband had gone off to Los Pilarcitos. I, however, was determined that the villain Gutiérrez should be punished for repaying us so cruelly for the courtesies that my husband and everyone else at my home had extended to him.

Whenever Don José Castro (my daughter Josefa's godfather) would remember the things I did to help make the revolt a success, he would laugh so hard. Truthfully, I did not do much. However, the revolt did free us from people who wanted to treat us more despotically than what we had ever experienced during the absolute rule of the Spanish governors. That Gutiérrez was a Spaniard by birth and an immoral man who set a dreadful example. But since he was the highest official, we had to tolerate him, until he became totally insufferable.

After the government had been partially established with Alvarado at its head, he and Castro headed south with all the troops. They left my brother,

José de Jesús Pico, as commander of Monterey, but he had no troops whatsoever to support him.

A number of inhabitants from Mexico, including some convicts from Guadalajara for whom Monterey was their jail, took advantage of that situation and recaptured the *castillo* and the plaza in July or August 1837. They believed that the Mexicans, who were scattered at the ranchos and whom the surgeon Manuel Alva had gone to win over, would run to their aid. But they were disappointed, because nobody came. At the time of the counter-revolt, Commander José de Jesús Pico was away from the capital. As soon as he found out what had happened from the communications that I and others had sent him, he began to muster forces to go and reclaim the plaza.

When Monterey was seized by the Mexicans that first afternoon, all or at least some of the Mexicans sent for the Californio families' Indian cooks. The relatives of these Indians were with Alvarado and Castro. The Mexicans promised to give the Indian cooks whatever was looted from their masters' homes. My house was the first one to be sacked that night. Several others were robbed as well.

Peregrino, our Indian cook, was a very big man and had served me faithfully for eight years. He was incited by them to commit outrages against us. He grabbed my husband's pointed, crowned officer's hat, which he had never worn, and put it on. He strapped a sabre to his waist, dragged it along the floor, and came out shouting, "Long live Mexico! Death to Alvarado!" He was looking for money, so he tore up all the books he found in the house, knocked down the candlesticks, took the clothing out of the trunks, and turned over the mattresses. He, along with seven others who came into my house, believed that we had money hidden somewhere.

While the looting was going on that night, my brother Francisco arrived in Monterey on horseback, along with Isidro Villa and several others. They came to my house first. Peregrino tried to pull my brother down from his horse. Francisco, who was lame, had his crutch with him and used it to strike Peregrino and knock him down. My brother's companions used their lariats to lasso some of the other Indians. They threw them all out of the house. The Indians were badly beaten and half dead. Later, I personally treated a number of the wounded as well as those who had been beaten. They were ignorant people and not as guilty as the villains who had incited them to commit those bad acts.

The following morning, my brother returned with José María Villavicencio, some Californio troops, and Graham and his riflemen. They quickly retook the *castillo* and the plaza.

My husband had left for Santa Bárbara with Señor Alvarado and Castro. When we received the news in Monterey that Santa Bárbara had pronounced in favor of the revolt, we, the women who supported the cause, went as a group to the *castillo*. There we made preparations to celebrate that event and appointed Plácida our commander. She was the wife of *Alférez* Lázaro Piña, who had gone to Santa Bárbara with Alvarado and the others. Men who were experts in handling artillery were appointed to help. After everything was ready, there was a twenty-one-gun salute.

ON NOVEMBER 22, 1818, early in the morning, two large, armed ships arrived. I was at my great-aunt Doña María Antonia Lugo's house at the time. I was born on January 8, 1811, so I was about seven years old when this happened. My great-aunt was the wife of Sergeant Don Ignacio Vallejo. Before the ships anchored, they began to bombard the *castillo*. There was so much fear and confusion that nobody really knew what they were doing. Even mothers lost their children. Some of the children were not found until two or three days later. The families were in such a hurry to leave Monterey that by six or seven o'clock that same morning they already had gotten as far as the Salinas River. I was one of the missing children. I did not know how I had become separated from my aunt, but fortunately I spotted Doña Trinidad Soto, my mother's *comadre,* and I accompanied her to Mission San Antonio. After much searching, my family finally found me four days later. To give you an idea of the confusion, the families were so scattered about and distressed that it took many men on horseback to bring them all together. They also had to find out if any people were still missing or had stayed behind in Monterey.

Once there was enough light, from Buenavista we could see the huge cloud of smoke from the presidio fire. The enemy, who were insurgents from the revolutionary provinces of Buenos Aires, had all come ashore. They looted the presidio and then set it on fire. Our troops had retreated to the Rancho de la Nación with Governor Solá. My father was the administrator, or person in charge, of the rancho. From there, they went to San Antonio.

As soon as the families saw the cloud of smoke, they began to walk more slowly, until they arrived at Mission Soledad. They prepared *carretas* and supplies there. We stayed at San Antonio until the beginning of April. After that, the families began to leave, each heading to their own destination. The entire Vallejo family, as well as the García and Soto families, joined my mother at the Rancho de la Nación. There were many other families, but I

Top: Mission San Antonio in 1875. Courtesy of the California Historical Society, FN-36288.
Bottom: Mission Soledad. Courtesy of the California History Room, California State Library,
Sacramento, California

do not remember their names. They all stayed at the ranch house, which
was very large. There were other houses at the rancho and they occupied
them, too.

The reason I was in Monterey with my aunt was so I could go to school.
Doña María Antonia Buelna was the teacher who taught the girls, and Corporal Miguel Archuleta was the teacher who taught the boys.

There was a custom in Monterey on Sundays. As soon as Mass was
over, the Father would sit down on the governor's bench in church and
ask the girls questions about what he had preached. He wanted to see if
we had understood him. Then, nuts, figs, raisins, hazelnuts, and other
things would be handed out to all the girls. The girls who demonstrated

This 1836 school book was composed by José Mariano Romero, who came to California with the Híjar-Padrés party in 1834 and taught school in Monterey. Courtesy of the Seaver Center for Western History Research, Natural History Museum of Los Angeles County, Los Angeles, California

that they had learned the most were the ones appointed to hand out the treats. The whole time that Rosalía Vallejo and I were in school, we were chosen to hand out the treats. We both studied very hard so that we could win prizes.

At school, they taught us how to read and write and also the four rules of arithmetic with whole numbers. Many girls did not complete even those basic subjects because their mothers would take them out of school, almost always to marry them off. The bad custom existed of marrying off very young girls whenever men asked for their hand. I was in school only until the age of fourteen, which is when my mother took me to the rancho to show me how to work. I got married when I was fifteen years and eight months old.

In 1822 we were living in Monterey. We attended the grand fiestas to celebrate the changing of the flag. I remember the tremendous emotion expressed by the Spaniards, especially by the missionary Fathers, because of that event. The Fathers never adjusted to the change, and soon a number of them began to collect funds to leave the country. It was said that at that time, Don José de la Guerra y Noriega was the *síndico* for the missionaries and managed their treasury. He held this position for many years.

I saw *Canónigo* Don Agustín Fernández de San Vicente at the home of Don Mariano Estrada. They had prepared a grand banquet for him. He was an obese man of average height with rosy-colored skin. I do not remember anything about his age. He brought quite an entourage with him. Everyone was very eager to meet a man of such great importance. A *canónigo* had never been seen in California before, and least of all a person who had so much power, as he seemed to have, to direct the fate of the country.

I also remember that around that time a very rich man arrived. Everyone called him the *Intendente*.

At the feasts to celebrate the changing of the flag, there were salvos, processions, mock battles, an oath to support independence, parties, dances, bullfights, and other activities that lasted for three days or more.

Solá continued on as governor until the *junta territorial* elected him delegate to the Mexican parliament. He was ill for a few months and stayed at my mother's house on the rancho. He was quite taken by the way the Californios had welcomed independence. Solá left for Mexico at the end of 1822 or the beginning of 1823. Don Luis Antonio Argüello, captain of the San Francisco garrison, was selected by the officers and members of the *junta territorial* to succeed Solá as acting governor. Luis Antonio Argüello was the son of Don José Darío Argüello, who was also acting governor of Alta California before Solá became governor. Don José later held the office of governor in Baja California.

Don Luis Argüello was dearly loved in Monterey and in all of California. The *diputación* preferred Argüello over Don José de la Guerra because, even though Captain Guerra had seniority, he was a Spaniard.

I remember when the Spanish ship *Asia* entered Monterey in 1825 and surrendered. There were many sailors and soldiers aboard that ship. I saw the men a number of times when they came ashore. They behaved very well. Some of them would take horses and go out into the countryside. But since they were not horseback riders, the horses would throw them off. Those men would spew forth horrible, blasphemous language against God. This was something that we were not used to in California. The ship was sent to Acapulco under the command of Don Juan Malarín, but several crew members remained in California. At the present time, there are three families here in San Luis Obispo who are descendants of those men. A few years later, in 1840, 1841, and 1842, one of the men, Don Vicente Cané, became the administrator of San Luis Obispo.

The administrators of the missions had authority over the Indians and managed the temporal interests of the mission they had been assigned to. In 1840, when I was traveling from Monterey to San Luis Obispo, I passed by four missions. Don Salvador Espinosa was in charge of Soledad. My brother Don Jesús Pico was in charge of San Antonio. Inocente García was the only one in charge of San Miguel from the time of secularization until there were no longer any Indians or material assets left at the mission.

García was the one who did away with everything. My husband told García many times that his bad management of Mission San Miguel as well as his looting of the assets for his own personal gain had destroyed the mission. My family and I spent three days resting at Mission San Miguel and I was able to see the disorder that reigned.

The fourth mission that I am referring to is San Luis Obispo. When I arrived there, Juan Pablo Ayala was the administrator. Shortly after, he turned it over to Don Vicente Cané. He, too, used up the mission's material assets. He took goods and other possessions from the mission to establish his own rancho. Cané was the person who tore down the mission buildings. He took everything that could be salvaged, such as beams, roof tiles, furniture, and even droves of oxen, to his rancho.

When my husband and I went to establish Rancho San Miguelito we took an order from Governor Alvarado to the administrators of Missions San Miguel and San Luis. They were supposed to provide us with Indians, plows, oxen, and other resources for our work. We would, of course, pay a fair price for them. We were unable to obtain assistance from the administrators for more than two or three months because they considered themselves the all-powerful owners of the missions and would do whatever they pleased.

In 1825 Captain Argüello was relieved of command by Lieutenant Colonel of Engineers Don José María Echeandía. He arrived with the title *Jefe Político y Comandante*. I knew him well in Monterey. He was tall, slim, well-mannered, very refined, and friendly. He was very fond of dances and other amusements. He quickly returned to San Diego and established his residence there.

During Señor Echeandía's administration, there were two military revolts. The first was motivated by nothing more than that the troops were not being treated as they should be. The second revolt definitely could have caused a general uproar in the country, even leading to the expulsion of the governor.

The soldiers were only given rice and dried meat. They called this "eating Moorish style." My *compadre* Pablo Véjar told me one day, "Let's lock up all the officers and make them eat Moorish style and see how they like it." They arrested the officers and gave them the same food that the soldiers had to eat. The entire company abandoned the presidio and took their weapons with them. They stayed away for quite some time. I do not know who persuaded them to return. They lined up in formation in front of my house because I had always helped them with whatever I had. Don Romualdo Pacheco came to the house to urge them to return to their posts. He promised them better treatment from that point on.

Señor Pacheco was eloquent and chose his words very carefully. My husband then told the soldiers they should heed Señor Pacheco's good advice and take into consideration the eloquent and courteous manner in which it had been offered. All the soldiers were armed and reluctant to enter Monterey. After more than an hour and a half of urging on the part of Pacheco and my husband (who had been recently discharged that same year, 1828), the soldiers were persuaded to return. The soldiers showed their respect for Pacheco and followed him. He led the group, marching with his sword unsheathed, and entered the plaza. My house was located about three hundred *varas* to the east of the presidio gate, so I was able to see them enter. Véjar was the principal ringleader of that revolt because he was a rebellious and brave man. My brother José de Jesús, who was a boy at that time and had been a soldier for only about a year, saw himself caught up in that revolt.

An order then came from the commander general to arrest the leaders and those men most closely involved. Others were arrested and held at the presidio, and charges were brought against them. They were held under arrest for about a year. During that time, they were threatened with death: one out of five or ten men would be selected to die by luck of the draw. However, I believe that was said merely to intimidate them.

The following year, 1829, there was a very serious uprising. All the officers in Monterey were arrested and the rebels seized everything. The rebels were in league with the soldiers from all the companies at the other presidios. They appointed Don Joaquín Solís as their leader. Solís was a convict and a very crude man. He was big and fat. It was said that former *Subcomisario* Don José María Herrera had formulated the plan. I do not remember the circumstances surrounding that revolt very well because I was sick at the time. I only know that the revolt failed and charges were brought against the leaders. They were sent back to Tepic to be tried. They were accused of planning to raise the Spanish flag again in California. There was information indicating that they had conspired with a number of Spaniards. Among these Spaniards were some missionary Fathers. Father Luis Martínez of San Luis Obispo was named, in particular. It is true that the rebels were aided by missionary Fathers at several missions, but I do not believe that the idea ever crossed the minds of the soldiers or the missionaries to reestablish Spanish control. That is how it was viewed in Mexico. The accused were neither returned to California nor was any punishment meted out to them in Mexico. Instead, they were forced to continue serving as soldiers. Only two or three of the men sent to Mexico returned.

In November 1831, Don José María Avila came from Los Angeles and stopped at my house in Monterey. The reason he came was to lodge a complaint with *Jefe Político* Don Manuel Victoria. Charges had been brought against Avila by a Señor Nieto as a result of a swordfight between the two of them. Nieto was severely wounded on his head. In the ensuing trial against Avila, Victoria sentenced him to pay a fine of two thousand pesos. He was also exiled to San Francisco to work on public projects. At that time, San Francisco was a desert. Avila went to appeal the sentence or at least try to get the sentence of exile commuted to a monetary punishment, since he was a rich man. He told us why he stopped at our home: his appeal had been denied. He was very sad and did not leave the house during the three days he stayed with us. He then said that he would be returning to Los Angeles because he would rather die than go and work on public projects at the San Francisco presidio. He somewhat insinuated that he was going to start a revolt as soon as he arrived in Los Angeles.[9]

A few days later, when word was received that a revolt in the south had broken out, Señor Victoria very quickly prepared to march south. Since my husband and I had a stockpile of supplies ready, that same day Victoria sent one of his officers to ask us to prepare provisions for him so he could leave at dawn. The provisions were prepared that night, and Señor Victoria left before daybreak with a squad of fifteen or twenty men. Later we received news about Victoria's clash with the rebels from the south and that he was badly wounded. We also learned of the deaths of José María Avila and Don Romualdo Pacheco, and other events that occurred until the time Victoria was shipped off to Mexico.

Avila's death was a source of great sorrow throughout California and most especially for his family. My husband was his nephew, and Avila highly respected both of us. He always treated us with great affection. He would give us wine and other fruits of the vine as gifts.

During his tenure, Señor Victoria was a veritable despot. He had three men shot in Monterey and had another man shot in San Francisco. The men in Monterey had committed petty thefts. One of them, a young Indian boy who could not have been more than seventeen years old, stole some buttons from the government warehouse. The people of Monterey were terribly anxious, because nobody knew how far Victoria would take his predilection for killing. There were other people who had provoked the ire of Victoria for various reasons. They all lived in danger as long as he remained there. He had no friends, received no invitations, and did not attend fiestas like the other *jefes* who had preceded him. However, he did take good care of the troops. Surely he did this to keep them on his side.

(Señora Avila promised to return to add some more recollections, but one must assume that the fulfillment of her religious obligations as well as her physical ailments prevented her from doing so. So as not to linger further, this work comes to a close today.)

San Luis Obispo
April 19, 1878

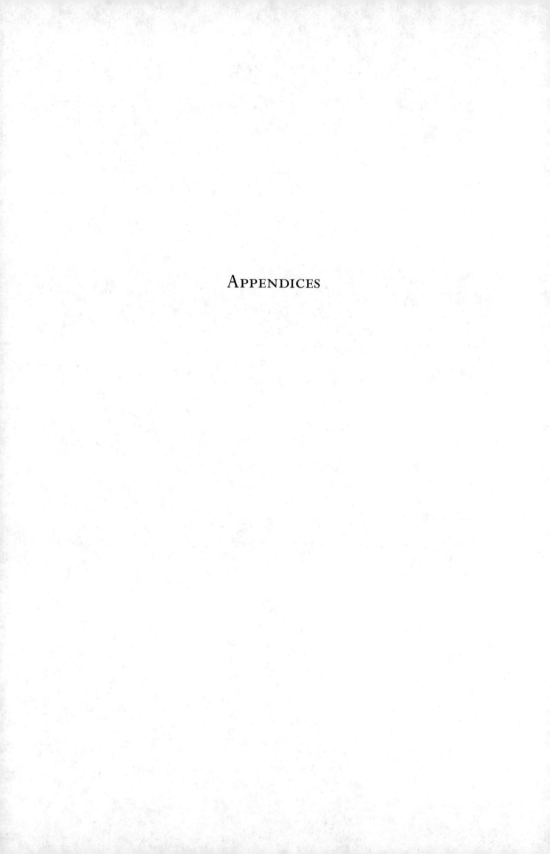

APPENDICES

Excerpts from "Ramblings in California" by Henry Cerruti

After I had been writing for Mr. Bancroft for the space of four months I received from General M. G. Vallejo, the potentate of Lachryma Montis, an invitation to visit Sonoma and write the history of California from the year 1813 to 1849. As a matter of course I did not delay the preparations for my voyage, and the next day I embarked on the steamer *Antelope* bound for Lakeville. While on the steamer my attention was called to a party of native Californians who, grouped in a corner not far distant from the bar room of the steamer, were quietly engaged discussing the topics of the day. On seeing so many natives of the country whose history I had been deputed to write, I did not hesitate to approach the abovementioned individuals, and,

Guillermo Fitch, son of Josefa Carrillo and Henry Fitch. He became the first Californio interviewed in connection with the Bancroft history project when Cerruti spoke to him in March 1874. Courtesy of the Sonoma County Library, Santa Rosa Central Branch, Santa Rosa, California

having saluted them in true California style, gave them an invitation to come to the bar and help me to break the then projected local option law. "Will a duck swim?" is an ancient saying; a true one in all probability, but not truer than the California proverb "Drink today and die tomorrow." Acting on this my newly acquired acquaintances, six in number, duly answered to their names at the call of the dispenser of rot-gut.

After they had swallowed their allotted share I begged of them to supply me with information as to the ancient times of California, and Mr. Guillermo Fitch and Blas Piña, both intelligent persons, endowed with a good dose of common sense, came forward and volunteered to dictate a few pages. The narrative of these gentlemen I considered interesting, and I assure you I felt sorry that the arrival of the *Antelope* at Lakeville should have deprived me of the pleasure of continuing noting down events which up to date have never been given to the public....

[*Cerrutti reaches Vallejo's home and has his first conversation with him. We pick up the narrative at the very end of that conversation.*]

...Moreover, I added that I had made the trip to Sonoma by request of Mr. Bancroft, who had directed me to obtain, either by purchase or in any other manner, as many original documents referring to California's early days as I could lay my hands upon. I likewise stated that it was part of my duty to interview every old settler living in the country. The term "old settlers" included every white man who had settled in California prior to 1850, and every native Californian upwards of sixty years of age...

After sleeping four hours I awoke refreshed in mind and body, and having performed my ablutions I went downstairs for the purpose of surveying the town of Sonoma. But ere I had walked three steps I met a portly man who, leaning on a stout cane, came slowly along dragging with evident pain his wounded limbs. I judged him to be a native Californian upwards of sixty years of age, and therefore I said to him, *"Hermosa manaña, caballero."* He answered, *"De veras, el día es hermoso."*

Having thus become acquainted, I moved to adjourn to the Union Hotel for the purpose of having a friendly chat, and both together retraced our steps toward the house of my friend Oettl, who in a twinkle placed before us a bottle of white wine and a couple of glasses. For the wine he charged one dollar, a very moderate price indeed if we stop to consider that white wine is to be had in Sonoma at forty cents a gallon, and even at that low price is a drug on the market. While discussing the merits of the innocent beverage that made Father Noah dizzy, I ascertained that my newly acquired friend was Major Salvador Vallejo, a citizen of California, born in Monterey in 1814. The Major, like a true son of Mars, soon became talkative and in less than one hour had related the principal events of his chequered life.

It was indeed amusing to listen to his narrative of bygone days, and he narrated many an adventure of Indian and backwoods life. He told me how fortune had frowned upon him, how his countless acres of good land had passed into strange hands, how rascally were the bankers, lawyers, and judges who from 1847 to 1853 ruled California, and of how the Cunninghams, Duanes, Mulligans, and Estells stuffed the ballot boxes. In fact he narrated so many strange things that interested me to such a degree that when we parted I begged the pleasure of his company at breakfast on the following day. I do not hesitate to say that though that morning we had met as strangers, when we bid adieu to each other we were sworn friends. It is my belief that between soldiers exists a species of masonry that, though unseen in the outward intercourse of everyday life, is felt inwardly and sends through the body an electric sensation that sets every feeling in motion. How to account for it is beyond my limited intelligence, and, therefore, I shall leave it to wiser heads to solve the mystery....

About eleven o'clock I repaired to the sitting room, where I wrote in an intelligible shape the items I had obtained from Messrs. Piña and Fitch while on board the *Antelope*. I had hardly written six pages when two gentlemen entered my improvised sanctum for the purpose of examining some charts. Their presence did not interfere with my writings, so I kept on scribbling until one of the two said, "When in 1849 I was keeper of the county jail of Marysville..." Having heard that much, I knew that I then stood in the presence of a pioneer, so without a formal introduction I made known to him the object of my visit to Sonoma and requested that he would place me in possession of every remarkable event that had transpired in California since his arrival. Mr. Vooster, for such was the name of the gentleman I had addressed, made some excuses and in a firm but polite manner declined the honor of being the narrator of an embryo history. He, however, gave me a formal introduction to his younger companion, who proved to be Captain McLaughlin, an officer of the United States Army and a good Indian fighter, who had long lived on the borders of California, Arizona, and New Mexico while in command of a troop of cavalry. The captain proved to be a fine fellow, full of fun, sociable, and bred to good manners....

[Cerrutti describes various activities around Sonoma, including interviews with a few of the men he met. We pick up the account as he describes a visit to Vallejo's house on the next day.]

...The General was engaged in conversation with a lively little woman about forty-five years of age, who, on being made aware of the mission which Mr. Bancroft had entrusted to me, volunteered to dictate a few items of her experiences in California. Of course I accepted the offer and took from her sweet lips the following narrative:

"My name is Sinforiana Cárdenas. I was born in 1830 in the town of Hermosillo, State of Sonora. I left Mazatlán on the 12th day of August, 1850, and reached San Francisco on the 8th day of October the same year. On landing I perceived only a few houses, for that unhappy city had been reduced to ashes a few days previously. I landed from the Mexican vessel which brought me to California in company with a family called Ayunse, which was composed of father, mother, two boys, ten girls, and a cousin of theirs called Guadalupe Muñoz. We remained one day in San Francisco, and on the following afternoon we took passage on a steamer bound to Stockton. The wind was fair, the sea was smooth and everything seemed favorable, but shortly after we left Benicia one of the boilers of the steamer blew up and left us at the mercy of the winds and waves. The captain, however, after taking care of the maimed and wounded, rigged a jury mast and by skillfully handling his disabled steamer succeeded in bringing her to an anchor close by Benicia.

"That fine town that is now celebrated for its colleges and many other things was then only a miserable farm house surrounded by four or five small shanties tenanted by Negroes and Indians. Our captain managed, however, to rig a temporary sleeping place by sending on shore tarpaulins, worn-out sails, and a good number of blankets; provisions were also sent us from the steamer. In this manner we spent the night and a good part of the following day, when to our relief and joy the opposition steamer hove in sight and, having been transferred to her, we landed safely in Stockton at midnight of the same day.

"We removed to the Hotel de México, where by good luck we obtained lodgings, and the next day we went in search of a house sufficiently commodious to accommodate our party. But though we inquired of everybody we came across to point out a good large house that could be rented, we obtained only negative answers, for though Stockton was then a flourishing California town, with gardens properly delineated, any number of dance houses, gambling saloons, and a theater, it did not contain one single pri-

Mariano Guadalupe Vallejo and family members at Sonoma. Courtesy of the California Historical Society, FN-30504

vate dwelling large enough to accommodate a numerous family. The buildings were mostly made of wood, furniture was then very scarce, servants could not be had for either love or money, and the ladies if inclined to sport white petticoats had to do their own washing. The Chinese, who a few years afterward like the locusts of Egypt invaded our state, had not yet settled among us. This scarcity of workingmen and house servants compelled the rich to work in spite of their wealth.

"To tell the truth, in those days California did not contain a single poor man or woman, for the mines produced immensely. The mining implements could easily be purchased on credit, provisions though quoted at a very high price were also sold on long terms, and I believe that I am not exaggerating when I make the assertion that in 1850 every inhabitant of California was rich. After a couple of days of vain search Mr. Ayunse resolved to build a house for his own use, and I, who during two days had already received four offers of marriage, consented to marry Mr. Fowler, then a good-looking young man full of bright prospects and a good share of cash. Shortly after I had been united in the bonds of matrimony to Mr. Fowler I removed to Sonoma county, where we purchased a farm and engaged extensively in the raising of grapes. This speculation paid but very poorly, my husband lost his sight and his senses, and today I find myself surrounded by fourteen children, a demented husband, and only by hard work can I make both ends meet. However, I have full faith in Providence, and I abstain from repining against the fate decreed me." After completing her narrative Madame Fowler bid adieu to General Vallejo, bowed politely to me and, having entered her carriage, was soon out of sight.

On finding myself tete-a-tete with General Vallejo, I suggested the propriety of his dictating something having reference to the early days of California. He did not object and forthwith proceeded to describe the funeral ceremonies which took place in the Mission of Soledad when, in 1814, Governor Arrillaga was buried. The General can, when so inclined, dictate very fluently, but it often happens that, when he is engaged in the description of some important event, some person steps in to crave favors and thereby causes the General to lose the thread of his narrative. During the first morning I spent at Lachryma Montis, four boys came in begging oranges for their sick relatives. Of course, General Vallejo sent every one of the little beggars to the garden with a strict injunction to gather the fruit without spoiling the trees. How far the request was obeyed I cannot tell, because I was writing in the front part of the house, and the orange grove is situated in an opposite direction.

Having transferred to paper about four pages of dictation, I broached to General Vallejo the propriety of supplying me with documents which I could copy at night in my sanctum. The reply I received was rather discouraging, and it showed plainly that he had no desire to allow his documents to go out of his hands. However, after a while I convinced him of the propriety of doing something to conciliate the goodwill of Mr. Bancroft, and, perceiving that I could not be put off with a negative answer, he at last consented to allow me to take to the hotel a small bundle of "doc" which happened to be at hand. Having only folded the papers loaned me to copy, I proceeded to the dining room, where a good repast was spread on the table.

The conversation during the meal was quite spirited and occasionally enlivened by some witty repartee of Madame Vallejo who, whenever a favorable opportunity presented itself, would fire a full broadside at the Bear Flag crowd, to whom, either justly or unjustly, she attributes the loss of a great part of her husband's estate. However, one thing is certain—the worthy trappers who in an unlucky moment hoisted the dreaded emblem of the bear on the plaza of Sonoma were not overnice when in need of any article to be had in the house of the next-door neighbor. They made but little difference between *meum* and *tuum,* and that such was the case is proven in many official documents and in the official correspondence addressed in the month of June, 1846, by Pío Pico, Governor of California, to Thomas O. Larkin, Esquire. Madame Vallejo described the greater number of the party as rough and uncouth, dressed like Spanish banditti, wearing caps

Four generations of Vallejo women. Right: Francisca Benicia Carrillo, wife of Mariano Guadalupe Vallejo. Left: Francisca Carrillo's daughter Epifania Vallejo Frisbie. Top: Epifania Frisbie's daughter Fannie Frisbie Sequeira. Bottom: Fannie Sequeira's daughter Juanita Sequeira. Courtesy of The Bancroft Library, University of California, Berkeley

made with coyote and wolf skins, and the greater part wearing buckskin pants that reached only to the knee. But leaving dress aside, I have no hesitation in saying that the description of the Bear Flag party as given by Madame Vallejo is in perfect consonance with truth and veracity.

After dinner I repaired to the room of my friend, Major Salvador Vallejo, who sleeps in a kind of room that no pen can accurately describe with any probability of making a true and reliable description. The Major's room can be called a library because it contains a good many books, but again I cannot call it a library because libraries are supposed to contain only books, while the Major's room contains weapons, modern and ancient, carpenter's implements, watchmaker's tools, blacksmith's hammers, a sleeping couch, and half a dozen demijohns always filled with good Sonoma wine. By the bye, I have forgotten to mention the famous tin cup in which the gallant Major serves out the delicious nectar to his visitors, many of whom have expressed wonder that "mine host" should not have at hand a glass. I told the Major that everybody expressed surprise at being made to drink wine out of a worn-out tin cup, and the answer I received is the following:

"About thirty-nine years ago I left Sonoma at the head of a body of troops for the purpose of capturing the noted Indian murderer, Zampay, and, while traveling, the horse that packed my rough earthenware fell down a precipice. Of course he got killed and his load was forever lost to me. When suppertime arrived we had plenty of fresh meat—deer meat and ducks. We roasted it, and after sprinkling a little salt over it we ate it, but feeling thirsty and having nothing at hand that could hold water, I cursed my ill luck and of course my officers and soldiers were not slow in following my example. In this emergency my orderly, Manuel Cantua, came toward me holding in his hand the identical tin pan in which I serve wine to my visitors. I assure you that if a vision from Heaven had vouchsafed me eternal years of eternal bliss I would not have felt happier. I incontinently snatched it from his hand, dipped it in a brook running close by, then I passed it round to officers and men, and, when everybody had imbibed satisfactorily, I fastened the blessed cup around the holster of my pistol, used it throughout the campaign, and on my return to Sonoma hung it over the chimney corner of my dwelling. I have preserved it till now, and I hope that the blessed cup will be buried with me in my coffin."

[We pick up the narrative a few days later, after Cerrutti has just finished interviewing David Burris, who had arrived in California in 1849.]
…After Mr. Burris had bid me adieu I went to the residence of Major Salvador Vallejo, who was so condescending as to accompany me to the hut where dwelt Isidora, Princess of Solano. The Princess is fully five feet ten inches tall and is rather stout. She has sunken eyes, small hands and feet, and long, slightly gray hair, and though verging on ninety years of age she is very nimble. On being introduced to her I did my best to engage her in conversation, but to no purpose. She was rather shy, and had it not been that Major Vallejo assured her that I was one of her people, an innate enemy of the Bostons—Princess Solano calls the natives of North America "Bostons"—she would to all certainty have refused to answer my questions. But having received from the Major an insight into the business on which I was bent, she laid aside her fears and accepted a drink from the bottle of brandy I had brought with me. Her History, as related by herself, may be seen in the book called *Dictation by Pioneers.*

When we were about to depart, the Princess Solano went to her sleeping room and presently came forth holding in her hand a bag containing several strings of beads made out of bones and shells, a belt about six inches wide made from the same material and many other articles of adornment worn by Indian women in ancient days. She assured me that those things constituted the whole of her wedding dress. I offered to purchase the whole and laid a ten-dollar gold piece on the table, but she laughed at me and felt indignant at my presumption. Nothing daunted, I offered her another drink and begged her to introduce me to her son who happened to be in the courtyard cleaning fish. She called Bill—the name of the young prince—and he came forward. I had the opportunity of conversing with him, and I found him an intelligent man about thirty years of age, well learned in the art of reading and writing, tolerably well versed in the mysteries of the Catholic Church, of which he is a constant attendant, strongly in favor of local option, and always ready to censure his mother, who is a decided worshipper of Bacchus. Bill has a few thousand dollars deposited in the San Francisco banks, but being very fond of his aged mother, he prefers to remain by her and watch over her in her old age. He greatly deprecates the drunken habits of the Princess, but is powerless in effecting a reform.

When Bill returned to his fish-cleaning business I offered the Princess another drink and again broached the subject of selling me her wedding dress. I offered her twenty-four dollars and the rest of the brandy contained in the bottle. She accepted my offer, and I thus became the happy possessor of a sacred relic of days gone by. Having paid the cash and noted in my portfolio the story of the Princess, I retraced my steps toward the residence of Salvador Vallejo, thanked him for having been so condescending with me, and then went home, where I wrote down in an intelligible style the record of my interview with Isidora and her son.

[In June Cerrutti takes a trip to San Francisco and then to San José.]
...A few days after my arrival in San Francisco I visited San José, well supplied with letters of introduction from General Vallejo. My first steps on reaching that city were directed toward the Bernal farm, where dwelt an aged gentleman who goes by the name of Francisco Peralta but whose real name I could not ascertain. I gave him a letter of introduction from General Vallejo; he read it three or four times, and then went to a drawer and from among some rags pulled out a splendid English translation of the voyages of Father Font. He took off the dust from the manuscript and handed it to me. I looked at it a few moments for the purpose of making sure that I held the right document, then unbuttoned my overcoat, and placed the diary in my bosom. "What are you doing, my friend?" shouted Peralta. I replied, "I am putting the document in a safe place. I have to travel tonight and am afraid the evening dew may get it damp." He looked astonished and then said, "I will not allow you to take it away. General Vallejo requested that I should allow you to copy it. That I am willing to do, but as to giving you my Font, that is out of the question." As I had brought along with me a bottle of the best brandy, I called for a corkscrew and a couple of glasses,

and, having lighted a cigar, I presented my companion with a real Havana. He accepted it, and we were soon engaged in conversation.

[Peralta offers Cerrutti a series of reflections on San José history.]
...I then tried to induce Mr. Peralta to give me a few details about himself, but to no purpose. I kept on filling his glass till the bottle was emptied; but I gained nothing by the trick, because every time he toasted he drank the health of General Vallejo, and of course I could not conveniently refuse to keep him company. The clock of the farmhouse having struck two, I bid adieu to Mr. Peralta, unfastened my horse that had remained tied to a post for five hours, and returned to San José. Of course I brought along with me the venerable "Father Font."

I have heard that Peralta a few days later wrote to General Vallejo a letter in which he said that I had stolen the manuscript from him. He wrote a falsehood, well knowing it to be such at the time he wrote. To speak plainly I will observe that the person, who like Mr. Peralta goes under an assumed name, is not much to be trusted. His secret, however, is known to General Vallejo, and should I be allowed to live long enough I will surely discover it because I have a peculiar way of acquiring knowledge of things and persons—things which I ought to know—and surely no person will gainsay my right to know everything that is to be known about the social position of my defamer....

Mission Santa Clara in 1849, *by Andrew P. Hill. Courtesy of the Santa Clara University Archives*

...On my return to San José...I allowed myself two hours of rest, after which I dressed for the day and took the cars that run between San José and Santa Clara with the object of visiting the great college located in the charming valley of that name.

With reverential awe, cast-down eyes, and studied demeanor of meekness I entered the edifice of learning. As soon as the gate closed behind me, I took off my hat and addressed the porter, whom I requested to send my card to the Reverend Father Director. Having said that much, I entered the parlor, opened a prayer book that happened to be at hand, and began to read the *miserere mei Deus secundum magnam misericordiam tuam*. These lines recalled to my mind many gloomy thoughts, for the last time I had sung these solemn sentences was at the funeral of President Melgarejo, the man who had been to me a second father.

But I was not allowed much time for reflection, because presently a tall priest of pleasing countenance entered the parlor, beckoned me to a chair, and in a voice that reflected kindness and goodwill begged me to explain the object which had procured for him the pleasure of my visit. I then announced myself as the representative of the great historian, H. Bancroft, and notified him that my object in visiting the college was for the purpose of having a fair view of the library and of examining the manuscripts it contained. I likewise assured him that, though the history was not written by a member of the Church of Rome, yet in it nothing derogatory to the Catholic Faith would be found. I added, however, that the bigoted priests who had destroyed the Aztecs' paintings, monuments, and hieroglyphics, which ought to have been preserved for the benefit of posterity, would be censured in due form, and their grave sin against science commented upon with the severity required. He reflected a moment and then said, "I see no reason why I should object to having the truth made known. History is the light of truth and when an impartial writer undertakes to write the history of a country, we must not conceal a single fact of public interest." After saying this he left the room. In about two minutes he returned, accompanied by the priest who had charge of the college library. He introduced his subordinate to me and then added, "Father Jacobo will be happy to place at your disposal every book and manuscript we possess."

The Father Superior having retired, I engaged in conversation with the librarian, who forthwith proceeded to the library. There I perceived many thousands of books arranged upon shelves, but found only few manuscripts. Among the manuscripts I discovered one of about eight hundred pages which contained a detailed account of the founding of every church built in Mexico and Guatemala. The manuscript was not complete, for the first eighty pages were missing. There were also a few pages of a diary kept by one of the first settlers of San Diego, but the rest of the diary was missing. I copied a few pages from this manuscript, tied together every document I judged would be of interest to Mr. Bancroft, delivered the package to the father librarian, and begged him to see the Father Superior and request his permission to forward the bundle to San Francisco. He started to fulfill my request, and assured me that though he had no hope of success, because it was against the rules of the college, he would make known my wishes to his chief.

He was absent half an hour, when he returned bearing a negative answer. Among other things, he said that the manuscripts I wanted to send away did not belong to the college, but were the property of some pious person who had placed them under their charge with instructions not to let the papers go out of their possession. I felt convinced that my reverend countryman was telling me the truth, so I abstained from urging my petition. I limited myself to the single request that he would be so kind as to keep in a separate place the package I had prepared for the purpose of sending to San Francisco to be copied. He agreed to it, and I embraced him Italian-style and then directed my steps toward the residence of Mr. Argüello.

I rang the bell of the stately dwelling in which the descendant of governors dwelt, and, having been ushered into the presence of Mr. Argüello, I stated to him the object of my visit. He listened to me with the air of one anxious to impress upon my mind the idea that I stood in the presence of a very great man. When I concluded my introductory remarks he said, "Well, well. In all this large house, by far the best one in Santa Clara, there does not exist a single scrap of paper that could be useful to an historian. I once found a great many documents that had been the property of my grandfather, and some belonging to my father, but I have set fire to them. I did not like the idea of encumbering my fine dwelling with boxes containing trash, so I got rid of the rubbish by burning the whole lot." Before Mr. Argüello had uttered four words I felt convinced that I stood in the presence of a self-conceited fool.

With people of that class it is useless to waste sound arguments and good reasoning. I knew it to be the case by experience, and therefore, without uttering another word except the commonplace compliments, I left the "best house in Santa Clara" and took the road that leads to the telegraph office. There I addressed a telegram to General Mariano G. Vallejo requesting his presence in Santa Clara. I took that step because I believed that Mr.

Argüello had told me lies, for I thought it so strange that a son who had reached the age of fifty years should be so stupid as to burn the family archives. I also began to fear that my plain talk had given offense. Therefore, I ventured to send for the good friend of Mr. Bancroft and the admirer of his perseverance, hoping that the high respect in which Mr. Argüello held General Vallejo would induce him to place at his disposal any documents he might have in the house.

[Cerrutti goes to interview an "aged Indian," José María Flores.]
...I took my departure from his house, jumped into the car that runs between Santa Clara and San José, and arrived in the latter city in time to meet General Vallejo, who in answer to my summons had taken the train and had come to give me a helping hand in trying to get possession of the documents of the Argüello family. In company with General Vallejo I returned to Santa Clara where we put up at the Cameron House, the best hotel in the place, where you pay high prices for everything you get and that which is served out to you is of a rather inferior quality. Mr. Cameron is a good-natured man, dresses in a peculiar style, and wears his hair in long ringlets that hang halfway down his neck. I said but little to him because I dislike effeminate men, but I believe, however, that Cameron is endowed with a good heart.

Next morning being Sunday, General Vallejo and I posted ourselves near the door of the church, and there General Vallejo passed the commonplace compliments with the friends of his youth. Among the persons who extended him a most cordial welcome I noted the widow of Luis Antonio Argüello, once governor of California. She embraced the General according to the good old Spanish style, reminded him that her husband had always been very kind to him when he was a young man without fame or fortune, inquired very anxiously about every member of the Vallejo family, and concluded by extending an invitation to dine in her house. The invitation was also extended to me, whom General Vallejo had introduced to her as a "promising young soldier who had done splendid work in the cause of republicanism as understood by sensible persons."

...We then went to the Argüello mansion, where the old dame received us with marked pleasure. Though immensely wealthy, she was dressed in a very simple style: Her body was covered with a black dress without ornaments of any kind and her head with a Spanish mantilla of a dark color. Her hair, as white as the snow and as rare as gold ounces in my pocketbook, hung loosely over her shoulders, and in her right hand she held a fan of dark color. I cannot undertake to give a detailed description of her face. Suffice it to say that it resembled a baked apple, but this is not to be wondered at because her advanced age prevented her from sporting rosy cheeks, and her well-known good sense was an insurmountable barrier to her trying to embellish herself by using dye, cosmetics, or colored arsenic.

As soon as we were duly installed in her large but scantily furnished parlor, she opened the conversation with the following remarks: "I am very much pleased, Guadalupe (the Christian name of General Vallejo), to see you in my house. I have often heard of you, and you are always well spoken of by our people. The notable men of our days are nearly all gone, and there remain only Alvarado, Pacheco, and you. The rest are either gone to their long account or have degenerated. Sorry, sorry indeed am I to see our race disappearing, but God's will be done.

"Religion also has lost greatly, but this does not surprise me, because ever since November, 1792, when Captain Vancouver visited California, the faith of our people has been dwindling, till now there is little if any remaining. It is true that we live in larger houses, that instead of sailing in canoes made of rushes and dry grass we now can go up and down our rivers in handsome steamers, and instead of the double-edged paddles our Costeños Indians used, coal and iron are made to do their work. But do you think, Guadalupe, that our race is as happy now as it used to be during the time in which my husband ruled the country? I fear not. They have been scattered to the four winds of heaven, their acres of fertile land have passed into strange hands, their cattle have either been stolen one by one, or by the thousand as General James M. Estell did with the whole of your stock. And what is still more to be regretted, instead of our being the rulers of the strangers who have taken up their residences in our towns, they rule us in the same manner that the owner of a large farm rules his slaves. Our sweet Castilian tongue has given place to the unpronounceable English jargon— bless the Almighty I have not learned it. Our good laws are not taken into consideration when we appeal to them for protection. Things are changed indeed, and I regret to say the change has not improved our condition, but the will of God be done."

General Vallejo, who had listened attentively to every word said by the aged Mrs. Governor Argüello, tried to refute her arguments. He called her attention to the fact that the present houses were more commodious than the adobe houses formerly in use. He recalled to her mind the fact that during her husband's administration furniture was not to be seen in the dwellings of the poor, and but few articles in the houses of the middle classes. No doubt General Vallejo intended to bring forward his favorite theme—the great improvements in the education of the lower classes— for I have repeatedly heard him bestow praises upon the Americans for having introduced in the country the present school system. But our hostess stopped him short, saying that she preferred the adobe buildings to the wooden ones and assigned as a reason that adobe houses even in the warmest weather offered a cool retreat, while wooden ones became so warm as to make them very uncomfortable. As to furniture she claimed that the poor people did not feel the want of it, because they did not know its use. She added that the Argüello, Amesti, Alvarado, de la Guerra, and several other families of note had possessed since 1824 handsome bureaus, large looking glasses, and tables inlaid with shells which sailing vessels brought from China or from Peru.

What more she would have said, I venture not to surmise, but, one of her servants having notified her that dinner was ready, she took hold of the arm of General Vallejo and requested him to lead the way to the dining room. I followed mechanically and only entered the dining room out of respect to General Vallejo. I did not relish the idea of coming in contact with the oldest son of Governor Argüello, a man for whom I felt a decided contempt from the very first moment I spoke with him. The first thing which met my eyes as soon as I stood inside of the dining room was the señor. There was the identical fool who had burned the family archives. There he was wearing eyeglasses and bowing to General Vallejo, whom he said he felt extremely pleased to see in his house—he ought to have said his mother's house. Argüello was uttering falsehoods, knowing them to be such. I say so advisedly, for if he was so glad to see General Vallejo in his mother's house, why had he hidden his insignificant person in the dining room? Why did he abstain from coming in the parlor to welcome the man who had been a true and trusty friend of his father? But enough of this unworthy son of a worthy father!

When we had taken our places at the table a scanty repast was served out to us, and already the dinner was becoming a thing of the past and not a word had been uttered. I felt sheepish, but I had no remedy at hand, so I concluded to chew the cud of disappointment till dinner was over. Presently they placed upon the table some sweetmeats, and I perceived that "four-eyed Argüello" was watching my actions. I therefore said, "Madame Argüello, yesterday I asked your oldest son to allow me to copy the family archives, but he assured me that the archives and every other document of early days had been burned by his orders. Can it be possible?" She assured me that I had been told the truth, and as she called to witness the Blessed Virgin I felt convinced that such was the case. General Vallejo then asked if any documents remained in her possession. She replied, "Not a line, everything has been burnt." While we were engaged in conversation, a young man about sixteen years of age, son of "four-eyed Argüello," left the table without saying a word of excuse either to his grandmother or guests, and went into the streets. I could not help admiring the impudence of the ill-bred youth who was so deaf to the calling of good manners, but when I stopped to consider who his father was I ceased wondering.

Shortly after dinner we bid adieu to the pious old lady, the only member of the Argüello family (the Santa Clara Argüellos) who is endowed with intelligence and bred to good and easy manners.

...The General expressed himself as very much dissatisfied with his visit to San José and Santa Clara and told me that he would feel ashamed to return to San Francisco without bringing along with him a good many documents. He then proposed that we two should take a trip to Monterey, where he was certain of meeting with better success. I coincided with his views and begged of him to delay his voyage for a day or two so as to give me time to send for funds. To this he objected, and pulling out from his pockets two hundred dollars he handed me one hundred, saying, "Let us divide our capital, and should either of us run short of funds in Monterey, I will get what we may need from my sisters." I pocketed the five twenties my kind friend had given me and prepared for the journey. My writing satchel being handy I took it along with me, purchased a dozen paper collars, a ten-cent handkerchief, and jumped into the stage, where I found General Vallejo engaged in conversation with a short, stout lady dressed in black. She did all the talking, for just then she happened to be in a loquacious mood. I soon ascertained that she was the widow of the Hon. D. R. Ashley, one of the boys who had arrived in California with Colonel Stevenson, and a gentleman who had filled in this, and in the neighboring state of Nevada, positions of high responsibility.

Having been introduced to the gay widow, I improved the occasion for the purpose of fostering the interests of my friend, H. H. Bancroft, and in a roundabout manner I obtained from her the promise that she would place in my hands every one of the documents referring to the early history of California, which she admitted having inherited from her deceased "lord and master." This promise she fulfilled one month afterward, and in justice to her I will state that "her papers" were of high historical interest. But it is my belief that they ought to be placed in the archives of the State, where everybody could have access to them, and not be locked up in a drawer of a private family.

The stage brought us to the depot of the railroad, where we got on board the cars, and at one o'clock in the afternoon we reached Salinas City. There we found the stage ready to take us to Monterey, but as the vehicle was an old-fashioned one, a perfect stranger to the comforts so highly prized by travelers, General Vallejo ordered a carriage to be prepared to convey him, Madame Ashley, and me to Monterey, which place we reached at five o'clock. When the driver presented the bill to the General, he coolly asked twelve dollars, which amount was instantly given him by my liberal companion. I believe five dollars would have been quite enough because the stage owners only charge passengers seventy-five cents for the trip. The stage driver had reached Monterey upward of one hour ahead of us and had imparted the news of the arrival of General Vallejo at Salinas on his way to his birthplace.

As soon as it was known that the ex-Comandante General would soon arrive in town, the inhabitants collected in groups at the house of Mrs. Jacob P. Leese, sister of General Vallejo, so that when he reached that abode he found himself surrounded by many of his ancient companions in arms, among whom I recognized Jacinto Rodríguez, who holding a cane under his left arm, his hat in his right hand, came forward saying, "My dear General, please forgive my attire, for since I finished my work at the convention which framed the constitution, I have not paid much attention to my appearance, and you can understand this very well, for great men are aware of the sudden changes in fortune to which those who take part in framing constitutions are exposed. I assure you that if the people should call upon me another time for public duties, I would not serve again. I sacrificed myself once, but they will not get me a second time."

Another of the bystanders whom I recognized was Don José Abrego, a stout old gentleman about fifty-five years of age, born in Mexico and arrived in California with the celebrated colony brought to this country by Messrs. Híjar and Padrés. By trade he was a hatter, but, having shortly after his arrival contracted marriage with the oldest daughter of Don Raymundo Estrada, one of the most influential and richest of the native Californians, and by that marriage having also become related to Governor Juan B. Alvarado, he obtained the office of Treasurer of the Department of California. This position he filled for a period of eight years, during which it is said he acted in an honorable manner. Notwithstanding his great age, Mr. Abrego is active and tends daily to his store and slaughterhouse.

I engaged in conversation with him and learned that though he had witnessed six revolutions since his arrival in California he never took part in
them. He also told me that at the time an election was held in Monterey for
the purpose of sending delegates to the convention that framed the Constitution of the State of California, his name, unknown to him, had been
placed at the head of the list of the persons to be voted for on election day,
but he had objected to accepting that office because he thought it wrong to
transfer his allegiance to the United States so soon after the defeat of the
Mexicans. I inquired of him whether he believed that California had gained
by the change of rulers, and he replied, "In some things we have gained, but
in others we have lost heavily. Education has greatly advanced since then,
but morality has decreased to an alarming extent. Before the arrival of
Commodore Stockton in Monterey, on an average each married couple
raised from ten to twelve children. Some marriages raised as many as
twenty-four, but nowadays two babies for each marriage, I believe, would
be the proper estimate throughout the state."

I also noticed the sons of Joaquín Gómez, a wealthy Mexican miner
who, driven to despair in the mother country by the bad conduct of his
faithless wife, had emigrated to California with his children. The son of that
broken-hearted man, called Vicente Gómez, no sooner perceived General
Vallejo than he grabbed the hand of the friend of his deceased father and
said, "It does my heart good, Don Guadalupe, to see you. I often think of
you and would feel greatly pleased to see you take up your residence in our
midst."

There were many more of the native Californians, whose names I did
not learn. When I entered the parlor of Mrs. Jacob P. Leese, I was welcomed by that lady and her amiable daughters in a manner that recalled to
my mind the hospitality for which the native Californians were far-famed
throughout the world. In her salon I noticed many bureau lamps, tables,
pictures, and boxes of Chinese make. I made bold to inquire the reason
why she preferred Chinese furniture to French or American. She replied
that in the olden times she was not allowed to choose, that French or
American furniture was not to be had in the country, and therefore she had
no choice but to furnish her apartments with articles of Chinese make. The
yard and porch of her house were paved with whale bones (vertebrae). Her
servants were two Indian girls whose mother had also been employed in
Mrs. Leese's house and when dying had requested her mistress to take care
of her children.

I engaged Mrs. Leese in conversation for the purpose of discovering her feelings in regard to the changes which had taken place in California since the arrival of the Americans, and to my sorrow I discovered that she disliked the whole race, and I may add that she has good grounds for complaint. She, the sister of the most wealthy Californians, had married an American who had squandered her dowry and then had deserted her, leaving to her charge four young daughters and two sons. She had also, through decisions of the State courts and through squatters, lost the greater part of her landed property. Aside from these reasons she had been roughly treated by the Bear Flag party, who in 1846 had imprisoned two of her brothers and husband and had repeatedly plundered her deposit of provisions. I tried to dispel the prejudices she entertained against the Americans, but my efforts were of no avail. She has suffered too long and too deeply to forget or forgive her wrongs. Her daughters have been educated in the highest branches of grammar and music and speak English very well, but Mrs. Leese always insists that they shall converse in the Spanish language when in her presence. The very sound of the English language causes her to shudder.

[Cerrutti interviews a number of people in Monterey, including David Spence, José Abrego, and Vicente Gómez.]

...I directed my steps to the house of the widow of Don Feliciano Soberanes and mother of Mrs. Gabriela Cambuston, relict of the lamented Enrique Cambuston who in 1839 40 and '41 taught school in Monterey. When I reached the house of Madame Soberanes, I was welcomed by an aged lady about seventy-six years of age who mistook me for a land speculator and without ceremony offered me a seat in her parlor. (During the time I was in Monterey a good many persons from San José and San Francisco visited the ancient capital for the purpose of investing in lands but found it impossible to transact business with the owners of building lots who actually believed that the railroad, which was just then being built for the purpose of connecting Monterey with Salinas City, would fill with gold the pockets of every landowner—an erroneous idea which, if persisted in, will prevent businessmen from settling in that seaport.)

I did not make any effort to undeceive her, and she went on to state how her husband had purchased at auction the Mission of Soledad and the Rancho of San Lorenzo, how the American judges had refused to grant him patents for his lands, and how hard she had had to struggle for the purpose of raising and educating her nine sons and four daughters, the whole of whom were still living, some in California and some abroad. She added that if I was anxious to rent a piece of ground for the purpose of building a residence or a store she would cheerfully rent me a piece of ground. I asked on what terms, and she replied that if I would build on her land a brick building and pay her a monthly rent of three hundred dollars she would allow me the use of her large yard. Considering that the land in question was only worth five hundred dollars at most, I could not help laughing at the coolness of the proposition. Not wishing, however, to displease her, I asked for time to consider her proposal and proceeded to ask her a few questions as to important events which had transpired in Monterey during her lifetime.

[The interview with "Madame Soberanes," María Antonia Rodríguez de Soberanes, which is recorded by Cerrutti at this point in "Ramblings in California," partly in English and partly in Spanish, is in this volume.]
...Being hungry, I bid adieu to Mrs. Soberanes and her amiable daughter and retraced my steps to the Washington Hotel, a large adobe building where I spent the night, and on the following morning I accompanied General Vallejo on board the steamer *Senator* bound for Santa Cruz and San Francisco.

"Report of Labors in Archives and Procuring Material for History of California, 1876–9" by Thomas Savage

[The manuscript begins with this loose page about the Archives of the Bishop, Joseph Sadoc Alemany.]

Archiepiscopal Archives.

Correspondence of Missionaries.

Being informed that the Most Rev.d Joseph S. Alemany, Archbishop of San Francisco, had in his possession a large quantity of valuable MSS connected with the history of the Catholic Church in Cal., which had been gathered and presented to it by Dr. Taylor; one evening in April 1876, Mr. Bancroft, accompanied by Thomas Savage, paid a visit to the Archbishop, to obtain, if possible, the loan of those documents, or at least permission for copying or making extracts from them, to be utilized in his History of California.

Archbishop Alemany would on no consideration permit the papers to leave his house, but kindly acceded to extracts being made from them, and placed his own private office at the disposal of Mr. Bancroft or of such person as he might entrust the work to.

The Archbishop was at first somewhat indisposed to place these church documents at the service of any one, unless he were well known as one of its warm friends.

Archivo del Arzobispado—Cartas de los Misioneros de California.

I. II. III.^{1} III.^{2} IV.^{1} IV.^{2} V. 1772–1849.

[Here begins the continuous narrative section of the manuscript.]

Archives of the United States Surveyor General's Office. San Francisco

The great task of epitomizing these archives, for the Bancroft Library, was begun by Thomas Savage with 10 or 12 assistants on, the 15th of May 1876.

The work of abstracting nearly 300 volumes of MSS, ranging from 700 to 1900 pages each, aside from a considerable quantity of unbound documents, much of the writing faded by time or difficult to decipher or understand, owing to bad penmanship, or worse grammar, at first appeared like an endless one requiring the expenditure of a fortune. It was accomplished, however, within 10 months, at an expense of nearly $10,000. Had all the documents been copied it is doubtful that 35 or 40,000$ would have met the cost.

Those archives had been gathered by order of the U.S. Government in 1851, from all parts of California, and placed in charge of the U.S. Surveyor Gen. at San Francisco, and the immediate custody of R. C. Hopkins. A little late[r] Hon. E. M. Stanton came with full powers from Washington, to attend to land and other affairs for the Government. He ordered those archives to be forthwith bound into books. The work was so hurriedly done that no attempt at chronological arrangement was thought of. The documents were merely thrown together, bound and paged. And yet some division of the volumes was effected, purporting to give the places the documents had been brought from, and the epochs and years they embraced. But the whole is a mere jumble from beginning to end. Some idea of their condition may be formed from the fact that in volumes marked as of late years, were found very important official letters of the earliest times of California, even as far back as 1770. Indeed, the archives, as they now stand, would be useless for finding facts connected with any given period of California History. Any such effort would be like trying to find a needle in a haystack.

Mr. Stanton ought not, perhaps, to be blamed for such a state of things. He, doubtless, had much to attend to within a short time, and resolved, at all events, to save the archives from being tampered with, a thing likely to happen if they were left longer in a loose state.

Among Mr. Savage's assistants were the three who had become quite expert at the Archbishop's. Eight or ten others had to be trained to the work—several educated young men tried and gave it up. After a while there were men enough possessed of the requisite efficiency for the duty entrusted to them, and who could fairly earn their compensation.

It will be readily understood that among that large mass of documents, there was a considerable portion of no value whatever, but which could not be ignored or set aside till after being read, or at least glanced over—Of the useful portion the substance had to be carefully extracted, and written down concisely tho' clearly—But if the document or any part of it was

Hubert Howe Bancroft as a young man. Courtesy of The Bancroft Library, University of California, Berkeley

important enough to be copied, it was taken down verbatim et literatim. What was of no practical use was left out.

To the inexperienced all this may appear easy—but men who have had occasion to make researches among old records will bear witness that a peculiar fitness and training is needed for the operation.

Contents of the archives—Official correspondence of the Superior and other authorities, civil and financial, military and ecclesiastic, of Mexico and the Californias from the foundation of the first mission in 1769, and even a little farther back, to the time California was admitted into the American Union as a State—also the Spanish and Mex^n records of military forces and their accounts—thus embracing the periods of Spanish and Mexican domination, as well as that of the U.S. military and civil adminis-tration from the time the country fell into the hands of the Americans in 1846. The record may not, indeed, be called complete, but affords an immense amount of material, which only required perseverance and the expenditure of money to be brought into use.

But before the work could be undertaken a few negotiations had to be gone thro'. During some time expectation had been entertained that Mr.

R. C. Hopkins, the Custodian of the Archives, would have extracted the data for Mr. Bancroft. It soon became evident, however, to himself and everyone else, that he alone could not have accomplished it in many years, even if his official and other business hadn't demanded all his attention.

The matter was then referred to H.G. Rollins Esq, the Surveyor Gen., for permission to occupy a portion of his premises. Mr. Rollins answered that it would be impossible to obtain the information desired amid the continual confusion of the office, and suggested a plan which promised to be advantageous—that Mr. Bancroft should rent a room in one of the buildings close at hand, and he would allow the records to be taken there for the work, considering them as still in the custody of his office. This plan was adopted, and a spacious room taken in the Blumenberg Building opposite the Surveyor General's, where after adopting precautions for the better security of the books, the work was commenced, and proceeded with for nearly a month—It was then concluded that the records would be as secure, if not more so, at the Bancroft Library, and they were accordingly transferred to the latter.

But on the 19th of June Mr. Hopkins very excitedly said that he could no longer allow the documents to be taken out of the archives, as remarks were being made, and some one had even hinted an intention of reporting to the Gov[t] at Washington that the archives were out of the Surveyor General's custody. He agreed to let Mr. Bancroft finish the books in his possession, but positively refused to allow any more taken out.

After a few remarks from Mr. Henry L. Oak, the Librarian, Hopkins calmed down and became quite accommodating. He finally stated that several clerks had been discharged from the Surveyor General's office, and from the 1st of July there would be room for 8 or 10, perhaps more, writers to work there—in the meantime he would allow Mr. Bancroft to have documents to keep his force at work till the end of the month.

The new arrangement was perfected, and Mr. Savage with his assistants occupied a room in the Surveyor General's premises, having the free use of the books and other documents, under Mr. Hopkins' nominal control, till the task was concluded toward the end of February or first part of March, 1877.

Such is the history of that enterprise resulting in 63 neatly bound books, which at the same time that they show the original divisions of volumes, titles, sub-titles, and years, contain the substance of the Cal. archives in the office of the U.S. Surveyor General at San Francisco.

The Bancroft Company building, on Market Street in San Francisco. Courtesy of The Bancroft Library, University of California, Berkeley

Researches in Monterey, Santa Clara, and Santa Cruz Counties.

Work in the Surveyor General's office being done, most of the men who had been employed were discharged, and Mr. Savage again took his place in the Library. Three or four of his best assistants, however, had been retained, who for a month or thereabouts were employed at certain unfinished abstracts at the Library.

There were many other archives, less important than those in San Francisco, only because less in number, which it seemed now best to epitomize, and for two reasons. First, the material was needed immediately, that notes might be taken from it for the History; and secondly, by retaining, say three of the most rapid and efficient of the men employed at the Surveyor General's office, Mr. Savage could have much better help in the performance of other similar labor than by any possibility could be secured from an army of inexperienced copyists at any future time. So it was settled that he should proceed to the counties of Monterey, Santa Cruz, and Santa Clara immediately and bring to as rapid completion as possible work of every kind in that direction. He was not only to get abstracts from government and church records, but also dictations on California events from old natives and others willing or able to contribute the same, and such old documents as he might find in private hands.

In order to ascertain what there might be in that direction, about the middle of March 1877 he visited the towns of Santa Clara, San José, and Salinas, searched the public archives in the last two named cities, and those of the Jesuit College and Parish Church of Santa Clara, and becoming satisfied that much important material could be there obtained, he made the necessary arrangements with the custodians of the respective collections to render it available for Mr. Bancroft's purpose. That done he returned to San Francisco, the journey having occupied about four days.

On the 20th of March he started for Salinas taking with him three assistants—viz, Emilio Piña, Rosendo V. Corona, and Vicente P. Gómez—to make abstracts from the records in the County Recorder's Office. Recorder Jacob R. Leese and his deputies facilitated operations as much as possible, allowing Mr. Savage to occupy a part of the premises for his work four weeks.

During this time, Gómez was occupied in visiting such native Californians as lived in that vicinity who could furnish desirable information, for the purpose of inducing them to narrate to Mr. Savage their recollections. To expedite this work S. rented a spacious room opposite the Recorder's, where he could take down those narratives, and at the same time watch the labors of his assistants.

He succeeded in obtaining dictations from several Californians, the most notable one of whom was Captain Don Francisco Arce. This gentleman came from his native country, Lower California, when still a boy, and in later years occupied prominent positions under the Mexican admin., in California, and subsequently took part on the Mexican side in several battles in the Valley of Mexico betw. the United States and Mexican armies.

Capt. Arce had been prejudiced against Mr. Bancroft; because a certain person of whom he entertained a very low opinion had once applied to him, on Mr. Bancroft's behalf, for a gift or loan of his old documents, and he thought it strange Mr. Bancroft should make use of such requests instead of applying direct to him, he had considered himself treated disrespectfully—but on being assured that the fellow's act had been unauthorized, in fact wholly unknown to Mr. Bancroft, he became mollified, and at once promised to furnish not only a narrative but such old historical papers on California as he possessed.

Unfortunately, Arce was then in great affliction—a daughter first budding into womanhood was then bed ridden in the last stage of consumption, and indeed, a few days later Death relieved her of further suffering. However, so soon as the father's grief was somewhat assuaged, he began the fulfillment of his promise with the delivery of a lot of important old papers; and subsequently, as his business permitted, dictated to Mr. Savage about seventy pages of his recollections.

Captain Arce's memory was found to be much clouded, a fact of which he was aware, attributing it to a severe kick by a mule he received some years before in Lower California, leaving a deep scar in his forehead.

He also accompanied Mr. Savage to the San Zenobio ranch at González, the residence of Capt. Francisco Rico, who had been a prominent man in the American war and in some of the political disturbances preceding it—from him were obtained in about eight hours' time 54 pages of most desirable historical data. Rico would have given more had he not been obliged to absent himself the next morning.

Several other persons promised to furnish their reminiscences, but were not ready at the time, among them Don Estevan de la Torre. Another, named Cantúa who was an officer in the Natividad fight, and received a severe wound, also promised his narration but death in his family prevented compliance.

After the work on the archives at the Recorder's office had been completed, Corona and Piña, being of no further use there, were dispatched to San Francisco, and Mr. Savage with Gómez repaired to Monterey, where they confidently expected to possess themselves of much historical information. They were not disappointed, as is witnessed in the books of narratives of Don Florencio Serrano and Don Estevan de la Torre (of 234 and 220 pages respectively), besides others of lesser note among the Californians and recollections by John Chamberlain, William Wiggins, and James Meadows.

The last named was one of the prisoners sent from California to Mexico in 1840—he was visited at his ranch 7½ miles from Monterey, and gave his account of the circumstances connected with the arrest of foreigners in that year, their treatment in California, on the passage to San Blas, and in Tepic—also, like Chamberlain, of the part he took in the war, against Governor Micheltorena.

Mr. Wiggins' narrative, tho' short, is also interesting to history.

Mr. Savage's absence from San Francisco was from March 20th to May 17th, during which time he secured about 700 pages of original material, besides some lots of old documents, and the abstracts from the records at Salinas. On his way back he tarried part of a day in San José to further complete arrangements for the work to be done there.

The total expense of that expedition was of about 600$.——

2ⁿᵈ trip. Started May 21ˢᵗ for San José with the same three assistants. By the kindness of Mayor Murphy Mr. Savage was allowed the use of a large room in the City Hall building, opposite the City Clerk's office, to which he was permitted by the last named officer to remove the bound records (6 volumes) as they were needed.

It must be recorded here that in San José, as in Salinas, and later in Santa Cruz, the use of pen and ink was interdicted in the offices except by the officers in charge or their employees. Lead pencil had therefore to be used in making extracts.

Every thing of historical value, not already possessed by the Bancroft Library, was duly taken out.

Besides the bound records there were some 2500 loose documents, every one of which was examined, and notes or copies taken from a large number of them, by Mr. Savage himself in the Clerk's office, for the official would not allow of their being taken out of it. He may, therefore, say that the Bancroft Library now has every important item of San José history from the foundation of the town to the time that the Mexican system ceased and the present American regime was inaugurated.

Extracts from the few papers existing in the Jesuit College of Santa Clara, and also from the old mission records in charge of the Parish priest, which were placed at Mr. Savage's disposal upon the kind recommendation of Archbishop Alemany, were likewise made.

During the sojourn of one month in San José, narratives of more or less extent were written down, furnished by several Californians and others both in San José and Santa Clara. Five days of that month (June) were extremely trying, the heat being intense—yet Mr. Savage walked under the broiling sun several times a day to and from Eusebio Galindo's house situated a long distance from the Santa Clara terminus of the railroad— Galindo, a man 45 years old, contributed 71 pages.

It may be asserted that no Californian who could furnish something, was forgotten. The result of those labors appear in several books standing on the shelves of the Library.

Mr. Savage had also the good fortune to obtain the loan from the heirs of the late Antonio Suñol, of a collection of letters from John A. Sutter at New Helvetia to said Suñol, from which extracts were taken.

Mariano Malarín Esq. lent Mr. Savage a bound collection of 38 numbers of the first newspaper published in California—the *Californian* of Monterey, preserved by the late David Spence—from about half of which the extracts were taken at San José and from the rest at Santa Cruz, working early and late. This work contains abt 170 pp of MSS.

After the work had been terminated at San José and the sister town, Corona and Piña were sent back to San Francisco, and Mr. Savage with Gómez transferred themselves in the Stage to Santa Cruz.

His object in visiting that city was to search the archives of the old town of Branciforte, and the records of Santa Cruz mission, and take extracts from them—likewise to obtain a dictation in California history, from the aged native Californian José María Amador, a son of Pedro Amador, one of the soldiers who founded San Diego and Monterey, and for many years was the Sergeant of the San Francisco presidial company. It was understood that José María Amador was a resident of Santa Cruz, had a good memory, and the will to contribute all he knew on the events that had passed in his country during his lifetime. But it turned out that he resided near Watsonville in the same county.

Mr. Savage and his assistant stayed two weeks in Santa Cruz—in that time he made abstracts from the numerous old papers, mostly of Branciforte, in the County Clerk's office, for which Mr. Mc Kinney, the Clerk, afforded him every facility.

After taking out every useful fact from the mission books, and from a considerable quantity of loose official letters of the old times, which Rev.d Father Hawes then in charge of the parish, during Rev. Father Adam, the Pastor's absence in Europe, had placed at his disposal, Mr. Savage concluded to pay a flying visit to Watsonville. Gómez had taken down a few short dictations from old native Californians, containing their personal experiences.

There being no further work for Gómez, he returned to his home in Monterey.

No time was lost in procuring the whereabouts of the aged Amador, who was reported to be 96 years old; but the record of his baptism at the San Francisco mission afterward showed that assertion, as well as his own to Mr. Savage to be incorrect—that record said that Amador was not born till the 18th of Dec. 1794, or thirteen years later than was supposed he was, however, old enough to have witnessed events which occurred in Cal. during the life of the first generation born in the country—probably the only living man whose father was one of its first founders. The old man was in great poverty on a ranch 4½ miles from the town, under the care of his youngest daughter who is married and has many children. On being requested to narrate the events which occurred in the country during the Spanish and Mexican occupation etc.—he promptly acceded without demanding any remuneration or gratuity. During five or six days he related all events in which he participated, and much other important matter, forming a volume of 229 pages—every word of which was written down by Savage, who for that purpose rode out to the ranch in the morning and returned in the evening to town. Of course nice things in the way of edibles were daily taken to the old gentleman and the children, and occasionally a bottle of Old Bourbon to warm his heart.

Amador couldn't move much, his left side being partially paralyzed, but his mind seemed quite clear and his cheerfulness under adversity was truly remarkable.

Here was found an old Santa Cruz mission Indian, quite an intelligent man who had been one of its musicians—from him considerable information was elicited on mission life during and after the management of the old Spanish Padres, and on occurrences there.

Whilst on the spot, Savage visited Mr. Job Francis Dye, an old pioneer living about ½ mile from Corralitos, which is some seven miles from Watsonville, to obtain a dictation from him. This necessitated taking up quarters for a day and a couple of nights in the so-called hotel of Corralitos—no complaint will he utter against the accommodations or the food—they were probably the best the host and hostess could then afford—but he hopes for better luck in his future wanderings.

Dye dictated a few pages, and added a scrap book containing articles he had contributed to the Santa Cruz Sentinel on Cal. affairs.

That week's work was hard indeed, owing to the prevailing heat, and the clouds of dust raised by the teams conveying lumber, during that year of severe drought.

On the way back, Savage stopped at San José and returned to Mr. Malarín his volume of the "Californian." The Sutter-Suñol letters had been previously sent to Mr. Echevarría of San José from whom they had been borrowed.

On the 17th of July, Savage was in San Francisco after an absence of one month and twenty-seven days having incurred in that trip the expense of some $450—for conveyances, wages, gratuities, fees etc.

[At this point, two pages are missing from the manuscript.]

...passengers now bound for San Luis, took a stroll on the pier. Arrived at Santa Bárbara the same day at 9 P.M.—The Captain told the passengers he would remain there 45 minutes at most, which deterred everybody from visiting the city—the boat stopped, however, fully two hours. In San Buenaventura at about 1.30 A.M. of the 8th, and at Santa Mónica between 7 and 8 of same morning—by 9 o'clock the passengers had arrived by rail at Los Angeles.

Mr. Savage lost no time in looking up the parties for whom he had letters—some were absent from the city, others attending to their business, Ex. Govr Downey couldn't be found during the day, but the letter was sent to his house, and that same evening Mr. Savage had the pleasure of meeting him at the Fair and after quite a friendly greeting, the ex-Govr gave Mr. Savage the assurance that he would do all in his power to render the latter's mission a success. The Hon. Ignacio Sepúlveda, District Judge, was likewise extremely kind and promised his cooperation, a promise that he fully carried out, and his influence was undoubtedly valuable in several instances, as will be made to appear in the course of this narrative.

Mr. Savage had little time to occupy on anything but the work that had brought him there. He couldn't but notice, however, the perfect confidence with which the sea lions from the rocks in the roadstead of Santa Mónica had seen the steamer pass near them—they seemed conscious that she held no enemy of theirs—the beach of Santa Mónica called his attention for its beauty. Los Angeles presented the appearance of progress on all quarters, and indeed, it was generally conceded that the old town had awakened from the old lethargy, and in the last seven or eight years taken large strides in the way of improvement, materially as well as intellectually.

The man whose services were most needed (Ex. Gov' Pico), was at his ranch, but soon returned, and was waited upon at once—he promised to take the matter in hand vigorously, and labor diligently with Mr. Savage six hours daily from the 10th at 9 A.M. He complied with his promise, in some measure, and that day filled 30 pages with incidents of his youth before he launched out into public life—but it was evident he knew nothing of California history back of 1826. He also furnished other convenient information to write—that the collection of papers of Agustín Olvera, who for many years had been the Secretary, and later a member of the California Assembly, before the U. States firmly held the country, were in possession of his son Carlos at the Rancho de los Malarines in the Chualar, between Soledad and Monterey; of which item a note was duly made for future action—that

José Matías Moreno, the last Government Secretary when he (Pico) was Governor, who accompanied him on his flight into Lower California (1846), was dead; and the widow, it was believed, had some interesting papers which he had unsuccessfully applied to her for—Note was also made of these facts with the hope that it would not be lost. The old ex-Gov[r] likewise offered his cooperation to secure useful data from various quarters.

Mr. Savage hadn't been many days in Los Angeles without becoming satisfied there were several men in the city and its vicinity from whom could be obtained not only dictations but valuable old documents, and didn't fail to avail himself of the influence of such men as Govr Downey, Judge Sepúlveda and Govr Pico. Others of less weight, apparently, also rendered good aid—It was necessary, however, to finish with Pico first, as he might be called away at any moment, or his enthusiasm evaporate.

The work had thus far promised well—willingness to cooperate on the part of those called upon, fairly cool weather, and tolerably good health—with these advantages the results couldn't but be at least satisfactory.

Govr Pico continued his dictation, but slowly, being constantly interrupted by business calls, and yet took up all Mr. Savage's time—some days he would stop suddenly, to attend court, or to go to his ranch; and Mr. Savage could attend to nothing else. Fortunately, Antonio F. Coronel had lent him his father Ignacio Coronel's papers, and Sheriff Alexander some of the late Manuel Requena, which occupied some hours, during Pico's absences, in making abstracts from.

A considerable time was also employed in looking up collections known to exist, and which couldn't be passed by unnoticed.

The late Judge Benjamin Hayes had borrowed from Mr. Alexander, son in law of Requena, a lot of old papers, and from Coronel another batch—among the former, Mellus' Diary. Hayes had pounced upon the book, and was at work upon it and those papers when death overtook him at his sister's (Dr. Griffin's wife) in Los Angeles. Every effort was made by Mr. Alexander, during Savage's sojourn in that city, to recover his property and Coronel's, without success—and the matter had to be dropped for the time being, until the Judge's son could be visited at his residence near San Luis Rey.

Col. John J. Warner, then a Notary Public, was repeatedly called on for his MSS which he had promised. He had neglected the work owing to ill health, and a suspicion that seemed to lurk in his mind of his Recollections not being appreciated—his mind was disabused on that point, and he then manifested greater interest promising to re-commence his labor.*

---

*He finally delivered the Book to Mr. Savage on the 12th of Nov., and it was forwarded to the Bancroft Library the next day.

Pico continued his dictations, off and on, during two weeks, causing much loss of valuable time. Patience has its limit, and this was reached at last, when Mr. Savage concluded to close at the 200th page. He must confess tho', that if Pico occupied too much time, he gave a good deal of history, and a mass of important documents of his own and of his brother, the late Gen. Andrés Pico, all of which were duly forwarded to the Bancroft Library.

In connection with papers of the late Andrés Pico, Eulogio Celis of Los Angeles promised Mr. Savage to procure him some more documents of the deceased, said to be in possession of Rómulo Pico—he was led to believe that the latter might have the missing books etc of the mission San Fernando. Pío Pico positively asserted that he hadn't them—the Bishop had sought for them in vain—Mr. Savage in these negotiations could have no direct intercourse with Rómulo Pico, who, if he had any papers of Andrés Pico, would have strenuously denied it, or run the risk of a criminal prosecution if he was proved by Pío Pico, the administrator of the estate, to have them after the Courts had peremptorily commanded him to turn over to the Administrator everything belonging to deceased. On the other side, it was necessary that ex-Gov' Pico shouldn't even suspect that Mr. Savage held any relations with Rómulo—that suspicion would have forfeited him Pío Pico's good will, which he couldn't afford to lose at that stage of the business. But the whole thing fell through because Celis left Los Angeles

Eulogio Celis. Courtesy of the Seaver Center for Western History Research, Natural History Museum of Los Angeles County, Los Angeles, California

for the North and didn't return as long as Mr. Savage was in the South, and Rómulo Pico couldn't be found when looked for.

Among the acquaintances made here was Don José Arnaz, an old Spaniard, and one of the earliest pioneers, residing on his estate near San Buenaventura—he promised his reminiscences to Mr. Savage when the latter should visit the above named place.

Borrowed from Justice of the Peace Pedro C. Carrillo a few papers of his father the late ex-Govr Carlos Antº Carrillo, from which copies or extracts were taken, as Mr. Carrillo wouldn't give away the originals.

Oct 25ᵗʰ began to write down the dictation of José del Carmen Lugo. This gentleman was introduced to Mr. Savage by Mr. Dolores Sepúlveda, an uncle of Judge Sepúlveda, as one who knew much on his country's history, and as a man of character and truthfulness—who was connected by blood with the best Californian families, had been in easy circumstances, but now was reduced to the greatest poverty, because he had placed too much trust in others. Señor Lugo had to be offered a small gratuity for his time, but disappointed expectations. His ignorance of history and of almost everything was soon discovered. According to his own statement he had not read a book or written a line from the age of 16 to the time he was elected Regidor of Los Angeles in 1839, when reading and writing, acquired in boyhood came again into requisition. For all his ignorance he was chosen *Alcalde* in 1849, a couple of years after the country had begun to be Americanized. From him were obtained 130 pages, by no means devoid of interest—finished Oct 30ᵗʰ.

Señor Lugo was not at all the most ignorant on history of California that was found among old settlers in Los Angeles. Mr. Francis P. F. Temple came to the country in 1841, and knew absolutely nothing—he tried to dictate and broke down at every moment, and the attempt had to be given up. He assured Mr. Savage of better success, if he would apply to Felipe Lugo, and offered to accompany him to Lugo's ranch. This Lugo was a brother of José del Carmen; his ranch was on the line traversed by the U.S. forces when they came to occupy Los Angeles. He had been a soldier as far back as under the domination of old Spain—found he talked too slowly, couldn't come to town—that he would have to be waited on at his ranch during several days at an expense of about 3$ per day for conveyance, besides whisky to keep his heart warm, and perhaps candy for the grandchildren—with slight probability of his furnishing but very little matter worth having—His information would cost too much time and money, and must be slighted.

Antonio Coronel and members of his family in Los Angeles, nineteenth century. Courtesy of The Bancroft Library, University of California, Berkeley

Many in that vicinity might have given their own experiences, having been in the fights of 1846 and 1847, but some were slippery, promised attendance and violated their word more than once; others lived too far and couldn't be reached without much expense; and a few were unreliable for various causes. There was one who shall be nameless, out of regard to his connections who are highly respectable—he was known as the champion liar, who on a first attempt at uttering a truth would have choked. He was Pío Pico's man of all work—After all, most of them could have given only a few pages. Mr. Savage tried to employ an assistant, but even there he was disappointed. Juan Toro, who had been one of Judge Hayes' Assistants in searching the archives, promised to aid, but for sickness in his family or other causes, never did anything.

One of the men to whom much commendation was due, Antonio F Coronel, formerly Treasurer of this State, not only devoted much of his time during several days in dictating (at his vineyard, near Los Angeles) 264 pages on historical events, manners, and customs, concluded on the 16th of November; but presented, at various times, to the Bancroft Library a large number of documents relating to California and Mexico. Mr. Savage could not speak too highly of the kindness and hospitality he received at the house of Mr. Coronel and his family. To Coronel's recommendation is likewise to be credited some portion of the success Mr. Savage met with elsewhere, and to Judge Sepúlveda's introduction this valuable cooperator.

Stephen C. Foster, at one time one of the most prominent men in Los Angeles, but now poor and almost beneath the notice of the respectable class; except as they might employ him at arranging archives or some such work for which he is especially fitted, was asked to write his own remembrances, and to assist at taking down those of others—He would do neither, declaring his time was all engaged—he finally, consented to devote three evenings—a promise that he did not carry out fully—for he never again made his appearance after dictating some 60 pages.

Tried unsuccessfully to obtain at least a short narrative from D^n Cristóbal Aguilar, a friend of Coronel's, and a man of good standing who had been about four times Alcalde of Los Angeles. He had no time to spare.

On or about the 15th of November Mr. Savage called on Right Rev.d Francis Mora, Bishop Coadjutor of the Catholic Diocese, for permission to make extracts from books and documents in the Episcopal Archives. Bishop Mora gave at first a prompt refusal, as if (judging from his manner) the pretension was a preposterous one, and almost sacrilegious to grant it. After a short discussion of the subject the Bishop went in to consult his superior Bishop Amat, and after a while returned as complacent as any one could wish him to be—The result was that he with his own "consecrated" hands pulled out 12 MSS Books, tied them with a rope, and then allowed Mr. Savage to take them to his quarters, by the mere signing of a receipt— One of the books was an incomplete record of land grants in San Luis Obispo. The other eleven were the Libros de Patentes of the missions San Buenaventura, Soledad, San Miguel, San Antonio, San Diego, San Juan Bautista, La Purísima, Santa Inés, San Luis Obispo, and Santa Cruz. Whatever was found useful in these books and not existing already in the Bancroft Library, was abstracted, and the books duly returned to the Bishop on the 19th.

Bishop Mora was also kind enough to provide Mr. Savage with a letter authorizing all the priests in charge of old mission records, within the Diocese, to place them at his disposal to take out all the material he might deem available.

The work in Los Angeles being about done, Mr. Savage now decided to visit Don Manuel Domínguez at his ranch near San Pedro—This was the 19th of November—He carried warm letters of introduction from Judge Sepúlveda to Domínguez' son-in-law Mr. Carson, and from Coronel and Arnaz to Domínguez himself—The old gentleman received his visitor with the utmost kindness, and did all in his power to make the time pass agreeably; but most positively declined to furnish any information, pleading that for many years he had been out of public life, and his memory had become very much weakened by age and disease—that for these reasons he would not make statements which might be incorrect and mislead the historian— he would upon no consideration have his name coupled with false asser- tions—He took this stand and no amount of argument from Mr. Savage backed by Mr. Carson could make the old gentleman swerve from his pur- pose—He added that he had no documents of a public nature. This was a real disappointment for his information had been counted upon as amongst the most desirable because coming from one of his high standing for char- acter and integrity, as well as wealth. This Mr. Domínguez had been many years in responsible positions. Regidor, *Alcalde*, Prefect, and one of the Delegates that in 1849 formed the Constitution of the State of California. He had been for some years past leading a retired life on account of blind- ness, one of the few Californians possessed of real wealth, free from debt, enjoying almost unlimited credit, intelligent, and respected by all who knew him. Such was the man whose evidence on Calif[a] events was wanted and couldn't be got, owing to his extreme sensitiveness—There was noth- ing for it but to thank Mr. Domínguez and family for their hospitality and go back crestfallen to Los Angeles.

No mention has been made of social enjoyments whilst in Los Angeles, for the reason that he had none worth mentioning—his whole time nearly from early morning till late in the evening was devoted to his work.

VISIT TO SAN GABRIEL, SPADRA, AND POMONA

Arrived at the old San Gabriel Mission on the afternoon of Nov. 21. Early the next morning, began to look around—first, the Parish Priest Father Joaquín Bot, a Catalán speaking English very well, and quite obliging—He allowed the old mission books to be taken to Mr. Savage's room—work on them immediately commenced—good to fall back upon when not occu- pied at other tasks, and for the evening.

Much alarm felt all around about a drought—the weather delightful— Delayed by indisposition from doing anything out of the room till the 24th inclusive. Next day visited Hon. Benj. D. Wilson at his residence of Lake Vineyard, about two miles from the mission, and made arrangements to take down his recollections, beginning on the 25th, but for reasons beyond Savage's control this work was not begun till the 28th.

On the 25th also paid a visit to Hon. E. J. C. Kewen, a neighbor of Mr. Wilson's, to see about the book he was preparing on Nicaragua. Col.

Kewen already had betw. 70 and 80 pages written clear, and a large collection of notes. He said the work would be in two parts; the first of about 100 pages, to give a retrospective view of that country before William Walker's advent, and the second, the Walker Administration, campaign &c. The colonel's labors had been stopped because the writer was prostrate with paralysis nearly two years—one whole year confined to his bed. Since the improvement of his health he opened a law office at Los Angeles, which he daily attended, except on Sundays, devoting evenings and Sundays to the Nicaragua task, and working at it diligently. He hoped to have it ready within a reasonable time for Mr. Bancroft.

The task of taking down Mr. Wilson's dictation occupied from 28th Nov. to 6th of Dec.*, holy days not included; during which time he furnished 113 pages of most interesting observations on New Mexico which he had visited as early as 1833, and on California, of which he was a pioneer since 1841. A great pity that he couldn't devote more time, for he must have had material in his head for 500 pages. He was first married to a native Californian lady, a Yorba, by whom he had a daughter (Mrs. Shorb)—by his second wife, an American, he had two interesting daughters. The old gentleman and his family showed themselves hospitable and kind, he was in easy circumstances, had a wife and three daughters living, four grandchildren, and hoped (to quote his own words) "to pass the remainder of my (his) days in peace with God and man, as well as with myself (himself)." Alas! his life was not to be spared but a few months longer!

Separate from the main narrative Mr. Wilson gave Mr. Savage in a few pages some facts on Isaac Graham, and John A. Sutter before they came to California, declaring those statements to be true, and such as he could swear to, for he was an eye-witness of the events therein detailed. But, he disliked to have his name coupled with any publication of those facts, specifically as to those relating to Sutter, because, as he said, he ought to have had the moral courage to make them known to all the world when the Legislature of California voted to Sutter a pension, and ordered his portrait placed in one of the Legislative Chambers. He (Wilson) was then a member of the State Senate, and ought to have spoken, but was deterred by the idea that any thing uttered against Sutter would have been, then, ill received. But he believed one of Sutter's victims, (Capt Charles Blummer), to be still living in New Mexico (Santa Fe), a highly respectable man, who might be called on to testify to the facts.

---

*Dec. 1 the work was suspended at 1:30 P.M. by a rush of members of his family and friends who had come to congratulate Mr. Wilson on his 66th birthday.

At such times as Mr. Savage was not engaged with Mr. Wilson, he obtained a statement from Victoriano Vega, an old, indigent Mexican, who came to California in 1834, and had many years served as a solider both in this country, and in the frontier of Lower California. Though only of 64 pages, Vega's narrative contains much that is interesting.

A short dictation of 34 pages was likewise obtained from the centenarian Eulalia Pérez, twice widow, first of Guillén, and next of Mariné—She expressed herself quite clearly for a woman whose age might be between 100 and 112 years, and was accused of being as old as 136 to 142! She had been for many years the *llavera* or Stewardess of the San Gabriel mission, and was questioned only upon mission life, characteristics of Padres, manner, and customs of the Californians in her early days, and other topics like these, upon which she could give information, as relating to her daily duties when still able to perform them. With a little perseverance, for the old lady was almost as deaf as a door post, straight answers were received, and they threw considerable light upon such subjects.

It was about this time difficult to get rid of catarrhs, with a temperature of 38° in the morning and 72° at noon, to have another great fall in the evening, accompanied on occasions with heavy wind and a d—l of a dust.

One of the parties that Mr. Savage was particularly recommend to see was Moncy, a Scotchman, residing in San Gabriel, said to possess vast knowledge of California, and on almost every subject. Called on Money, the "Doctor" or herbalist, who showed him monstrous maps, and piles of MSS, all his own work upon every known and unknown subject from the beginning of the world, and maybe of an earlier time—together with a MSS mission book. On being asked if he would furnish his recollections, he declined to do it unless all those maps and MSS, the mission book inclusive, were purchased from him for 1000$!, which encumbered tender of service was of course not accepted. The mission book contained important statistics, was the property of the San Gabriel Church, and subsequently recovered by Mr. Savage, and after extracts had been taken from it with Father Bot's permission, was returned to the Church. "Doctor" Money was believed by some people to be a profound thinker, a "well of science", but maybe set down as both a humbug and a lunatic—in early life he is said to have been a taxidermist and then drifted into a herbalist—the knowledge of the qualities of herbs he used in the cure of diseases, when regular physicians were not to be found in California; he may have been more or less successful, and, hence the handle of "Doctor" added by some to his name.

Michael White being absent at Pomona must be put off for a few days.

Visited Los Angeles Dec. 9th, posted documents to the Library, back at San Gabriel the same evening, and on the next day proceeded in the afternoon by rail to Spadra, which had been at one time the terminus of the railroad. A fine large hotel had been kept there which now received only a stray passenger and appeared to be a lodging place for laborers. A beautiful, spacious building surrounded by orange and other fruit trees, vineyards &c. The town itself small and perfectly dull. The object of this visit was to take down the recollections of an old soldier, upward of 70 years of age, named Pablo Véjar, who had become famous among his countrymen, in connection with military mutinies for which he was sent a prisoner to Mexico, escaped from there and returned, and during the American war took part in several fights, one of them that of San Pascual in which he was the only Californian taken prisoner by Gen. Kearny's force.

Véjar lived at the ranch of his brother Ricardo, about four miles from the town of Spadra, and both were in very great poverty, and with large families to support. Ricardo Véjar had some years before possessed a fortune of about $400,000.—now he told Mr. Savage he was too much ashamed to invite him into his hovel, and arranged that he should meet Pablo at his son Francisco's, a short distance off.

Mr. Savage had a letter of introduction to Ricardo from his cousin ex-Govr Pico. A little incident occurred in connection with this letter. When Pico was called upon for it, he was engaged, and desired Mr. Savage to dictate one in as warm terms as he chose, and his boy would write it for him to sign. Rather awkward to dictate a warm epistle in one's own favor, but it was done, confining the contents to the business on hand, and Pico signed it. When the letter was presented to Ricardo Véjar, outside of his house, he said that he couldn't read and desired Mr. Savage to do it. Another awkward predicament—but there was no help for it.

Pablo Véjar's narrative of 90 pages was taken on the 11th, 12th and 13th of December—his time was compensated for.

On the last day, on the way to Véjar's place, Mr. Savage's life was in great jeopardy. The man who drove the horses was relating stories to a young man seated betw. him and Savage, and was almost on the point of crossing a railroad bridge when he heard the train coming at full speed without the slightest warning having been given. The horses were turned double quick, but they became greatly excited, and as the train was passing (now making all possible noise), they wanted to back against it. The train passed, however, without doing damage, and the horses were driven plump against a fence—they continued terribly excited and unruly for some time till the young man seeing an opportunity, jumped down, and from the other side of the fence succeeded in detaching them from the wagon, when they became somewhat quiet. After a while they were harnessed on, and were going along still indisposed to mind the reins when some dogs rushed out barking at them, which maddened them a second time almost beyond control. It was with very great difficulty that the driver, a man of good presence of mind, and strong arm, kept them well in hand.

Early on the morning of the 14th took the train for Pomona, to see Michael C. White, generally known among the Californians by his translated name Miguel Blanco. An Englishman by birth, he came to the Pacific coast as early as 1817, when a boy of about 15 years, landing at San José del Cabo in Lower California, and never returned to his country. In 1828 he came to Upper California and settled, marrying in 1831 a daughter of Eulalia Perez Mariné, the *llavera* of San Gabriel mission, by Guillén her first husband.

White was temporarily sojourning at the place of his son-in-law Ignacio Alvarado, a short distance from Pomona, where he was visited at once. The old man was then in feeble health, and with his mind much disturbed by pecuniary troubles, as his ranch of San Isidro at San Gabriel was about to be taken from him by creditors. But he cheerfully assented to dictate his recollections, beginning forthwith, as his stay at the farm would be only for three or four days.

That 14th day of December was a very stormy one—the rain poured in torrents and the wind blew a perfect gale—mud was formed ankle deep. But neither unpropitious weather nor mud could deter Mr. Savage from attending to his duties, and he walked to and from the Alvarado farm four times a day during the three days that White's dictation lasted. White's narrative, an interesting one, indeed, bears the title of "California all the way back to 1828."

The town of Pomona possessed elements of wealth which were being developed. It was said that the failure of the bank of Workman, Temple, &c. had had a very injurious effect on the place, as the settlers had in it the funds which they had appropriated for improvements.

There being nothing more to do here on the morning of the 17th returned to San Gabriel—tarried here to procure the mission book in Money's hands—got it, and tried to obtain Father Bot's permission to send it to San Francisco as it contained statistical data from 1775 to 1832, the extracting of which would detain him too long in the place—he didn't feel authorized to grant it; but allowed that the book should be taken to Los Angeles, where the Bishop might possibly accede. But on arriving at Los

Angeles the same difficulty occurred. Bishop Mora couldn't be spoken to till the 19th, and he declined to let the book go out of the Diocese—so the day had to be employed in making abstracts from it, after which it was safely returned to Father Bot without loss of time; the Bishop had given the assurance that the priest would gladly furnish any information in his power to Mr. Bancroft.

There have been heavy rains, making roads impassable, destroying bridges, and delaying trains from North and South—People much encouraged *[The rest of this sentence is illegible.]*

After obtaining some letters of introduction to facilitate operations farther south, that same afternoon took the train for Downey City, intending to obtain, by recommendation of ex-Govr Downey, the reminiscences of José María Romero, a Californian aged about 90. Next morning early went to see Romero at Old Los Nietos, seven miles distant—devoted to him part of the 20th and 21st, but after writing down some twenty pages, drawn from him with the utmost difficulty, became convinced that his memory was very weak—he could not remember a single date, not even that of his birth. All his friends said he possessed a large stock of knowledge on events and men, which was quite possible, and if one lived with him, and noted down his recollections as he happened to utter them from day to day, much might have been got from him, but of course that would occupy too much time and cost too much money. So, Mr. Savage returned to Downey City in the afternoon. That same evening, (21st) took the train for Santa Ana, the terminus of the Southern Railroad; after supper about seven had taken his seat in the Stage for San Juan Capistrano, where he arrived between 12 and 1 o'clock—took lodging for the rest of the night at the hotel; next morning after breakfast transferred himself to more comfortable quarters provided him through the exceeding kindness of Mark A. Forster and Doctor Crane.

Father Mut, the Parish Priest being absent most of the day, the old mission books could not be got till quite late. The work of abstracting from them was begun on Sunday 23[d].

Mr. John Forster, the proprietor of the Santa Margarita estate, from whom some historical facts were expected, arrived at San Juan in the night of the 22[d]. As Mr. Savage had two good letters for him—one from Judge Sepúlveda—he called to present them accompanied by Don Juan Avila, an uncle of the Judge and Mr. Forster's compadre and friend, as well as family connection by the marriage of one of Forster's sons with one of Avila's daughters. A cordial reception was extended to the visitor, with a warm request to call at the Santa Margarita, where he (Mr. F) would be happy to impart all the information he might possess, adding that he couldn't undertake it in Capistrano as he had a good deal of business to demand his whole attention three days, and his return home as soon as possible.

Made inquiries from Father Mut and Mr. Forster for the books of baptisms, marriages and burials of San Luis Rey mission, and obtained no satisfaction. Mut referred to Forster and the latter denied all knowledge of their whereabouts. The loss of those records and those of San Fernando leaves a void in mission archives.

Remained in Capistrano till the 28th, making extracts from the mission books—took down also some dictation of Don Juan Avila. This gentleman was found to be very genial, and quite intelligent though he had not had in his youth the advantages of education. He had some years previously owned a very spacious mansion in the town, where he dispensed hospitality in true old Californian style, and of which the charred ruins were yet to be seen, to remind the owner and his numerous friends of a past that probably will never be revived.

During this week there have been some heavy rains, but they don't seem to do good enough. The drought is a reality as yet, and the prospects are bad. So think the weather wise. God grant that their predictions may not come to pass—for a second year of drought means the ruin of thousands of families.

Arrived at Santa Margarita Dec. 29th about noon from Las Flores— found Mr. Forster quite unwell, and unable to attend to business. An unfortunate circumstance that caused delay—Sunday 30th nothing done. Visited San Luis Rey, 7 miles from the ranch, in hopes of meeting Chauncey Hayes—was disappointed, and went back.

On 31 Dec. Mr. Forster dictated 30 pages—on January 1st he had to go back to Capistrano intending to return the next day, but didn't till the evening of the 3d. Feasting on new year's day, and the hospitality of Mr. and Mrs. Forster and the rest of the family at all events couldn't be surpassed— it was very pleasant, to say the least, but the work of gathering history was in a measure at a stand still.

The time was not, however, entirely lost—obtained more narrative from Don Juan Avila, and some very interesting pages from Michael Kraszewski on lawlessness at San Juan Capistrano in 1856.

Was promised by Chauncey Hayes he would soon pack up and send to Mr. Bancroft, as a gift, all papers and scraps of a historical nature left by his father.

Don Juan Bandini, whom Mr. Savage had met in Los Angeles, offer'd to send him to San Diego forthwith a collection of official letters etc of his deceased father.

Will these parties carry out their promises? It is to be hoped they will—but after receiving so many promises from others, and seeing them carried off by the wind, Mr. Savage began to be somewhat skeptical.

Mr. Forster completed 55 pages—a good deal of their contents new evidence on historical events, but the whole was little enough considering the delay and expense incurred to get it.

On 5th of January 1878 concluded to wait no longer, but to go to San Luis Rey, sleep there that night, and start the next morning early at 6 on the stage for San Diego.

The drought playing havoc on the stock everywhere—The Santa Margarita has lost nearly 2000 head of cattle.

The 45 miles between San Luis Rey and San Diego were traveled in 9 ½ hours, arriving at the new town at about 3.30 PM on the 6th of January. Next morning went to look for Father Ubach at North San Diego, but as bad luck would have it he had gone to Julian to be absent several days, and his assistant, Father Pujol, couldn't let Mr. Savage have the mission books.

At this time there was no hotel or lodging house, or restaurant in the old place—One bakery and grocery, and another shop, and one small bar-room were the only public houses open, besides the Post Office. The town was almost dead and the new one not thriving very much. Every one expecting to be enriched if the Texas Pacific railroad is built.

Juan Bandini and his daughter Margarita in the 1850s. Courtesy of The Bancroft Library, University of California, Berkeley

Father Pujol was kind enough to present Mr. Savage to some native Californians, from whom interesting narratives, as well as points were obtained—Thus were the statements of Doña Juana Machado (Mrs. Ridington) and Doña Felipa Osuna, widow of Juan María Marrón, secured together with a few old documents.

Fortunately at this time a species of hotel was opened in North San Diego, which was quite a convenience for operations in the town.

Don José María Estudillo also kindly furnished, at his hospitable country residence, some pages of his recollections on events, and men, trade in the old Mexican times &c—Also allowed copies to be made of a few of his late father's documents.

In the mean time Father Ubach returned from Julian, and lent Mr. Savage the old mission records to get from them such items as he needed.

Met with much better luck in San Diego even than was expected. Mrs. Moreno, widow of the last Government Secretary of Pico's administration, happened to be on a visit to old San Diego, and had here a trunk full of her deceased husband's papers which she allowed Mr. Savage to search, and to borrow all he might deem useful for Mr. Bancroft's purpose. Father Ubach and Don Manuel C. Rojo the widow's attorney tried to dissuade him from the search assuring him they had examined the contents of the trunk, and there was nothing of interest to history in it. But he made the search, (January 11th) among 3000 or more letters and memoranda, was rewarded by finding a considerable lot of important documents on the two Californias. The lady acted very cleverly in the matter, for she returned the very next day to her ranch in Guadalupe (Lower California) leaving her documents in Mr. Savage's possession. This was indeed a piece of condescension for she looked upon her late husband's papers as a treasure. A peculiarity of Moreno was that of endorsing every letter "a mi archivo—apuntes para la historia" or other words to the same effect. Most of those papers had no historical facts or important information. The papers were indeed interesting in a historical point of view—Moreno had not only been Secretary in Upper California but taken part in the war against the United States in 1846 and for several years was the *Jefe Político* of the whole region called Northern Frontier of Lower California—But the question arose—were those all the documents on California that the widow Moreno had? Father Ubach seemed to think she might have more, which, perhaps, might be secured in return for a consideration—and Señor Rojo, on giving some points upon Moreno's public life, which was well known to him, said that when Pico and Moreno were on their way to Mulegé in Lower California, "they left behind the archives of the government in some place which is unknown." Had that treasure ever been disinterred?

Another stroke of good fortune was to have induced Don Narciso Botello, for a moderate allowance to come to North San Diego, and give his account of public affairs in which he was an active participant from 1833 to 1847. His narrative of nearly 200 pages (written down in 5 days), is full of information on historical events, manners and customs, education, judicial procedures in criminal and civil causes, etc. It is one of the most important contributions, coming from a man of character who held some of the most responsible positions, and who spoke of that on which he was well informed.

Mr. Botello even after the change of flag was Justice of the Peace by popular choice in Los Angeles, 1858—reelected in 1859, and commissioned a Notary Public by Govr Downey. But now the poor old gentleman is very much reduced in his pecuniary circumstances. Bad luck has followed his every effort to secure him a competency for his old age. He assured Mr. Savage that all his old papers were destroyed by fire, when his house was burned down with all its contents, leaving him without even clothes but those he had on.

A letter came to Father Ubach from Juan Bandini requesting him to explain to Mr. Savage his inability for the time being to carry out his promise about his father's official papers, as they were mixed up with thousands of private letters, and his agricultural business demanded close attention just then. Mr. S. resolved to make his return trip by land—and thus by his chances of seeing both Chauncey Hayes and Bandini, and hold them, if possible, to their promises. Besides, the weather had been so stormy on the coast that there was no certainty when other gales might come on, and prevent the coast steamer from entering Wilmington or Santa Mónica, the most convenient road steads to land and take rail for Los Angeles.

Mr. Savage was tempted to visit the Tía Juana ranch on the Lower California line, and have an interview with the widow of Captain Santiago Argüello, for whom he had letters, but time pressed, the roads were almost impassable, and some well informed persons assured him the lady was much enfeebled, her memory very weak, and that she had no documents.

All the work to be done in North San Diego being finished on the 27th, visited the new town (South San Diego) on the 28th, and deposited all the material collected, (some 600 or more pages) with the Express of Wells Fargo and C° for safe delivery at the Library in San Francisco. Jany 29th At 10 A.M. on the stage to begin the homeward trip. Arrived at San Luis Rey at 6.30 P.M. Next day obtained from Chauncey Hayes at his ranch 5 miles distant two cases pretty well crammed with MSS and newspaper slips, every one of which contained some information on the Californias, or other part of the Pacific coast—They were taken to San Luis under a heavy rain, which however did no damage. After some carpentering to render the cases secure, arranged for their being conveyed to South San Diego, and shipped there for San Francisco.

Bandini's place, 6 miles distant, not visited because it was learned reliably that he was absent in Los Angeles.

Rode this day (31st) 12 miles, which added to the 45 of yesterday, and 33 to be gone over in the night make 90. Tiresome work, particularly the last part which must be done in a rickety wagon without a boot, open on all sides, and devoid of any thing to rest the back on. The road all along from San Diego was very much cut up by the heavy rains, and passenger (Savage being the only one) and baggage had a lively dance from 6.30 P.M. to between 12 and 1. Six mortal hours. Fortunately, it wasn't all to be bad— the weather was pleasant.

Ignacio del Valle. Courtesy of the California History Room, California State Library, Sacramento, California

Resolved to rest one day in San Juan Capistrano and, if possible, get a narration from an old Californian named Blas Aguilar. After some search, discovered the man, plied him with questions, and elicited nothing—his memory was entirely unreliable. Looked after others and met with no better success.

Being too tired to proceed that night to Santa Ana in the Stage, next day left San Juan carrying a lively remembrance of the kindness received there from Judge Egan, Dr. Crane, Pablo Pryor, Don Juan Avila, Father Mut, and others. The 22 miles to Santa Ana were traveled without any mishap; arrived some time in the afternoon. A very promising place is Santa Ana, endowed with a semi-tropical climate and a fertile country—It seems destined to have a bright future. Slept here the night, and the next morning by 10 was in Los Angeles. Visited Mr. Coronel to see if he had found more old documents—he had not, but promised to send whatever he could rake up this same afternoon. It seems he could discover only a few books on Mexican laws which he sent to Mr. Savage.

Feb. 3 at 1 P.M. took the train for Newhall, where he transferred himself to the Stage, bound to Don Ignacio del Valle's famous ranch Camulos, 18 miles distant. This journey was a very hard one, owing to the bad condition of the road. Mr. Savage had a warm letter of recommendation from del Valle's dearest friend Judge Sepúlveda, and was of course received with the cordiality for which del Valle has ever been noted. The gentleman and his lady and other members of the family not only were hospitable exerting themselves to render the visit pleasant, but taking a deep interest in the work of Mr. Bancroft, ransacked drawers, boxes, &c, and placed their papers at Mr. Savage's disposal. Several originals were given, others were copied or extracted from.

Mr. del Valle came to California very young, and served many years as an officer of the Army, and in several civil positions, and after California became a part of the American Union as a State, he served in her Legislature—at all times commanding the respect and esteem of all who knew him for his high character, affability and ready wit. He was well off in worldly goods, possessing a valuable ranch, where some of the best California wine and brandy are made. He has a numerous family, and takes the greatest interest in their education having two able teachers—a lady and gentleman, residing on the estate for the portion who are still of the age to receive instruction.

The gentleman pleaded a weak memory and an unwillingness to impart information which might prove to be erroneous; but he gave way to Mr.

Savage's request, and on the 4th began dictating some of his recollections, which he continued until the 7th, when he shut down declaring his stock of knowledge on California history to be exhausted. Indeed, it was very evident that Mr. del Valle's memory couldn't aid his good desire to please. In the afternoon at 5 ready to take the stage for San Buenaventura, when it was found to be entirely full—There was no help for it, but to wait for the next day's—the only thing regrettable about it being the loss of time—Life at Camulos was a patriarchal one; hard to be compelled to leave it.

Next evening after a cordial God speed, quitted hospitable Camulos on the Stage at 5.15 with one fellow passenger inside, one Mr. Savage was really glad to meet so soon again—Bishop Mora—He, like the writer, was bound to San Buenaventura, preferring the long journey by land because there was no certainty of the Steamer entering the place after the storms had carried away the wharf. Thirty-eight miles of plain to traverse, but the road maltreated by the heavy rains, and the constantly passing vehicles.

Supper at Santa Paula and away to San Buenaventura—arrived at 12.30—last part of the road was fair, the stage good, the driver careful;

Lucrecia del Valle at Rancho Camulos. Courtesy of the Seaver Center for Western History Research, Natural History Museum of Los Angeles County, Los Angeles, California

with these advantages and a tolerably clear moon, the journey was rather pleasant than otherwise.

Lodged at the new house with the high sounding name of "Palace Hotel"—room spacious and nicely furnished, with view on the sea—Hueneme light-house in sight.

Had no difficulty in getting the mission books with the Bishop's favor, and the kindness of the Parish Priest—Father Farrelly, a kind-hearted, gentlemanly and jolly good fellow.

Made the acquaintance of several gentlemen connected with the Guerra and other respectable California families, who promised their aid in the way of letters and their friends in Santa Bárbara.

After some delay and a visit to Don José Arnaz' ranch, received the unpleasant notification that he must go off to Los Angeles at once, but would return in 3 or 4 days. This was unlucky, for the rains continued pouring down heavily and Señor Arnaz was weather bound at Los Angeles. Stages were very irregular in their services, and mails delayed from all directions but the temperature was extremely agreeable. There were no amusements for several days no beef was to be had in the town—very little mutton and very little pork—no fresh fish tho' upon the broad Pacific.

During Arnaz' absence worked at the mission books, took down a short statement of the Californian Ramon Valdés, who gave some interesting items—tried to obtain another from Raimundo Olivas, an old soldier of 78 years of age owning a ranch some 3 miles from the town—was overtaken by a torrent of rain on the way to his place—he solemnly promised to be on hand for the purpose in town, but broke his word—which was, of course, a misfortune, but not a surprise, several others having acted in the same manner. It was really a pity, nevertheless, for the man seemed to have a fresh memory, and considerable information on California affairs.

Just as all prospect of Arnaz' immediate return had become very small, he came back on the evening of the 21st of February. Waited on him at his ranch on the 22d, and found him much fatigued and unwell—promised to be in town the next morning to dictate his memoirs. He did come late and concluded it were best that Mr. Savage should take up his quarters at the Santa Ana ranch (his residence) seven miles from San Buenaventura, which was done, and 95 pages were written down on Feb. 24th, 25th, and 26th, much of the material being on trade, customs etc, Mr. Arnaz and family conducting themselves as the truly generous and genteel folks that they are. On the 27th Mr. Savage intended coming away, but the heavy rains of the past days had so swollen the San Antonio arroyo—a stream to be crossed three times on the way to town—that he was obliged to tarry there another day—the Stage from Nordoff failed to pass.

March 1st Took the stage for Santa Bárbara—the first half of the journey, mostly along the beach, was quite difficult—some distance with the waves striking the stage. For nearly two miles the stage had to go over or around large boulders—Should have alighted and walked this distance in preference, but lameness from rheumatism precluded it—that rheumatism was caused by a cold on the left foot, just where some days before it received a blow at San Luis Rey causing a little limping—the foot had been very painful three or four days. Reached Santa Bárbara safe and sound that afternoon.

For several days mail communications with the North and South were much deranged by bad weather. The wharf of the place had been carried off some days ago. Passed the first week as a lodger and boarder at Raffow's, but after that took lodgings at Cook's building, State St corner of Carrillo, together with Mr. E. F. Murray, who was then engaged in making extracts from the late Capt. de la Guerra's Collection, loaned for the purpose by Hon. Thomas Dibblee, administrator of the Estate.

Mr. Dibblee, though very friendly disposed to Mr. Bancroft, didn't then feel authorized to give those papers away, as he held them only as a portion of the property of the late Captain's heirs. Neither would he assent to any of the papers leaving Santa Bárbara. Mr. Savage had numerous letters which he presented to their respective addresses as soon as possible, and then set himself down to work in earnest early and late, from 8 A.M. to 10 or 11 P.M. nearly every day, including Sundays.

Obtained the mission books, and worked on them when no other business was on hand. When these abstracts were ready on 17th of March forwarded them to San Francisco. Tried to get dictations from the two living sons of Captain de la Guerra, but failed; one of them was disabled by sickness and died during Mr. Savage's sojourn in the place. The other, Capt. Antonio María de la Guerra had lost a part of the roof of his mouth and was blind. He declined making any statement alleging ignorance of events in his youth many years of which he had spent in Chile. For their sister, Angustias (Mrs. Ord) Mr. Savage had letters from their other sister, Teresa (Mrs. Hartnell), and from Santiago de la Guerra—No other difficulty was encountered in procuring Mrs. Ord's narrative, except from delay inevitably caused by her brother's fatal illness. She did, however, as circumstances permitted, make a contribution of 156 pp finished April 4—very valuable data. From other parties received, likewise, good substantial matter—viz:

Augustin Janssens 223 pages of dictation, and the loan of a considerable number of official documents in connection with the U.S. campaign in California and other subjects—from Doña Apolinaria Lorenzana, then blind and indigent, who was one of the Foundling children sent to California by the Viceroy of Mexico in the beginning of the 19ᵗʰ century, 48 pages giving some good matter on the history of San Diego town and mission etc.—from Rafael González, an old soldier who had been at one time *Alcalde* of Santa Bárbara 36 pages.

From the widows of Captains Domingo Carrillo and José Carrillo,* several important original documents; they may be termed a small *bonanza*.

Mr. Savage also made abstracts from a very large quantity of the de la Guerra collection—read hundreds upon hundreds of letters &c, and took note of every useful item.

Judge Huse of Santa Bárbara promised to procure some papers of the Carrillo family, but nothing came of it. The fact was that a son of Don Domingo Carrillo had actually destroyed a large collection of papers which had been in his father's possession, excepting the few that the widow Doña Concepción Pico de Carrillo managed to save. The same foolish thing was done by a daughter of Lieut. Col. Gumersindo Flores, who figured considerably in California from 1834 to 1847. That lady regretted the act, when its heinousness was made clear to her, but it was too late.

Many useful public documents have been smoked up in the form of cigarettes, and others wantonly destroyed, or allowed to decay.

Considerable effort was made to ascertain if there were extant any papers of the Moraga family—all proved in vain. It was said there was a diary of Lieut. Gabriel Moraga which for some reason connected with the new Almaden case, was sent north together with other papers.

Father Romo, the Guardian of the Franciscan convent at the old Santa Bárbara mission, with his usual goodness and enlightenment, furnished Mr. Savage many points of interest.

Toward the last days of Mr. Savage's stay in Santa Bárbara, Mr. Dibblee was so kind as to lend him a quantity of very important papers which he had reserved from Mr. Murray—he did more—actually allowed the privilege of taking them to San Luis Obispo under a solemn promise to return them as soon as possible.

The results of the labor done in Santa Bárbara from March 2ᵈ to April 4ᵗʰ were: about 400 pages of dictations, over 2000 documents and the mission

---

*The former Concepción Pico, sister of ex-Govʳ Pico. The latter, Dolores Domínguez.

books examined from which 200 pages, more or less were extracted—and the original papers presented by Madame Carrillo. It is to be regretted that a good deal of time was wasted in vain searches for collections supposed to exist and to be procurable. The satisfaction remains, however, that every endeavor was made to get whatever there might be useful for the history.

The place couldn't be said to have been exhausted of material—there were a few of the earliest American pioneers, who could supply much; but they were necessarily left for a future day.*

On the evening of the 4th of April took passage on the elegant Steamer "Orizava" for San Luis Obispo. It was a rather difficult thing to get on board—the inner portion of the wharf having been carried away some time before, the passengers had to be conveyed to the outer portion, at which the ship was hauled, in a large launch—each person was carried on a man's back through the heavy surf and dumped, so to speak, into the launch. However, all was accomplished without accident and the passengers made comfortable for the night on the ship, and arrived at Port Harford early in the morning of the 5th. After a short delay the train took them to San Luis Obispo.

Immediately called on Father Roussel, the Catholic Priest, who was very courteous, and forthwith placed at the writer's command the Record books of the missions San Luis Obispo and San Miguel in his charge.

Previous to leaving Santa Bárbara news arrived there of the death of Don Mariano Bonilla—thus, two of the most important men, whose knowledge of California affairs was extensive, quitted this mortal coil within a short time of each other—Bonilla and Francisco de la Guerra—The former was regularly educated for the law, came from Mexico in 1834, and for a number of years and while the Superior Court of Justice existed in California during Mexican times, was its Secretary—he also held several positions before and after the American occupation—His widow and daughters were left almost destitute of means for their support.

Francisco de la Guerra, a son of the veteran Captain José de la Guerra, had been a member of the Assembly, and figured in the negotiations between Andrés Pico, commander of the California forces, and Col. Frémont, which terminated all further struggles on the part of the Californians and Mexicans in the country against the inevitable.

Mr. Savage had very strong letters to Mrs. Wilson (Govr Pacheco's mother), José de Jesús Pico, and others, and promised himself a tolerably

---

*Their copious statements were subsequently obtained by Mr. Murray. The secular archives of Sta Bárbara, for Mexican times, were stolen [illegible] ago from Clerk [illegible]'s premises.

good harvest in this place. The results were not all that he expected, even with allowances, and yet some very good material was secured.

Mrs. Wilson asked to be excused from giving any statement, owing to the shattered condition of her nervous system, which allowed of no exertion on her part.

Don Joaquín Estrada promised, and failed to comply—he might have said a good deal, had he felt disposed. The widow Bonilla searched for papers and gave the few she found. All her husband's documents were destroyed or blown away some years before when they lived on his ranch, and a heavy gale accompanied with rain injured the house carrying off the roof &c.

Mr. Charles Dana offered to search at the family ranch for his father's papers—he feared, however, that most of the old Mexican documents had been smoked up by the herders. Whether this was so or not, the gentleman never furnished any papers. But Mr. Savage owed him the favor of procuring the old Mexican secular archives, which the County Recorder did not know existed in his office. Their number was considerable, but many were circulars, of which the Bancroft Library already had copies—For all that, they yielded about 26 pages of extracts.

Doña Maria Inocenta Pico, widow of Miguel Avila, owner of the ranch on Port Harford and of property in the town of Avila, furnished 31 important pages of narrative, and a good lot of old documents, some of them partly charred. Her husband had been *alcalde* and Judge, noted as a preserver of public documents, of which he had a large collection when his house was burned down, and a large part of his papers destroyed. José de Jesus Pico gave 78 pages and a couple of original documents—a very meager contribution from a man that had participated in many of the most prominent events in California during his life, and should have supplied at least 200 pages. But the smallest favor thankfully received &c. The fact is the old man's memory has been much weakened by pecuniary troubles, and maybe, by a little excess in the use of spirituous liquors.

Inocente García, an old soldier, who for many years had been a *major-domo* of the San Juan Bautista mission, and lastly the Administrator of San Miguel, under whose management it became thoroughly secularized (the *modus operandi* of which he explains), furnished 110 pages.

Canuto Boronda, and Ignacio Ezquer (the latter's wife said to be a daughter of ex-Govr Alvarado) dictated 24 and 33 pages respectively.

In the midst of all that work and all the time endeavoring to procure more, abstracts were made from the papers loaned in Santa Bárbara by Mr. Dibblee.

The stage stop in San Luis Obispo. Savage took the stage from San Luis Obispo to Jolon in April 1878. Reproduced by permission of the Huntington Library, San Marino, California

Strenuous efforts were made to ascertain the whereabouts of the books of the Vigilance Committee—inquiries were made from men that had belonged to the committee and made no secret of it, but without learning anything satisfactory.

Met Padre Ambris, the Curate of San Antonio, and made arrangements with him for the books of that mission and of La Soledad. As to loose documents he at first denied the existence of any in his possession, but finally confessed that he had them "bien guardados en la sacristía."

Examined two collections of newspapers and found nothing in them worth noting down.

Had the good fortune to obtain from the widow of Hon. Walter Murray his long Diary of Col. Stevenson's Regiment (to which he belonged) from New York to San Francisco, and of the campaign of a certain portion of it under Lieut. Col. Burton in Lower California, a most interesting contribution to the history of the American occupation of the two Californias. The lady, in addition to much kindness from herself and family, allowed Mr. Savage to bring the book to San Francisco, and return it when convenient, as she wished to retain the original for Judge Murray's young son.

And now every thing that could be done in the place was already accomplished—this had been amid much difficulty and interruption, caused part of the time by the festivities of the Holy Week, at other times by unpropitious weather, and not seldom by procrastination.

On the 14th of April Mr. Savage accompanied by José de Jesús Pico proceeded in the train to the ranch of the latter's sister, Señora de Avila; the train didn't stop at Avila, but carried them to the pier at Port Harford—after inquiry found there was no certainty of the train going back to town till night—to save time, they walked back, passed over several trestle-work bridges at fearful heights over chasms—the footing was very narrow and slippery—at the time it was raining, hailing, and blowing quite a gale—then to avoid the last bridge which was the longest and most perilous, walked 3½ miles under the heavy rain, opening their way through thick bushes, and waded an arroyo. Of course on arriving at Mrs. Avila's both were in a sorry plight. Life was really imperiled on that travel over the bridges, but the time was saved, work was done at writing, and examining papers—the train did not go back till 8 P.M. to San Luis, and Mrs. Avila wouldn't permit them to leave on it.

After placing every thing that was to go to San Francisco in charge of Wells, Fargo & Co.'s Express, secured a seat in the Stage for Jolon, 5 or 6 miles from San Antonio. Just as Mr. Savage's baggage was on the stage, and he on the point of taking his seat, was advised that Doña Modesta Castro, the widow of the former Comandante General of California, José Castro, was expected in town that day. She had been living, (about 24 miles from town) at the Nipomo Ranch, her daughter being the wife of William Dana, and Mr. Savage had endeavored to procure some narrative from her, thro some member of her family, but it was all unavailing. It would have been perhaps, but fair, to obtain from the widow something in Castro's favor, as so much has been said against him. But those who should have done the needful towards it, didn't seem to manifest any interest. Saw three of Castro's sons in the place—one, Estevan, who had been interested in mines, and at one time a member of the California Legislature, was now for some days a City Policeman, which position he resigned—the other two brothers had no social standing.

Traveled all day the 1st of May, on the Stage, through Paso de Robles, where the passengers partook of breakfast—the place has mineral baths, and its whole aspect was neat and pleasant, as far as it was possible to judge in the few minutes allowed to breakfast and look about. Arrived at Jolon (45 miles from San Luis Obispo) in 12½ hours travel.

On the 2d rode over to the mission, and learned that the old Indian Padre Ambris had gone off to Soledad intending to return in one or two days.

Top: A group of Native Californians outside Mission San Antonio in 1875, three years before Savage visited there. Courtesy of the California Historical Society, FN-36290

Bottom: A Native Californian, Perfecta Encinal, and her family at Mission San Antonio during restoration activities in 1903. Courtesy of the California Historical Society, FN-36289

There was nothing to do about it but to await his coming, as the books and papers couldn't be had till then. Whilst at the mission inspecting the buildings, a large portion of which was in ruins, and surroundings had a taste of the quality of the ants of San Antonio, in the form of bites, two in the back of the neck and another in the forehead—the pain caused was severe and lasting, as the burning had not disappeared entirely the next day altho' cool water and deposits of ammonia, were constantly applied. The weather was hot, and Jolon afforded no means of spending time agreeably. The house accommodations are tolerable. Whilst waiting, did some translation of the genealogy of Capt. de la Guerra's parents, by request of Mr. Dibblee of Santa Bárbara.

As bad luck would have it, Padre Ambris didn't come back till the evening of the 5th. On his passing Jolon, Mr. Savage spoke to him—and the next morning as soon as he could procure a wagon repaired to the mission, and got its books as well as those of La Soledad. The priest gave him also a lot of old letters, sermons, and other documents. Among the ruins under the roof were found buried under mounds of mud fragments more or less preserved of numerous official letters—all that were tolerably legible or had authorized signatures were secured for the Bancroft Library—The search was repeated on the 9th when he went to return the books, and it was rewarded with the finding of more such material. This last day the Priest was stung in his bald head by bees, and Mr. Savage again bitten by ants—Padre Ambris had a small bottle containing a preparation of *yerba de la víbora* (snake's master), which he applied to his own head, and to the spot where Mr. Savage had been bitten, and the smarting pain disappeared as if by magic.

Saw one of the old mission Indians, and tried to get information from him, but he proved to be almost an imbecile—being asked if it was true that the old missionary P. Juan Sancho, had been really the despot and cruel man some had represented him, the old Indian twice exclaimed, Ah, Padre Sancho! Ah, Padre Sancho! and looked as if he were then writhing under the lash that Sancho was so fond, it is traditionally given, of applying to his dusky wards.

It was here that the venerable ex-Prefect Sarría died and was buried by Padre Mercado in 1835. According to Father Ambris, Mercado told him a long time afterward that previous to leaving the mission he opened Sarría's grave and discovered the body to be in a perfect state of preservation—but the habit having been destroyed, he wrapped the remains in a new one. Ambris added that several years later, Bishop Amat being at the mission, he (the curate) suggested the idea of reopening the grave to see if the body was still undecayed; but the Bishop discountenanced it. Mr. Savage asked permission to open the grave, and would have paid the expense to do it, but the Padre refused it, not wishing to incur the censure of his Prelate.

On the 9th all work being finished, in the evening took the stage for Los Coches, where he arrived about 2 o'clock, having traveled some 40 miles. Slept here the rest of the night, and after an early breakfast took the train at Soledad for Chualar, it being important to see a gentleman named Carlos Olvera, about the collection of papers of his father Agustín Olvera, of whom evil tongues had reported that he appropriated to himself or hid the minutes of the last sessions of the *Excelentísima Asamblea,* of which he was Secretary and a member.

Chualar Station is within sight of Olvera's house in the "rancho de los Malarines," but the Salinas river was between them, and it was most difficult to procure a vehicle or horse to go across—no one would let his horse go over from fear of the quicksand—after some hours of useless exertion, fortune favored. Don Urbano Malarín, brother-in-law and neighbor of Olvera, came over. Mr. Savage and he had become acquainted the previous year at Monterey—Malarín procured a horse; and that same afternoon they waded the Salinas and reached Olvera's in safety, where Mr. Savage was received and treated very hospitably, and passed the night—Mr. Olvera is a gentleman who enjoys a good reputation for character and integrity, and on receiving his assurance that he would examine his papers and send to the Library in San Francisco, as a loan, all such as had any bearing on history, Mr. Savage felt that his promise was not like that of some others who had disregarded their offers as soon as his back was turned.

Next morning under the kind guidance of Mr. Malarín, returned to Chualar, and took the train for Salinas, arriving there about noon. About 3 P.M. started on the Stage for Monterey to see Vicente Gómez, and learn from him what old men there were in the region of San Juan, Hollister, Gilroy &c. from whom dictations could be got. It was Saturday. Gómez suggested Felipe Arce, and Don Rafael Pinto, and one or two others who were not easily accessible, and not important.

Spent Sunday in Monterey, and on Monday morning returned to Salinas—took the train for Sargent, and from thence per stage to San Juan Bautista, arriving in the afternoon. Bad luck again—the Parish priest— Father Rubio had gone off to Los Angeles to attend the funeral of his Prelate, Bishop Amat. Was soon expected, but some days passed, and he didn't come, nor would his assistant allow the mission books to be touched. During stay in San Juan had a serious attack of illness, about four days, tho' the first two were the worst ones. Felipe Arce proved to be an old man who had been a soldier under the Spanish and Mexican domination—quite an imbecile from old age and family troubles.

In the mean time having made a trip to Hollister and seen Rafael Pinto, who was a little unwell, but promised to relate all he remembered in two or three days when he should feel better, finding after further waiting at San Juan that Father Rubio wouldn't be back yet for some days, concluded to take up quarters at Hollister, and write down Señor Pinto's narrative, taking advantage of his temporary sojourn, where he was on a visit to his married daughter, his residence being on his ranch in vicinity of Watsonville.

Pinto was Collector of San Francisco at the time of the American occupation, tho' he was not in the place at the time the U.S. flag was hoisted over it. Discovered that he possessed many valuable papers that the Society of Pioneers, thro Hon. Philip A. Roach had been after, and he refused to let them have—finally consenting to give them the Custom House flag. He assured Mr. Savage that some of the papers had been destroyed, but he still had a good collection, which in a few days when he returned to Watsonville he would send to the Bancroft Library. In the mean time he dictated 106 pages of his recollections, which were finished in the afternoon of the 23^d of May. Next day at 2.15 P.M. by train to Tres Pinos. At this place took short narratives of two brothers Germán, one from young Estolano Larios on life and adventures of his father, and one quite interesting from an old Indian named Julio César who was born in the mission of San Luis Rey.

On the evening of the 28th received a telegram from San Juan advising the return of Father Rubio—next morning went in a buggy to the old mission, and made arrangements with the Priest to work on his books the next morning—the abstracts were made in about seven or eight hours, and were it not for the necessity of having complete records of the missions, wouldn't be worth the time and money expended to procure them.

San Juan was at one time the centre of the cattle trade of California, where the drivers from the South brought their stock and purchasers from the North met. It was then a lively place, and its principal hotel is said to have set the best table in the State—Business was brisk, and amusements, especially gambling, contributed to bring a large concourse of people to the town, money passing freely from hand to hand. But that is a thing of the past—railroads have killed San Juan, and were it not for the few excursionists from Hollister that visit it, the place would be almost as quiet as a cemetery.

There were no old Mexican archives to be found either at San Juan Bautista (or, as it was named during the administration of Gov.ʳ Alvarado, San Juan de Castro)* or at Hollister. The county of San Benito being recently formed by detaching it from that of Monterey, the archives of San Juan are together with those of the latter county at Salinas.

May 31.ˢᵗ At 8 A.M. departed for Hollister to take the train for Gilroy, that being the most convenient route as to time, tho' a trifle more expensive. It afforded also an opportunity to visit Don Rafael Pinto, and refresh his memory as to his collection of documents. Got another assurance from him, and went on to Gilroy.

On the 1st of June took a narrative of 33 pages from an old Californian named Justo Larios, and not having been able to find other parties that were supposed able to make contributions, the next day (Sunday) left on the train for San José—tarried there till early next morning, and proceeded to San Francisco, where he arrived safely after an absence of 8 months less three days, during which time there was incurred an expense of between fifteen and sixteen hundred dollars for salary, traveling charges of all kinds, board, gratuities &c &c.

Since his return to San Francisco Mr. Savage has obtained at trifling expense dictations and old documents from various quarters, making probably over 600 pages.

He visited the ex-missions of San Rafael, San José, and San Francisco (generally called Mission Dolores), and made abstracts from their old Record Books. So that the Bancroft Library possessed copies and abstracts from all but two of the 21 missions, the missing ones being San Fernando and San Luis Rey.

It is supposed there must be at least five collections of documents existing that Mr. Bancroft has not had access to—those of the two Argüello branches (Luis and Santiago's), Estudillo, Pacheco, and Covarrubias.

The writer does not know where the two Argüello collections may be.

It is understood ex-Gov.ʳ Romualdo Pacheco has the papers of his father the Captain of the same name. He promised to let Mr. Bancroft have the use of them, but the promise has remained unfulfilled.

The collection of General José M. Covarrubias must be in the hands of the widow, or of his son, the Sheriff of Santa Bárbara. This gentleman promised the writer at that place to search among the old papers, and lend Mr. Bancroft for his historical purposes such as he might find containing historical matter; but to the date of writing this—Sept. 17. 1879—no such papers have come to hand.

Its present official name is South San Juan.

Top: Mission Dolores in the nineteenth century. Bottom: Mission San José in the nineteenth century. Both images courtesy of the Seaver Center for Western History Research, Natural History Museum of Los Angeles County, Los Angeles, California.

That of the Estudillo family is missing. Mr. Savage understood that they were in possession of Hon. J. G. Estudillo, the State Treasurer, and lost no time, on his return to San Francisco, in making application for the same. Mr. Estudillo replied on the 17 of July 1878, it would afford him much pleasure to comply with Mr. Bancroft's wishes, but unfortunately he had not such papers, nor had he ever seen them. Indeed, he believed they were scattered and lost many years before.

With unfeigned satisfaction it is recorded here that Carlos Olvera of Chualar, and Rafael Pinto of Watsonville, faithfully carried out their promises in due time. Their collections contain much valuable matter that the history of California would not have been complete without. They form good sized volumes—

During his travels Mr. Savage made every possible effort to procure the needed material. He applied to all persons, reasonably accessible and supposed to be able to furnish it, and regrets to say that he found quite a number who were totally indifferent to the country's history being written or left unwritten, and who couldn't be induced to devote any time to the subject— each one pleaded of course, some plausible reason—such as bad memory, ill-health, business &c. Their testimony had, therefore, to remain unrecorded. Some few would have been willing enough to dictate, but their statements were not worth having, being unreliable, for one reason or another.

There were found some old men and women that would speak fluently on events they professed to have witnessed or obtained from good sources. To one uninformed on the country's history their talk appears sound enough and even interesting. But to one who has gathered his information from the best authorities, and read nearly all the official documents issued since the foundation of the first settlement, and even back of that, the effect is quite different. The latter finds that such chroniclers are not only unable to furnish dates in most cases, but that their descriptions of events are jumbled.

The fact is that the majority of those men were illiterate common soldiers who had no means of learning any thing, beyond what passed under their own eyes, but from hearsay, rumor, or tradition transmitted to them by word of mouth—We know how much weight must be given to all that. They might speak of some Indian fight they were in, or of the modes of life in their youth, or of some other subject that their uneducated minds could understand; but to treat of government policy or any other matters of similar import is beyond their depth.

The experience of searching the records in Sacramento, and making abstracts from books, early newspapers, charts &c, existing in the State Library there, had been resolved upon for some time past, and not effected because of other pressing business. As the gathering of that material could be no longer delayed, Mr. Savage left for that city, via Vallejo, on the afternoon of July 8th 1879. The next day a little after 10 A.M. was at work taking notes from the "Californian," newspaper published in San Francisco in 1847, being the second volume of the paper of the same name that was issued in Monterey since shortly after the occupation by the United States forces in 1846. This work was finished on the 16th.

During that time examined the old archives at the offices of the Secretary of State, and County Clerk, postponing for a few days the taking of them in hand. Took notes also from the "California Star," and "Cal. Star and Californian"—all the notes from the three Journals were forwarded to San Francisco on the 17th of July—and began to extract from the "Placer Times" of Sacramento.

The next day (18th) took notes from the old archives at the County Clerk's, being the records of the Court of first Instance, and the Criminal Court, before the American Judicial system had been established—Examined several books, from which but little useful matter was obtained. The Mexican records at the Secretary of State's office were voluminous, but were copies of original land grants and documents therewith connected which exist in the office of the U.S. Surveyor General at San Francisco, and of course, there was no need of taking notes from them.

After finishing with the "Placer Times" about the 25th, began work on the "Transcript", and "Placer Times & Transcript"; but stopped it, to take out all useful matter in Horace Culver's Sacramento City Directory, issued January 1851, understood to be the only copy (or possibly one of two) existing.

Finally, having obtained from the Board of Trustees permission to take to San Francisco the books called for from the Bancroft Library, on Mr. Bancroft's guarantee, they were forwarded.

Mr. Savage not having any further cause to remain in Sacramento, where the heat had been almost unbearable nearly all the time of his sojourn there, returned to San Francisco in the afternoon of the 31st, taking with him the book he was working on. During that visit to finish the work, he had to labor assiduously from early morning till 10 P.M. almost daily—

Before closing these remarks he desires to state that to the enlightened kindness of Mr. Cravens, the Librarian, and of the County Clerk, he was indebted for facilities to fulfill the commission entrusted to him. Mr. Secretary of State Beck and his assistant were also ready to do his part toward the same end.

Bancroft Library
San Francisco, Cal.
Sept. 17 1879
Thos Savage

Original Transcript of Interview of Rosalía Vallejo by Henry Cerruti

History of the Bear Party *by Mrs. R. Leese*
Narrative of Mrs. Rosalia Leese who witnessed the hoisting of the bear flag in Sonoma on the 14th of June 1846.

Q. Please madam Leese, tell me what you know with reference to the hoisting of the Bear Flag in Sonoma.
A. About half past five in the morning of June 14th 1846, an old gentleman called Don Pepe de la Rosa came to my house and notified me that a band of seventy two rough looking desperadoes, many of them runaway sailors from whale ships had surrounded the house of General Vallejo and had arrested him, Captain Salvador Vallejo and Victor Prudón. On hearing this alarming piece of intelligence, I dressed in a hurry and hastened to the streets for the purpose of ascertaining the truth of such report—the first thing which met my eyes was Colonel Prudón hastening to the rescue of Captain Salvador Vallejo, whom a ruffian called Benjamin Kelsey was trying to murder in cold blood. I don't believe that you can give a different name to the killing of an unarmed prisoner by a stalwart bully who had seventy men of his own ilk at his back. The timely arrival of Prudón saved the life of the defenseless Captain whom the companions of Kelsey hurried off towards the party under Doctor Semple to all appearance the least inhuman of that godforsaken crowd. I also perceived ex-Commander General Vallejo dressed in the uniform of a general of the Mexican army, a prisoner of a large group of rough looking men, some wearing on their heads caps made with the skins of coyotes or wolfs, some wearing slouched hats full of holes, some wearing straw hats as black as charcoal. The majority of this marauding band wore buck-skin pants, some blue pants that reached only to the knees, several had no shirts, shoes were only to be seen on the feet of fifteen or twenty among the whole lot.

After some parleying among themselves, a great many of them mounted their horses and escorted General Vallejo, Captain Salvador Vallejo, Colonel Victor Prudón and my husband Jacob Leese to Sacramento where they were delivered to the tender mercy of the arch fiend John A. Sutter, a man who though married in Europe where he had left a wife and several children, was living in open concubinage with two black women whom he had brought in his vessel from the Sandwich Islands.

After General Vallejo had been hurried away, the remaining robbers hoisted in the square of Sonoma, on the flag staff that was standing in the corner of the plaza near the old mission church, a piece of linen about the size of a large towel, in it was painted a red bear and a lone star. It is fair to presume that John C. Frémont, the man who had planned the wholesale robbery of California, though an officer of the United States army, was afraid to compromise the honor of his government if his party pursued their thieving operations under the flag, that lovers of liberty throughout the world hold dear, hence his reason for resorting to the adoption of a flag unknown to civilized nations. As soon as the flag of the Bear had been hoisted, the robbers interpreter, Solís (formerly a servant of my husband) notified me that I was a prisoner, and he pointed towards four ill-looking desperadoes who stood near me with drawn pistols. Resistance being useless, I yielded and at their request gave them the key of the storehouse of my husband. No sooner I gave them the key, they called their friends and began ransacking the storehouse where were deposited provisions and liquor sufficient to feed two hundred men during two years. Few days after the departure of my husband, arrived in Sonoma John C. Frémont, who as he then said, came for the sole and only purpose of arranging matters so as to give general satisfaction, and protect every one against extortion or oppression. That man, whom many paid writers have dubbed with many an endearing epitet was a great coward. I say so with good reason—hear me—on the 20th of June, news reached Sonoma that Captain Padilla at the head of one hundred men was coming to the rescue of Sonoma, no sooner Fremont heard this than he sent for me and ordered me to address Padilla a letter requesting him to return to San José, and not to approach Sonoma. I flatly refused, but Frémont, who was bent on having his way, told me that he would burn our houses with us inside of them if I refused to address Padilla in the manner he wished me to do so, ("mandaré quemar las casas con ustedes adentro si Padilla se acerca a Sonoma"). I consented, not for the purpose of saving my life, but being then in the family way, I had no right to endanger the life of my unborn baby, moreover I judged that a man who had already gone so far would not stop at anything which may be a barrier to his ends, and being desirous of saving trouble to my countrywomen, I wrote the fatal letter which induced Captain Padilla to retrace his steps— while on the alert for Padilla, Frémont changed his shining uniform for a blue blouse, put away his hat and wrapped his head with a common handkerchief—he adopted this fantastic style of dress for the purpose of avoiding recognition. Is this the conduct becoming a brave man?

During the whole time Frémont and his gang were in Sonoma, robberies were very common. Ladies dared not go out for a walk unless escorted by their husband and brothers. Among my maid servants I had a young Indian girl about seventeen years of age; and I assure you that many a time John C. Frémont sent me orders to deliver her to the officers of the barracks, but by resorting to artifices I managed to save the unhappy girl from the fate decreed to her by the lawless band who had imprisoned my husband. During the whole time of my husband's imprisonment I forwarded him delicacies and gold, but the recreant Sutter, who on more than one occasion had been compelled to acknowledge the superiority of Mr. Leese, arranged matters so that during the two months of his imprisonment he never received a single dollar. He kept him during one whole week sleeping on the bare floor, and appointed as jailer of this room in which he was confined an uncouth Missourian who whenever he opened the door insulted the prisoners, whom a band of ungrateful horse thieves, trappers and runaway sailors had deprived of their liberty. I could relate many a misdeed of the Bear Flag crowd, but not wishing to detain you any longer I will close with the remark that those hated men inspired me with such a large dosis of hate against their race, that though twenty eight years have elapsed since that time, I have not yet forgotten the insults they heaped upon me, and not being desirous of coming in contact with them I have abstained from learning their language.

Monterey—June 27th 1874
Por Rosalía de Leese.
Rosana Leese.

Original Transcript of Interview of Dorotea Valdez by Henry Cerruti

Reminiscences of Dorotea Valdez with reference to Governor Arrillaga. Arrival of man of war Asia. Destruction of Monterey by the pirates under Captn Hipolito Bouchard. Appearance of Solano in Monterey. Doings of David Spencer Esq. Conduct of Micheltorena. Some items about Yankees in general. etc.

My father was called Juan Bautista Valdez, he came to upper California with Captain Rivera, the first settler of the city of San Diego, and afterwards emigrated to Monterey where I was born in 1793, and I have witnessed every event which have transpired since that time, but being a woman was denied the privilege of mixing in politics or in business, my education has been very limited, yet my memory is good, and being aware of the fact that you are the emissary of a learned man, bent on a noble object, namely writing a reliable history of this country, I will with great pleasure give you the benefit of my recollections, you can at leisure proceed to ask me questions.

Q: Do you remember the funeral of Gov. Arrillaga? (1814)
Answer: I do, his Excellency lies buried in the ex-mission of Soledad, his funeral was a very imposing one, and was witnessed by hundred of good citizens of Spain, the missionaries of four missions and a great many Indians, and every soldier belonging then to the Presidio of Monterey—at his funeral José el Cantor and upward of four hundred neophytes kept up a continuous singing of the miserere. By way of digression I will observe, that José el Cantor, though then a young indian was an excellent singer, understood music and Latin of the church as well as any priest. After governor Arrillaga was buried, a monument was raised over his grave, and during many years afterwards on the 2^d day of November hundreds of Indians and many white men and women visited his grave for the purpose of placing flowers over it. The mission of Soledad is now in ruins, only a part of the church exists, yet I can point out the place where Arrillaga was buried, for I have often prayed in front of his tomb.

Q: Was you in Monterey when the Spanish man of war "Asia" arrived from Peru? (1825)
A: I don't remember the year in which that event took place, but I remember the day in which Captain Martinez landed in a large boat which

contained six stout "gachupines" arrived with shining cutlasses; those chaps were dressed in white pants and wore good shoes. When the ship "Asia" was first seen by the look-out (vijia) at the fort, Governor Argüello, whose father was governor Arrillaga, believing that the large ship had hostile intentions, ordered all the old men, children and women to go to the woods, and prepared himself for a good fight. (In my opinion, would have been madness for him to offer resistance to the "Asia" a vessel that mounted upward of fifty guns, had a crew of nearly one thousand men, while he could not have mustered more than two hundred men, beside the guns of the fort, and the weapons of his soldiers were of the very poorest kind) but when Captain Martinez came on shore and saluted him with great politeness, Governor Argüello took him inside the walls of the Presidio, and I remember well that during the time that the ship was in port Gov. Argüello and Captn Martinez used to walk out every evening arm in arm—two days after the Captain of the large war vessel had taken up his abode at the Presidio, about five hundred or more of the sailors came on shore and built themselves temporary houses with the sails of their ship. They also built a large oven in which they baked bread. The sailors of this ship were mostly Spaniards who had been a great many years engaged in fighting in the coast of Peru and Chile. They behaved very well, paid in good Spanish coin for everything they purchased, and showed a great spirit of liberality by giving away to the Californians and neophytes many sacks of sugar, an article then very scarce in Monterey and which at the time sold for four bits a pound and when very scarce even at one dollar for a pound of twelve ounces. After the sailors had remained on shore nineteen days they returned to the big ship which was then sent away to some of the ports on the pacific. I do not now exactly remember whether she was taken to Mazatlán or Acapulco, but this much I know, that, she was placed under the command of a Peruvian sea captain called D^n Juan Malarín who as a reward for this service, which he performed to the satisfaction of the Mexican government, was made first lieutenant of the Mexican navy. Captain Malarín died in 1849 leaving eleven children, eight daughters and three sons, the whole of whom are now living, some reside in Monterey and others in Santa Clara county. Some of the sailors of the *Asia* were granted permission to remain on shore, and their descendants might be found among the oldest and most esteemed families of Californians. I must not forget to mention that during the early days of this country, in fact until the arrival of the Americans, our population increased very rapidly. It was then not an unusual thing to see a mother leading to church twenty four children all begotten by the same husband, and I am not far from the mark, when I state that the average number of children raised by one mother was rather above than below the number of eleven; but since the Americans have taken possession of this country, sterility has become very common, because the American women are too fond of visiting doctors and swallowing medicines. Este es un delito que Dios no perdona.

Q:Was you in Monterey when Captain Hipolito arrived in command of two pirate vessels? (1818)
A: I was living in the presidio with the family of governor Sola; I cannot describe the battle which took place, nor the manner in which the Presidio of Monterey was sacked, because early in the morning of that fatal day, Governor Sola ordered the women old men and children to be driven to the woods. I assure you that they drove us away in a hurry for the greater part of us went away almost naked, and among the whole lot there were but two persons who wore shoes, none had dresses. I remember one smart girl who ran away carrying on her head a cora (basket) filled with boiled beans. It was indeed funny to see her long hair streaming in the wind with grease running down from her neck and other parts of her body. As soon as the runners which Governor Sola had sent to the missions nearest Monterey notifying them that the non-combatants of Monterey had gone to the "Rancho del Rey" the good fathers and the wealthy people of the surrounding country sent us food and clothing. After remaining two days in the "Rancho del Rey" we returned to this place, but instead of houses we only found smouldering ruins. The hated pirates had sacked our dwellings and afterwards burned everything they could lay their hands upon, yet our people "hicieron buena cara a un mal que ya no tenia remedio" and with the assistance of carpenters, blacksmiths, and many neophytes in less than four months our city looked as smart as before the arrival of the pirate captain.

Q: Was you in Monterey when the indians from Sonoma visited Monterey?
A: At the time Solano visited Monterey, I was residing with Madam Prudencia Amesti and I took particular notice of the tall figure of that dark coloured savage, who was dressed like the people of my race; his many followers however were dressed like indians, and wore feathers round their heads, many of them were tattooed round their wrists, arms and legs— their presence we disliked very much because their conduct was really

overbearing. Solano and his indians were all mounted on fine horses, all had achimas but few of them had saddles. They wore long hair, carried their bows and arrows, and their appearance was such as to inspire fear. I really believed them to be devils let loose from hell. Not every one of the indians had a dark colour like Solano, some had white skins, but the majority looked very red in the face. I heard my mistress say, that the arrival of these savages in Monterey, was a plague sent by god, for the purpose of punishing us for our sins. Solano did not remain long in Monterey, he was prevailed upon to return to Sonoma, by Governor Alvarado and D^n Pablo de la Guerra, at that time a very influential citizen of this country and one of the chiefs of the custom house.

Q: Can you tell me something about D^n David Spencer?
A: Of course I can—I have known him since 1824 when he arrived from Europe for the purpose of serving the large firm of foreigners that had purchased the products of the missions. I knew him when he did business on his own account. I was present at his wedding. I assisted his wife when inside of one week she buried one grand-daughter, one grand-son and the only son of D^n David. I have known him when he was a high officer of the government of Mexico and I assure you that myself and countrymen have the greatest respect for him. We consider him very honest. (Though is known to me that in the early days of California, say from 1834 to 1842 Mr Spencer did considerable smuggling yet this does not detract one inch from the good standing of Mr Spencer, because in those days smuggling was all the go and no man could have made a single dollar without resorting to some kind of sharp practice, because every commercial transaction was done on long credit, duties were high, and money very scarce except in the coffers of the missionaries) and we only regret that the bump of generosity is not fully developed in his head. Since the death of his only son, Mr Spencer has taken charge of his three grand-sons and is having them educated by the italians priests that keep a boys school in Santa Clara. They are fine boys full of promises.

Q: Do you know Mr Jacks?
A: "El Señor Jacks es el dueño del pueblo" I consider him a very mean man, a cunning rascal, a pious hypocrite, "miserable cual ninguno" he even denies his own wife and children the comforts of life—at present Jacks consider himself a millionaire, but as soon as the rail-road will begin to run, many

strangers will come and settle in our midst and then, rest assured, he will get his desserts; all we want is a smart lawyer to take away from him the lands of the pueblo, lands which no person had right to give away, because said lands did not belong to the American authorities who contracted the debts for whose payment were sold, but were the property of every man, woman and child born in our town: when the lands now owned by David Jacks were the property of the town, wood could be had by gathering it; our horses and cattle fed everywhere and no person ever troubled them, but since this bad man got possession of our property, he has fenced everywhere, and even the celebrated "pozo" (well) where the "insurgentes" first landed in 1818 is now under fence. Mr Jacks is an innate enemy of everything having relation to our ancient history; he even attempted to get possession of the crops planted near the bridge in 1770 by father Junipero who on the seventh day of June of that year said his first mass under the live oak near which the crops now stand.

Q: *Were you ever acquainted with General Micheltorena?*
A: I have known General Micheltorena, he was a very good man, a great deal better than we deserved, however he had the misfortune to arrive in a very bad time, and to lead an army composed almost of robbers and cowards, he ruled but very little time because driven by hunger he was compelled to surrender his army to the native Californians, but I am certain that if Micheltorena had been given an equal opportunity he would have whipped his enemies. This unfortunate General came to the country in a very bad epoc. I heard him say that General Vallejo had sent for him, had made him very good promises and when he arrived here, denied him his support. I believe every word General Micheltorena said, because he was by far the best and most popular man of the two. Every poor man could get lands free from General Micheltorena, every man was allowed the privilege of addressing him in the street and he did justice to every one he came in contact with; while General Vallejo whenever he came to Monterey he placed some of his Sonoma savages in front of the door of his house, and compelled every passerby to take off their hats,——mind me the people were compelled to make a salute to the house, and not to the general, who being inside could not know who were the persons who had passed in front of his dwelling. General Micheltorena was a tall man, of very light complexion, always shaved clean, when in California was about forty eight years of age, but looked a great deal younger. I consider him a very much

abused man, he came to this country at the special request of the most prominent men of California, and no sooner had he arrived than everybody turned against him, he however behaved with bravery and prudence, and his surrender is to be attributed to a desire on his part to avoid bloodshed. After Micheltorena surrendered in Los Angeles, Pío Pico became governor and José Castro Commander General. The interests and private views of these two gentlemen being antagonistic, bad feelings prevailed to an alarming extent among the inhabitants of the southern and northern Californias. Pio Pico used every means in his power for the purpose of removing the Custom House from Monterey to San Pedro, the port of Los Angeles, and Castro wanted it in San Francisco. D^n Pio Pico was intriguing with Forbes for the purpose of obtaining an english protectorate, and Castro guided by General Vallejo was doing his best for the purpose of having the country annexed to the United States. To make a long story short, I will conclude by saying that if the Americans had not taken the country in 1846, in 1847 every native Californian would have been killed in civil war; the feeling of hate was very bitter, good men preached in vain for nobody was willing to listen to the voice of reason.

Q: Was you in Monterey when Commodore Sloat hoisted the American flag in Monterey?
A: Though at time of the arrival of Com^{dr} Sloat in Monterey I resided in Soledad, I remember having heard people say, that the Commodore was in port several days before he made up his mind to take the place; he hoped that the people of California would make a revolution against Mexico, and request his assistance in securing their independence. He was led to believe that such would be the case by Mr Larkin: I also heard that he hoisted the American flag, because he was informed that the english emissaries were ready to deliver the country to England as soon as an english man of war should arrive in port. Commodore Sloat when he took the place on the 6th day of July 1846 only landed one hundred and sixty men who hoisted the American flag on the flag staffs of the Custom House, government house and Fort (the Fort was good for nothing) the soldiers landed by the Commodore behaved very well, but the rabble that afterwards came with Captn Fremont acted more like thieves than soldiers. Captain Fremont never presented himself before the enemy, and his partners stole horses, saddles, aguardiente, and everything else they could lay their hands upon. I have heard my countrymen curse the soldiers of Micheltorena but I assure you,

that they were gentlemen compared with the trappers which Fremont brought to Monterey.

Monterey, June 27, 1874

José Abrego, Esq.ʳ
Please peruse the few pages of history dictated to me by Dorotea Valdez and let me know if the contents are in consonance with truth and veracity.
Respectfully your obt. Serv.ʳ
Henry Cerruti

Monterey, June 28, 1874
Los hechos referidos por Dorotea Valdes creo son muy cerca de la verdad.
Su Afm. S.
José Abrego

Biographical Sketches of Historical Figures

José Ramón Abella was born near Zaragoza, Spain, in 1764. He came to New Spain as a Franciscan in 1795 and entered Alta California at Santa Bárbara in 1798. He served at San Francisco from that date until 1819, and during that time participated in two important exploratory journeys into the interior of California. After his stay at San Francisco he moved to Mission San Carlos at Carmel, where he remained until 1833. When, at the request of the Mexican government, a group of friars from the missionary college of Guadalupe, in Zacatecas, replaced the Spanish friars in the northern Alta California missions, he moved south to San Luis Obispo, where he ministered until 1841. He died at Santa Inés in 1842. (Geiger, *Franciscan Missionaries*, 3–6)

José Abrego came to Alta California in 1834 with the Híjar-Padrés colony. He became a merchant in Monterey and held a variety of political offices. He served as treasurer of the territory from 1839 to 1846. After the war, he continued as a merchant in Monterey until his death in 1878. One of his sons, Abimael, married Adelaida Leese, daughter of Rosalía Vallejo. (Bancroft, *California*, 2:686; Northrop, *Spanish-Mexican Families*, 2:1)

José Antonio Aguirre was born in about 1793 in Spain. He established a very successful trading concern in Guaymas, Mexico, and engaged in the California coastal trade. He lived in Santa Bárbara from at least 1838, and married María del Rosario Estudillo. He was still living in Santa Bárbara in the 1850s. (Bancroft, *California*, 2:688)

Gervasio Alipás was involved in the San Diego phase of the movement against Governor Victoria in 1831. He was executed by the Los Angeles vigilantes in 1836. (Bancroft, *California*, 2:690)

José Alipaz was a resident of San Juan Capistrano and a leader of the resistance to the Americans in southern California in 1846–1847. (Bancroft, *California*, 2:690)

José Altimira was born in Barcelona in 1787. He entered the Franciscan order and was ordained a priest in his homeland. He arrived in Monterey in 1820 and was assigned to Mission San Francisco but quickly grew to dislike the cold, damp climate. In apparent complicity with Luis Argüello, he petitioned the *diputación* in 1823 to transfer the missions in San Francisco and San Rafael to a new site in Sonoma. When the *diputación* approved, Altimira quickly established the mission. His superiors strongly objected to this, and finally a compromise was reached whereby all three missions, including Altimira's new mission, San Francisco Solano, were allowed to remain active. He stayed there until 1826, when Indians burned the mission, and retreated to San Rafael with a small band of neophytes. He was then posted to Missions San Carlos and San Buenaventura. He secretly fled Alta California with Father Antonio Ripoll in 1828. He was last reported to be in the Canary Islands in 1860. (Geiger, *Franciscan Missionaries*, 6–10)

Manuel Alva came to Alta California with Governor Figueroa in 1833 as a surgeon for the military. He took part in the revolt against Juan Bautista Alvarado in 1837 and sided with Carlos Carrillo in 1838. He left Alta California in about 1840. (Bancroft, *California*, 2:692)

Francisco Javier Alvarado was born in 1808, the son of María Ignacia Amador and Francisco Javier Alvarado, who served as a soldier and official at San Diego and Santa Bárbara from 1780 until his death in 1818. The younger Alvarado served as *alcalde* of Los Angeles in 1835 and as a substitute member of the *diputación* in 1833 and 1837. (Bancroft, *California*, 2:692)

Juan Bautista Alvarado, the son of José Francisco Alvarado and María Josefa Vallejo, was born in Monterey in 1809. His father died shortly after his birth, and his mother married José Raimundo Estrada, brother of José Mariano Estrada. Alvarado served as secretary of the *diputación* from 1828 to 1834 and was a member of that body for the next three years. During that period he also worked in the Monterey Customs House. He led the revolution against Nicolás Gutiérrez in 1836 and served as governor until 1842. He was a leader in the movement against Micheltorena in 1844–1845 and was subsequently appointed administrator of the Customs House at Monterey. He died in 1882. (Bancroft, *California,* 2:693–694; Mathes, "Juan Bautista Alvarado," in Alvarado, *Vignettes,* vii–xiv; Meier, *Mexican American Biographies,* 5; Sánchez, "Juan Bautista Alvarado," *Crítica,* 76)

María Ignacia Amador was born at Loreto, Baja California, in 1770. She came to Alta California with her father, Pedro Amador (a veteran of the 1769 Portolá expedition), in 1784 and married soldier Francisco Javier Alvarado around 1787. She died in 1851. (Bancroft, *California,* 2:584–585, 692; Northrop, *Spanish-Mexican Families,* 1:6–8, 34)

José Amesti was a native of the Basque region of Spain. He came to Alta California in 1822 and became a merchant based in Monterey. He married Mariano Guadalupe Vallejo's older sister Prudencia in 1823. He served in public office, including as *alcalde* in 1844. He was granted Rancho Corralitos in Santa Cruz in that same year. In 1846, his horses, saddles, and blankets on the rancho were seized by Frémont's men. He died around 1856. (Bancroft, *California,* 2:696; 5:358–359)

Juan Amorós was born in Porrera, Spain, in 1773. He became a Franciscan in 1791 and arrived in California in 1804. He worked at Mission San Carlos until 1819, and from then until his death in 1832 he ministered at Mission San Rafael. While at San Rafael he kept a close eye on the Russians at Fort Ross and reported frequently on their movements to the political authorities. (Geiger, *Franciscan Missionaries,* 11–13)

Antonio Apalátegui was born around 1801. A clerk, he was part of the Híjar-Padrés colonization effort in 1834. He was apparently refused a position by Governor Figueroa and took part in a movement against him in Los Angeles in 1835. He was exiled for his part in the affair. (Bancroft, *California,* 2:699)

Buenaventura Araujo, a Mexican naval captain, came to California with the Híjar-Padrés group in 1834. He was expelled and sent back to Mexico by Governor Figueroa. (Bancroft, *California,* 2:699)

Francisco Araujo arrived in Alta California as a soldier with Governor Figueroa in 1833 and served for a time in Monterey. In 1836 he was commander of the vigilante armed force in Los Angeles. He may have been sent out of the territory by Governor Chico. (Bancroft, *California,* 2:699)

Miguel Gerónimo Archuleta was born in 1779. He served in the military in San Francisco and in Monterey, where he became a schoolmaster. He died in 1822. (Bancroft, *California,* 2:700; Northrop, *Spanish-Mexican Families,* 2:12–13)

Gervasio Argüello was born in 1786. He was the son of José Darío Argüello and María Ignacia Moraga. He served at San Francisco from 1807 to 1817, and he was *habilitado* for most of that period. He was married to Encarnación Bernal. In 1816 he was appointed *habilitado general* of the Californias and moved to Mexico City. He served in that office until 1832, when he retired and moved to Guadalajara. (Bancroft, *California,* 2:701)

José Darío Argüello was a native of Querétaro, New Spain. He joined the army at around the age of twenty and arrived in California in 1781. He served as commander in both San Francisco and Monterey in the 1790s and early 1800s. He became acting governor upon the death of José Joaquín de Arrillaga and was named to the same office in Baja California when Pablo Vicente de Solá was appointed governor of Alta California. He held that office until 1822, when, after San José del Cabo and Loreto were sacked by insurgents, he moved to Guadalajara, where he died in the late 1820s. (Bancroft, *California,* 2:701)

Luis Antonio Argüello was born in San Francisco in 1784. His father, José Darío Argüello, was then serving with the military at the Santa Bárbara presidio. Luis Argüello entered the military at an early age and quickly rose through the ranks, no doubt aided by his father's eminence. A cadet in 1799, he became a lieutenant in 1806, and by 1818 he had become captain of the garrison at San Francisco. He was selected acting governor in 1822 and held that office until the appointment of José María Echeandía in 1825. After leaving office he filled a number of military offices but apparently began drinking heavily and died at San Francisco in 1830. (Bancroft, *California,* 3:9–13)

Santiago Argüello, younger brother of Gervasio and Luis Antonio Argüello, was born at Monterey in 1791. He entered the military at an early age and served at Santa Bárbara from 1806 to 1817 and at San Francisco from 1817 to 1827, when he was transferred to San Diego, where he served as commander and as a member of the *diputación.* He retired from the military in 1834 and served as *alcalde* of San Diego in 1836, acting against Juan Bautista Alvarado. He was commissioner of Mission San Juan Capistrano from 1838 to 1840 and prefect of Los Angeles from 1840 to 1843. He received a number of land grants and died in 1862 on his rancho, Tijuana, near the California-Mexico border. His wife was Pilar Ortega. (Bancroft, *California,* 2:702)

José Joaquín de Arrillaga was born at Aya, Guipúzcoa, Spain, in 1750. He entered the army at an early age and served in northern Mexico and Texas in the 1780s and 1790s. He was appointed lieutenant governor of the Californias in 1783 and served as interim governor from 1792 to 1794. The governments of Alta and Baja California were separated in 1804, and he was appointed the first governor of Alta California in that same year. He served until his death in 1814. Bancroft portrayed him as a competent official, one who could obey orders so well and tactfully that he made no enemies, but who also lacked originality, vision, and "enthusiastic confidence in the future of the province." (Bancroft, *California,* 2:204–207)

Felipe Arroyo de la Cuesta was born in Cubo, Burgos, Spain, in 1780. He became a Franciscan in 1796 and arrived in California in 1808, serving at Mission San Juan Bautista until 1833. While there, he compiled an extensive vocabulary of the Mutsun language and composed music and hymns. He died at Santa Inés in 1840. (Geiger, *Franciscan Missionaries,* 19–24)

Anastacio Avila was the son of Cornelio Avila, a native of Sinaloa who settled in Los Angeles in 1783, and María Isabel Urquídez. He was born about 1776. He served as *regidor* in Los Angles in 1810 and as *alcalde* there from 1820 to 1821. He was granted Rancho Tajuanta in 1843. He died in 1850. (Bancroft, *California,* 2:705; Northrop, *Spanish-Mexican Families,* 1:56)

Antonio Avila was a convict who arrived in California in 1825 after having been convicted of robbery and murder in Puebla. He sided with the authorities in the Solís revolt and again in 1832, in the apparent hope of gaining an early release. His hope was unrealized and he remained in California until about 1838. (Bancroft, *California,* 2:705)

Antonio Ignacio Avila was the son of Cornelio Avila and brother of Anastacio Avila. In 1804 he married Rosa María Ruiz. In 1822 he was granted Rancho Sausal Redondo on the Pacific coast, directly north of Los Palos Verdes. Between 1835 and 1848, he often served as *juez de campo*. He died in 1858. (Bancroft, *California,* 2:705)

Bruno Ignacio Avila, another son of Cornelio Avila and María Isabel Urquídez, was born in 1788 and settled at Los Angeles. He married María Rosalía Serrano and then, after her death, María Balbina Duarte. (Bancroft, *California,* 2:705; Northrop, *Spanish-Mexican Families,* 1:56)

Francisco José Avila, also a son of Cornelio Avila and María Isabel Urquídez, was born in 1772. He was a soldier at Santa Bárbara and served as *alcalde* in Los Angeles in 1810. He was granted Rancho Ciénegas in 1823. He died in 1832. (Bancroft, *California,* 2:705; Northrop, *Spanish-Mexican Families,* 1:55)

José María Avila, a native of Sinaloa, and another son of Cornelio Avila and Isabel Urquídez, became the owner of extensive property in Alta California and was elected *alcalde* of Los Angeles in 1825, but he was evidently suspended for overbearing behavior. He was jailed by Vicente Sánchez in 1831 and killed later that year in the battle of Cahuenga. (Bancroft, *California,* 2:705; 3:207)

Juan Avila, the son of Antonio Ignacio Avila and Rosa María Ruiz, was born in 1812. He served as judge in both Los Angeles and San Juan Capistrano and was granted Rancho Niguel in 1842. (Bancroft, *California,* 2:705–706; Northrop, *Spanish-Mexican Families,* 1:54)

Juan Pablo Ayala was born in 1803. He served in the military at Santa Bárbara, where he was acting *comandante* in 1845. He was administrator of San Luis Obispo from 1839 to 1840. (Bancroft, *California,* 2:706; Northrop, *Spanish-Mexican Families,* 2:21–22)

Juan Bandini was born in Perú in 1800 and came to Alta California with his father, a trader, in the 1820s. He served in the *diputación* in 1827, in the customs service for four years after that, and was active in the movement against Governor Victoria in 1831. In 1833 he represented Alta California in the Mexican congress and became involved in the colonization efforts being organized at the time. He headed the Cosmopolitan Company, a trading concern established in conjunction with the Híjar-Padrés venture, which failed when its supply ship was wrecked. He opposed Juan Bautista Alvarado from 1837 to 1838 but was later appointed administrator at San Gabriel. In the 1840s he was *síndico* of Los Angeles and secretary to Governor Pío Pico. He died in Los Angeles in 1859. (Bancroft, *California,* 2:709–10)

José Barona was born at Villanueva del Conde, Spain, in 1764. He entered the Franciscans in 1783 and arrived in the Americas in 1798. He served at Mission San Diego from then until 1811 and at Mission San Juan Capistrano from 1811 until his death in 1831. He was at San Juan Capistrano for the devastating earthquake of 1812 and for the sacking of the mission by Bouchard's forces in 1818. (Geiger, *Franciscan Missionaries,* 26–28)

Fabiano Barreto lived in Monterey and was granted Rancho Pescadero in 1836. (Bancroft, *California,* 2:711)

Leonardo Díaz Barroso was sent to Alta California in 1830 as a lieutenant and was soon promoted to captain. He was at Los Angeles in 1831 and saw action during the military campaigns of 1832. He returned to Mexico in 1833. (Bancroft, *California,* 2:711)

José Mariano Bonilla came to California in 1834 with the Híjar-Padrés colony. He was a teacher in Santa Bárbara, where he also was a clerk at a number of public offices. He married María Dolores García in 1838. He was granted Rancho Huerhuero in 1842 and served in a variety of offices in San Luis Obispo before and after the American conquest. (Bancroft, *California*, 2:724; Northrop, *Spanish-Mexican Families*, 2:95)

Gerónimo Boscana was born in Mallorca, Spain, in 1776. He joined the Franciscans and came to America in 1803. He was assigned to California in 1806 and served at Missions San Luis Rey, San Juan Capistrano, and San Gabriel. His ethnographic study of the southern California native religion Chinigchinich was the only work of its kind written by a California missionary. A version of it was first published in Alfred Robinson's *Life in California* (1846) and it has been republished a number of times since. He died at San Gabriel. (Geiger, *Franciscan Missionaries*, 29–32)

Hipólito Bouchard was born around 1785 in St. Tropez, France. By 1811 he was sailing and fighting on behalf of the revolutionaries of the La Plata River region in modern Argentina. In July 1817 he was given command of the *Argentina* and set out to circumnavigate the globe. By August 1818 he had reached Hawai'i and from there proceeded to raid the coast of Alta California. On his return to South America, the *Argentina* was used as a transport vessel for San Martín's 1820 expedition to Perú. At the conclusion of the campaign Bouchard was given some land in Perú, where he settled. He died there in January 1837, killed by one of his slaves. (Ratto, *Bouchard*)

María Antonia Buelna was born in 1806. The daughter of José Antonio Buelna and Mariá Antonia Tapia, she was a teacher in Monterey. Her father had also been a teacher in Monterey and San José. (Northrop, *Spanish-Mexican Families*, 1:91–92)

María Hilaria Buelna, born in 1801, was an older sister of María Antonia Buelna. She was listed in the 1836 Monterey census as single. (Pico, *Cosas* [Los Californianos edition], 71; Northrop, *Spanish-Mexican Families*, 1:92)

Pedro Cabot was born in Mallorca in 1777. He became a Franciscan in 1796 and came to California in 1804. He worked at Mission San Antonio for thirty years and then briefly at Missions San Miguel and San Fernando. He also was a secretary to Father Vicente Sarría for some of his official visitations to various missions. He died at San Fernando in 1836 as he was preparing to leave California. (Geiger, *Franciscan Missionaries*, 34–36)

Vicente Cané was a Spanish sailor who arrived in Monterey with the Asia in 1825. He remained in California and married Josefa Buitrón in 1828. He was granted Rancho San Bernardo in 1840 and served as a judge in San Luis Obispo in 1841. (Bancroft, *California*, 2:741; Northrop, *Spanish-Mexican Families*, 1:98)

Juan Ignacio Cantúa was born in 1828. The son of Vicente Cantúa, a Monterey landowner, he was active against the Americans in 1846. (Bancroft, *California*, 2:741; Northrop, *Spanish-Mexican Families*, 2:44)

Anastasio Carrillo was born at Santa Bárbara in 1788. His father was José Raymundo Carrillo, and his mother was María Tomasa Ignacia Lugo. He entered the military at an early age. He engaged in many expeditions against the Indians during the 1820s. He retired from the military in 1836 but negotiated with Juan Bautista Alvarado in the south in 1837. He served on the *diputación* in 1839. He was married to Concepción García. He received a number of land grants, including an 1845 grant to Rancho Cieneguitas, a few miles west of Santa Bárbara. (Bancroft, *California*, 2:743; 3:518–519)

Carlos Antonio Carrillo, a brother of Anastasio and José Antonio Carrillo, was born at Santa Bárbara in 1783. He served in the military at Monterey and Santa Bárbara from 1797 to 1825. In 1828 he served in the *diputación*, and he was a delegate to the Mexican congress from 1831 to 1832. He served again in the *diputación* in the mid-1830s. In 1837 he was appointed governor of Alta California, but he was never able to force Juan Bautista Alvarado from office. He died in 1852. (Bancroft, *California*, 2:743)

José Antonio Carrillo, brother of Anastasio and Carlos Antonio Carrillo, was born in San Francisco in 1796. He served in the *diputación* from 1822 to 1824, as Echeandía's secretary in 1826, and as Los Angeles *alcalde* in 1827. He was exiled to Baja California in 1831 as a result of a quarrel with Los Angeles *alcalde* Vicente Sánchez. From 1831 to 1832 he opposed Governor Victoria and favored Pío Pico. After serving as a delegate to the Mexican congress, he opposed Juan Bautista Alvarado in 1837 and was jailed at Sonoma as a result. He participated in the resistance to the North American invasion in 1846 and signed the Treaty of Cahuenga in 1847. He attended the Constitutional Convention in 1849 and died in 1862. (Bancroft, *California*, 2:745)

José Raymundo Carrillo was born in Loreto, Baja California, around 1749. He served at San Diego and Santa Bárbara for a number of years before being promoted to lieutenant in 1800. In the same year, he was made commander of Monterey. He became commander of the Santa Bárbara presidio in 1802 and was appointed captain and commander at San Diego in 1806. He died in 1809. His wife was María Tomasa Ignacia Lugo. (Bancroft, *California*, 2:100–101)

José María Castañares was born in Puebla, New Spain, and came to Alta California in 1833 to clerk for Rafael González at the Customs House. He was married to Ana González, Rafael's daughter. His affair with Ildefonsa González, the wife of José María Herrera, caused a sensation in Monterey in 1836 and he soon went to Mexico. He returned to Alta California in 1840 and served on the staff of the *tribunal*. He went back to Mexico in 1845 and remained there. (Bancroft, *California*, 2:748)

Juan Castañeda, a Mexican officer serving in Baja California, came to Alta California in 1837 with José Antonio Carrillo. He played a major role in the Carrillo fight against Juan Bautista Alvarado. In 1839 he was named secretary to General Mariano Guadalupe Vallejo, who sent him on a mission to Mexico City. He returned to Alta California in 1842, perhaps with Governor Micheltorena. He testified in some land cases in the 1850s. (Bancroft, *California*, 2:748–749)

José Castro, the son of José Tiburcio Castro, was born around 1810. He served in the *diputación* in the 1830s and was acting governor for four months after the death of José Figueroa in 1835. He took part in the resistance to both Mariano Chico and Nicolás Gutiérrez in 1836 and served again as acting governor after Gutiérrez's expulsion. He took an active role against the foreigners' revolt in 1840 and also against Micheltorena in 1845. After Micheltorena's exile, he became military commander and led part of the resistance against the North Americans. He fled to Mexico in 1846, returned to Alta California in 1848, and then returned to Mexico in 1853. He was appointed military commander of Baja California in 1856 and held that office until he was killed in 1860. (Bancroft, *California*, 2:751–752)

José Tiburcio Castro was a native of Sinaloa, New Spain. His father, Macario, was a soldier at San Diego and San José. Tiburcio followed in his father's path and entered the military. He also served as *alcalde* of both San José and Monterey in the 1820s and as a member of the *diputación* in the 1830s. He participated in the movement against Governor Victoria in 1831. In the later 1830s he was the administrator at Mission San Juan Bautista. He died in 1841. (Bancroft, *California*, 2:752–753; Northrup, *Spanish-Mexican Families*, 1:106)

Manuel de Jesús Castro was the son of Simeón Castro and María Antonia Pico. Born in Monterey in 1821, he served as secretary to the prefect of Monterey from 1842 to 1844. He was one of the instigators of the revolt against Micheltorena. He was made prefect of Monterey in 1845 and supported Pío Pico against José Castro. He fought with José María Flores in 1846 and fled to Mexico in 1847. From 1852 until his death he lived mainly in San Francisco. (Bancroft, *California*, 2:753)

Magín Matías Catalá was a native of Catalonia. He went to Mexico in 1786 and to Alta California in 1793. After a brief stay at San Francisco, he moved to Mission Santa Clara in 1794. He worked there until his death in 1830. He suffered greatly from rheumatism and toward the end of his life, although he could only hobble feebly as he visited the sick, he insisted on continuing his work, gaining a reputation as "the holy man of Santa Clara." (Geiger, *Franciscan Missionaries*, 42–46; Engelhardt, *The Holy Man of Santa Clara*)

José (Joseph) Chapman, an American, was a member of Bouchard's crew. He was taken prisoner in Monterey and settled in California. He built grist mills at Missions Santa Inés and San Gabriel. He married Guadalupe Ortega in 1822 and they had five children. He did a variety of carpentry tasks for the missionaries and eventually moved to Santa Bárbara. He died in 1849. (Schuetz-Miller, *Building and Builders*, 130–131)

José Antonio Chávez came to California with Governor José Figueroa in 1833. Many Californios believed that he was a son of the governor. He was active in the movements against both Micheltorena in 1845 and the Americans the next year. He left California in 1848 and became active in the affairs of Baja California. (Bancroft, *California*, 2:758)

Mariano Chico was born in 1796 in Guanajuato, New Spain. He served in the Mexican congress and was appointed governor of Alta California in December 1835. Arriving in April 1836, he was expelled by the Californios on July 31 of that same year. He later served as governor of Guanajuato in 1846 and participated in the war against the North American invasion. He died in 1850. (Bancroft, *California*, 2:759; *Diccionario Porrúa*, 464)

John B. R. Cooper, a native of the Alderney Islands in the English Channel, arrived in Massachusetts as a young boy. He first came to California in 1823 as master of the Boston vessel *Rover*. He settled in California as a merchant in 1826, married Encarnación Vallejo the next year, and became active in public affairs. He received a number of land grants during the Mexican period. He divided his time between living in Monterey and making trading voyages in the Pacific. He died in 1872. (Woolfenden and Elkinton, *Cooper*; Bancroft, *California*, 2:100–101)

Antonio José Cot was a Spanish trader based in Lima. He was a partner of Juan Ignacio Mancisidor. He settled in Alta California in 1822 but left in 1830, returning in 1835 to become a resident of the Los Angeles area. He purchased San Luis Rey in 1846 and died around 1860. (Bancroft, *California*, 2:769)

Francisco Atanasio Cota was born in 1787. He married María de Jesús Olivera in 1811 at Mission Santa Bárbara. He served as administrator and *comisionado* at Santa Inés from 1837 to 1841 and was granted Rancho Santa Rosa in 1839. He died in 1851. (Bancroft, *California*, 2:769; Northrop, *Spanish-Mexican Families*, 1:111–113)

Leonardo Cota was born in about 1816. He was a leader of the resistance to the Americans in southern California in 1846 and 1847. In 1847 he married María Inés de los Dolores Yorba. He died in 1887. (Bancroft, *California*, 2:769; Northrop, *Spanish-Mexican Families*, 2:62–63)

María Luisa Cota was born at Loreto in Baja California about 1776. She married José María Claudio López, also a native of Baja California, at Mission San Gabriel in 1789. They were settlers in Los Angeles in 1811, and he served as *mayordomo* for Mission San Gabriel from 1821 to 1830. In 1826 he was also *alcalde* of Los Angeles. López died in 1833, and María Luisa Cota died in 1851. (Northrop, *Spanish-Mexican Families*, 2:146–147)

Ignacio Delgado, an *alférez*, came to California in 1819 and served generally around Santa Bárbara. He either died or left California around 1827. (Bancroft, *California*, 2:778)

Manuel Domínguez was the son of Cristóbal Domínguez, a San Diego soldier from before 1800. He served on the Los Angeles *ayuntamiento* in 1829 and as *alcalde* in 1832. He opposed Juan Bautista Alvarado in 1837 and was second *alcalde* of Los Angeles in 1839. The North Americans occupied his rancho at San Pedro in 1846. In 1849 he was a member of the Constitutional Convention. He died in the early 1880s. (Bancroft, *California*, 2:783)

Narciso Durán was born in 1776 at Castelló de Ampurias in Catalonia, Spain. He arrived in Alta California in 1806 and served at Mission San José from that date until 1833. At San José he organized the neophytes into a mission choir, wrote an elaborate choir book, and composed the music for two Masses himself. Alfred Robinson heard the choir in 1831 and called the music "well-executed." Also at San José, Durán extended hospitality to Jedediah Smith and Kit Carson, among others. He became president of the missions in 1825, but his stand against the emancipation of the Native Californians made him unacceptable to the Mexican officials and he stepped down in 1827. Nonetheless, he was elected president again in 1830 and was appointed vice-commissary prefect soon after. In 1833 when, at the request of the Mexican government, a group of friars from the missionary college of Guadalupe, in Zacatecas, replaced the Spanish friars in the northern Alta California missions, Durán went to Santa Bárbara, where he remained until his death in 1846. He served as president of the Fernandino missions until 1838, when he was chosen commissary prefect. He remained in that office the rest of his days. (Geiger, *Franciscan Missionaries*, 68–75)

José María Echeandía, a lieutenant colonel of engineers, was engaged in surveying the boundaries of the newly created Federal District in Mexico when he was appointed political and military governor of Baja and Alta California in 1825. He disliked the chilly and foggy climate of northern California and made his headquarters in San Diego. Little is known about him except for his service in Alta California. He returned to Mexico in 1833 and was reported to be practicing his profession as an engineer in the 1850s. He died sometime before 1871. (Bancroft, *California*, 3:243–245; Hutchinson, *Frontier Settlement*, 124–125)

Salvador María Espinosa was born in 1798. He married María Josefa Lugarda Castro in 1814. He served in a number of public offices in Monterey, including *alcalde* and *regidor*. He also served as administrator at Soledad from 1836 to 1839. (Bancroft, *California*, 2:792; Northrop, *Spanish-Mexican Families*, 1:138–139)

Estanislao was a member of the Lakisamne tribe of the Central Valley of Alta California, about fifty miles east of Mission San José. He was the indigenous *alcalde* there, an indication that he enjoyed the favor of the local clergy. Juan Bautista Alvarado said that Estanislao was able to read and write. Along with a number of companions he refused to return to the mission after visiting his *ranchería* following the 1828 harvest. His forces defeated those of veteran fighter José Sánchez in 1829, before being defeated by a combined Monterey–San Francisco expedition led by Mariano Guadalupe Vallejo. Estanislao was pardoned after this and continued to live at Mission San José until his death in the 1830s. The only physical description of him comes from Juan Bojorques, decades after his death: "He was about 6 feet tall, his skin was more white than bronze, he was very muscular like a horse….born and raised at Mission San José, employed as a vaquero and a trainer of mules." (Osio, *Alta California,* 89–94; Alvarado, "Historia de California," 1:52; Bojorques, "Recuerdos," 21)

Tomás Eleuterio Esténaga was born in Vizcaya, Spain, in 1790. He was ordained in Mexico around 1810 and came to Alta California in 1820. He worked at San Francisco until 1833. When the Zacatecan friars took over the northern missions, he was assigned to San Gabriel, where he presided over the decline of that once flourishing institution. Discouraged, he left Alta California in 1835, but returned a year later. He died in 1847. (Geiger, *Franciscan Missionaries,* 78–81)

José Ramón Estrada was the son of José Mariano Estrada. Born in 1811, he hunted otter in the early 1830s, was the grantee of El Toro rancho outside of Monterey in 1835, and served as *alcalde* at Monterey in 1836. He served as administrator of Mission Santa Clara in the late 1830s, and as a member of the departmental *junta* from 1842 to 1845. Like his father, he dropped from public view after 1845. (Bancroft, *California,* 2:793)

José Antonio Estudillo was the son of José María Estudillo and Gertrudis Horcasitas. He was born in 1803 and married María Victoria Domínguez. He served in a variety of public offices in San Diego under both Mexican and American rule. In 1842, he was granted Rancho San Jacinto. He died in 1852. (Bancroft, *California,* 2:793–794; Northrop, *Spanish-Mexican Families,* 2:81–83)

José María Estudillo was born in Spain around 1772 and came to Baja California in 1795. He served in the military there and was assigned to Monterey in 1806 as a lieutenant. He served there, sometimes as *comandante,* until he was promoted to captain and assigned to command San Diego in 1827. He died in 1830. He was married to Gertrudis Horcasitas and they were the California founders of the significant Estudillo family. (Bancroft, *California,* 2:542)

Narciso Fabregat, a Spanish lieutenant, came to Alta California in 1819 with the Mazatlán squadron, which was sent to protect the province after the Bouchard raid. He served mainly at Santa Bárbara, where he eventually became a trader. (Bancroft, *California,* 2:733)

José Fernández was born in Spain around 1803. Before arriving in Alta California aboard a French ship in 1818, he had been living in Lima. A sailor by trade, he became an artillery soldier and served at San Francisco from 1819 to 1827. He then settled in San José, where he served as secretary to the *ayuntamiento* and as *síndico.* He fought with José Castro against the North Americans in 1846 and then lived in Santa Clara until his death in the mid-1870s. (Bancroft, *California,* 3:737)

José Fernández del Campo arrived in California in 1828 and served as artillery commander at Monterey. He was arrested in the Solís revolt and died in 1831. (Bancroft, *California,* 3:737)

Agustín Fernández de San Vicente, a priest from Durango, was sent by Agustín de Iturbide to manage the change of government from Spain to Mexico in Baja and Alta California. He arranged the appointment of Luis Argüello as governor. He had the reputation of being a bon vivant and gambler. In 1825 he was appointed vicar in New Mexico. (Bancroft, *California,* 3:737)

José Figueroa was born in 1792 in Jonacatepec, New Spain. He participated in the Wars of Independence, fighting with José María Morelos and Vicente Guerrero. He served as military commander of Cuernavaca in 1823 and in the congress of the state of Mexico in 1824. In 1824 he was appointed military commander of Sonora and Sinaloa, where he subdued rebellions of the Yaqui and Mayo peoples. He arrived in Alta California as governor in 1833 and served there until his death in 1835. He is best known for the secularization of the missions and for his opposition to the Híjar-Padrés colonization effort of 1834. (Hutchinson, *Frontier Settlement,* 154–155)

Gumersindo Flores, a Mexican solider, came to California with the Híjar-Padrés group. He served in the military at San Francisco and as commander at both Monterey and Santa Bárbara. After the war he lived in Santa Bárbara, where he was shot in 1860. (Bancroft, *California,* 3:741)

José María Flores came to Alta California in 1842 as Governor Micheltorena's secretary. He was sent to Mexico in 1844 but returned the next year. In 1846 he directed Californio resistance in the last phase of the war against the North Americans. He returned to Mexico in January 1847 and remained in the Mexican army, becoming a general. He died in 1866. (Bancroft, *California,* 3:741; Layne, "José María Flores")

James Alexander Forbes was born in 1804 in Scotland. He arrived in Alta California in 1831, after having been rescued from a shipwreck by a vessel heading for San Francisco. He lived as a trader and farmer in the Santa Clara Valley and married Ana María Galindo. In 1842 he was appointed British vice consul at Monterey. After the conquest, most of his wealth was eaten up in litigation concerning the New Almaden mine in San José. He died in Oakland in 1881. (Bancroft, *California,* 3:743)

John Forster, an Englishman, came to California as a ship's master and trader in 1833. He married Isidora Pico, sister of Pío and Andrés Pico, in 1837 and received a number of land grants. He purchased the former mission of San Juan Capistrano in 1845 and was in charge of San Luis Rey for a time in 1846. He was involved in extensive litigation over land claims in the 1860s and 1870s. He died in 1884. (Jensen, "John Forster"; Gray, *Forster v. Pico*)

Buenaventura Fortuny was born in Moster, Spain, in 1774. He joined the Franciscans in 1792 and arrived in California in 1806. He was assigned to Mission San José, where he remained until 1826. While there, he accompanied José Antonio Sánchez on an expedition into the Central Valley. He also worked at Missions San Francisco Solano, San Diego, San Luis Rey, and San Buenaventura, where he died in 1840. (Geiger, *Franciscan Missionaries,* 89–91)

John Charles Frémont was born in Georgia in 1813. He was a lieutenant in the United States Army Corps and made journeys to Oregon in 1842 and California in 1843 and 1844. He appeared at Sutter's Fort in the winter of 1845 and then, claiming to be short on supplies, at Monterey in January of 1846. He was active in the conquest and accepted the surrender of Andrés Pico at Cahuenga. He served California in the U.S. Senate and was the first Republican candidate for president in 1856. After serving in the Civil War, he spent the rest of his life as a territorial governor and as a promoter of various Western development projects. (Hart, *Companion,* 172–173)

James Gadsden, an American diplomat, was appointed minister to Mexico in 1853. He negotiated the purchase of land now in southern Arizona and southern New Mexico from the Mexican government in 1853: the United States paid Mexico $15 million for almost thirty thousand square miles. (Lamar, ed., *New Encyclopedia of the American West,* 417)

William A. Gale was a Boston trader. He first visited California in 1810 as a clerk on board the *Albatross* and returned in 1822 on board the *Sachem* to initiate the hide-and-tallow trade on behalf of the Boston firm of Bryant and Sturgis. He visited California a number of times, eventually marrying María Francisca Marcelina Estudillo at San Diego on May 21, 1827. He died in Massachusetts in 1841. Because of his spectacles, he was popularly known as *"Cuatro Ojos"* (four eyes). (Bancroft, *California,* 3:750–751; Rhoades, "Foreigners," 87–88)

Juan Gallardo, a shoemaker from Mexico, was a leader of the Apalátegui revolt in Los Angeles in 1835. He served as *alcalde* there in 1846. (Bancroft, *California,* 3:751)

Inocente García was born in 1791. He served in the military at Monterey and then became a trader at San Juan Bautista. He took part in the movement against Nicolás Gutiérrez in 1836 and was the administrator of San Miguel from 1837 to 1845. He died in 1878. (Bancroft, *California,* 3:752–753; Northrop, *Spanish-Mexican Families,* 1:163; Pico, *Cosas* [Los Californianos edition], 73)

Francisco García Diego y Moreno was born in Jalisco in 1785. He joined the Franciscans at Our Lady of Guadalupe College near Zacatecas and was ordained a priest in 1808. He became vicar of the college in 1832. When the Mexican government turned the northern Alta California missions over to the Zacatecan friars, he headed north, arriving in Monterey in 1833. He became the first Bishop of California, in 1840, and established his residence in Santa Bárbara. His tenure as a bishop was difficult, and he died in 1846. (Geiger, *Franciscan Missionaries,* 98–103)

Antonio Garra was a Cupeño chief living near Rancho Agua Caliente, east of San Diego. In 1851 he attempted to organize a pan-tribal resistance to the American presence. His force attacked and burned the house on the rancho in 1851. Tensions between the Cupeños and Cahuillas wrecked the uprising and Garra was captured and executed in San Diego in 1852. (Phillips, *Chiefs and Challengers*)

Luis Gil y Taboada was born in Guanajuato, Mexico, in 1773. He joined the Franciscans in Michoacán in 1792 and came to California in 1801. He worked at a variety of missions in the Chumash region, including Santa Inés, Santa Bárbara, La Purísima, and San Luis Obispo. He was said to have learned the local languages well. He was also the founding priest at Mission San Rafael. He died in 1833. (Geiger, *Franciscan Missionaries,* 104–106)

Archibald Gillespie was born in Pennsylvania in 1812 and was a lieutenant in the U.S. Marines in 1846. He arrived at Monterey in April of that year on a mission to assist Larkin in persuading the Californios to join the United States. He also delivered a secret message to Frémont which appears to have encouraged Frémont to become more belligerent. Gillespie served in the military during the conquest. His arbitrary behavior while he was in charge of the Los Angeles garrison sparked a Californio revolt. He was wounded at San Pascual. He spent most of the rest of his life in California and died in 1873. (Hart, *Companion,* 186)

Manuel Gómez, an artillery soldier, came to Alta California in 1816 and served at San Francisco and Monterey. He was promoted to lieutenant for his part in trying to defend Monterey from Bouchard. He returned to Mexico in 1822. (Bancroft, *California,* 2:470)

Rafael Gómez was born around 1800. A Mexican lawyer, he came to California as *asesor* in 1830. He served on the Monterey *ayuntamiento* in 1835 and on the *diputación* the following year. At the end of the 1830s he was killed by a horse on his rancho, Tularcitos, near Santa Clara. (Bancroft, *California*, 3:759)

Vicente Perfecto Gómez was the son of José Joaquín Gómez, a trader and public official in Monterey. Vicente served as a clerk to Governor Micheltorena. He said that he had been granted a rancho in 1844, but the courts rejected the claim. He was in charge of Mission San Antonio for a brief time in 1846 and 1847. He worked for Thomas Savage in the 1870s. Along with Blas Piña and Rosendo Corona, he accompanied Savage to Salinas in March 1877 to copy documents at the Recorder's Office there, and he also conducted ten interviews of Californios. He died in 1884. (Bancroft, *California*, 3:759)

Macedonio González, a Mexican soldier, participated in a number of campaigns against the indigenous peoples on the Baja California frontier. He took part in the movement against Juan Bautista Alvarado in 1837 and was imprisoned for a time at Sonoma. He eventually settled in Alta California, and Bancroft reports that he was living in San Diego in 1864. (Bancroft, *California*, 3:760)

Miguel González was a Mexican artillery captain who served at Monterey from 1825 to 1830. (Bancroft, *California*, 3:760–761)

Rafael González came to California in 1833 as a customs administrator, served as *alcalde* of Monterey in 1835, and worked at the Customs House from 1837 to 1846. He was granted Rancho San Justo and served in some other public offices in the Monterey area. He died in 1868. (Bancroft, *California*, 3:761)

Teodoro González arrived in California in 1825. He settled at Monterey as a sea otter hunter. He married Guadalupe Villaruel, the mother of Francisco Rico. He served as *regidor* and acting *alcalde* in 1836 during the difficulties with Governor Chico. He was granted Rancho Rincón de la Puente and Rancho San José y Sur Chiquita. (Bancroft, *California*, 3:761)

Francisco González de Ibarra was born in Navarra, Spain, in 1782. A Franciscan, he came to California in 1819 and served at Mission San Fernando from 1820 to 1833. Discouraged by secularization, he abandoned the missions for a time but returned and served at Mission San Luis Rey. There he had a difficult time coping with Pío Pico's administration, and he died in 1842. (Geiger, *Franciscan Missionaries*, 110–113)

José María de Jesús González Rubio was born in Guadalajara in 1804. He was ordained a Franciscan priest in 1827 and arrived in California with the rest of the pioneer friars from Zacatecas in 1833. He served at Mission San José until 1842. He became secretary to Bishop García Diego in 1842. When the bishop died in 1846, he became head of the Church in California. In the late 1850s, he became involved in a dispute between Bishop Thaddeus Amat and the Franciscans. He died in 1875. (Neri, *Hispanic Catholicism;* Geiger, *Franciscan Missionaries*, 113–120)

Isaac Graham was born in Kentucky and moved west as a fur trapper in the 1820s. He entered Alta California from New Mexico in 1833 and settled at Natividad, outside of Monterey. He seems to have operated a distillery there that catered to hunters and deserting sailors. He supported Juan Bautista Alvarado in 1836. Accused of leading a rebellion against the Alta California government in 1840, he was sent to Mexico City for punishment. Upon his return he settled near

Santa Cruz, where he operated a sawmill. He supported Governor Micheltorena in 1844 and 1845 and continued to live at Santa Cruz until his death in 1863. (Bancroft, *California,* 3:762–763)

José Antonio de la Guerra, a son of José de la Guerra y Noriega and María Antonia Carrillo, and brother of Angustias de la Guerra and Teresa de la Guerra Hartnell (whose testimonios appear in this volume), was born in 1805. He was a cadet in the Santa Bárbara military from 1818 to 1828. He married María Concepción Ortega. He was a *síndico* and *alcalde* in Santa Bárbara in the 1830s and a member of the *diputación* in 1835 and 1836. He served as captain of the port at Santa Bárbara from 1837 to 1840 and as administrator at Mission La Purísima in 1841 and 1842. After the conquest he continued to live in the Santa Bárbara area and served as sheriff of San Luis Obispo. (Bancroft, *California,* 3:768–769)

Pablo de la Guerra, also a son of José de la Guerra y Noriega and María Antonia Carrillo, was born in 1819. He attended his brother-in-law William Hartnell's school in Monterey and worked at the Customs House in that city from 1838 until the American invasion. He later served in the 1849 Constitutional Convention and as a member of the California state senate. He died in 1874. (Bancroft, *California,* 3:769; Pubols, "Fathers of the Pueblo")

José de la Guerra y Noriega was born in Spain in 1779. He left for Mexico in the 1790s to work in his uncle's store and soon after that entered the military. He arrived in Alta California in 1801, where he served until 1806 in Monterey. In that year he was made lieutenant at Santa Bárbara and soon moved to San Diego, where he remained until 1809. By acting as his uncle's commercial agent in Alta California, he was able to improve his financial condition greatly. He was promoted to commander of the Santa Bárbara presidio in 1815, in which position he remained until 1842, when he retired from the military. He died in 1858. (Thompson, *El Gran Capitán*)

Nicolás Gutiérrez came to Alta California as a captain in 1833 with Governor Figueroa. He was promoted to lieutenant colonel in that same year and acted as *comisionado* for the secularization of Mission San Gabriel from 1834 to 1836. He served as acting governor after the death of Figueroa in 1835 and again after the expulsion of Mariano Chico the next year. Juan Bautista Alvarado expelled Gutiérrez at the end of 1836; little is known of his later career. (Bancroft, *California,* 3:772)

William Edward Petty Hartnell was born in Lancashire, England, in 1798. In 1819 he left for South America to clerk for the firm of Begg and Co., and he arrived in California in 1822. In partnership with a fellow Begg clerk, Hugh McCullough of Scotland, he formed McCullough, Hartnell, and Co. and did a large business with the missions in the 1820s. On April 30, 1825, he married María Teresa de la Guerra, whose testimonio appears in this volume. Business reverses in the late 1820s forced the dissolution of his partnership with McCullough, and Hartnell supported himself with a variety of enterprises. He received a grant for Rancho Alisal, outside of Monterey. In the mid-1830s he opened a short-lived school in Monterey. In 1839 Juan Bautista Alvarado appointed him *visitador general* of the missions. He worked at the Customs House in the 1840s and made a brief trip to Hawai'i shortly after the North American invasion. Employed by the North Americans as an interpreter and translator in the late 1840s and early 1850s, he died in 1854. (Dakin, *The Lives of William Hartnell*)

José María Herrera came to Alta California with José María Echeandía in 1825 as *comisario*. He later became involved in controversies with Echeandía and was exiled for alleged involvement in the Solís revolt. He returned to Alta California in 1834 with the Híjar-Padrés party as secretary of Juan Bandini's Cosmopolitan Company. He avoided further controversy, although his wife, Ildefonsa González, became romantically involved with José María Castañares. Herrera left Alta California in 1836 and may have been *contador* of the Customs House at Guaymas in 1839. (Bancroft, *California,* 3:466; Hutchinson, *Frontier Settlement,* 203)

José Leonardo Higuera married María Antonia Guillén, daughter of Eulalia Pérez, whose testimonio appears in this volume, in 1830 at Mission San Gabriel. He was involved in the revolt against Archibald Gillespie in Los Angeles in 1846. (Bancroft, *California,* 3:784, 5:308; Northrop, *Spanish-Mexican Families,* 2:117)

Juan José Higuera was born in Santa Bárbara in 1787. He married María Marta de la Luz Salazar in 1800 and they had six children. He lived in the Los Angeles and Santa Bárbara areas and died in 1826. He was buried at Mission San Gabriel. (Northrop, *Spanish-Mexican Families,* 2:128–129; Bancroft, *California,* 3:784)

José María Híjar was born around 1793 in Guadalajara and served for many years in the Jalisco state congress, where he most likely became acquainted with Valentín Gómez Farías. When Gómez Farías got a bill authorizing a colonization effort for Alta California passed by the Mexican congress, Híjar was appointed director of the colony and *jefe político* of Alta California. Political change in Mexico prevented his assuming the political office, and the colony ran afoul of Governor Figueroa and the Californios. He was sent back to Mexico in 1835. Ironically, he returned to Alta California in 1845 as a member of a Mexican commission and died that year in Los Angeles. (Hutchinson, *Frontier Settlement,* 184–185, 374–375)

Gil Ibarra was born in San Diego in 1784. He served as *síndico* of Los Angeles in 1831 and as *alcalde* there from 1836 to 1837. He opposed Juan Bautista Alvarado and, like many of Alvarado's erstwhile opponents, he was granted a rancho, in 1841. (Bancroft, *California,* 4:688)

Juan María Ibarra, a lieutenant in the army, came to Alta California with the Mazatlán squadron in 1819. He was stationed at San Diego from 1821 to 1830. He supported Zamorano in 1832 and was commander at Santa Bárbara from 1833 to 1836. He left Alta California in 1836. (Bancroft, *California,* 4:688)

William Brown Ide was born in 1896 in Massachusetts and came overland to California in 1845. He settled near Sonoma and was a leader of the Bear Flag revolt. He became bitter when Frémont took control of the movement in the summer but served as a private in the California battalion during the war. He returned to Sonoma and served as a surveyor there and as a public official in Colusa. He died in 1852. (Warner, *Bear Flag,* 150–174))

David Jacks was born in Scotland in 1822 and came to California in 1849. He settled in Monterey and began to acquire real estate in the region. In 1859, Monterey was forced to put its pueblo lands up for auction to pay Delos R. Ashley, the lawyer who had successfully argued the city's claim before the U.S. land commission. Ashley and Jacks purchased the lands for a bit over $1,000. Ashley sold out his share to Jacks in 1869 and Jacks became the largest landholder and developer in the region. He died in 1909. (Bestor, *David Jacks*)

Antonio Jayme was born in Mallorca in 1757 and entered the Franciscans there. He arrived in California in 1795 and ministered at Mission Soledad from 1776 to 1821. His weakened physical condition resulted in his being sent to Mission Santa Bárbara, where he was assigned to minister when he was able to do so. He was spared by the Chumash during the 1824 revolt and died in 1829. (Geiger, *Franciscan Missionaries,* 126–127)

Antonio Jimeno was born in Mexico City and entered the Colegio de San Fernando there. He came to California in 1827 with his brother, Fray José Joaquín Jimeno. After brief service at Mission Santa Cruz, he was assigned to Mission Santa Bárbara, where he ministered from 1829 to 1858. After the gold rush, he became involved in a series of disputes between the bishop and some of the friars. He returned to Mexico City in 1859 and died in 1876. (Geiger, *Franciscan Missionaries,* 129–130)

José Joaquín Jimeno accompanied his brother Antonio to California in 1827. He served at Missions San Luis Rey, Santa Cruz, and Santa Inés. He became president of the missions from San Miguel to San Diego in 1838. In 1844 he became head of a seminary that opened at Santa Inés. After the gold rush, he served at Mission San Gabriel and then as superior of a Franciscan college in Santa Bárbara. He died in Santa Bárbara in 1856. (Geiger, *Franciscan Missionaries,* 131–134)

Manuel Jimeno Casarín was born in New Spain. He came to Alta California in 1828 as *sub-comisario* and *contador* at the Customs House. Two of his brothers, José Joaquín and Antonio, were Franciscan missionaries in Alta California. Manuel held a large number of public offices; he was *síndico* and *alcalde* at Monterey, and a member of the *diputación.* He was Governor Alvarado's secretary and filled the same office for Governor Micheltorena. In the early 1830s he married Angustias de la Guerra, whose testimonio appears in this volume. He returned to Mexico in 1853 and died that same year. (Bancroft, *California,* 4:692)

Thomas ap Catesby Jones was born in Virginia in 1790 and was commander of the United States Navy Pacific Squadron in 1842. He took Monterey in that year because he thought war had broken out between the United States and Mexico. The United States apologized for the incident and briefly relieved him of command but restored it to him quickly. He died in 1859. (Hart, *Companion,* 250)

Stephen Watts Kearny was born in New Jersey in 1794. A career soldier, he served in the army in the War of 1812 and later commanded the Army of the West in 1846. He also served as military governor at Santa Fe. After crossing overland to California he was defeated at the battle of San Pascual on December 6, 1846. He died two years later, in St. Louis, after having served in Mexico as governor in Veracruz and Mexico City. (Clarke, *Stephen Watts Kearny*)

Benjamin Kelsey, a native of Kentucky, came overland to California in 1841. In 1843 he went to Oregon but returned the next year. He settled in the Napa Valley as a hunter and was a member of the Bear Flag revolt. After the war, he moved to Humboldt County, then to Texas, and finally settled in southern California. He died in 1889. (Warner, *Bear Flag Revolt,* 222–233; Bancroft, *California,* 4:698)

Thomas Oliver Larkin was born in Massachusetts in 1802 and came to Alta California in 1832. He lived in Monterey as a trader. He supported Juan Bautista Alvarado in 1836 and was appointed U.S. consul eight years later. In 1845 President Polk and Secretary of State Buchanan made him a confidential agent to try to bring Alta California peacefully into the United States. He died in San Francisco in 1858. (Hague and Langum, *Thomas O. Larkin*)

Cesáreo Lataillade, a Spaniard of French descent, came to California in 1842 as a member of a Mexican trading company. He settled in Santa Bárbara and married María Antonia de la Guerra in 1845. He accidentally shot and killed himself in 1849. (Bancroft, *California,* 4:708)

Jacob Primer Leese was born in 1809 in Ohio. He traded along the Santa Fe trail in the early 1830s and moved in Alta California in 1834. He lived in Yerba Buena (San Francisco) from 1836 to 1841, when he moved to Sonoma. He married Rosalía Vallejo, the sister of Mariano Guadalupe Vallejo. Her testimonio appears in this volume. In 1846 he was captured by the Bear Flaggers. He was vice president of the Society of California Pioneers in 1855. In 1864 he was granted almost two-thirds of Baja California as part of a colonization enterprise. After the failure of this project he left California in 1865 and did not return until his old age. He died in 1892. (Hart, *Companion,* 274; Martínez, *Historia,* 406–412)

Miguel García Lobato, a Mexican lieutenant of engineers, served in California from about 1825 to 1830. (Bancroft, *California,* 4:716)

Juan Malarín, a Peruvian of Italian extraction, first arrived in Alta California in 1820 as master of the vessel *Señoriano.* He returned in 1824 as master of the *Apolonia.* As a result of his returning the *Asia* to Mexico for Luis Antonio Argüello, he was made a lieutenant in the Mexican navy. He married Josefa Estrada and made his home in Monterey, where he served on the *tribunal superior* in the 1840s. He died in 1849. (Bancroft, *California,* 4:728)

Juan Ignacio Mancisidor, a Spaniard, visited California from 1822 to 1823 as supercargo of the vessel *ColonelYoung.* He was a partner of Antonio José Cot. He returned in 1825 on the *Thomas Nowlan* and settled in Los Angeles. He left California in 1830. (Bancroft, *California,* 4:729)

Bill Marshall, an American from Rhode Island, deserted from a whaling ship at San Diego in 1845. He managed Rancho Agua Caliente in 1846. He married the daughter of Cupeño chief José Nocar and was implicated in the Garra uprising. He was executed in San Diego in 1852. (Bibb, "William Marshall")

Fernando Martín was a native of Robledillo, Spain, who worked as a preacher for eleven years at Ciudad Rodrigo before volunteering for the California missions. He was assigned to Mission San Diego in 1811 and remained there for the rest of his life. He was instrumental in establishing the *asistencia* of Santa Isabela. He died in 1838. (Geiger, Franciscan Missionaries 147–149)

Juan Martín was born in Villastor, Spain, in 1770. He joined the Franciscans in 1787 and came to California in 1794. He was briefly stationed at Missions San Gabriel and La Purísima before going to San Miguel in 1797. He remained there until his death in 1824. In 1804 he accompanied a military expedition into the San Joaquín Valley, and he reported that the native peoples there were anxious for baptism. His pleas to Governor Arrillaga to open a mission there were unsuccessful. (Geiger, *Franciscan Missionaries,* 149–150)

Ignacio Martínez was born in Mexico City in 1774 and came to Alta California around 1800. He served at Santa Bárbara and San Diego before being sent to San Francisco as a lieutenant in 1817. He succeeded Luis Antonio Argüello as commander in 1822 and acted in that capacity until 1827. From 1828 to 1831 he had various stints as acting commander and commander. He retired from the military in 1831 and then held a number of public offices, such as *alcalde* of San Francisco, member of the *diputación,* and *regidor* at San José. He owned a large ranch, Pinole, in Contra Costa, across the bay from San Francisco. He died before 1852. (Bancroft, *California,* 4:733)

William Mervine was born in 1791 and served as captain of the USS *Cyane* in 1846. He occupied Monterey in July and was sent south to relieve Gillespie in Los Angeles in October. He was defeated by the Californios in this attempt. He served as commander of the U.S. Pacific Fleet from 1855 to 1857 and as a captain in the Civil War. He died in 1868. (Hart, *Companion*, 314; Bancroft, *California*, 4:739)

Manuel Micheltorena was a native of Oaxaca, New Spain. Little is known of his career before 1840, when he was involved in suppressing a revolt in Mexico City. Appointed governor of Alta California in 1842, he arrived with some three hundred soldiers, many of whom were reported to be ex-convicts and all of whom were thoroughly disliked by the Californios. He attempted to restore undistributed mission lands and property to the Church but was generally unsuccessful. He was expelled in 1845, fought against the North Americans in 1846, and served as a member of the Mexican congress in 1847. In 1850 he was *comandante general* of Yucatán. He died in 1853. (Bancroft, *California*, 4:740)

José Matías Moreno, a native of Baja California, came to Alta California in 1844 and served as secretary to Governor Pío Pico in 1846. After the war he moved to San Diego for a time and settled on his ranch in northern Baja California. He served as head of the northern district of Baja California and died in 1869. (Bancroft, *California*, 4:745)

Juan Moreno was born in 1790 at Montenegro, Spain. He joined the Franciscans in Mexico and came to California in 1827. He served at six different missions, generally for a few years at each. He died at Santa Inés in 1845. (Geiger, *Franciscan Missionaries*, 157–158)

Rafael de Jesús Moreno was born in Mexico in 1795 and entered the Franciscans in 1817. He came to California with Governor Figueroa in 1833. He was the president of the missionaries who were sent from Zacatecas to replace the Spanish priests in the northern Alta California missions. He soon became involved in a dispute with Mariano Guadalupe Vallejo, with Vallejo holding him responsible for an attack on a group of friendly Indians. He died in 1839. (Geiger, *Franciscan Missionaries*, 158–160)

Antonio Ruiz de la Mota had served in the Mexican military but came to California as a convict around 1825. He was released around 1833 and became a *mayordomo* for Manuel Jimeno Casarín, first husband of Angustias de la Guerra, whose testimonio appears in this volume. He returned to Mexico in 1853, but she brought him back in 1856. After his return, he settled near Santa Cruz. His two sons were named Antonio and Maximiano. (Bancroft, *California*, 4:747)

Juan Antonio Muñoz, a Mexican artillery captain, came to California in 1832. He was stationed at Monterey until he left in 1836. His wife was Manuela Cruz and they had three children. (Bancroft, *California*, 3:467; 4:748)

José Pedro Narváez, a Mexican naval officer, served as captain of the port of Monterey from 1839 to 1844. He was granted the Rancho Paso de Robles, which he sold to Petronilo Ríos (husband of Catarina Avila, whose testimonio appears in this volume). In 1846 he served under José Castro. (Ohles, *Lands of San Miguel*, 56–59; Bancroft, *California*, 4:752)

Bernardo Navarrete, a lieutenant in the Mexican army, came to Alta California with Figueroa in 1833. He served at Monterey and left Alta California with Nicolás Gutiérrez in 1836. (Bancroft, *California*, 4:752)

Luis del Castillo Negrete, a Spaniard, came to California with the Híjar-Padrés colony in 1834. He became the district judge for the territory and later served as an advisor to Nicolás Gutiérrez. He left California in 1836. He later served as an officer of the Baja California government. He died in 1843. (Bancroft, *California,* 3:466)

Manuel del Castillo Negrete was the *comandante general* in Jalisco in 1840 and the brother of Luis del Castillo Negrete, who had served in Alta California as an advisor to Governor Gutiérrez. (Bancroft, *California,* 3:466; 4:30)

Francisco Noriega, a captain, came to Alta California with Governor Micheltorena in 1842. (Bancroft, *California,* 4:754)

Joaquín Pascual Nuez was born in Luco, Spain, in 1785, and entered the Franciscans in 1800. He arrived in the Americas in 1810 and in California two years later. He served at Mission San Fernando and then at Mission San Gabriel from 1814 to 1821. He accompanied a military expedition in 1819 that was sent to punish the Mojave Indians for raids against San Gabriel neophytes. He died at San Gabriel in 1821. (Geiger, *Franciscan Missionaries,* 166–167)

Vicente Pascual Oliva was born in Aragón, Spain, and joined the Franciscans in 1799. He arrived in California in 1813. After a series of brief assignments, he served at Mission San Diego from 1820 to 1846, with a two-year stay at Mission San Luis Rey in 1832 and 1833. In 1846 he went to Mission San Juan Capistrano, where he died in 1848. (Geiger, *Franciscan Missionaries,* 168–170)

James Ord came to California with his brother Lieutenant Edward O. C. Ord during the Mexican War. A civilian, he served as an army doctor. He settled in California after the war and married Angustias de la Guerra, whose testimonio appears in this volume, in 1856. They had one daughter, Rebeca, and were divorced in 1875. Ord later served as an army surgeon in Arizona and San Francisco. (Bancroft, *California,* 4:759)

Blas Ordaz was from the area near Burgos, Spain, and came to Mexico in 1819. He entered the Colegio de San Fernando in Mexico City that same year. He worked at Mission San Francisco in 1820 and 1821 and accompanied Luis Antonio Argüello on an 1821 journey to northern Alta California. He worked at a number of missions, chiefly Santa Inés (1824 to 1833) and San Fernando (1837 to 1847). He remained in Alta California through the American invasion and died at Mission San Gabriel in 1850. (Geiger, *Franciscan Missionaries,* 208–210, 170–174)

Gaspar Oreña, a Spanish trader, arrived in California in 1843. He married María Antonia de la Guerra in 1854. (Bancroft, *California,* 5:759–760)

José Joaquín Ortega, the son of José María Ortega and María Francisca López, was a member of the *diputación* in the early 1830s. He married María Pico, the sister of Pío and Andrés Pico. He served as administrator of Mission San Diego from 1835 to 1840 and as *mayordomo* of Mission San Luis Rey from 1843 to 1845. (Bancroft, *California,* 4:760)

Romualdo Pacheco was born in Guanajuato, New Spain. Like José María Echeandía, he was in the engineering corps. He accompanied Echeandía to California when the latter was appointed governor in 1825. From 1827 to 1828 he served as aide-de-camp and acting commander at Monterey. He served as acting commander at Santa Bárbara from 1828 to 1829. He was killed while fighting in support of Governor Victoria at the battle of Cahuenga in 1831.

His son, also named Romualdo, became governor of California in 1875. (Bancroft, *California,* 4:764; Genini and Hitchman, *Romualdo Pacheco,* 3–13)

Juan Nepomuceno Padilla was a barber and saloon keeper in Yerba Buena (San Francisco) in the 1840s. He led a band of irregular cavalrymen who resisted the Bear Flag revolt. The band was accused of killing and mutilating two of the Bear Flaggers near Santa Rosa. His adobe house was burned in retaliation. (Bancroft, *California,* 4:765; Warner, *Bear Flag Revolt,* 242–246, 403)

José María Padrés, a native of Puebla, was a member of the engineering corps in the military. He accompanied Echeandía in 1825 but was posted to Baja California. In 1827 he served in the Mexican congress. He came to Alta California in 1830 as *ayudante inspector.* An ardent proponent of the secularization of the missions, he was sent back to Mexico by Governor Victoria in 1831. He returned to Alta California in 1834 with the Híjar-Padrés colonizing effort started by Valentín Goméz Farías. He became embroiled in a bitter controversy with Governor Figueroa and the Californio elite and was sent back to Mexico in 1835. Nothing is known of his later life. (Hutchinson, *Frontier Settlement,* 182–184, 370–379)

Mariano Payeras was born in Mallorca in 1769. After entering the Franciscans in 1784, he arrived in California in 1796. He served at Mission Soledad for five years and then briefly at San Diego before going to La Purísima in 1804. He remained there until his death in 1823. He was at La Purísima when it was destroyed by the 1812 earthquake, and he chose the new site for the complex. He served as president of the missions from 1815 to 1820. (Payeras, *Writings of Payeras;* Geiger, *Franciscan Missionaries,* 184–189)

Miguel Pedrorena was a Spaniard who came to California in 1837 as the agent for a Lima trading company. He settled in San Diego and married María Antonia Estudillo. He was granted Rancho San Jacinto Nuevo in 1845, and she was granted Rancho El Cajón the next year. A strong supporter of the Americans in 1845, he served in the California Constitutional Convention in 1849. He died in 1850. (Bancroft, *California,* 4:770)

Cosme Peña, a lawyer, came to Alta California with the Híjar-Padrés colonization party in 1834, with an appointment as *asesor* to succeed Rafael Gómez. He sided with Juan Bautista Alvarado in 1836 and was made his secretary. He later affiliated with Angel Ramírez and was imprisoned at Sonoma. He left Alta California in 1839. (Bancroft, *California,* 3:594; 4:771)

José Antonio Peña was an artillery soldier at San Francisco and served as a teacher there as well. He also seems to have taught at Santa Clara and San José. He was granted Rancho Rincón de San Francisquito in 1841. He was married to Gertrudis Lorenzana, who had come to California in 1800 in the same group with Apolinaria Lorenzana, whose testimonio appears in this volume. (Bancroft, *California,* 4:771–772)

Antonio Peyri was born in 1769 in Catalonia, Spain. He was ordained a priest in 1793. He arrived at San Francisco in 1796 and was the founder of Mission San Luis Rey in 1798. Under his leadership the mission was said to produce the best wine in Alta California. He remained there until he left Alta California for Rome in 1832. He took two Indian boys, Pablo Tac and Agapito Amamix, with him, and intended to have them study for the priesthood. Both died during their studies. Peyri himself, regretting that he had left California, died in Spain. (Geiger, *Franciscan Missionaries,* 192–196)

Andrés Pico, the son of José María Pico of Sinaloa and María Eustaquia Gutiérrez of Sonora, was born in San Diego in 1810. In the late 1830s he was active in the southern opposition to Juan Bautista Alvarado and was arrested and sent to Sonoma. From 1839 to 1842 he served as *alférez* at San Diego. He undertook a mission to Mexico for Governor Micheltorena in 1844. On his return he continued to serve in the military, mainly in the Los Angeles area. He commanded the Californios in their victory over the North Americans at San Pascual and later negotiated the Treaty of Cahuenga with Frémont. He was elected to the state assembly in 1851, served in the state senate from 1860 to 1861, and died in 1876. (Bancroft, *California,* 4:776–777; Meier, *Mexican American Biographies,* 176–177)

José Antonio Pico was born in 1794 in San Diego. Brother of Andrés and Pío Pico, he was the eldest son of José María Pico and María Eustaquia Gutiérrez. He served in the military at San Diego and was *comisionado* at San Juan Capistrano from 1834 to 1846. He left the military in 1843 and died in San Diego in 1871. (Bancroft, *California,* 4:777)

José de Jesús Pico, the son of José Dolores Pico and Isabel Cota, was born at Monterey in 1807. He sided with Joaquín Solís from 1828 to 1829 and with Juan Bautista Alvarado from 1836 to 1838. He was one of the instigators of the revolt against Micheltorena in 1844, fought with Flores in 1846, and later served in the California assembly, in 1853. (Bancroft, *California,* 4:777–778)

Pío Pico, older brother of Andrés, was born at San Gabriel in 1801. He served in the *diputación* in 1828, and as a *vocal,* he was one of the leaders of the opposition to Governor Victoria in 1831. He served as one of the acting governors in 1832. He was a leader in the 1836–1837 opposition to Juan Bautista Alvarado. He served as the administrator of Mission San Luis Rey from 1834 to 1840. After the expulsion of Micheltorena, he became *jefe político,* and in that capacity frequently quarreled with José Castro, the *jefe militar.* He fled to Mexico in 1845 but returned to southern California in 1848 and lived in Los Angeles until his death in 1894. (Pico, *Don Pío Pico's Historical Narrative;* Bancroft, *California,* 4:778–779; Meier, *Mexican American Biographies,* 177–178)

Lázaro Piña was a Mexican artillery soldier. He served at Monterey and Sonoma and was granted Rancho Agua Caliente in 1840. He married Plácida Villela in 1823. When war with the United States broke out, he returned to Mexico, where he was killed at the battle of Cerro Gordo in April 1847. (Bancroft, *California,* 4:780)

Rodrigo del Pliego came to California as a soldier in 1825. He served at Monterey, Santa Bárbara, and San Diego as an *alférez.* Governor Victoria took him to Monterey in 1831 and he served on Victoria's staff. He left California with Victoria in January 1832. (Bancroft, *California,* 3:211–212)

Louis Pombert, a Canadian, was a member of Jedediah Smith's trapping party. He left Smith in 1827 and settled in the Monterey area, and joined the foreigners' movements led by Isaac Graham. He married María Filomena de Carmen Rudecinda Pico in 1830. (Bancroft, *California,* 4:782; Northrop, *Spanish-Mexican Families,* 2:207)

Pablo de la Portilla arrived in San Diego in 1819 with the Mazatlán troops and was stationed there until 1838. He was made commander of the garrison in 1831 and in that year opposed Governor Victoria. He was charged with secularizing Mission San Luis Rey from 1833 to 1835. In 1836 he backed Mariano Chico and opposed Juan Bautista Alvarado. In 1838 he enlisted under the banner of Carlos Carrillo and after Carrillo's defeat he left Alta California. He was stationed in Guaymas in 1846. (Bancroft, *California,* 4:782)

Víctor Prudón was born in France around 1809 and went to Mexico in 1827. He arrived in California as a teacher with the Híjar-Padrés colonization group in 1834. He married Teodosia Bojorques. He served as president of the Los Angeles vigilantes in 1836 and as Governor Alvarado's secretary from 1837 to 1838. He worked in the same capacity for Mariano Vallejo in 1841 and served as Vallejo's emissary to Mexico in 1842. He was arrested with Vallejo by the Bear Flag soldiers in 1846. His whereabouts after 1853 are unknown. (Bancroft, *California,* 4:784–785; Rhoades, "Foreigners," 70–71)

José Lorenzo de la Concepción Quijas was most likely a native of Ecuador. He entered the Franciscan College of Nuestra Señora de Guadalupe in Zacatecas after having been a muleteer and a trader. He came to California in 1833 and served at Missions San Francisco, San Francisco Solano at Sonoma, San Rafael, and San José. He was reputed to be a heavy drinker. He was appointed vice-commisary prefect of the missions in 1843 and quickly became involved in a series of jurisdictional disputes with Bishop García Diego y Moreno. He left California in 1844. (Geiger, *Franciscan Missionaries,* 200–203)

Angel Ramírez, a friar who had left his order around 1820, had participated in the wars of independence. Apparently a friend of Valentín Gómez Farías, he arrived in Alta California in 1834 as administrator of the Customs House. He served in that capacity until 1836, when Juan Bautista Alvarado removed him. He was arrested in July 1837 and died at Mission San Luis Obispo in 1840. (Bancroft, *California,* 3:587–588)

José María Ramírez came to California in 1825 with Governor Echeandía and was assigned to San Diego. He took part in the movement against Governor Victoria in 1831. He was a *comisionado* for the secularization of Mission San Diego. He received some land around Los Angeles and was active in the 1846–1847 resistance to the Americans. (Bancroft, *California,* 5:687–688)

William Reed, an Englishman, came to California in 1837. He served two years as a pilot aboard the vessel *California* and then settled near San Miguel. He and Petronilo Ríos were granted the ex-mission in 1846. He married María Antonia Vallejo. He and his family were killed at the mission in December 1848. (Bancroft, *California,* 5:690)

Manuel Requena was a trader from Yucatán, Mexico, who arrived in Alta California in 1834. He married Gertrudis Guirado. He served as *alcalde* of Los Angeles in 1836 and was active in the opposition to Juan Bautista Alvarado from 1836 to 1838. He served in the departmental *junta* from 1839 to 1841 and again as *alcalde* in 1844. In the first two decades of U.S. rule he often was a member of the Los Angeles city council. He died in 1876. (Bancroft, *California,* 5:691–692; Meier, *Mexican American Biographies,* 189)

Francisco Rico was born in Guadalajara in 1826 but moved to Monterey while still a child. He worked at the Customs House. He was active against Micheltorena in 1845 and against the Americans the next year. He was involved in the negotiations with Frémont that led to the Treaty of Cahuenga. (Bancroft, *California,* 5:695; Northrop, *Spanish-Mexican Families,* 2:226–228)

Antonio Ripoll was born at Palma, Mallorca, in 1785. After being ordained a priest, he reached New Spain in 1810 and San Diego in 1812. He worked at Missions La Purísima, Santa

Inés, and San Miguel. He trained a company of local indigenous people to fight Bouchard in 1818 and was at Santa Bárbara when the 1824 Chumash revolt broke out. He accompanied Father Vicente Sarría on the Portilla expedition to bring the Chumash fugitives back to the missions. He secretly left Alta California with Father José Altimira in 1828. He was last reported as being on Mallorca in 1832. (Geiger, *Franciscan Missionaries,* 207–208)

Alfred Robinson was born in Massachusetts in 1806 and came to California in 1829 as a clerk for Bryant and Sturgis Co., the same enterprise for which William A. Gale worked. He engaged in the hide-and-tallow trade for a number of years and in 1836 married Ana María de la Guerra, daughter of José de la Guerra y Noriega of Santa Bárbara (and sister of Teresa and Angustias de la Guerra, whose testimonios appear in this volume). He returned to the East in 1842 and four years later anonymously published *Life in California,* which became a standard North American account of Mexican Alta California. Robinson returned to California in 1849 as an agent for the Pacific Mail Steamship Co. He lived in Santa Bárbara and San Francisco for the remainder of his life, dying in 1895. (Bancroft, *California,* 5:698; Rhoades, "Foreigners," 72–74)

Juan José Rocha came to Alta California with Governor Echeandía in 1825. He was posted to Monterey, serving as *alférez* there. He was acting commander during the Solís revolt and was jailed by the rebels. He served as administrator of Missions San Juan Capistrano and San Gabriel in the 1830s and was active in the movement against Juan Bautista Alvarado in 1837. The date of his death is uncertain. (Bancroft, *California,* 5:699)

Antonio Catarino Rodríguez was a native of San Luis Potosí, Mexico, and came to Alta California in 1809. He worked for nine years at Mission San Luis Obispo, then went to La Purísima. He died at San Luis Obispo in 1824. (Geiger, *Franciscan Missionaries,* 208–210)

Manuel Rodríguez came to California from Mexico in 1795 and was named *habilitado* for the San Diego presidio in 1798, and *comandante* two years later. He became *habilitado general* for California in 1807 and moved to Mexico City, where he died in 1810. (Bancroft, *California,* 2:98)

Domingo Antonio Romero served as *alcalde* in Los Angeles in 1835. (Bancroft, *California,* 5:703)

José (Pepe) de la Rosa came to California in 1834 with the Híjar-Padrés party. Like many of the colonists, he settled in the Sonoma area. A printer by trade, he worked as a handyman for Vallejo, mending clothes and tinware. He served as Sonoma *alcalde* in 1845. In 1846 Vallejo sent him to Yerba Buena to alert John B. Montgomery, captain of the *Portsmouth,* about the Bear Flag incident and to seek the captain's intervention on Vallejo's behalf. Montgomery refused to become involved. (Koegel, "Mexican-American Music," 66–72; Bancroft, *California,* 5:704)

John Rowland came to California as a leader of the Rowland-Workman immigration party in 1841. He settled in southern California and received a grant of Rancho La Puente, south of Los Angeles, in 1842. He died in 1873. (Bancroft, *California,* 5:705)

Francisco María Ruiz was born in Loreto, Baja California, about 1754. He enlisted in the military in about 1780 and was sent as a sergeant to Santa Bárbara in 1795. He was promoted to *alférez* in 1801 and to lieutenant in 1805. He became *comandante* of San Diego in 1806 and retired from that post as a captain in 1827. He was granted Rancho Peñasquitos over the objections of the missionaries in 1823. He died in San Diego in 1839. (Bancroft, *California,* 2:540–541)

Josefa Antonia Sal was born in 1787 in Monterey. Her parents were Hermenegildo Sal, who was *habilitado* and *comandante* of the presidio there, and María Josefa Amezquita. In 1805 she married Mariano Mercado, a soldier, at Mission Dolores in San Francisco. He was transferred to San Diego, where he served in the military and as a schoolteacher until his death in 1814. (Northrop, *Spanish-Mexican Families*, 1:300–301; Bancroft, *California*, 1:678–680; 4:738)

Juan Salazar was the head of the mission guard at San Fernando in 1823 and served as interim *habilitado* at Santa Bárbara and San Diego in the late 1820s. He was promoted to *alférez* in the 1830s and once served as acting *comandante* at San Diego. (Bancroft, *California*, 5:709)

Francisco Sánchez was the son of José Antonio Sánchez. He was a soldier of the San Francisco company from 1824 and continued to serve in military and civilian offices in the San Francisco area. In 1846, he was acting commander there and commanded the Mexican troops at Santa Clara the following January. He lived in San Francisco and San Mateo after the conquest, serving on the San Francisco Board of Supervisors in 1850. He died in 1862. (Regnery, *The Battle of Santa Clara*, 141–142; Bancroft, *California*, 5:710)

José Antonio Sánchez, a native of Sinaloa, Mexico, was a member of the military company at San Francisco in the 1790s. He received various promotions until he rose to command the San Francisco garrison from 1829 to 1833. He had a reputation as a skilled fighter against the indigenous peoples and participated in more than twenty campaigns against them. He retired in 1836 and died seven years later. (Bancroft, *California*, 5:710)

José Bernardo Sánchez was born in Robledillo, Spain, and came to California as a missionary in 1804. He served at San Diego from 1804 to 1820, then at Mission La Purísima for a year, and at Mission San Gabriel from 1821 until his death in 1833. He was elected president of the missions in 1827, and as part of his duties, he directed the ecclesiastical inquiry into the wedding of Josefa Carrillo and Henry Fitch (described in the testimonio of Josefa Carrillo). (Geiger, *Franciscan Missionaries*, 217–222)

Vicente Sánchez held a variety of public offices in Los Angeles during the Mexican period. He was present in Los Angeles as early as 1814 and *alcalde* in 1826 and 1831. He also served in the *diputación* in 1828. In 1831 Governor Victoria backed him against the *ayuntamiento*, which wanted to depose him, and Sánchez managed to send José Antonio Carrillo into exile. He served as *alcalde* again in 1845. (Bancroft, *California*, 5:711)

Juan Bautista Sancho was born in Mallorca in 1772 and became a Franciscan in 1791. He arrived in California in 1804 and served at Mission San Antonio until his death in 1830. Sancho was an accomplished musician. He organized a native orchestra and composed liturgical music for them while at the mission. He also appears to have had a good grasp of the local language. (Russell, "Fray Juan Bautista Sancho;" Geiger, *Franciscan Missionaries*, 223–225)

Vicente Francisco de Sarría was a native of Spain and had taught at the Franciscan establishment in Bilbao before arriving in Mexico in 1804 and in Alta California in 1809. He worked at Mission San Carlos in Carmel until 1828. He served as prefect of the missions from 1812 to 1818 and from 1824 to 1830. He became embroiled in a dispute with the government for refusing to take the oath supporting the constitution of 1824, and in that same year he was involved with the expedition to the interior against the Chumash Indians. In 1828 he was moved to Mission Soledad, where he stayed until his death in 1835. (Bancroft, *California*, 2:396–397; Engelhardt, *Missions and Missionaries*, 2:3–4; 4:815; Geiger, *Franciscan Missionaries*, 228–235, 297)

José María Segura, a Mexican captain, came to Alta California with Governor Micheltorena in 1842 and remained in California after Micheltorena left. He was active against the Americans in the Los Angeles area in 1846 and left California with José María Flores. (Bancroft, *California*, 5:715)

Robert Semple, a native of Kentucky, came overland to California in 1845. He worked as a carpenter at Sutter's Fort and became a leader of the Bear Flag revolt. After the war, he became copublisher of the *Californian*, the first newspaper published in California. He speculated in land around the San Francisco Bay Area and served as president of the Constitutional Convention in Monterey in 1849. He moved to Colusa County and died in 1854 after a fall from a horse. (Warner, *Bear Flag Revolt*, 107–123; Bancroft, *California*, 5:715)

José Francisco de Paula Señán was born in Barcelona in 1760 and entered the Franciscans in 1774. He arrived in California in 1787 and served at Mission San Carlos until 1795, when ill health caused him to return to Mexico. He came back to California in 1798 and ministered at Mission San Buenaventura until his death in 1823. He also served two three-year terms as president of the missions, from 1812 to 1815 and 1820 to 1823. (Geiger, *Franciscan Missionaries*, 235–239)

Francisco Sepúlveda was born around 1790 and settled in Los Angeles in 1815. He served on the *ayuntamiento* and as acting *alcalde* in 1825. He was commissioner for Mission San Juan Capistrano from 1836 to 1837 and was granted a rancho in 1839. (Bancroft, *California*, 5:716)

José Sepúlveda was born in 1803. He married María Francisca de Paula Avila. He served on the Los Angeles *ayuntamiento* in 1833, as *alcalde* in 1837, and on the *ayuntamiento* again in 1839. From Juan Bautista Alvarado he received two land grants, Ciénega de las Ranas and Rancho San Joaquín. He served as subprefect in 1845 and died in 1875. (Bancroft, *California*, 5:716; Wittenburg, "Three Generations," 220–243)

José Dolores Sepúlveda was born in 1793, the son of Juan José Sepúlveda and María Tomasa Gutiérrez. He married María Ignacia Avila in 1813 and was killed in the Chumash revolt in 1824. (Northrop, *Spanish-Mexican Families*, 1:316)

Florencio Serrano came to California with the Híjar-Padrés colony in 1834. He was employed as a teacher and a government clerk in Monterey. He also served as *alcalde* of Monterey both before and after the American takeover. He died in 1877. (Bancroft, *California*, 5:716–717)

José Antonio Serrano was the son of Leandro Serrano and María Presentación Yorba. He was granted Rancho Pauma in 1844 and fought at San Pascual in 1846. (Bancroft, *California*, 5:717)

Patrick Short, a native of Ireland, was a member of the Congregation of the Sacred Hearts of Jesus and Mary who came to California from Hawai'i in 1832. He worked with William Hartnell (husband of Teresa de la Guerra, whose testimonio appears in this volume) at the school the two of them administered in Monterey during the mid-1830s. After the school closed he went to Valparaíso in Chile and died there in 1870. (Bancroft, *California*, 5:719)

John Drake Sloat was born in New York in 1781. He joined the U.S. navy in 1800 and by 1844 had risen to commander of the United States Pacific Fleet. He took possession of Monterey on June 7, 1846, but left the command in California to Stockton at the end of July and returned east. He commanded the Norfolk navy yard from 1848 to 1850. He retired in 1855 and died in 1867. (Hart, *Companion,* 478–479)

Feliciano Soberanes was born in 1788 at Monterey, where he lived his entire life. He served as a *regidor* there in 1829 and was granted Rancho Alisal in 1834. Soberanes served as *alcalde* at Monterey in 1838 and 1839 and was granted another rancho, San Lorenzo, in 1841. In that same year he was also named as administrator of the ex-mission of Soledad, and he served in that capacity until 1845. He died in 1868. His wife was María Antonia Rodríguez, whose testimonio appears in this volume. (Bancroft, *California,* 5:726; Northrop, *Spanish–Mexican Families,* 2:266–268)

Pablo Vicente de Solá was born in Vizcaya, Spain. The date of his arrival in the New World is unknown, but he was sufficiently well-established by 1805 as a captain in the military to be appointed temporary *habilitado general* of the Californias. He served in that office until 1807. He rose to the rank of lieutenant colonel by the time he was appointed governor in 1814. A brother of his, Faustino Solá, was a Franciscan and had served in the Alta California missions—at San Luis Obispo and at San Francisco—from 1786 to 1790. The governor's appearance was reported as "normal height, heavy build, short neck, large and somewhat long head, wide face, very few teeth, hair almost white, with a deep and calm voice." He served as governor until 1822. After his return to Mexico he served on the Commission for the Development of the Californias. (Bancroft, *California,* 2:470–473; 5:727; Geiger, *Franciscan Missionaries,* 274; Hutchinson, *Frontier Settlement,* 117; Torre, *Reminiscencias,* 3)

Joaquín Solís was a leader in the 1829 revolt in which a number of soldiers rose up to protest their lack of pay. Little is known about him. He had apparently fought in the war of independence and then turned to crime. He was sentenced to California in 1825. He was living outside of Monterey at the time of the revolt. In 1830 he was sent back to Mexico. (Bancroft, *California,* 3:68–69)

David Spence was born in Scotland around 1798. He came to Alta California in September 1824 to manage a meat-packing plant in Monterey for Begg and Co. He went into business for himself in 1827, and in 1829 he married Adelaida Estrada, daughter of Mariano Estrada. He served as *alcalde* of Monterey in 1835 and was on the *diputación* in the following year. He was *juez de paz* in 1839. He also served in some public offices after Alta California became part of the United States. He died in 1875. (Bancroft, *California,* 5:730–731)

Abel Stearns was born in Massachusetts in 1798 and moved to Mexico in 1826. After becoming a naturalized Mexican citizen he moved to Alta California in 1829. Unsuccessful in his attempt to obtain a land grant, he was active against Governor Victoria in 1831 and settled in Los Angeles as a trader in 1833. There he married Arcadia Bandini, daughter of Juan Bandini. He served as *síndico* in the first half of 1836 and supported Juan Bautista Alvarado over the next few years. He was also active against Governor Micheltorena and worked with Larkin for Alta California to join the United States. He became a large landowner and participated in the Constitutional Convention of 1849 and held various offices thereafter. He died in San Francisco in 1871. (Bancroft, *California,* 5:732–733)

John Stewart was born in 1811. He first came to California in 1835 on the *Pilgrim,* on which he was a shipmate of Richard Henry Dana. He settled in San Diego and married Rosa, a sister of Juana Machado, whose testimonio appears in this volume. He died in 1892. (Brandes, ed. "Times Gone By," 229)

Robert Field Stockton was born in New Jersey in 1795. He joined the U.S. navy as a young man and served in the War of 1812. He arrived in Monterey in command of the USS *Congress* in July 1846 and soon after was appointed as commander to succeed Sloat. He resigned in 1847 and returned east. He served as a United States senator from New Jersey from 1851 to 1853 and died in 1866. (Hart, *Companion*, 503; Bancroft, *California*, 5:735)

José María del Refugio Suárez del Real was born in New Spain about 1804. Ordained in 1831, he was a member of the first group of Zacatecan Franciscans to enter Alta California with Figueroa in 1833. He served at Mission San Carlos from that date until 1843; during that time he had additional responsibilities in the city of Monterey, where he bought a house in 1837. In 1844 he moved to Mission Santa Clara, serving there until he left for Mexico in 1851. He was believed to have engaged in sexual peccadilloes in both Monterey and Santa Clara. He left the Franciscans upon his return to Mexico and served as a parish priest at San José del Cabo in 1853. The date of his death is unknown. (Geiger, *Franciscan Missionaries*, 249–251)

Francisco Suñer was born at Olat, Spain, in 1764. He entered the Franciscans in 1779 and came to California in 1808. He served at Missions San Carlos, San Juan Capistrano, San Luis Rey, Santa Bárbara, and San Buenaventura. His brusque manner made him a somewhat unpopular missionary. He lost most of his sight in 1825 and died in 1831. (Geiger, *Franciscan Missionaries*, 252–253)

John Sutter was born in Germany in 1803 and, after failing in business in Switzerland and traveling in northern Mexico as well as Alaska and Hawai'i, settled in Alta California. He received a huge grant in the Sacramento Valley from Juan Bautista Alvarado, who was seeking to check the influence of Vallejo. Using indigenous laborers practically as serfs, he turned New Helvetia into an almost feudal estate. In 1845 he assisted Micheltorena against the rebels and later supported the North American invasion. He was a member of the Constitutional Convention in 1849, the year after gold was discovered on his property. By the mid-1850s squatters had taken most of his land, but he was able to survive on a pension that the California legislature awarded him. When that was not renewed in 1878, he moved to Lititz, Pennsylvania, where he died in 1880. (Hart, *Companion*, 508)

Rafael Téllez came to Alta California as a lieutenant colonel with Micheltorena in 1842 and left in 1844. He later became acting commander at Mazatlán and was in that position when the North Americans captured the city in 1848. He died later that year. (Bancroft, *California*, 5:744)

Ignacio Tenorio was a wealthy South American who retired to California around 1815 to live with the friars at the missions. He died in 1831 and was buried by Father Zalvidea. (Bancroft, *California*, 5:745)

Joaquín de la Torre was the son of José Joaquín de la Torre and María de los Angeles Cota. He was a member of the Monterey military company, and in 1840 he was one of the guard who accompanied the Graham exiles to Mexico. In 1846 he fought at Olompali. He was killed by a bandit he was trying to arrest near Santa Bárbara in 1855. (Bancroft, *California*, 5:750)

Francisco Torres was born around 1806 in Guadalajara, Mexico. A physician, he was also the secretary for and a teacher at the Institute of Public Instruction in his home city. In June 1833 he wrote a long letter to the official government paper in Mexico City about the precautions that might be employed against the Asiatic cholera that had recently broken out there. He accompanied the Híjar-Padrés colony to California and was accused of directing an insurrection against the government in Los Angeles. He was exiled in 1835. (Hutchinson, *Frontier Settlement,* 353–354)

Juan José Tovar, a Mexican captain, came to California from Sonora in 1838 in support of Carlos Carrillo. He left the same year. (Bancroft, *California,* 5:748; Harding, *Zamorano,* 211–250)

Román Francisco Fernández de Ulibarrí was born in Vitoria, Spain, in 1773. After entering the Franciscans in 1794, he arrived in California in 1809. He worked at Missions San Juan Bautista, Santa Inés, and San Fernando. Sarría wrote that he could be too "zealous" toward the mission Indians. He died in 1821. (Geiger, *Franciscan Missionaries,* 86)

Francisco Xavier de la Concepción Uría was born near Pamplona, Spain, in 1770. He arrived in Mexico in 1795 and was sent to Alta California at the end of the following year. He worked at Missions Santa Bárbara, La Purísima, and San Fernando until 1805, when he returned to the Colegio de San Fernando. He came back to Alta California in 1808 and, after a short time at Mission Santa Cruz, worked for many years among the Chumash at Mission Santa Inés. After the 1824 revolt he worked at Santa Bárbara, Soledad, and San Buenaventura. He died at Santa Bárbara in 1834. (Geiger, *Franciscan Missionaries,* 257–259)

Antonio del Valle, a lieutenant in the army, arrived in Alta California in 1819 and served at San Francisco in the early 1820s. He was jailed for a few years in the mid-1820s, apparently as a result of a quarrel with Luis Antonio Argüello. In 1832 he supported Zamorano and in 1834 was commissioner at San Fernando. He opposed Juan Bautista Alvarado in 1836 and supported Carlos Carrillo two years later. He was granted Rancho San Francisco, about thirty miles west of Mission San Buenaventura, in 1839. He died in 1841. (Bancroft, *California,* 5:755)

Ignacio del Valle was the son of Antonio del Valle. He came to California in 1825 with Echeandía and served at Santa Bárbara and San Diego in the late 1820s. In 1831 and 1832 he opposed both Governor Victoria and Agustín Vicente Zamorano. In 1836 he supported Nicolás Gutiérrez against Juan Bautista Alvarado. Two years later he supported Carlos Carrillo and had to go into brief exile as a result. After his father's death he lived on the family rancho and continued to fill various Mexican public offices in the 1840s and Los Angeles municipal offices in the early 1850s. He died in 1880. (Bancroft, *California,* 5:755–756)

Ignacio Vallejo, founder of the Vallejo dynasty in Alta California, was born in Jalisco, Mexico, in 1748. He entered the army at an early age and arrived in San Diego in 1774. He worked at Missions San Luis Obispo and San Carlos in the 1780s. After re-enlisting in 1787, he was promoted to corporal in 1789 and to sergeant in 1805. He died in Monterey in 1831. He and his wife, María Antonia Lugo, had thirteen children. (Bancroft, *California,* 5:756)

José de Jesús Vallejo, a son of Ignacio Vallejo and María Antonia Lugo and the older brother of Mariano Guadalupe Vallejo, was born in San José in 1798. He was an active participant in the defense of Monterey against Bouchard. He later held various military and civilian offices in Alta California, including the position of administrator of Mission San José after 1836. After the North American conquest he remained at Mission San José, serving for a time as postmaster there. He died in 1882. (Bancroft, *California,* 5:757)

Mariano Guadalupe Vallejo was born in Monterey in 1808. He entered the military in 1824 and was promoted to *alférez* in 1827. He was involved in a number of expeditions against the indigenous peoples of Alta California, notably against Estanislao in 1829, when his victory was marred by summary executions and a brutal massacre. He served in the *diputación* in the early 1830s and as commander of San Francisco from 1831 to 1834. In 1832 he married Francisca Benicia Carrillo. He founded the Sonoma pueblo in 1835, and from that time generally remained in the northern part of Alta California. Juan Bautista Alvarado appointed him military commander in 1836, and he held that position until the arrival of Micheltorena in 1842. Even though he was not unfriendly to the notion of a North American takeover of Alta California, he was arrested by the Bear Flaggers in 1846. After his release he became one of the leading proponents of cooperation with the new authorities. He served in the Constitutional Convention in 1849 and the state senate the following year. As the California resident best known to both Californios and North Americans, he was instrumental in persuading a number of his fellow Californios to cooperate with the research of Hubert Howe Bancroft and his staff, although he was not always pleased with the portrayal of his people in the pages of the seven volume *History of California*. He lived at Sonoma until his death in 1890. (McKittrick, *Vallejo*; Bancroft, *California*, 5:757–759; Meier, *Mexican American Biographies*, 232–233; Sánchez, "Mariano Guadalupe Vallejo," *Crítica*, 138)

Salvador Vallejo, a son of Ignacio Vallejo and María Antonia Lugo and the younger brother of Mariano Guadalupe Vallejo, was born in Monterey in 1814. In 1836 his brother made him captain of the militia at Sonoma, and he engaged in many campaigns against the indigenous peoples in the area. He was married to María de la Luz Carrillo. He served as *juez de paz* and as administrator of Mission San Francisco Solano. He was held prisoner by the Bear Flaggers in 1846. During the Civil War he served in Arizona. Later he lived with his brother at Sonoma, until his death in 1876. (Bancroft, *California*, 5:759; McKittrick, "Salvador Vallejo"; Sánchez, "Salvador Vallejo," *Crítica*, 92)

Pablo Véjar was born in 1802. He served in the military in San Diego and Monterey. In 1827 he married Mariana de Jesús Féliz, a half sister of María Inocenta Pico, whose testimonio appears in this volume. He was a participant in the Solís revolt and was expelled from California in 1830. He returned in 1833 and settled in southern California. (Bancroft, *California*, 5:761; Pico, *Cosas* [Los Californianos edition], 74)

José Viader arrived in Mexico in 1795 from Catalonia, Spain, and came to Alta California in 1796. He was assigned to Mission Santa Clara in that year and remained there until he left for his native Spain in 1833. He and Magín Matías Catalá worked together for three decades. During that time, Viader was generally in charge of the temporal concerns of the mission. (Geiger, *Franciscan Missionaries*, 263–265)

Manuel Victoria was born in Tecpan, Mexico. An infantry officer, in 1829 he requested an appointment in Baja California for reasons of health, and he was appointed governor there. In 1830 Alta California was added to his responsibilities. He assumed office on January 31, 1831, less than a month after Echeandía's secularization decree. He became involved in a series of disputes with the Californios, and the *diputación* organized a movement against him within a few months of his arrival. He defeated a rebel army in December 1831 at Cahuenga, near Los Angeles, but he was so badly wounded that he had to leave for Mexico. Little is known of his later career. (Hutchinson, *Frontier Settlement*, 142–150)

José María Villavicencio was born in 1800 in Monterey. He was heavily involved in the movement against Nicolás Gutiérrez in 1836. He served as administrator of the former missions of San Antonio and San Fernando. He was granted Rancho Corral de Piedra in the San Luis Obispo area in 1841, and he was active against the Americans in 1846. (Bancroft, *California*, 5:763; Northrop, *Spanish-Mexican Families*, 1:360)

Plácida Villela married Lázaro Piña in 1823. She was the daughter of Marcos Villela and Viridiana Carrillo, a mission Indian. (Pico, *Cosas* [Los Californianos edition], 71)

José Viñals was born at Villafranca, Spain, in 1759 and became a Franciscan in 1776. He came to California in 1798. He served at Mission San Carlos until 1804, when he asked to return to Mexico. He did so at the end of the year. (Geiger, *Franciscan Missionaries,* 265–266)

Enrique Virmond was a German resident of Acapulco who engaged in extensive trade along the Pacific coast of California. (Bancroft, *California,* 5:764)

Marcos Antonio Vitoria was born at Vitoria, Spain, in 1760. He came to California in 1805 and spent his entire missionary career in the Chumash region, at Missions Santa Bárbara, San Buenaventura, San Fernando, La Purísima, and Santa Inés. His personal life was apparently quite virtuous, but his practical abilities as a missionary were generally not praised by his Franciscan colleagues. He died in 1836. (Geiger, *Franciscan Missionaries,* 212–214)

Michael White, a native of Ireland and a sailor, visited Baja California as early as 1817 and engaged in trading voyages on the coast after that. He settled in Alta California in 1829. He built a boat for Mission San Gabriel in the early 1830s and in 1831 married María del Rosario, a daughter of Eulalia Pérez, whose testimonio appears in this volume. He was granted Rancho Muscupiabe in San Bernardino County in 1843. He died in 1885. (Bancroft, *California,* 5:773)

George Yount was a trapper from North Carolina who came to Alta California in 1831. He hunted sea otters off the Santa Bárbara Channel Islands and in San Francisco Bay. He moved to the area north of San Francisco in 1835 and worked for Mariano Guadalupe Vallejo at Sonoma. In the following year he received a land grant, Rancho Caymus, in the Napa Valley, where he lived as a hunter and trapper until his death in 1865. (Hart, *Companion,* 573; Bancroft, *California,* 5:783)

José María Zalvidea, a native of Bilbao, Spain, came to California in 1805. He served at Mission San Gabriel from 1806 to 1827, then at Mission San Juan Capistrano until 1842, and finally at Mission San Luis Rey until 1846. He was reputed to be an excellent administrator, especially at San Gabriel. He suffered from asthma and exhibited a number of personal peculiarities during his later years. He died at San Luis Rey in 1846, as he was about to be transported to San Juan Capistrano in a *carreta*. (Geiger, *Franciscan Missionaries,* 266–269)

Agustín Vicente Zamorano was born in San Agustín, Florida, in 1798. His father, a soldier, was assigned in 1809 to New Spain, where Agustín entered the military in 1821. He joined the engineering corps in 1824 and accompanied Echeandía to Alta California in the following year. He served as the governor's secretary for five years and was made commander at Monterey in 1831. After Manuel Victoria left Alta California, Zamorano was one of three de facto *jefes* who ruled until the arrival of Figueroa in 1833. He was Figueroa's secretary for two years and operated the first printing press in Alta California. In 1835 he was made commander of San Diego. He became involved in the movement against Juan Bautista Alvarado from 1836 to 1837, and when that failed, he left for Mexico. He returned to Alta California with Micheltorena in 1842 but died shortly after arriving in San Diego. (Harding, *Don Agustín V. Zamorano*)

Chronology of Events in Early California

Bouchard Raid (1818)—Hipólito Bouchard, a French-born privateer sailing for the United Provinces of the Río de la Plata, the anti-Spanish independence movement in Argentina, raided the Alta California coast in the fall of 1818. He sacked and burned Monterey. Governor Pablo Vicente de Solá ordered the town evacuated and the residents took refuge at the Rancho del Rey, near Salinas. Bouchard also landed at Refugio, Santa Bárbara, and San Juan Capistrano, where his men looted the mission, before heading south. (Uhrowczik, *Burning of Monterey*)

Chumash Revolt (1824)—In February 1824, an organized revolt broke out against the missions of Santa Inés, La Purísima, and Santa Bárbara, all of which had large Chumash populations. The rebels burned most of the Santa Inés complex, although they spared the church. They then withdrew to La Purísima, where they forced the garrison to surrender. Another group briefly seized Santa Bárbara. The rebels eventually withdrew to Buena Vista Lake, about sixty miles east of Santa Bárbara. They beat back the first military expedition sent to bring them back. A second expedition, accompanied by Fathers Vicente Sarría and Antonio Ripoll, convinced them to return to their missions. This was the largest organized revolt against the missions in the history of Alta California. (Sandos, "Levantamiento")

Arrival of the Asia (1825)—In 1825, three Spanish warships arrived in Alta California. The *Asia* and the *Constante* arrived at Monterey, while the *Aquiles* landed at Santa Bárbara. The three ships were part of a Spanish fleet that was fighting in the Pacific against vessels of the South American republics who had declared their independence from Spain. The crews mutinied off the Mariana Islands and put José Martínez, commander of the *Constante,* in charge of the *Asia,* the largest of the ships. He guided them back to California, where they surrendered to Governor Argüello at Monterey. Juan Malarín was put in charge of transporting the *Asia* to Mexico. (Osio, *Alta California,* 75–83)

Revolt of Estanislao (1829)—Estanislao, an *alcalde* at Mission San José, and a group of his fellow mission Indians refused to return to the mission after a regularly scheduled break to visit relatives and friends in the Central Valley. The group defeated the first expedition sent out to retrieve them. The second expedition was commanded by Mariano Guadalupe Vallejo. He was unable to dislodge Estanislao's group in two separate attacks. After the second attack, the military massacred a good number of captives it had taken, and then declared victory and returned home. Estanislao himself returned to the mission some time later. (Osio, *Alta California,* 89–94)

Solís Revolt (1829)—In 1829, a group of soldiers at the Monterey presidio who had not been paid for some time rebelled against their commanders and the customs officials. The rebels jailed a number of people, including Mariano Guadalupe Vallejo and Angustias de la Guerra's future husband Manuel Jimeno Casarín. Under the leadership of Joaquín Solís, a ranchero living nearby, the rebels marched south, but they were defeated by Governor Echeandía's forces in a skirmish near Santa Bárbara. (Bancroft, *California,* 3:67–85; Osio, *Alta California,* 94–98)

Expulsion of Governor Victoria (1831)—After Governor Manuel Victoria halted the preliminary secularization process that had been put in motion by his predecessor, José de Echeandía, and refused to call the elected *diputación* into session, a revolt against him broke out. It was centered in San Diego. Victoria marched south against the rebels. At the battle of Cahuenga, Victoria was wounded and Romualdo Pacheco, from his side, and José María Avila, on the rebel side, were killed. Victoria left California shortly afterward. (Bancroft, *California*, 3:181–215; Osio, *Alta California*, 106–113)

Secularization of the Missions (1833)—Secularization was the process by which the missions were turned into parish churches. The Mexican congress passed a law mandating this transformation in 1833. The missions' extensive lands and ranchos were supposed to be distributed to the Indians, with surplus lands to be given to the settlers. The missions were put under the control of civil administrators, who were to supervise the process. Very few Indians actually received any land. (Haas, "Emancipation"; Ivey, "Secularization")

Híjar-Padrés Colony (1834)—This was the one attempt by the Mexican government to send colonists to California to increase the population and thus render it more secure against Russia, England, and the United States. The project was supported by the liberal Mexican vice president, Valentín Gómez Farías. Over two hundred people arrived in California with the colony. The Californio elite, which saw the colonists as unwelcome competitors for the mission lands, refused to recognize the colony's leadership. Many of the colonists eventually settled in California, and a good number of them made substantial contributions to its development. (Hutchinson, *Frontier Settlement*)

Revolt against Governor Chico (1836)—After the death of the popular Governor José Figueroa, the Mexican government appointed Mariano Chico governor of California. His mandate was to introduce the new centralist administration that was being inaugurated in Mexico by Antonio López de Santa Anna. He also brought with him a woman who was not his wife, with whom he lived. For these political and personal reasons, the Californios expelled him after only a few months in office. (Bancroft, *California*, 3:414–444)

Revolt against Governor Gutiérrez (1836)—When Mariano Chico left, he appointed Nicolás Gutiérrez, a military man, to succeed him. Since he had the same powers as Chico, the Californios did not like him any more than they had liked Chico. An armed revolt in the Monterey area led to his expulsion at the end of the year. (Bancroft, *California*, 3:445–477)

Alvarado-Carrillo Disputes (1836–1838)—After the expulsion of Gutiérrez, the Monterey-based rebels supported Juan Bautista Alvarado as governor. This selection was not well received in southern Alta California, and Alvarado and José Castro marched there to force that region to accept him. In the meantime the Mexican government appointed Carlos Antonio Carrillo as governor, and the southerners supported him. A series of minor military engagements between the forces of Alvarado and Carrillo lasted for the next few years. Finally, Mexican emissary Andrés Castillero, dispatched by the authorities in Baja California, negotiated a settlement, and Alvarado was accepted as governor both by the southerners and the government in Mexico City. (Bancroft, *California*, 3:478–578)

The Taking of Monterey by Jones (1842)—In October 1842, Thomas ap Catesby Jones, commander of the United States Pacific Fleet, sailed into Monterey and captured it without a fight. Under the mistaken belief that war had broken out between the United States and Mexico, Jones had wanted to seize California before the British or the French got a chance to do so. When he discovered that there was no war, he apologized and left. (Osio, *Alta California*, 208–210; Smith, "Thomas ap Catesby Jones")

Expulsion of Governor Micheltorena (1845)—Manuel Micheltorena was appointed governor of California by the Mexican government in 1842. He was personally popular, but the rowdy behavior of his troops irritated many Californios, and his moves toward restoring control of some mission lands to the priests greatly upset the rancho elite. A military confrontation between him and rebel forces ended peacefully in 1844, but he was forcibly expelled the next year. Pío Pico became the territory's political leader, and José Castro the military head. (Bancroft, *California,* 4:454–517)

Bear Flag Revolt (1846)—In June 1846 a group of Americans living around Sonoma and Sutter's Fort stormed into the Sonoma plaza and arrested Mariano Guadalupe Vallejo, his brother Salvador and his secretary, Víctor Prudón, and Rosalía Vallejo's husband, Jacob P. Leese. The group proclaimed a short-lived California Republic. The primitive flag one of them stitched together gave the movement its name, the Bear Flag revolt. They sent the four detainees to Sutter's Fort, where John C. Frémont kept them under arrest for the next six weeks. On July 7, Commodore John Drake Sloat captured Monterey, and the Bear Flag revolt was absorbed into the larger war. (Warner, *Men of the Bear Flag Revolt*)

The War in California (1846–1847)—After the capture of Monterey, most of the military activity took place in the southern part of Alta California, although there were two significant engagements in the north.

The first, in the north, was the battle of Natividad, which took place on November 16, 1846, outside of San Juan Bautista. The Californios and the Americans fought each other to a standoff, although the Americans suffered higher casualties than did the Californios. The battle of Santa Clara occurred on January 2, 1847. A group of Californios, incensed at the plundering of their ranchos, had seized Washington Bartlett, *alcalde* of San Francisco, and five or six others. American marines came to the scene and joined the battle. After a brief engagement an armistice was arranged and the American authorities agreed to respect the Californios' property. (Harlow, *California Conquered,* 195–197; Regnery, *The Battle of Santa Clara*)

In the south, both Pío Pico and José Castro left Los Angeles the night of August 10 and the Americans soon took possession of the city. Archibald Gillespie was made military commander of the southern area. His rule in Los Angeles was harsh, and resistance to his regime grew. José María Flores led that resistance, and Gillespie was forced to leave Los Angeles and set up headquarters in San Pedro on September 30. An American attempt to retake Los Angeles was thwarted by the Californios, led by José Antonio Carrillo, outside of San Pedro on the rancho of Manuel Domínguez, on October 9. This battle is often referred to as "the Battle of the Old Woman's Gun," since the Californio forces employed a cannon which supposedly had been buried in Ignacia Reyes's garden. Frémont managed to come south, escaping an ambush which had been set for him at Gaviota by marching through the San Marcos pass instead. General Stephen Watts Kearny marched overland from New Mexico, and his dragoons were defeated by the Californios under Andrés Pico at the battle of San Pascual on December 6. A few days later, Kearny did manage to reach San Diego, where Sloat's successor Robert Stockton had set up his headquarters. Kearny bested the Californio forces at San Gabriel on January 8 and at La Mesa on January 9. His troops entered Los Angles on January 10, and the Californios surrendered to Frémont at Cahuenga on January 13. (Harlow, *California Conquered,* 159–218)

Pauma Killings (1846)—A few days after the battle of San Pascual, a group of eleven Californios who were at Rancho Pauma, owned by José Antonio Serrano, were captured and killed by a group of Luiseño Indians. The killings may have been in reprisal for the recent killings of some Luiseños. José María Flores sent a force headed by José del Carmen Lugo in pursuit of the Luiseños. This force killed thirty-eight Luiseños and Cupeños at the Luiseño ranchería of Aguanga, northeast of San Diego. (Griswold del Castillo, "The U.S.–Mexican War in San Diego, 1846–1847")

Governors of Alta California and Important Events during Their Governorships

1815–1821: Governorship of Pablo Vicente de Solá
1818: Arrival of the privateer Hipólito Bouchard in Monterey

1822–1825: Governorship of Luis Antonio Argüello
1824: Chumash revolt

1825–1831: Governorship of José María de Echeandía
1825: Arrival of the *Asia* at Monterey
1827–1830: Intrigues of Solís and Herrera
1829: Revolt of Estanislao
1831 (January): Echeandía's secularization decree

1831–1832: Governorship of Manuel Victoria
1831: Movement against Victoria
1831 (December): Battle of Cahuenga
1832 (January): Departure of Victoria

1832–1833: Governorship of Pío Pico (1832, Acting), José María de Echeandía (in the south), Agustín Vicente Zamorano (in the north)

1833–1835: Governorship of José Figueroa
1833: Arrival of friars from Zacatecas
1833: Secularization of the missions
1834: Arrival of Híjar-Padrés colony

1835–1836: Governorship of José Castro (Acting)

1836 (January 2–May 3): Governorship of Nicolás Gutiérrez (Acting)

1836 (May 3–July 31): Governorship of Mariano Chico

1836 (August 1–November 5): Governorship of Nicolás Gutiérrez (Acting)
1836 (November): Alvarado revolt against Gutiérrez

1836–1842: Governorship of Juan Bautista Alvarado
1837 (January): Opposition to Alvarado in Los Angeles
1837 (May): Opposition to Alvarado in San Diego
1837 (May): Arrival of Andrés Castillero
1837 (June): Appointment of Carlos Carrillo as governor
1838 (March): Battle of San Buenaventura
1838 (August): Departure of Castillero for Mexico City
1838 (November): Return of Castillero from Mexico City
1840: Isaac Graham revolt

1841: Tensions between Alvarado and Mariano Guadalupe Vallejo
1842: Víctor Prudón and Manuel Castañares mission to Mexico City

1842–1845: Governorship of Manuel Micheltorena

1842 (October): Thomas ap Catesby Jones seizes Monterey
1845 (February): Battle of Cahuenga; departure of Micheltorena

1845–1846: Governorship of Pío Pico (in the south) and José Castro (in the north)

1846 (March): John C. Frémont outside of Monterey
1846 (April): Arrival of Archibald Gillespie
1846 (June): Bear Flag revolt
1846 (September): Gillespie abandons Los Angeles
1846 (October): William Mervine driven away from Los Angeles
1846 (December): Battle of San Pascual
1847 (January): Battle of San Gabriel; Treaty of Cahuenga

NOTES

NOTES TO PROLOGUE

1. The description of the Real Casa de Expósitos is largely taken from the Casa's constitution, which was reprinted in León, *La obstetricia en México,* 610–612, 663–668. We thank Carmen Boone de Aguilar for bringing this volume to our attention.
2. Archivo General de la Nación (Mexico City) Californias, tomo 41, p. 21, consulted on microfilm at The Bancroft Library.

NOTES TO INTRODUCTION

1. "Narrative of William Fitch taken on board of steamer M.S. Latham on her voyage from San Francisco to Donahue," The Bancroft Library, C-E 67:3.
2. Sánchez, *Telling Identities,* 7.
3. Owens, "Magnificent Fraud."
4. Bancroft, *Literary Industries,* 368, 375, 444–445.
5. Bancroft, *California,* 3:759.
6. Bancroft, *Literary Industries,* 259; Oak, "Estimate," in Henry Lebbeus Oak Papers, The Bancroft Library, C-B 386, Part II, Folder 6.
7. Bowman, "History of the Provincial Archives."
8. In these totals we are counting only those interviews that were classified as discrete interviews back at the library in San Francisco. Cerruti also interviewed a number of other people whose testimonios he did not write up as separate documents, embedding them instead in his manuscript "Ramblings in California." In this volume, we are including one of the interviews from "Ramblings." This is a conversation with María Antonia Rodríguez in Monterey.
9. Genaro Padilla and Rosaura Sánchez have both written quite perceptively on the interview process. See Padilla, *My History, Not Yours* and Sánchez, *Telling Identities.* See also Bouvier, "Framing the Female Voice."
10. The indigenous peoples of the Californias lived in small groups which, though often connected culturally, were usually autonomous politically. Because the word "tribe" connotes a large, cohesive group of the type found elsewhere in North America, we have avoided it here.
11. Osio, *History of Alta California,* 243.
12. See, for instance, Armitage, ed., *Women's Oral History,* and Perdue, ed., *Sifters,* for a representative sample of some of this recent work.
13. A small sampling of some recent work that has employed these testimonios would include Bouvier, *Women and the Conquest;* Castañeda, "Gender, Race, and Culture"; Casas, "In Consideration"; Chávez-García, *Negotiating Conquest;* and Hurtado, *Intimate Frontiers.*
14. The 1956 translation has recently been republished. See Ord, *California Recollections,* 114. The editor of the republished volume corrects this particular error in an endnote.

NOTES TO ISIDORA FILOMENA TESTIMONIO

1. Isidora tended, for instance, not to conjugate verbs, but to use the infinitive form. This, along with some of the other ways she spoke, clearly marked her as a second-language learner.

2. On Mission San Francisco Solano, see Smilie, *The Sonoma Mission*. Studies on Vallejo are numerous. Much of the information here comes from Rosenus, *Vallejo*, and Tays, "Vallejo and Sonoma."

3. The information about the Suisuns and Chief Solano in this and the next few paragraphs comes from an unpublished paper by Randall Milliken, "Ethnographic and Ethnohistorical Context for the Archaeological Investigation of the Suisun Plain, Solano County, California." We are very grateful to Randy for sharing this paper and his knowledge of the Suisuns and Solano with us. We also thank Edward Castillo for sharing his own work on Isidora and her people with us.

4. See Cook, *The Epidemic of 1830–1833 in California and Oregon;* Cook, "Smallpox in Spanish Mexican California, 1770–1845"; and Preston, "Portents of Plague from California's Protohistoric Period."

5. Lothrop, "Indian Campaigns," 188; Peterson, "Career of Solano," 25; Silliman, *Lost Laborers,* 45–46; Bancroft, *California,* 4:70–74.

6. Peterson, "Career of Solano," 41; Milliken, "Ethnographic and Ethnohistorical Context"; Land Case 396, Northern District (Suisun). This and all other land cases were consulted at The Bancroft Library.

7. Lothrop, "Indian Campaigns," 196–198; Tays, "Vallejo and Sonoma," 17.2: 155–156.

8. Vallejo, *Derivation and Definition;* Land Grant Case 396, Northern District (Suisun).

9. Lachryma Montis was the name of Mariano Guadalupe Vallejo's Sonoma landholdings.

10. The indigenous names in this paragraph are Cerruti's phonetic renderings of the words that Isidora used. They most likely refer both to a specific group and to the area around which that group lived. Some of the names are to be found in the San Francisco Solano mission baptismal records. They indicate there what the padres termed the "gentile *ranchería*," the village from which the baptized person came. See, for instance, Johnson, "Patwin," 350, and Bancroft, *California,* 2:506 and 4:72. On the native peoples of the region, see Johnson, "Patwin;" Kroeber, *Patwin;* Beard, *Wappo;* and Dillon, *Napa Valley's Natives.* At the end of the next paragraph, Isidora may be referring to an episode in which Vallejo wanted to execute a captured chief named Zampay but was dissuaded from doing so by Solano. See Lothrop, "Indian Campaigns," 188.

11. The word "Churucto" was Cerruti's phonetic rendering of what he heard her say. Her home village was probably the settlement of Churup on Cache Creek. See Johnson, "Patwin," 350.

12. Sutter had spent five months in Hawai'i before he arrived in California. The woman to whom Isidora refers here was named Manaiki. Sutter brought her from Hawai'i. See Breault, *Sutter in Hawaii;* Engstrand, "Sutter," 81–82; and Dillon, *Sutter,* 94–95. By *"Joaquinero,"* Isidora means the peoples of the Central Valley. Indigenous peoples from central California were involved in every aspect of Sutter's establishment at New Helvetia. Sutter settled near the boundary between the Nisenan and Miwok peoples of the Sierra Nevada and foothills, and he was able at times to pit indigenous groups against each other to his own advantage. On the question of Sutter and his Indian neighbors, see Hurtado, "The Indian Business." Sutter and Vallejo were thus rivals on the northern frontier and Solano's relations with the Indians who worked for Sutter could work to Vallejo's advantage. Solano's intelligence about Sutter's cruel treatment of his indigenous workers, for instance, provided Vallejo with the information he used to denounce Sutter to the authorities. See Dillon, *Sutter,* 124.

13. We have not been able to identify these two foods.

14. This is perhaps an example of Isidora's lack of complete fluency in Spanish. The context makes it clear that she was referring to healers *(curanderos),* but she used the word *astrólogos,* which means astrologers.

NOTES

Notes to Rosalía Vallejo Testimonio

1. Family information about the Vallejos is generally taken from Emparán, *Vallejos of California,* Rosenus, *Vallejo,* and Northrop, *Spanish-Mexican Families,* 2:308–311. The Alvarado citation is from his "Historia de California," 3:50–51.
2. Tays, "Vallejo," 16.4:352–353; Emparán, *Vallejos of California,* 186. See also Sánchez, *Telling Identities,* 216; Casas, "In Consideration," 164.
3. Land Case 237, Northern District (Cañada de Guadalupe); Land Case 285, Northern District (Cañada de Guadalupe); Land Case 50, Northern District (Huichica); Land Case 396, Northern District (Suisun).
4. Hague and Langum, *Larkin,* 196–197, 207.
5. Martínez, *Lower California,* 389–494; Piñera Ramírez, ed., *Panorama histórico,* 201–207.
6. Juan Padilla and Ramón Carrillo were in command of a group of Californio horsemen in the vicinity of Sonoma. On the night of June 14, as Vallejo, the other prisoners, and their guards were spending the night at Manuel Vaca's rancho on their way to Sutter's Fort, Vicente Juárez, a member of Padilla and Carrillo's band, made contact with Vallejo and offered to help him escape. Fearing retaliation against his family, who were still under the control of the rebels at Sonoma, Vallejo refused the offer. See Rosenus, *Vallejo,* 118.
7. In his rendition of the testimonio, Cerruti reproduced this sentence in Spanish: *Mandaré quemar las casas con ustedes adentro si Padilla se acerca a Sonoma.* (I will order the houses burned with you inside if Padilla approaches Sonoma.) He did this probably because he found it such an extreme statement. He wanted those who read the interview to have no doubt that these were the exact words Rosalía Vallejo used in reporting what she insisted Frémont said.
8. While it was a short-lived affair, the Bear Flag rebellion did have its grisly aspects. A few days after the seizure of Sonoma, two of the rebels, Thomas Cowie and George Fowler, were sent to seek gunpowder from Moses Carson, who was the *mayordomo* for absentee owner Henry Fitch at Rancho Satiyomi, about twenty miles northwest of Sonoma. The two men were captured by Padilla and Carrillo's forces and were killed near the Carrillo establishment, Rancho Cabeza de Santa Rosa. Word quickly spread among the rebels that the two men had been mutilated, although the actual circumstances of their deaths are uncertain. See Bancroft, *California* 5:160–164; Warner, *Bear Flag,* 242–247. Frémont was at Sutter's Fort when the Bear Flag rebellion broke out. He remained in that vicinity until June 25, when he went to Sonoma with a party of some one hundred and thirty men. He headed toward San Rafael in pursuit of the band led by Padilla and Carrillo. This group had been reinforced by another force sent by José Castro and commanded by Joaquín de la Torre. This new force and the Bear Flaggers had engaged in a battle near Olómpali on June 23. Frémont's party hurried to San Rafael, but the Californios had already left. However, they did spot three civilians, José Berryessa and two brothers, Francisco and Ramón de Haro. The three were shot in cold blood, in retaliation for the killing of Cowie and Fowler a few days earlier. The killing was apparently carried out by Moses Carson's brother Kit, who was scouting for Frémont. Frémont's party then returned to Sonoma, because of intelligence that de la Torre was planning to attack Sonoma. It was most likely at this juncture, with both sides having already killed prisoners and with Frémont fearing that he had been outmaneuvered by the Californios, that Frémont would have made his threat to Rosalía Vallejo. (Roberts, *A Newer World,* 170; Guild and Carter, *Carson,* 154) But the intelligence turned out to be false. It had been deliberately planted by the Californios to get Frémont to retire from the field and return to Sonoma. The Californios used the occasion to escape across the bay. Frémont then went to Yerba Buena, where he spiked the abandoned cannons at the old *castillo* near the Golden Gate. He then returned to Sonoma in time for a Fourth of July party. On July 5, he formally brought the Bear Flaggers under his control, and he returned to Sacramento on the next day. See Harlow, *California Conquered,* 108–110.

9. Rosana Leese was Rosalía Vallejo's twenty-three-year-old daughter, and she was probably present at the interview.

NOTES TO DOROTEA VALDEZ TESTIMONIO

1. Information about Juan Bautista Valdez is in Crosby, *Gateway,* 170.
2. It would be tempting, but overly speculative, to identify her with a woman named simply "Dorotea" who was listed as an "Indian" in both the 1860 and 1870 federal censuses for Monterey. Her age was reported as seventy in 1860, and eighty-eight in 1870. She was said to be a "laborer" in 1860 and reported as "keeping house" in 1870. In both years, she was the companion of a man identified as an "Indian," Venturo.
3. Rosenus, *Vallejo,* 25–27, 47; Osio, *Alta California,* 202–207.
4. It is difficult to know whether she specifically referred to Spaniards here. She may well have simply used the normal phrase *gente de razón* ("people of reason"), which generally connoted non-Indians. Cerruti may have translated that into "good Spanish citizens."
5. On José el Cantor, see Hackel, *Children of Coyote,* 413–417.
6. *Gachupín* is derived from the Náhuatl word *cacchopini*. *Cactli* means "shoe" and *chopini* means "to kick," so the combination *cacchopini* or *gachupín* means "a man who kicks," i.e., someone wearing spurs. Historically, the term *gachupín* referred to Spaniards during and after the conquest of Mexico.
7. There may have been a class component to family size in Mexican Alta California, with more children in elite families than in other families in the territory. Using data compiled by Northrop, Gloria Ricci Lothrop calculated an average family size of about 8.8 children (see Lothrop, "Rancheras"). Local studies, which include samples of women and families who were perhaps more representative than Northrop was able to investigate, have tended to show slightly smaller families. For instance, Katharine Meyer Lockhart found that fertility in San José was "higher than comparable figures for many populations during the same time period." The average number of children per marriage over the Spanish and Mexican period was a bit under eight. (Lockhart, "Demographic Profile," 60–67). In an investigation of Santa Bárbara and Los Angeles, Gloria Miranda has found that the average family sizes there were smaller. In 1834 Santa Bárbara families had 4.4 children, and Los Angeles families 3.9. In addition, over the Mexican period the average age of women at marriage slightly increased (Miranda, "Hispano-Mexican Childrearing Practices," 308, and *"Gente de Razón* Marriage Patterns," 7). The infant mortality rate is also an important demographic variable. Robert Wayne Eversole has found that it was comparatively low throughout the Mexican period (Eversole, "Towns in Mexican Alta California," 169–178).
8. Cerruti rendered this in Spanish *("Este es un delito que Dios no perdona")* and did not translate it into English.
9. A *jáquima* ("hackamore" in English) is a rope or rawhide halter with a wide band that can be lowered over a horse's eyes. Hackamores are used in breaking horses to a bridle. The word in English is a corruption of the Spanish word.

NOTES TO MARÍA ANTONIA RODRÍGUEZ TESTIMONIO

1. Northrop, *Spanish-American Families,* 1:285–286, 2:266–273; Schuetz-Miller, *Building and Builders,* 88–91.
2. Manuel Gómez was artillery commander at Monterey when Bouchard attacked. At one point he ordered José de Jesús Vallejo to cease firing at Bouchard's ships. That decision was

subsequently severely criticized by many Californios. The more extreme criticism, which
María Antonia Rodríguez reflected in her comments here, spilled over into accusations that
he was a traitor. According to this version, he had secretly sent Bouchard the plans of the
Monterey defenses, and he had a cousin in Bouchard's crew. Governor Solá, noting that
Gómez's own house had been hit by the insurgents, dismissed the criticism and recommended that Gómez be promoted to lieutenant. The promotion took effect the following
year. Gómez remained in Alta California until he returned to México in 1822, after he had
married into the Estudillo family. See Bancroft, *California,* 2:230, 470; 3:759.

3. This land was near the Punta de Pinos in Monterey. See Clark, *Monterey County Place Names,* 460.
4. Rancho Refugio, west of Santa Bárbara, was owned by the Ortega family. It was a well-
    known center of smuggling during the Spanish period. See José de Jesús Vallejo, "Historical
    Reminiscences," 11; Ogden, *California Sea Otter Trade,* 78.
5. According to another Californio, Antonio Coronel, "The *jarabe* is the national dance of the
    Mexican people. It is variable in its composition, because it has a diversity of tunes and
    popular songs mixed together; it is varied in its music and is difficult to dance well, for
    every change of tune or piece requires new movements. Therefore, it is a dance which was
    only danced by those persons who knew how to perform it. The *tecolero* (master of cere-
    monies), knowing who could dance it, would choose one man and one lady and arrange
    them in place. The dancers would begin to dance, and in the intervals of instrumental
    music when the dancers would rest, the singer would improvise and sing a quatrain based
    on the music that was being played." Koegel, "Mexican-American Music," 150.
6. Cerruti wrote this sentence in English.

NOTES TO TERESA DE LA GUERRA TESTIMONIO

1. On the de la Guerra family genealogy, see Pubols, "de la Guerra Family," 602–609.
2. On Hartnell, see Dakin, *Lives of Hartnell.*
3. These papers have recently been published. See Hartnell, *Diary and Copybook.*
4. Land Case 362, Northern District (Cosumnes).
5. For the troubles faced by settlers in the Monterey area because of raids by various indige-
    nous peoples in the late 1830s, see Broadbent, "Conflict at Monterey," and Bancroft,
    California, 3:693.
6. William H. Aspinwall of the New York merchant firm Howland and Aspinwall organized
    the Pacific Mail Steamship Company in 1848 and received a government contract to carry
    mail between Panama and Oregon. Aspinwall also organized the Panama Rail Company to
    transport people and goods across the isthmus. Henry Chauncey, a New York capitalist,
    provided some of the funding for these ventures. Robinson was the first agent for the
    Steamship Company in San Francisco. The rail line was completed in 1855 and the combi-
    nation of rail and ship service was able to thwart the attempts of Cornelius Vanderbilt to
    develop a competing transportation corridor across Nicaragua. Vanderbilt did gain the gov-
    ernment contract for a year in 1859 after Aspinwall had retired, but he and the Pacific Mail
    Steamship Company agreed to a truce in 1860. By its terms, Vanderbilt agreed to operate
    only in the Atlantic, and the Pacific Mail only in the Pacific. See Kemble, *The Panama Route.*
7. On the de la Guerra family's use of patriarchy in Santa Bárbara in the 1850s, see Pubols,
    "Fathers of the Pueblo."
8. David Leese was a son of Rosalía Vallejo.

NOTES TO JOSEFA CARRILLO TESTIMONIO

1. Bolton, ed., *Anza's California Expeditions,* 4:138–139.
2. Northrop, *Spanish-American Families,* 1:200–202; 2:46–48.
3. Ibid., 2:46–48; "Documentos para la historia de California 1826–1850. Originales y copiados de los Archivos del Condado de San Diego por Benjamin Hayes," C-A 70, 1:21–22, The Bancroft Library.
4. Beebe and Senkewicz, eds. *Lands of Promise and Despair,* 341–342.
5. Ibid., 355–359.
6. The documents relating to the elopement and the subsequent investigations are in two places: the Santa Bárbara Mission Archive-Library, where the files on the ecclesiastical investigation at San Gabriel are in the California Mission Documents collection under the year 1830, and The Bancroft Library, where other documents relating to the affair were obtained from Josefa Carrillo when Cerruti interviewed her in 1875. These are grouped under C-E 67, item 10 B. See also Miller, "Henry Delano Fitch," 13–27, 225–236.
7. Northrop, *Spanish-American Families,* 2:86–88; "Documentos para la historia...por Benjamin Hayes," The Bancroft Library, C-A 70:1, 141; Miller, "Henry Delano Fitch," 82–83.
8. Land Case 52, Northern District (Satiyomi); Miller, "Henry Delano Fitch," 196.
9. Correspondence between Josefa and a variety of people relating to these events is in the Fitch papers at The Bancroft Library, C-B 55, folders 697, 600, 601, 608–612, 614, and 619.
10. John Temple to Mrs. Fitch, July 5, 1850, Fitch Papers, The Bancroft Library, C-B 55, folder 620.
11. Miller, "Henry Delano Fitch," 210–212.
12. Alexander, *Sonoma Valley Legacy,* 37–41; Hayes, "Emigrant Notes," 4:721.
13. *Carne Humana* means "human flesh." Bale received his grant in 1841. See Pérez, *Land Grants,* 61.
14. *Río de los Putos* means "River of the Sons of Bitches."
15. Pico's paternal grandmother was María Feliciana Arballo. She was also Josefa Carrillo's maternal grandmother.
16. According to Dr. W. Michael Mathes, *pisco* is the Peruvian equivalent of tequila, and it is a grape *aguardiente (grappa).* It is usually drunk with lemon and sugar. *Ica* is the big grape-growing area of Peru. We thank Mike for sharing this information with us.

NOTES TO CATARINA AVILA TESTIMONIO

1. Northrop, *Spanish-Mexican Families,* 1:192–194.
2. Ohles, *Lands of Mission San Miguel,* 23–33.
3. Land Case 306, Southern District (San Bernabé); Land Case 351, Southern District (Paso de Robles); Ohles, *Lands of Mission San Miguel,* 37–43.
4. Ohles, *Lands of Mission San Miguel,* 73–84, 237.
5. The murders at Mission San Miguel are treated in Secrest, *California Desperadoes,* 3–27; Ohles, *Mission Lands of San Miguel,* 52–55; and Johnson, *Mysteries of the Murders.*
6. At the time, Catarina and her husband were probably staying at their adobe on the Estrella River, about six miles from the mission. See Ohles, *Lands of Mission San Miguel,* 54.

NOTES TO EULALIA PÉREZ TESTIMONIO

1. Leslie, *California,* 259.
2. Northrop, *Spanish-Mexican Families,* 2:116–118.

3. McKenzie, "The San Pascual Grant," 34–41; Nunis, ed., *Southern California Local History,* 107–112; Land Case 173, Southern District (San Pascual [Garfias]).

4. Antonio Grájera was the commander at San Diego from 1793 to 1799. See Bancroft, *California,* 1:676.

5. Father Fernando was Fernando Martín, who served at Mission San Diego from 1811 to 1838. See Geiger, *Franciscan Missionaries,* 147–149.

6. Father Sánchez would have been familiar with the historical and literary roots of the surname "Tenorio." The reference to Ignacio Tenorio as the "king's judge" might refer to the Spanish prelate Pedro Tenorio, Archbishop of Toledo from 1375 to 1399. This archbishop was very influential during the reigns of Enrique II, Juan I, and Enrique III and was the head of the council of regency during the reign of Enrique III. Father Sánchez might also have been alluding to the Tenorio family members who are protagonists in Tirso de Molina's play *El burlador de Sevilla,* written in 1615. In this play, the father and uncle of Don Juan Tenorio have important roles as members of the king's inner circle of advisors or judges.

7. The word in Spanish is *sayasaya.* See Perissinotto, Rudolph, and Miller, *Documenting Everyday Life in Early Spanish California,* 85, fn 42.

8. *Tafilete,* named after a region in Morocco, is a shiny, burnished leather from goatskin or calfskin, considerably thinner than the more commonly requested cordoban. See Perissinotto, Rudolph, and Miller, *Documenting Everyday Life in Early Spanish California,* 315, fn 163.

9. Traces are the two lines that connect the horse's harness to the coach.

10. "Vicar Forane" was someone who, in the absence of a resident bishop, was delegated by the appropriate bishop (in this case the bishop of Sonora) to exercise certain ecclesiastical powers that were normally within the jurisdiction of a bishop. Overseeing questions about the validity of marriages was one such power. As president of the missions, Sánchez was also Vicar Forane. See Geiger, *Franciscan Missionaries,* 215–222.

11. Pío Pico was born on May 5, 1801, at Mission San Gabriel.

12. This was José Antonio Ramírez, a master carpenter and stonecutter. He was originally from Jalisco, in New Spain, and came to California in 1792. He worked on many construction projects in California, including a number of missions and the church at the pueblo of Los Angeles. He died in Los Angeles in 1827. See Schuetz-Miller, *Building and Builders,* 85–87.

13. They were Pablo Tac and Antonio Amamix. They both died before finishing their studies in Rome. Tac's memoir, which he wrote in Rome, is an important source for Indian life at San Luis Rey. See Hewes, "Indian Life and Customs at Mission San Luis Rey."

14. A *guaje* is a gourd.

15. Antonio Coronel dictated his reminiscences, "Cosas de California," to Savage in 1877. In his testimonio, Coronel provides a vivid account of the dances and dance music of early California. Professor John Koegel has included Coronel's descriptions in his two-volume dissertation, "Mexican-American Music in Nineteenth-Century Southern California: The Lummis Wax Cylinder Collection at the Southwest Museum, Los Angeles." According to Koegel, the word *sones* means "tunes." In addition, Coronel states that some of the dances were called *sones.* Coronel says, "Even though they were the same style as the other dances, they differed in melody, lyrics, and formality." Koegel points out that "the principal *sones* of the *jarabe* include *El pantorico* and *El caballo.* Many of the titles of the *jarabe* tunes make references to animals. These references usually relate to the choreography of the particular dance, which often imitates the characteristic movements of the animal referred to in the title." See Koegel, "Mexican-American Music," 154–155.

16. José Lugo was another Californio who contributed to the Bancroft project. His testimonio, "Vida de un ranchero" (1877), includes brief descriptions of dances and music in early

California. Lugo describes the *jarabe* in this way: "The *jarabe* was danced by a man and a woman. After dancing for a short time, the woman would sit down and another woman would step forward, then another, and another, until the man had to let another man take his place." Koegel, "Mexican-American Music," 152.

17. According to Lugo, in "*El pontorico*, or Sinaloa, a woman danced alone." Koegel's analysis is that *El pontorico* was probably a *jarabe* tune that had some connection with eighteenth-century Mexican or Spanish popular dances that had their origin in the theater. Koegel, "Mexican-American Music," 152, 161.

18. Lugo says that *El medio catorce* "was a top-hat dance that a man usually danced alone, although a man and woman sometimes danced it together." Koegel, "Mexican-American Music," 152.

19. *El fandango* was "danced by a man and a woman. During the dance, suddenly the music would be interrupted by a song and an old man would shout, '*Bomba al hombre*' (give the man your attention). The man who was dancing had to say a poem or a verse to his partner, generally of an amorous nature, according to the whim or intelligence of the dancer. The musicians began again to play and sing another verse and refrain, the music stopped, the same word was repeated, and this time the lady had to say a verse to the gentleman. If she failed to do this, because of shyness or lack of poetic ability, the man filled in the space, reciting another verse." Coronel, as quoted in Koegel, "Mexican-American Music," 153.

20. According to Koegel, *La zorrita* was one of the early California dances in which the choreography mimics the motions of the animal for which the dance is named. The person singing *La zorrita* is free to add new and original verses to the tune according to ability. The singer, therefore, is like the little fox who goes out and brings back any fruit or vegetable she wishes. See Koegel, "Mexican-American Music," 175–176.

21. Coronel says that *El caballo* was a favorite dance of the old women in the pueblo. "It was danced by a man and a woman. After the music started, the two began to sway back and forth, making passes from one side to the other. When the singers sang their verse, the dancers made figures with their handkerchiefs, and at a pre-arranged time, the woman picked up the front of her petticoat with her hands, to form a wing, as if mounted on a horse. The gentleman would grasp his handkerchief at two edges to show that he was the horse, and in this position both dancers made a horse-like movement to the melody of the music. Koegel, "Mexican-American Music," 151.

22. The *tecolero* is the master of ceremonies.

23. These three terms refer to card-game terminology. The *caballo*, or horse, in the Spanish deck of cards corresponds to the queen in an English deck. The *jota* is a jack. The *malilla* or manille are the highest cards of each suit. In a Spanish deck, this would be a nine.

24. Coronel says that *La zorrita* was "danced by couples as in the *jota*, with the difference that in the first verse, instead of the couples making the figures, the men made gestures to the women, according to the content of the verses. During the refrain, the two couples across from each other would form a chain of hands between the four of them; a second refrain would mark the time when the men were to give a skip, a touch of hands, and a clap. They would change their hand movements depending on the meaning of the verses. The dancers made gestures that described the verse. The dancers took part in the song." Koegel, "Mexican-American Music," 145.

NOTES TO JUANA MACHADO TESTIMONIO

1. Mason, *Census of 1790*, 39–40; Northrop, *Spanish-Mexican Families*, 1:342–343.
2. Bancroft, *California*, 5:754; Northrop, *Spanish-Mexican Families*, 1:219–220.

3. Brandes, ed., "Times Gone By," 197; Bancroft, *California*, 2:690; 3:417–419, 431–432.
4. Bancroft consistently spells the name "Ridington." See Bancroft, *California*, 5:695. Also Brandes, ed., "Times Gone By," 227.
5. Smythe, *San Diego*, 276.
6. Menéndez was the same priest who had been scheduled to perform the wedding of Josefa Carrillo and Henry Fitch.
7. Pala, Las Flores, and Temécula were all related to Mission San Luis Rey. Pala, about fifteen miles northeast of the mission, was the site of a mission granary in 1810. An *asistencia*, or mission outpost, was located there from 1815 to 1829. Temécula, slightly north of Pala, was a mission rancho. Las Flores, to the north of Temécula, was organized as an Indian pueblo in 1823, and it served as a cattle ranch for the mission. See Brandes, ed., "Times Gone By," 219.
8. Jacum is about fifty miles east of San Diego, close to the present U.S.–Mexican border.
9. The Rancho de la Nación was a government ranch whose purpose was to supply the presidio. It was directly east of San Diego.
10. Pico Silvas was married to Juana's sister María Antonia. See Northrop, *Spanish-Mexican Families*, 1:222.
11. Juan María Osuna was Felipa Osuna's father. In 1805 he was briefly held captive by Joseph O'Cain, the captain of a North American ship that was hunting sea otters off of Ensenada. See Pourade, *Time of the Bells*, 104.
12. San José del Cabo was sacked in 1822 by forces under the British commander Cochrane. See Carlos López Urrutia, *La escuadra chilena*.
13. Short jacket.
14. Nankeen is a type of cotton cloth, usually yellow in color. Originally it was manufactured and imported from Nankin, China. Duck is a closely woven, heavy cotton fabric.
15. Brandes, ed., "Times Gone By," (239–240), has collected what information can be gathered on these people, about most of whom, unfortunately, little is known. Francisco Basualdo was an artilleryman who served at Santa Bárbara and San Diego. He was married to Ignacia López. (See also Northrop, *Spanish-Mexican Families*, 1:202.) Ramón Aguilar was about fifteen years old, and a brother-in-law of José Antonio Serrano, the owner of the rancho. Santos Alipaz was a thirteen-year-old nephew of Serrano. Domínguez was apparently named Francisco Pancho Domínguez. Santiago Osuna was a younger brother of Felipa Osuna (Northrop, *Spanish-Mexican Families*, 1:264). José María Alvarado was married to Lugarda Osuna, a younger sister of Felipa Osuna. After her husband's death, Lugarda Osuna married Juana Machado's younger brother Jesús (Northrop, *Spanish-Mexican Families*, 1:222, 264). Juan José López was born in 1786 at San Juan Capistrano. He married María Eduviges Arce in San Diego in 1806. He served as a soldier at San Diego for many years and was granted Rancho Cañada de San Vicente in 1845 (Northrop, *Spanish-Mexican Families*, 1:202–204). Manuel Serrano was the twenty-year-old brother of José Antonio Serrano. Eustaquio Ruiz was the son of Joaquín Ruiz of Las Bolsas, in the Los Angeles area.
16. Juana Machado's younger brother Rafael, who was born in 1826, later married María Presentación de Alta Gracia Osuna (Northrop, *Spanish-Mexican Families*, 1:222).

Notes to Felipa Osuna Testimonio

1. Crosby, *Gateway to Alta California*, 161.
2. Northrop, *Spanish-Mexican Families*, 1:262–265; Land Case 238, Southern District (Agua Hedionda).
3. Bancroft, *California*, 5:730, 762.

4. Land Case 238, Southern District (Agua Hedionda).
5. Hayes, "Emigrant Notes," 4:721.
6. She was referring to Francisco González de Ibarra, who died in 1842.
7. Magdalena Baca said, "*Ahora esta misión es mía.*" Felipa Osuna de Marrón was mocking Baca by exaggerating the pronunciation of the word "*mía*" to make it sound like the "meow" or "*miau*"(Spanish) of a cat.
8. Jesús Machado was a younger brother of Juana Machado. In 1850 he married Lugarda Osuna, Felipa's widowed sister (Northrop, *Spanish-Mexican Families,* 1:221, 264).
9. At the Battle of San Pascual, Captain Benjamin D. Moore first shot at Andrés Pico, the Californio commander, but he missed. Moore then charged at Pico with his sword, but he was killed by the lances of several Californio soldiers who were near Pico. Lieutenant Thomas C. Hammond came to assist Moore, but he was also struck by a lance, and he died two hours later. See Harlow, *California Conquered,* 185.

NOTES TO APOLINARIA LORENZANA TESTIMONIO

1. Engelhardt, *Santa Bárbara,* 397.
2. Land Case 48, Southern District (Jamachá); Land Case 266, Southern District (Cañada de los Coches).
3. In July 1846 a group of Mormons heading west was recruited into the U.S. army at Council Bluffs, Iowa. Initially numbering about five hundred men, the battalion marched to Santa Fe and then San Diego, where it arrived in January 1847 and set up headquarters at the former mission. The battalion was ordered to San Luis Rey at the beginning of February. See Harlow, *California Conquered,* 247, Engelhardt, *San Diego,* 257–258, and Bancroft, *California* 5:469–498.
4. Apolinaria Lorenzana to José Joaquín Jimeno, January 25, 1848, California Mission Documents, Santa Bárbara Mission Archive-Library; Engelhardt, *San Luis Rey,* 224–225; Geiger, *Franciscan Missionaries,* 170.
5. Van Wormer, "Legal Hocus-Pocus"; Huntington Library Manuscript HM 44696.
6. By "mother," she was referring to María de Jesús Lorenzana, the teacher who accompanied the children to Monterey.
7. Fillet is net or lace with a simple pattern of squares. From Old Provencal *filat,* meaning "made of threads."

NOTES TO ANGUSTIAS DE LA GUERRA TESTIMONIO

1. Pubols, "De la Guerra Family," 174–176, 602–609; Pubols, "Casa de la Guerra," 89, 91.
2. Pubols, "De la Guerra Family," 246.
3. Bancroft, *California,* 4:692.
4. Pérez, *Land Grants,* 69, 87, 97.
5. Joseph Sadoc Alemany to José de la Guerra, November 5, 1851, de la Guerra Papers, Santa Bárbara Mission Archive-Library.
6. Pubols, "Casa de la Guerra," 67.
7. Pablo de la Guerra to Josefa de la Guerra, December 9, 1854; Pablo de le Guerra to Antonio María de la Guerra, December 9, 1854; Antonio Jimeno to Pablo de la Guerra, April 4, 1855; all in the de la Guerra Papers, Santa Bárbara Mission Archive-Library.

8. Pubols, "Casa de la Guerra," 76–77; José de la Guerra to Angustias de la Guerra, December 20, 1856, de la Guerra Papers, Santa Bárbara Mission Archive-Library; Thompson, *El Gran Capitán,* 157; José Antonio de la Guerra and brothers to Angustias de la Guerra, July 8, 1858; Bill of Dr. James Ord, January 1, 1861; Antonio María de la Guerra to Pablo de la Guerra, Nov. 11, 1866; all in the de la Guerra Papers, Santa Bárbara Mission Archive-Library.
9. John Peshine to Holy Cross Cemetery, January 5, 1919; James Murphy (Holy Cross Cemetery) to John Peshine, January 1919, de la Guerra Papers, Santa Bárbara Mission Archive-Library.
10. On October 6, 1818, Captain Henry Gyzelaar of the American ship *Clarion* arrived at Santa Bárbara with the news that two insurgent ships were being outfitted in Hawai'i for an expedition against Alta California. Guerra y Noriega informed Governor Solá of the news, and the governor ordered increased vigilance. See Bancroft, *California,* 2:222–224.
11. A number of convicts were sent to Santa Cruz Island, in the Santa Bárbara Channel. See Bancroft, *California* 3:48.
12. In 1833 a group of Mexican friars from the Franciscan Colegio de Nuestra Señora de Guadalupe in Zacatecas arrived in California to take over the northern group of missions—from San Francisco Solano to San Carlos—from the Spanish friars from the Colegio Apostólico de San Fernando in Mexico City. The Fernandinos had founded and administered all the Alta California missions up to then.
13. The borage plant *(Borago officinalis)* is native to southern Europe and northern Africa. It has hairy leaves and star-shaped blue flowers. The young leaves taste like cucumber and are sometimes used as seasoning.
14. A tsunami formed off the coast of central California on December 21, 1812. See Bancroft, *California,* 2:201.
15. The painting to which Angustias de la Guerra referred was entitled *Reception of the Count of La Pérouse* by Gaspar Duché de Vancy, a painter on the French expedition that visited Monterey in 1786. It was given as a present to Father Fermín Francisco de Lasuén, and the friars kept it in Monterey. As Angustias de la Guerra said, the painting is now lost; however, it was copied three times, each slightly differently, by members of a Spanish scientific expedition that visited Monterey a few years later. Those three copies have survived and are at the Museo Naval in Madrid. See Sotos Serrano, *Los pintores,* 2:196–197. Angustias de la Guerra is correct that neither Serra nor Amorós was depicted, since Serra was dead and Amorós had not yet arrived in California. Noriega, however, was stationed at San Carlos when La Pérouse visited (Geiger, *Franciscan Missionaries,* 165–166).
16. This brief revolt is described in Osio, *History of Alta California,* 130–131.
17. The *vihuela* is a small guitar that was very popular in the sixteenth century, before it was superseded by the guitar.
18. This means that he asked them to assume some of his administrative duties as bishop.
19. This is the version of the Spanish song *"Destino fatal"* that appears in Koegel, "Mexican-American Music," 2:151L.

Destino fatal	*Fatal Destiny*
Destino fatal, me aleja de tu hogar.	Fatal destiny keeps me from your home.
La suerte impía, me aleja de mirarte.	Unspeakable luck keeps me from gazing upon you.
Mas no por eso dejaré de amarte,	But that will not stop me from loving you,
martirio cruel el que juzga la razón.	Cruel martyrdom for the one who asks why.

Las horas pasan dejándome en dolor.	The hours go by leaving me to my sorrow.
Esa tu ausencia me causa mi martirio.	Your absence causes my martyrdom.
Y si no fuera todo un delirio,	And if it were only an illusion,
martirio cruel el que juzga la razón.	Cruel martyrdom for the one who asks why.
Esas caricias que antes me hacías	Those caresses that you used to give me
me hacen llenar el sueño de confianza.	Are my inspiration when I sleep.
Y recuerdo que dice la esperanza	And I continue to hope
que tú sola de mi amor disfrutarás.	That you alone will be my love.
Tu pecho ardiente puro y divino	Your passionate breast, pure and divine
un amor fino debió sentir.	Should have felt a tender love.
Y al contemplarte, mujer hermosa,	And every thought of you, my beauty,
un fuego soso llegó hasta mí.	Kindled a constant flame in me.

20. *Turrón* is almond nougat and *biznaga* is a candy made from barrel cactus that is crystalized with sugar. It was a sacred plant of the Aztecs.
21. As Angustias de la Guerra indicated in her testimonio, the relationship between herself and her husband's brothers was very close. Here she refers to her brother-in-law Father Antonio Jimeno as her "brother."
22. A bullion knot is an embroidery stitch.
23. A *cacastle* (the word comes from Náhuatl) refers to an open, slatted crate made of rough-hewn branches, used to transport small livestock or dry goods. The use of Indian words is an indication of the relevance of the Mexican origin of the settlers. (Perissinotto, Rudolph, and Miller, *Documenting Everyday Life*, 93).
24. *Cuajada* is curd. It is similar to cottage cheese.
25. The word *mudo* means mute.
26. Angustias de la Guerra abbreviated some information about the feast that her brother-in-law hosted. It was a breakfast, not a luncheon or dinner. According to Louise Pubols, Angustias's father hosted a one o'clock luncheon and that came later. "After a dawn ceremony, the missionary hosted breakfast, then organized a procession to lead the new couple to the casa de la Guerra." (Pubols, "De la Guerra Family," 200–201).
27. *Olla podrida* is a type of Spanish stew.
28. *Islay* is the hollyleaf cherry, *Prunus ilicifolia*. It was a favorite Indian food. (Gudde, *California Place Names*, 180)
29. *Cacomite* or *Tigridia pavonia* is rich in starch and is boiled and used for food. From "Materia Médica from the New Pharmacopoeia, Part 4," *American Journal of Pharmacy* 57.8 (August 1985):4.

Notes to María Inocenta Pico Testimonio

1. Northrop, *Spanish-Mexican Families*, 2:206.
2. Mason, *Census of 1790*, 33; Crosby, *Gateway to Alta California*, 161; Northrop, *Spanish-Mexican Families*, 1:262–263.
3. Bancroft, *California*, 4:777; Northrop, *Spanish-Mexican Families*, 1:116–117, 2:205–207.
4. Northrop, *Spanish-Mexican Families*, 1:59; Bancroft, *California*, 2:706.

5. Krieger, *San Luis Obispo,* 52–57; Land Case 37, Southern District (San Miguelito).

6. Miguel Avila to Pablo de la Guerra, January 14, 1857, and January 24, 1860, de la Guerra Papers, Santa Bárbara Mission Archive-Library.

7. *San Luis Obispo Tribune,* cited in Angel, ed., *Thompson and West's History of San Luis Obispo County,* 350.

8. Probably Fabiano Barreto.

9. According to Bancroft, Avila was jailed in Los Angeles around 1831. There is some reference in the archives to trouble between him and a man named Nieto, but the specifics of the affair are vague. See Bancroft, *California,* 3:207.

LIST OF ILLUSTRATIONS

GLOSSARY

abalorios Glass beads

administrador The person in charge of a mission after secularization

adobe A sun-dried brick made of sand, clay, and straw; a dwelling or construction made of these bricks

aguardiente Hard liquor

Alabado A Latin hymn the missionaries taught the Indians as part of morning prayer

alcalde A local magistrate, usually a member of the municipal council; the chief executive officer of a pueblo. He possessed a combination of executive and judicial authority.

alcalde (Indian) The highest-ranking neophyte in the mission hierarchy. He was supposed to be elected by the neophytes, and he possessed a real, if limited, authority in supervising mission Indians and in maintaining order.

alcalde mayor A chief magistrate in charge of a district; a regional governmental post combining judicial, administrative, and tax-collecting duties; subordinate to the *gobernador* of the region

alférez An ensign; the lowest-ranked military officer, approximately equal to today's rank of second lieutenant

alguacil A sheriff or constable

amole Soapweed, also called soaproot

arroyo A creek or stream

asesor A legal adviser to the government; a lawyer appointed to advise the judge in the conduct of legal proceedings

asistencia Mission outpost, usually with a chapel, which a priest would occasionally visit to conduct religious services

atole A cooked mixture of water and ground, dried grains; a staple mission food

ayudante de plaza An officer at a specific locale who received his orders directly from the general or another superior. Other titles included *ayudante general, ayudante inspector,* and *ayudante de campo.*

ayuntamiento A municipal corporation in charge of administering and governing a town; a town council

bits A bit is equal to one-eighth of a dollar. Used only in even multiples: two bits equal twenty-five cents.

Californio Regional name for a non-Indian inhabitant of California. All *gente de razón* reared— or later, born and reared—in California were Californios. The term was used in Antigua California from 1700 on and came into popular use in Alta California by the 1820s, with the growth of the first generation of California-born Mexicans.

canónigo A member of the clergy attached to a cathedral or other major church

cañada A gully or ravine

carreta A two-wheeled cart

castillo A fortress or coastal defense battery

chamizales Thatched huts

cholo A derogatory term for a *mestizo,* or person of mixed European and Indian heritage *chupín* A short jacket

comandante Commandant or commander

comisaría Commissariat or branch of the army in charge of providing food and other supplies for the troops

comisario The officer in charge of the warehouse

comisionado Noncommissioned soldier (usually a sergeant or corporal) appointed by the commander of the presidio to serve as a liaison between the presidio and the towns or missions. Duties included supervising the *alcalde* and exercising military and judicial authority. With secularization, the *comisionado* also became the temporary supervisor of former missions.

comadre Godmother, in relation to a child's godfather or parents: to a child's godfather, the *comadre* is the fellow godparent; to the child's parents, the *comadre* is the godmother of their child.

compadre Godfather, in relation to a child's godmother or parents (see *comadre*). *Compadre* also means protector, benefactor, or very close friend.

cuera From the word *cuero,* which means "hide" or "leather." A heavy, knee-length, usually sleeveless jacket made of up to seven layers of buckskin or cowhide and bound at the edges with a strong seam. This distinctive armor garment gave the presidio soldier the name by which he was known for more than two centuries: *soldado de cuera.*

cuna crib, or foundling child

curandera (o) A practitioner of folk medicine

diputación territorial The elected assembly, which usually met at Monterey during the Mexican period in California. A consultative body to the governor of the territory.

diputado A delegate or member of the *diputación territorial;* also the territorial/departmental delegate to the lower chamber of the Mexican national congress

Don/Doña A title of respect. In California it was accorded to any Spaniard, officer, or person from an important, respected family. Used before the first name. Can also be used to express extreme respect or extreme disdain.

elector de partido District elector

escolta The escort or squad of soldiers assigned to protect a missionary at a mission

fanega A dry measure of weight, the equivalent of about 1.6 bushels; also a land measurement, *fanega de sembradura,* equivalent to 8.8 acres

fiscal A public prosecutor

Fernandinos Term used to refer to the Franciscans who came to California from the Colegio Apostólico de San Fernando in Mexico City

fresno Ash tree

gachupín During and after the conquest of Mexico, a Spaniard. Derived from the Náhuatl word *cacchopini: cactli* means "shoe" and *chopini* means "to kick," so the combination, *cacchopini* (or *gachupín*), means "a man who kicks," i.e., someone wearing spurs.

gente de razón Literally, "people with the capacity to reason"; any non-Indian

gentile A non-Christian Indian

Guadalupanos Term used to refer to the Franciscans who came to California from the Colegio de Guadalupe de Zacatecas *habilitado general* An officer in a Spanish regiment charged with its supplies or money; a quartermaster, supply master, or paymaster

hacienda As a unit of measurement, equivalent to five square leagues, or 21,690 acres. Also, very large estates were generally called *haciendas*. Variable factors defining *haciendas* included capital, labor, land, markets, technology, and social recognition.

hijo del país Native son

intendente Quartermaster general

jacal Hut or crude dwelling

jáquima Hackamore

jara Dart or arrow

jefe Leader, head, or superior; followed by adjectives such as *militar, político, principal,* and *superior*

Joaquinero An Indian from the San Joaquín Valley

juez de paz Judge or justice of the peace; replaced the office of *alcalde* in some areas after 1836. Combined municipal and judicial powers within the pueblo.

juez de primera instancia Judge of the first instance; a judge presiding in a lower court

juez suplente A substitute judge

junta A congress, an assembly, a council; any meeting of persons to speak about business; a group used to administer or govern, usually ad interim

lavandera A washerwoman

legua A standard Spanish measure of distance (a league), approximately 2.6 miles

licenciado A university degree usually held by priests and lawyers in canon or civil-criminal law

llavera (o) The keeper of the keys at a mission

matanza A slaughter of herd animals

matrona The woman who supervised the single Indian women in the *monjerío*

mayordomo A foreman or supervisor of a mission under the priest, or of a ranch under the owner; majordomo

mestizo A person of mixed European and Indian heritage

monjerío The separate living quarters at a mission for single Indian women

neophyte Term used to describe the Christian mission Indians

padrino Godfather, sponsor, or best man at a wedding

paisano Fellow countryman

pajales Indian word for rabbit skins

Pastorela A religious play performed at Christmas

peso The monetary unit of Spanish America. In the first half of the nineteenth century, a peso was roughly equivalent to one U.S. dollar or two Russian rubles.

pinole Parched corn, ground and mixed with sugar and water for a drink (also refers to the ground seeds of other plants)

plaza Town square, fortified town, or military base

pozole A thick soup of cornmeal, beans, hominy, marrowbones, and scraps of meat

pozolera Mission kitchen. *Pozolera (o)* can also mean the person who cooks in the *pozolera*.

presidio A frontier military garrison; the fortified location and community of such a garrison *pueblo* The populace; a village or town; the smallest municipal entity, possessing an *ayuntamiento,* or town council

ranchería An Indian village or settlement. The Spanish usually used the term to refer to non-Christian Indians. It is now a common term in English for small communities of Alta California Indians.

ranchero Rancher

rancho An estate granted, under a variety of laws, to an individual. In common usage, a rancho was usually an estate devoted generally to the raising of cattle. A rancho usually covered approximately four square miles, but some covered up to thirty square miles. A rancho could also be one of the units of a *hacienda,* in which case it would be run by a *mayordomo* responsible to the *hacendado.* The size and specific characteristics of ranchos varied according to the region in which they were located. Variables included labor, land, production for market or subsistence, availability of water, and climate.

Rancho del Rey A rancho operated by the local presidio for the support of the soldiers and their families

Rancho Nacional The name given to the Ranchos del Rey after Mexican independence

reata A rope made of braided rawhide or leather, used for roping cattle and other chores

rebozo A shawl or wrap

regidor A member of the *ayuntamiento*

sala A sitting or reception room

Salve Regina A prayer to the Virgin Mary

secretaría Secretariat, government department, or office of the secretary

silicio A flint-tipped whip

síndico A public attorney or advocate/representative of a mission

sínodos Annual stipends paid to the missionaries by the government of New Spain. In Alta California these stipends were financed from the Pious Fund, an endowment originally established by the Jesuits in the eighteenth century to support the Baja California misisons.

tecolero Master of ceremonies at a dance

Te Deum Laudamus A traditional Latin hymn of praise to God

temescal A sweat lodge

teniente A lieutenant, or the officer who was second in command of a military unit

testimonio Personal reminiscence

tribunal superior The highest judicial body in Alta California

tule Any of several grassy or reed-like plants growing in the marshy lowlands of the western United States. The Spanish word derived from Náhuatl *tullin.*

vaquero A cowboy. In Mexican California they were generally indigenous people, frequently from Baja California, who tended the large stock herds under the direction of a *mayordomo.*

vara A measure of length, approximately thirty-three inches

vocal Member of the assembly

BIBLIOGRAPHY

Alexander, James B. *Sonoma Valley Legacy: Histories and Sites of 70 Historic Adobes in and around the Sonoma Valley*. Sonoma, Calif.: Sonoma Valley Historical Society, 1986.

Alvarado, Juan Bautista. *Vignettes of Early California: Childhood Reminiscences of Juan Bautista Alvarado*. Translated by John H. R. Polk with an introduction and notes by W. Michael Mathes. San Francisco: Book Club of California, 1982.

————. "Historia de California." 5 vols. 1876. The Bancroft Library, C-D 1–5.

Amador, José María. *California Voices: The Oral Memoirs of José María Amador and Lorenzo Asisara*. Trans. and ed. Gregorio Mora-Torres. Denton, Tex.: University of North Texas Press, 2005.

Angel, Myron, ed. Introduction by Louisiana Clayton Dart. *Reproduction of Thompson and West's History of San Luis Obispo County, California, with Illustrations and Biographical Sketches of its Prominent Men and Pioneers*. Berkeley: Howell-North Books, 1966.

Armitage, Susan H., ed., with Patricia Hart and Karen Weathermon. *Women's Oral History: The Frontiers Reader*. Lincoln: University of Nebraska Press, 2002.

Bakken, Gordon Morris. "Mexican and American Land Policy: A Conflict of Cultures." *Southern California Quarterly* 75 (3–4), 1993: 237–262.

Bancroft, Hubert Howe. *History of California*. 7 vols. San Francisco: The History Company, 1884–1890.

————. *California Pastoral*. San Francisco: The History Company, 1888.

————. *Literary Industries*. San Francisco: The History Company, 1890.

Bastain, Beverly E. "'I Heartily Regret That I Ever Touched a Title in California': Henry Wager Halleck, the Californios, and the Clash of Legal Cultures." *California History* 72(4), 1993/1994: 310–323.

Beard, Yolande S. *The Wappo: A Report. With Drawings by the Author*. Banning, Calif.: Malki Museum Press, 1979.

Beebe, Rose Marie, and Robert M. Senkewicz, eds. "The End of the 1824 Chumash Revolt in Alta California: Fr. Vicente Sarría's Account," *The Americas* 53(3), 1996: 273–283.

————. *Lands of Promise and Despair: Chronicles of Early California, 1535–1846*. Berkeley and Santa Clara, Calif.: Heyday Books and Santa Clara University, 2001.

————. *Guía de Manuscritos Concernientes a Baja California en las Colecciones de la Biblioteca Bancroft*. Berkeley: University of California Library, 2002.

Bestor, Arthur Eugene. *David Jacks of Monterey and Lee L. Jacks, His Daughter*. With a foreword by Donald Bertrand Tresidder. Stanford, Calif.: Stanford University Press, 1945.

Bibb, Leland E. "William Marshall, 'The Wickedest Man in California': A Reappraisal." *Journal of San Diego History* 22(1), 1976: 11–25.

Blanco, Antonio. *La lengua española en la historia de California*. Madrid: Cultura Hispánica, 1971.

Blevins, Juliette, and Victor Golla. "A New Mission Indian Manuscript from the San Francisco Bay Area." *Boletín: The Journal of the California Mission Studies Association* 22(1), 2005: 33–61.

Bojorques, Juan. "Recuerdos sobre la historia de California." 1877. The Bancroft Library, C-D 46.

Bolton, Herbert Eugene, ed. *Anza's California Expeditions*. 5 vols. Berkeley: University of California Press, 1926–1930.

Bouvier, Virginia M. "Framing the Female Voice: The Bancroft Narratives of Apolinaria Lorenzana, Angustias de la Guerra Ord and Eulalia Pérez." In *Recovering the U.S. Hispanic*

Literary Heritage, Vol. III, ed. María Herrera-Sobek and Virginia Sánchez Korrol. Houston: Arte Público Press, 2000: 138–152.

Bouvier, Virginia Marie. *Women and the Conquest of California, 1542–1840: Codes of Silence.* Tucson: University of Arizona Press, 2001.

Bowman, J. N. "History of the Provincial Archives of California." *Southern California Quarterly* 64(1), 1982: 1–97.

Brandes, Raymond S., intro. and trans. "'Times Gone By in Alta California': Recollections of Señora Doña Juana Machado Alipás de Ridington." *Historical Society of Southern California Quarterly* 41(3), 1959: 195–240.

Breault, William J. *John A. Sutter in Hawaii and California, 1838–1839.* Rancho Cordova, Calif.: Landmark Enterprises, 1998.

Broadbent, Sylvia. "Conflict at Monterey: Indian Horse Raiding, 1820–1850." *Journal of California Anthropology* 1, 1974: 86–101.

Carrico, Richard L., and Florence C. Shipek. "Indian Labor in San Diego County, California, 1850–1900." In *Native Americans and Wage Labor: Ethnohistorical Perspectives,* ed. Alice Little field and Martha C. Knack. Norman: University of Oklahoma Press, 1996: 198–217

Casas, María Raquel. "'In Consideration of His Being Married to a Daughter of the Land': Interethnic Marriages in Alta, California, 1825–1875." Ph.D. diss., Yale University, 1998.

Castañeda, Antonia I. "Gender, Race, and Culture: Mexican Women in the Historiography of Frontier California." In *Chicana Leadership: The Frontiers Reader,* ed. Yolanda Flores Niemann, with Susan H. Armitage. Lincoln and London: University of Nebraska Press, 2002: 144–178.

———. "Presidarias y Pobladores: Spanish-Mexican Women in Frontier Monterey, Alta California, 1770–1821." Ph.D. diss., Stanford University, 1990.

Cerruti, Henry. *Ramblings in California: The Adventures of Henry Cerruti.* Ed. Margaret Mollins and Virginia E. Thickens. Berkeley: The Friends of the Bancroft Library, 1954.

Chávez-García, Miroslava. *Negotiating Conquest: Gender and Power in California, 1770s to 1880s.* Tucson: University of Arizona Press, 2004.

Churchill, Charles B. *Adventurers and Prophets: American Autobiographers in Mexican California, 1828–1847.* Spokane: The Arthur H. Clark Company, 1995.

Clark, Donald Thomas. *Monterey County Place Names: A Geographical Dictionary.* Carmel Valley, Calif.: Kestrel Press, 1991.

Clarke, Dwight L. *Stephen Watts Kearny: Soldier of the West.* Norman: University of Oklahoma Press, 1961.

Cole, Martin, and Henry Welcome. *Don Pío Pico's Historical Narrative.* Trans. Arthur P. Botello. Glendale, Calif.: The Arthur H. Clark Co., 1970.

Cook, Sherburne F. *The Epidemic of 1830–1833 in California and Oregon.* University of California Publications in American Archaeology and Ethnology 43(3). Berkeley: University of California Press, 1955.

———. "Smallpox in Spanish Mexican California, 1770–1845." *Bulletin of the History of Medicine* 8(2), 1939: 151–191.

Cowan, Robert G. *Ranchos of California: A List of Spanish Concessions 1775–1822 and Mexican Grants 1822–1846.* Los Angeles: Historical Society of Southern California, 1977.

Crosby, Harry W. *Gateway to Alta California: The Expedition to San Diego, 1769.* San Diego: Sunbelt Publications, 2003.

————. *Antigua California: Mission and Colony on the Peninsular Frontier, 1697–1768.* Albuquerque: University of New Mexico Press, 1994.

Cutter, Donald, trans. and ed. *The Writings of Mariano Payeras.* Santa Bárbara: Bellerophon Books, 1995.

Dakin, Susanna Bryant. *The Lives of William Hartnell.* Stanford, Calif.: Stanford University Press, 1984.

————. *Rose, or Rose Thorn? Three Women of Spanish California.* Berkeley: The Friends of The Bancroft Library, 1963.

Dillon, Richard H. *Napa Valley's Natives.* Fairfield, Calif.: J. Stevenson Publisher, in cooperation with the Napa County Historical Society, 2001.

————. *Captain John Sutter: Sacramento Valley's Sainted Sinner.* Santa Cruz, Calif.: Western Tanager Press, 1981.

Duggan, Marie Christine. "Laws of the Market vs. Laws of God: Scholastic Doctrine and the Early California Economy." *History of Political Economy* 37(2), 2005: 343–370.

————. *The Chumash and the Presidio of Santa Bárbara: Evolution of a Relationship.* Santa Bárbara: Santa Bárbara Trust for Historic Preservation, 2004.

————. "Market and Church on the Mexican Frontier: Alta California, 1769–1832." Ph.D. diss., New School for Social Research, 2000.

Ebright, Malcolm. *Land Grants and Lawsuits in Northern New Mexico.* Albuquerque: University of New Mexico Press, 1994.

Emparán, Madie Brown. *The Vallejos of California.* San Francisco: Gleeson Library Associates, University of San Francisco, 1968.

Engelhardt, Zephyrin, O.F.M. *Santa Bárbara Mission.* San Francisco: The James H. Barry Company, 1923.

————. *San Luis Rey Mission.* San Francisco: The James H. Barry Company, 1921.

————. *San Diego Mission.* San Francisco: The James H. Barry Company, 1920.

————. *The Missions and Missionaries of California.* 4 vols. San Francisco: The James H. Barry Company, 1908–1916.

————. *The Holy Man of Santa Clara; or, The Life, Virtues and Miracles of Fr. Magín Catalá, O.F.M.* San Francisco: The James H. Barry Co. 1909.

Engstrand, Iris H. W. "John Sutter: A Biographical Examination." In *John Sutter and a Wider West,* ed. Kenneth N. Owens. Lincoln and London: University of Nebraska Press, 1994: 76–92.

————. "The Legal Heritage of Spanish California." *Southern California Quarterly* 75(3–4), 1993: 205–236.

————. "An Enduring Legacy: California Ranches in Historical Perspectives." *Journal of the West* 27(3), 1988: 36–47.

————. "The Transit of Venus in 1769: Launching Pad for European Exploration in the Pacific During the Late Eighteenth Century." *Boletín: The Journal of the California Mission Studies Association* 22(2), 2004: 36–48.

Ettinger, Catherine R. " Spaces of Change: Architecture and the Creation of a New Society in the California Missions." *Boletín: The Journal of the California Mission Studies Association* 21(1), 2004: 23–44.

Eversole, Robert W. "Towns in Mexican Alta California: A Social History of Monterey, San José, Santa Bárbara, and Los Angeles, 1822–1846." Ph.D. diss., University of California, San Diego, 1986.

Farris, Glenn J. "A Peace Treaty between Mariano Vallejo and Satiyomi Chief Succara." Paper presented at the Fifth California Indian Conference, Humboldt State University, Arcata, October 13, 1989.

Farris, Glenn, Maurice Hodgson, and Andrew David, eds. Annotated by Glenn Farris. "The California Journal of Lt. Edward Belcher aboard the H.M.S. *Blossom* in 1826 and 1827." *Boletín: The Journal of the California Mission Studies Association* 21(1), 2004: 45–67.

Fischer, Christiane. "Women in California in the Early 1850s." *Southern California Quarterly* 60(3), 1978: 231–253.

Fischer, Vivian C., trans. and ed. *Three Memoirs of Mexican California, by Carlos N. Híjar, Eulalia Pérez, Agustín Escobar, as Recorded in 1877 by Thomas Savage.* Berkeley: The Friends of the Bancroft Library, 1988.

Francis, Jessie Davies. *An Economic and Social History of Mexican California, 1822–1846.* New York: Arno Press, 1976.

Frost, Elsa Cecilia. *El arte de la traición o los problemas de la traducción.* Mexico: Universidad Nacional Autónoma de México, 2000.

García, Mario T. "The Californios of San Diego and the Politics of Accommodation, 1846–1860." *Aztlán* 6(1), 1975: 69–85.

———. "Merchants and Dons: San Diego's Attempt at Modernization, 1850–1860." *Journal of San Diego History* 21(1), 1975: 52–80.

Gates, Paul Wallace. *Land and Law in California.* Ames: Iowa State University Press, 1991.

Geiger, Maynard, O.F.M. *Franciscan Missionaries in Hispanic California, 1769–1848: A Biographical Dictionary.* San Marino: The Huntington Library, 1969.

Genini, Ronald, and Richard Hitchman. *Romualdo Pacheco: A Californio in Two Eras.* San Francisco: Book Club of California, 1985.

González, Michael J. *This Small City Will Be a Mexican Paradise: Exploring the Origins of Mexican Culture in Los Angeles, 1821–1846.* Albuquerque: University of New Mexico Press, 2005.

Gray, Paul Bryan. *Forster vs. Pico: The Struggle for the Rancho Santa Margarita.* Spokane, Wash.: Arthur H. Clark Co., 1998.

Griswold del Castillo, Richard. "Neither Activists Nor Victims: Mexican Women's Historical Discourse: The Case of San Diego, 1820–1850." *California History* 74(3), 1995: 230–243.

———. *The Treaty of Guadalupe Hidalgo: A Legacy of Conflict.* Norman: University of Oklahoma Press, 1990.

———. "Patriarchy and the Status of Women in the Late Nineteenth Century Southwest." In *The Mexican and Mexican American Experience in the 19th Century*, ed. Jaime E. Rodríguez. Tempe, Ariz.: Bilingual Press/Editorial Bilingüe, 1989: 85–99.

———. "The Del Valle Family and the Fantasy Heritage." California History 59(1), 1980: 2–15.

Gudde, Erwin G. *California Place Names.* Revised 4th edition. Berkeley: University of California Press, 1998.

Guild, Thelma S. and Harvey L. Carter. *Kit Carson: A Pattern for Heroes.* Lincoln: University of Nebraska Press, 1984.

Gutiérrez, Ramon A., and Richard J. Orsi, eds. *Contested Eden, California Before the Gold Rush.* Berkeley: Published in association with the California Historical Society by the University of California Press, 1998.

Haas, Lisbeth. "Emancipation and the Meaning of Freedom in Mexican California." *Boletín: The Journal of the California Mission Studies Association* 20(1), 2003: 11–22.

———. *Conquests and Historical Identities in California, 1769–1936*. Berkeley: University of California Press, 1995.

Hackel, Steven W. *Children of Coyote, Missionaries of Saint Francis: Indian-Spanish Relations in Colonial California, 1769–1850*. Chapel Hill: Published for the Omohundro Institute of Early American History and Culture, Williamsburg, Virginia, by the University of North Carolina Press, 2005.

Haggard, J. Villasana. *Handbook for Translators of Spanish Historical Documents*. Oklahoma City: Semco Color Press, 1941.

Hague, Harlan, and David J. Langum. *Thomas O. Larkin: A Life of Patriotism and Profit in Old California*. Norman: University of Oklahoma Press, 1990.

Harding, George L. *Don Agustín Zamorano: Statesman, Soldier, Craftsman, and California's First Printer*. Los Angeles: The Zamorano Club, 1934.

Hargis, Donald E. "Native Californians in the Constitutional Convention of 1849." *Historical Society of Southern California Quarterly* 36(1), 1956: 3–13.

Harlow, Neal. *California Conquered: The Annexation of a Mexican Province*. Berkeley: University of California Press, 1989.

Hart, James D. *A Companion to California*. Berkeley: University of California Press, 1987.

Hartnell, William E. P. *The Diary and Copybook of William E. P. Hartnell, Visitador General of the Missions of Alta California in 1839 and 1840*, trans. Starr Pait Gurcke, ed. Glenn J. Farris. Santa Clara, Calif., and Spokane, Wash.: California Mission Studies Association and The Arthur H. Clark Company, 2004.

Hayes, Benjamin Ignatius, "Emigrant Notes." 4 vols. 1875. The Bancroft Library, C-E 62.

Heizer, Robert F., ed. *The Archaeology of the Napa Region*. University of California Publications, Anthropological Records 12(6). Berkeley: University of California Press, 1953.

Hernández, Salomé. "No Settlement Without Women: Three Spanish California Settlement Schemes, 1790–1800." *Southern California Quarterly* 72(3), 1990: 203–233.

Hewes, Gordon and Minna. "Indian Life and Customs at Mission San Luis Rey." *The Americas* 9(1), 1952–53: 87–106.

Honig, Sasha. "Yokuts, Spaniards, and Californios in the Southern San Joaquín Valley." *Boletín: The Journal of the California Mission Studies Association* 20(1), 2003: 50–62.

Hughes, Charles. "The Decline of the Californios: The Case of San Diego, 1846–1856." *Journal of San Diego History* 21(3), 1975: 1–31.

Hurtado, Albert L. *Intimate Frontiers: Sex, Gender, and Culture in Old California. Histories of the American Frontier*. Albuquerque: University of New Mexico Press, 1999.

———. "John A. Sutter and the Indian Business." In *John Sutter and a Wider West*, ed. Kenneth N. Owens. Lincoln and London: University of Nebraska Press, 1994: 51–75.

———. "Sexuality in California's Franciscan Missions: Cultural Perceptions and Sad Realities." *California History* 71(3), 1992: 371–385.

———. *Indian Survival on the California Frontier*. New Haven: Yale University Press, 1988.

Hutchinson, C. Alan. *Frontier Settlement in Mexican California: The Híjar-Padrés Colony and Its Origins, 1769–1835*. New Haven and London: Yale University Press, 1969.

Hyer, Joel R. *"We Are Not Savages": Native Americans in Southern California and the Pala Reservation, 1840–1920*. East Lansing, Mich.: Michigan State University Press, 2001.

Ivey, James E. "Secularization in California and Texas." *Boletín: The Journal of the California Mission Studies Association* 20(1), 2003: 23–36.

Jackson, Robert H. *Missions and the Frontiers of Spanish America: A Comparative Study of the Impact of Environmental, Economic, Political, and Socio-Cultural Variations on the Missions in the Río de la Plata Region and on the Northern Frontier of New Spain*. Scottsdale, Ariz.: Pentacle Press, 2005.

———. *Indian Population Decline: The Missions of Northwestern New Spain, 1687–1840*. Albuquerque: University of New Mexico Press, 1994.

Jackson, Robert H., and Edward Castillo. *Indians, Franciscans and Spanish Colonization: The Impact of the Mission System on California Indians*. Albuquerque: University of New Mexico Press, 1995.

Jensen, James M. "John Forster—A California Ranchero." *California Historical Society Quarterly* 48(1), 1969: 37–44.

Johnson, Charles H., Jr. *Mysteries of the Murders at Mission San Miguel*. Paso Robles, Calif.: The Mission Press, 1997.

Johnson, Patti J. "Patwin." In *Handbook of North American Indians*. Gen. ed. William C. Sturtevant. Vol. 8, *California*, ed. Robert F. Heizer. Washington, D.C.: Smithsonian Institution, 1978:350–360.

Jones, Oakah, Jr. *Los Paisanos: Spanish Settlers on the Northern Frontier of New Spain*. Norman: University of Oklahoma Press, 1979.

Jore, Leonce. "The Fathers of the Congregation of the Sacred Hearts (called Picpus) in California." Trans. L. Jay Oliva. *Southern California Quarterly* 46(4), 1964: 293–313.

Kemble, John Haskell. *The Panama Route, 1848–1869*. Berkeley and Los Angeles: University of California Press, 1943.

Killea, Lucy Lytle. "The Political History of a Mexican Pueblo: San Diego from 1825 to 1845." *Journal of San Diego History* 12(3), July 1966: 5–35 and 12(4), Oct. 1966: 19–41.

Koegel, John. "Mexican-American Music in Nineteenth-Century Southern California: The Lummis Wax Collection at the Southwest Museum, Los Angeles." Ph.D. diss., The Claremont Graduate School, 1994.

Krieger, Daniel E. *San Luis Obispo County: Looking Backward into the Middle Kingdom*. Chatsworth, Calif.: Windsor Publications, 1988.

Kroeber, A. L. *The Patwin and their Neighbors*. University of California Publications in American Archaeology and Ethnology 29(4). Berkeley: University of California Press, 1932.

Lamar, Howard R., ed. *The New Encyclopedia of the American West*. New Haven: Yale University Press, 1998.

Langum, David J. "Sin, Sex and Separation in Mexican California: Her Domestic Relations Law." *The Californians* 5(3), 1987: 44–50.

———. "Californio Women and the Image of Virtue." *Southern California Quarterly* 59(1), 1977: 245–250.

Layne, J. Gregg. "José María Flores: California's Great Mexican Patriot." *Historical Society of Southern California Quarterly* 17(1), 1935: 23–27.

León, Nicolás. *La obstetricia en México*. Mexico: Tip. de la Vda. de Francisco Díaz de León, Sucrs., 1910.

Leslie, Mrs. Frank. *California: A Pleasure Trip from Gotham to the Golden Gate*. New York: G. W. Carleton and Co., 1877.

Lightfoot, Kent G. *Indians, Missionaries, and Merchants: The Legacy of Colonial Encounters on the California Frontiers*. Berkeley and London: University of California Press, 2005.

Lightfoot, Kent G.; Malcolm Margolin; Keith Douglass Warner, O.F.M.; John R. Johnson; and Julia Costello. "Symposium: *Indians, Missionaries, and Merchants: The Legacy of Colonial Encounters on the California Frontiers.*"*Boletín: The Journal of the California Mission Studies Association* 22(1), 2005: 62–86.

Lockhart, Katharine Meyer. "A Demographic Profile of an Alta California Pueblo: San José de Guadalupe, 1777–1850." Ph.D. diss., University of Colorado, 1986.

López Urrutia, Carlos. *La escuadra chilena en México (1822): los cosarios chilenos y argentinos en los mares del norte.* Buenos Aires: Editorial F. de Aguirre, 1971.

Lorenzana, Apolinaria. "Memories of La Beata: Doña Apolinaria Lorenzana." Trans. Barbara C. Quintana. Introduction by Gloria Ricci Lothrop. *The Californians* 8(1), 1991: 15–25.

Lothrop, Gloria Ricci. "Rancheras and the Land: Women and Property Rights in Hispanic California." *Southern California Quarterly* 76(1), 1994: 59–84.

Lothrop, Marion Lydia. "The Indian Campaigns of General M. G. Vallejo, Defender of the Northern Frontier of California." *Quarterly of the Society of California Pioneers* 9, 1932: 161–205.

———. "Mariano Guadalupe Vallejo: Defender of the Northern Frontier of California." Ph.D. diss., University of California, 1927.

Low, M. Clyde, "Chief Solano: The Legend Examined." Paper presented at the California Indian Conference, University of California, Los Angeles, October 6, 1995.

Machado, Juana. "'Times Gone By in Alta California': Recollections of Señora Doña Juana Machado Alipás de Ridington." Trans. Raymond S. Brandes. Intro. Gloria Ricci Lothrop. *The Californians* 8(4), 1990:43–51.

Martínez, Pablo L. *Guía familiar de Baja California, 1700–1900.* Mexico: Editorial Baja California, 1965.

———. *A History of Lower California.* Mexico: Editorial Baja California, 1960.

Mason, William. "Indian-Mexican Cultural Exchange in the Los Angeles Area, 1781–1834." *Aztlán* 15(1), 1984: 123–144.

Mason, William M. *The Census of 1790: A Demographic History of Colonial California.* Menlo Park, Calif.: Ballena Press, 1998.

McCawley, William. *The First Angelinos: The Gabrielino Indians of Los Angeles.* Menlo Park, Calif.: Ballena Press, 1996.

McCormack, Brian Timothy. "Marriage, Ethnic Identity, and the Politics of Conversion in Alta California, 1769–1834." Ph.D. diss., University of California, San Diego, 2000.

McKenzie, Roderick Clayton. "The San Pascual Grant: The Sequent Occupation of a Portion of the San Gabriel Arcángel Mission Lands through Two Centuries." Ph.D. diss., University of California, Los Angeles, 1972.

McKittrick, Myrtle M. "Salvador Vallejo." *California Historical Society Quarterly* 29(4), 1950:309–331.

———. *Vallejo: Son of California.* Portland: Binfords and Mort, 1944.

Meier, Matt S. *Mexican-American Biographies: A Historical Dictionary, 1836–1987.* Westport, Conn.: Greenwood Press, 1988.

Mendoza, Rubén G. "Sacrament of the Sun: Eschatological Architecture and Solar Geometry in a California Mission." *Boletín: The Journal of the California Mission Studies Association* 22(1), 2005: 87–110.

Miller, Robert Ryal. *Juan Alvarado: Governor of California, 1836–1842.* Norman: University of Oklahoma Press, 1998.

Miller, Ronald Lee. "Henry Delano Fitch: A Yankee Trader in California, 1826–1849." Ph.D. diss., University of Southern California, 1972.

Milliken, Randall. *A Time of Little Choice: The Disintegration of Tribal Culture in the San Francisco Bay Area, 1769–1810*. Menlo Park, Calif.: Ballena Press, 1995.

————. "Ethnographic and Ethnohistorical Context for the Archaeological Investigation of the Suisun Plain, Solano County, California." Unpublished paper.

Miranda, Gloria. "Racial and Cultural Dimensions in *Gente de Razón* Status in Spanish and Mexican California." *Southern California Quarterly* 70(3), 1988: 265–278.

————. "Hispano-Mexican Childrearing Practices in Pre-American Santa Bárbara." *Southern California Quarterly* 65(4), 1983: 307–320.

————. "*Gente de Razón* Marriage Patterns in Spanish and Mexican California: A Case Study of Santa Bárbara and Los Angeles." *Southern California Quarterly* 63(1), 1981: 1–21.

Monroy, Douglas. "They Didn't Call Them 'Padre' for Nothing: Patriarchy in Hispanic California." In *Between Borders: Essays on Mexicana/Chicana History*, ed. Adelaide R. Del Castillo. Encino, Calif.: Floricanto Press, 1990: 433–445

————. *Thrown Among Strangers: The Making of Mexican Culture in Frontier California*. Berkeley: University of California Press, 1990.

Morton, Michelle E. "Utopian and Dystopian Visions of California in the Historical Imagination." Ph.D. diss., University of California, Santa Cruz, 2005.

Neri, Michael. *Hispanic Catholicism in Transitional California: The Life of José González Rubio, O.F.M. (1804–1875)*. Berkeley: Academy of American Franciscan History, 1997.

Northrop, Marie E. *Spanish-Mexican Families of Early California. Vol. III. Los Pobladores de la Reina de Los Angeles*. Burbank, Calif.: Southern California Genealogical Society, 2004.

————. *Spanish-Mexican Families of Early California, 1769–1850*. Vol. II. Burbank, Calif.: Southern California Genealogical Society, 1984.

————. *Spanish-Mexican Families of Early California, 1769–1850*. Vol. I. New Orleans: Polyanthos, 1976.

Nunis, Doyce B. "Medicine in Hispanic California." *Southern California Quarterly* 76(1), 1994: 31–57.

————. *A Commentary on Alfred Robinson and His Life in California*. Los Angeles: R. J. Hoffman, 1970.

————. *The Trials of Isaac Graham*. Los Angeles: Dawson's Book Shop, 1967.

Nunis, Doyce B., ed. *Southern California Local History: A Gathering of the Writings of W. W. Robinson*. Los Angeles: Historical Society of Southern California, 1993.

Ogden, Adele. *The California Sea Otter Trade, 1784–1848*. Berkeley: University of California Press, 1941.

Ohles, Wallace V. *The Lands of Mission San Miguel*. Fresno, Calif.: Word Dancer Press, 1997.

Ord, Angustias de la Guerra. *The California Recollections of Angustias de la Guerra Ord (Occurrences in Hispanic California) as Dictated by Angustias de la Guerra Ord to Thomas Savage in 1878*. Ed. Giorgio Perissinotto. Bilingual Edition. Washington, D.C.: Academy of American Franciscan History, in collaboration with the Santa Bárbara Trust for Historic Preservation. 2004.

————. *Occurrences in Hispanic California*. Trans. and ed. Francis Price and William E. Ellison. Washington, D.C.: Academy of American Franciscan History, 1956.

Osio, Antonio María. *The History of Alta California: A Memoir of Mexican California.* Trans., ann., ed. Rose Marie Beebe and Robert M. Senkewicz. Madison: University of Wisconsin Press, 1996.

Osuna de Marrón, Felipa. *The Reminiscences of Felipa Osuna de Marrón.* Trans. Silvia Rangel and Aleida Rico. Introduction by Gloria Ricci Lothrop. *The Californians* 13(1), 1996: 22–29.

Owens, Kenneth N. "Magnificent Fraud: Ivan Petrov's Docufiction on Russian Fur Hunters and California Missions." *The Californians* 8(2), 1990: 25–29.

Paddison, Joshua, ed. *A World Transformed: Firsthand Accounts of California Before the Gold Rush.* Berkeley: Heyday Books, 1999.

Padilla, Genaro M. *My History, Not Yours: The Formation of Mexican American Autobiography.* Madison: University of Wisconsin Press, 1993.

Pauley, Kenneth, ed., *Rancho Days in Southern California: An Anthology with New Perspectives.* Los Angeles: Westerners, Los Angeles Corral, 1997.

Perdue, Theda, ed. *Sifters: Native American Women's Lives.* Oxford and New York: Oxford University Press, 2001.

Pérez, Crisóstomo N. *Land Grants in Alta California.* Rancho Cordova, Calif.: Landmark Enterprises, 1996.

Pérez, Eulalia. "*Una vieja y sus recuerdos.* The Reminiscences of Eulalia Pérez." Trans. Ruth Rodríguez. Introduction by Gloria Ricci Lothrop. *The Californians* 11(6), 1994: 22–29.

Perissinotto, Giorgio, ed. Principal researchers Catherine E. Rudolph and Elaine Miller. *Documenting Everyday Life in Early Spanish California: The Santa Bárbara Presidio Memorias y Facturas, 1779–1810.* Santa Bárbara: Santa Bárbara Trust for Historic Preservation, 1998.

Peterson, Marcus Edmund. "The Career of Solano, Chief of the Suisuns." M.A. thesis, University of California, 1957.

Phillips, George Harwood. *Bringing Them Under Subjection: California's Tejón Indian Reservation and Beyond, 1852–1864.* Lincoln: University of Nebraska Press, 2004.

———. *Indians and Indian Agents: The Origins of the Reservation System in California, 1849–1852.* Norman: University of Oklahoma Press, 1997.

———. *Indians and Intruders in Central California, 1769–1849.* Norman: University of Oklahoma Press, 1993.

———. *Chiefs and Challengers: Indian Resistance and Cooperation in Southern California.* Berkeley: University of California Press, 1975.

Pico de Avila, María Inocenta. *Cosas de California. Things of California.* Ed. Mary Triplett Ayers, Maurice and Marcy Bandy, and Rudecinda Lo Buglio. Transcr. Donald T. Garate. Trans. Mary Triplett Ayers, Maurice and Marcy Bandy, Carmen Boone de Aguilar, William K. Boone Canovas, Antoinette Egan, and Donald T. Garate. San Diego: Los Californianos, 2002.

Piñera Ramírez, David, ed. *Panorama histórico de Baja California.* Tijuana: Centro de Investigaciones Históricas, Universidad Nacional Autónoma de México, Universidad Autónoma de Baja California, 1983.

Pitt, Leonard. *The Decline of the Californios: A Social History of Spanish-Speaking Californians, 1846–1890.* Berkeley and Los Angeles: University of California Press, 1970.

Pourade, Richard F. *Time of the Bells: The History of San Diego.* San Diego: Union-Tribune Pub. Co., 1961.

Preston, William L. "Portents of Plague from California's Protohistoric Period." *Ethnohistory* 49(1), 2002: 69–121.

Pubols, Louise. "Fathers of the Pueblo: Patriarchy and Power in Mexican California, 1800–1880." In *Continental Crossroads: Remapping U.S.–Mexico Borderlands History*, ed. Samuel Truett and Elliot Young. Durham, N.C. and London: Duke University Press, 2004: 67–93.

————. "The de la Guerra Family: Patriarchy and the Political Economy of California, 1800–1850." Ph.D. diss., University of Wisconsin, 2000.

————. "The Casa de la Guerra: Family and Community in Nineteenth Century Santa Bárbara." M.A. thesis, University of California, Santa Bárbara, 1991.

Ratto, Hector R. *Capitán de navío Hipólito Bouchard*. Buenos Aires: Secretaría de Estado de Marina, 1961

Rawls, James J. *Indians of California: The Changing Image*. Norman and London: University of Oklahoma Press, 1984.

Regnery, Dorothy F. *The Battle of Santa Clara, January 2, 1847*. San José: Smith and McKay Print Company, 1978.

Reyes, Barbara O. "Nineteenth Century California as Engendered Space: The Public/Private Lives of Women of the Californias." Ph.D. diss., University of California, San Diego, 2000.

Rhoades, Elizabeth R. "Foreigners in Southern California During the Mexican Period." M.A. thesis, University of California, 1924.

Ríos-Bustamente, Antonio. *Mexican Los Angeles: A Narrative and Pictoral History*. Encino, Calif.: Floricanto Press, 1992.

Roberts, David. *A Newer World: Kit Carson, John C. Frémont, and the Claiming of the American West*. New York: Simon and Schuster, 2000.

Robinson, W. W. *Land in California, The Story of Mission Lands, Ranchos, Squatters, Mining Claims, Railroad Grants, Land Scrip, Homesteads*. Berkeley and Los Angeles: University of California Press, 1948.

————. *Ranchos Become Cities*. Pasadena, Calif.: San Pasqual Press, 1939.

Rojas, Lauro de. "California in 1844 as Hartnell Saw It." *California Historical Society Quarterly* 17(1), 1938: 21–27.

Roselund, Nels. "Three Eras of Construction at the San Juan Capistrano Mission Church: 1800, 1900, and 2000." *Boletín: The Journal of the California Mission Studies Association* 22(1), 2005: 9–24.

Rosenus, Alan. *General M. G. Vallejo and the Advent of the Americans: A Biography*. Albuquerque: University of New Mexico Press, 1995.

Russell, Craig. "Fray Juan Bautista Sancho: Tracing the Origins of California's First Composer and the Early Mission Style." *Boletín: The Journal of the California Mission Studies Association* 21(1, 2), 2004: 68–103, 4–35.

Sánchez, Rosaura. "Nineteenth-Century Californio Narratives: The Hubert H. Bancroft Collection." In *Recovering the U.S. Hispanic Literary Heritage*, ed. Ramón A. Gutiérrez and Genaro Padilla. Houston: Arte Público Press, 1993: 279–292

————. *Telling Identities: The Californio Testimonios*. Minneapolis and London: University of Minnesota Press, 1995.

Sánchez, Rosaura, Beatrice Pita, and Bárbara Reyes, eds. *Nineteenth Century Californio Testimonials*. Crítica monograph series 68. La Jolla, Calif.: UCSD Ethnic Studies/Third World Studies. 1994.

Sandos, James. *Converting California: Indians and Franciscans in the Missions*. New Haven: Yale University Press, 2004.

———. "Christianization Among the Chumash: An Ethnohistoric Perspective." *American Indian Quarterly* 15(1), 1991: 65–89.

———. "Levantamiento! The 1824 Chumash Uprising Reconsidered." *Southern California Quarterly* 67(2), 1985: 109–133.

Sandos, James A., Edward Castillo, Joseph P. Chinnici, O.F.M., Lisbeth Haas, and William John Summers. "Symposium: *Converting California: Indians and Franciscans in the Missions*." *Boletín: The Journal of the California Mission Studies Association* 21(2), 2004: 49–72.

Santamaría, Francisco J. *Diccionario de Mejicanismos*. Mexico: Editorial Porrúa, 2000.

Schafer, Robert G., and Christopher Loomis. "Preserving the Jewel of the Missions: San Juan Capistrano's Great Stone Church, 1806–2004." *Boletín: The Journal of the California Mission Studies Association* 22(1), 2005: 3–8.

Schuetz-Miller, Mardith K. *Building and Builders in Hispanic California, 1769–1850*. Tucson: Southwestern Mission Research Center, and Santa Bárbara: Santa Bárbara Trust for Historic Preservation Presidio Research Publication, 1994.

Secrest, William B. *California Desperadoes: Stories of the Early California Outlaws in Their Own Words*. Clovis, Calif.: Word Dancer Press, 2000.

Servín, Manuel P. "California's Hispanic Heritage: A View into the Spanish Myth." In *New Spain's Northern Frontier*, ed. David J. Weber. Albuquerque: University of New Mexico Press, 1979.

———. "The Secularization of the California Missions: A Reappraisal." *Historical Society of Southern California Quarterly* 47(2), 1965: 133–149.

Silliman, Stephen W. *Lost Laborers in Colonial California: Native Americans and the Archaeology of Rancho Petaluma*. Tucson: University of Arizona Press, 2004.

———. "Missions Aborted: California Indian Life on Nineteenth-Century Ranchos, 1834–1848." *Boletín: The Journal of the California Mission Studies Association* 21(1), 2004: 3–22.

Smead, Robert N. *Cowboy Talk: A Dictionary of Spanish Terms from the American West*. Norman: University of Oklahoma Press, 2004.

Smilie, Robert S. *The Sonoma Mission, San Francisco Solano de Sonoma: The Founding, Ruin and Restoration of California's 21st Mission*. Fresno, Calif.: Valley Publishers, 1975.

Smith, Gene A. "The War That Wasn't: Thomas ap Catesby Jones' Seizure of Monterey." *California History* 66(2), 1987: 105–113.

Smythe, William E. *History of San Diego, 1542–1908: An Account of the Rise and Progress of the Pioneer Settlement on the Pacific Coast of the United States*. San Diego: History Co., 1907.

Solano, Isidora Filomena. "Reminiscences of a Princess: Isidora Solano." Trans. Sandra Villanueva Guerrero. Introduction by Gloria Ricci Lothrop. *The Californians* 11(3), 1993: 24–28.

Sotos Serrano, Carmen. *Los pintores de la expedición de Alejandro Malaspina*. 2 vols. Madrid: Real Academia de la Historia, 1982.

Street, Richard Steven. *Beasts of the Field: A Narrative History of California Farm Workers, 1769–1913*. Stanford, Calif.: Stanford University Press, 2004.

Swanson, Craig Arthur. "Vanguards of Continental Expansion: Americans in Alta California, 1790–1846." Ph.D. diss., University of Maryland, College Park, 2000.

Tays, George. "Mariano Guadalupe Vallejo and Sonoma." *California Historical Society Quarterly* 16, 1937: 99–121, 216–254, 348–372; *California Historical Society Quarterly* 17, 1938: 50–73, 141–167, 219–242.

————. "Revolutionary California: The Political History of California during the Mexican Period, 1822–1846." Ph.D. diss., University of California Berkeley, 1932.

Thompson, Joseph, O.F.M. *El Gran Capitán: José de la Guerra*. Los Angeles: Franciscan Fathers of California, 1961.

Torre, Esteban de la. "Remininscencias." 1878. The Bancroft Library, C–D 163.

Uhrowczik, Peter. *The Burning of Monterey: The 1818 Attack on California by the Privateer Bouchard*. Los Gatos, Calif.: CYRIL Books, 2001.

Vallejo, Mariano Guadalupe. *Report of a Visit to Fort Ross and Bodega Bay in April 1833*. Trans. Glenn Farris and Rose Marie Beebe, ann. Glenn Farris. Bakersfield, Calif.: California Mission Studies Association, 2000.

————. *Derivation and Definition of the Names of the Several Counties of California. Report of General Mariano G. Vallejo to the First Legislative Session. In Senate, April 16, 1850*. Sacramento: State Printing Office, n.d.

Vallejo, José de Jesús, "Historical Reminiscences of California." Trans. Brother Henry De Groote, ed. Elinor Butler. 1875. The Bancroft Library, C-D 16.

Van Wormer, Stephen. "'Legal Hocus-Pocus:' The Subdivison of Jamacha Rancho." *The Journal of San Diego History*, 30(2), 1984.

Voss, Barbara L. "Culture Contact and Colonial Practices: Archaeological Traces of Daily Life in Early San Francisco." *Boletín: The Journal of the California Mission Studies Association* 20(1), 2003: 63–77.

Warner, Barbara R. *The Men of the California Bear Flag Revolt and Their Heritage*. Sonoma, Calif.: The Arthur H. Clark Company for the Sonoma Valley Historical Society, 1996.

Weber, David J. *Bárbaros: Spaniards and their Savages in the Age of Enlightenment*. New Haven and London: Yale University Press, 2005.

————. *The Spanish Frontier in North America*. New Haven and London: Yale University Press, 1992.

————. *The Mexican Frontier, 1821–1846: The American Southwest under Mexico*. Albuquerque: University of New Mexico Press, 1982.

Weber, Francis J. *The California Missions: As Others Saw Them (1786–1842)*. Los Angeles: Dawson's Book Shop, 1972.

————. "John Thomas Doyle, Pious Fund Historiographer." *Southern California Quarterly* 49(3), 1967: 297–303.

————. "Los Angeles Chancery Archives." *The Americas* 21(4), April 1965: 410–420.

————. *A Biographical Sketch of Right Reverend Francisco García Diego y Moreno, First Bishop of the Californias, 1785–1846*. Los Angeles: Borromeo Guild, 1961.

Wittenburg, Mary Joseph, S.N.D. "Three Generations of the Sepúlveda Family in Southern California." *Southern California Quarterly* 73(3), 1991: 197–250.

Woolfenden, John, and Amelie Elkinton. *Cooper: Juan Bautista Rogers Cooper, Sea Captain, Adventurer, Ranchero, and Early California Pioneer, 1791–1872*. Pacific Grove, Calif.: Boxwood Press, 1983.

INDEX

Bandini, Juan (son), 363, 366
Barona, José, 236, 398
Barreto, Fabián, 305, 398, 441n8
Barroso, Leonardo Díaz, 106, 398
Bastida, María Jacinta de la, 297-8
Basualdo, Francisco, 142, 437n15
Battle of San Pascual, 120, 141-3, 157-8, 162, 360, 426, 428, 438n9
Bear Flag rebellion, 9, 19-21, 25-9, 33, 326-7, 339, 385-7, 426
Births:
birthrates, 36, 432n7, 124; midwifery, 88-9, 98, 110
Bonilla, José Mariano, 232, 303, 373, 399
Boscana, Gerónimo, 111, 236, 399
Bouchard, Hipólito, 33-6, 45, 125, 199, 202-4, 388, 390, 399, 424, 427, 432n2
Buelna, Félix, xxvi
Buelna, María Antonia, 311, 399
Buelna, María Hilaria, 307, 399
Cabot, Pedro, 226, 236, 399
Californio culture:
celebrations/festivities/pastimes, 32, 34, 219, 232, 255, 263, 277-8, 290-91, 293-5, 313; dances, 47-8, 133-4, 255, 258, 263-4, 274, 277-9, 289-91, 293, 295, 313-4, 324, 433n5, 435-6nn15-21, 24; dress, 164, 126-8, 172, 282, 287; food, 281-2, 288; dwellings, 13, 282-3, music/song, 34, 47, 113-16, Pastorela, 139, 192
Camacho (indigenous leader), 130, 185-6, 188
Cambustón, Henri, 42, 44, 339
Cané, Vicente, 313-4, 399
Cantúa, Juan Ignacio, 266-7, 347, 399
Cardero, José, 97, 228
Carrancio (indigenous leader), 131
Carrillo, Anastacio, 205, 207, 283, 399
Carrillo, Carlos Antonio, 138-9, 202, 208, 242, 247-53, 354, 400, 425, 427
Carrillo, Domingo, 72, 78, 242, 372
Carrillo, Joaquín, 16, 68
Carrillo, Joaquín Víctor, 68
Carrillo, José, 89, 93

Carrillo, José Antonio, 116, 128, 140, 220-3, 244, 248-53, 400, 426
Carrillo, José Raymundo, xvi, 50-1, 55, 165, 170-1, 201, 400
Carrillo, Josefa, xx, xxiii, xxvi, xxviii, 68-84, 109, 131, 145, 161, 166, 286, 437n6
Carrillo, Francisca Benicia, 16, 19-20, 25, 326-7
Carrillo, Manuelita, 286
Carrillo, María, 252
Carrillo, María Antonia, 50-1, 55, 116, 194, 201
Carrillo, Pedro C., 156, 354
Carrillo, Ramón, 431n6, 431n8
Carrillo, Ramona, 216-17, 286
Carrillo, Raymundo, 242
Cartucho (indigenous leader), 125, 131, 189
Castañares, José María, 257, 400, 428
Castañeda, Juan, 250, 400
Castro, Ana Josefa, 42, 44
Castro, Joaquín Isidro, 42, 44
Castro, José, xxxv, 40, 139-40, 200, 240, 246-56, 260-3, 265-6, 302, 305-10, 376, 393, 400, 427-8, 431n8
Castro, José Tiburcio, 306, 401
Castro, Manuel, 87, 266, 273, 401
Castro, Modesta, 376
Catalá, Magín Matías, 237, 401
Cattle, 63, 87, 109, 126, 152-3, 158, 175, 183-90, 234-5, 283
Chapman, Joseph, 109, 112, 203, 401
Chávez, José Antonio, 199, 266-70, 401
Chico, Mariano, 57, 62, 137-8, 240-6, 401, 427
Cholos, 46, 139-40, 259-61
Chumash rebellion, xxxii, 58, 205-9, 283
Colonization efforts, 127, 137, 166, 170, 222
Commerce/trade, 12, 37, 40, 46, 51, 56-7, 59, 78, 81-2, 120, 174, 211, 235, 302
Convicts sent to California, 126, 213-4, 309
Cooper, John, 56, 73, 83, 303, 401
Corona, Rosendo V., 346-7, 349
Cot, Antonio José, 218, 401
Cota, Antonia Rosalía, 94-5, 99

ABOUT THE AUTHORS

Rose Marie Beebe is a Professor of Spanish at Santa Clara University. She is, with Robert M. Senkewicz, editor of *Lands of Promise and Despair: Chronicles of Early California, 1535–1846* (2001) and translator, editor, and annotator of *The History of Alta California by Antonio María Osio* (1996), which received the Norman Neuerburg Award from the Historical Society of Southern California. They also jointly edited *Guide to the Manuscripts Concerning Baja California in the Collections of The Bancroft Library* (2002). Beebe served as president of the California Mission Studies Association from 2001 to 2005.

Robert M. Senkewicz is a Professor of history at Santa Clara University. He is the author of *Vigilantes in Gold Rush San Francisco* (1985).

Beebe and Senkewicz are co-editors of *Boletín: The Journal of the California Mission Studies Association*. They are also the co-directors of the California Studies Initiative at Santa Clara University.

Photograph by Steven Taddei and Chrisanne Beebe

The Bancroft Library

The Bancroft Library is the primary special collections library at the University of California, Berkeley. One of the largest and most heavily used libraries of manuscripts, rare books, and unique materials in the United States, Bancroft supports major research and instructional activities. The library's largest resource is the Bancroft Collection of Western Americana, which was begun by Hubert Howe Bancroft in the 1860s and which documents through primary and secondary resources in a variety of formats the social, political, economic, and cultural history of the region from the western plains states to the Pacific coast and from Panama to Alaska, with greatest emphasis on California and Mexico from the late eighteenth century to the present. The Bancroft Library is also home to the Rare Book and Literary Manuscript Collections, the Regional Oral History Office, the History of Science and Technology Collections, the Mark Twain Papers and Project, the University Archives, the Pictorial Collections, and the Center for the Tebtunis Papyri. For more information, see the library's website at http://bancroft.berkeley.edu.

For information on the Friends of The Bancroft Library, to make a gift or donation, or if you have other questions, please contact:

Friends of The Bancroft Library
University of California, Berkeley
Berkeley, Calfornia 94720-6000
(510) 642-3782

HEYDAY INSTITUTE

Since its founding in 1974, Heyday Books has occupied a unique niche in the publishing world, specializing in books that foster an understanding of California history, literature, art, environment, social issues, and culture. We are a 501(c)(3) nonprofit organization committed to providing a platform for writers, poets, artists, scholars, and storytellers who help keep California's diverse legacy alive.

We are grateful for the generous funding we've received for our publications and programs during the past year from various foundations and more than three hundred individuals. Major recent supporters include: Anonymous; Anthony Andreas, Jr.; Arroyo Fund; Barnes & Noble bookstores; Bay Tree Fund; California Association of Resource Conservation Districts; California Oak Foundation; Candelaria Fund; CANfit; Columbia Foundation; Colusa Indian Community Council; Wallace Alexander Gerbode Foundation; Richard & Rhoda Goldman Fund; Evelyn & Walter Haas, Jr. Fund; Walter & Elise Haas Fund; Hopland Band of Pomo Indians; James Irvine Foundation; Guy Lampard & Suzanne Badenhoop; Jeff Lustig; George Frederick Jewett Foundation; LEF Foundation; David Mas Masumoto; James McClatchy; Michael McCone; Gordon & Betty Moore Foundation; Morongo Band of Mission Indians; National Endowment for the Arts; National Park Service; Ed Penhoet; Rim of the World Interpretive Association; Riverside/San Bernardino County Indian Health; River Rock Casino; Alan Rosenus; John-Austin Saviano/Moore Foundation; Sandy Cold Shapero; Ernest & June Siva; L. J. Skaggs and Mary C. Skaggs Foundation; Swinerton Family Fund; Susan Swig Watkins; and the Harold & Alma White Memorial Fund.

For more information about Heyday Institute, our publications and programs, please visit our website at www.heydaybooks.com.